Selecting Effective Treatments
Revised Edition

*A Comprehensive, Systematic Guide
to Treating Mental Disorders*

Linda Seligman

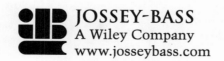

JOSSEY-BASS
A Wiley Company
www.josseybass.com

*This book is dedicated to my father, Irving Goldberg (1904–1994),
who always encouraged my writing and scholarship, and to my mother,
Florence Scolnick Goldberg (1908–1996), who was never quite sure
why I wanted to write books but was proud of me anyhow.*

Published by

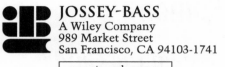 **JOSSEY-BASS**
A Wiley Company
989 Market Street
San Francisco, CA 94103-1741

www.josseybass.com

Copyright © 1998 by John Wiley & Sons, Inc. 2000

Jossey-Bass is a registered trademark of John Wiley & Sons, Inc.

Jossey-Bass books and products are available through most bookstores. To contact Jossey-Bass directly, call (888) 378-2537, fax to (800) 605-2665, or visit our website at www.josseybass.com.

Substantial discounts on bulk quantities of Jossey-Bass books are available to corporations, professional associations, and other organizations. For details and discount information, contact the special sales department at Jossey-Bass.

We at Jossey-Bass strive to use the most environmentally sensitive paper stocks available to us. Our publications are printed on acid-free recycled stock whenever possible, and our paper always meets or exceeds minimum GPO and EPA requirements.

Library of Congress Cataloging-in-Publication Data

Seligman, Linda.
    Selecting effective treatments : a comprehensive, systematic guide
to treating mental disorders / Linda Seligman.—Rev. ed.
        p.   cm.
    Includes bibliographical references and index.
    ISBN 0-7879-4307-X
    1. Mental illness—Treatment.   2. Psychiatry—Differential
therapeutics.   3. Psychotherapy.   I. Title.
RC480.S342   1998
616.89'1—dc21
                                                                98-17919

REVISED EDITION
PB Printing
10 9 8 7

CONTENTS

PREFACE

The landmark research of Smith, Glass, and Miller (1980), along with other research, gave the definitive affirmative answer to the question of whether psychotherapy has any value. Research in the decade that followed turned to differential therapeutics, seeking to determine which approaches to psychotherapy are effective in treating which mental disorders, under what conditions, with which clients, and to what ends.

Our understanding about the differential diagnosis of mental disorders has advanced greatly over the past twenty years. In 1994 these advances culminated in the publication of the fourth edition of the *Diagnostic and Statistical Manual of Mental Disorders,* or *DSM-IV.* But understanding of differential therapeutics has lagged behind. Many books have been published that focus on one particular disorder, espouse one preferred mode of treatment, or offer a compendium of articles by different authors, but few volumes have presented a systematic, research-based approach to the treatment of mental disorders. As a result, approaches to treatment are often haphazard, with clinicians relying on familiar or comfortable models rather than on treatments that have demonstrated the greatest effectiveness.

In this volume, the second edition of *Selecting Effective Treatments,* I present an overview of the major types of mental disorders, accompanied by treatment models that are structured, comprehensive, grounded in research, and likely to be effective. Knowledge about differential therapeutics for mental disorders certainly has advanced over the decade since work was begun on the first edition of the book. But if this area of inquiry has moved out of its infancy, it still seems to be in its adolescence, and there is much still to be learned about the effective treatment of mental disorders. The information in this book, by offering clinicians the possibility of a better understanding of the major mental disorders, should enable them to provide more effective treatment to their clients. Use of the guidelines provided in the book should also increase psychotherapists' accountability and enable them to deal more effectively with the intricacies of third-party payments and peer review.

This volume is not intended to be a "cookbook," nor is it intended to restrict clinicians to a narrow range of techniques. Neither does it advocate the universal application of a particular technique or theoretical model: research does not support such a circumscribed view of therapy, and such an approach would not promote the optimal use of each therapist's special talents. Rather, this book seeks to increase clinicians' understanding of the symptoms and dynamics of mental disorders and to provide a range of treatment options for each disorder, allowing clinicians to blend their own therapeutic strengths and preferences with those approaches that have demonstrated effectiveness.

AUDIENCE

Most of the existing books on treatment of mental disorders were written from a medical perspective, but most treatment of mental disorders is provided by psychologists, counselors, and social workers. Therefore, this book fills a gap in the literature by focusing on the needs of nonmedical mental health practitioners (psychologists, counselors, and social workers) and by recognizing the increasingly important part they play in treating mental disorders. The book is also addressed to students in these fields who have at least a basic understanding of approaches to counseling and psychotherapy.

Clinicians, researchers, and educators in the mental health fields should all be able to use this book in their work. Clinicians in particular who read the book can expect to gain a deeper understanding of the complexities of diagnosis, as well as of *DSM-IV.* They will be able to develop sound treatment plans and will gain greater confidence and credibility, which should help them treat their clients more knowledgeably and more effectively. Some information has been provided about the usefulness of medication for the various mental disorders, but this information is included primarily to help clinicians determine when a referral for medication is in order and to assist them in anticipating the impact that medication is likely to have on their clients.

ORGANIZATION

Selecting Effective Treatments is organized into ten chapters, and its format is intended to facilitate readers' understanding and application of the information that the book contains. Chapter One introduces the reader to the process of treatment planning. It discusses the importance of systematic and effective treatment planning and presents the *Client Map,* a structured approach to treatment planning. After summarizing the literature on the effectiveness of the various approaches to psychotherapy and examining the decisions that must be made as part of treatment planning, the chapter looks at the client, the therapist, and their relationship, exploring those personal and interpersonal variables that maximize the likelihood of effective treatment.

In Chapters Two through Nine, the mental disorders have been grouped into eight broad categories. Within each of these chapters, the material on each mental disorder has been organized into five sections:

- A description of the disorder
- An overview of the characteristics that typify people with the disorder
- An overview of the qualities of style and personality that typify clinicians likely to be successful in treating the disorder
- A review of the research on treatment of the disorder
- Information on the prognosis for the disorder

This format should enable readers to understand the differences and similarities among the disorders, as well as their dynamics and treatment. At the end of each of these eight chapters, treatment information included in the chapter is summarized and organized according to the Client Map. A case study is also provided, which includes a treatment plan that follows the Client Map. (All case studies appearing in the book have been created on the basis of composite characters, to protect the privacy of actual clients.) Each of these eight chapters also includes a brief list of recommended readings.

Chapter Two, completely new to this edition, discusses the diagnosis and treatment of those mental disorders that usually are first diagnosed in infancy, childhood, or adolescence. With the addition of this chapter, *Selecting Effective Treatments* is now fully compatible with *DSM-IV,* presenting information on the treatment of nearly all the mental disorders in that manual. Chapter Three examines situationally-precipitated conditions and disorders, the mildest of the *DSM* categories. These conditions and disorders involve problems of adjustment and coping. Chapter Four considers Mood Disorders, which are characterized primarily by depressed or extremely elevated moods. Chapter Five examines Anxiety Disorders, expressed in troubling anxiety and fearfulness. Chapter Six focuses on disorders of behavior and impulse control. These include Substance-Related Disorders, Eating Disorders, Sexual and Gender Identity Disorders, other Impulse-Control Disorders, and Sleep Disorders.

Chapter Seven examines disorders in which physical and psychological factors combine. These include Somatoform Disorders, Factitious Disorders, Delirium, Dementia, Amnestic and other Cognitive Disorders, and Mental Disorders Due to a General Medical Condition. That chapter also emphasizes the importance of treatment collaboration between medical and nonmedical practitioners in treating these disorders.

Personality Disorders, their nature and their treatment, are the focus of Chapter Eight. These are long-standing and often treatment-resistant disorders, and this chapter is designed to help clinicians ameliorate them.

Chapter Nine focuses on those mental disorders that involve impairment in awareness of reality, the Psychotic and Dissociative Disorders. The chapter examines their differences and similarities as well as effective interventions in their treatment. The book concludes with Chapter Ten, which discusses the future of diagnosis and treatment planning.

ACKNOWLEDGMENTS

I received a great deal of personal and professional support in writing this book. I am especially appreciative of the following people:

Mittie Quinn, M.A., N.C.S.P., is a licensed school psychologist, an expert in the diagnosis and treatment of mental disorders in children and adolescents, and the coauthor of Chapter Two. She is currently in private practice in the Washington, D.C., area, where she also is a consultant to the Fairfax County Public School System and leads parent education seminars on child development and girls' self-esteem.

Carol J. Kaffenberger, M.Ed., educator and elementary school counselor for twenty-five years, is currently a Ph.D. candidate and my graduate assistant at George Mason University. Her encouragement and help with the research and writing of this book, as well as her contributions to my other professional projects, have been invaluable to me.

Stephanie A. Hardenburg, M.A., L.P.C., is in private practice, specializing in marriage and family counseling, and is also a Ph.D. candidate at George Mason University. Her assistance with this book, particularly her knowledge of Impulse-Control Disorders, made a significant contribution.

The administrators of the Graduate School of Education at George Mason University, particularly Dr. Gary Galluzzo, Dr. Gustavo A. Mellander, and Dr. Martin Ford, provided encouragement and time that facilitated my completion of this book.

My husband, Dr. Robert M. Zeskind, reminded me with his warmth and his sense of humor that writing is only one important part of life.

May 1998   Linda Seligman
Fairfax, Virginia

CHAPTER ONE

Introduction to Effective Treatment Planning

A usually quiet and withdrawn young woman became verbally abusive to her supervisor and warned him that if she were not promoted to a job commensurate with her outstanding abilities, she was going to "come back with a gun." A few weeks earlier, she had a brief consultation with a psychiatrist, who diagnosed her as having a Major Depressive Disorder and prescribed antidepressant medication.

A man who had been a capable and hardworking accountant was referred to an employee assistance counselor because of a sudden and extreme decline in his performance. After some brief and unsuccessful efforts were made to re-motivate the man, he was fired from his job.

A woman had been treated with years of unsuccessful psychoanalysis during which she had been told that her difficulty in concentrating and her chaotic lifestyle reflected her efforts to avoid dealing with her early losses.

THE IMPORTANCE OF SYSTEMATIC
AND EFFECTIVE TREATMENT PLANNING

Poor clinical understanding, inaccurate diagnosis, and inappropriate treatment contributed to all of the situations just described. The first woman had a history of both manic and depressive episodes; in fact, she had Bipolar Disorder, and the antidepressant medication contributed to the development of a manic episode. The man was suffering from a Cognitive Disorder, which had resulted from a head injury incurred in a bicycling accident. The second woman had Attention-Deficit/Hyperactivity Disorder and responded well to a combination of behavior therapy and medication. These examples, all drawn from the experience of actual clients of mine, make clear the importance of accurate diagnosis and treatment planning.

The primary goal of diagnosis and treatment planning is to help psychotherapists from all disciplines, psychologists, counselors, social workers, psychiatrists, and psychiatric nurses make sound therapeutic decisions so that we can help our clients ameliorate their difficulties, feel better about themselves and their lives, and achieve their goals. A need for accountability as well as for effectiveness mandates systematic treatment planning.

As health care costs have risen, the growth and impact of managed care have escalated, and third-party payers increasingly require mental health professionals to describe and justify their treatment plans. Case managers, who are usually other mental health practitioners, review treatment plans and determine whether they are appropriate. If a treatment plan does not seem sound, third-party payments may be denied or withheld until a more appropriate plan is submitted. Clearly, the therapist's knowledge of treatment planning is an essential element of people's ability to afford the psychotherapy they need.

Requests for accountability also come from mental health agencies and clinics, from counseling centers at schools, hospitals, and residential facilities where therapy is done, and from funding agencies. Financial support is rarely adequate for mental health services in these settings, and therapists often must provide documentation of the services' effectiveness before they can obtain continued funding.

Unfortunately, treatment planning is sometimes viewed as a process that must be carried out for no better reason than to satisfy bureaucratic requirements. That may in fact be the underlying motive in some cases, but the fundamental reason for treatment planning is to facilitate effective treatment. The purpose of this book, as the Preface has already outlined, is to provide the most up-to-date information available on *differential therapeutics*—that is, the study of which treatment approaches are most likely to be effective in treating each of the mental disorders. The book seeks to facilitate the process of treatment planning by linking knowledge about treatments to information about diagnoses, which are usually made with the *Diagnostic and Statistical Manual of Mental Disorders,* now in its fourth edition and also known as *DSM-IV* (American Psychiatric Association, 1994a).

This book is not designed to present a rigid formula for treatment planning; the state of the art does not allow that, and even if it were possible it probably would not be desirable. Therapeutic effectiveness depends not only on the application of well-supported methods of intervention but also on such indefinable and intricate ingredients as the purity of the therapist's style, the expertise and training of the therapist, the personalities of therapist and client, their demographic characteristics, and the alliance between the two of them. Therefore, this book presents information not just on the mental disorders and their appropriate treatment but also on the probable nature of the people suffering from each disorder, those characteristics on the part of the therapist that are likely to contribute to effective treatment, and the prognosis for the treatment of each disorder.

In therapy there are many roads to the same goal. This book seeks to point out which roads are likely to be smooth and rewarding and which are full of ruts and barriers. Plotting the actual course is up to the therapist and the client. Systematic treatment planning allows the clinician to map the therapeutic journey, revise the route as necessary, and repeat the trip with others if it turns out to be worthwhile, all without compromising the spontaneity of the traveler or the guide.

RESEARCH ON THE EFFECTIVENESS OF PSYCHOTHERAPY

In the 1950s and 1960s, Eysenck (1952, 1966) reviewed a group of studies on psychotherapy outcomes and concluded that therapy is not effective. This startling finding triggered a series of studies designed to conduct a more thorough investigation into the question of whether therapy is effective.

Meltzoll and Kornreich (1970) reviewed a large number of outcome studies. Of fifty-seven studies that they viewed as adequately designed, forty-eight, or 84 percent, yielded evidence of therapy's effectiveness. Of forty-four questionable studies, however, only one-third yielded such evidence. Therefore, not surprisingly, the quality of an outcome study's design and execution seems important in any assessment of the true impact of therapy. Luborsky, Singer, and Luborsky's (1975) review of thirty-three outcome studies yielded similar results. They concluded that "controlled comparative studies indicate that a high percentage of patients who go through any of these psychotherapies gain from them" (p. 1003).

The most definitive earlier study on the effectiveness of psychotherapy was conducted by Smith, Glass, and Miller (1980). These researchers used a sophisticated meta-analysis to do a numerical summary of the results of every controlled study they could locate on psychotherapy outcomes—a total of 475 studies conducted before 1977. They conclude that "the average person who received therapy is better off at the end of it than 80 percent of those who do not" (p. 87). Smith and colleagues concluded that the effect of therapy was clearly substantial. Their research also examines many aspects of the therapeutic process, including the type of therapy, the relationship between diagnosis and treatment outcome, the relationship between client characteristics and treatment outcome, treatment duration, treatment setting, and medication. These findings will be discussed later in this chapter.

The findings of Smith, Glass, and Miller have been substantiated by a subsequent analysis of their data. Andrews and Harvey (1981) found that the condition of the typical psychotherapy client was better than the condition of 77 percent of the people in an untreated control group who were measured at the same time as the clients. They also found only a small rate of relapse within the first two years after treatment.

The verdict on the outcome of psychotherapy seems positive: for most people, therapy is more effective at ameliorating emotional disorders than is no treatment at all. Where do we go from here? Vanden Bos (1986), perceiving the research to have focused too much on outcomes and not enough on process, has suggested that comparative research is needed. Such research, he says, should explore the relative advantages and disadvantages of alternative treatment strategies for people with different disorders, and it should also explore the therapeutically relevant qualities of the client, the therapist, and their interaction. Study of the therapeutic process contains many challenges, however, and even the best-defined therapy is difficult to reproduce because of its interactive nature. Other challenges inherent in the process of conducting research on therapy's effectiveness include the large number of client-related variables, variations in therapists' expertise, variation in the severity of disorders, participant and observer bias, the questionable ethics of establishing true control and placebo groups, and the difficulty of assessing how much progress has been made.

Lambert and Cattani-Thompson (1996) sum up the current research by stating, "The research literature clearly shows that counseling is effective in relation to no-treatment and placebo conditions. The effects of counseling seem to be relatively lasting. These effects are attained in relatively brief time periods, with the percentage of clients who show substantial improvement increasing as the number of counseling sessions increases. There continues to be little evidence of specific efficacy for particular techniques or counseling theories, and a small portion of clients seem to deteriorate while undergoing, and perhaps because of, counseling interventions" (p. 601). These conclusions do not pertain exclusively to the counseling of adults. According to Kazdin (1995), "The meta-analyses have shown that treatment with children and adolescents is effective and parallels the outcomes achieved in therapy with adults" (p. 258).

Conclusions similar to these have been drawn by Martin Seligman (1995), who conducted what he describes as "the most extensive study of psychotherapy effectiveness on record" (p. 969). Seligman's survey, conducted under the auspices of *Consumer Reports,* obtained responses from more than five thousand people who had sought help for emotional difficulties. Effectiveness was determined by assessment of satisfaction, specific improvement in symptoms or complaints, and global improvement. The study found that 87 percent of those who had started out feeling "very poor" described themselves as feeling "very good," "good," or "at least so-so" at the end of treatment, and that the same levels of improvement were also achieved by 92 percent of those who had started out feeling "fairly poor." Clearly, rates of improvement are high, and rates of decline or no change are relatively low (about 10 percent in most studies, a proportion encompassing the most severely disturbed clients). Seligman concludes that "patients benefitted very substantially from psychotherapy . . . [and] no specific modality of psychotherapy did better than any other for any disorder" (p. 965). Thus studies conducted in the 1990s have substantiated and expanded on the 1980 study by Smith, Glass, and Miller, although much is still unknown. Stiles, Shapiro, and Elliott (1986) have observed that "most reviews of psychotherapy outcome research show little or no differential effectiveness of different psychotherapies" (p.165). As Perry, Frances, and Clarkin (1985) have stated, "Too often, patients receive the treatment known best to, or practiced primarily by, the first person they consult rather than that from which they might best benefit" (p. xviii). These studies imply that the field of differential therapeutics has not progressed much, but that is only partially true.

DETERMINANTS OF TREATMENT OUTCOME

Psychotherapy outcome seems to be determined by four clusters of variables:

1. *Therapist-related variables,* including such factors as age, gender, ethnicity, education and training, theoretical orientation, and counseling style

2. *Client-related variables,* including demographic factors, diagnosis and symptoms, motivation for and expectations of treatment, history, support systems, ability to form relationships and collaborate with the therapist, personality, and the natural course of the client's disorder

3. *The therapeutic alliance,* including the ability of the therapist and the client to agree on goals and treatment procedures, the match between therapist- and client-related variables, and their interaction

4. *Treatment variables,* including the theories that guide the treatment, the techniques used, medication, the treatment setting and context, the frequency and duration of treatment, and such adjuncts to treatment as self-help groups

Maximization of the therapy's effectiveness should take account of all four clusters of variables.

The remainder of this chapter presents an integrated model for treatment planning that will help therapists think systematically about that process and explores the factors to be considered in structuring treatment. These factors include, among others, the modality of treatment (group, individual, or family), the theoretical framework for treatment, the duration of treatment, and the treatment setting. The chapter goes on to summarize the available research on the first three clusters of variables (therapist-related variables, client-related variables, and the therapeutic alliance).

The chapters that follow focus primarily on the fourth cluster of variables (treatment variables), to help therapists deepen their understanding of the mental disorders discussed in *DSM-IV* and their effective treatment. Because this book is designed to help clinicians move beyond the assumption that therapy is effective and on to an exploration of what works for whom, the large and growing body of literature on that subject is reviewed here. Some of the conclusions drawn from the literature are tentative, but they should provide a basis for future research into treatment planning, as well as for the development of treatment plans themselves.

AN INTEGRATED MODEL FOR TREATMENT PLANNING

The integrated model presented here in skeleton form lists the five major elements (items I through V) that structure the information in the following eight chapters. Clinicians, when they are assessing particular clients or disorders, often do not have information about all the categories and subcategories in this outline, but effective use of the model does not depend on complete information. Indeed, gaps in the therapist's knowledge, as well as in the information available on a client, can actually be used to guide the development of a treatment plan and to indicate areas needing further research or investigation.

I. *Description of Disorder*
  A. *Diagnosis.* DSM-IV comprises the accepted system for classifying mental disorders in the United States, as well as in many other countries. Its nomenclature will be used as the standard throughout this book. Many people have two or more coexisting diagnoses, and common examples of comorbidity will be discussed.
  B. *Epidemiology.* The area of epidemiology includes both the *incidence* (number of new cases) and the *prevalence* (number of existing cases at a given time) of a disorder. Acute disorders tend to have a higher incidence; chronic disorders, a higher prevalence. Approximately 32 to 50 percent of Americans will have some type of mental disorder during their lifetimes, although only about 25 percent of these people will seek

help from a psychotherapist (Maxmen & Ward, 1995). In general, the more common the disorder and the better established the diagnosis, the more is known about its treatment (because there has been greater opportunity for research on the disorder).

C. *Primary and secondary symptoms.* A mental disorder is typically comprised of a cluster of symptoms, both *primary* and *secondary,* or underlying. (The primary symptoms are those that must be present to meet the criteria for diagnosis; for this book, *DSM-IV* is used as the major source of information on symptoms.) Comparison of a disorder's standard symptoms with a person's presenting symptoms is important in individualizing a treatment plan so that it meets the needs of that particular person.

D. *Typical onset, course, and duration of the disorder.* This information can be useful to clients as well as to the clinician who is engaged in treatment planning. Disorders vary widely in terms of their course. For example, some disorders, such as Schizophrenia, typically are chronic and need extended follow-up; others, like Major Depressive Disorder, tend to run a circumscribed course but frequently recur. In general, a disorder that has a brief duration, and whose onset has quickly followed a precipitating event, has a better prognosis than a disorder that has a slow, insidious onset and no clear precipitant.

II. *Typical Client Characteristics.* The purpose of this section is to provide typical profiles of people with particular mental disorders. These profiles can facilitate diagnostic interviewing, alerting clinicians to client patterns that are likely to be present. By comparing these profiles with information gathered on individual clients, therapists can also identify areas that need exploration and can gain insight into clients' readiness for treatment, types of treatment that are most likely to be effective, adjunct and referral sources that may be useful, and prognoses. The following client characteristics, among others, are typically relevant to treatment.

A. *Genetic and other predisposing factors.* In this section, common etiologies of disorders are discussed. Many disorders tend to follow a genetic or familial pattern; these disorders or related ones are often found in a client's family (Schizophrenia and Bipolar Disorders are examples of disorders that are heritable). Identification of these patterns can enable clinicians to plan treatments that take account of environmental or family dynamics contributing to the development of a disorder. A family history of a disorder may also imply a biological element to its transmission, suggesting that medication may enhance treatment. Developmental patterns (such as the age at which a disorder is most likely to emerge) and predisposing factors (such as a precipitating incident or a background common to those who suffer from the disorder) also provide data useful in determining treatment plans. That information can also facilitate the formulation of plans to prevent relapse.

B. *Demographics.* Information about such areas as the typical social and economic environment, marital status, and family constellation of someone with a given disorder is included in this section.

C. *Source of referral and apparent motivation for treatment.* Clues to a person's probable response to treatment are often provided by the nature of the referral. For example, a client who has sought therapy on the recommendation of a career counselor with whom she has worked successfully is likely to have a more intrinsic motivation to change than is someone who has been ordered into treatment by the courts.

D. *Treatment history.* Information on previous treatment is important in determining what treatments are likely to be helpful. For example, a long treatment history, especially one including numerous treatment failures, suggests a poor prognosis, but perhaps that outcome can be averted if a treatment is provided that is different from those that have failed.

E. *Personality profile.* Clients' personality profiles are obtained through psychological assessment, interviews, or observation by clinicians. Typical interpersonal and intrapsychic dynamics of clients with each mental disorder will be considered in later chapters and include such aspects as cognitions, affect, behavior, defenses, and lifestyle.

F. *Developmental history.* A review of the client's background, including such areas as family relationships, work history, social and leisure activities, and medical conditions, usually provides valuable information on that person's strengths and areas of difficulty. If the client's successes and failures, support systems, and coping mechanisms are considered when treatment is planned, the treatment is likely to be more effective.

III. *Preferred Therapist Characteristics.* This section reviews the available information on therapist-related variables that are relevant to the treatment of a particular disorder or client. Such information may include the therapist's experience, theoretical orientation, and training; the therapist's personal and professional qualities; and the relationship between the client's and the clinician's personalities and backgrounds.

IV. *Intervention Strategies.* In this section, what is known about the effective treatment of a disorder is reviewed. Recommendations about treatment strategies are made, and areas where information is lacking are discussed.

A. *Approaches to psychotherapy.* This section contains a review of the literature on those approaches to therapy that seem to work best with the disorder under consideration. Details on the dimensions listed here are provided later in this chapter; for now, let us note that the following dimensions of the therapeutic process have been found to be important in treatment planning and, according to the information available (Seligman, 1996a), may be considered in this section.

1. Psychotherapeutic theories and techniques
2. Therapist's implementation of these theories and techniques (including level of directiveness, exploration, support, structure, and confrontation)
3. Balance of focus—affective, behavioral, cognitive
4. Modality of treatment—individual, family, group

B. *Medication.* The question of whether medication enhances or is necessary in the treatment of a particular disorder is considered in this section. Although the focus of this book is the treatment of mental disorders by nonmedical clinicians, who emphasize psychotherapy rather than drugs to effect change, for some disorders a combination of medication and psychotherapy is usually more effective than either one alone. Nonmedical therapists must be aware of these findings so that they can refer clients with such disorders for medical evaluation or provide treatment in collaboration with a psychiatrist or other medical specialist.

C. *Duration and pacing of treatment.* This section focuses on the typical length of treatment necessary for ameliorating a disorder and on the swiftness of the therapeutic pace.

D. *Treatment setting.* Inpatient settings, partial hospitalization or day treatment, and outpatient settings all have their place in the treatment of mental disorders.

E. *Adjunct services.* These services include social and personal growth activities, support and self-help groups (such as Alcoholics Anonymous), leisure and exercise groups, professional and governmental services (such as legal aid and subsidized housing), and psychoeducational services (such as assertiveness training and education on effective parenting) that may enhance the effectiveness of psychotherapy.

V. *Prognosis.* This section provides information on how much change or improvement can be expected in a person experiencing the disorder under consideration, how rapidly progress is likely to occur, the likelihood of relapse, and the overall prognosis.

THE CLIENT MAP

The major elements of the treatment plan discussed in this chapter have been organized into a structured and systematic model for treatment planning, the Client Map. The steps of this treatment plan are represented by the acronym formed from the first letter in each of the twelve steps: DO A CLIENT MAP. This acronym facilitates recall of the parts of the plan, reflects the plan's purpose, and guides its development. A clinician who supplies information about the following twelve items will have created the Client Map, a treatment plan for working with a particular client:

DO A CLIENT MAP

Diagnosis

Objectives of treatment

Assessments (for example, neurological or personality tests)

Clinician characteristics

Location of treatment

Interventions to be used

Emphasis of treatment (for example, level of directiveness; level of supportiveness; cognitive, behavioral, or affective emphasis)

Numbers (that is, the number of people in treatment: individual, family, or group)

Timing (frequency, pacing, duration)

Medications needed

Adjunct services

Prognosis

The format represented by the DO A CLIENT MAP acronym is used throughout this book to illustrate the process of treatment planning for sample cases.

DIMENSIONS OF TREATMENT PLANNING

In general, treatment planning moves from the nature of the disorder through consideration of the client's characteristics and on to the treatment approach. That will be the sequence followed throughout most of this book. In the present section, however, the focus will be primarily on the approach to treatment and what is known about its impact on mental disorders. The parts of the Client Map considered here are Location, Interventions, Emphasis, Numbers, Timing, and Medications; Clinician characteristics are discussed later in this chapter, along with client-related variables and the therapeutic alliance, and in subsequent chapters Diagnosis, Assessment, specific information on Interventions, and Prognosis are discussed for each disorder.

Location

Research on selection of treatment settings is fairly limited. In general, the treatment location will be determined by the following considerations (Seligman, 1996a):

1. Diagnosis, and the nature and severity of the symptoms
2. Danger that clients present to themselves and others
3. Objectives of treatment
4. Cost of treatment, and the client's financial resources
5. Client's support systems, living situation, and ability to keep scheduled appointments
6. Nature and effectiveness of previous treatments
7. Preferences of the client and of significant others

As for where treatment actually tends to take place, Schwartz and Schwartzburg (1976) found that psychiatric hospitalizations were accounted for by people diagnosed with Schizophrenia (27 percent), Mood Disorders (22.5 percent), and Substance-Related Disorders (21 percent), with the remaining 29.5 percent accounted for by people diagnosed with a broad range of other disorders. These figures do not seem to have changed much over the years, although inpatient treatment of Substance-Related Disorders is probably less common.

Perry et al. (1985) see selection of treatment setting as related primarily to the goal of the therapy rather than to a disorder's severity. In some cases, there may even be a negative relationship between severity of the disorder and duration of hospitalization. For example, more demanding goals are usually set for people with Anorexia Nervosa or Alcohol Dependence who were functioning fairly well before or during their disorders than are likely to be set for people with chronic Schizophrenia and poor adjustment, and the more demanding goals may require a longer hospitalization.

Frances, Clarkin, and Perry (1984) also recommend giving consideration to the client's preferences and motivation, given that many disorders can be treated successfully in more than one setting. For example, severe Major Depressive Disorder can be treated initially with intensive hospitalization, partial hospitalization, or outpatient crisis intervention. Treatment of Substance Dependence can be accomplished through inpatient treatment, day treatment, or intensive outpatient programs combined with the client's participation in self-help groups.

The decision about the treatment setting, like many of the other decisions that must be made as part of treatment planning, calls on clinical judgment because the literature gives only sketchy guidelines. In general, however, inpatient treatment is indicated for people who need a high level of supervision because of suicidal or homicidal ideation, bizarre behavior, or inability to care for themselves. Hospitalization is most likely to be needed for people diagnosed as having Psychotic Disorders, Major Depressive Disorder, severe Eating Disorders, Substance Dependence, or Bipolar Disorders. Some studies indicate that a brief hospital stay followed by aftercare is more therapeutic than a longer stay. In general, the most efficient, least confining treatment setting should be used to reduce the stigma associated with treatment, maintain the client's independence and connection to the community, and reduce costs.

Interventions

Once the clinician has identified the treatment setting for a particular client, the next step probably will be to determine the specific approaches and techniques that will guide treatment. A vast array of psychotherapeutic approaches is available to clinicians: according to Kazdin (1986), more than four hundred psychotherapies have been advanced. Therapies seem to have more similarities than differences, however. Lambert and Bergin (1994) have identified three common factors that are associated with a positive outcome, no matter which therapy is used:

1. Support factors, including the therapeutic alliance, trust, structure, and reassurance

2. Learning factors, including feedback, insight, advice, affective expression, and cognitive restructuring

3. Action factors, including reality testing, modeling, changing behavior, facing fears, and working through

Perry et al. (1985), in a similar vein, have identified nine elements or strategies that they believe are common to almost all psychotherapeutic approaches:

1. Establishing and maintaining a positive therapeutic relationship

2. Providing support via reality testing, suggestions, structure, confirmation, acceptance, validation, and communication of a sense of optimism and confidence

3. Providing information and education

4. Reducing painful feelings, especially anxiety and depression

5. Decreasing specific maladaptive behaviors

6. Modifying specific misperceptions

7. Helping people put their concerns in context and make sense of them

8. Expanding emotional awareness

9. Enhancing interpersonal effectiveness

Karasu (1986) has presented yet another useful framework. According to Karasu, all approaches to therapy involve three therapeutic change agents: affective experiencing, cognitive mastery, and behavioral regulation. Approaches differ, however, in terms of the relative attention given to these three vehicles for change.

Although different terminology is used, leading to different sets of commonalities, these studies suggest that there are not really hundreds of discrete approaches to psychotherapy but instead many variations on a far smaller number of well-established themes. The existence of so many commonalities among therapeutic approaches raises an interesting issue: Are the differences among therapies genuine, and do these therapies have differential effectiveness? Or is any apparent differential effectiveness among therapies due more to particular therapists' effectiveness, if not to the chemistry of particular therapeutic relationships? This issue should be borne in mind when the research on the impact of the major approaches to therapy is reviewed.

Earlier in this chapter, the overall effectiveness of psychotherapy was discussed. The findings of Lambert, Shapiro, and Bergin (1986) seem typical: outcome research suggests that 66 percent of clients improve, 26 percent are unchanged, and 8 percent are worse after therapy. Once it was established that most people benefit from psychotherapy, the fundamental question became "What forms of psychotherapy are most effective, and what are the common ingredients of their greater effectiveness?" Although there are still no conclusive answers, a considerable body of research addresses this question, beginning with the work of Smith, Glass, and Miller (1980).

The Study by Smith, Glass, and Miller. A synthesis of the very rich data of the Smith et al. study (1980) suggests the following conclusions about the major approaches to psychotherapy:

1. The behavioral approaches tend to be highly effective with a broad range of disorders and are particularly powerful in dealing with fear/anxiety, Specific Phobias, global adjustment, depression, and vocational-personal development. Systematic desensitization, a form of behavior therapy, achieved a relatively high effect score in the treatment of fear/anxiety, emotional-somatic complaints, and global adjustment.

2. The cognitive therapies also have a broad range of effectiveness and a particularly strong impact in the treatment of fear/anxiety, global adjustment, and Specific Phobias. In general, Smith, Glass, and Miller find the cognitive therapies to be somewhat more powerful than the behavioral approaches, although Shapiro and Shapiro (1982) have found little difference in effectiveness between these two forms of therapy. A combination of the two, cognitive-behavioral therapy, also seems effective with some disorders, notably disorders of social behavior, simple phobias, fear/anxiety, and global adjustment.

3. The dynamic, dynamic-eclectic, and psychodynamic approaches to counseling seem nearly as effective as the behavioral and cognitive approaches and are especially effective with social, career, or academic concerns, with fear/anxiety, with criminal behavior, with addictions, and with emotional-somatic complaints.

4. Research on the person-centered or humanistic approach has not shown the positive outcomes of the cognitive or behavioral approaches, partly because there has been less systematic research on the person-centered model than on the cognitive and behavioral approaches. Nevertheless, the person-centered approach does seem to make an important contribution to building self-esteem.

5. Only limited research was available to Smith, Glass, and Miller on the effectiveness of the developmental approaches. These approaches do seem to ameliorate vocational-personal concerns but do not demonstrate a high overall level of effectiveness.

6. Smith, Glass, and Miller find that the effect size of many of the psychotherapies (psychodynamic, person-centered, vocational-personal developmental, cognitive-behavioral, and implosion therapy) is not affected by whether a client is neurotic, psychotic, or phobic, but that placebo treatment and systematic desensitization are more effective at treating simple phobias than at treating neurotic disorders. Behavior modification is more effective in treating psychoses and simple phobias than in treating neurotic disorders. Rational-emotive therapy, by contrast, is more effective in the treatment of phobias than in the treatment of neuroses, and dynamic-eclectic therapy is more effective with neurotic than with psychotic disorders.

These results, although helpful to the process of treatment planning, should be interpreted cautiously. The findings are not based on one large, well-planned experimental study but rather on a meta-analysis of the data from more than four hundred studies. Moreover, the findings were published nearly two decades ago. Consequently, there were many gaps in the information available to Smith, Glass, and Miller, and if their study omits any one approach to therapy, the omission may mean only that their research was conducted at a time when not enough work had been done on the effectiveness of that approach to yield meaningful data. Indeed, Smith, Glass, and Miller themselves are cautious in interpreting their own data. They conclude, "Different types of psychotherapy (verbal or behavioral; psychodynamic, client-centered, or systematic desensitization) do not produce different types or degrees of benefit" (p. 184). Luborsky et al. (1975) agree, summing up the comparative research as yielding a "Dodo Bird verdict" (the Dodo, in Lewis Carroll's classic *Alice's Adventures in Wonderland,* concludes that everyone has won and must have a prize).

Smith, Glass, and Miller's own reaction to their accumulation of data is to recommend a treatment approach that they call "pluralism," which they describe as "the more intelligent alternative to eclecticism" (p. 185). What they mean by pluralism is an approach to treatment planning that will combine methods in a logical, systematic way so as to maximize the chances of a positive therapeutic impact, a method that seems preferable to a "cookbook" approach dictating specific types of therapy for specific disorders. Subsequent surveys of practice have reflected this shift toward pluralism (or "eclecticism," as it is more commonly and less precisely known). For example, in a survey of psychologists, 44.2 percent described their primary theoretical orientation as eclectic (Wogan & Norcross, 1983). Integrated and eclectic models that have been developed include Lazarus's multimodal therapy (Lazarus, 1989), systematic eclectic psychotherapy (Beutler & Consoli, 1993), developmental counseling and therapy (Ivey & Rigazio-Digilio, 1991), actualizing therapy (Brammer, Shostrom, & Abrego, 1989), and adaptive counseling and therapy (Howard, Nance, & Myers, 1987). These are all promising, but their effectiveness is not yet well substantiated.

Other Research on the Effectiveness of Psychotherapeutic Approaches. Despite the shift toward eclecticism that occurred during the 1980s, research in the 1990s has continued to explore the appropriate use of specific approaches to psychotherapy, as well as ways of tailoring eclectic models to particular clients and disorders. There has been an increase in the use of manualized therapy, which provides clear and specific guidelines and interventions for particular disorders. In addition, many continue to question the value of eclecticism. As Beutler and Consoli (1993, p. 417), for example, write of the "Dodo Bird verdict" discussed earlier, "Unfortunately, this conclusion has been retained at the expense of a careful inspection of the clinically appealing possibility that there are subtypes of clients who, if disaggregated from pooled samples, may in fact respond with varying levels of benefit to different psychotherapists."

A study by Lyddon (1989) lends support to the concept of attending to clients' preferences and personal styles and to matching clients with clinical approaches. Lyddon looks at the relationship between people's dominant ways of knowing (rationalism, metaphorism, and empiricism) and their preferences for three counseling approaches (rationalist, constructivist, and behavioral). Each of the three groups preferred an approach that matched its own way of knowing: the rationalist thinkers preferred Ellis's rational-emotive therapy (Ellis & Greiger, 1986), those with a metaphoric viewpoint preferred the constructivist model of counseling, and the empirical thinkers preferred behavioral counseling. In addition, matching clients with approaches seems to lead both clients and counselors to rate each other more favorably, as well as leading to greater interpersonal attraction and to more effective treatments.

Another study with intriguing implications was conducted by Luborsky et al. (1985). They studied nine therapists who were treating 110 male veterans on methadone maintenance because of drug misuse. Three of the therapists provided supportive-expressive (SE) counseling with medication. Three provided cognitive-behavioral (CB) psychotherapy with medication. Three provided only drug counseling (DC). Although all the client groups improved, large differences were found among the outcomes. Overall, the SE treatment was more effective than the CB treatment, which was more effective than the DC treatment. The addition of medication to therapy, as well as the establishment of a positive therapeutic relationship, seemed to increase the likelihood of a positive outcome.

One of the most interesting findings of this study is the observation that purity of technique (close adherence to prescribed techniques as presented in a manual) is significantly correlated with outcome. This finding seems to conflict with the recommendation of Smith et al. (1980), who advocate pluralism in therapy, and with the tendency of most therapists to identify themselves as eclectic practitioners (Howard et al., 1987). A question not answered by Luborsky and his colleagues (1985) is whether the use of a relatively pure model of therapy promotes a positive outcome or whether therapy that is already moving in a positive direction facilitates the application of a pure model because the therapist does not need to innovate or experiment in order to effect progress.

Frances et al. (1984) see advantages as well as disadvantages in integrated treatment. The advantages they cite include the synergism in some treatment combinations, the ability to focus different interventions on different target symptoms, the dilution of the transference via a team approach, and the inducing of changes in different areas at different rates of speed, with progress in one area optimally paving the way for progress in another. The disadvantages they observe in the eclectic model include the possibility of negative interactions among therapies, conflict or lack of clear direction or responsibility (especially if more than one therapist is involved), higher costs, the possibility of increased dependence on the part of clients or of an exaggeration of the client's perception of a disorder's severity, confusion about what is really helping the client, and the risk of detracting from a holistic picture of the client.

A growing number of studies, to be discussed in later chapters with reference to specific disorders, assess the effectiveness of therapies across orientations. Although some studies focus on only one or two approaches, they also provide useful information on the effectiveness of the various psychotherapies. In general, the desirable psychotherapeutic approaches for a particular client or disorder are those that demonstrate a high likelihood of addressing relevant problems, of maximizing the client's motivation, of helping the therapist and the client achieve the treatment goals, of overcoming obstacles, of consolidating gains, and of reducing the likelihood of a relapse (Beutler & Consoli, 1993).

Psychoanalysis. Few studies are available on the effectiveness of psychoanalysis, partly because the lengthy and intense nature of the process means that each analyst can treat only a small number of clients. Nevertheless, one of the most thorough studies of psychotherapeutic effectiveness does focus on clients treated with psychoanalysis.

The Psychotherapy Research Project (PRP) of the Menninger Foundation collected data for thirty years (1954–1984) on a cohort of forty-two former patients
(Wallerstein, 1986) whose primary diagnoses had been "severe symptom neuroses, severe character neuroses, impulse neuroses (alcohol, addictive, sexual),
narcissistic and borderline personality disorders" (p. 91). Most also had anxiety and/or depression, uncontrolled aggression, sexual difficulties, somatic
symptoms, and marital problems. Twenty-three had been hospitalized at some
time, generally for problems of substance use. Half of the forty-two patients had
been treated with psychoanalysis and half with "equally long-term expressive
and supportive psychoanalytic psychotherapies" (p. vii), approaches that have
a more limited focus than psychoanalysis and that do not seek to evoke a full
transference. Length of treatment for the group in psychoanalysis had ranged
from seven months to ten years, with an average of five and two-thirds years
and 1,017 hours in treatment (five sessions per week). The group assigned to
other forms of psychotherapy averaged four and one-third years and 316 hours
in treatment (one to three sessions per week).

In general, those who had been selected for psychoanalysis were initially
functioning at a higher level, although outcomes were very similar for both
groups, with 63 percent of the psychoanalysis group and 58 percent of the other
group having good or moderate outcomes. Those diagnosed as having hysteric
or phobic disorders generally improved, whereas those diagnosed as paranoid,
borderline, or obese were unlikely to have improved. Adolescent and female patients typically improved, whereas patients who were themselves employed in
the helping professions were often resistant to treatment and generally did not
show good improvement. A high percentage of those with good results had
what Wallerstein (1986) termed "transference cures," whereby clients were
strongly motivated to change by their wishes to please their therapists. The education and information that were provided during treatment seemed to be important positive ingredients, even though they were not usually viewed as major
components of intensive psychotherapy. The former patients' ability to engage
in successful conflict resolution was also associated with improvement, but insight did not seem to be necessary in order for positive change to occur. Improvement typically had continued at follow-up, and regression was noted in
fewer than one-quarter of the clients (primarily those who had not had good
initial outcomes).

Since the time of the Menninger study, therapists have generally been moving away from prolonged psychoanalysis and other treatments of long duration,
and toward the development of briefer psychotherapies. Nevertheless, the Menninger study provides a useful basis of comparison. It also furnishes some support for the principles and procedures of psychoanalysis, as well as some
information on the sort of client (typically a young client with a nonpsychotic
disorder of moderate severity) who responds best to this treatment approach.
Also useful, if perhaps discouraging, is the realization that in some cases even

the most intensive treatments fail to work: approximately 40 percent of the clients in the Menninger study showed little or no improvement.

Psychodynamic Psychotherapy. In recent years, as the use of long-term psychodynamic approaches has declined, briefer psychodynamic psychotherapy has gained in popularity. The psychodynamic approach to treatment borrows heavily from the psychoanalytic model, but treatment under this approach takes less time, is more directive, and focuses more on specific problems. According to Frances et al. (1984), the psychodynamic approach is best suited to people who are suffering from intrapsychic conflicts and are seeking personality change in at least one area. The ideal clients for this approach are motivated, straightforward, willing to make a commitment to therapy, psychologically minded, able to tolerate and discuss painful feelings, intelligent, verbal, and in possession of relatively high ego strength. They are motivated toward insight, have a history of shared and meaningful relationships, are able to benefit from interpretation, and have a significant focal concern. In addition, they have no urgent concerns and are unlikely to regress or become psychologically disabled.

Crits-Christoph (1992) conducted a meta-analysis of eleven studies of short-term dynamic psychotherapy, at least twelve sessions in length. People treated with brief psychodynamic psychotherapy showed large effect sizes relative to people with similar disorders who were on waiting lists for treatment. Moreover, for a wide range of disorders, brief psychodynamic psychotherapy was equally effective as treatment via other psychotherapies and medication.

Typical outcomes of brief dynamic therapy include symptom relief, improved relationships, better self-esteem, greater insight and self-awareness, better problem-solving ability, and a sense of accomplishment (Budman, 1981). The approach seems to provide a corrective emotional experience for people who are not severely dysfunctional but who may be suffering from Depressive Disorders, Anxiety Disorders (especially Posttraumatic Stress Disorder), Adjustment Disorder, stress, bereavement, and mild to moderate Personality Disorders (Goldfried, Greenberg, & Marmar, 1990). This approach is not recommended for treatment of severe depression that seems to have a biochemical basis, for Schizophrenia, for long-term substance misuse, and for Borderline or other severe Personality Disorders.

Behavior Therapy. Wilson (1981) views behavior therapy as capable of effecting improvement in overall psychological functioning as well as in target symptoms. No studies have shown that symptom substitution—that is, the shifting of the focus of a problem from one symptom to another—takes place after successful behavior therapy. On the contrary, studies have yielded evidence of spontaneous improvement in untreated symptoms after successful behavior therapy that has focused on one symptom.

Many studies over the last twenty years have substantiated the value of behavior therapy. For example, Wilson (1981) has found that people with Phobias show considerable improvement after no more than about six sessions of participant modeling or of graduated, in vivo exposure to the feared object. Seligman (1995) reports that exposure is helpful in relieving symptoms of Obsessive-Compulsive Disorder and that systematic desensitization relieves symptoms of Specific Phobias. Flooding, along with medication, has been shown to effect significant improvement in Agoraphobia.

Goldfried et al. (1990) conclude that behavior therapy is effective in the treatment of stress, depression, suicidal behavior, Conduct Disorders, Mental Retardation, Substance-Related Disorders, and family conflicts, as well as in relapse prevention. Other disorders, including Impulse-Control Disorders, Sexual Dysfunctions, Paraphilias, some Sleep Disorders, and Anxiety Disorders, are also likely to respond well to behavioral therapy. The people most likely to benefit from behavior therapy are motivated to change, follow through on homework assignments or self-help programs, and have friends and family members who are supportive of their efforts to change. Clients who are action-oriented seem to respond particularly well to behavior therapy (Lambert, 1982, p. 33). Clearly, the literature contains many positive reports of behavior therapy's effectiveness.

Nevertheless, assessment of this treatment approach's effectiveness is complicated by its many techniques and variations. For example, duration of treatment and specific techniques are critical variables in determinations of how effective behavior therapy is. For example, one two-hour session of in vivo exposure seems to be more effective than four half-hour sessions, and flooding can actually increase anxiety if it is not maintained long enough for the anxiety reaction to subside. Moreover, in the treatment of Phobias, Obsessive-Compulsive Disorder, and Sexual Disorders, performance-based in vivo exposure methods are more likely to be more effective than methods employing imaginal symbolic procedures. It seems clear that support is better than confrontation in promoting clients' adherence to treatment plans in behavior therapy, but more research will be needed before it can be determined exactly how this powerful treatment approach can best be used.

Cognitive Therapy. Cognitive therapy, developed by Beck and his colleagues (Beck, Rush, Shaw, & Emery, 1979) and by Ellis (Ellis & Greiger, 1986), is used primarily for the treatment of Adjustment Disorder, Anxiety Disorders, and Depressive Disorders, although in recent years its use has expanded to include Personality Disorders and other kinds of disorders. Cognitive therapy assumes that people's thoughts are a dynamic representation of how they view themselves, their world, their past, and their future (in other words, their phenomenal field). Cognitive structures are viewed as the major determinants of people's affective states and behavioral patterns. Through cognitive therapy, people are helped to become aware of their cognitive distortions and to correct their dysfunctional automatic thoughts and schemas, a correction that leads to clinical improvement. The focus of the treatment is on the present, and homework assignments are important. Cognitive therapy is often combined with behavior therapy, with the earlier rivalry between these two approaches having apparently evolved into mutual appreciation and recognition of the value of their integration.

Beck et al. (1979) reviewed eight studies of the effectiveness of cognitive therapy and found cognitive and cognitive-behavioral therapy superior both to no treatment at all and to other approaches to treating depression at every level of severity. Nevertheless, Beck and his colleagues also conclude that cognitive therapy is not indicated in the presence of a family history of Bipolar Disorder or if there is a coexisting diagnosis of Schizophrenia, Cognitive Disorder, or Mental Retardation. Seligman (1995) finds cognitive therapy effective and better than medication as a treatment for Bulimia Nervosa. Johnson et al. (1994) conclude that rational-emotive therapy, Ellis's cognitively based approach, is successful in reducing depression, automatic negative thinking, irrational thinking, and general pathology in people with mild to moderate unipolar depression. Hayes, Castonguay, and Goldfried (1996) have found that cognitive therapy that addresses interpersonal and developmental domains as well as thinking patterns is associated with more improvement, a longer time without relapse, and better overall functioning than is a purely cognitive approach.

Other Approaches to Psychotherapy. Although most of the empirical research on psychotherapy's effectiveness has focused on the psychodynamic, behavioral, and cognitive approaches, other approaches may also be effective, especially when they are thoughtfully integrated into these three. Logic, as well as the limited research available on other models, suggests the following recommendations:

1. Supportive, humanistic, and person-centered models are useful with well-functioning people who are interested in personal growth and development and who have relatively minor concerns. These approaches can also help consolidate gains and promote adjustment and self-esteem in people whose primary treatment is medication.

2. Adlerian approaches, which have recently grown in popularity, are particularly useful in treating behavioral disorders of children, family and other interpersonal conflicts, mild depression and anxiety, and concerns focused on goals and direction.

3. Gestalt therapy, another model geared primarily to people who are relatively well-functioning, features empty-chair and two-chair dialogue techniques that can be useful in helping people resolve conflicts (Goldfried et al., 1990). This approach also seems likely to help people who channel their concerns into somatic symptoms, as well as people who are experiencing mild depression and anxiety.

4. Existential psychotherapy, yet another of the approaches best suited to relatively well-functioning people with mild depression, mild anxiety, or situational concerns that raise questions about the meaning and direction of their lives, is often useful for people coping with life-threatening illnesses.

No Treatment. Despite the demonstrated effectiveness of therapy, 30 to 40 percent of people who receive psychotherapy do not show clear benefits from that process. Little research is available on the iatrogenic or negative effects of psychotherapy, but Frances et al. (1984) offer some guidelines for determining when no treatment may be the best recommendation. They suggest that the "no treatment" option be considered for the following groups of people:

1. People at risk for a negative response to treatment (for example, people with severe narcissistic, borderline, masochistic, or oppositional personality patterns and a history of treatment failures, as well as people who want to support a lawsuit or a disability claim and thus may have an investment in failing to make progress)

2. People at risk for no response (for example, people who are poorly motivated and not incapacitated, people with Malingering or Factitious Disorder, and those who seem likely to become infantilized by the therapeutic process)

3. People likely to show spontaneous improvement (for example, healthy people in crisis or with minor concerns)

4. People likely to benefit from strategic use of the "no treatment" recommendation (for example, people with oppositional patterns who are refusing treatment, and people whose adaptive defenses would be supported by a recommendation of no treatment)

The "no treatment" recommendation is intended to protect clients from harm, prevent clients and therapists from wasting their time, delay therapy until clients are more receptive to it, support prior gains, and give people the message that they can survive without therapy. Although this option may make theoretical sense, clinicians do not seem to use it with any frequency, at least partly because of the great difficulty of predicting who will *not* benefit from therapy and the risk involved in discouraging a person from beginning therapy when he or she may really be able to make good use of it. Nevertheless, therapists may want to give more consideration to this recommendation, especially in light of the current emphasis on short-term productive treatment.

Current State of the Art. Perry et al. (1985) encourage clinicians to continue their efforts to determine the most effective treatment approaches by reviewing the literature on particular disorders and by generalizing from available studies and cases. They conclude, "It is sad but true that it will be a long time before treatment selection in psychiatry will have a solid foundation" (p. 361). Progress has been made in the past fifteen years, but the prediction made by Perry and his colleagues seems on target: differential therapeutics has grown from infancy to adolescence, but considerable research is still needed in this area.

Some of the reasons for the lack of clarity with respect to treatment recommendations are obvious. The challenges of conducting research on something as ill defined and variable as psychotherapy, without also jeopardizing people's right to the best possible treatment, are enormous. In addition, as discussed earlier, the various therapies have many underlying similarities, and perhaps these are more important than their overt differences, tending to blur distinctions and thereby leading to inconclusive research. Moreover, as we shall see, client- and therapist-related variables seem to be at least as important as those variables involved in the particular approach to therapy. In the foreseeable future, research can be expected to go on examining the many approaches to psychotherapy, as well as client- and therapist-related variables and their interaction, and the field can be expected to continue evolving.

Emphasis

The multitude of approaches to psychotherapy reflects only one aspect of the diversity that exists in treatment interventions. Variation in the implementation of therapies also greatly increases the diversity of approaches. Clinicians adapt models of psychotherapy to their own personal styles and individualize treatments to meet the needs of particular clients. Therefore, the application of an approach to psychotherapy differs from one therapeutic relationship to another. Beutler (1991) catalogues as treatment variables the following potentially important dimensions of psychotherapy (p. 227):

- Insight-oriented versus action-oriented
- Directive (therapist-guided) versus evocative (therapist-stimulated)
- Systemic versus person-centered
- Supportive versus insight-oriented
- Group versus individual
- Multidimensional versus unidimensional
- Short-term versus long-term
- Open-ended versus closed-ended
- Growth-oriented versus symptom-oriented
- Planned versus spontaneous
- Entailing homework versus not entailing homework

In psychotherapy, the nature of some of these variables will be determined by the theoretical framework that is chosen; the nature of others must be determined by the individual therapist.

Directiveness Versus Evocativeness. Beutler and Consoli (1993) describe therapeutic interventions as either directive or evocative. Little research has been conducted on this variable, which exists on a continuum extending from humanistic, experiential, and person-centered models of therapy to structured and directive models of the behavioral and cognitive therapy. Nevertheless, clinicians have drawn tentative conclusions regarding when it is appropriate for therapists to be directive and when it is appropriate for clients to be encouraged to structure and guide sessions. The following list describes this continuum and suggests its appropriate application:

Directive	*Evocative*
Therapist-directed	Client-directed
Structured	Amount of structure varies and depends on client
Goals: change in maladaptive behavior; symptom reduction; environmental change; development of new skills; problem solving; building of confidence in therapy	Goals: development of self-awareness; reduced identity confusion; increased sense of direction; promotion of independence; building of self-confidence
Recommended for clients who are willing to take direction from others or unable to establish own direction; motivated primarily to achieve specific limited goals; severely disturbed, dysfunctional, fragile; in crisis or experiencing pressing problems; having difficulty setting boundaries, especially in therapy	Recommended for clients who are capable of establishing own direction; guided by broad, far-reaching goals; functioning acceptably but not up to potential; not in crisis; able to establish limits and appropriate interpersonal boundaries, in and out of therapy

Perry et al. (1985) view the directive approach as encompassing such techniques as systematic desensitization; flooding; positive reinforcement, including token economies, contingency contracting, and extinction; strategic techniques, such as suggestion, paradox and metaphor; humor; homework assignments; and cognitive techniques. In all these approaches the therapist assumes an authoritative stance, clearly defines target concerns, and designs a specific program to change overt and covert symptoms.

The evocative, experiential, or person-centered model, by contrast, avoids what some view as manipulation of clients by focusing on the therapist-client interaction and allowing the client to guide the therapeutic process. That approach emphasizes catharsis and abreaction; ventilation; empathy and reflection of feeling; support; affection; praise; and unconditional positive regard.

There are also approaches that fall in the middle of the directive/evocative continuum. Psychoanalysis, for example, is characterized by a therapist who is clearly an authority figure, but such psychoanalytic techniques as free association are evocative or experiential.

Anne and Bettie have similar presenting problems. Each is a woman in her early twenties who has sought counseling after a broken engagement, but their circumstances and their views of therapy are very different and warrant different levels of directiveness.

Anne is in her second month of an unplanned pregnancy. She is receiving little help from her family or from her former fiancé. She is unemployed and is living with a single friend who has two children. Anne is not sure what she wants to do about her pregnancy and has been using alcohol as a way to avoid thinking about her difficulties. She has not had previous therapy and is uncertain of why the nurse with whom she spoke at an abortion clinic has referred her to a counselor, although she is motivated to get some help.

Bettie's situation is quite different. Although she too is depressed that her former fiancé ended their engagement, she views this as a time to review her goals. She believes that she focused too much of her time and energy on her fiancé and has neglected her career and her education. She is interested in returning to college, learning more about some of her aptitudes and preferences, and establishing a better balance between her social life and her career. At the same time, she is angry that she feels a need for therapy, and her disappointment in her former fiancé has led her to feel mistrustful of others.

Anne does not have the leisure or the sense of direction for an evocative approach. She needs a directive therapist, not to tell her what to do about her pregnancy, but to give her a structure for expediting her decision making and helping her gain some control of her life. Bettie, by contrast, would be more amenable to experiential or person-centered therapy, which would afford her the opportunity to engage in self-examination and goal setting.

In general, a directive approach has been correlated with goal attainment (Green & Herget, 1991), whereas an evocative approach seems most likely to be successful with people who are self-directed and perhaps also somewhat resistant to help (Beutler & Consoli, 1993).

Exploration Versus Support. This is another dimension that has received little but theoretical examination in the literature. Nevertheless, it is often cited as an important aspect of treatment (Frances et al., 1984; Horowitz, Marmar, Weiss, De Witt, & Rosenbaum, 1984; Wallerstein, 1986).

The dimension of exploration versus support, like the dimension of directiveness versus evocativeness, also exists on a continuum. Approaches that emphasize exploration typically are probing, interpretive, and analytic, stressing the importance of insight, growth, and an understanding of past influences and patterns. By contrast, approaches that emphasize support tend to be present-oriented, symptom-focused, and more action-oriented. Psychoanalysis and psychodynamic psychotherapy, using such techniques as free association, analysis of transference, examination of dreams, and interpretation, emphasize exploration. The other end of the continuum is represented by the behavioral model, with its focus on the present, on circumscribed and measurable changes, and on reinforcement of positive coping mechanisms. Models at each end of the continuum, of course, as well as those in the middle, inevitably include both exploration and support. They are distinguished by the balance between exploration and support rather than by the absence of one or the other. The person-centered model, for example, has both exploratory and supportive elements.

One of the few studies of this dimension of therapy is the one by Wallerstein (1986), who concludes that insight is not always necessary for change. In 45 percent of the cases he examined, changes that were achieved seemed to go beyond the amount of insight that was attained, whereas insight surpassed discerned change in only 7 percent of these cases. Overall, Wallerstein concludes, supportive therapy was more effective in these cases than had been expected, and it did not seem to be less effective than exploratory therapy.

Other research on this dimension has been contradictory, perhaps because the variables were not clearly and similarly defined. For example, Allen, Coyne, Colson, and Horwitz (1996) have found that therapists using high levels of interpretation and clarification were more successful at establishing collaborative therapeutic relationships than therapists who emphasized advice and praise. By contrast, Svartberg and Stiles (1994) have found that support is a key element of establishing a positive therapeutic alliance and that transference interpretations correlate negatively with outcome.

The following list organizes information on this continuum:

Exploration	*Support*
Seeks to eliminate barriers to growth	Builds on existing defenses, coping skills, and strengths
Focuses on the past as well as on the present, seeking patterns	Focuses on the present
Provides challenge and stimulus for change, in an accepting context	Provides acceptance, protection, reassurance, empathy
Encourages client's interpretations, insight	Encourages client's understanding, information gathering
Goals: growth and development; increased understanding of intrapsychic conflict; development of new resources	Goals: symptom reduction; improved functioning; increased self-acceptance; strengthening of existing resources
Recommended for clients who are not in crisis and have some sound coping skills; are highly motivated, well organized, reasonably healthy, in contact with reality; are insightful,	Recommended for clients who are in crisis and are functioning poorly; are resistant, fragile, highly dysfunctional, in poor contact with reality; are action-oriented; are

psychologically minded, verbal; are internally controlled and like to see change as a result of their own efforts	externally controlled and see change as other-directed

Bettie and Anne, the clients discussed earlier, need different levels of exploration. Bettie, a strong client who is interested in personal growth and introspection, is a good candidate for an approach that is at least moderately probing in nature, such as psychodynamic therapy. Anne, by contrast, needs a more supportive approach that will help to reduce the stress she is experiencing and enable her to draw on her existing strengths to cope with her situation.

Although most therapists probably make intuitive judgments of whether their clients will benefit from high or low levels of exploration, more research on this dimension would also facilitate effective treatment planning.

Numbers

Where the literature comparing individual, group, and family psychotherapy is concerned, research is once again limited. Smith et al. (1980) found no significant differences in the impacts of these modalities. Another study, by Pilkonis, Imber, Lewis, and Rubinsky (1984), randomly assigned sixty-four outpatients to individual, group, or conjoint therapy with experienced clinicians. The clients' diagnoses included Mood, Anxiety, Adjustment, and Personality Disorders. They were seen for an average of 26.8 therapy sessions. All the modalities of treatment focused on helping the outpatients develop cognitive or affective insight. The sample as a whole demonstrated significant improvement in symptoms, target complaints, self-awareness, and interpersonal and family functioning. That improvement was maintained at follow-up after thirty-one weeks, but the study yielded no clear evidence of any one treatment modality's superiority; any differences seemed to be due more to the therapist, the client, and the nature of the client-therapist match than to the modality of treatment. Nevertheless, individual therapy seemed to have been most successful in increasing self-awareness in clients from lower socioeconomic groups, whereas group and family counseling were better at lessening interpersonal problems in the more chronically ill clients.

Individual Psychotherapy. Individual psychotherapy certainly has demonstrated its effectiveness. Clarkin, Frances, and Perry (1992) recommend individual therapy as the modality of choice for people whose intrapsychic difficulties cause them repetitive life problems, for people in crisis or those with urgent concerns, for people with problems that might cause them distress or embarrassment in a group setting, and for people who are vulnerable, passive, and low in self-esteem. Although individual therapy is generally a safe choice, it does have certain limitations. It does not offer the client the opportunity to receive feedback from anyone but the therapist, it gives the therapist only one source of information about the client, it encourages transference reactions, and it offers only a limited opportunity to try out new interpersonal behaviors in therapy sessions.

Group Psychotherapy. Efforts have been made to determine what makes group therapy effective and to compare the impact of group and individual therapy. Bloch, Crouch, and Reibstein (1981), reviewing the literature on group psychotherapy published between 1955 and 1979, sought to discover the therapeutic factors and processes contributing to clients' improvement. The research on self-disclosure, insight, catharsis, interaction, and acceptance/cohesiveness all yielded ambiguous results. Perhaps both the nature of the group and the client- and therapist-related variables are so powerful in determining outcome that few conclusions can be drawn about group therapy in general.

Group therapy does, however, seem to be effective from both the cost and outcome standpoints. In general, studies find its impact to be comparable to that of individual therapy. Fenster (1993) suggests that group psychotherapy usually should be the treatment of choice for interpersonal problems, including loneliness, competitiveness, shyness, aggressiveness, and withdrawal, as well as for people who have problems with intimacy and authority. Group therapy offers an environment more like everyday life and therefore provides an arena for interaction and learning from others. Group therapy can promote self-esteem, reduce resistance, and diffuse feelings of differentness and shame.

In deciding whether a particular person is likely to benefit from group psychotherapy, the therapist needs to consider not only the impact of the group on the client but also the impact of the client on the group. Ideal clients for group therapy seem to be those who are motivated, aware of their interpersonal difficulties, able to take responsibility for their concerns, and able to give and accept feedback. People who are extremely aggressive, confused, self-centered, or fearful of others may have a harmful impact on group interaction and are unlikely to derive much benefit from that process. If group therapy is used at all with clients like these, it probably should be deferred until they have made noticeable progress in individual or family psychotherapy.

Therapy groups may be either heterogeneous (composed of individuals with different problems) or homogeneous (composed of individuals with similar problems). Homogeneous groups seem particularly effective with such concerns as Impulse-Control Disorders, Substance-Related Disorders, Conduct Disorders, most Personality Disorders, Eating Disorders, Posttraumatic Stress Disorder, Pain and other Somatoform Disorders, chronic mental illness, Bipolar Disorders, Mental Retardation, and Phobias. People with these disorders and problems can learn coping skills from each other, benefit from feedback and modeling, and receive support and validation.

Family Therapy. Research has demonstrated that couples therapy and family therapy are effective in general and may be superior to alternative treatment modalities for some problems and disorders (Pinsof, Wynne, & Hambright, 1996). Nevertheless, the research has not yet fully clarified which disorders and clients are most likely to benefit from family therapy.

Family therapy has both strengths and limitations. It can promote improved family dynamics and interaction, allow the therapist a clearer picture of the clients and their environment, and reduce both resistance and the stigmatizing of the identified patient. At the same time, family therapy can also become a stressful and derogatory experience, may not succeed in effecting intrapsychic change, may increase fear and guilt, and may lead to less openness and more withholding than individual therapy does. Family therapy, of course, is often indicated for problems that stem from, are affected by, or have an impact on the family system. Children and adolescents seen for therapy will usually have family therapy as a component of their treatment. Clients with disorders like Schizophrenia and Major Depressive Disorder, in which there is a correlation between the likelihood of relapse and the family environment, typically benefit from family therapy. People with Substance-Related Disorders, Bipolar Disorders, and Obsessive-Compulsive Disorder that seem to have a genetic or familial component are also likely to benefit from family therapy.

Research continues on the appropriate uses of these treatment modalities, but most of the information in the literature about the respective strengths and benefits of the three primary modalities of therapy—individual, group, and family—is inferential. The following list summarizes this information, showing the client groups for which each of the modalities is recommended:

Individual Counseling	*Group Therapy*	*Family Therapy*
Highly anxious, withdrawn, isolated, or introverted clients; people who have difficulty with ambiguity; people seeking help with intrapsychic concerns; extremely suspicious, guarded, hostile, paranoid, or destructive clients who have difficulty with trust; people seeking independence and individualization; those with very inti-	Anxious clients with authority concerns; people with pervasive personality dysfunction who have made progress in individual therapy; people with interpersonal concerns; people who may feel stigmatized or scapegoated as a result of individual therapy (such as the identified patient in a family); people who are likely	Clients who have problems with family structure; people with intergenerational or other family conflicts; families with communication problems; families needing consolidation; acting-out adolescents; families with limited resources, when more than one family member needs help; families with no severe pathology;

mate or idiosyncratic concerns; those with concerns of very long duration in which improvement rather than maintenance is sought; people in crisis

to give the therapist excessive power; people who need reality testing and group feedback; those with specific behavioral concerns (such as Eating Disorders or Alcohol Dependence) that are shared with other group members; people with limited financial resources; people who have been through traumatic experiences

children; families with a member who has a chronic or recurrent mental disorder

Timing

In addition to determining the degree of directiveness and exploration, the modality of counseling, and the therapeutic approaches and techniques that will be used, the clinician must also decide how frequently to schedule a client's appointments, how long each session should be, and approximately how long a particular client will need to be in treatment. The typical client is seen once a week for a session of forty-five to fifty minutes in length, but the frequency of therapy sessions can vary. One session every other week is often used in supportive therapy, particularly toward the end of treatment, whereas clients in psychoanalysis commonly have five sessions per week. The duration of therapy varies widely, of course, and is often difficult to predict.

The available research offers some help in making decisions about frequency and duration, and many studies compare long-term treatment with short-term treatment for a broad range of disorders. Orlinsky and Howard (1986), for example, conducted meta-analyses of studies that looked at the relationship between length of therapy and therapeutic outcome. They conclude that total number of sessions—and, to a lesser extent, duration of treatment—are positively correlated with therapeutic benefit. Not all studies show the same relationship, however, and a small number show a curvilinear relationship between outcome and number of sessions. Nevertheless, Seligman's (1995) large-scale naturalistic study found that people who had received more than six months of psychotherapy showed more improvement in work, relationships, enjoyment of life, and personal growth than those who had received less treatment. He concludes that "long-term treatment did considerably better than short-term treatment" (p. 965).

In the research of Smith et al. (1980), involving meta-analysis of 475 studies on the effect of psychotherapy, clients were seen for an average of 17.8 sessions, with the number of sessions ranging from one to one hundred. These researchers found no clear relationship between treatment duration and improvement. A reanalysis of the Smith et al. data by Andrews and Harvey (1981) did yield an average effect size of 0.68 for brief therapy (zero to nine hours), 0.73 for short therapy (ten to nineteen hours), and 0.86 for longer therapy (twenty to one hundred hours), but the differences among these figures were not significant. The Smith et al. meta-analysis found clients to have made the greatest progress during the first seven sessions and between the nineteenth and twenty-fifth sessions.

A meta-analysis by Bloom (1981) found that single-session episodes of care were quite common, especially among clients from lower socioeconomic groups. In general, 30 to 35 percent of clients seen at family counseling agencies, 25 to 30 percent of clients seen at community mental health centers, and 15 percent of clients seen at university-based mental health centers received only one counseling session, sometimes because of the therapist's recommendation and sometimes because of what may be perceived as premature termination on the client's part. Nevertheless, one study included in Bloom's meta-analysis found that two-thirds of clients who had received only one therapy session felt that they had been helped. Bloom concludes that "a single contact, virtually regardless of the nature of that contact, appears to have salutary consequences" (p. 179). In fact, Howard, Kopta, Krause, and Orlinsky (1986) found that 10 to 18 percent of clients improved before the first session just by virtue of having made contact with a potential source of help. These researchers also found that, overall, approximately 50 percent of clients showed measurable improvement after eight sessions of therapy, 75 percent after twenty-six sessions, and 85 percent after one year of treatment.

A study by Kadera, Lambert, and Andrews (1996), however, yielded less optimistic results. At the end of this study, 33 percent of the participants had recovered, 25 percent had improved, 37 percent were unchanged, and 5 percent had deteriorated. These researchers found that the average time for recovery was eleven sessions (with 76 percent of those who would recover doing do by the thirteenth session), and that all who were going to recover had done so by the twenty-fifth session.

These studies are informative but incomplete: typically, short-term therapy is not just less long-term therapy; the goals, the treatment interventions, the disorders, and the clients themselves are likely to differ. Therefore, research of this kind must at least consider the presenting disorders and concerns when the research question is one of determining outcomes on the basis of therapy's duration.

Current research on the duration of psychotherapy usually presents findings in terms of the therapy dose, with an effective dose (ED) expressed as a percentage of clients whose symptoms were significantly improved after a given number of sessions. Kopta, Howard, Lowry, and Beutler (1994), for example, studied the effective dose in eight hundred clients who had acute distress, chronic distress, and characterological symptoms and who had received unlimited counseling. These researchers found that for acute anxiety and distress, ED50—the point at which 50 percent had received an effective enough dose to show significant improvement—was five sessions, and that 68 to 95 percent had shown significant improvement after fifty-two sessions. For clients experiencing anxiety, phobias, depression, interpersonal sensitivity, or chronic distress, ED50 was fourteen sessions, with 60 to 86 percent showing improvement after fifty-two sessions. For those with characterological symptoms, ED50 was more than eighteen sessions, with 59 percent showing improvement after fifty-two sessions. Most of those with Paranoid, Schizoid, Schizotypal, or Borderline Personality Disorders had not evidenced significant improvement within fifty-two sessions.

Short-Term Therapy. Today's emphasis on short-term therapy has increased the importance of studying the approaches to brief treatment and determining the clients for whom they are suitable. Many studies (Foa, Hearst-Ikeda, & Perry, 1995; Piper, Azim, McCallum, & Joyce, 1990; Piper, Debbane, Bienvenu, & Garant, 1984) have demonstrated that short-term treatment can have a significant and lasting positive impact, but that is only the case for some clients and some disorders.

Frances et al. (1984) suggest that the following circumstances serve to increase the duration of therapy, whereas their converse will tend to shorten therapy:

- The presence of a chronic disorder
- The client's poor functioning before the onset of the presenting concerns
- Ambitious or unclear treatment goals
- Motivation for an enduring therapeutic relationship
- The client's expectation that change will be a lengthy process
- The therapist's expectation that there will be many target symptoms
- The absence of an acute precipitant
- Extensive economic resources
- A therapist whose geographical location is convenient for the client
- A client between the ages of twenty-five and fifty
- Emphasis on an exploratory and/or psychoanalytic approach to therapy
- A maintenance (rather than reparative) setting
- A heterogeneous group as the treatment modality

Other researchers' findings are generally compatible with these. Littrell, Malia, and Vanderwood (1995), for example, view short-term cognitive therapy as appropriate when problems are related to stress, dysfunctional behaviors, academic problems, interpersonal difficulties, and career concerns. Luborsky et al. (1996) recommend brief psychodynamic psychotherapy for both chronic and nonchronic depression. Talley (1992) emphasizes the importance of clients for short-term treatment being mentally and emotionally accessible to the therapist and being able to engage easily in a therapeutic alliance. Hoglend et al. (1993) view people who have had a pretreatment history of mutually satisfying, caring, sharing, and intimate relationships as suitable candidates for short-term therapy. People who are motivated, who do not have characterological problems, and who have a focal concern or crisis, a positive history, good ego functioning, and a sound ability to relate well to others and express their emotions typically make good clients for short-term therapy.

People for whom short-term therapy usually is not indicated are those who are very hostile, paranoid, or psychotic or who have long-standing, severe problems. Eating Disorders, Bipolar Disorders, Dysthymic Disorder, Borderline Personality Disorder, and Antisocial Personality Disorder are examples of disorders that generally do not respond well to short-term therapy.

In general, short-term therapy seems likely to be effective with a substantial percentage of clients (approximately 75 percent); in fact, time-limited treatment can encourage people to be more focused and make more rapid progress (Lambert & Cattani-Thompson, 1996). Again, however, candidates for this approach to treatment must be carefully selected.

Frequency and Length of Sessions. Research on the frequency and length of sessions is rather sparse. Frances et al. (1984) reviewed a group of studies on this topic and found that most yielded little significant information. At least one study, however, did find that clients who were seen twice a week did less well than clients who were seen once a week, partly because the more severely disturbed clients had difficulty handling the intensity of the twice-a-week relationship. Lambert et al. (1986) recommend monthly sessions as "booster shots" to maintain progress. Research does not support the superiority of the fifty-minute hour, and variations on that standard seem to be increasing, with sessions of twenty to thirty minutes being used to monitor progress and provide support, and with sessions of several hours' duration being used for family counseling and to curtail clients' avoidance of difficult issues.

The literature on the duration and frequency of treatment is contradictory and often methodologically flawed (for example, by the failure to control for severity of disturbance). In general, however, most studies do not indicate that longer treatment has a clear advantage over briefer therapy. In light of the added cost (in terms of money, time, and emotional investment) entailed by longer treatment, the research suggests that brief therapy should be the treatment of choice for most clients. At the same time, no harm has been shown to come from longer treatment. In some cases, moreover, extended treatment and treatment with sessions more frequent than once a week have been found advantageous (Orlinsky & Howard, 1978).

Medications

This book, as already mentioned, is directed primarily toward nonmedical clinicians, who do not themselves prescribe medication as part of the treatment they provide. Nevertheless, nonmedical clinicians who understand the role that medication can play in the treatment of mental disorders will know when a client's progress can be accelerated by collaboration with a physician.

The research on the relative impacts of psychotherapy and medication is unclear. According to Goldfried et al. (1990), "Some comparisons of psychotherapy and drug treatment have suggested that combined treatment may present definite advantages over either treatment alone, . . . others have shown no differences between psychotherapy and psychotherapy plus medication at termination, . . . and still others have shown advantages at follow-up for patients who received cognitive-behavioral therapy" (p. 675). Seligman (1995), in his large-scale study, based on client self-reports, concludes that, in general, "psychotherapy alone did not differ in effectiveness from medication plus psychotherapy" (p. 965). Despite this overall finding, some studies see a definite advantage to combining psychotherapy with medication. For example, Luborsky et al. (1985) found that medication enhanced the effectiveness of the psychotherapy provided to clients in a methadone maintenance program; May, Tuma, and Dixon (1976) observed a similar outcome in their study of the treatment of hospitalized clients diagnosed with Schizophrenia.

Medication and psychotherapy often have different effects on a given mental disorder. Klerman, Dimascio, and Weissman (1974), in a study of the treatment of moderately depressed female outpatients, found that amitriptyline significantly reduced relapse rates but had no effect on social adjustment, whereas supportive psychotherapy did not prevent relapse, although it did improve social adjustment, work performance, and family communication, and it did reduce feelings of stress, resentment, and dissatisfaction. Karasu (1982) summarizes the differential effects of psychotherapy and medication as follows: drugs have a major impact on symptom formation and affective distress, whereas therapy improves interpersonal relations and social adjustment.

Kendall and Lipman (1991) have found clients generally more receptive to psychotherapy than to medication. They have also found that psychotherapy and medication have a synergistic relationship, especially in the treatment of Major Depressive Disorder: the medication acts first and, by energizing clients and promoting some optimism, enables them to make better use of psychotherapy; and the impact of the therapy in turn promotes compliance with the recommended drug treatment. According to these researchers, the drugs are particularly helpful in reducing the likelihood of relapse and in treating vegetative symptoms, and the psychotherapy aids with many facets of adjustment and coping. Although the effects of the therapy may take longer to appear than the effects of the medication, the effects of the therapy are likely to last longer. When the question is whether medication should be used, most clinicians seem to agree with Perry et al. (1985): "To increase compliance and to enhance the placebo effect, somatic treatments should always be provided within the context of a therapeutic relationship" (p. 363). Medication seems most useful for disorders involving debilitating anxiety, endogenous (melancholic) depression, mania, or psychosis; therapy seems more effective in treating problems involving adjustment, behavior, relationships, mild to moderate anxiety, reactive depression, and Personality Disorders. Many disorders in the second group, however (including Eating Disorders, some Personality Disorders, and Impulse-Control Disorders), are often accompanied by underlying depression. Medication is increasingly being used to relieve the underlying symptoms and enhance the impact of psychotherapy on the presenting problems and the principal diagnosis.

Psychotropic medications can be divided into the following groups (Seligman, 1996a):

1. *Antipsychotic medications.* These drugs are primarily for the treatment of Schizophrenia and other disorders involving delusions and hallucinations. People with Tourette's Disorder, Pervasive Developmental Disorder, and severe Cognitive Disorders also tend to benefit from the use of these drugs. This category includes the phenothiazines (such as Thorazine, Prolixin, Mellaril, and Stelazine), as well as such other antipsychotic drugs as clozaril (Clozapine), haloperidol (Haldol), and risperidone (Risperdal).

2. *Antidepressant medications.* These drugs fall into the following groups: (a) *Tricyclic and heterocyclic antidepressants* seem to facilitate the treatment of moderate to severe Major Depressive Disorder (especially with Melancholia), Enuresis, Trichotillomania, panic attacks, bipolar depression, and Eating, Sleep, and Obsessive-Compulsive Disorders. Examples of this type of drug include imipramine (Tofranil), clomipramine (Anafranil), and amitriptyline (Elavil). (b) *Monoamine oxidase inhibitors (MAOIs),* such as Nardil and Parnate, tend to be effective with atypical depressions, severe phobias, Anxiety Disorders, Panic Disorder, obsessional thinking, Hypochondriasis, and Depersonalization Disorder. They are also used to treat disorders that have not responded to other antidepressant medication. (c) *Selective serotonin reuptake inhibitors (SSRIs)* are newer than the preceding two groups of antidepressant medications and seem to be growing in use. These drugs are effective in the treatment of depression, as well as with such disorders as Eating and Somatoform Disorders that are accompanied by underlying

depression (Maxmen & Ward, 1995). This category includes fluoxetine (Prozac), sertraline (Zoloft), and paroxetine (Paxil). (d) *Bupropion* (Wellbutrin), *nefazodone* (Serzone), and *venlafaxine* (Effexor) are other, relatively new, antidepressant drugs.

3. *Lithium.* This drug is effective in reducing symptoms of mania, depression, and mood instability. It is used for treatment of Bipolar Disorders, Cyclothymic Disorder, and Schizoaffective Disorder.

4. *Benzodiazepine/antianxiety drugs.* These medications are used for reduction of anxiety, panic attacks, and insomnia. They also can facilitate withdrawal from drugs or alcohol and can enhance the impact of antipsychotic medication. Examples of these drugs are alprazolam (Xanax), lorazepam (Ativan), and diazepam (Valium).

5. *Other drugs.* Additional drugs helpful in the treatment of mental disorders include methylphenidate (Ritalin), for the treatment of Attention-Deficit/Hyperactivity Disorders, and Antabuse and Methadone, for prevention of relapse into misuse of alcohol and narcotics, respectively.

Electroconvulsive therapy (ECT) should also be mentioned here because of its beneficial use in the treatment of severe depression, particularly when psychotherapy and medication have failed, and especially when the depression is characterized by Melancholia.

The Smith et al. (1980) study, cited earlier, entailed a review of 112 studies on the use of medication in the treatment of emotional disorders. These researchers state, "When the two therapies [psychotherapeutic treatment and medication] are combined, the net benefits are less than the sum of their separate benefits" but more than the benefits of either treatment modality alone (p. 188), particularly in the treatment of psychotic disorders. This conclusion continues to hold true today.

Examples of Treatment Planning: Bettie and Anne

Application of the preceding information on treatment planning to the cases of Bettie and Anne should clarify the type of treatment likely to benefit each of them. Although both women are coping with broken engagements, Anne is also dealing with an unplanned pregnancy, and she has used alcohol and avoidance as coping mechanisms. Bettie, by contrast, has more self-confidence and more personal resources, and she views her unexpected change in plans as an opportunity for personal growth.

Both women probably would benefit from short-term therapy. Bettie should be seen weekly. Anne should be seen more frequently, until she has resolved her immediate crisis and dealt successfully with her alcohol use. Bettie is more self-directed. Although she does evidence some cognitive dysfunction, resistance, and mild depression, Bettie may respond well to a modified form of person-centered therapy that encourages her to develop her self-confidence and her self-awareness and to establish goals and direction, as well as interpersonal skills. Anne, by contrast, is less motivated toward self-exploration and is primarily interested in resolving her immediate concerns. Her therapy will probably focus more on cognitive-behavioral areas, emphasizing decision making and behavioral change.

Anne seems likely to respond best to individual therapy because she is in crisis, must make a rapid decision about her pregnancy, and is not currently interested in personal growth and development. Bettie, however, would probably benefit from either individual or group psychotherapy, or from a combination of the two—perhaps short-term individual therapy followed by participation in a personal growth group for women or a psychotherapy group for young adults.

Neither Anne nor Bettie seems to need medication, although Anne's therapist should make sure that Anne is receiving any necessary medical care. Both Anne and Bettie are capable of self-regulation and are in touch with reality. An outpatient treatment setting, such as a community mental health center or a private practice, seems an appropriate location for treatment. Adjunct services, such as Alcoholics Anonymous and even inpatient treatment, may need to be considered for Anne if her alcohol misuse is severe enough.

After their immediate concerns have been resolved, both Bettie and Anne may decide to continue treatment, but their goals are likely to differ. Bettie will probably seek to improve her relationship skills, to clarify her goals and direction, and to enhance her self-esteem. Anne will probably need to develop better coping mechanisms and greater independence.

The research on therapeutic variables does not yield definitive descriptions of the exact types of psychotherapy that would be best for each of these women. Nevertheless, it does offer guidelines for designing a treatment plan likely to be effective with each of them. The rest of this chapter and the rest of the book provide a closer look at the dynamics of the relationship between client and therapist, the relationship between those dynamics and the effects of therapy, and the relationship between a client's diagnosis and the treatment selected for that client.

THERAPIST- AND CLIENT-RELATED VARIABLES

The previous sections of this chapter have reviewed the literature on the effectiveness of psychotherapy in general, as well as on the effectiveness of particular approaches to psychotherapy. Although psychotherapy itself has been found generally effective, the research on the differential effectiveness of the various psychotherapies is rather inconclusive, perhaps because therapy is an inexact science. Moreover, even with the advent of manuals that direct the therapeutic process and give it some uniformity and consistency, therapy inevitably varies widely because it depends on the nature of the therapist, the client, and their interaction. As Pilkonis et al. (1984) conclude, differences in outcome may be due more to the therapist, the client, and their fit than to aspects of the particular therapeutic model being used. The ability to maximize the effectiveness of psychotherapy, then, will require an understanding not only of the therapeutic models and techniques being used but also of the client and the clinician. This chapter will now review and discuss the literature about the therapeutically relevant characteristics of the clinician, the client, and their interaction. These variables may be at least as important in determining the outcome of therapy as the specific model of therapy that is used.

Therapist-Related Variables

Najavits and Weiss (1994) believe that therapists' personal contributions to therapeutic outcomes outweigh what is contributed by their theoretical orientations. They support this position with their finding that therapists' success rates vary greatly; for example, in one study that these writers examined, therapists' rates of successful outcomes ranged from 25 percent to 100 percent of clients treated. They have also found that premature termination rates vary widely from therapist to therapist. Luborsky et al. (1985) agree with this finding: "The therapist is not simply the transmitter of a standard therapeutic agent. Rather, the therapist is an important, independent agent of change with the ability to magnify or reduce the effects of a therapy" (p. 609). The literature on therapists' effectiveness can be organized into three categories: research dealing with demographic characteristics of therapists; research concerning therapists' professional backgrounds; and research on therapists' personal, relational, and therapeutic backgrounds, styles, and values.

Variables Related to the Therapist's Demographic Characteristics. The literature lends modest support to the idea that similarity between the therapist and the client is associated with a beneficial outcome (Kendall & Lipman, 1991). At the same time, Beck (1988) concludes that the findings on this kind of match are inconclusive: "Effective therapy can be obtained through other means, such as appropriate counselor attitudes, values, sensitivity, and orientation to subcultures, without sex and ethnic matching" (p. 12). Research does provide some limited guidance on the issue of matching.

Gender. The gender of the therapist and the gender-based interactions between therapist and client seem likely to have an impact on the development of the therapeutic relationship. Mogul (1982) finds evidence to indicate that clients are more satisfied with female than with male therapists and suggests that selection of the therapist by gender in light of the client's history may contribute to therapeutic effectiveness. For example, to facilitate the resolution of issues connected with early life experiences, a client can be assigned a therapist of the same gender as a parent lost in childhood or as the parent with whom the patient has had moderate (but not disabling) conflict. Mogul also suggests that women who have been victims of rape or incest may work better with female therapists and that adolescents may be more comfortable with same-sex therapists. Beutler, Crago, and Arizmendi (1986) likewise have found that the therapist's being female contributed to therapeutic effectiveness; so does gender matching between client and therapist, especially if the therapist does not communicate attitudes that promote gender stereotyping. They have also found that clients who have expressed a preference for therapist of one gender or the other tend to respond better when treatment is provided by a therapist of the preferred gender.

Perry et al. (1985) make related suggestions: "Treatment aimed at character change should probably be conducted by a therapist whose sex presents the most difficulties for the patient, whereas treatments designed to alleviate symptoms should most often be conducted by a therapist whose sex poses the least problems for the patient" (p. 364).

Beck's (1988) research has yielded some interesting findings on the relationship of the therapist's gender to the outcomes of therapy. Beck found that female therapists had better outcomes when two or more family members were seen together. Other findings of Beck's research are that younger clients responded especially well to family counseling with a female therapist; that treatment of parenting difficulties via individual therapy was most successful when client and therapist were of the same gender, whereas treatment of marital difficulties via individual therapy was most successful with a therapist of the opposite gender; and that both male and female adults with personality problems responded better to female therapists. Beck concludes that the women clients in his research were more aware of possible gender-related power issues in relationships, and that both genders tended to see female therapists as more nurturing, caring, and expressive than male therapists.

Beck (1988) has also found that many clients in group counseling initially viewed female clinicians as less powerful and less influential than male clinicians but that this perception was corrected over time, becoming more closely aligned with the therapists' actual behavior than with their gender. In the long run, the gender of therapists leading groups was not a significant determinant either of the therapist's perceived influence or of the therapist's effectiveness.

Mogul (1982) concludes that although the gender of the therapist may be important to individual clients and is worth considering (especially in short-term counseling, where rapid establishment of a positive therapeutic alliance is important), "no specific conclusions as to optimal patient-therapist matches on the basis of therapist sex appear warranted" (p. 1). This general conclusion seems sound in light of the limited research on this variable, although in individual cases consideration of a potential therapist's gender may be called for.

Age. In a comparative study of professional and paraprofessional therapists, Berman and Norton (1985) address the variables of the therapist's and the client's age and the relationship between their ages. Their finding is that older, professional therapists worked better with older clients, whereas paraprofessionals had a slight edge over the older professionals in their effectiveness with younger clients. These findings raise the possibility that age similarity may contribute to therapeutic effectiveness, and that the older clients' more positive response to the older, professional therapists may reflect these clients' greater respect for those therapists' credentials and education.

By contrast, Beck (1988) has found that clients under the age of fifty-five preferred therapists who were either older or within ten years of the clients' ages; clients older than fifty-five tended to prefer therapists who were at least ten years younger. These findings may not really contradict those just presented but may reflect differences in how the researchers grouped clients by age. Beck has also found that clinicians with at least ten years' experience were more successful in treating family relationship problems than were clinicians with less experience. This finding seems to be explained partly by a drop in therapists' positive outcomes (perhaps related to burnout or to the acquisition of challenging clients) that often occurs between a therapist's fourth and tenth years of experience.

In general, clients seem to prefer clinicians who are mature enough to have had considerable experience in their field and who are in touch with clients' age-related and developmental issues but who do not seem too old to be out of touch with modern developments in the profession.

Ethnicity and Socioeconomic Status. Lambert (1982) has found no clear evidence that the therapist's race, or similarity in the therapist's and the client's race, affects therapeutic outcomes. Lambert has also noted, however, that African American clients leave therapy at higher than usual rates when they are working with white therapists, which suggests that in some circumstances race may indeed be a factor in determining therapeutic outcomes. Smith et al. (1980) have found a small positive correlation between outcome and client-therapist similarity in terms of education and socioeconomic status. This finding, however, may simply indicate that clients of higher education and socioeconomic status benefit from counseling more than those of lower status, or it may reflect a sampling bias in that most therapists probably do not come from lower-class backgrounds.

A meta-analysis conducted by Coleman, Wampold, and Casali (1995) found that ethnicity is not a factor in the perceived competence of therapists, but that people who belong to ethnic minority groups are more likely to prefer ethnically similar therapists. Moreover, according to Hess and Street (1991), "Several studies have demonstrated that subjects express a greater preference for, engage in more self-exploration with, and are better understood by counselors of their same ethnic background than by those whose background differs from their own" (p. 71). Minority clients' degree of assimilation to the majority culture also seems to be a moderating variable in the relationship between these clients' and their therapists' ethnicity, on the one hand, and therapeutic outcomes, on the other. Coleman et al. (1995) conclude that those minority clients who are not highly assimilated to the majority culture have more negative attitudes toward therapy and are more likely to prefer ethnically similar therapists. By contrast, according to Sue, Ivey, and Pedersen (1996), minority clients who are highly assimilated to the majority culture sometimes feel stereotyped if they are automatically assigned to ethnically similar therapists. Ethnic matching between client and therapist does seem to be indicated in some cases, but the research generally suggests that therapists who attend to issues of culture as well as to their clients' wants and expectations in therapy are likely to be successful with both ethnically similar and ethnically different clients.

Variables Related to the Therapist's Professional Background. Studies on the impact on outcome of the therapist's training, experience, and professional affiliation are unclear and often contradictory. Parloff (1986) has found no clear correlation between the length of the therapist's experience and therapeutic outcomes. Lambert (1982), however, has found that the therapist's experience has a "reliable relationship to outcome" (p. 60). Perhaps this apparent contradiction can be explained by more specific findings, which suggest complicated interactions among the client's diagnosis, the treatment approach, and the clinician's experience. Beck (1988) has found that therapists with graduate-level preparation are more successful in treating family relationship problems, whereas therapists without that training are more successful in treating other problems, perhaps because they are more practical and down-to-earth in their approaches. Beck's findings, reported earlier, about some therapists' drop in effectiveness are also relevant with respect to the importance of the therapist's experience and training. Schneider's (1992) study concludes that, in general, the therapist's experience is most likely to make a positive difference with a difficult client.

Beutler et al. (1986) have found no relationship between the therapist's discipline and therapeutic outcomes. In fact, Berman and Norton (1985) have found that, overall, professionals and paraprofessionals are equally effective. Nevertheless, Greenspan and Kulish's (1985) study of 273 clients who terminated treatment prematurely, but after at least six months, indicates that therapists with Ph.D. degrees and personal experience of psychotherapy have lower rates of premature termination by clients than do therapists with M.D. or M.S.W. degrees. Seligman (1995), however, reports that psychologists, psychiatrists, and social workers do not differ in their therapeutic effectiveness. So far no conclusive relationship has been found between the length of the therapist's training, the therapist's personal experience of psychotherapy, and the therapist's professional discipline, on the one hand, and therapeutic outcomes, on the other.

Variables Related to the Therapist's Personal Background. A small but growing body of literature suggests that the therapist's personal background and experience are determinants of the therapeutic alliance and of therapeutic outcomes. Poal and Weisz (1989), for example, have found the number of childhood problems reported by therapists to be positively related to improvement in the problems of children treated by them. Watts, Trusty, Canada, and Harvill (1995) studied novice counselors and found a significant positive correlation between the counselors' effectiveness and their having negative perceptions of their own early family experience, negative memories of their opposite-sex parent, and less positive perceptions of their parents' relationship and of parent-child interactions: the lower the perceived "autonomy and intimacy in early childhood experiences," the higher the "interpersonal-facilitation skill level" in these counselors (p. 105). Whether these findings can be explained by the counselors' increased empathy, their greater awareness of personal problems, or the growth that accompanied the resolution of these early problems has not been determined, but the research does seem to suggest that therapists who have had more difficulties as children use those experiences in some way to become better therapists.

Strupp (1981) looked at the interaction between the therapist's skill and what he calls "human qualities" and at the impact that this interaction has on therapeutic outcomes. He suggests that the human qualities of the therapist are less important in work with clients who have good ego strength and who are motivated than they are in work with clients who are resistant and low in ego strength. He also observes that therapists who are high in human qualities and low in technical skills still obtain moderate outcomes, but that therapists who are high in technical skills and low in human qualities tend to obtain poor outcomes. Human qualities, then, are not sufficient to effect optimal gains in therapy, but they do seem to be a necessary ingredient of that process.

More research has been conducted on therapists' personal characteristics and styles than on their personal experiences and professional backgrounds. The following characteristics, attitudes, and approaches on the part of therapists have been found to be correlated with therapists' effectiveness:

1. Having personal/psychological maturity and well-being (Schneider, 1992)

2. Communicating empathy and understanding to clients (Lambert and Cattani-Thompson, 1996)

3. Manifesting high ethical standards

4. Being authoritative rather than authoritarian, and freeing rather than controlling clients (Hyman & Woog, 1989)

5. Having strong interpersonal skills; communicating warmth, caring, respect, acceptance, and a helping, reassuring, and protecting attitude; affirming rather than blaming clients (Najavits & Weiss, 1994)

6. Having a capacity for self-criticism and an awareness of their own limitations, but not being easily discouraged; continuously searching for the best ways to help clients

7. Empowering clients and supporting their autonomy and their use of resources

8. Being tolerant of diversity, ambiguity, and complexity; being open-minded and flexible; not needing to control clients or their choices (Hyman & Woog, 1989)

9. Being self-actualized, self-fulfilled, creative, committed to self-development, responsible, and able to cope effectively with their own stress

10. Being authentic and genuine, and having credibility

11. Focusing on people and processes, not on rules (McLeod & McLeod, 1993)

12. Being optimistic and hopeful, having positive expectations for the treatment process, and being able to engender those feelings in clients (Miller, Hubble, & Duncan, 1997)

13. Being actively engaged with and receptive to clients, and giving some structure and focus to the treatment process (Green & Herget, 1991)

These findings support the importance of the core conditions identified by Carkhuff and Berenson (1977), Rogers (1951), and others in effecting improvement, regardless of the therapist's theoretical orientation. The findings suggest that the therapist who is emotionally healthy, active, optimistic, expressive, straightforward yet supportive, involved, and in charge of the therapeutic process, and who is also able to temper that stance with encouragement of responsibility on the part of the client, is the one most likely to achieve a positive outcome.

Morgan et al. (1982) have observed that therapists seem to have a good sense of those clients with whom they can work effectively, and that when therapists can choose their clients, the outcomes are better than those that are the results of random assignment. Therefore, therapists' assessment of their likelihood of success with a given client should be included in the list of variables that seem to predict therapeutic effectiveness.

Client-Related Variables

No matter how wisely the therapist selects an intervention strategy, and no matter how abundantly the therapist demonstrates the personal and professional qualities that are positively correlated with a good outcome, the therapy will not be effective if the client is not ready or able to benefit from the therapeutic strategy and the therapist's positive qualities. In fact, Stiles, Shapiro, and Elliott (1986) and Lambert and Cattani-Thompson (1996) believe that the key to therapeutic effectiveness is more likely to be found in the client or in the therapeutic alliance than in the therapist. Attention should be given, then, to those qualities in clients that are correlated with effective treatment.

Variables Related to the Client's Assessment. The development of a treatment plan for a given client begins with a thorough understanding of that person. Formats for intake interviews and mental status examinations are readily available elsewhere (Seligman, 1996a) and are beyond the scope of this volume, but a brief and useful overview of relevant aspects of the client is provided by Longabough, Fowler, Stout, and Kriebel (1983). They suggest gathering data on the following dimensions:

- Demographic characteristics
- Physical characteristics
- Behavior
- Affect
- Thinking and learning style
- Intimate relationships
- Social behavior
- Lifestyle
- Role in therapy
- Environment
- Any other relevant areas

Maxmen and Ward (1995) elaborate by describing the following important steps in client assessment:

- Obtaining a history
- Evaluating the client's mental status
- Collecting auxiliary data (for example, by using psychological tests and medical evaluations)

- Summarizing the principal findings
- Making a diagnosis
- Establishing the prognosis
- Developing a biopsychosocial formulation
- Planning the treatment

Therapists seem to be making more use of diagnostic interviews, inventories, and rating scales. In the preliminary stages of therapy, these help the clinician gather information on the client's diagnosis and dynamics. In the termination stages, they provide information on progress and outcome. Projective testing is also sometimes used in gaining an understanding of clients. The literature offers many assessment tools, developed in recent years, that can play an important role in screening clients (Sexton, 1995). The following are some of the most useful:

1. *Structured diagnostic interviews,* such as the NIMH Diagnostic Interview Schedule, the Schedule for Affective Disorders and Schizophrenia, the Brief Psychiatric Rating Scale, and the Symptom Checklist 90

2. *General personality inventories,* including the Minnesota Multiphasic Personality Inventory, the Millon Clinical Multiaxial Inventory, the Millon Adolescent Personality Inventory, the California Psychological Inventory, and the High School, Children's, and Early School Personality Questionnaire

3. *Inventories for assessing specific symptoms,* including the Beck Depression Inventory, the Beck Anxiety Inventory, the Hamilton Rating Scale for Depression, the State-Trait Anxiety Inventory, the Michigan Alcoholism Screening Test, the Elementary Guidance Behavior Rating Scale, and the Eating Disorders Inventory

Assessment is an important component of the treatment planning process and should be done with care. Effective treatment planning is probably impossible unless the clinician has made an accurate diagnosis and has a good understanding of the client's development, concerns, strengths, and difficulties.

Variables Related to the Client's Demographic and Personal Characteristics. On the National Comorbidity Survey (NCS), a structured interview administered to a national sample of people between the ages of fifteen and fifty-four, nearly 50 percent of respondents reported at least one mental disorder during their lifetimes, and close to 30 percent had experienced such a disorder during the previous twelve months (Kessler et al., 1994). Of those who had experienced at least one disorder, 56 percent had experienced two or more over their lifetimes. The most common disorders included Major Depressive Disorder, Alcohol Dependence, and Social and Specific Phobias. Fewer than 40 percent of those people who had experienced mental disorders had received professional help for those disorders.

What distinguishes people who seek help for their concerns and who benefit in the process from people who do not? Those who do seek treatment are more likely to be female, college-educated, and from the middle to upper classes, and they are more likely to have reasonable expectations for how therapy can help them. People who continue in therapy tend to be more dependable, more intelligent, better educated, less likely to have a history of antisocial behavior, and more anxious and dissatisfied with themselves than those who leave therapy prematurely (Garfield, 1986).

African American clients, as well as those under the age of forty, are more likely to fail to keep therapy appointments, whereas both African American clients and lower socioeconomic clients are more likely to drop out of therapy. Those who refuse treatment are more likely to be younger, to have been told by someone else to seek therapy, to be receiving third-party payments for treatment, to have an acute nonpsychotic situational concern (such as a family or interpersonal problem or a reactive depression), to have had fewer prior episodes of emotional disorders, and to have had no prior therapy (Greenspan & Kulish, 1985; Hoffman, 1985; Rabin, Kaslow, & Rehm, 1985).

Lambert's (1982) review of the literature finds no clear relationship between outcome and the client's age, race, or gender. Other research, however, has yielded different findings. Smith et al. (1980), for example, believe that females benefit more than males from therapy. They have also found a curvilinear relationship between age and effect size, with clients between the ages of nineteen and twenty-two benefiting from therapy more than both older and younger clients. Pilkonis et al. (1984), in their study of sixty-four outpatients, find that lower socioeconomic status and chronicity of the emotional disorder are predictive of a poorer outcome.

Many personal characteristics in clients have been found to be correlated with outcomes. Beutler et al. (1986) have found that people who are open, in touch with their emotions, and able to express their thoughts and feelings in therapy have positive prognoses. Garfield (1986) has found a correlation between anxiety and positive outcome, as well as between outcome and likability of the client. A high tolerance for frustration and anxiety, as well as low levels of guilt or self-destructive behavior, have also been associated with a good prognosis (Wallerstein, 1986). According to Seligman (1995), the immediacy of the client's affective expression has been found to have a particularly strong correlation with outcome; the likelihood of a positive outcome is also increased if the client demonstrates good ego strength, becomes an active participant in treatment, and can take responsibility for problems rather than viewing them as external sources of difficulty. Moreover, according to Miller et al. (1997), people with positive pretreatment functioning, awareness of their difficulties, positive expectations of change, stable lifestyles, and good support systems seem better able to make good use of therapy.

Research on the relationship between outcomes and clients' personal characteristics is suggestive but not yet conclusive. Overall, however, the indications are that therapy is particularly effective with white females who are intelligent, motivated, expressive, and not severely dysfunctional. Therapy can be very helpful to people who do not fit this description, of course, but these findings point out some of psychotherapy's limitations, as well as the difficulty of adapting the therapeutic process to the needs of a particular client.

Variables Related to the Client's Diagnosis. The diagnosis, of course, is another factor relevant to outcome. In general, the more severe and long-standing the disorder (for example, Schizophrenia and the Personality Disorders), the poorer the prognosis. People with circumscribed, reactive, brief, situational problems, such as Adjustment Disorder and some Mood and Anxiety Disorders, tend to have better treatment outcomes. People with more than one comorbid diagnosis seem to be particularly resistant and challenging clients (Najavits & Weiss, 1994). Typically, a person who was at a lower level of functioning before therapy is still at a lower level after therapy than a person who was at a higher level before therapy, even though both may have improved. Kendall and Lipman (1991) have found that people who respond rapidly to psychotherapy are more likely to find homework assignments useful and to maintain their gains after the end of treatment.

Variables Related to the Client's Perceptions of Psychotherapy. Horowitz, Marmar, Weiss, and colleagues (1984), in an extensive review of the literature, conclude, "What has emerged as the most consistent process predictor of improvement is the patient's subjective perception of the therapist-offered relationship" (p. 439). The research suggests that people who perceive their therapists as helping them, who have positive perceptions of their therapists' skills and facilitative attitudes, and who see themselves engaged in teamwork with their therapists are likely to show more benefits from therapy than people who do not share those perceptions. Therefore, clients' perceptions of the therapeutic process seem to play a very important role in determining outcomes.

Variables Related to the Client's Readiness for Treatment. People enter therapy with a broad range of expectations and attitudes. The well-known self-fulfilling prophecy seems to hold true: people who expect positive and realistic outcomes from therapy, and whose expectations are congruent with those of their therapists, are more likely to achieve those outcomes, whereas those who are resistant to change are less likely to benefit from therapy (Beutler et al., 1986). Perry et al. (1985) suggest that attending to the preferences that clients express for treatment (such as for specific forms of treatment, or for specific conditions of treatment like place, cost, time, and frequency, or for particular types of therapists) should increase clients' positive expectations for therapy and therefore should also increase the likelihood of positive outcomes.

Howard et al. (1987) also address the issue of the client's readiness for therapy, which they define as having three components: motivation, ability, and self-confidence. They believe that the client with a high degree of readiness is active and relatively independent, has a broad repertoire of behaviors, has mature and enduring interests, can take a broad outlook that includes the past as well as the present and the future, is able to relate to others as equals or superiors, and has adequate self-control and a good sense of self.

These researchers and others have also developed models for matching the therapist's style to the client's readiness. According to Howard et al. (1987), clients with very low levels of readiness need therapists with a strong power base who emphasize "telling" and who are high in directiveness and low in support (for example, rational-emotive or behavior therapists). Clients with moderately low levels of readiness are most likely to benefit from a "teaching" approach, in which both directiveness and support are high (as in the approach of reality therapists or Adlerian therapists). Those with moderately high levels of readiness tend to respond best to therapy that emphasizes "understanding" and is low in directiveness but high in support (for example, person-centered therapy), whereas clients with high readiness are capable of benefiting from therapists who observe and who delegate responsibility to them, providing only limited directiveness and support (for example, psychodynamic psychotherapists). Beutler and Consoli (1993) suggest that people who cope by acting out respond best to therapists with an external and behavioral focus, whereas those who internalize their difficulties need therapists who can promote insight, awareness, and interpersonal functioning. The concept of matching client to therapist seems useful in the effort to help the therapist individualize the treatment plan, maximize the readiness of the clients, and promote a positive therapeutic alliance.

A process called *role induction* also seems helpful in the development of attitudes in clients that are conducive to a positive outcome. In role induction, clients are oriented to the therapeutic process and are given clear information on what is expected of them, what the therapist can offer, and what therapy will probably be like. The client's engagement in the therapeutic process is a variable that is correlated with a positive therapeutic outcome, and role induction seems likely to increase the client's engagement (Nelson & Neufeldt, 1996).

Variables Related to the Therapeutic Alliance

In addition to research on the impact that therapist- and client-related variables have on therapeutic outcomes, research has been conducted on the interactive and synergistic effect that the therapist-client relationship, or therapeutic alliance, has on outcomes. Luborsky, Barber, and Crits-Christoph (1990) reviewed a number of studies on that topic and report that nearly all demonstrate measures of the therapeutic alliance as being significant predictors of therapeutic outcomes. According to Green and Herget (1991, p. 321), "Evidence is mounting that therapist relationship skills and strength of the therapeutic alliance are the most powerful predictors of client outcome across many therapeutic orientations." Krupnick (1996) has found that the therapeutic alliance is important regardless of whether the primary intervention is psychotherapy or medication.

Clients' perceptions of the quality of the therapeutic alliance are formed early and tend to be stable. They are more highly correlated with therapeutic outcome than therapists' or observers' perceptions of the quality of the therapeutic alliance (Horvath & Symonds, 1991).

Many qualities are associated with a positive therapeutic alliance and therefore with an optimistic prognosis. A positive therapeutic climate and a feeling of mutual warmth, affection, affirmation, and respect have been found to contribute to a positive outcome (Waterhouse & Strupp, 1984). Nelson and Neufeldt (1996) have found that the development of a productive working alliance is facilitated by role induction, by open disclosure of the therapist's background and procedures, by the therapist's and the client's agreement on realistic goals and tasks, and by the therapist's asking the client for feedback. Miller et al. (1997) emphasize the importance of the client's having a positive perception of the therapist, of the client's belief that the focus is on his or her goals and expectations, and on the client's being comfortable with the pace of treatment; also important is the ability of the client and the therapist to view themselves as engaged in a common endeavor likely to succeed.

Beck (1988) has found specific types of therapist-client combinations to be associated with a positive therapeutic alliance and with superior results in treatment; in fact, these combinations seem to be more important than individual characteristics of the client or the therapist considered in isolation. Many studies have tried to identify the nature of these combinations (some of that research is discussed earlier in this section), but the research is unclear with respect to whether similarity or difference between client and therapist is more desirable.

Beck (1988) has found that difference in the therapist's and the client's life experience is associated with a positive therapeutic alliance and with a positive outcome. According to Beck, life experiences very similar to those of the client may lead the therapist to lose objectivity, set unrealistic goals, and draw premature conclusions. Lambert (1982) takes a similar view, suggesting that complementary matching of therapist and client (for example, the combination of a directive therapist with a passive client) is positively correlated with a successful outcome. At the same time, however, several other researchers have found therapist-client similarity to be positively related to a successful outcome (Garfield, 1986). Both conclusions have logical appeal. Similarity between the therapist and the client seems likely to promote the rapid establishment of a comfortable working alliance in which goals and values are compatible, but complementary matching can offer the client an important learning experience through the therapist's modeling ways of behaving and coping that are unfamiliar to the client. The circumstances determining whether the therapist's and the client's similarity or their difference is more likely to enhance the therapeutic alliance is an intriguing and potentially fruitful area of research that warrants further study.

The client's identification with the therapist is another factor relevant to outcome. Beutler et al. (1986) conclude, "There is apparently a decided tendency for successful therapy dyads to be associated with the patients' acquiring therapists' belief systems, both about religious and moral attitudes and about more general concepts as well" (p. 275). This is consistent with the finding that similarity seems to improve outcomes, but it does raise some philosophical questions—for example, is a major element of therapy the process of promoting middle-class values in clients?

Research consistently indicates that the therapeutic alliance is a necessary but not sufficient condition for effecting desired changes and positive therapeutic outcomes. Horvath and Symonds (1991, p. 139) conclude that a successful therapeutic alliance makes it possible for the patient to accept and follow the treatment faithfully, and that it bridges the gap between process and outcome. The conditions conducive to a positive therapeutic alliance have been discussed earlier in this chapter, but therapists should not limit their attention to those conditions; they should also attend to clients' preferences. The client's perceptions are a key contributor to the quality of the therapeutic alliance, and so the client's ability to select the sort of therapist he or she prefers should contribute greatly to the establishment of a positive alliance.

※

This chapter has presented an outline for a comprehensive treatment plan. It has also reviewed the literature on the dimensions of effective therapy and on the contributions that the qualities of the therapist, the qualities of the client, and the interaction between therapist and client can make to therapeutic outcomes. The next eight chapters describe the various mental disorders and report research on treatment models that have been found to be effective with those disorders. That information, in combination with the information presented in this chapter, should help clinicians maximize the success of their efforts to help clients in psychotherapy.

CHAPTER TWO

Mental Disorders in Infants, Children, and Adolescents

S hannon's first arrest occurred when she was nine years old and was caught stealing a videotape from a local store, but her parents had been receiving complaints about her since kindergarten. She frequently pushed and hit younger children and took their toys. She tore up flowers and bushes in the neighbors' garden and threw eggs at their house. When the neighbors complained to her parents, Shannon and some friends retaliated by stealing the neighbors' mailbox and breaking bottles in their driveway.

At school, Shannon had trouble staying in her seat. She frequently interrupted other children and the teacher. She rarely completed her schoolwork independently, and she often lost her assignments.

Shannon's parents were concerned, but they both had experienced similar problems in school, and both had left high school without graduating. Both were employed to support the family (Shannon and two older children), the mother as a school bus driver and the father as a mechanic. Parental supervision was limited; the oldest child, age sixteen, watched Shannon and her brother after school.

Shannon's history reflects symptoms of disruptive behavior and attention deficit. These are common symptoms of mental disorders among children and adolescents.

Note: This chapter was written in collaboration with Mittie Quinn, M.A., N.C.S.P.

OVERVIEW OF MENTAL DISORDERS IN INFANTS, CHILDREN, AND ADOLESCENTS

The need for mental health services for the nation's youth is evident in statistics published by the Carnegie Council on Adolescent Development (1995). According to this report, one-fourth of the eighth graders surveyed said that they drink alcohol. The firearm-related homicide rate for children between the ages of ten and fourteen more than doubled between 1985 and 1992. Research repeatedly indicates that the best way to reduce the incidence and severity of mental disorders is prevention. Therefore, early identification and effective treatment of emotional problems is critical in reducing the overall prevalence and severity of mental disorders.

Unlike the mental disorders discussed in other chapters of this book, which are related to one another by their similarity of symptoms, those discussed in this chapter are linked by their early age of onset. This chapter addresses the thirteen major categories of Disorders Usually First Diagnosed in Infancy, Childhood, or Adolescence, as listed in the fourth edition of the *Diagnostic and Statistical Manual of Mental Disorders,* or *DSM-IV* (American Psychiatric Association, 1994a). The chapter also briefly reviews childhood presentations of some disorders discussed elsewhere in the book. Although the disorders discussed in this chapter usually begin in childhood, many often continue into adulthood. Therefore, the information in this chapter will be relevant to all therapists.

Description of the Disorders

From 5 to 15 percent of children between the ages of nine and ten suffer from emotional or behavioral disorders severe enough to interfere with their daily functioning (Brandenburg, Friedman, & Silver, 1990). Only about 10 percent of these children receive treatment, however. Boys between the ages of four and twelve have more emotional difficulties than girls in that age group, whereas girls between twelve and sixteen years of age have more mental disorders than their male counterparts do (Offord & Fleming, 1991).

Many theories have been advanced about the etiology of childhood mental disorders. Psychodynamic theorists typically describe these disorders as developmental fixations or regressions and attribute them to early childhood conflicts or experiences. Medical models look for neurological or genetic causes. Behavioral theory posits that these disorders are the results of learned experiences. Social learning theorists consider the impact of environmental factors on the child. Developmental theorists look at age-related patterns and deviations from those patterns (Johnson, Rasbury, & Siegel, 1986).

All these theories are relevant to an understanding of the full spectrum of mental disorders in young people. For example, Mental Retardation reflects a deviation from age-appropriate levels of cognitive development, and some of the Pervasive Developmental Disorders are characterized by a regression in language and social development. Other disorders, such as Rett's Disorder, have neurological, biological, or genetic determinants. Conduct Disorder often is linked to chaotic and antisocial family patterns.

A great deal of attention has been given recently to the impact that attachment has on development. Bowlby (1969/1982) describes attachment as a process: a child produces behaviors in reaction to stress, and these behaviors in turn elicit other behaviors from the caregiver that reestablish a sense of security for the child, usually through physical closeness or proximity (Lyons-Ruth, Zeanah, & Benoit, 1996). Bowlby's theory suggests that the quality of all subsequent interpersonal relationships is affected by the nature of attachment relationships formed during infancy. Other findings suggest that insecure attachment during the early years can affect children's cognitive and social development (Hersen & Ammerman, 1995) and may even affect their skills as adults in parenting the next generation (Zeanah & Emde, 1994).

Children typically are referred for psychotherapy when their behaviors or symptoms interfere with their daily functioning or with the functioning of their families. Problems in school, such as inattention, misbehavior, or academic deficits, often prompt teachers or school counselors to suggest therapy. Academic problems often coexist with social-emotional problems like insecure attachment, inappropriate peer relationships, aggression, social isolation, low self-esteem, and lack of motivation. The family members of children with difficulties like these are frequently experiencing considerable stress and change themselves and may be struggling with their own mental disorders. Therefore, the therapist working with a child usually has targets of intervention in addition to the child—namely, the school, the family, and the environment. The therapist needs to be knowledgeable about social, educational, and community resources for children and families. The therapist also needs to be an excellent diagnostician because comorbidity and confusing presentations (such as a Depressive Disorder masked by anger and a Bipolar Disorder that looks like hyperactivity) are common in childhood mental disorders.

Typical Client Characteristics

An epidemiological study conducted by the National Institutes of Mental Health (1990) estimates 12 percent of American children as being in need of mental health services. This figure represents approximately 7.5 million children in the United States. Only 10 to 20 percent of those children are believed to be receiving the type of treatment they need, however.

By definition, mental disorders in youth have an onset prior to the age of eighteen. Unlike adults, who may come to therapists without a diagnosis, children with mental disorders are often diagnosed in medical or educational settings. Their diagnoses usually address their major symptoms but may overlook comorbid disorders, and so the therapist should be alert to additional symptoms that may require complex treatment planning.

Children with mental disorders vary in appearance. Some, for example, have obvious physical anomalies. Children with certain disorders of neurobiological etiology, such as Rett's Disorder or Down's Syndrome, typically have associated physical characteristics like microcephaly, short stature, or atypical facial structure. By contrast, children with disorders of a psychosocial etiology, such as Conduct or Separation Anxiety Disorders, usually evidence no external physical symptoms.

Because children present differently in different settings, therapists should collect information from multiple sources in order to make accurate diagnoses. The collection of information should always include input from teachers and parents. There is a variety of checklists available that categorize behaviors according to *DSM-IV.* The Conners Teacher and Parent Rating Scales (Conners, 1990), the Achenbach Child Behavior Checklist (Achenbach, 1991), and the Behavior Assessment System for Children (BASC) (Reynolds & Kamphaus, 1992) are three tools for facilitating the collection and organization of information. Each assesses such characteristics as anxiety, depressive symptoms, hyperactivity, inattention, impulsivity, atypical thoughts, aggressive or delinquent behaviors, and somatic complaints.

Therapy with children almost always involves contact with their families because a disorder and its concomitant behaviors will both affect and be affected by family life. The impact of financial and emotional stressors, transitions, and family relationships on a child's emotional health should all be assessed. Additional services may be required to provide treatment, support, and resources to siblings and parents, who may have their own emotional difficulties.

Preferred Therapist Characteristics

Therapists working with children should have a broad range of professional and personal skills. They must be patient and calm. They should have a clear understanding of their own values and of their own childhood and parenting experiences. As neutral adults, therapists typically receive negative and positive transference of the feelings that children have for their parents. Children may refuse to talk, make insulting and disparaging statements to their therapists, or even attack their therapists physically. Children may also relate to therapists in seductive or manipulative ways. Therapists' countertransference reactions to these behaviors may interfere with treatment unless the therapists carefully monitor and understand their feelings and use them only in ways that are therapeutic. Therapists may also need to manage their own rage in response to child abuse and their need to save children from their caretakers.

In addition to basic psychotherapy skills, therapists who work with children must have sound knowledge of human development over the life span. One of therapists' most important tasks will be to distinguish between age-appropriate and atypical behaviors: some of the disorders discussed in this chapter are characterized by behaviors that may be developmentally appropriate at some ages but clinically significant at others. In Attention-Deficit Disorder, for example, one task of the clinician is to determine how much activity is typical for the client's chronological age.

Collaboration with other professionals is another important task for therapists working with children. Young people who come for therapy may also have been seen by physicians, psychiatrists, school counselors, social workers, speech therapists, and family therapists. Ongoing consultation and collaboration with other professionals will be crucial to providing the most effective and efficient treatment. At the same time, however, too many helpers can fragment the treatment, and so therapists may need to assume a case management role in order to coordinate services for children and their families and in order to ensure that all the treatment providers have shared and congruent goals.

Parenting a child with a mental disorder can evoke feelings of failure, frustration, sadness, anger, and helplessness. The child's needs may also overwhelm the family, impairing its functioning and family relationships. Therefore, therapists working with children must give empathy and support to families as well as guidance about parenting, information about the particular disorders involved, and referrals for family therapy and other ancillary services.

Intervention Strategies

Treatment planning for children is a very complex task; individual psychotherapy is rarely the sole treatment modality. Children experience at least two systems—the family and the school—that affect their behaviors and emotional well-being. A therapist may be seeing a child for individual therapy while the child also is involved in special education, family therapy, medical treatment, and the workings of the juvenile justice system. Treatment of the child will usually require contact and cooperation with all the agencies and professionals concerned.

Direct intervention strategies may include individual, group, and family therapy or consultation, as discussed in the following paragraphs. Other sections of this chapter discuss treatment modalities in greater detail.

Individual Therapy. Johnson et al. (1986) suggest that the structure of individual therapy—regularly scheduled sessions of fixed length and frequency that are conducted at a stable location—is in itself an important intervention. This kind of structure can give children a positive experience with clear limits and boundaries, as well as an environment in which trust and safety can readily be established.

Play is often the therapeutic modality used to help children express themselves and modify their behaviors. Play therapy can be conducted in either group or individual treatment settings. Play therapists have an assortment of toys, games, and art supplies and assume that children will seek out the toys and activities that are appropriate to their emotional needs. In the same way that physical, cognitive, and social-emotional development follow predictable patterns, play progresses through developmental stages. An understanding of the stages of play can provide therapists with a useful frame of reference for understanding children.

The process of play therapy varies and will depend on the theoretical orientation of the therapist. In person-centered play therapy, for example, children are allowed free expression in their play, and therapists reflect feelings, assuming that this process will be therapeutic in itself and that children have the ability to solve their own problems (Johnson et al., 1986). In psychodynamic play therapy, therapists interpret the symbolism in the play: the assumption here is that what is unconscious is brought into consciousness, and that the child's ego is able to resolve unconscious psychic conflicts. Social learning theorists view play therapy as an opportunity for therapists to teach prosocial play behaviors and for children to practice appropriate social interactions.

Because adolescents may be able to participate in the traditional fifty minutes of talk therapy, individual therapy for adolescents is similar to therapy for adults. Cognitive-behavioral, psychodynamic, person-centered, eclectic, and other approaches can be used with adolescents who have sufficient ego strength and cognitive functioning to benefit from these methods of intervention. If the adolescent has significant Expressive Language Disorders or Mental Retardation, however, some accommodations may be necessary so that accessible interventions can be provided.

Group Therapy. Group therapy is often used in addition to individual therapy, particularly for disorders in which social skills are impaired (Kaplan, Sadock, & Grebb, 1994). Group therapy can address behavioral difficulties, educational and social problems, or intrapsychic issues. Therapeutic groups can also be a source of peer support and relationships. The group format usually involves shared discussion about the personal issues of group members, with an exchange of feedback.

Many approaches to group therapy have been developed on the basis of different theoretical models, as well as on the basis of children's varying needs. For example, person-centered group therapy may be effective for children with mild behavior problems or emotional immaturity (Johnson et al., 1986). Children with severe disruptive behavior disorders, however, typically require groups that have more structure and emphasize behavioral change. Other types of structured groups are those established with the purpose of helping members work toward a common goal. For example, training groups for teaching social skills develop members' communication skills through a carefully sequenced set of lessons. Anger management (Glick & Goldstein, 1987) and problem solving (Kazdin, Siegel, & Bass, 1992) are other areas where structured therapeutic groups can benefit young clients. Training in these areas, based on cognitive-behavioral theory, teaches such skills as recognizing and labeling affect, managing stress, using relaxation techniques, understanding appropriate interpersonal distance, starting and stopping conversations, identifying problems, and evaluating alternative solutions.

Not all children should be involved in group therapy, however. Yalom (1995) recommends screening children for group readiness, and Dishion and Andrews (1995) suggest that the problem behaviors of adolescents with Conduct Disorders may actually increase with exposure to others who have similar problems. Moreover, children who are actively experiencing psychotic thoughts are usually not appropriate candidates for group therapy.

Family Interventions. On the assumption that a child's or an adolescent's behavior is shaped by the family, therapists often involve families in children's treatment. The goal of this kind of intervention is to change those interactions among family members that may be contributing to or sustaining a troubled child's difficulties. Structural family therapy, for example, seeks to develop appropriate boundaries between family members and subsystems. Another therapeutic goal in this model of therapy is the empowering of adults to take on the responsibilities of parenting. Interactional models focus on improving communication skills among family members. The parents, the troubled child, and the siblings may be guided in making "I" statements and in rephrasing content or expressing emotions in constructive ways; modeling and role playing are often used to achieve this goal. The particular approach to family therapy will be determined by the nature of the family's dynamics and difficulties and the child's disorder.

Parental psychoeducation may also be used to complement a child's treatment. In this approach, information is presented to the parents about their child's disorder, and methods are suggested for creating positive change. Psychoeducation often involves a prescribed curriculum, presented over a series of sessions; two examples of such curricula, widely available through community agencies, are Systematic Training for Effective Parenting (STEP) (Dinkmeyer, 1975) and Parent Effectiveness Training.

Psychotherapy for one or both parents or for siblings, in addition to couples counseling, may also be suggested. Filial therapy, which teaches parents to engage in child-centered play, is a new approach being implemented in some settings (Guerney, 1993). Sibling therapy may also be included in the treatment plan developed for a child.

The issue of confidentiality with children is complicated because the family is an integral part of the treatment, if only in a supportive way (for example, in family members' provision of transportation or payment). Therapists need to clarify the boundaries and limits of confidentiality with the child as well as with the other family members before therapy begins. What information will be communicated to parents, as well as how that communication will occur, should be agreed on during the planning phase of treatment. These negotiations will be especially important when the child is a mature adolescent.

Other Interventions. The development of behavioral programs for use at home or in school is frequently an integral part of psychotherapy with children. Symptoms that may require this type of intervention include repetitive or habitual behaviors, impulsive or off-task behaviors that interfere with the completion of schoolwork, and self-injurious behaviors. The establishment of behavioral interventions requires carefully planned collaboration and is rarely effective without the support and involvement of the adults in a child's daily life.

Psychotropic medication is increasingly used with children; methylphenidate (Ritalin) for Attention-Deficit Disorder is particularly common. The positive effects of Ritalin have been documented repeatedly, but its use continues to be a source of debate among physicians and psychotherapists (Quinn, 1997). Other medications commonly used with children include Dexadrine and Cylert (for Attention-Deficit Disorder), antidepressants like Zoloft, and neuroleptics like haloperidol (Haldol, for Tic or Psychotic Disorders). Therapists working with children should be aware of the potential drug therapies and their side effects.

Residential or day treatment programs and hospitalization are interventions for severe disorders in young clients. These also may be necessary for children who pose a danger to themselves or to others. Residential treatment programs are sometimes used in the treatment of children with severe or profound Mental Retardation, Conduct Disorders, or Psychotic Disorders that do not respond to outpatient or pharmacological interventions.

Prognosis

Outcome research for mental disorders in children and adolescents is a fairly recent phenomenon. Limited information is available, and many questions still need to be answered. Most research provides information only on short-term outcomes (Serketich & Dumas, 1996). Nevertheless, one meta-analysis of these outcome studies does indicate that psychotherapy is significantly better than no treatment at all (Weisz et al., 1995). The same meta-analysis has found that behavioral interventions generally yield outcomes that are more positive than those for nonbehavioral treatments, and that adolescent girls demonstrate better outcomes than those for children in any other age/gender group. Outcome research for specific disorders is considered in the relevant sections of this chapter.

MENTAL RETARDATION

Description of the Disorder

Mental Retardation has a pervasive impact on cognitive, emotional, and social development. As a result, its presence has significant implications for treatment planning at all ages. Historically, Mental Retardation has been diagnosed from results of individual intelligence tests, such as the Wechsler scales and the Stanford-Binet; level of social functioning has also been incorporated recently into the diagnosis. According to *DSM-IV*, the criteria for diagnosis of Mental Retardation include onset prior to age eighteen, subaverage intellectual functioning (IQ below 70), and impaired adaptive functioning in at least two areas, such as communication, social skills, and work.

The impact of this disorder on a child's life and the prognosis for improvement in functioning are significantly correlated with the degree of intellectual impairment. Performance on standardized IQ tests determines the subcategory of retardation. *Mild* retardation reflects an IQ score in the range of 50–55 to 70, two to three standard deviations below the mean. *Moderate* retardation reflects an IQ score in the range of 35–40 to 50–55, or three to four standard deviations below the mean. *Severe* retardation reflects an IQ score in the range of 20–25 to 35–40, or four to five standard deviations below the mean. *Profound* retardation reflects an IQ score below the range of 20–25. Because of the many physical anomalies that may be associated with severe and profound levels of retardation, children with those low levels of functioning can be identified during infancy. By contrast, mild to moderate levels of retardation may not be diagnosed until children begin school.

The evaluation of functioning or adaptive behavior is a less precise process. Assessment tools like the Vineland Adaptive Behavior Scales are often used to quantify these skills (Sparrow, Balla, & Cicchetti, 1984). These scales provide an assessment of a person's life skills on the basis of reports made by caretakers and teachers, or on the basis of direct observations made by the evaluator. The scales provide an assessment of communication, social functioning, daily living, and motor skill development. Wide variations in a child's functioning raise questions about distorted reporting or about the possibility that cultural factors are interfering with functioning.

Mental Retardation usually is diagnosed during infancy or childhood. Recent estimates suggest that approximately 1 percent of the general population can be diagnosed with Mental Retardation (National Institutes of Mental Health, 1990). Boys are three times more likely than girls to be diagnosed with Mental Retardation (Dulmus & Wodarski, 1996). Approximately 25 to 50 percent of people with Mental Retardation have identifiable biological causes for the disorder, such as genetic and chromosomal abnormalities, prenatal and perinatal difficulties, or acquired childhood diseases (King & Noshpitz, 1991). Down's Syndrome is the most widely known genetic type of mild or moderate retardation. Severe and profound retardation commonly have a neurological origin and may be associated with more than two hundred physical disorders, including cerebral palsy, epilepsy, and sensory disorders (Baumeister & Baumeister, 1995).

Cultural and familial factors account for 50 to 75 percent of people diagnosed with Mental Retardation. This subtype is characterized by lack of identifiable biological causes (Baumeister & Baumeister, 1995) and is thought to be the result of some combination of inherited cognitive impairment and environmental deprivation. Mild and moderate retardation is fifteen times more common among children from the lowest socioeconomic class than among children from other classes (Harris, 1995), and this correlation with socioeconomic status has led to questions about the validity of these diagnoses. The issue is confounded by the fact that children with mild retardation often demonstrate age-appropriate behaviors at home but developmentally inappropriate behaviors at school. As the population of the United States becomes increasingly diverse, therapists will need to exercise caution in diagnosing Mental Retardation. The therapist should make a thorough examination of clients' cultural and socioeconomic contexts and of their nonacademic functioning. The therapist will also have to determine whether the assessment tools being used are culturally biased.

Typical Client Characteristics

The characteristics of children, adolescents, and adults with Mental Retardation vary greatly and depend on their level of impairment and on their environment. These clients often present with aggressive, overactive, or self-injurious behavior (Kronenberger & Meyer, 1996). Because of their cognitive limitations, they tend to be concrete in their thinking, reasoning, and problem solving. Developmental delays are common, with such milestones as walking and talking generally appearing later than average. Learning of new tasks requires more practice and guidance for people with Mental Retardation than for their chronological counterparts.

Children with moderate to mild levels of retardation may not exhibit atypical behaviors in all environments. They often master self-care, as well as social and job skills. Children with mild levels of retardation may demonstrate highly adaptive behaviors in nonacademic settings. Their cognitive deficits may become apparent only when they are placed in situations that require higher-order reasoning skills, such as reading, writing, or mathematics. To learn these skills, the children usually require special education, which adapts the curriculum to their learning needs.

A child with a severe or profound level of retardation will frequently exhibit significant motor deficiencies in addition to cognitive impairment. The child may require a wheelchair for mobility and may require assistance with feeding, toileting, and self-care. Speech and language deficiencies may necessitate a facilitated communication device, such as a picture board or word cards.

Comorbid psychological and physical disorders are common among this population. Children with Mental Retardation are three to ten times more likely than people in the general population to experience serious emotional difficulties in addition to their disorder (Baumeister & Baumeister, 1995). In recent years, Fetal Alcohol Syndrome has received increasing attention from the medical and research communities. Children with this medical condition may present with Mental Retardation, Attention-Deficit/Hyperactivity Disorder (ADHD), and diverse learning problems (Don & Rourke, 1995; Niccols, 1994). Heart arrhythmias and respiratory ailments are common among children with Down's Syndrome.

Preferred Therapist Characteristics

Therapists working with people diagnosed with Mental Retardation must be able to establish realistic goals and accept limited progress. They must be knowledgeable about human development and the correlation between intellectual level and development in thinking, communication, and social and motor skills (Harris, 1995). They should exhibit patience and genuineness in their interactions with people with Mental Retardation.

Therapists must also have excellent collaborative skills (Bregman & Gerdtz, 1995). The presence of comorbid disorders is particularly likely in people with severe and profound levels of retardation and will necessitate a team-based treatment approach. Moreover, stress and problems in the family or the environment tend to exacerbate the symptoms of Mental Retardation, decreasing the person's ability to cope, and these factors will also require identification and amelioration. Therapists must work closely with the families of people with Mental Retardation, and so therapists' understanding and appreciation of the particular challenges that parents experience in bringing up a child with Mental Retardation will facilitate the ongoing treatment of this population.

People with Mental Retardation probably will need treatment into adulthood to help them achieve as much independence as possible. Therefore, therapists may serve as long-term case managers, coordinating a variety of services and playing a role as advocates for these clients.

Intervention Strategies

Early intervention is essential to the treatment of children with Mental Retardation. Special education, home health care, language stimulation, and social skills training at an early age can have a great impact on treatment outcomes.

A developmental approach, which takes account of children's cognitive age rather than their chronological age and sets goals on the basis of individual abilities and needs, is crucial to working with children with Mental Retardation.

Nezu and Nezu (1994) recommend that therapists working with people diagnosed with Mental Retardation adopt a five-step problem-solving approach to therapy:

- Identifying beliefs and assumptions
- Defining problems
- Generating alternative solutions
- Evaluating options
- Implementing solutions

The first two steps are particularly important because people with Mental Retardation may not be cognizant of their own difficulties and may need help in identifying aspects of functioning that need attention.

Many people with mild or moderate levels of retardation have the potential to function in socially appropriate ways if they are provided with adequate training. King and Noshpitz (1991) suggest that family, group, and individual psychotherapy can all be effective in promoting these clients' positive self-regard and improving their social and occupational skills. A behavioral approach is most often used to help people diagnosed with Mental Retardation develop appropriate social interaction and self-help skills, such as dressing, taking a bus, and grocery shopping. Learning skills for self-help and daily living is a critical goal for children and adults with mild to moderate levels of Mental Retardation and can make the difference between a life of dependence and a life of productivity.

Most children with severe and profound levels of retardation will ultimately reside in public institutions. Therapists involved in their treatment can contribute to these clients' quality of life by helping them develop recreational interests and interpersonal relationships. Sturmey (1995) has used behavior management strategies with adults with profound levels of retardation; when the number of positive social interactions initiated by the staff was increased, the maladaptive behaviors of adults with Mental Retardation were significantly decreased.

Behavior modification has long been viewed as the treatment modality of choice for Mental Retardation and has been especially helpful in decreasing self-injurious behaviors (Baumeister & Baumeister, 1995; Harris, 1995). Some disagreement does exist over the efficacy of behavioral methods, however. For example, Harris (1995) reports that stereotypical and noncompliant behaviors generally respond well to behavioral treatment, with a success rate of 65 to 75 percent, but a recent meta-analysis of interventions (Scotti, Evans, Meyer, & Walker, 1991) indicates that approximately 40 to 50 percent of the studies reviewed were reporting questionable effectiveness for behavioral interventions.

Therefore, the effectiveness of behavioral interventions should be carefully monitored, especially if negative reinforcers or aversive stimuli are being used.

Nezu and Nezu (1994), having reviewed the treatment literature for people with mild to moderate levels of retardation, find few of the studies they surveyed to be well designed. They report social learning and cognitive-behavioral strategies as having had the most promising results, but few such studies were conducted in outpatient settings.

Hurley (1989) identifies a variety of therapeutic adaptations that may need to be implemented in work with this population. These adaptations include having therapists match their approach to the cognitive and developmental levels of the client, be directive and concrete, take an eclectic approach to the choice of treatment modalities, involve the family, and recognize their own personal biases about people with Mental Retardation. Hurley also suggests that rational-emotive therapy may help children with Mental Retardation acknowledge not only their limitations but also the contributions they are capable of making to society. Another accommodation is to adjust therapeutic timing. Stavrakaki and Klein (1986) suggest that twice-weekly sessions of thirty to forty-five minutes may be particularly effective for people with short attention spans. Sessions that are shorter and more frequent also address the need of many people with Mental Retardation to have information repeated so that their learning will be facilitated.

Family counseling may be indicated, to improve parent-child interactions and educate families about services available in the community. Harris (1995) suggests that families of children with Mental Retardation receive supportive therapy, particularly when the initial diagnosis is made and at times when changes or adaptations for the child are required. Marital problems are common among parents of children with Mental Retardation and may also require intervention, as may issues of loss and grief that are similar to those experienced by parents during bereavement.

Hizen Parenting Skill Training, a program similar to the Parent Management Training model developed by Patterson (1982), was introduced to a group of Japanese parents of children with Mental Retardation (Menta et al., 1995). In a ten-session psychoeducational format, the parents were given information on child development and on basic techniques of behavior change, including positive and negative reinforcement and shaping. The group members also provided support for one another. The children's skills and behavior problems, and the mothers' parenting skills and levels of stress and depression, were measured as dependent variables at the beginning of the training and at regular intervals during the subsequent year. Improvements were noted in all the dependent variables.

Psychopharmacology plays an increasingly important role in the control of symptoms such as aggression, agitation, and hyperactivity associated with Mental Retardation (Baumeister & Baumeister, 1995; Stewart, Myers, Burket, & Lyles, 1990). Haloperidol (Haldol) and thioridazine (Mellaril), medications often used in the treatment of psychotic disorders, have been used to reduce aggressive behaviors in children with Mental Retardation (Kronenberger & Meyer, 1996).

Case management for people with Mental Retardation is often an important part of treatment planning, particularly for adolescents and young adults. Advocacy with schools, agencies, and families and facilitation of appropriate job placement are tasks that may be included in a treatment plan, as may coordination of a multimodal treatment team.

Prognosis

Mental Retardation has implications for a person's entire life span. Adults with a mild level of retardation often live independently and maintain jobs with minimal supervision. People with a moderate level of retardation may ultimately be able to live independently in group-home settings and gain employment in sheltered workshops. Social skills training, career counseling, and development of self-awareness skills may all facilitate these clients' efforts at being independent. Therapists working with children and adults who have severe and profound levels of Mental Retardation may be able to effect many positive changes. For example, the use of behavioral techniques to reduce self-injurious acts is likely to be successful. Regardless of the degree of retardation, therapists can make a difference in improving the lives of people diagnosed with Mental Retardation.

LEARNING, MOTOR SKILLS, AND COMMUNICATION DISORDERS

Description of the Disorders

Learning, Motor Skills, and Communication Disorders are identified in children whose levels of functioning are significantly below expectations in the pertinent skill areas. The expectations are based on the children's age, cognitive abilities, and education, and their level of functioning is judged to be interfering with their achievement or daily activities. According to *DSM-IV,* a determination that a child's level of functioning is significantly below expectations is made if the child's score on achievement tests is more than two standard deviations below the child's IQ. Functioning is measured with such standardized assessments as the Woodcock Johnson–Revised Tests of Achievement (Woodcock & Johnson, 1989) or the Wechsler Individual Achievement Test (Wechsler, 1992).

Disorders of Mathematics, Reading, and Written Expression are characterized by significant difficulties in those areas of academic functioning. These disorders must be distinguished from underachievement caused by normal variations, lack of opportunity, poor teaching, or cultural factors. Deficiencies of vision or hearing should be ruled out as causes of impairment before Learning Disorders are diagnosed. The category of Learning Disorders Not Otherwise Specified describes academic deficits that do not meet the criteria for specific Learning Disorders. This diagnosis may be used when a child exhibits academic deficits in more than one academic area, or when the deficits do not reach the required degree of significance (two standard deviations below age- and ability-based expectations).

Developmental Coordination Disorder is the diagnosis for motor coordination substantially below age- and intelligence-based expectations. This diagnosis should not be made if symptoms are due to a medical condition (American Psychiatric Association, 1994a).

DSM-IV describes four types of Communication Disorders: Expressive Language Disorder, Mixed Receptive-Expressive Language Disorder, Phonological Disorder, and Stuttering. Children with the first two disorders demonstrate language development that is significantly below expectations based on nonverbal ability and that interferes with academic progress. Phonological Disorder is "failure to use developmentally expected speech sounds that are appropriate for age and dialect" (American Psychiatric Association, 1994a, p. 61); lisping is an example. Stuttering reflects problems with speech fluency that interfere with a child's ability to communicate or make good academic progress.

The causes of Learning, Motor Skills, and Communication Disorders currently are thought to be related to neurocerebral atypia, which may result from exposure to perinatal or neonatal insult (Johnson, 1995). Lead poisoning or head traumas in childhood may contribute to Learning Disorders. Silver (1991) also reports correlations between Learning Disorders and low birth weight, maternal smoking or alcohol use during pregnancy, and exposure to other toxins.

Family patterns of learning disabilities have long been recognized. Approximately 35 to 45 percent of boys with Learning Disorders have at least one parent who had similar learning problems (Maughan & Yule, 1994), and recent studies have identified strong genetic links to such reading subskills as phonology (Olson et al., 1991). Features associated with Learning Disorders include low socioeconomic status, poor self-esteem, depression, and perceptual deficiencies (Silver, 1992). As a result of these concomitant problems, differential diagnosis may be difficult, and treatment may require both educational and psychological interventions.

Typical Client Characteristics

DSM-IV estimates the prevalence of Learning Disorders at approximately 5 percent. They usually become evident in the early elementary school years. Children with these disorders often are unhappy in school, have negative self-images and social difficulties, and show increased likelihood of dropping out of school. Depression, as well as Attention-Deficit and Disruptive Behavior Disorders, will often coexist with Learning Disorders.

Reading Disorders are found in approximately 4 percent of school-age children, and of that group, 60 to 80 percent are boys. Children with Reading Disorders may have difficulty decoding unknown words, memorizing vocabulary lists, and comprehending written passages.

According to *DSM-IV*, approximately 1 percent of school-age children can be diagnosed with Mathematics Disorders; Maxmen and Ward (1995) suggest that the actual prevalence is 6 percent. Boys are four times more likely than girls to be diagnosed with Mathematics Disorders than with Reading Disorders. Children with mathematics-related deficiencies may have difficulty with conceptual math, calculation, or both.

Disorders of Written Expression are rarely found in isolation; another Learning Disorder is also present in most cases (American Psychiatric Association, 1994a; Silver, 1992). The difficulties associated with Disorders of Written Expression are typically reflected in multiple areas, which include handwriting, spelling, grammar, and the creation of prose.

Children with Developmental Coordination Disorder usually appear clumsy and have delays in achieving developmental milestones. This disorder is often accompanied by a Communication Disorder.

Language Disorders resemble Learning Disorders in terms of prevalence, gender ratio, and familial patterns. They typically appear during the preschool years. Although they often disappear spontaneously, they can still cause considerable academic and social impairment.

Preferred Therapist Characteristics

Therapists working with children who have Learning Disorders must be able to take a broad view of their clients, determining and assessing a range of possible contributing factors and coexisting mental disorders. Therapists should be able to evaluate children's perceptual and cognitive processes as well as their emotional functioning. Children with significant language deficits may require non-verbal approaches to therapy, such as play therapy or activity-group therapy.

Intervention Strategies

The primary interventions for children with Learning Disorders will occur at school. The major goal will be the remediation of learning and skill deficits (Johnson, 1995). A child who demonstrates significant underachievement (more than two standard deviations below measured ability) may be eligible for special education. An individualized education plan, developed by the school according to the requirements of Public Law 94–142 (the Education of All Handicapped Children Act), will specify the educational goals that the school is to address. This kind of plan is similar to a treatment plan in a mental health setting: it identifies areas of weakness, sets strategies for improving areas of deficit, and establishes observable goal behaviors. These plans often include social and emotional goals, such as improved interpersonal relationships, increased on-task behaviors, and decreased inappropriate language. School counselors and psychotherapists usually collaborate with special education teachers in treating children with these disorders.

The goals of psychotherapy for children with Learning, Motor Skills, and Communication Disorders typically focus on improving self-confidence, interpersonal behaviors, and school adjustment. Silver (1992) suggests that essential goals of treatment will include identifying and building on the children's strengths as well as educating the children and their families about Learning Disorders and their impact on school, family, and social functioning. Parents often feel anger and disappointment about their children's academic performance, and those feelings must receive attention. Once academic issues are addressed, and once the family and the child have a better understanding of the Learning Disorder and its impact on them, the child's behavioral problems may disappear spontaneously (Silver, 1995).

Children with Learning Disorders frequently come for counseling because of problems with their interpersonal skills. The same perceptual difficulties that impair academic learning can interfere with a child's comprehension of social information and may result in inappropriate social behaviors (Silver, 1995). Therapy may be required to teach social skills. Goldstein (1997) and others describe social skills training programs with curricula based on cognitive-behavioral models. These training programs teach such social skills as understanding social space, behaviors associated with making a personal approach, attending and communication skills, and understanding the nature of social interactions. The lessons are primarily didactic but are typically given in small-group settings so as to facilitate practice and feedback.

Counselors and therapists are occasionally asked to instruct children in learning strategies. Children with Learning Disorders frequently demonstrate distinctive preferences in learning style and may need individualized help in acquiring new ways to learn. Clinicians can use cognitive-behavioral approaches to help children understand their learning strengths and weaknesses and build on their abilities.

Therapists may also need to serve as advocates for children with their schools. This role may require a therapist to explain the learning strategies likely to work best for a particular child and to recommend an appropriate educational placement for the child.

Therapists are especially likely to see children with Learning Disorders or related disorders if there is a coexisting mental disorder. Treatment plans should take into account not just the coexisting mental disorder but also the academic, interpersonal, family, and self-esteem issues that typically accompany learning problems.

People in other professions also contribute to the treatment of children with Learning Disorders and related disorders. Communication and Coordination Disorders are almost always addressed through school-based programs. Children are routinely screened by speech and language therapists, who identify speech disorders and design treatments for correcting them. Motor Skill Disorders are addressed by other specialists, usually occupational or physical therapists, who use exercises to improve muscle tone, balance, range of motion, and fine motor coordination. Occupational therapists occasionally teach keyboarding skills, which facilitate a child's communication with teachers and with other children. Computer technology offers an invaluable aid for children with Motor Skills Disorders.

Prognosis

Although some early learning deficits are related to developmental delays and can improve with maturation, many such deficits continue to have a negative impact on functioning throughout adolescence and adulthood. Learning Disorders and related disorders, left undiagnosed and untreated, can lead to extreme frustration, loss of self-esteem, inadequate education, underemployment, and more serious mental disorders. Proactive interventions, including psychotherapy, individualized teaching strategies to accommodate different learning styles, and social skills training, can have a significant positive impact on children with these disorders (Silver, 1995).

PERVASIVE DEVELOPMENTAL DISORDERS

Description of the Disorders

The prevalence of Pervasive Developmental Disorders is approximately ten to twenty cases per ten thousand people (Lord & Rutter, 1994). Males with these disorders outnumber females by a ratio of approximately 2.5 to 1 (Harris, 1995; Sigman & Capps, 1997). *DSM-IV* describes four Pervasive Developmental Disorders (PDDs) differentiated by age, pattern of onset, and nature of symptoms:

- Autistic Disorder
- Rett's Disorder
- Childhood Disintegrative Disorder
- Asperger's Disorder

A fifth type listed by *DSM-IV* is Pervasive Developmental Disorder Not Otherwise Specified. All five have a great impact on neurological, emotional, linguistic, and, in some cases, physical development.

Degree of impairment and prognosis varies considerably for each disorder. Typically, children with Rett's Disorder and Childhood Disintegrative Disorder regress over time, whereas those with Autistic Disorder and Asperger's Disorder may improve. An accurate diagnosis will aid in the development of appropriate treatment plans.

Children with PDDs typically have deficits in socialization, communication, and behavior (American Psychiatric Association, 1994a; Maxmen & Ward, 1995; Volkmar, 1991). They tend to avoid contact with others, and they have poor social skills, as well as a limited capacity for empathy. Their speech is often limited or atypical, and they have difficulty sustaining a conversation. Most lack initiative and may exhibit rigid, stereotyped, repetitive behaviors, such as rocking, flapping, or head banging. Children diagnosed with PDDs tend to under- or over-react to sensory stimuli and have difficulty with change and variations from their regular routines. Although some have strong intellectual or other abilities, most children with PDDs can also be diagnosed with Mental Retardation (Maxmen & Ward, 1995). Moreover, a variety of general medical conditions, including chromosomal abnormalities and chronic infections, can be found in children with PDDs.

Studies of neurophysiological and neurochemical correlates of these disorders are inconclusive (Lord & Rutter, 1994), and the etiology of Pervasive Developmental Disorders remains unclear. Sigman and Capps (1997) suggest that Autistic Disorder is related to deficits in cognitive and affective skill development, and strong evidence of a genetic component has been found in recent studies of twins and families. One such study (Smalley, 1991) reports that, among monozygotic twins, 60 percent both had Autistic Disorder, by contrast with a comparison group of dizygotic twins in which only 5 percent both had the disorder. Family studies also report that the incidence of Autistic Disorder among siblings of children with that disorder is fifty times greater than in the general population (Silliman, Campbell, & Mitchell, 1989).

A diagnosis of PDD can be facilitated by the use of behavioral rating scales. For example, the Child Autism Rating Scale (Schopler, Reichler, De Vellis, & Daly, 1991) assesses children's performance in fifteen different domains: relating to people, imitation, emotional response, body use, object use, adaptation to change, visual response, listening response, sensory response, fear or nervousness, verbal communication, nonverbal communication, activity level, intellectual functioning, and general impressions. The Checklist for Autism in Toddlers (Baron-Cohen, Allen, & Gillberg, 1992) identifies early signs of the disorder by assessing imaginative play, social interest, social play, indication of interest through pointing, and following of another's gaze (Sigman & Capps, 1997). The Pervasive Developmental Disorders have many similarities, but each is diagnosed on the basis of distinguishing characteristics.

Autistic Disorder

Autistic Disorder, found in two to five of every ten thousand people, is characterized by significant deficits in socialization, communication, and behavior (American Psychiatric Association, 1994a; Sigman & Capps, 1997). Social difficulties are reflected by limited initiation of social interaction or conversation, lack of interest in other people, dysfunctional emotions, poor skills in imitating affective expressions, and limited empathy.

The degree of impairment in communication skills varies widely among people with Autistic Disorder. Some are mute, whereas others do eventually develop age-appropriate language skills; nearly all, however, have problems with the use of narrative language and with comprehension, and they tend to show abnormalities in spoken language. These problems further impair their socialization.

Children with Autistic Disorder rarely engage in make-believe play that mimics human activity. Their play more often exhibits repetitive, stereotyped interactions with inanimate objects. As these children grow older, this play activity may evolve into obsessional interest in mechanical objects, time schedules, or factual data. Children with Autistic Disorder may also exhibit characteristic physical movements (hand flapping, rocking), fascination with moving things (such as ceiling fans and light switches), aggressive and hyperactive behavior, abnormalities in sleeping and eating, and a preoccupation with some narrow interest (lights, trains, meteorology). Another characteristic of Autistic Disorder is onset before the age of three, typically with no period of normal development. Mental retardation accompanies this diagnosis in 75 percent of all cases (Sigman & Capps, 1997).

Gillberg, Gillberg, and Steffenberg (1992) have found that children with Autistic Disorder are often firstborn or only children. Rutter, Bailey, Bolton, and Le Couteur (1993) have found children with Autistic Disorder particularly likely to have relatives who exhibit cognitive deficits, usually involving language delays, and who have been diagnosed with Asperger's Disorder.

Rett's Disorder

Rett's Disorder is characterized by a period of normal development during the first five to forty-eight months of life. This period is followed by progressive loss of abilities and ultimately by severe or profound retardation (Campbell, Cueva, & Hallin, 1996). To date, only females with this disorder have been identified.

Children with this disorder exhibit deceleration of head growth, stereotypical hand movements (usually hand wringing or hand washing), lack of social involvement, poorly coordinated gait or trunk movements, Mental Retardation, and severely impaired language development (American Psychiatric Association, 1994a). This disorder is estimated to affect one in ten thousand females (Rett Syndrome Diagnostic Criteria Work Group, 1988).

Childhood Disintegrative Disorder

Children diagnosed with Childhood Disintegrative Disorder manifest apparently normal development until at least the age of two. At some point between the ages of two and ten, however, they exhibit significant regression of functioning in at least two of the following areas:

- Language
- Social skills

- Elimination
- Play
- Motor skills

Children with this extremely rare disorder eventually exhibit social, communication, and behavioral deficits that are similar to those of children with Autistic Disorders. Severe Mental Retardation also usually accompanies Childhood Disintegrative Disorder (Campbell, Cueva, & Hallin, 1996).

Asperger's Disorder

Like Autistic Disorder, Asperger's Disorder is typified by impaired social skills and repetitive or stereotypical behaviors. Unlike Autistic Disorder, however, Asperger's Disorder typically does not involve significant delays in the development of language, oral communication, or cognitive functioning (American Psychiatric Association, 1994a). Children with this disorder also often develop age-appropriate self-help skills. Although these children have limited skills in social interaction, they may derive some pleasure from interpersonal situations (Lord & Rutter, 1994). Asperger's Disorder is more common in males, and onset is somewhat later than in Autistic Disorder (American Psychiatric Association, 1994a).

Typical Client Characteristics

Children with PDDs are characterized by their atypical social behaviors. They generally exhibit flat affect, poor eye contact, and minimal social speech. They do not demonstrate the social behaviors that one expects in children of their age. They typically do not seek parental attention and do not engage in imitative or interactive play (Harris, 1995). Although the quality of their social skills continues to be atypical, their social skills may improve with age or circumstances. For example, children with Autistic Disorder may exhibit episodes of heightened relationship skills when they feel distress at being separated from their parents, or they may experience enjoyment of an activity (Lord & Rutter, 1994).

Other characteristics of people with PDDs vary and depend on the specific disorder; most of the available research focuses on people with Autistic Disorder. Autistic speech typically exhibits such atypical features as echolalia, or rote repetition of what others have said. Older children with autism may develop fairly complex speech, but they continue to have difficulty participating in social conversation because they miss social and conversational cues. Children with Autistic Disorder and Asperger's Disorder often have difficulty with transitions or changes in routine. Their stereotypic behaviors may become exaggerated at times of transition, or when they experience increased stress.

Having a first-degree relative with a PDD typically carries a profound impact for the family. Siblings often have peer problems, feel lonely, and are concerned about their brother or sister who has the disorder (Bagenholm & Gillberg, 1991). Marital difficulties commonly develop as the parents of the child focus their energies on the often fruitless search for a remedy.

Preferred Therapist Characteristics

Therapists working with children who have PDDs must be familiar with the distinctions among these disorders. At present, treatments and prognoses for the different types of PDD vary greatly. Therapists need patience and an ability to identify with these children. Campbell, Schopler, Mesibov, and Sanchez (1995) suggest that therapists must work especially hard to develop rapport and trust. Grandin (1995) and Campbell, Cueva, and Hallin (1996) report that the therapist's gaining an understanding of the things that are meaningful to the child with a Pervasive Developmental Disorder, as well as the therapist's developing an understanding of the child's idiosyncratic viewpoint, can provide the foundation for developing a relationship.

Intervention Strategies

Lord and Rutter (1994) recommend four treatment goals for children with PDDs:

1. Fostering the development of social and communication skills
2. Enhancing learning and problem solving
3. Decreasing behaviors that interfere with learning
4. Helping the family cope with the disorder

Because of the pervasive nature of the symptoms, treatment is multifaceted and usually requires collaboration by many health care providers (Awad, 1995; Campbell, Cueva, & Hallin, 1996). Children with Pervasive Development Disorders are usually involved in special education, speech and language therapy, and physical therapy. Those with Rett's Disorder or Childhood Disintegrative Disorder may also be under the care of physicians, neurologists, or other medical specialists. Consultation with other service providers, as well as case management of this broad spectrum of services, may fall to the therapist.

Historically, the treatment approach used for children with Autistic Disorder was psychodynamic, but research on outcomes has not supported the effectiveness of that approach with this population (Campbell, Cueva, & Hallin, 1996). Current findings indicate that behavioral approaches are generally more effective. Typical goals of behavioral treatment are to reduce or avoid the fear and anxiety that can heighten stereotypical behaviors, to eliminate or prevent repetitive and stereotypical activities, and to stimulate development of age-appropriate skills. Di Lalla and Rogers (1994) have found that negative emotionality in people with PDDs decreased in response to treatment over a six-month period. Volkmar (1991) finds that the interventions most effective with these clients are behavioral techniques like positive reinforcement, time-out, overcorrection, punishment, and substitution of new skills through a program of shaping and rewarding more socially appropriate behaviors.

Lovaas (1987) reports on one promising behavioral program in which nineteen children with Autistic Disorder began treatment before the age of four. Interventions included one-to-one behavior modification for forty hours a week for two years. Goals of the program included the diminishing of negative behaviors (such as rocking, flapping, and repetitive noises) and the increasing of socially appropriate skills (such as making eye contact, answering social questions, and engaging in play). According to Lovaas, the researchers involved in this study reported that 47 percent of the children were able to enter a regular first-grade class and demonstrated considerable gains in IQ scores; a positive long-term impact of this treatment has also been reported (McEachin, Smith, & Lovaas, 1993), although other researchers have not been able to replicate these results. The costs and the intensity of such a program are high but must be weighed against the potential costs of lifelong residential placement.

Other approaches have also demonstrated some effectiveness. Campbell, Cueva, and Hallin (1996), for example, have found that children with Autistic Disorders who had good cognitive abilities were able to benefit from a relationship-oriented and cognitive-behavioral model of individual counseling. By communicating understanding, the therapists built rapport and were then able to use cognitive-behavioral therapies to teach the children more adaptive methods of communication and social interaction. The model included teaching the children such communication skills as making eye contact and allowing an appropriate amount of personal space, as well as helping them understand typical topics of interest for children in their age group. Children with Autistic Disorder and Asperger's Disorder are particularly likely to respond to individual therapies that address social skills and social communication (Sigman & Capps, 1997).

Structured training programs have also demonstrated some improvement of skills in people with PDDs. For example, Mesibov (1984) developed a social skills training program that included peer tutoring, after-school activities, and weekly social groups for adolescents with Autistic Disorder. These groups took a social learning approach and emphasized modeling, immediate feedback, and positive reinforcement. Specific social goals were targeted and included making appropriate eye contact and recognizing interpersonal space or distance.

In addition to behavioral treatment, people with PDDs typically require a variety of adjunct services, which may include speech and language training and residential placement. Medication is sometimes also helpful (Campbell et al.,

1995; Campbell, Cueva, & Hallin, 1996), particularly if self-injurious behaviors are not responsive to behavior modification. Methylphenidate (Ritalin) and neuroleptics like haloperidol (Haldol) have been used with some success to reduce symptoms associated with these disorders.

A variety of other innovative treatments have been used with these clients, but to date the value of these treatments has not been conclusively demonstrated. Grandin (1995), for example, developed a device, called the Squeeze Machine, that attempts to desensitize children with Autistic Disorder to physical contact. An approach known as Facilitated Communication has also been used to aid these children in their attempts to communicate. It involves holding a child's hand above a keyboard or letterboard and assisting the child's efforts to point to various letters and, eventually, to spell out words. Some case studies have reported success with this technique, but empirical support has not been forthcoming (Sigman & Capps, 1997), and some writers have expressed concern about whether the resulting communications reflect the child's or the facilitator's words (Mesibov, 1995).

Family consultation, as well as supportive therapy for parents and siblings, should usually be included in the treatment of children with PDDs. Couples or sibling therapy can also be beneficial as a means of providing emotional support and useful information about the development of the disorder (Sigman & Capps, 1997). Higashi Daily Life Therapy (Lord & Rutter, 1994) is a highly structured behavioral training program that teaches parents to be cotherapists. In this model, the parents are trained to implement behavioral techniques (such as shaping and extinction of behaviors) in the home setting. The sense of isolation felt by families of children with PDDs may also be reduced if informative publications and networking resources are provided. The Autism Society of America has local chapters throughout the country, and the Rett's Syndrome Association disseminates information from its headquarters. Both groups also have sites on the Internet.

Prognosis

In a review of outcome studies, Gillberg (1991) found that some children diagnosed with Autistic Disorder had become able to lead independent lives as adults, but that about two-thirds of children with the disorder went on to require care throughout their lives. Prognoses for people with the other Pervasive Developmental Disorders are variable. For those with Asperger's Disorder, the prognosis is excellent; many live independent lives. Residential treatment is probable for those with Rett's Disorder and Childhood Degenerative Disorder because of those disorders' progressive nature. For all PDDs, early intervention appears to be the most important factor in a positive outcome (Campbell, Schopler, Cueva, & Hallin, 1996; McEachin et al., 1993).

ATTENTION-DEFICIT DISORDERS AND DISRUPTIVE BEHAVIOR DISORDERS

Overview of the Disorders

Attention-Deficit Disorders and Disruptive Behavior Disorders listed in *DSM-IV* include Attention-Deficit/Hyperactivity Disorder, Conduct Disorder, and Oppositional Defiant Disorder, as well as Disruptive Behavior Disorder Not Otherwise Specified. These disorders present therapists with a considerable challenge. Children with these disorders have high rates of comorbidity (Arnold & Jensen, 1995), need a variety of collaborative interventions (Pelham, 1994), and often are resistant to treatment.

Attention-Deficit Disorders are found in as many as 50 percent of the children seen for psychotherapy (Cantwell, 1996). Children with Oppositional Defiant Disorder and Conduct Disorder often have comorbid attention deficits, and many children with Attention-Deficit Disorders or Conduct Disorder have concomitant Learning Disorders. To be effective, diagnosis and treatment must address these dual diagnoses.

Attention-Deficit/Hyperactivity Disorder

Description of the Disorder

DSM-IV divides Attention-Deficit/Hyperactivity Disorder (ADHD) into three subtypes:

- Predominantly Hyperactive-Impulsive Type
- Predominantly Inattentive Type
- Combined Type

By definition, ADHD has an onset prior to age seven, is present in two or more settings (such as at home and in school), and interferes with social, academic, or occupational functioning. The person with this disorder also exhibits six or more symptoms of hyperactivity/impulsivity or inattentiveness that have persisted for at least six months (American Psychiatric Association, 1994a). Symptoms of inattention include failure to give close attention to details, difficulty sustaining attention, poor follow-through on instructions, failure to finish work, difficulty organizing tasks, misplacement of things, distraction by extraneous stimuli, and forgetfulness. Hyperactive-impulsive characteristics are more visible, and so this diagnosis is usually identified at a younger age. Hyperactive-impulsive behaviors include fidgeting, running about, difficulty playing quietly, acting as if driven by a motor, talking excessively, blurting answers, and interrupting.

The diagnosis of ADHD can be made from an evaluation of the child's history (King & Noshpitz, 1991). A more thorough evaluation includes medical, cognitive, and achievement assessments, as well as parents' and teachers' input on behavior rating scales (Cantwell, 1996). The inclusion of a Continuous Performance Test (CPT) has recently been recommended as a measure of the child's or adolescent's ability to sustain a focus on monotonous and repetitive tasks (Kronenberger & Meyer, 1996); CPTs have been found to distinguish between children with ADHD and those without the disorder (Loge, Staton, & Beatty, 1990).

Behavior checklists provide an assessment of attentional deficits. The Conners Teacher and Parent Rating Scales (Conners, 1990), the Achenbach Child Behavior Checklist (CBCL) Parent, Teacher and Youth Self-Report forms (Achenbach, 1991), and the Behavior Assessment System for Children (BASC) (Reynolds & Kamphaus, 1992) all use a 4-point Likert-type scale to assess a range of behaviors. The Conners instrument is frequently used by physicians to monitor the effects of medication. The CBCL and the BASC evaluate a broader spectrum of comorbid symptoms, such as depression, anxiety, atypical thoughts, and delinquent and withdrawn behaviors. The BASC includes a scale that allows the therapist to check the validity of responses and that facilitates assessment of the Predominantly Inattentive Type of ADHD.

Magnetic resonance imaging (MRI) and positron emission tomography (PET) technology have been used to study neurological activity in people with ADHD (Semrud-Clikeman et al., 1994). Preliminary results reveal significant brain abnormalities that may ultimately allow the diagnosis of ADHD to be based on direct assessment of brain functioning. At this time, however, these procedures are being used solely for research purposes.

In recent years a dramatic increase in the diagnosis of ADHD has been reported, raising questions about the accuracy of these diagnoses. One difficulty with the diagnosis of this disorder is its reliance on a history derived from teachers' and parents' reports. Negative relationships between the child and these adults may skew these assessments. Moreover, the requirement that the identified behaviors be more frequent and more severe than those found in children at comparable developmental levels is sufficiently vague to create diagnostic problems, particularly in children of preschool age.

The current prevalence rates for ADHD range from 3 percent to 5 percent of children (Cantwell, 1996; Wolraich et al., 1996). Until recently, boys were believed to be two to ten times more likely to have this disorder than girls (Barkley, 1990), but the inclusion of the Predominantly Inattentive Type in *DSM-IV* may reduce this gender discrepancy. There have been more females than males among subjects diagnosed with ADHD in adulthood (Wender, 1987).

Comorbidity of ADHD with Learning Disorders, Oppositional Defiant Disorder, and Conduct Disorder is fairly common (Barkley, 1996). Current research suggests a causal relationship among ADHD, Oppositional Defiant Disorder, and Conduct Disorder (Biederman et al., 1996). Anxiety and Tic Disorders have been found to coexist with ADHD as well, although the nature of the relationship is less clear. Hyperactive behaviors can also be an expression of the manic phase of a Bipolar Disorder.

Typical Client Characteristics

Symptomatic behaviors vary and depend on the age at presentation and the type of ADHD. The common feature in elementary school–age children with ADHD is difficulty in sustaining attention, particularly during long, monotonous, repetitive tasks. (These children can usually focus their attention on tasks that include small instructional units or fast-paced multisensory presentations.) Other common symptoms include poor impulse control, restlessness, and overactivity. Children may also exhibit noncompliant and antisocial behaviors related to their impulsivity.

Impulsive behaviors typically impair functioning in many areas. They can result in poor interpersonal relationships and academic difficulties. Barkley, Anastopoulos, Guevremont, and Fletcher (1991) report that 20 to 30 percent of children with ADHD have comorbid Learning Disorders. Children with ADHD also are at greater risk for accidental injury and may experience significant sleep problems. As a result of all these difficulties, children with ADHD commonly manifest poor social skills and low self-esteem. Family conflict and discomfort at school are also frequent results of these children's behaviors.

ADHD was once thought to be a disorder of childhood that would abate as a child reached adolescence (King & Noshpitz, 1991). However, current research portrays it as a lifelong disorder for many; 30 to 50 percent of children with ADHD will be symptomatic through adolescence and adulthood (Mash & Barkley, 1996). But the symptoms of the disorder typically change. Hyperactivity is unusual among adolescents with ADHD; restlessness, poorly organized schoolwork, failure to complete independent work, and high-risk behaviors are more common indicators of this disorder in teenagers (Cantwell, 1996; Rapport, 1995; Weiss & Hechtman, 1986).

For the diagnosis of ADHD to be made in adults, symptoms must date back to childhood. Hallowell and Ratey (1994) list the following twenty diagnostic criteria for a diagnosis of adult ADHD, with the presence of fifteen or more considered to be significant:

> a sense of not meeting one's goals, difficulty getting organized, chronic procrastination, multiple ongoing simultaneous projects, blurting out inappropriate comments, frequent searches for high stimulation, intolerance of boredom, distractibility, creativity, trouble following proper procedures, low frustration tolerance, impulsive behaviors, a tendency to worry, a sense of insecurity, mood swings, restlessness, a tendency toward addictive behavior, chronic problems

with self-esteem, inaccurate self-observation, and a family history of ADHD or Bipolar Disorders [pp. 73–74].

Research has shown compelling evidence of a greater prevalence of ADHD among members of the same family. Barkley et al. (1991) have found that 20 to 32 percent of first-degree relatives of children diagnosed with ADHD also exhibit characteristics of that disorder, and studies of twins confirm a genetic component of ADHD. First-degree relatives have also been found to have an elevated incidence of depression, alcohol misuse, conduct-related problems, and antisocial disorders (Biederman, Newcorn, & Sprich, 1991). Thus a child with ADHD often has parents and siblings with the disorder, which may lead to a chaotic home environment and make it difficult for the parents to establish the clear guidelines needed by a child with ADHD.

Preferred Therapist Characteristics

Hyperactive behavior typically affects the therapeutic relationship, just as it affects the child's daily life. The therapist needs to present a calm and patient demeanor, to avoid escalating the excitable behaviors of a child with ADHD. Many transference and countertransference issues can arise as a result of the emotional volatility in a child with this disorder (Lewis, 1991). To be effective, therapists must be clear about their own emotional issues and able to distinguish them from those of the child.

Children with ADHD frequently experience negative interactions with others, particularly adults, as a result of their impulsive and sometimes noncompliant behaviors (Barkley, 1996). Consequently, the development of a trusting, accepting relationship with the therapist will be a critical element of treatment. Therapy can be enhanced by the provision of a structured setting where boundaries of time and safety are clearly established by the therapist.

Therapists who work with children with ADHD also need a clear developmental yardstick against which to measure these children's activity and impulsivity. They also need to keep abreast of the rapidly evolving research on ADHD.

Intervention Strategies

Therapists working with children with ADHD rely primarily on behavioral interventions. Behavioral treatments for children with ADHD are based on operant conditioning, the shaping of behavior through the use of positive reinforcers. Treatment most often addresses the behaviors of staying on task, completing work, and following directions (Rapport, 1995). These interventions are demanding of time and resources; they involve teaching, practice, encouragement, reinforcement, and monitoring, and they require cooperation on the part of these children's teachers and parents.

Cognitive-behavioral models of treatment have been used to improve social skills in people with ADHD and to provide training for parents (Cousins &

Weiss, 1993; Rapport, 1995). Social skills training programs teach behaviors that can improve interpersonal relationships. Skills like identifying personal space, starting and maintaining a conversation, identifying the main idea of a conversation, and accepting and giving compliments are all addressed in these programs.

Training can also help parents recognize and encourage socially competent behavior, teach self-evaluation strategies, model good communication skills, and provide consistent rewards and consequences (Anastopoulos, Shelton, Du Paul, & Guevremont, 1993; Cousins & Weiss, 1993). Newby, Fischer, and Roman (1991), for example, describe a home intervention plan that educated parents about ADHD, about the negative family interactions that it may elicit, about the importance of positive attention, and about the implementation of behavior management techniques that use positive reinforcement. Programs like Systematic Training for Effective Parenting (STEP) (Dinkmeyer, 1975) and support groups like Children with Attention Deficit Disorders (CHADD) or Adults with Deficit Attention (ADDA) may also be useful.

School interventions in the treatment of ADHD are important as well and usually consist of behavioral techniques. Interventions that offer praise for appropriate behaviors and ignore those that are inappropriate have been shown to be effective (Du Paul, Guevremont, & Barkley, 1992). The teacher's attention or proximity, used as a reinforcer, can be another powerful tool in the treatment plan (Kronenberger & Meyer, 1996). Consistent and regular communication among parents, teachers, and therapists is also an integral part of treatment, so that desirable behaviors will be reinforced in multiple settings.

Ideally, children with ADHD will ultimately monitor their own behaviors. Timing devices called Attention Training Systems (Rapport, 1995) have been available since the early 1980s. Based on classical conditioning theory, these devices ring an alarm at specified intervals. When the alarm rings, the child self-monitors and records behaviors. This approach has the potential of developing lifelong self-awareness; unfortunately, however, these devices have not yet proved their effectiveness (Whalen & Henker, 1991). Token economies have been effective with children with ADHD, even with children who have not responded to other behavioral interventions (Du Paul et al., 1992). In this approach, children earn tokens or points for appropriate behaviors, accumulate the tokens or points, and exchange them for rewards. This system can be cumbersome, but, if well designed, can be beneficial to all the children in the classroom or in the home (Kronenberger & Meyer, 1996).

Timeouts and reprimands (usually verbal) can serve as negative reinforcers for inappropriate behaviors. A timeout involves removing the child from the classroom or home activity for a short period; the assumption is that reducing the amount of stimulation and the availability of positive reinforcers will lead to a decrease in negative behaviors. Support for the effectiveness of these two interventions has been mixed (Kronenberger & Meyer, 1996); used effectively, however, these tools of operant conditioning may well have a positive impact on the behaviors of children with ADHD (Abramowitz & O'Leary, 1991).

Other psychotherapeutic approaches have also played a role in the treatment of ADHD. Individual psychotherapy has been used to address low self-esteem or comorbid Anxiety or Mood Disorders (Fonagy & Target, 1994). Group therapy, focusing on improving communication skills, recognition of nonverbal messages, and appropriate approach behaviors, has promoted social skill development in children with ADHD. Dietary restrictions or adjustments, such as elimination of sugar and chemicals from the diet (Carter et al., 1993; Wolraich et al., 1996), and biofeedback (Tansey, 1993) have also been used. These approaches may be helpful, but minimal outcome research is available to support their effectiveness.

Psychostimulant medication for ADHD has been the focus of considerable research over the past ten years. Effective drugs are thought to stimulate the production of the neurochemicals that facilitate brain functioning. Contrary to the popular misconception that these children are hypersensitive or hyper-attentive, neurodevelopmental research suggests that ADHD is actually a problem of underarousal (Barkley, 1996). Methylphenidate (Ritalin) and dextroamphet-amine (Dexadrine) are the drugs prescribed most frequently; approximately 75 percent of children with ADHD will respond positively to one of these (Cantwell, 1996; King & Noshpitz, 1991). Pemoline (Cylert) demonstrates some advantages for adolescents in terms of its longer-lasting effects and its fewer behavioral side effects (Pelham, Swanson, Furman, & Schwindt, 1995), but use of this medication with young children can present dangers.

Meta-analyses of research on psychostimulants to treat ADHD have consistently found that hyperactive, restless, and impulsive behaviors, as well as disruptive, aggressive, and socially inappropriate actions, diminish in response to treatment (Klein, 1993; Whalen & Henker, 1991). Rapport, Denney, Du Paul, and Gardner (1994) have reported improved performance on cognitive tests of attention, vigilance, reaction time, visual and verbal learning, and short-term memory among children with ADHD who were treated with psychostimulant medication. Increased attention to tasks and completion of work frequently lead to improved academic performance.

Therapists may become involved in monitoring clients' reactions to medication and should be in contact with prescribing physicians. The most common side effects of medication for treating ADHD are decreased appetite and insomnia (Rapoport & Castellanos, 1996). Less common side effects include weight loss, abdominal pain, and headaches. Suppression of growth, particularly in older children, occurs rarely and generally does not occur when low doses of medication are used. In some cases, facial or motor tics may develop. Cantwell (1996) suggests that medication for ADHD may be contraindicated when there is a history of Tic Disorders.

Not all children with ADHD need to take medication. Rapoport and Castellanos (1996) suggest that the decision be based on the severity of the symptoms; on the preferences of the parents and the child; on the ability of the child, the parents, and the school to cope with the disorder; and on the success or failure of alternative treatments.

Prognosis

The studies by Pelham et al. (1993) present an optimistic long-term prognosis for treatment of ADHD. These findings have been supported by many other studies. For example, Whalen and Henker (1991) have found behavior modification effective in reducing off-task and distractible behaviors. Du Paul et al. (1992) report that token economies, when well designed and well implemented, also decrease inappropriate, off-task behaviors. According to Mannuzza et al. (1993), 75 percent of adults previously diagnosed with ADHD were later found to have normal global functioning.

Studies cited earlier support the benefits of psychostimulant medication. In effecting a positive outcome, Ialongo et al. (1993), however, examining the additive effects of psychostimulant and cognitive-behavioral therapies, including parental training and clients' self-monitoring, have found no evidence to support the superiority of combined therapies. Klein (1993) suggests that this outcome has to do with the amount of coordination and cooperation required in implementing these plans effectively. Nevertheless, and despite these equivocal results, integrated treatments continue to be the accepted treatment approach for this disorder (Cantwell, 1996; Erk, 1997; Klein, 1993).

Disruptive Behavior Disorders

DSM-IV describes two Disruptive Behavior Disorders: Conduct Disorder and Oppositional Defiant Disorder. These disorders, typical clients, and preferred therapists for each disorder will be discussed separately. The disorders will be considered together in sections on intervention strategies and prognosis.

Description of the Disorders

Conduct Disorder. Conduct Disorder is one of the most frequently encountered diagnoses in settings that provide therapy to young clients: one-third to one-half the children seen for treatment in mental health clinics present with symptoms of Conduct Disorder (Kazdin, 1989). Estimates of the prevalence of Conduct Disorder vary and depend on the population sampled but range from 6 percent to 16 percent of males under the age of eighteen. Its prevalence among females is significantly less, with estimates ranging from 2 percent to 9 percent (American Psychiatric Association, 1994a).

A diagnosis of Conduct Disorder requires the presence of repetitive and persistent violations of the basic rights of others or violations of major age-appropriate societal norms or rules. *DSM-IV* lists fifteen behaviors, divided into four main groups—aggression against people and animals, destruction of property, deceitfulness or theft, and serious violations of rules—that characterize Conduct Disorder. For a diagnosis of this disorder, three or more of these behaviors must have been present during the previous twelve months, with at least one during the previous six months. As with all mental disorders, the disturbance must cause clinically significant impairment in social, academic, or occupational functioning.

Conduct Disorder is divided into childhood-onset and adolescent-onset types. A diagnosis of childhood-onset type is made when at least one manifestation of this disorder occurred prior to the child's reaching the age of ten. Adolescent-onset type is diagnosed if no characteristics of the disorder appeared before age ten. According to Webster-Stratton and Dahl (1995), the prognosis for the childhood-onset type is worse than for the adolescent-onset type. By the age of eighteen, Conduct Disorder has often evolved into Antisocial Personality Disorder, particularly if the Conduct Disorder began early and continued through adolescence.

The prevalence of Conduct Disorder has increased over the past few decades, a circumstance that leads professionals to speculate on the impacts of societal and environmental changes. Clinicians are cautioned to assess context when making this diagnosis; behaviors considered to be disordered may be appropriately protective in a given environment or culture. Although the diagnosis may still be appropriate, the interventions and the prognosis are likely to vary.

Comorbidity with other disorders often occurs and complicates the diagnosis of Conduct Disorder. Comorbid disorders are also often masked by the prominence of the antisocial behaviors. Arredondo and Butler (1994), for example, have found that forty-one of fifty-seven adolescents receiving inpatient treatment for Conduct Disorder also met the criteria for a Mood Disorder. Moreover, 84 to 96 percent of children with Conduct Disorder meet the criteria for Oppositional Defiant Disorder, 45 to 70 percent of children with Conduct Disorder have ADHD (Kazdin, 1997), and comorbidity with Anxiety Disorders may also occur (Walker et al., 1991). Substance misuse (Lavin & Rifkin, 1993), low verbal intelligence, reading deficits, and other Learning Disorders also are common (Warr-Leeper, Wright, & Mack, 1994).

Research based on attachment theory (Bowlby, 1969/1982) and social cognitive processes has changed the understanding of behavioral disorders. Impairments in relationship skills, as well as the biased attributions about hostility that are found among children with these diagnoses (for example, the belief that random provocations are directed at them), have been explained as impairments in attachment and social cognition. This perspective has had an impact on treatment models, as will be seen in the section on interventions.

Oppositional Defiant Disorder. Oppositional Defiant Disorder (ODD) is described as a pattern of negativistic, hostile, and defiant behavior lasting at least six months. According to *DSM-IV,* characteristic behaviors include losing one's temper, arguing with adults, defying or refusing to comply with adults' requests, deliberately annoying people, being angry and resentful, being easily annoyed by others, blaming others for one's own negative behavior, and being vindictive. At younger ages, ODD may be manifested by temper tantrums, kicking, power struggles with parents, disobedience, screaming, and low tolerance for frustration (Rey, 1993). Common complaints from the parents of older children with this disorder are that the children argue, threaten, show disrespect for adults, destroy property in a rage, refuse to cooperate, and are stubborn.

These symptoms often appear to be an exacerbation of typical childhood misbehaviors. The diagnosis of ODD is made when these behaviors are of greater frequency, duration, and intensity than would be expected for the child's age and when they cause social, occupational, and academic impairment (Kronenberger & Meyer, 1996). Often these children come to the attention of school counselors and therapists when the oppositional behaviors interfere with functioning at school. Until then, parents may not recognize the behaviors as being unusual. Behaviors of children with ODD sometimes worsen as the result of a cycle of negative reinforcement: when a child with oppositional behaviors acts inappropriately, an adult reacts with hostility or frustration, and the child responds by escalating the negative behaviors.

Estimates of the prevalence of Oppositional Defiant Disorder vary greatly: it is thought to occur in 2 to 16 percent of children (American Psychiatric Association, 1994a). ODD is positively correlated with low socioeconomic status and urban location. This disorder usually begins by the age of eight, with peak prevalence occurring between the ages of eight and eleven (Maxmen & Ward, 1995). Before the age of twelve, boys diagnosed with ODD outnumber girls, but the rates seem to equalize after the age of twelve.

Typical Client Characteristics

Conduct Disorder. *DSM-III-R* (American Psychiatric Association, 1987) distinguishes between *socialized* youths, whose conduct-disordered behaviors occur in a peer group, and *undersocialized* youths, who act in isolation. Those who are socialized are influenced by peer pressure to continue their antisocial behaviors, and so therapists need to recognize the importance of combating the impact of peer pressure on these clients. Undersocialized boys have a particularly poor prognosis (Kronenberger & Meyer, 1996).

Inappropriate behaviors can be categorized as either overt or covert. Overt behaviors, such as theft, assault, and the setting of fires, have direct impacts on others. These behaviors are more often exhibited by males (American Psychiatric

Association, 1994a). Covert behaviors, exemplified by cutting oneself, lying, shoplifting, or truancy, are more often exhibited by females with Conduct Disorder.

Children and adolescents with Conduct Disorder have difficulty developing satisfactory interpersonal relationships. They lack empathy, are hostile toward adults, dominate other children, and, as adolescents, typically have numerous sexual partners. Cruelty to animals and other sadistic behaviors may be present and are predictors of poor long-term outcomes. These relationship deficits are thought to have a connection with early problems in attachment (Bowlby, 1969/1982). The negative, hostile behaviors of children with Conduct Disorder keep others away or evoke equally hostile responses, and a negative pattern is perpetuated. Evidence suggests that this cycle of negative and insecure attachments continues into succeeding generations (Zeanah & Emde, 1994).

A careful analysis of the families, environments, and skills of those with Conduct Disorder is necessary to the development of appropriate treatment plans. Diamond, Serrano, Dickey, and Sonis (1996) report that parents of young people with Conduct Disorder have a high incidence of psychopathology themselves and that their symptoms include depression, antisocial behaviors, and aggression. Mothers are particularly likely to exhibit symptoms of depression and feelings of isolation. These parental characteristics are correlated with premature termination of the children's treatment and with increased likelihood that the children's disruptive behaviors will return after treatment has ended (Webster-Stratton & Dahl, 1995).

Children with Conduct Disorder often come from large families, live in substandard housing, and attend school in disadvantaged settings (Kazdin, 1995). Families that include a child with Conduct Disorder have reported from two to four times more stressors in their lives than nonclinical controls (Webster-Stratton & Dahl, 1995). Unemployment among the parents of children with Conduct Disorder is common, and parents are likely to display open conflict. Harsh and inconsistent discipline, criminal behavior, substance misuse, and poor parental supervision have also been identified as common among families of young people diagnosed with Conduct Disorder (Kazdin, 1997).

In school settings, children who meet the criteria for Conduct Disorder typically have both academic and disciplinary problems. Language-processing deficits are common and may interfere with comprehension and with the processing of social information (Warr-Leeper et al., 1994).

Oppositional Defiant Disorder. Young people diagnosed with ODD have low tolerance for frustration or delayed gratification, and they expect their demands to be granted immediately. Although ODD may coexist with a diagnosis of Conduct Disorder, those diagnosed only with ODD do not evidence the cunning and calculating behaviors associated with Conduct Disorder. They have stronger interpersonal bonds and are more successful in social situations.

Many children with ODD exhibit aggressive behaviors. The presence of aggression in preschool children has been identified as a significant risk indicator, associated with poor problem-solving skills, negative self-statements, and biased attributions (Dodge & Frame, 1982; Dodge & Newman, 1981) as well as with later development of Conduct Disorder (Loeber, Green, Keenan, & Lahey, 1995), substance misuse, delinquency, and failure in school (Kendall, 1993). Another characteristic of aggressive children is their tendency to be hypervigilant and to perceive hostility among those around them, a perception that leads them to retaliate with hostile acts (Kendall, 1993; Offord & Bennett, 1994).

Comorbidity with ADHD is common. ODD is also associated with Learning and Communication Disorders. Impulsive behaviors typical of children with ADHD may intensify oppositional behaviors and contribute to poor social judgment and faulty decision making. If ADHD is present, its treatment is essential to the successful treatment of ODD.

Parents of children with ODD are more likely to report marital discord (Schachar & Wachsmuth, 1990), and mothers are more likely to report personal distress, as well as less satisfaction with their marriages (Barkley et al., 1991). Mothers of adolescents with ADHD and ODD also exhibit greater negative interactions with their children during neutral discussions.

Preferred Therapist Characteristics

Conduct Disorder. Working with a child or an adolescent who has Conduct Disorder is challenging. Transference and countertransference are likely to occur. The client's disruptive or provocative behaviors may stir up unresolved conflicts or negative feelings from the therapist's own youth. Therapists should not engage in win-lose battles, should not always believe what they hear, should not fear manipulation, and should not become trapped in the idea that the child simply needs more love. Because of the frequency of comorbid disorders, therapists must have excellent diagnostic skills so that concomitant symptoms can be identified. Therapists may also become involved with the legal system or with court-ordered services and so must have knowledge of those systems. Therapists' expertise appears to be an important predictor of successful treatment outcomes for clients with Conduct Disorder (Kazdin, 1993).

Oppositional Defiant Disorder. Clients with ODD typically transfer their negative feelings toward authority, as well as their perceptions of hostility in the environment, to their therapists. Therapists working with young clients diagnosed with ODD must have great patience and be cognizant of their own feelings about control, anger, defiance, and misbehavior. Therapists must also recognize their own countertransference issues so as to prevent these from having a negative impact on treatment (Lewis, 1991).

King and Noshpitz (1991) suggest that therapists for these children must be dedicated and available and able to provide a consistent relationship during long-term treatment, if that kind of treatment is indicated. Therapists also need knowledge of behavioral therapies, family therapy, and psychoeducation, and they may be called on to develop behavioral strategies for changing negative behaviors and to provide training in social skills and problem solving.

Intervention Strategies

Most of the treatment literature considers Conduct Disorder and Oppositional Defiant Disorder to be on a continuum of disorders that involve the externalizing of dysfunctional behavior. From the standpoint of the therapist, the primary difference between these two disorders is that the prognosis for ODD is more promising. Therefore, treatment planning for that disorder should emphasize prevention.

The multiplicity of problems and contributing factors that are involved in these disorders, and particularly in Conduct Disorder, makes their treatment extremely complex. Multiple modalities and systems must often be involved. The treatment of children with Conduct Disorder, for example, may involve professionals from other agencies, such as those connected with law enforcement, the judicial system, and social services. In almost all cases, advocacy and consultation with school systems is indicated.

The first step in devising a treatment plan for young persons with Conduct Disorder or ODD is to assess the degree of danger the children pose to themselves or others and to evaluate the impact that the environment may be having on their continued development (King & Noshpitz, 1991). Behavior checklists like the Achenbach Child Behavior Checklist (CBCL) (Achenbach, 1991) or the Behavior Assessment System for Children (BASC) (Reynolds & Kamphaus, 1992) are useful in identifying the parents' perceptions and the severity of the child's behaviors. If the client has a clear suicide plan or intends to harm others, parents or appropriate authorities must be notified, and residential treatment should be considered. The psychological status of the parents and the parents' perceptions of the child's behaviors may also be so impaired that the home is not an appropriate setting for the child. Alternative placement may be necessary if the child's relationship to the parent is aggressive or characterized by mutual abuse.

Information regarding behaviors observed at school should also be considered. Low self-esteem related to poor academic performance may exacerbate problems. The Conners Teacher Rating Scale (Conners, 1990) and the teacher versions of the CBCL (Achenbach, 1991) and BASC (Reynolds & Kamphaus, 1992) enable teachers to provide information about children's delinquent and aggressive behaviors, as well as about their hyperactive, inattentive, somatic, depressive, and other behaviors. The importance of including reports from multiple informants in the diagnostic assessment of ODD and Conduct Disorder is highlighted by Hart, Lahey, Loeber, and Hanson (1994), who have found reports from teachers to have the strongest correlation with criterion behaviors observed in 177 boys between the ages of seven and twelve in a clinic setting; reports from parents and other children were less valid.

The next step in the assessment process is to rule out comorbid disorders that may be contributing to or compounding the effects of the primary disorder. The possibility of ADHD, Learning Disorders, thought disorders, a history of abuse, neurological difficulties, and other medical conditions should always be considered. Psychological testing is recommended and should include assessment of cognitive, perceptual, and social-emotional functioning. A neurologist can be consulted to rule out seizure activity, and a psychiatrist may be consulted regarding the advisability of medication. Among adolescents, the possibility of substance use also should be investigated. This lengthy diagnostic process can provide invaluable guidance in treatment.

As already mentioned, intervention strategies for children with Conduct Disorder and ODD often incorporate multiple modalities. Offord and Bennett (1994) and Kazdin (1997) report four types of interventions that offer promise in the treatment of those diagnosed with Conduct Disorder or ODD: individual therapies, parent or family interventions, school-based interventions, and community-based interventions. In some cases, pharmacological interventions are also used in addressing comorbid disorders, such as ADHD, Mood Disorders, and Anxiety Disorders. When behavior is dangerous or out of control, or when the home environment is unsafe, residential or day treatment also may be required.

Individual and Group Psychotherapy. Individual psychotherapy nearly always will be a part of the treatment plan for a young person diagnosed with Conduct Disorder or ODD. Many individual approaches have been developed to treat these disorders.

Social-cognitive approaches are based on the assumption that if thoughts can be changed, affect and behaviors can also be changed. Kazdin (1997) reviews problem-solving skills training (PSST), which teaches people to define a problem, identify goals, generate options, choose the best option, and evaluate the outcome (Kronenberger & Meyer, 1996). Techniques from social learning theory, such as modeling, role playing, reinforcement, and shaping of behaviors, enhance clients' ability to make decisions. PSST has been found to lead to significant reductions in parents' and teachers' ratings of children's aggressive behaviors, both immediately after treatment and one year later (Durlak, Fuhrman, & Lampman, 1991).

Reality therapy can provide a framework for challenging the distorted environmental perceptions often held by adolescents involved in or at risk for delinquent behavior. This approach, developed by Glasser (1990), is frequently used in day treatment or hospital settings. The therapeutic relationship and techniques like contracting and the use of rewards and consequences help clients meet their needs in healthy, positive ways.

Anger management training is another cognitive approach that has received some support. Lochman, White, and Wayland (1991), for example, taught elementary school–age boys strategies for coping with anger through self-talk, modeling, and role play. Each boy then developed a behavioral contract that was monitored by teachers and by the boys themselves. This goal setting was identified as an important motivational element in the treatment plan (Kronenberger & Meyer, 1996).

Fonagy and Target (1994) have evaluated the outcomes of psychodynamic psychotherapy for children with Disruptive Behavior Disorders and for children with such emotional disorders as Anxiety Disorders and Mood Disorders. Children with Anxiety Disorders and Mood Disorders exhibited significantly greater improvement than those with Disruptive Behavior Disorders, although 56 percent of those with ODD, 36 percent of those with ADHD, and 23 percent of those with Conduct Disorder did show some improvement. Early termination was a confounding variable: 31 percent of the children with disruptive behaviors terminated treatment within the first year.

The use of group therapy to treat both Conduct Disorder and ODD has demonstrated mixed results. Social skills training groups like those developed by Kazdin (1993) have been successful in decreasing the oppositional behaviors and increasing the prosocial behaviors of children with ODD. Therapy groups for adolescents with Conduct Disorder have been less successful. Dishion and Andrews (1995), who included a teenagers-only group in their comparison of treatment modalities, report that this intervention did result in a decrease in family conflict but that it also led to an increase in positive perceptions about drug use, as well as to increased smoking. The authors suggest that group therapy for adolescents with Conduct Disorder may not be appropriate because of the tendency for the group to bond and accept riskier behaviors as a norm. By contrast, Mendel (1995) reports somewhat decreased antisocial behavior for adolescents who received group therapy in a residential setting and suggests that the setting was crucial to the success of this treatment. Unfortunately, the question of generalization to outpatient behaviors was not addressed.

Family Interventions. Recent research has identified the treatment of parents as a key factor in successful outcomes for young people with Disruptive Behavior Disorders (Dishion & Andrews, 1995; Webster-Stratton & Dahl, 1995). Parent management training (PMT), developed by Patterson (1982), is the model for many current training programs for parents. PMT is a cognitive-behavioral approach that teaches skills like monitoring children's behaviors, maintaining discipline, and providing rewards. Outcome studies find PMT to have reduced children's aggression and increased their prosocial behaviors (Eisenstadt,

Eyberg, McNeil, & Newcomb, 1993), and these learned behaviors have been generalized to school settings. Improvements in siblings' behavior and decreased maternal stress and depression have also been beneficial side effects of PMT (Kazdin, 1997). McMahon (1994) has identified continuing benefits of PMT fourteen years after the original training.

Webster-Stratton (1989) developed a PMT-style program that used videotaped vignettes, role playing, a discussion group for parents, and peer support. In the basic curriculum, parents were taught to play with and praise their children, to set limits, and to provide discipline. The advanced curriculum taught such concepts such as timeouts, problem-solving, anger management, and communication skills. Webster-Stratton reports significant reduction of aggressive behaviors in 20 to 60 percent of clinic-referred children whose parents participated in the training (Webster-Stratton & Hammond, 1997). Prosocial behaviors reportedly were generalized to home and school settings. A third module was recently added to this program, teaching parents to become partners in their children's academic development by establishing learning routines and supporting homework and reading.

Functional Family Therapy (FFT) (Alexander & Parsons, 1982) is derived from PMT as well as from communication training and behavioral, structural, and systems theories of family therapy. FFT attempts to reduce defensiveness and blame and to develop positive interactions among family members. It has been implemented among adolescents with Conduct Disorder whose behaviors have resulted in court involvement. Positive outcome indicators include improved family communications and less involvement with the courts up to two and one-half years after treatment (Kazdin, 1997).

Henggeler and Borduin (1990) developed a treatment program, Multisystemic Family Therapy (MFT), that addressed the multiple contexts in which Conduct Disorder is manifested. MFT was used initially as a family intervention in a way similar to the way in which FFT has been used. Therapists, recognizing the adolescent as an integral member of other systems, introduced individual, peer, and school interventions that used some of the techniques already mentioned. This approach, used with adolescents exhibiting violent criminal behaviors, has reduced delinquency and emotional problems and has improved family functioning for adolescents with Disruptive Behavior Disorders (Kazdin, 1997).

One of the greatest challenges in treating these clients is the frequency with which parents terminate treatment prematurely. Kazdin (1990, 1997), evaluating parent dropouts from treatment, has found that those who left treatment early were no different, in terms of sex, age, IQ, child's diagnosis, maternal psychopathology, or number of parents in the home, from those who completed treatment. Parents who terminated treatment early reported continuing problems with their children's antisocial and aggressive behaviors, whereas the parents of children who had completed treatment reported an increase in functional behaviors at home, at school, and in the community.

Prinz and Miller (1994) supplement training groups for parents with discussions about such nonparenting issues as job stress, health problems, family disputes, and external demands. This kind of enhanced family treatment has brought a significant reduction in the number of parents who terminate treatment prematurely. Prinz and Miller also found parents' engagement in their children's treatment to be enhanced by the provision of training in the home, by the provision of transportation to treatment sessions, by flexible hours for treatment, and sensitivity to cultural differences.

School and Community Interventions. Kellam et al. (1991) addressed conduct problems through classroom interventions that were implemented by teachers. This model had two advantages: the model's use of presentations to all the children in a classroom eliminated any stigma associated with these interventions, and the model could be implemented without any reliance on parents' involvement. Research has identified improvements in reading and decreases in aggressive and shy behavior in the classroom as outcomes of these interventions.

In one promising outcome study, Zigler, Taussig, and Black (1992) surveyed nineteen-year-olds who had participated in preschool intervention programs that were begun in the 1960s and the 1970s. One program had randomly assigned three- and four-year-old low-income African American children to four groups: a group that received early childhood education, a group that received home visits by teachers, a group that had monthly parent-teacher meetings, and a group that received no intervention at all. The findings suggest that adolescents who were assigned in childhood to one of the intervention groups had higher rates of high school graduation and lower rates of arrest.

Pharmacological Interventions. According to a study by Abikoff and Klein (1992), medication in general does not substantially enhance the impact of other treatment modalities for young people with Disruptive Behavior Disorders. These authors have found, however, that some comorbid diagnoses (such as ADHD) do require medication. Medication is shown to have mixed success when violent behaviors are present (Kronenberger & Meyer, 1996).

Hospitalization and Day Treatment Programs. Sometimes a young person's behavior becomes sufficiently dangerous or uncontrollable to warrant placement in an intensive treatment setting. This is usually a short-term residential placement and can accomplish three goals (Kronenberger & Meyer, 1996):

1. It removes the young person from any peer or family pressure in his or her environment.

2. It interrupts the negative cycle of the person's behavior.

3. It provides a setting where intensive cognitive-behavioral or reality therapy can be conducted.

A residential setting also facilitates detoxification from drugs or alcohol and provides time and resources both for in-depth evaluation and for stabilization on medication.

Day treatment programs offer similar benefits to those available in hospital or residential settings, but they allow the young person to return home at night and are usually less costly than hospitalization. Day treatment programs typically are intensive, running from five to eight hours a day, five days per week. In addition to individual, group, and family therapy, these programs often include special education and behavioral consultation to develop individualized intervention plans. Day treatment programs have been found to reduce behaviors associated with Conduct Disorder and to improve social skills and family functioning (Grizenko, Papineau, & Sayegh, 1993).

Placement in a residential setting may be necessary when a negative or abusive family environment has been contributing to a client's problems. One residential program, the Response Program (Holland, Moretti, Verlaan, & Peterson, 1993), is based on Bowlby's theory of attachment. Its goal is to develop feelings of affiliation and mutuality with other residents, and adolescents participate in a variety of activities and therapies designed to achieve this goal. According to Holland, Moretti, Verlaan, and Peterson (1993), parents have reported fewer disordered behaviors twelve months after their children's completion of the program than were reported at intake. Glick and Goldstein's (1987) outpatient training in anger management has also been adapted for use in a residential program. Its goals are similar to those for the outpatient program and focus on the promotion of coping strategies other than aggression and anger. Young people participate in structured groups that teach anger control, social skills, and moral reasoning. Participants in these training programs have demonstrated improved socialization, as well as decreased impulsivity and acting-out behaviors (Durlak et al., 1991).

Although inpatient treatment is sometimes necessary for these clients, it should be recommended cautiously. Grizenko et al. (1993) have found that outcomes for residential settings are similar to those for day treatment programs. Given the substantially higher cost of residential programs, therapists and families must question the cost-effectiveness of this choice. Moreover, if attachment theory is correct, the removal of young people from their primary caregivers may interfere with their primary attachments, no matter how insecure those attachments may be. Placing adolescents in residential settings where they can bond with other conduct-disordered adolescents may also worsen their behaviors (Dishion & Andrews, 1995).

Factors in Successful Treatment. Many factors are associated with successful treatment of Disruptive Behavior Disorders. McMahon's (1994) meta-analysis has found outcome to be related to accuracy in diagnosing comorbid disorders. The duration of treatment and the therapist's expertise in treating Conduct Disorder also seem to be important predictors of a successful outcome (Kazdin, 1993). Cognitive-behavioral approaches that teach problem-solving techniques clearly decrease aggressive behaviors, but the effects are greatest in children who have achieved formal operational cognitive levels (approximately by the age of eleven) and in adolescents with strong ego functioning (Durlak et al., 1991; Kazdin, 1993). Dishion and Andrews (1995), focusing on high-risk children between the ages of eleven and fourteen, evaluated different intervention models that included the use of groups for parents, groups for teenagers, combined parent and teen groups, and self-directed workbooks. All these therapeutic interventions were largely effective, but those that featured parents' involvement demonstrated the most positive results.

Prognosis

Disruptive Behavior Disorders, especially Conduct Disorder, are sometimes thought of as having no cure (Diamond et al., 1996) or as having poor prognoses (Maxmen & Ward, 1995), but they certainly can show a positive response to treatment. Prognoses for these disorders appear to be best when there has been late onset, early intervention, and long-term intervention. Early intervention facilitates therapists' efforts to change cognitive structures, so that new ideas are generated and alternative choices are made (Kendall, 1993), and in Conduct Disorder with late or adolescent onset, children can draw on a history of appropriate behaviors. Intervention programs of at least a year's duration have demonstrated substantially better gains than has briefer treatment (Diamond et al., 1996). The most critical element of successful treatment for this population appears to be parents' participation in ongoing support and periodic retraining. Self-help movements like Tough Love can also be helpful to parents of children with Disruptive Behavior Disorders. Prevention, both for high-risk children who have not yet met the criteria for ODD or Conduct Disorder and for those who have had these disorders but have improved through therapy, is also essential in reducing the incidence and severity of these disorders.

FEEDING AND EATING DISORDERS
OF INFANCY OR EARLY CHILDHOOD

Description of the Disorders

DSM-IV category Feeding and Eating Disorders of Infancy or Early Childhood includes three disorders that interfere to a significant degree with a child's development, social functioning, or nutritional health: Pica, Rumination Disorder, and Feeding Disorder of Infancy or Early Childhood. The first two can also be diagnosed in adults but are much more common in children.

Pica is characterized by the consumption of nonnutritive substances for at least one month. The substances that are eaten vary across the life span. Infants and preschool children with this disorder typically eat items like paint, paper, hair, or cloth. Older children eat insects, plants, pebbles, or animal droppings. Clay or soil may be ingested by adolescents or adults with this disorder (American Psychiatric Association, 1994a). The diagnosis of Pica should not be made if the eating habits are consistent with the cultural values and beliefs of the child's family.

Pica often coexists with Mental Retardation or another mental disorder and becomes the focus of treatment only if it interferes with the child's functioning to a significant extent. Children with Pica usually do not present for treatment until a medical complication has resulted. Lead poisoning is a common complication of eating paint chips. Other resulting medical problems include obstructed bowels, intestinal perforations, or infections.

Rumination Disorder is found primarily in infants and in older children diagnosed with Mental Retardation. Typical age of onset of this uncommon disorder is three to twelve months. The symptoms include repeated regurgitation and remastication of food. The disorder develops after a period of normal eating and digesting and is not due to a general medical condition. Children with Rumination Disorder typically exhibit straining postures and sucking movements that facilitate the regurgitation. They appear to derive satisfaction from this activity, although they also are often irritable and hungry (American Psychiatric Association, 1994a). Most children recover spontaneously from this disorder, but it should be taken seriously when it occurs because death from malnutrition can result (Skuse, 1994).

Two subtypes of Rumination Disorder have been distinguished. The psychogenic subtype is reserved for those children who show no evidence of Mental Retardation. The etiology of psychogenic rumination is thought to be related to negative interactions between infants and caregivers, especially around feeding issues. The self-stimulating subtype is most likely to be found in children with Mental Retardation whose ruminative behaviors are linked to cognitive rather than social deficits (Kronenberger & Meyer, 1996).

Feeding Disorder of Infancy or Early Childhood is diagnosed when a child exhibits persistent failure to eat adequately and has not gained weight or has lost a significant amount of weight over a period of at least one month. The symptoms must not be related to a general medical condition or to a lack of available food. Onset must be before the age of six years and usually comes during the first year of life (American Psychiatric Association, 1994a). This disorder can lead to a medical condition: nonorganic failure to thrive. Families of children with Feeding Disorder of Infancy or Early Childhood often (but not always) exhibit such psychosocial contributory factors as low socioeconomic status, emotional disorders in the parents, high environmental stress, and abuse and neglect of the child (Lyons-Ruth et al., 1996). Feeding Disorder of Infancy or Early Childhood may be found in children who also have Reactive Attachment Disorder that is due to conflicts occurring in connection with feeding (Kronenberger & Meyer, 1996).

Typical Client Characteristics

Accurate data about the prevalence of these disorders is sparse because these disorders typically occur in conjunction with Mental Retardation, Pervasive Developmental Disorders, or other mental disorders and may not be coded separately. They are listed on Axis I only if they are prominent enough to require separate treatment.

Although Pica is sometimes diagnosed in pregnant women, it most often is found in preschool children and among children with severe emotional disturbances. Onset is usually between the ages of twelve and twenty-four months. The disorder is rare in adolescence or adulthood (Rapoport & Ismond, 1996). The prevalence of Pica is significantly greater among children with Mental Retardation (as high as 30 percent in that population) or Autistic Disorder (as high as 60 percent). Its prevalence is also higher among children with behavior disorders and among children from families with low socioeconomic status (Kronenberger & Meyer, 1996). No gender differences in prevalence have been identified (Marchi & Cohen, 1990). Children who have ingested chips of lead paint may exhibit the effects of lead poisoning, which include developmental delays, learning disabilities, and attention deficits (Skuse, 1994).

Children with Rumination Disorder, as already mentioned, usually have had a period of normal eating habits before the atypical eating behaviors appear. Some parents report a sour odor from these children's regurgitations (Rapoport & Ismond, 1996). Untreated, this disorder may result in weight loss, malnutrition, and even death. Dental caries may also develop from the repeated contact of the teeth with gastric acids (Skuse, 1994). Rumination Disorder is rare but occurs more often in males than in females (Lyons-Ruth et al., 1996).

Because Feeding and Eating Disorders of Infancy or Early Childhood is a new diagnostic category in *DSM-IV,* prevalence figures are not yet available. Nevertheless, nonorganic failure to thrive, a related medical diagnosis, accounts for an estimated 1 to 5 percent of pediatric hospital admissions (Lyons-Ruth et al., 1996).

Children with Feeding Disorder of Infancy or Early Childhood may be irritable and difficult to console. They may exhibit slowed growth patterns or sleep-wake cycle disturbances (Frank & Ziesel, 1988). Psychosocial problems, such as parental psychopathology, poor parent-child interactions, poverty, and neglect, are significant correlates of this disorder (Linscheid, 1992). Insecure attachment and negative interactions and emotions, including anger, sadness, and frustration, have been reported among children with the diagnosis of nonorganic failure to thrive (Lyons-Ruth et al., 1996).

Preferred Therapist Characteristics

Children with Feeding and Eating Disorders usually first present in medical settings when physical conditions have developed from their impaired eating. Therefore, therapists affiliated with hospitals are most likely to see children with these disorders, although the parents of these children may be seen in any treatment setting.

Therapists working with this population must be at ease with potentially life-threatening situations. Therapists must also be good collaborators, able to consult with and contribute to a team of medical professionals. Training in family systems and cognitive-behavioral approaches can help therapists deal with the familial correlates of these disorders, as well as with parents' resistance and with their anger about feeling blamed for their children's symptoms.

Intervention Strategies

In addition to medical monitoring, the primary treatment modality for children with Feeding and Eating Disorders is work with the family. Cognitive-behavioral and educational approaches are useful in addressing issues related to parenting. Provision of information on children's developmental and eating patterns is commonly the first step toward a positive outcome. Linscheid (1992) suggests providing the child with a parent substitute who can offer a warm, nurturing feeding environment while the parents receive counseling to address any issues that are interfering with their nurturing of the child.

Pica is often addressed through parental training in behavior management strategies. This kind of training promotes closer monitoring of the child's eating, as well as the use of behavioral rewards or punishments. Charts for recording the ingestion of appropriate foods can be developed and can be used with stickers or other rewards for the child's eating of appropriate nutritive substances. This approach is usually adequate for discouraging children from eating inappropriate substances (Kronenberger & Meyer, 1996).

Rumination Disorder is addressed primarily through family interventions designed to improve the parent-child relationship and provide the child with consistent nurturance and response. Cognitive-behavioral or educational therapies for parents, focused on attachment issues, child development, and parenting skills, can also be helpful. Parent-child therapy may be introduced to model and encourage more positive and supportive interactions between parent and child (Kronenberger & Meyer, 1996).

Other techniques have also proved helpful in treating Rumination Disorder. In life-threatening situations, behavioral modification with aversive stimuli may be necessary. For example, Rapoport and Ismond (1996) describe a case in which mild electric shocks were applied to the leg of an infant when rumination behaviors were exhibited; the symptoms were arrested within one week.

Researchers have found a relationship between the occurrence of rumination and the types of food provided (Linscheid, 1992); ruminating behaviors diminished in children with Mental Retardation when they were fed their preferred foods.

When Feeding Disorder of Infancy or Early Childhood is accompanied by failure to thrive, the treatment is similar to that for Reactive Attachment Disorder (discussed later in this chapter). If the disorder involves the child's refusal of food, then behavioral techniques can be helpful and may include positive reinforcement for eating, the modeling of positive eating behaviors, control of between-meal eating, and reduction of mealtime distractions (Kronenberger & Meyer, 1996).

The treatment of Anorexia Nervosa and Bulimia Nervosa is addressed in Chapter Six, but Maloney, McGuire, and Daniels (1988) and others have identified children as young as eight years old who are restricting their diets because of concern about body fat. Therefore, therapists working with children who have eating problems should be knowledgeable about Anorexia Nervosa and Bulimia Nervosa.

Prognosis

In the majority of cases, Feeding and Eating Disorders in young children remit after a few months of appropriate intervention. Nevertheless, Marchi and Cohen (1990) have found feeding problems in childhood to be a risk indicator for Eating Disorders in adolescence. Children with Pica were at significant risk for developing Bulimia Nervosa. Pica may also continue, especially if it is present in conjunction with Mental Retardation. Rumination Disorder in infants most often resolves by itself within a month or two, but chronic cases left untreated may result in death (American Psychiatric Association, 1994a; Linscheid, 1992).

TIC DISORDERS

Description of the Disorders

The disorders discussed in this section are typified by "sudden, rapid, recurrent, nonrhythmic, stereotyped motor movements or vocalizations" (Towbin & Cohen, 1996, p. 351). These symptoms typically worsen under stress and are less noticeable when the child is involved in an engrossing activity. The symptoms also diminish significantly during sleep. Examples of simple motor tics are eye blinking, neck jerking, facial grimacing, shrugging, or coughing. Simple vocal tics include clearing one's throat, grunting, sniffing, or barking. Complex motor and vocal tics incorporate complete actions or words that are repeated involuntarily and in rapid, staccato fashion. Complex motor tics include jumping, grooming, or smelling an object. A child with complex vocal tics may repeat sentences or phrases out of context. Other types of complex vocal tics include coprolalia (the use of socially unacceptable or obscene words), palilalia (repetition of one's own sounds or words), and echolalia (repetition of the sound, word, or phrase last heard). Tic Disorders are more common in boys.

A diagnosis of Tic Disorder is appropriate only if the onset of the disorder occurs prior to the age of eighteen, if the symptoms are not the result of drugs or a medical condition (such as Huntington's disease), and if the symptoms cause significant distress or impairment (American Psychiatric Association, 1994a). Towbin and Cohen (1996) report that Tic Disorders vary according to five properties:

1. Frequency (the number of tics that occur over a given period)
2. Complexity (the nature of the tic itself)
3. Intensity (the forcefulness of the tic, some tics being subtle while others seem almost explosive or violent)
4. Location (the parts of the body affected by the tic)
5. Duration (the length of time that tics persist in each episode)

Assessment according to these properties can be helpful in determining what type of disorder is involved, the exacerbating factors, and the appropriate treatment and its impact.

Tic Disorders have a higher incidence in children with certain coexisting disorders. Comings, Himes, and Comings (1990) suggest that Tic Disorders are related to other disorders with neuropsychiatric components, including Attention-Deficit/Hyperactivity Disorder, Learning Disorders, Pervasive Developmental Disorders, Anxiety Disorders, and Obsessive-Compulsive Disorder. Magnetic resonance imaging (MRI) studies of people with Tourette's Disorder have indicated neurological abnormalities (Singer et al., 1993), although a neurological basis for Tic Disorders is still not fully accepted (Kronenberger & Meyer, 1996). Motor tics are sometimes a side effect of the psychostimulants used in the treatment of ADHD; therefore, many clinicians do not prescribe psychostimulant medication for ADHD to children who have concurrent Tourette's Disorder (Towbin, Cohen, & Leckman, 1995). The spectrum of Tic Disorders includes those discussed in the following paragraphs.

Tourette's Disorder. Tourette's Disorder, named after Gilles de la Tourette, who first identified it, is diagnosed on the basis of tics that occur many times during a day and that combine multiple motor tics and one or more vocal tics. The motor and vocal tics need not occur simultaneously in order for this diagnosis to be made. The severity and the location of the tics may change over time, but the diagnostic criteria require that the symptoms occur for a period of at least one year, with no more than a three-month tic-free period (American Psychiatric Association, 1994a). People with this disorder usually also have relatives with the disorder.

Tourette's Disorder often begins with intermittent, simple eye blinking. Tics may present only a few times each week or may be almost constant. These involuntary movements have been reported to occur as frequently as one hundred or more times per minute (Leckman & Cohen, 1994). Over time, the tic behaviors usually become persistent (of higher frequency or longer duration) and occur at multiple sites on the body. The tics often interfere with academic or work performance and with social relationships. By the age of ten, children with Tourette's Disorder may be aware of "premonitory urges" (p. 455) that forewarn them of impending tics; a tic itself may be described as an itch or a tickle. Because of these premonitions, adolescents and adults may perceive their tics as at least partly voluntary. Usually by adolescence or early adulthood the frequency of the tics has been reduced, but there are cases of very disabling Tourette's Disorder found in adults.

Chronic Tic Disorder. Chronic Tic Disorder resembles Tourette's Disorder except that it involves single or complex motor *or* vocal tics (not both). The symptoms are also of lesser intensity and frequency than in Tourette's Disorder and are usually confined to the eyes, face, head, neck, and upper extremities. This disorder sometimes is comorbid with ADHD and is exacerbated by stress (Leckman & Cohen, 1994).

Transient Tic Disorder. Transient Tic Disorder resembles Chronic Tic Disorder except for its duration: it lasts at least four weeks but no longer than one year. Emotional tension is often the cause of simple Transient Tic Disorder (King & Noshpitz, 1991).

Prevalence of Tic Disorders. The prevalence of Chronic Tic Disorder and Transient Tic Disorder is not known. Many children with these disorders never come to the attention of the medical or mental health communities. Tourette's Disorder is estimated to occur in approximately four or five children per ten thousand, with cases in males outnumbering cases in females (American Psychiatric Association, 1994a). The age of onset may be anywhere from the age of two to the age of fifteen years, although the average age at onset is seven years (Towbin & Cohen, 1996).

Typical Client Characteristics

Stress is known to worsen all Tic Disorders (Shapiro, Shapiro, Young, & Feinberg, 1988) but not to cause Tourette's Disorder. Leckman and Cohen (1994) report cases of families who chastised children for tic-related behaviors and thereby increased stress, which in turn led to increased frequency and severity of tics; severe cases of Tourette's Disorder may be related to this pattern of family dynamics. Tic Disorders often have an impact on self-image and functioning. Social withdrawal may result from interactions with critical others who focus on the tic-related behaviors.

Preferred Therapist Characteristics

Therapists working with children who have severe Tic Disorders need skills in establishing positive and supportive working relationships, both with these young clients and with their parents. Tourette's Disorder in particular introduces stressors into family dynamics, and these stressors may in turn exacerbate the condition. Tourette's Disorder is often a lifelong disorder that requires ongoing support and advocacy from the therapist.

Intervention Strategies

The treatments of choice for Tic Disorders currently include a psychodynamic approach (to identify any underlying stressors), cognitive-behavioral methods of stress management, education of children and families about the disorder, advocacy with education professionals, and collaborative work with physicians if pharmacological interventions are necessary (Towbin et al., 1995). Choosing among these interventions requires careful analysis of the type of disorder that is involved, as well as analysis of any underlying stressors that may be exacerbating the disorder.

The initial goal of treatment is to educate the child and the parents about the nature of the disorder. Information about the course of the disorder, its potential concomitants, and the influence of stress on its symptoms should be presented in the early sessions (King & Noshpitz, 1991; Towbin et al., 1995). These sessions also provide the foundation for building a relationship with the child and the parents; this relationship will be important over the course of this disorder (Cohen, Ort, Leckman, & Hardin, 1988).

After having made these efforts to educate the family and establish a positive working relationship, the therapist should facilitate the collection of baseline data about the frequency of the tics. Sometimes the act of collecting the data is therapeutic in itself, and the frequency of the tics may diminish (King & Noshpitz, 1991). Baseline data guide the behavioral and environmental interventions, which constitute the next step in treatment.

Therapists or school counselors can suggest classroom modifications to reduce stress. These may include development of clear expectations, a low teacher-student ratio, predictable schedules, and contracts specifying rewards for behavioral control. Leckman and Cohen (1994) emphasize the importance of flexibility: perhaps the child can be allowed to leave the classroom when a tic occurs, or maybe academic requirements can be adjusted. School curricula that accommodate a variety of learning styles can allow children with Tourette's Disorder to use learning strategies that make use of their strengths.

Adolescents with this disorder benefit from career counseling, which can help them make plans to enter occupations where they are likely to succeed (Towbin et al., 1988). The creation of realistic expectations on the part of these adolescents, their parents, and their teachers may also have to be a treatment goal.

Behavioral techniques are often used to diminish tic-related behaviors. Self-monitoring, for example, involves children in recording the occurrence and frequency of tics (Kronenberger & Meyer, 1996). In relaxation training, children are taught to use methods like progressive relaxation of muscle groups, deep breathing, or imagery before or during episodes of tics. Massed practice is a behavioral technique in which a child or adolescent is instructed to perform a tic-related behavior repeatedly, and as quickly and intensely as possible, in order to gain some control over it (Azrin & Peterson, 1988). Habit-reversal training uses reinforcement and other behavioral techniques to enable people with Tic Disorders to recognize premonitory urges, become aware of the presence of tics, monitor their own behaviors during stress-inducing situations, use relaxation techniques, and perform competing behaviors that are incompatible with the performance of the tic-related behavior (Azrin & Peterson, 1990). This approach has achieved significant success in the treatment of Tourette's Disorder (Azrin & Peterson, 1992) and in the treatment of chronic motor or vocal tic disorders (Peterson, Campise, & Azrin, 1994).

Children with Tourette's Disorder sometimes benefit from individual therapy. Towbin et al. (1995) suggest that psychodynamic, cognitive, behavioral, and interpersonal models may all be successful with particular constellations of symptoms. For example, a psychodynamic or cognitive approach may help a child explore events that have led up to episodes of tics, and an understanding of those events may provide insights that can allow increased control over symptomatic behaviors. As another example, because the stress created by negative family interactions can increase the frequency of tics, and because blame from family members and teasing from peers can cause a child with Tourette's Disorder to assume the role of victim, interpersonal and family therapy can help the child and the family understand the disorder and the role that each family member plays in perpetuating negative dynamics and worsening the symptoms (Towbin et al., 1995). An adjunct to treatment that should be considered for the family is the Tourette's Syndrome Association, which provides many types of information, as well as family support networks all around the country (King & Noshpitz, 1991). The association can also be reached via the Internet. Because the therapist may need to be an advocate with school or employment personnel, educating these professionals about the disorder may also reduce the stress experienced in those environments by a child or adolescent with Tourette's Disorder.

Tourette's Disorder often has a negative impact on peer relationships, especially among children and adolescents. Children with Tourette's Disorder typically benefit from participation in social skills training groups, similar to those used for children with ADHD or Learning Disorders, that can help them develop skills in relaxation and play and can teach them appropriate behaviors for approaching others.

Pharmacological treatment usually is reserved for those clients who do not respond well to behavioral and environmental interventions. Haloperidol (Haldol) continues to be the most commonly used medication in the treatment of Tourette's Disorder (Erenberg, 1992), despite this drug's side effects, which may include sedation, tremors, constipation (Towbin & Cohen, 1996), depression, and cognitive blunting (King & Noshpitz, 1991). Tardive dyskinesia may also result from long-term use of haloperidol (Silva, Magee, & Friedhoff, 1993). In some cases, clonidine has been used because it elicits fewer side effects, and because this drug's effects last longer (King & Noshpitz, 1991). Two other drugs that are being investigated in the treatment of Tic Disorders are fluvoxamine (Prozac) and clonazepam (Klonopin), both of which seem to diminish the frequency of tics while yielding fewer side effects (Drtilkova, Balastikova, Lemanova, & Zak, 1994).

Prognosis

Peterson et al. (1994), reviewing outcome research on behavioral and pharmacological treatments for Tic Disorders, have found behavioral techniques to yield the greatest reduction in tic-related behaviors. Treatments using haloperidol reported a 50 to 60 percent reduction in tics, whereas those using clonidine yielded only a 25 percent reduction; by comparison, habit-reversal techniques showed a 90 percent reduction in tics. Behavioral interventions have many benefits in the treatment of this disorder but do require significant effort and time.

ENCOPRESIS

Description of the Disorder

Encopresis is defined by *DSM-IV* as "repeated passage of feces into inappropriate places, whether intentional or involuntary" (American Psychiatric Association, 1994a, p. 106). This diagnosis is applicable only if the person has a chronological or developmental level equivalent to at least four years of age and if the symptoms were presented at least once a month for a minimum of four months. The symptoms must not be due to a general medical condition or to a reaction to medications. In order to establish an appropriate treatment plan, the therapist should determine whether the child has ever had an extended period of continence before the onset of Encopresis.

DSM-IV distinguishes between Encopresis With and Without Constipation and Overflow Incontinence. These distinctions usually reflect differences in etiology and subsequent treatment. Harbeck-Weber and Peterson (1996) suggested that Encopresis Without Constipation can be divided into two types: chronic diarrhea/irritable bowel syndrome and manipulative soiling. Encopresis With Constipation often develops after an occurrence of severe constipation resulting from an illness or a change in the diet. The resulting impaction of fecal material can cause painful bowel movements, and anal fissures or irritations have also been reported as contributing factors (Pettei & Davidson, 1988); children develop a fear response and withhold feces in order to avoid painful bowel movements. This type of Encopresis accounts for 80 to 90 percent of all cases (Christopherson & Rapoff, 1992).

Historically, Encopresis Without Constipation has been viewed as a symptom of family conflicts (Shaffer & Waslick, 1996), whereas Encopresis With Constipation was believed to reflect poor toilet training or family stress (Levine, 1975). No empirical data exist to support these views, however. Encopresis Without Constipation seems better understood as the result of operant conditioning, in which the child receives reinforcement (usually increased attention from the parents) for soiling (Christopherson & Rapoff, 1992). Abrahamian and Lloyd-Still (1984) report significant emotional problems, usually caused by the Encopresis, in approximately 20 percent of children with the disorder.

The average age of attaining initial bowel control is 22.7 months (Shaffer & Waslick, 1995), and nearly all children in the United States are fully toilet trained by the age of five years. *DSM-IV* gives the prevalence of Encopresis among five-year-olds as 1 percent, and the disorder is rare beyond the age of sixteen (Shaffer & Waslick, 1996). Encopresis is more common in boys. Physiological abnormalities, such as spasms of the sphincter muscle, have been identified among encopretic youngsters and can leave them prone to constipation (Wald & Handen, 1987).

Typical Client Characteristics

Children exhibiting Encopresis Without Constipation often have other significant mental disorders, such as Mental Retardation, Conduct Disorder, or Oppositional Defiant Disorder. These children typically are manipulative and receive secondary gains from the soiling.

Children with both types of Encopresis may feel shame and low self-esteem related to their symptoms. Parental anger and rejection, as well as children's avoidance of social situations in which they may be embarrassed (such as overnights with friends), may further contribute to their distress and impairment. Smearing of feces (usually to hide the evidence) is sometimes present and can exacerbate negative family reactions.

Preferred Therapist Characteristics

The therapist will need good skills in establishing rapport with both the child and the parents and in collaborating with physicians. The child must feel secure with and trusting of the therapist in order for the treatment to be successful. Similarly, the relationship with the parents must enable them to feel support, as well as some relief from the guilt that parents of children with Encopresis often experience.

Intervention Strategies

The successful treatment of Encopresis requires collaboration among parents, the child, the therapist, and the physician. Nolan, Debelle, Oberflaid, and Coffey (1991) have found a combination of behavioral-educational therapy and medical management to lead to positive treatment responses among children exhibiting Encopresis With Constipation. The initial medical intervention involved purging the bowels with mineral oil, milk of magnesia, or stool softeners (Shaffer & Waslick, 1996). A behavioral program was then introduced by the therapist, incorporating a high-fiber diet, increased intake of fluids, and a feasible plan for regular toileting that could be followed consistently. The children and their parents also received education about the disorder. Boon and Singh (1991) have found that positive reinforcement involving rewards for appropriate toilet use can enhance treatment. To succeed, the overall treatment plan must be one to which the parents will subscribe and lend their support.

Some children with this disorder are resistant to treatment. Rockney et al. (1996), for example, found that 42 percent of the subjects treated at their clinic for Encopresis were not responsive to behavioral treatment that assumed fecal retention as being at the core of the problem: children who had Encopresis Without Constipation were less likely to respond to these interventions. In cases like these, psychodynamic approaches may be useful. Cuddy-Casey (1997) used play therapy with a child who was both enuretic and encopretic and achieved resolution of the Elimination Disorders in thirteen sessions. She suggests that persistent elimination problems may reflect power struggles with the parents or a history of toileting-associated trauma that may need intervention.

Prognosis

Encopresis may continue for some time, but it is rarely chronic (Shaffer & Waslick, 1995). When symptoms are long-lasting, comorbid mental disorders, such as Mental Retardation or Mood Disorders with psychotic features may result in the disorder's being resistant to treatment. Research has not suggested, however, that children with Encopresis are particularly likely to manifest other mental disorders (Loening-Baucke, Desch, & Wolraich, 1988).

ENURESIS

Description of the Disorder

Enuresis is the repeated voiding of urine into the bed or clothes and is considered to be clinically significant if it occurs at least twice per week during three consecutive months or if it interferes with the child's social or interpersonal functioning. In order for this diagnosis to be appropriate, the child must have both chronological and mental ages of at least five years, and the disorder must not be caused by a general medical condition.

The diagnosis, as well as its treatment and prognosis, will be clarified if the time of day when the symptoms typically appear can be determined. Diurnal Enuresis occurs during the daytime and is considered to be related to poor toilet training, social anxiety, or preoccupation with other activities (American Psychiatric Association, 1994a). Nocturnal Enuresis is more common, usually occurs during the REM stage of sleep, and may occur during deep sleep that prevents awareness of the need to urinate.

Coexisting mental disorders are more common in people with Enuresis than in those without this disorder, but no consistent evidence has been found to suggest any causal relationship between Enuresis and other mental disorders (Shaffer & Waslick, 1995). Furthermore, elimination of the Enuresis usually does not entail improvement in any concurrent mental disorders (Moffatt, Kato, & Pless, 1987), although it may ameliorate emotional and behavioral problems resulting from the stress and embarrassment caused by the Enuresis (Christopherson & Rapoff, 1992).

Secondary Enuresis, which follows a period of appropriate bladder control, is most likely to develop between the ages of five and eight (American Psychiatric Association, 1994a). The prevalence of the disorder decreases with increasing age (Christopherson & Rapoff, 1992): 7 percent of boys and 3 percent of girls have Enuresis at the age of five, whereas only 1 percent of males and even fewer females have the disorder at the age of eighteen. Boys are twice as likely as girls to experience Nocturnal Enuresis at the age of eleven or older (Shaffer, 1994). Diurnal Enuresis is more common among girls (Rapoport & Ismond, 1996). Children with Nocturnal Enuresis may also experience episodes of sleepwalking, Encopresis, and nightmares and may report dreams about urinating (Rapoport & Ismond, 1996).

Typical Client Characteristics

Enuresis can lead to anxiety for the child and may cause embarrassment, particularly around the occurrence of overnight visits to friends and family members.

Children may also experience lowered self-esteem as a result of this disorder. Parental anger may contribute to these negative emotions.

A family history of Enuresis is a predictor for this disorder to occur in children. One study found that 77 percent of children with two parents who had experienced Enuresis also had the disorder, whereas only 15 percent of children whose parents had no history of Enuresis were exhibiting the symptoms (Christopherson & Rapoff, 1992). Contextual factors should be considered in cases of Diurnal Enuresis because it is often related to anxiety around missing school activities or to a reluctance to use school toilets (Rapoport & Ismond, 1996).

Preferred Therapist Characteristics

The therapist should have a solid foundation in family dynamics and techniques of behavioral treatment. Much of the family's associated emotional distress can be alleviated if education about the disorder is provided, guilt is relieved, and symptoms are rapidly addressed with behavioral techniques that reduce the frequency of wetting. The therapist must be supportive and nonjudgmental about the causes of the disorder. Unless abuse or another severe problem or symptom is present, the focus should be on removing the symptoms.

Intervention Strategies

The initial phase of treatment for Enuresis involves establishing rapport with the family and the child. Education about the disorder and its treatment can diminish anxieties related to the disorder. The collection of baseline data may effect some change in the enuretic behaviors and will provide the necessary information for measuring progress. Psychodynamic approaches may be warranted, to address any underlying issues, but behavioral approaches to the Enuresis will be primary. Psychodynamic therapy has not been found effective in alleviating the symptoms of this disorder (Christopherson & Rapoff, 1992).

The bell-and-pad system or some variation on it will usually be the most effective form of therapy (Shaffer & Waslick, 1995). A popular version of this system involves an alarm worn on the body: a sensor is attached to a pad that is placed inside the child's pants, and the alarm is placed on the child's wrist or in a pocket. If the pad becomes wet, a sensor in the pad triggers the alarm. This system has the advantage of being useful both day and night. Butler, Brewin, and Forsythe (1990), in fact, report that this system has brought about an even faster reduction of symptoms in Nocturnal Enuresis than an alarm-and-pad system used in the child's bed, although Christopherson and Rapoff (1992) have found the bed-pad type of system preferable. This system reportedly has a cure rate of 50 to 100 percent (Butler et al., 1990).

A variation on this system, called Dry-Bed Training, was developed by Azrin, Sneed, and Foxx (1973). This version adds retention training to the bell-and-pad system. To date, it has been more successful than any other treatment modality (Ronen & Wozner, 1995). This approach is most successful with younger children (Dittman & Wolter, 1996). The duration of the treatment varies. Its length depends on the cognitive functioning of the child, as well as on the presence or absence of physical disabilities, but all children eventually do respond to this treatment (Boggs, Geffken, Johnson, & Silverstein, 1992). Approximately one-third of the children who have been treated may experience relapse within six months of treatment (Butler et al., 1990), but repetition of the treatment usually brings about successful resolution of any relapse.

Drugs, including antidiuretics, tricyclic antidepressants, and anticholinergic medications that may increase bladder capacity, have been used to treat Enuresis, but none has been shown to have enduring effects. Imipramine, an antidepressant, was found to reduce wetting frequency in 85 percent of children treated, but the symptoms returned within three months after the medication was discontinued (Rapoport et al., 1980).

Prognosis

Spontaneous remission occurs in many children with Enuresis. For those who do receive treatment, the classical conditioning method, represented by the bell-and-pad system and Dry-Bed Training, has been found superior to no treatment at all, to psychodynamic psychotherapy, and to medication. Other treatments may also be introduced, to support the family and to reduce anxiety and low self-esteem in the child, but the evidence indicates that these problems are likely to diminish once the Enuresis is resolved (Christopherson & Rapoff, 1992).

SEPARATION ANXIETY DISORDER

Description of the Disorder

Separation Anxiety Disorder is a common disorder among children. The essential characteristic of this disorder is excessive distress upon separation from primary attachment figures. Manifestations of that distress may include worry about caretakers being harmed, reluctance or refusal to go to school or be separated from caregivers, fear about being alone, repeated nightmares incorporating separation themes, and frequent somatic complaints linked to separation. For diagnosis, *DSM-IV* requires evidence of three or more of these symptoms for at least four weeks, with an onset prior to eighteen years of age.

In public, children with Separation Anxiety Disorder may cling to their parents. They often visit the school health clinic with minor physical complaints, or they ask to call home and have their parents come to retrieve them (Popper & Gherardi, 1996). As these children mature, the symptoms may change, with absenteeism and somatic complaints particularly prominent. Children with Separation Anxiety

Disorder frequently present with symptoms of other anxiety disorders and often report many specific fears, as well as feelings of sadness and of not being loved. The fear of getting lost is particularly common in these children (Albano, Chorpita, & Barlow, 1996). Separation Anxiety Disorder frequently coexists with Major Depressive Disorder (Last, Perrin, Hersen, & Kazdin, 1992), ADHD (Klein, Koplewicz, & Kanner, 1992), and Communication Disorders (Cantwell & Baker, 1989).

The etiology of Separation Anxiety Disorder varies. In some cases it is precipitated by a stressful event, such as a significant loss, separation from loved ones, or exposure to danger. This disorder may also stem from an insecure attachment to the primary caregiver, or it may occur in families in which a parent is emotionally dependent on the child (Kronenberger & Meyer, 1996), and it has been associated with enmeshed family relationships. As with many of the other disorders seen in childhood, a careful analysis of contextual and interpersonal factors is important in making a diagnosis and developing treatment plans.

Klein (1994) has found prevalence rates of Separation Anxiety Disorder ranging from 2 percent to 6.8 percent among children four to eighteen years old. Klein and Last (1989) have found this disorder reported as a contributing factor in 50 to 80 percent of school absences. Among children five to eighteen years old who presented for treatment of Anxiety Disorders, 33 percent had a primary diagnosis of Separation Anxiety Disorder (Last, Strauss, & Francis, 1987). Females seem more likely to present with this disorder than males, although some studies have found no gender differences (Albano et al., 1996).

Typical Client Characteristics

Popper and Gherardi (1996) report that the peak prevalence of this disorder occurs before adolescence and seems to be related to issues surrounding increasing independence and resultant changes in family relationships. Klein (1994) suggests that many children begin to exhibit these symptoms around the ages of five or six, when they enter school for the first time. Its onset is often insidious, with the child making innocent requests for physical closeness to the parent because of a physical complaint or a nightmare. The parent may unwittingly reinforce the fearful behavior by allowing the child to stay nearby. Stress may exacerbate the symptoms, and Separation Anxiety Disorder can take a chronic course if not treated early. Prevalence of the disorder diminishes in adolescence, and it appears to be the least common Anxiety Disorder in that age group (Kronenberger & Meyer, 1996).

Children with this disorder sometimes have academic and social problems related to their absenteeism, as well as discomfort with other children. Their fears may preclude their participation in social activities, and their lack of participation causes them to be separated from their peers.

Mothers of children with Separation Anxiety Disorder have a high prevalence of Anxiety or Depressive Disorders. Treatment for a child with this disorder frequently must also address the mother's disorders (Last et al., 1987). Lower socioeconomic status and lower levels of parental education have been associated with greater prevalence of Separation Anxiety Disorder. It also appears to be more common among Caucasian families (Albano et al., 1996).

Preferred Therapist Characteristics

The therapist is often the primary facilitator of the child's separation from the parent and must be confident and clear in that role. If the therapist presents any insecurity or uncertainty, the child and the parent will not receive the emotional support required for them to effect separation. According to King and Noshpitz (1991), "Clinicians permitting a child [with this disorder] to stay at home risk stagnation and false treatment alliance" (p. 258).

Intervention Strategies

Separation Anxiety Disorder can be classified as a phobic response, usually surrounding the fear of leaving the primary caregiver but occasionally related to fear of social situations. Consequently, the course of treatment for Separation Anxiety Disorder almost always includes the behavioral technique of systematic desensitization, highly effective in the treatment of Phobias. School counselors may become involved in the development and implementation of a plan for returning the child to school or shaping attendance behaviors by rewarding progressive approximations (bringing the child to the perimeter of the school property, to the front door, and finally to the classroom, and gradually extending the time that the child remains at school). Additional strategies that have been used in the treatment of this disorder include participant modeling of relaxation techniques and contracting for progressive improvement (Livingston, 1991). If the symptoms are of brief duration, a return to school may be sufficient treatment (Ollendick & Mayer, 1984). Children with chronic features of the disorder, however, such as a long history of absenteeism, many visits to the school clinic, or significant problems at school, may require additional treatment. After the return to school, individual and family psychotherapy, in addition to ongoing school consultation, can be implemented to address any underlying anxieties that may continue and that may shift to another manifestation or to another child in the family.

Family therapy as part of the treatment plan is particularly important when enmeshment is contributing to the disorder. Parents of children with Separation Anxiety Disorder may be dependent on their children or may be emotionally immature themselves. The goal of therapy in these cases would be to reestablish appropriate hierarchies and boundaries between the family subgroups. In severe cases, hospitalization may be required in order to force the separation that parent and child may be unable to accomplish (King & Noshpitz, 1991).

The use of medication in the treatment of Separation Anxiety Disorder is rare and is considered only in severe cases. Imipramine, a drug used successfully with Agoraphobia in adults, has been used with children (six to sixteen years old) with Separation Anxiety Disorder, but no superiority of Imipramine to a placebo has been found (Klein et al., 1992).

Prognosis

In a study by Last et al. (1992), 96 percent of children with Separation Anxiety Disorder recovered from their symptoms after treatment and remained free of the disorder one year later. Other studies, however, which were conducted in the 1960s and 1970s, found lower rates of success, with approximately one-third of children not returning to school (Klein, 1994). Public Law 94–142, the Education of All Handicapped Children Act, now requires schools to provide educational programs for all children, and this law may be partly responsible for this significant difference in outcome rates.

Lipsitz et al. (1994) have found that a significant number of adults with multiple anxieties report having had a history of childhood Separation Anxiety Disorder, a finding that suggests Separation Anxiety Disorder as a precursor of later anxiety disorders, especially Agoraphobia (King & Noshpitz, 1991; Klein, 1994). Children with Separation Anxiety Disorder are also at risk for developing Mood Disorders in adulthood (Popper & Gherardi, 1996), for continuing to be over-dependent and constricted, and for having poor peer relationships (Berg & Jackson, 1985).

SELECTIVE MUTISM

Description of the Disorder

Selective Mutism is characterized by a person's consistently not speaking in some social contexts, such as school, although the person does speak in other contexts, usually at home (Popper & Gherardi, 1996). Symptoms are not due to discomfort with the language. The minimum duration required for diagnosis of this disorder is one month. Black and Uhde (1995) found that 97 percent of their subjects diagnosed with Selective Mutism also had comorbid symptoms of Social Phobias, and 30 percent had Specific Phobias.

Kronenberger and Meyer (1996) describe children with four subtypes of Selective Mutism:

1. Children who are shy and fearful, with significant stranger anxiety
2. Children who are noncompliant and hostile

3. Children whose mutism is the result of a traumatic or upsetting event or experience

4. Children who have a symbiotic relationship with the primary caretaker and who are manipulative and controlling, although they sometimes seem shy

Each of these subtypes presents a different clinical picture and may respond to different methods of intervention.

Popper and Gherardi (1996) estimate that Selective Mutism occurs in approximately thirty to eighty people per one hundred thousand. Gender differences seem negligible, although girls are slightly more likely to present with this disorder. It usually begins before the age of five.

Typical Client Characteristics

Children with Selective Mutism often have academic and social difficulties. Teasing by peers is particularly common.

Family dysfunction is often implicated in this disorder. Silver (1989) describes mothers of children with this disorder as lonely, anxious, or depressed. The mothers also commonly exhibit overinvolvement or enmeshment with the child, which can alienate the father. In order to maintain this symbiotic relationship with the mother, the child rejects others via the mutism. Alternatively, the child's silence may reflect defiance and anger about the mother's behavior (Kronenberger & Meyer, 1996).

Preferred Therapist Characteristics

The therapist treating a child for Selective Mutism should be confident, consistent, calming, reassuring, and supportive. This stance is helpful to the parents, who are likely to be insecure and inconsistent in their communications to their child, and it will also help the child develop trust and feel comfortable speaking in novel settings. The therapist may need to serve as an advocate for the child, facilitating the establishment of a special education plan or initiating an evaluation of the child's school functioning, and so must be comfortable working collaboratively.

Intervention Strategies

Hadley (1994) suggests that appropriate treatment for this disorder should emphasize behavioral interventions aimed at increasing the child's communication and autonomy and at reducing enmeshment. Teaching social and other skills can also help reduce the child's feelings of fear and shyness and help the child learn to express needs more directly.

Several approaches have been used in encouraging children diagnosed with Selective Mutism to talk. Stimulus fading, a method similar to systematic desensitization, has had success with children who speak in some situations. In this approach, a person with whom the child does speak (often the mother) accompanies the child to the site where the child is mute. The child is gradually introduced to the feared situation while the parent withdraws. The child may also be rewarded for increasing communication and social interaction. These behaviors can then be generalized through shaping and reinforcement techniques.

Play therapy can also be useful in treating this disorder, especially if the child will not speak to the therapist or is in enmeshed relationships. The symbolic nature of play allows the child a nonverbal modality in which to safely process uncomfortable feelings and upsetting experiences that may be at the heart of the Selective Mutism.

Given the role that families play in the perpetuation of this disorder, intervention with the family is usually required. Structural family therapy is a logical choice because of its goal of restructuring family roles and relationships. This approach can engage and empower the nonenmeshed parent (usually the father) and establish appropriate boundaries and family hierarchies, with the parents in charge of the family (Kronenberger & Meyer, 1996). In some cases marital therapy, or individual therapy for one parent, is indicated so that issues in the parental relationship to the child can be addressed.

Other strategies are also being explored in the treatment of Selective Mutism. When fluoxetine (Prozac) has been used (Black & Uhde, 1994), parents have reported improvement, but teachers and clinicians working with the children have not; the typical child with this disorder does speak at home, and so these findings are not particularly encouraging. Strategies like relaxation and desensitization, which are used in treating Anxiety Disorders, have also been used with Selective Mutism (see Chapter Five for more information).

Prognosis

Most children receiving treatment for Selective Mutism recover within two to twelve months (Livingston, 1991). Popper and Gherardi (1996) report that approximately half the children with this disorder are able, after treatment, to talk in public by the age of ten. For young children with this disorder, then, the prognosis is relatively good, although the prognosis is less optimistic for those who still exhibit symptoms beyond the age of twelve (Livingston, 1991).

REACTIVE ATTACHMENT DISORDER

Description of the Disorder

Reactive Attachment Disorder is an uncommon disorder that begins before the age of five, and in which children manifest severe disturbance in social relatedness. Children with Reactive Attachment disorder are those whose attachment to their primary caregivers has been disrupted so that future relationships are also impaired. These children have experienced extremely poor care involving persistent disregard of their basic emotional or physical needs or repeated changes of primary caregiver, and it is this poor care that has caused the disturbance in social functioning (American Psychiatric Association, 1994a). Lieberman and Zeanah (1995) describe this as a disorder of deprivation or maltreatment.

DSM-IV delineates two subtypes of Reactive Attachment Disorder. The inhibited type characterizes children who seem extremely withdrawn, unresponsive, or hypervigilant. The disinhibited type characterizes children who demonstrate no preferential attachment to any caregiver but instead are excessively social and seek comfort indiscriminately. Children with this type of Reactive Attachment Disorder may even follow or seek solace from strangers.

Studies have considered the relationship of early attachment experiences to behaviors among preschool children. In many cases, children identified as hostile and aggressive have also manifested disordered attachment behaviors with their mothers. Therefore, Reactive Attachment Disorder may reflect the roots of Oppositional Defiant Disorder and Conduct Disorder (Lyons-Ruth et al., 1996), and early identification and treatment of Reactive Attachment Disorder may prevent the later development of ODD and Conduct Disorder.

Typical Client Characteristics

Reactive Attachment Disorder often coexists with the medical diagnosis of nonorganic failure to thrive and with Feeding Disorder of Infancy. Little information is available on the prevalence of Reactive Attachment Disorder, although, as previously mentioned, nonorganic failure to thrive accounts for an estimated 1 to 5 percent of pediatric hospital admissions (Lyons-Ruth et al., 1996). Children who fail to thrive typically lose significant amounts of weight, may appear malnourished, and exhibit delayed achievement of developmental milestones in addition to being unresponsive or inappropriately responsive to social stimuli.

Preferred Therapist Characteristics

Therapists working with children who have attachment disorders should understand the dynamics of the attachment process. Rebuilding a relationship between the child and the parents will be the primary goal of treatment. A psychodynamic or family systems conceptual framework for analyzing family dynamics is helpful in understanding this disorder and its treatment. One of the greatest challenges for therapists dealing with Reactive Attachment Disorder is managing their own negative feelings toward the caregivers and remaining supportive and empathic while still establishing appropriate guidelines and boundaries for childcare. The therapist must also be able to consult with and contribute to a team of medical professionals.

Intervention Strategies

Children with Reactive Attachment Disorder often present initially in hospital settings because of their failure to gain weight. Therefore, their treatment may begin with a medical diagnosis of failure to thrive (Kronenberger & Meyer, 1996). Treatment to ensure these children's safety and reverse their potentially life-threatening eating behaviors will also be included, as will attention to psychological stimulation. The introduction of such objects as crib toys, mobiles, and childproof mirrors is important. Another important element of treatment is the presence of a limited number of consistent caretakers. Sometimes the assignment of substitute parental figures is necessary so that the care vital to establishing positive and secure attachment relationships can be provided (Kronenberger & Meyer, 1996).

Once these children's immediate medical needs have been addressed, behavioral programs to improve feeding, eating, and caregiving routines are implemented. These are similar to the interventions used in treating Eating Disorders in young clients and include modeling appropriate eating behavior, limiting nonnutritive foods, and allowing children to play with food as a way of reducing any food aversions that may have developed. Of equal importance is training the caregivers to deal positively with these children. Ignoring oppositional behaviors and praising appropriate behaviors are two basic elements addressed by this training (Kronenberger & Meyer, 1996).

The next step in treating children with Reactive Attachment Disorder is to address those behaviors that interfere with the development of adequate and secure attachments (Kronenberger & Meyer, 1996; Zeanah & Emde, 1994). Initially, psychoeducation for the parents will focus on parenting skills and on the nature of positive attachment behaviors. Psychoeducation may be accompanied by parent-child dyad therapy, in which the therapist models positive interactions and facilitates parent-child play. The goal of this intervention is to improve parent-child interactions and attachments (Kronenberger & Meyer, 1996).

Additional goals address the assessment and development of attachment behaviors in the parents. Any abusive or neglectful behaviors certainly must be modified, and quickly. Marital or individual psychotherapy may also be in order. An assessment of the parents' relationships to their individual families of origin can provide the therapist with a baseline assessment of the parents' levels and styles of attachment. Research using the Adult Attachment Interview (Cowan, Cohn, Cowan, & Pearson, 1996) shows significant links between parental attachment and a child's externalizing and internalizing behaviors. This kind of information can stimulate therapeutic discussions with the parents. A cognitive-behavioral framework can be used to identify inappropriate thoughts and actions in the parenting process, and psychodynamic therapy can address unresolved issues from childhood that are interfering with the ability to parent.

Research based on Bowlby's theory of attachment has mushroomed in recent years; the way in which secure and insecure attachment patterns evolve and affect children's development is the focus of many studies. Speltz (1990) has developed a parental training program based on behavioral and attachment theory. This program has three phases, which address child development and appropriate expectations, parent-child play, and effective setting of limits. Although no conclusive outcome research is available for Speltz's program (Zeanah & Emde, 1994), it is similar to programs developed by Webster-Stratton (1989) that have received substantial empirical support.

Therapists must carefully monitor the family situations of children diagnosed with Reactive Attachment Disorder. In some cases, where no gains or changes have been made to improve the quality of childcare, "protective removal" of the child may be warranted (Kronenberger & Meyer, 1996, p. 493); the options include placing the child in foster care, with a relative, or in respite care. Establishing a consistent, safe environment that provides positive care and nurturing is essential to the alleviation of this disorder.

Prognosis

Research has demonstrated a connection between insecure attachment and subsequent behavior and impulse-control problems, poor peer relationships (Zeanah & Emde, 1994), and low self-esteem among six-year-olds (Cassidy, 1988). Clearly, early and effective intervention is indicated for Reactive Attachment Disorder. Interventions based on attachment theory are relatively new, however, and so only limited evaluation data are available. Nevertheless, the treatment of Reactive Attachment Disorder offers many possibilities for future research and holds promise as a key to successful early interventions for behavior disorders.

STEREOTYPIC MOVEMENT DISORDER

Description of the Disorder

Stereotypic Movement Disorder, according to *DSM-IV,* is characterized by repetitive, apparently intentional, driven, nonfunctional, and often self-injurious behaviors, such as hand waving, rocking, head banging, or self-biting. These behaviors persist for at least four weeks and interfere with normal activities.

Comorbidity with Mental Retardation and Pervasive Developmental Disorders is common (Rapoport & Ismond, 1996). Stereotypic Movement Disorder has also been identified in children diagnosed with Anxiety Disorders and Mood Disorders. As with most secondary disorders, Stereotypic Movement Disorder should be diagnosed only if it is so severe as to warrant separate treatment.

Typical Client Characteristics

Children with Stereotypic Movement Disorder exhibit the repetitive behaviors just described. These behaviors are voluntary, although the children may report that they cannot stop them. The behaviors, sometimes manifested by children who have inadequate social stimulation (Rapoport & Ismond, 1996), often begin after a stressful event and may continue despite chastisement from family members and teasing by peers. The family histories of children with Stereotypic Movement Disorder often include compulsive or other stereotypic behaviors (Rapoport & Ismond, 1996).

Preferred Therapist Characteristics

Therapists working with children with Stereotypic Movement Disorder should be aware of common comorbid disorders and their treatments. Behavioral strategies are typically the first line of treatment, and so therapists need a working knowledge of the basic elements of behavior change therapies. Skill in cognitive-behavioral or psychodynamic play therapy may also be helpful, as may family counseling and collaboration with physicians and educators. Therapists need to be calm and empathic with these clients, particularly if underlying anxiety or depression is present.

Intervention Strategies

Treatment for Stereotypic Movement Disorder is similar to that used for Tic Disorders and compulsive behaviors. Baseline data are collected, both to determine the initial frequency and timing of the targeted behaviors and to evaluate progress. Then a behavioral plan is developed for modifying behaviors. The plan may follow a classical model or a model based on operant conditioning.

The classical paradigm for conditioning pairs the stereotypic behavior with some aversive stimulus or competing behavior. This type of aversion or competition is intended to decrease the frequency of the targeted behavior. For example, a rubber band may be placed around a child's wrist, and the child is given instructions to pluck the band each time the stereotypic behavior begins. As another example, tape may be placed over the thumb of a child in order to interfere with the automatic nature of chronic thumbsucking. Operant conditioning uses both positive and negative reinforcers to change a targeted behavior. In the case of stereotypic movements, a chart may be developed and particular time periods may be delineated, with the child being rewarded with a sticker for each time period in which the behavior is not manifested; at the end of a week, the stickers can be redeemed for prizes. Therapists facilitate the development of these plans, but special education teachers often oversee their execution. Therefore, consultation between therapists and teachers may contribute to the effectiveness of the treatment.

If the stereotypic movements are related to a Mood Disorder or an Anxiety Disorder, person-centered or psychodynamic play therapy may be the treatment of choice. These treatments can help children identify the sources of their discomfort. When their distress is alleviated, the children may not need to manifest behavioral expressions of their distress.

Prognosis

Little information is available about the prognosis for Stereotypic Movement Disorder, perhaps because it is rarely the primary focus of treatment and usually accompanies more severe disorders. Successful reduction of targeted behaviors via behavior modification is likely, although this disorder may persist for years, sometimes with changes in its nature. This outcome is especially likely in people with severe or profound levels of Mental Retardation (American Psychiatric Association, 1994a).

ADDITIONAL MENTAL DISORDERS DIAGNOSED IN CHILDREN AND ADOLESCENTS

Many of the mental disorders considered in later chapters of this book are found in young clients, although they are far more prevalent in adults. The remainder of this chapter will discuss differences in the diagnosis and treatment of some of those disorders when they are found in children and adolescents. Discussion of some disorders will not follow the usual format of this book if information of particular relevance to children is unavailable in certain areas. Readers should also review later sections of this book to obtain a complete picture of these disorders.

Mood Disorders

Description of the Disorders

The diagnosis of Mood Disorders in childhood requires an understanding of child development and of age-related differences in presentations of this disorder. While reported feelings of sadness are characteristic of depression across all age ranges, children are more likely to exhibit externalized behaviors as an expression of their feelings. Carlson and Kashani (1988), for example, found that depressed preschoolers typically displayed a sad appearance, sulkiness, crying, and social withdrawal but also tended to somatize their depression and complain of physical aches and pains. School-age children experiencing depression were less likely to appear sad but were more likely to be irritable and to present somatic complaints. Nearly 25 percent of the children diagnosed with Depressive Disorders reported mood-congruent hallucinations, whereas 38 percent presented fighting and other disruptive behaviors. Adolescents' symptoms of depression are similar to those of adults and include sad feelings, social withdrawal, and, in about 10 percent of cases, mood-congruent hallucinations. Adolescents are less likely than younger children to complain of physical problems, to appear sad, and to cry, but irritability continues to be a characteristic complaint. Major Depressive Disorders in young people typically are of mild to moderate severity.

In young children, Separation Anxiety Disorder often is characterized by features of depression, including crying, sulkiness, irritability, and a sad appearance. Clinicians should be sure that Separation Anxiety Disorder is not misdiagnosed as a Depressive Disorder.

Bipolar Disorder is extremely rare among children and has not been identified in children under thirteen in any major studies (Kronenberger & Meyer, 1996). Recent research has raised questions about the potential overlap between the manic phase of a Bipolar Disorder and ADHD (Biederman et al., 1996). Therapists also should be aware that the mood swings characteristic of most adolescents can be mistaken for a Bipolar Disorder. The prevalence of Bipolar Disorders among adolescents is similar to that for adults, and treatment follows a similar course.

Typical Client Characteristics

Therapists working with children and adolescents often will encounter symptoms of Mood Disorders. Recent prevalence estimates of Major Depressive Disorders in young people range from 0.4 percent to 2.5 percent among children and from 0.4 percent to 8.3 percent among adolescents (Birmaher et al., 1996). Dysthymic Disorder is slightly less common, with an estimated 0.6 to 1.7 percent of children and 1.6 to 8 percent of adolescents meeting the criteria for this diagnosis. Wittchen, Knauper, and Kessler (1994) have found that adults with Major Depressive Disorders often report its onset during adolescence.

Gender differences among children with symptoms of Mood Disorders have not been found. Nevertheless, female adolescents are twice as likely as males to experience Major Depressive Disorders (Breslau et al., 1995).

The Children's Depression Inventory (CDI) may be useful in diagnosing depression in children between the ages of eight and seventeen (Kovacs, 1992). The CDI is a self-report instrument consisting of twenty-seven questions designed to identify depression; it can supplement interviews, and it can screen groups for the presence of depressive symptoms.

Intervention Strategies

Recommended treatment for children with Mood Disorders is similar to that for adults (see Chapter Four), but some programs and guidelines are especially pertinent to young clients with these disorders. Lewinsohn, Clarke, Hops, and Andrews (1990), for example, have designed the Coping with Depression Course for Depressed Adolescents, a sixteen-session psychoeducational group training that includes workbooks, readings, and quizzes. The premise of this course is that adolescents with poor social skills elicit negative responses from others, and that by learning specific social skills they can engage in more positive interactions, an outcome that in turn will have a positive impact on their emotions. The preliminary findings are encouraging: participants in the course have experienced significant decline in depressive symptoms by comparison to people on a waiting list, and these effects had continued at one-month follow-up.

Although medications are being used effectively in the treatment of Mood Disorders among adults, more caution is advised in their use with adolescents. Birmaher et al. (1996) have reviewed several studies and conclude that no significant differences have been found between placebo treatment of Mood Disorders in adolescents and treatment with tricyclic antidepressants. Selective serotonin reuptake inhibitors (SSRIs) like fluoxetine appear to be more effective. These authors caution that more research is needed in this area of pharmacology.

Prognosis

Interventions show promising results. Kovacs, Akiskal, Gatsonis, and Parrone (1994), for example, have found that psychoeducational programs presented to children diagnosed with Dysthymic Disorder were usually effective in preventing the development of a Major Depressive Disorder. Weisz et al. (1995) carried out a meta-analysis of outcome studies and found that children with depression who received psychotherapy were 77 percent more likely than controls to show improvement on posttreatment assessments and continued to be better off than 69 percent of the controls on follow-up assessments.

Psychosis

Description of the Disorder

Although rare, childhood-onset psychosis does occur. Approximately one child in ten thousand develops Schizophrenia, with males predominating (Remschmidt, Schulz, Martin, & Warnke, 1994). Since the publication of *DSM-III* (American Psychiatric Association, 1980), the criteria for Psychotic Disorders in children have been the same as those used for adults, with primary symptoms including hallucinations, loose associations, and illogical thinking. Volkmar (1996) reviewed five case studies of Childhood Schizophrenia and found auditory hallucinations to be the most frequent symptom, with delusions presented in approximately half the cases. Illogical conversation or thought patterns also were common.

The difficulty in applying this diagnosis to children is that loose associations and illogical thinking are not unusual before the age of seven (Volkmar, 1996). With older children, however, these symptoms should be taken quite seriously. (For additional information on Psychotic Disorders, see Chapter Nine.)

Typical Client Characteristics

Childhood-onset Schizophrenia is the most prevalent Psychotic Disorder in children. Onset before the age of six is extremely rare; nevertheless, histories of adults diagnosed with Schizophrenia often reveal the presence of unusual personality styles as well as language or motor problems in childhood (Werry, 1996). The frequency of Schizophrenia increases after the age of eleven until late adolescence, when it reaches adult prevalence rates (Volkmar, 1996).

Preferred Therapist Characteristics

Training and experience is similar to that required for working with adults with Psychotic Disorders. These disorders, like Mood Disorders, tend to be familial, and therapists need to be alert to the possibility that other family members also have Psychotic Disorders. A difficult aspect of the work with a family that has a child with psychosis is helping the family members cope with the uncertain prognosis of the disorder.

Intervention Strategies

The research on effective interventions for Psychotic Disorders in childhood is limited. As with adults, multiple treatment modalities are required. In addition to family therapy, treatment for children and adolescents should include special education. Therapists may become involved in the development of educational plans, which should incorporate social and emotional goals. Social skills training, the teaching of approach behaviors, interpersonal interaction, playing with peers, and effective communication should be included. Techniques of stress management may also be useful to young people diagnosed with Schizophrenia, given that high levels of stress have been found to increase dysfunctional thought patterns and the likelihood of psychotic episodes. Modification of the home environment, promotion of a positive attitude on the part of the parents, and training of the parents in effective coping strategies are all likely to be helpful. Additional useful psychoeducational family interventions could include teaching communication and problem-solving skills and providing specific factual information about the disorder and its treatment.

Prognosis

Bellack and Mueser (1993) report a fairly positive prognosis for young people diagnosed with Psychotic Disorders. They have found that children who received family interventions in addition to medication had a relapse rate of only 17 percent, by comparison with a relapse rate of 83 percent among a control group in which children received medication only.

Obsessive-Compulsive Disorder

Description of the Disorder

March and Leonard (1996) report that approximately one in two hundred children and adolescents meets the diagnostic criteria for Obsessive-Compulsive Disorder (OCD), manifesting symptoms similar to those of adults with the disorder. Most children with OCD present with obsessions about germs or disease and exhibit concomitant rituals of washing or checking. Other common obsessions include concern about harm to the self or others, sexual themes, or forbidden thoughts. Common compulsions, in addition to washing and checking, include touching, counting, hoarding, and repeating. A high rate of comorbid tic disorders has also been noted (Rapoport, Leonard, Swedo, & Lenane, 1993).

Typical Client Characteristics

The most frequent age of onset among young patients treated for OCD at the National Institutes of Mental Health was 7 years; the average age at onset was 10.2 years (March & Leonard, 1996). Rapoport et al. (1993) report that this disorder can start as early as age 2 and that it is more prevalent among boys. OCD and Tourette's Disorder are common among the family members of children with OCD. Epidemiological studies have identified no differences in prevalence among various ethnic groups (Rasmussen & Eisen, 1994).

Preferred Therapist Characteristics

Children with OCD can be manipulative and resistant to any change in their compulsive behaviors. As behavior changes are introduced, oppositional behavior may be exhibited in response to any limits placed on the targeted behaviors. Therefore, therapists working with children with OCD need to be empathic yet confident in their skills and the plans they develop. Therapists must also provide support to the parents of these children.

Intervention Strategies

Childhood OCD is treated as an Anxiety Disorder, and cognitive-behavioral interventions are emphasized. The primary intervention for OCD is exposure to obsessions, with prevention of compulsions, to promote systematic desensitization (March & Leonard, 1996). Inclusion of parents in the treatment is beneficial because the family often has developed maladaptive coping strategies for dealing with the distressed child (Rapoport et al., 1993). The use of other behavioral techniques, such as flooding, relaxation, extinction, and habit reversal, has also been attempted, although limited outcome data are available. (For additional discussion of the diagnosis and treatment of OCD, see Chapter Five.)

Posttraumatic Stress Disorder

The criteria for Posttraumatic Stress Disorder (PTSD) in children are the same as for adults (see Chapter Five). Children's distress may be manifested in slightly different ways, however, because of their different level of cognitive and emotional functioning. Nightmares are common among children with PTSD, although they may not be able to remember the content of the dreams. Flat affect or withdrawn behaviors are also typical of children with PTSD. They frequently are unable to talk about their traumatic experiences and can communicate them only through play (Kronenberger & Meyer, 1996).

In the past, children were thought to be resilient to the impact of traumatic events. Recent natural and other disasters, however, such as Hurricane Hugo and the California school sniper, have provided researchers with the opportunity to study children's reactions to traumatic stress (Yule, 1994). Using the Revised Children's Manifest Anxiety Scale (Reynolds & Richmond, 1978) and questionnaires assessing stress level, Lonigan et al. (1991) found that children exposed to a hurricane, by comparison with adults, reported significantly higher stress and stress reactions. Children exposed to repeated or chronic traumas, such as abuse, also exhibited more troubled behaviors. Famularo, Kinscherff, and Fenton (1990) have found that children who experienced traumas commonly exhibited detachment, sadness, restricted affect, and dissociative episodes. Inappropriate sexual behaviors are often exhibited by children who have experienced sexual abuse (Deblinger et al., 1989). Effective treatment of PTSD in children is similar to its treatment in adults. (For more information, see Chapter Five.)

Generalized Anxiety Disorder

Generalized Anxiety Disorder (GAD) may also present in young people. Children with GAD have concerns about many aspects of their lives. These children typically exhibit excessive worry or anxiety, difficulty controlling the worry, trouble concentrating, problems in sleeping, and muscle tension. They have difficulty relaxing and may exhibit exaggerated emotional responses to stressors. Frequently their anxiety is reflected in somatic complaints (Kronenberger & Meyer, 1996).

Comorbidity of GAD with other disorders is common. Last et al. (1987) have found Separation Anxiety Disorder to be present in 70 percent of children who had previously been diagnosed with GAD, and 35 percent met the criteria for both GAD and ADHD. Last et al. also report that the mean age of onset among children referred for treatment of GAD was approximately 13.4 years and that the prevalence of GAD was similar for both genders.

Assessment and treatment of children with GAD emphasizes behavioral strategies. The Revised Children's Manifest Anxiety Scale is often used in determining the extent of the anxiety and the specific issues that may underlie the disorder (Reynolds & Richman, 1978). This inventory provides a baseline that can be used to evaluate the success of treatment. The first approach to treatment is most often a plan for systematic desensitization. This plan can be designed by the therapist and implemented by the parents. (Additional information on the treatment of GAD can be found in Chapter Five.)

Phobias

Phobias are common among children, particularly Specific and Social Phobias, although they rarely are presented for treatment. In most cases, the children simply avoid whatever situations produce the phobic responses. Animal phobias are common in young children. Older children are more likely to exhibit blood- and injury-related phobias (Kronenberger & Meyer, 1996).

Treatment for Phobias in children is similar to that for other Anxiety Disorders. Behavioral treatments using systematic desensitization or relaxation training are the most frequent interventions. (Additional information about Phobias and their effective treatments is to be found in Chapter Five.)

TREATMENT RECOMMENDATIONS: CLIENT MAP

This chapter has focused on disorders that usually begin before the age of eighteen, as well as disorders that typically begin later but sometimes manifest earlier. Beyond their early age of onset, these disorders vary widely, although most are reflected by behavioral difficulties. The following general treatment recommendations, organized according to the format of the Client Map, are provided for the disorders discussed in this chapter.

Client Map

Diagnosis

Disorders usually first diagnosed during infancy, childhood, or adolescence

Objectives of Treatment

Eliminate conduct-disordered behavior

Improve academic functioning

Improve socialization and peer-group involvement

Promote family understanding of the disorder

Improve parenting and family functioning

Assessments

Assessment of intelligence and learning abilities often needed

Assessment of behaviors, fears, and mood

Clinician Characteristics

Skilled at providing support and building rapport while setting limits and overcoming resistance

Knowledgeable about developmental patterns and issues in children

Able to collaborate with family members, teachers, school counselors, and physicians

Location of Treatment

Usually outpatient

Day treatment centers increasingly available for troubled children

Interventions to Be Used

Behavioral therapy, especially reality therapy, emphasizing strategies for behavior change

Establishment of a baseline

Setting of realistic goals

Modification and tracking of behavior

Use of reinforcements and natural consequences

Education on the disorder for the child and the family

Training in communication and other skills

Play therapy (for young children)

Emphasis of Treatment

Structured but supportive

Primarily oriented toward the present

Numbers

Individual and family therapy

Peer-group counseling possibly helpful

Timing

Usually medium-term therapy, with a rapid pace

Medications Needed

Usually for ADHD, Tourette's Disorder, OCD, Psychotic Disorders, and severe forms of other disorders

Adjunct Services

Parent education

Rewarding activities for children

Prognosis

Varies according to the disorder

Client Map of Shannon

This chapter began with a description of Shannon, a nine-year-old girl who for several years had been displaying a broad range of behavioral and academic problems. As is common among children with Attention-Deficit and Disruptive Behavior Disorders, the parents had manifested similar symptoms as young-sters; they had difficulty appreciating the severity of Shannon's symptoms and helping her modify her behavior. The following client map outlines the treatment recommended for Shannon.

Diagnosis

Axis I: 312.8 Conduct Disorder, Childhood-Onset Type, Moderate

   314.01 Attention-Deficit/Hyperactivity Disorder, Predominantly Hyperactive-Impulsive Type, Moderate

Axis II: V71.09 No diagnosis on Axis II

Axis III: None reported

Axis IV: Arrest, academic problems, lack of adequate supervision

Axis V: Global assessment of functioning (GAF Scale): current GAF = 50

Objectives of Treatment

Eliminate conduct-disordered behavior

Improve attention and academic skills

Assessments

Assessment of intelligence and learning abilities

Conners Rating Scales

Clinician Characteristics

Skilled at building rapport, overcoming resistance, setting limits, using family interventions

Location of Treatment

Community mental health center

Interventions to Be Used

Reality therapy, emphasizing strategies for behavior change (to help with recognizing self-destructive nature of behavior)

Contract for behavior change

Help with recognizing triggers for impulsive behavior and substituting alternative behaviors

Training in other ways to get needs met

Setting of realistic goals in family and school meetings (for help in improving attention and academic achievement)

Reinforcement for positive behaviors

Emphasis of Treatment

Structured but supportive, primarily present-oriented

Numbers

Individual therapy with family involvement

Counseling group at school (to help in improving social skills and reinforcing positive changes)

Consultation with school counselor, teachers, and representatives of the justice system (to provide the experience of consequences for theft but also an avenue for demonstrating sincere efforts to change)

Timing

Medium- or long-term treatment, rapid pace

Medications Needed

Referral to a child psychiatrist for determination of whether medication is indicated for reducing symptoms of ADHD

Adjunct Services

Parent education

Involvement in some interesting, action-oriented pursuit likely to provide an experience of being successful

Possible involvement in a Big Sister program

Prognosis

Good, with parental cooperation; otherwise, fair.

Recommended Reading

Journals, including *Adolescence, Child Abuse and Neglect, Child Development, Developmental Psychology, Elementary School Guidance and Counseling, Journal of Abnormal Child Psychology, Journal of the American Academy of Child and Adolescent Psychiatry,* and *Journal of Clinical Child Psychiatry*

Kazdin, A. E. (1995). *Conduct disorders in childhood and adolescence.* Thousand Oaks, CA: Sage.

Kottman, T., & Schaefer, C. (Eds). (1993). *Play therapy in action: A casebook for practitioners.* Northvale, NJ: Aronson.

Mash, E. J., & Barkley, R. A. (1996). *Child psychopathology.* New York: Guilford Press.

Rapoport, J. L., & Ismond, D. R. (1996). *DSM-IV training guide for diagnosis of childhood disorders.* New York: Brunner/Mazel.

Rutter, M., Taylor, E., & Hersov, L. (Eds.). (1994). *Child and adolescent psychiatry: Modern approaches.* Cambridge, MA: Blackwell.

CHAPTER THREE

Situationally-Precipitated Conditions and Disorders

Beth H., a forty-seven-year-old divorced Jewish woman, sought counseling two weeks after a biopsy revealed that she had breast cancer. She reported that she had been consumed by fear and grief since her diagnosis and had been unable to make decisions about her treatment. The physicians had told her that she could choose either a mastectomy or a combination of removal of the tumor and the surrounding tissue along with thirty radiation treatments. Beth was terrified that the radiation itself would cause secondary cancers, and she viewed the mastectomy as the safer option. However, that choice was also frightening and confusing to her because she was apprehensive about the more extensive surgery and the resulting physical changes. Beth had explored the possibility of reconstructive surgery concurrent with her mastectomy. Once again, however, she had been confronted with an array of choices, all of them with risks and drawbacks. Beth's physicians cautioned her that putting the surgery off too long might worsen her prognosis, but her anxiety and her sorrow were preventing her from making a decision. Despite these worries, Beth continued to fulfill all her personal and professional responsibilities.

Beth reported that her life had been difficult over the past year but that she had been managing to keep it all under control. She and her husband had divorced a year before, and Beth had just begun to socialize as a single person. She had a successful career as a benefits manager for a county government. She also had a twelve-year-old daughter, Amanda, whom she described as the greatest joy in her life. She had several close women friends and maintained positive relationships with her father and her younger sister. She reported great enjoyment of outdoor activities, especially hiking, camping, and bird-watching.

Beth's diagnosis of cancer raised several powerful fears that were linked to her symptoms. Her mother had died of breast cancer at the age of fifty, and Beth feared that she too would die and not see her daughter grow up. She was also apprehensive that, even if she did survive, the diagnosis and the subsequent surgery would prevent her from developing close intimate relationships and marrying again. She was terrified that her disease was hereditary and that her daughter would inherit this legacy. Finally, she was fearful that she would need chemotherapy after the surgery. Beth reported that she had successfully coped with many problems over the course of her life but had never before felt so hopeless and worried.

Beth is an emotionally healthy woman who has functioned well throughout her life. She has good relationships with family and friends, rewarding interests, and a usually optimistic view of her life and of herself. The diagnosis of breast cancer, however, especially coming not long after her divorce, raised many fears about her future and left her feeling anxious and discouraged. Beth was experiencing an Adjustment Disorder With Mixed Anxiety and Depressed Mood. This chapter will focus on both Adjustment Disorder and Other Conditions That May Be a Focus of Clinical Attention (formerly known as the V-Code Conditions). These typically are the mildest categories of symptoms described in the fourth edition of the *Diagnostic and Statistical Manual of Mental Disorders,* or *DSM-IV* (American Psychiatric Association, 1994a).

OVERVIEW OF SITUATIONALLY-PRECIPITATED CONDITIONS AND DISORDERS

Description of the Disorders

Both categories of disorder—Other Conditions and Adjustment Disorders—usually have an identifiable precipitant or cause and are often relatively mild and transient, especially if the person has no other mental disorders. Causes are most likely to be such common life events or circumstances as relocation, divorce, a death, or retirement. Any emotional symptoms that result are clearly connected to the precipitant, although the client may react with some generalized dysfunction.

Several other disorders in *DSM-IV* (such as Brief Psychotic Disorder, or Major Depressive Disorder without melancholic features) also tend to be precipitated by an external stressor, but the severity of the symptoms in those disorders may obscure the role of the precipitant, and it is the symptoms themselves rather than stressful life circumstances that become the focus of treatment, at least initially. For Adjustment Disorders and Other Conditions, however, the precipitant and its impact on the person's lifestyle and adjustment are usually the primary focus of treatment; the emotional upset and dysfunctional behavior resulting from the precipitant receive secondary attention. In treating these disorders and conditions, clinicians commonly assume that if the individuals can gain a realistic view of the precipitant, adapt to and manage the changes it has produced, and increase their sense of control over their life and their responses, then any dysfunctional symptoms accompanying the stressful life change will spontaneously be alleviated, if not eliminated.

Sometimes clinicians have difficulty determining whether a person is experiencing an Other Condition or an Adjustment Disorder. Adjustment Disorders by definition result in noticeable impairment or dysfunction and/or marked distress beyond what would be expected in reaction to the stressor (American Psychiatric Association, 1994a). Other Conditions are normal or expectable reactions to life events and are therefore not viewed as mental disorders, although the Conditions are associated with some upset or dysfunction that may be alleviated by psychotherapy. Beth, for example, was immobilized by symptoms of apprehension and depression, which reflected an Adjustment Disorder. Had she been saddened and worried by the diagnosis of cancer but nevertheless in control and able to make appropriate medical decisions, she would have been described as experiencing an Other Condition or Phase of Life Problem.

Both Adjustment Disorders and Other Conditions tend to be relatively brief in duration. If there is a long-standing cause or precipitant, however (such as abuse, below-average intellectual functioning, or treatment via neuroleptic medications), the Adjustment Disorder or Other Condition may be enduring.

Strain (1995) suggests a five-level taxonomic structure clarifying the relative levels of severity of these two categories:

1. Normal state

2. Problem-level diagnoses (for example, the Conditions)

3. Adjustment Disorder

4. Minor disorder or Not Otherwise Specified diagnosis

5. Major disorder

In other words, the Conditions represent more dysfunction than what is considered normal, but not enough for a diagnosis of a mental disorder, whereas an Adjustment Disorder is viewed as the mildest type of mental disorder listed in *DSM-IV.*

Typical Client Characteristics

Nearly everyone has experienced either an Adjustment Disorder or an Other Condition or both. They occur at all levels of mental health, intelligence, affluence, and psychological sophistication. Their symptoms may be triggered by a broad range of transitions and changes such as mistreatment and abuse, diagnosis of a life-threatening illness, or relocation and may reflect and be related to common problems of living such as occupational dissatisfaction, marital conflict, or caretaking of an ill or elderly parent. Although few people go through life without experiencing a Condition or an Adjustment Disorder, some people—especially those who have effective coping mechanisms and ways of handling stress, those who have support systems and confidants, those who have a record of successfully coping with previous stressors, and those whose functioning is good overall—are less likely to be troubled by these problems. People are also typically more successful at handling stressful life circumstances if those events are not severely disruptive and if there are not multiple stressors. The impact of stressors seems to be additive, so that a major stressor (such as diagnosis of a life-threatening illness) accompanied by several minor stressors (such as relocation and a new job) is probably going to have a much greater impact than an isolated major stressor.

Preferred Therapist Characteristics

People with Adjustment Disorders or Other Conditions typically work best with therapists who are supportive, affirming, collaborative, and empathic and who provide the stimulus, direction, and skills needed for the clients to mobilize themselves and use their resources more effectively. Treatment is typically short-term and focused on helping people cope more effectively with the stressful changes or circumstances. Therapists should be comfortable with brief, structured interventions that may involve teaching and referral to outside sources of help and information but that are unlikely to involve extended exploration. Therapists should also be comfortable dealing with persons in crisis who may be feeling overwhelmed, discouraged, and even suicidal. Because Adjustment Disorders and Other Conditions may stand alone or be accompanied by a broad range of other disorders, therapists need to be skilled diagnosticians so that they can determine quickly whether coexisting mental disorders are present that may interfere with the clients' efforts to cope.

Intervention Strategies

Treatment for these disorders and Conditions varies and depends on the nature of the associated crisis or life circumstance and on the presence of any coexisting disorders. In general, however, treatment will be designed to provide people a clear understanding of what is going on in their lives, of their reactions to those situations, and of their options. People's current resources and coping mechanisms provide the foundation for treatment, and efforts will be made to increase clients' awareness of existing strengths, to build on those strengths, and to help them develop new coping skills if those are needed. For example, individuals with a Partner Relational Problem might be taught to improve their communication skills, clarify their expectations of their partners, and seek a mutually agreed-on and rewarding relationship. People who have experienced the death of a loved one will usually need help in expressing and managing their grief, in dealing with the impact the loss has had on their lives, and in establishing new and realistic goals, directions, friends, and activities.

Therapists will typically seek to build rapport quickly so that they can function as collaborators, helping and guiding these clients toward mobilizing their resources, gathering information, and coping effectively with stressors. Normalizing people's troubled reactions, if that is warranted, can be helpful. A support group composed of others who are dealing with similar life circumstances can reduce feelings of aloneness and differentness and can help individuals accept and understand their responses to the stressor, obtain information about it, and learn ways to cope effectively with it. Support groups for people coping with cancer, for people who have experienced the death of a loved one, and for people going through marital separation or divorce are widely available and can greatly enhance the process of therapy.

Prognosis

The prognosis is excellent for returning people with Adjustment Disorders and Other Conditions to their previous levels of functioning. In fact, some people seem to function even better afterward because of the self-confidence they have gained from handling their situations effectively and because of the skills they have developed or improved over the course of therapy. Therefore, treatment of Adjustment Disorders and Other Conditions is often a growth-promoting experience for clients. At the same time, however, if a stressor is unremitting, if the person is unsuccessful in coping with the stressor, or if the person already has emotional difficulties, the symptoms may not abate or may even evolve into a more significant mental disorder.

ADJUSTMENT DISORDERS

Description of the Disorders

The category of Adjustment Disorders is the less prevalent of the two discussed in this chapter. According to *DSM-IV* (American Psychiatric Association, 1994a), "The essential feature of an Adjustment Disorder is the development of clinically significant emotional or behavioral symptoms in response to an identifiable psychosocial stressor or stressors. The symptoms must develop within 3 months after the onset of the stressor(s)" (p. 623). Precipitating stressors may be of any severity and may include traumas.

Adjustment Disorders are one of the very few *DSM* diagnoses that are by definition time-limited. This diagnosis can be maintained for a maximum of six months after the termination of the precipitating stressor. If symptoms persist beyond this period, the diagnosis must be changed. Nevertheless, because many precipitants (such as a disabling medical condition or a dangerous environment) are chronic and enduring, this diagnosis may be maintained for many months or even for years. An Adjustment Disorder that remits within six months is described as Acute; one that lasts longer is classified as Chronic.

The category of Adjustment Disorders is sometimes thought of as a residual category, one that is not used if the symptoms also meet the criteria for another mental disorder. The diagnosis of Adjustment Disorder typically stands alone on Axis I of a multiaxial assessment but can be used along with the diagnosis of another mental disorder if the development of the Adjustment Disorder is separate from the development of the other mental disorder. For example, a person with a preexisting Somatization Disorder might develop symptoms of an Adjustment Disorder after a marital separation.

A wide variety of stressors can precipitate an Adjustment Disorder. Stressors may be single events (such as the end of a relationship or the loss of a job) or multiple events (such as diagnosis of an illness and concurrent marital conflict). The stressors may be circumscribed events, recurrent events (such as relapses of an illness), or continuous circumstances (such as poverty or a conflicted relationship). The most common stressors for adults are marital difficulties, divorce or separation, financial problems, and relocation; for adolescents the most common stressors are school-related problems, parental divorce or rejection, and substance abuse (Maxmen & Ward, 1995). Because the impacts of stressors tend to be additive, assessment should look beyond the presenting concern to determine what other circumstances may be affecting a person.

The reaction to the stressor, rather than the presence of the stressor itself, is what determines whether a person has an Adjustment Disorder. A significant stressor (such as the loss of one's home in a flood) may have little impact on one person, whereas a relatively minor stressor (such as the end of a brief dating relationship in adolescence) may evoke a very strong reaction in another person. An Adjustment Disorder seems particularly likely to develop when a stressor touches on an area of vulnerability for the client and leads to an adverse reaction.

Adjustment Disorders differ from Other Conditions in being characterized by impaired functioning or reactions exceeding those that would normally be expected—in other words, by what Strain (1995) describes as an overwhelming psychological response to a stressor. A Condition, by contrast, refers to a context, a problem, or a situation rather than to excessive reactions and symptoms.

DSM-IV specifies six types of Adjustment Disorders. When this diagnosis is made, the clinician should specify whether the type is Adjustment Disorder with Depressed Mood, with Anxiety, with Mixed Anxiety and Depressed Mood, with Disturbance of Conduct, with Mixed Disturbance of Emotions and

Conduct, or Unspecified. Examples of the Unspecified type include adjustment problems characterized by work inhibition or mild physical symptoms without an apparent medical cause. Depression and anxiety are the most common accompaniments of Adjustment Disorders in adults, whereas disturbances of conduct are particularly common among adolescents with Adjustment Disorders (Maxmen & Ward, 1995). Behaviors like vandalism, reckless driving, fighting, and truancy are typical of youth with Adjustment Disorders, and this kind of disorder may be confused with Conduct Disorder if a careful history is not taken. Some Adjustment Disorders are severe enough to warrant hospitalization.

Maxmen and Ward (1995) report that approximately 10 percent of adults develop an Adjustment Disorder. The prevalence and severity of this type of disorder are typically greater in adolescents, with as many as one-third experiencing an Adjustment Disorder. Nevertheless, because many people with an Adjustment Disorder do not seek treatment and experience spontaneous remission of symptoms, its incidence is difficult to assess and may be considerably higher than these estimates.

Some sources indicate that Adjustment Disorders affect males and females equally (American Psychiatric Association, 1994a), whereas other sources indicate that, especially among people hospitalized for this disorder, single women are overrepresented (Despland, Monod, & Ferrero, 1995; Kaplan, Sadock, & Grebb, 1994). According to Marttunen, Aro, Henriksson, and Lonnqvist (1994), adolescent males with this diagnosis seem to have the highest likelihood of committing suicide. The same researchers have found such acts of suicide to have been generally precipitated by some interpersonal loss or conflict, whereas the people who committed suicide were characterized by narcissistic traits and tendencies to withdraw.

Typical Client Characteristics

Adjustment Disorders occur in all types of people but seem to be more prevalent in those who have limited resources and support systems, poor or underdeveloped coping mechanisms, little experience in dealing effectively with previous stressful events, and multiple stressors. Adjustment Disorders are particularly common among people who are coping with life-threatening illnesses. Oxman, Barrett, Freeman, and Manheimer (1994) have found that, among a sample of older adults anticipating cardiac surgery, 50.7 percent had an Adjustment Disorder related to their medical condition and its treatment. Similarly, Massie and Holland (1990) have found a high incidence of Adjustment Disorders among people hospitalized because of a diagnosis of cancer. Other factors, in addition to poor physical health, that seem to predispose people to develop an Adjustment Disorder include financial difficulties, a history of Mood Disorders or Alcohol-Related Disorders, family conflict, poorly controlled physical pain, and feelings of loss of control. Sleep disturbance resulting from stressors also seems to put people at risk for the development of an Adjustment Disorder (Cartwright & Wood, 1991).

Preferred Therapist Characteristics

Most people with Adjustment Disorders have a relatively high level of previous functioning. They probably are capable of handling the stressors themselves but are daunted by the stressors' suddenness or by their own lack of resources and self-esteem. Therapists should communicate confidence that these clients, with some support and direction, will be able to resolve their problems themselves. This optimistic attitude should serve to strengthen people's coping mechanisms and encourage them to face the stressors with a hopeful outlook.

Intervention Strategies

Most Adjustment Disorders improve spontaneously without treatment when stressors are removed or attenuated, but therapy can facilitate recovery. It can hasten improvement, provide coping skills and adaptive mechanisms to avert future crises, and minimize poor choices and self-destructive behaviors that may have adverse consequences (Maxmen & Ward, 1995). As necessary, therapy also can address long-standing maladaptive emotional and behavioral patterns.

A flexible crisis-intervention model probably best characterizes the therapy usually recommended for the treatment of Adjustment Disorders. This model of therapy would focus both on relieving the acute symptoms that clients are experiencing and on promoting clients' adaptation to and ability to cope with the stressors. Therapy would also support the clients' strengths, paying little attention to past problems unless these problems suggested patterns that had to be addressed in the effort to promote effective coping with current stressors. Education and information are usually part of the treatment and are intended to help people take a realistic look at their situations and become aware of options and resources that may be useful. The following are typical steps in crisis intervention:

1. Understanding the problem
2. Viewing the problem in context, to clarify the issues and the client's strengths
3. Contracting with the client for change, to mobilize and empower the client
4. Applying interventions to promote affective, cognitive, and behavioral changes in the client
5. Reinforcing and solidifying gains
6. Terminating treatment and following up (Wells & Giannetti, 1990)

The overriding goal of this brief, problem-focused orientation to treatment is to return people to previous or higher levels of functioning and to change some of their self-destructive behaviors and reactions so that the chances of a recurrence are reduced with the next life change. Maxmen and Ward (1995) report that more than half of people with Adjustment Disorders who were treated with a brief crisis-intervention model completed treatment in four weeks or even less time.

A wide variety of interventions have been suggested for treatment of Adjustment Disorders. The specific interventions employed depend on the symptoms associated with the particular Adjustment Disorder as well as on the nature of the stressors and the theoretical orientation of the therapist. For example, to cite just a few of the diverse approaches that can be used, people with depressive symptoms probably will respond to techniques borrowed from cognitive and interpersonal therapy (see Chapter Four), people experiencing anxiety probably will benefit from learning how to use relaxation techniques (see Chapter Five), and people with problems of conduct are likely to respond to behavioral therapy (see Chapters Two and Six). Because approximately one-third of people with Adjustment Disorder, particularly adolescents, have suicidal thoughts, preventing suicide must of course be a priority of treatment.

Moretti, Feldman, and Shaw (1990) and Noshpitz and Coddington (1990) describe the use of time-limited cognitive therapy (usually twenty or fewer sessions) in treating Adjustment Disorders. The first few sessions focus on assessment of the problem, building rapport, and explaining the goals of cognitive therapy. The sessions then focus on helping people see how the precipitating stressors have led to dysfunctional feelings and distorted thinking and on helping people modify their thinking and the associated feelings. Treatment concludes with efforts to help people use what they have learned in therapy in order to develop more successful ways of dealing with life crises.

Behavioral interventions like relaxation, bibliotherapy, assertiveness training, and visual imagery are often combined with cognitive interventions in the treatment of this disorder so that beliefs as well as behaviors can be changed. An example of a cognitive-behavioral approach to treatment is suggested by Gutsch (1988), who views Adjustment Disorders as stress-related disorders and recommends stress inoculation as an approach to treatment. Gutsch's model includes the following four phases:

1. Understanding stress in general and the specific stressor in question
2. Developing coping strategies (for example, relaxation, decision making)
3. Applying coping strategies to current problems
4. Assessing and revising strategies, as necessary, and reinforcing the self for successes

Gutsch also suggests a multifaceted approach to teaching coping mechanisms. This approach involves using such techniques as modeling, role playing, and cognitive rehearsal.

Brief psychodynamically oriented psychotherapy also seems to be a useful approach in treating Adjustment Disorders (Koss & Butcher, 1986). That approach does involve interpretation and the use of positive transference, two techniques that are usually associated with long-term treatment. Because brief psychodynamic psychotherapy typically focuses on a single concern presented by the client, however, treatment can be both crisis-oriented (involving environmental manipulation and crisis resolution) and insight-oriented (promoting understanding of the connection between the impact of the crisis and the client's personality dynamics).

The therapist using brief psychodynamic psychotherapy typically is supportive, active, flexible, and goal-directed, working in a time-limited context (nearly always fewer than twenty-five sessions) to restore the client's previous level of equilibrium. This model seems particularly well suited to problems of acute onset experienced by people with positive prior adjustment and a good ability to relate to others and engage in a therapeutic relationship. Ideally, such clients are also verbal, psychologically minded, and highly motivated to benefit from treatment.

According to Koss and Butcher (1986), studies of treatment in which brief psychodynamic psychotherapy was used show improvement in more than 70 percent of clients, but they also indicate that more than half of these clients later return for additional treatment. Rather than deterioration, however, this finding may reflect a desire for further growth and an appreciation of the benefits of psychotherapy. Brief psychodynamically oriented psychotherapy seems likely to be helpful in quickening the pace of people's ability to deal with disconcerting life changes and in effecting immediate improvement.

Solution-focused therapy is another brief approach that is likely to be effective in the treatment of Adjustment Disorders. Developed by de Shazer (1991) and others, this approach emphasizes health, positive reframing, and rapid resolution of problems. Its hallmark is de Shazer's Miracle Question (p. 113): "Suppose that one night there is a miracle and while you were sleeping the problem that brought you to therapy is solved. How would you know? What would be different? What will you notice different the next morning that will tell you that there has been a miracle?" This question helps people focus on goals that are likely to lead to the resolution of the precipitants of their difficulties.

The therapist's understanding of the specific nature of the crisis that has led to the development of an Adjustment Disorder can guide the selection of appropriate treatment interventions. Environmental manipulation such as a change of residence, a job transfer, hired help for a new baby, or reorganization of shared duties at home or at work can be useful. Bibliotherapy—the assignment of books written by others who have knowledge about concerns similar to the client's—can provide useful information and a clearer perspective; for example, excellent books are available on such specific stressors as cancer (Spiegel, 1993), divorce (Viorst, 1986), and career changes (Bolles, 1996), as well as on handling other crises and disappointments (Schlossberg & Robinson, 1996). Tools for promoting self-awareness and clarifying options include developing a chronology of important life events and taking inventories of interests or marital satisfaction. The Myers-Briggs Type Indicator (Myers & McCauley, 1985) and the Lifestyle Assessment Questionnaire (National Wellness Institute, 1983) can also help people understand why they are having difficulty with particular situations, what resources they may be able to draw on, and what options they have.

Group therapy can be a useful addition to treatment. It can provide a support system, teach and reinforce coping mechanisms, improve self-esteem, and promote reality testing through group members' sharing their perceptions of the client's situation. Groups composed of people going through similar life circumstances such as cancer, marital separation or divorce, or bereavement can be particularly helpful. Group therapy typically does not provide crisis intervention, however, and so it may not be a sufficient response to the urgency of a client's situation. A combination of group and individual therapy can be particularly useful to people with Adjustment Disorders: the individual therapy addresses the immediate crisis, and the group therapy provides support and an arena for testing new ideas and behaviors. If group therapy is used alone, leaders should help people avoid inappropriate self-blame, focus on the reality of their situations, and take responsibility for acting to resolve their difficulties (Noshpitz & Coddington, 1990).

If a stressor involves the client's family, directly or indirectly, at least a few sessions of family therapy may be useful in solidifying the support that the person is receiving, ensuring that the person's efforts to cope with the stressor are not being undermined by the family, and dealing with any family circumstances that may be related to the stressful situation. Any problems involving secondary gains from the extra attention that people may be receiving when they are in crisis can also be identified and addressed in family therapy (Kaplan et al., 1994).

Medication is usually not necessary in the treatment of Adjustment Disorders, although in some cases medication may help people manage anxiety or depression. Any use of medication should be time-limited and symptom-focused, however, and it should be perceived as secondary to the therapy.

People with Adjustment Disorders should be encouraged to resume their former lifestyle, to expect a return to normal functioning in a relatively short time, and to deal with the stressor as expeditiously as possible. Typically, the longer a person avoids dealing with a stressful situation, the more difficult it will be for the person to handle the situation effectively. Therefore, timing is an important variable in treatment. Early detection of Adjustment Disorders seems to enhance the likelihood of a positive prognosis, and so it is unfortunate that many people with these relatively mild disorders do not seek treatment for their symptoms (Meyer, 1983).

Prognosis

Of all the disorders, the prognosis for treatment of Adjustment Disorders is one of the most positive and is particularly good for adults. Among people diagnosed with Adjustment Disorders in response to cardiac surgery, for example, 69 percent had recovered from the disorder at six-month follow-up (Oxman et al., 1994). According to Maxmen and Ward (1995), follow-up studies of people treated for this disorder indicate that 59 to 71 percent of them were functioning well enough three to five years after treatment, although only 44 percent of the adolescents who had been treated were functioning successfully. Andreasen and Hoenk (1983) conducted a five-year follow-up of one hundred adults and adolescents diagnosed as having Adjustment Disorders and found that 79 percent seemed to be well at follow-up, although 8 percent had developed intervening problems, most commonly Alcohol Abuse or severe depression. Although Andreasen and Hoenk conclude that the overall prognosis for treatment of Adjustment Disorders is excellent, they report that the prognosis is relatively less good for males and for individuals with behavioral symptoms or comorbid disorders.

People with Adjustment Disorders tend to seek subsequent psychotherapy. Whether this pattern reflects an incomplete recovery from the Adjustment Disorder, a subsequent Adjustment Disorder, the onset of another disorder, or simply a wish for more personal growth is not clear from the literature, but it does highlight the importance of including a preventive component in the treatment of Adjustment Disorders.

OTHER CONDITIONS THAT MAY
BE A FOCUS OF CLINICAL ATTENTION

Description of the Conditions

The various Conditions discussed here encompass concerns that may well be amenable to psychotherapy but that are not in themselves mental disorders (unlike Adjustment Disorders). People with these Conditions may not have any mental disorders. They may have coexisting mental disorders that are unrelated to the Other Condition, or they may have mental disorders that are related to the Other Condition, but the Condition is listed on the multiaxial assessment because it is severe enough to warrant separate attention.

These three possibilities can be illustrated by three hypothetical clients who seek counseling after losing a job. Each of these clients would be described as having an Occupational Problem (a Condition). The first client is a well-functioning person with no coexisting mental disorders who lost her job because the company went out of business; now she needs help in locating new employment. The second person lost his job for the same reason and has no mental disorders related to his unemployment but reports that he cannot seek employment requiring outdoor work because of his extreme fear of snakes; he would be described as having an Occupational Problem and a coexisting but unrelated mental disorder, Specific Phobia. The third person lost her job because her use of alcohol led to frequent absences; she would have a coexisting and related diagnosis of Alcohol Dependence.

Not all current stressors are listed as Conditions on Axis I of a multiaxial assessment; Axis IV is the usual place to list the stressors. Axis I should be reserved for circumstances that are so severe as to merit special clinical attention. *DSM-IV* lists the Conditions described in the following sections.

Psychological Factors Affecting Medical Condition

In this Condition, psychological symptoms, maladaptive behaviors, a mental disorder, or other psychological factors are having a negative impact on a person's medically verified illness or physical disorder (specified on Axis III). The psychological factor may be increasing the risk of complications. It may also be an exacerbation or a poor outcome of the medical condition. When this condition is listed, both the psychological factor and the medical condition are named. For example, if a person with lung cancer (coded on Axis III as Neoplasm, Malignant, Lung, Primary) continues smoking against medical advice, that person's multiaxial assessment would also include, on Axis I, Maladaptive Health Behaviors Affecting Malignant Lung Neoplasm. Psychological Factors Affecting Medical Condition often reflects a negative cycle in which a medical condition causes stress, physical discomfort, and worry, which in turn leads to emotions and behaviors that worsen the person's physical disorder.

Medication-Induced Movement Disorders

This category includes Neuroleptic-Induced Parkinsonism, Neuroleptic Malignant Syndrome, Neuroleptic-Induced Acute Dystonia, Neuroleptic-Induced Acute Akathisia, Neuroleptic-Induced Tardive Dyskinesia, Medication-Induced Postural Tremor, and Medication-Induced Movement Disorder Not Otherwise Specified. All these Conditions describe symptoms that manifest themselves physiologically and are side-effects of medication (usually neuroleptic drugs). Consequently, many people with these Conditions have a comorbid diagnosis of a Psychotic Disorder. These movement disorders include a considerable array of symptoms, among them rigid muscle tone, a pill-rolling tremor, a masklike facial appearance (Parkinsonism), muscle contractions causing abnormal movements and postures (Dystonia), restlessness and anxiety (Akathisia), and involuntary movements of the face, tongue, or limbs (Tardive Dyskinesia). Many of these symptoms are irreversible.

Adverse Effects of Medication Not Otherwise Specified

This Condition is similarly caused by medication but encompasses symptoms other than movement, such as hypotension and sexual dysfunction.

Relational Problems

This broad category includes Relational Problem Related to a Mental Disorder or General Medical Condition (such as an adolescent daughter's withdrawal from her mother, who is coping with breast cancer), Parent-Child Relational Problem, Partner Relational Problem, Sibling Relational Problem, and Relational Problem Not Otherwise Specified (such as problems with colleagues, friends, or in-laws). These descriptors are used to label interpersonal difficulties significant enough to warrant clinical attention. Such difficulties may be related to poor communication skills, weak parenting skills (such as difficulty in maintaining discipline), over- or underinvestment in relationships, lack of empathy and caring for others, or family changes and role conflicts.

Problems Related to Abuse or Neglect

Conditions in this category, new in *DSM-IV,* include Physical Abuse of Child, Sexual Abuse of Child, Neglect of Child, Physical Abuse of Adult, and Sexual Abuse of Adult. These descriptors are used both for the survivors and the perpetrators of abuse; different code numbers indicate the distinction. These Conditions are often accompanied by coexisting and related mental disorders, such as Antisocial Personality Disorder or Alcohol Abuse for the perpetrator and Post-traumatic Stress Disorder or Borderline Personality Disorder for the survivor.

Reports of abuse or neglect have increased 49 percent since 1986 (De Angelis, 1997). In 1995, nearly one million children were found to have been abused or neglected, and an additional two million unsubstantiated reports were received.

Perpetrators of abuse are often themselves victims of abuse. They also typically repeat the pattern of abuse, even after an arrest. Egami, Ford, Greenfield, and Crum (1996) have found that 59 percent of those who abused and 69 percent of those who neglected had received a diagnosis of a mental disorder at some time during their lives, most often a Mood Disorder, an Anxiety Disorder, or an Alcohol Use Disorder.

Survivors of abuse manifest a broad range of reactions; no consistent pattern of postabuse adjustment has been identified (Powell & Wagner, 1991). Some may emerge from the experience without significant emotional difficulties, but it is more common for symptoms like depression, self-destructive behavior, anxiety, withdrawal, repressed anger, substance misuse, dysfunctional and abusive relationships, shame, and low self-esteem to be present. In extreme cases, children as well as elderly and disabled people may die or suffer permanent physical impairment as a result of abuse. Support, as well as more active therapeutic interventions, has been shown to make a difference in restoring or preserving the emotional health of children who have been abused (Reyes, Kokotovic, & Cosden, 1996). Clearly, abuse and neglect are Conditions that merit intensive treatment, both for the survivors and for the perpetrators.

Additional Conditions That May Be a Focus of Clinical Attention

This broad and diverse group includes the following Conditions:

1. Noncompliance with Treatment is refusal to follow treatment recommendations for either a mental disorder or a medical condition. Many factors may contribute to the development of this Condition. For example, the original medical condition or mental disorder may have been misdiagnosed or not fully explained to the person, and so his or her motivation to comply with treatment has been reduced, or a mental disorder (perhaps even the one being treated) may be interfering with the person's interest in treatment. As another example, people with Bipolar Disorders sometime enjoy their manic or hypomanic episodes, and so they resist treatment. The appeal of secondary gains may also counteract the benefits of successful treatment. A thorough evaluation of people with this Condition, as well as a thorough evaluation of these people's families and their occupational and environmental contexts, is important to a full understanding of this Condition's dynamics.

2. Malingering is defined as the deliberate production of symptoms for the purpose of gaining some external benefit, such as a military discharge or disability payments. This Condition sometimes accompanies a diagnosis of Antisocial Personality Disorder. People with this Condition are often involved in lawsuits or have other legal problems. They may be uncooperative and withholding in treatment in an effort to avoid full disclosure that might jeopardize external benefits. Malingering is more common among men than among women (Kaplan et al., 1994). With Malingering, as with many of the Other Conditions, a thorough understanding of the context is important, as is corroborative information from other sources if it can be obtained. The Structured Interview of Reported Symptoms is a useful tool for detecting feigned symptoms (Rogers, Kropp, Bagby, & Dickens, 1992). Clinicians do seem quite skilled at detecting Malingering, but this descriptor should still be used with caution (Bourg, Connor, & Landis, 1995).

3. Adult, Childhood, or Adolescent Antisocial Behavior is used to label both isolated acts and repeated patterns of illegal behavior not due to a mental disorder. Patterns of antisocial behavior associated with this condition generally begin in adulthood and are accompanied by a relatively stable lifestyle, so that

the person does not meet the criteria for Antisocial Personality Disorder. Clinicians should be careful to rule out not only Antisocial Personality Disorder but also Conduct Disorder, Substance Use Disorders, or another Impulse-Control Disorder before concluding that this Condition is present. People with this Condition often have accompanying financial, occupational, and relationship problems and tend to misuse drugs and alcohol.

4. Borderline Intellectual Functioning is coded on Axis II and reflects an IQ in the 71–84 range, below normal but above the criteria for Mental Retardation. Interpersonal difficulties, adjustment difficulties, and other behavioral difficulties are often found in people with this Condition, just as they are in people diagnosed with Mental Retardation. This Condition is found in 6 to 7 percent of the population (Kaplan et al., 1994).

5. Age-Related Cognitive Decline is characterized by cognitive impairment and decline that are within normal limits. The decline is significant enough to cause distress but not significant enough to meet the criteria for Dementia. People with this Condition may have difficulty remembering other people's names or keeping appointments or solving complex problems, but they do not forget such information as their own names and addresses. Fears that they are developing Dementia may lead them to seek assessment and treatment. Neurological and psychological evaluations, including assessment of memory and verbal fluency, can help determine whether this Condition or a more serious disorder is present.

6. Bereavement is a response to the death of a loved one. Common symptoms include sadness, regret about actions taken around the time of the death, anxiety, mild somatic symptoms, loss of appetite, and difficulty sleeping. These symptoms may subsequently be diagnosed as a Major Depressive Disorder if they are long-standing (usually more than two months), if they cause severe impairment, and if they include such signs of a Major Depression as strong feelings of guilt and worthlessness, suicidal ideation and preoccupation with death, psychomotor retardation, or loss of contact with reality (other than seeing or hearing the deceased). People with few support systems and those with coexisting medical problems are at particularly high risk for severe reactions to a death. Responses to death vary widely among cultures, and so a client's background, ethnicity, and religious beliefs should be considered when a diagnosis related to a death is made.

7. Academic Problem reflects difficulties in scholastic achievement that are not due to a mental disorder (such as a Learning Disorder, a Communication Disorder, or Mental Retardation). Children and adolescents, of course, are most likely to present with this Condition, which may involve such issues as poor study skills, little interest in school subjects or achievement, or a poor image of their own academic abilities.

8. Occupational Problem includes such concerns as career choice and dissatisfaction, job loss or change, demotion, or difficulty fulfilling the requirements of a job. High stress, reduced self-esteem, insecurity, anger, resentment, and fears about the future may accompany this Condition (Seligman, 1994). McCarroll, Orman, and Lundy (1993) have found that two Conditions, Occupational Problem and Phase of Life Problem, explained the concerns of 51 percent of people seen for treatment in a military outpatient clinic. Career counseling and assessment can be helpful both in clarifying the concerns of people with this Condition and helping them resolve those concerns.

9. Identity Problem encompasses a variety of doubts about self-image or direction and involves such issues as sexual orientation, morals and values, friendships, group loyalties, and long-term goals. These concerns are most likely to emerge during middle and late adolescence but also are common in adults going through a sort of midlife reevaluation. People with an external locus of control, as well as those going through a life change, a family breakup, a loss, a challenging developmental task, or a values conflict with others, are especially prone to identity problems.

10. Religious or Spiritual Problem reflects issues related to a loss of faith, questions about religious beliefs or affiliation, problems associated with conversion to another faith, or other spiritual concerns. Consultation with a spiritual or religious adviser as well as with a psychotherapist may help people cope more successfully with these concerns. Religious and spiritual beliefs can be very important in helping people find meaning and direction in their lives and maintain good self-esteem and interpersonal relationships.

11. Acculturation Problem focuses on issues related to a move from one culture to another. It may entail such concerns as balancing loyalty to one's culture of origin with an interest in adopting one's current culture, feeling alienated and isolated in the new culture, longing for one's former home or culture, or experiencing family conflicts (among families whose members acculturate differently after immigration).

12. Phase of Life Problem includes such circumstances as illness, divorce, retirement, graduation, marriage, the birth of a baby, a job change, or other life change. It is distinguished from Adjustment Disorder in terms of the nature and severity of the person's reaction to the change; Adjustment Disorder reflects more difficulty and emotional dysfunction in response to the change.

The Conditions just listed are problems in living that are experienced by most people. Often these Conditions go untreated, and people manage to deal with them with varying degrees of success. People with these Conditions who do not have coexisting mental disorders are typically in good contact with reality, and their reactions seem consistent with the stressors or life circumstances they are experiencing. Nevertheless, they may be experiencing considerable unhappiness and dissatisfaction with their lives and may benefit from therapy.

Typical Client Characteristics

Because the Other Conditions can be found in the entire range of clients, few generalizations can be made about people with these Conditions. Those who seek therapy are likely to have fewer support systems and less effective coping skills. Beyond that, however, all that can be said is that these people are struggling with particular life circumstances that will need to be addressed in therapy.

Preferred Therapist Characteristics

Therapist variables indicated for treatment of Other Conditions vary little from those indicated for treatment of Adjustment Disorders. People probably will respond best to therapists who are supportive and flexible and yet who challenge them to grow and develop. Therapists should encourage these clients to take responsibility for their own treatment when that is possible but should also provide direction, resources, and information as needed (Gutsch, 1988; Maxmen & Ward, 1995). The therapist should maintain an attitude that is optimistic and that anticipates fairly rapid progress. With the Conditions, as with Adjustment Disorders, clinicians must be astute diagnosticians so that they can ascertain quickly whether coexisting mental disorders are present; that factor will determine the specific nature of a particular client's treatment.

Intervention Strategies

Treatment for the Conditions is typically similar to treatment for Adjustment Disorders. The major difference is that less attention probably will be paid to the client's emotional, social, and occupational dysfunction, and more attention will be paid to the presenting concerns and the person's existing strengths and coping abilities, especially if no coexisting mental disorders have been identified. People can benefit from support and from the reassurance of having their reactions normalized. People experiencing these Conditions typically need education and information about their situations and about the options available to them. Environmental changes can be useful, as can the inclusion in therapy of others who are involved in the problem (for example, family members, friends, or business colleagues). Brief approaches to treatment are emphasized.

No controlled studies have been located on the overall treatment of the Conditions, but suggestions can be inferred from studies of treatment for specific types of Conditions and from information on the treatment of related disorders. Specific approaches to therapy have been developed or adapted to ameliorate some of the Conditions. For example, a large body of literature is available on theories and techniques of career counseling that can guide therapy for people coping with occupational problems (Seligman, 1994). Career counseling typically promotes information seeking and decision making, teaches such skills as interviewing and résumé writing (Myers, 1986), and promotes self-awareness and career maturity. Bibliotherapy (especially reading about occupations) and informational interviewing for the purpose of learning about job roles can accelerate the process of therapy.

Family therapy is likely to be useful for most people coping with relationship problems and family change and conflict. Many books are available to familiarize therapists and clients with patterns of family change and effective ways of dealing with those patterns. These books include *The Changing Family Life Cycle* (Carter & McGoldrick, 1988), *Divorce Busting* (Weiner-Davis, 1992), and *Time for a Better Marriage* (Dinkmeyer & Carlson, 1984).

An approach to both group and individual therapy that is cognitive-behavioral in nature and is geared to the developmental level of the client has been found effective in helping people with Borderline Intellectual Functioning (Paxon, 1995). Multimodal therapy has also demonstrated effectiveness with these clients, as well as with people who have experienced abuse and neglect (Martin-Causey & Hinkle, 1995).

Techniques that address the mind-body connection, such as biofeedback, relaxation, and encouragement of a healthy lifestyle, can help people with Psychological Factors Affecting Medical Condition (Seligman, 1996b). Collaborative treatment, in which therapist and physician work together, is also indicated for these clients, as well as for people coping with Medication-Induced Movement Disorders.

People with long-standing antisocial behavior typically benefit from counseling in a homogeneous group setting. That environment can facilitate their receiving feedback and learning and practicing new ways to meet their goals and cope with stress.

Kaplan et al. (1994) recommend not confronting people who are Malingering. Psychotherapy that addresses the underlying reasons for the feigned symptoms may enable people to eventually give up the symptoms without pressure or embarrassment.

Support groups can be particularly helpful to people coping with the Conditions listed in *DSM-IV;* sometimes these groups provide all the treatment that is needed. Therapy or self-help groups composed of people with similar life circumstances such as bereavement, retirement, a recent marriage, or abuse can be particularly useful in offering information and modeling coping mechanisms as well as in providing feedback and support. Nonprofessional, socially oriented groups like Parents Without Partners can also be useful adjuncts to treatment.

Courses designed to develop such skills as parenting, assertiveness, and studying can be useful to people with these Conditions. The group environment of the classes can also offer support and encouragement while normalizing concerns.

Many people coping with these Conditions will have coexisting mental disorders, of course, particularly people who are perpetrators or survivors of abuse or neglect. The treatments recommended for the coexisting mental disorders (see the relevant chapters in this book) should become part of the help that is provided to these people.

Prognosis

The prognosis for treatment of most of these Conditions, if they stand alone, is quite good, although the diversity of Conditions and of people manifesting these Conditions mandates caution in generalizing. Figures are available, however, to support a positive prognosis for some Conditions. For example, studies of the effectiveness of career counseling indicate a success rate ranging from 73 percent to 93 percent; the exact figure depends on length of time between treatment and follow-up (Myers, 1986). Horowitz, Marmar, Weiss, and colleagues (1984) surveyed the impact of time-limited dynamic psychotherapy on fifty-two people coping with Bereavement and found that outcomes were generally favorable in terms of symptom relief and social and occupational functioning. Those people who benefited the most from treatment had the highest pretreatment levels of functioning and self-concept and were motivated to receive treatment. Borderline Intellectual Functioning, Medication-Induced Movement Disorder, and Age-Related Cognitive Decline are not likely to improve much in response to therapy, but treatment of these Conditions may well have a positive impact on the outlook and coping abilities of people with these Conditions. People with long-standing antisocial behavior will also often not have a positive response to treatment. Nevertheless, most Conditions that are short-term and that have developed in response to specific precipitants (such as a death or a relocation) are likely to have an excellent prognosis, especially if they are not accompanied by other mental disorders.

TREATMENT RECOMMENDATIONS: CLIENT MAP

The following list organizes the recommendations made in this chapter for the treatment of Situationally-Precipitated Conditions and Disorders (Adjustment Disorders and Other Conditions) according to the Client Map format.

Client Map

Diagnoses

Adjustment Disorders

Other Conditions That May Be a Focus of Clinical Attention

Objectives of Treatment

Increase knowledge of the situation

Promote information gathering

Relieve symptoms

Improve coping

Promote use of support

Restore at least prior level of functioning

Assessments

Measures of transient anxiety, depression, and stress

Clinician Characteristics

Flexible yet structured

Present-oriented

Optimistic

Skilled in diagnosis and treatment of a broad range of disorders

Location of Treatment

Outpatient

Interventions to Be Used

Empowerment of client

Crisis intervention

Bibliotherapy

Brief psychodynamically oriented psychotherapy

Cognitive-behavioral therapy

Stress management

Skill development

Other short-term or active approaches

Emphasis of Treatment

Moderate emphasis on support

Probing only when relevant to current concerns

Focus to be determined by specific precipitant and response

Numbers

Usually individual therapy

Concurrent or later group therapy sometimes indicated

Family sessions sometimes indicated

Timing

Usually brief duration and rapid pace

Timing may need modification in the presence of coexisting mental disorders

Medications Needed

Usually not needed

Adjunct Services

Inventories to clarify goals and direction

Education and information

Support groups

Possibly environmental manipulation

Prognosis

Excellent if cause or precipitant can be changed, especially if no underlying mental disorder is present

Client Map of Beth H.

This chapter began with the case of Beth H., a forty-seven-year-old woman who had been diagnosed with breast cancer. Short-term counseling helped Beth decide to have a mastectomy, with immediate reconstruction, to facilitate her rapid return to work and help her maintain her positive body image. Fortunately, chemotherapy was not needed. Beth became involved with a support group that helped normalize her feelings and provided information, role models, and encouragement. After the immediate medical crisis was over, Beth continued to receive some therapy to help her establish rewarding goals and directions for herself and implement health- and lifestyle-related goals. Like most clients with Adjustment Disorders, Beth needed only some short-term counseling to help her mobilize her resources, make decisions, and establish a rewarding direction for herself. The self-awareness, support systems, and coping strategies she gained from the therapeutic process should enable her to cope more effectively with future life transitions. This chapter concludes with a client map of Beth.

Diagnosis

Axis I: 309.28 Adjustment Disorder with Mixed Anxiety and Depressed Mood

Axis II: V71.09 No diagnosis on Axis II

Axis III: 174.9 Neoplasm (malignant, breast)

Axis IV: Diagnosis and treatment of breast cancer, divorce

Axis V: Global Assessment of Functioning (GAF Scale): current GAF = 72

Objectives of Treatment

Reduce anxiety and depression related to cancer diagnosis

Help client make sound decisions about her medical treatment

Promote establishment of a healthy lifestyle

Continue client's efforts to cope with her divorce and develop a rewarding lifestyle

Help client resume previous level of functioning

Assessments

Measure of Adjustment to Cancer Scale

Profile of Mood States

Clinician Characteristics

Supportive and accepting yet action-oriented

Knowledgeable about cancer and the mind-body connection

Location of Treatment

Outpatient

Interventions to Be Used

Cognitive-behavioral therapy, designed to promote a fighting spirit, normalize reactions, and empower the client

Bibliotherapy on reactions to cancer and treatment options

Analysis and modification of dysfunctional cognitions

Use of information-gathering and decision-making strategies

Identification and mobilization of previously successful coping mechanisms

Visual imagery and relaxation

Emphasis of Treatment

High emphasis on supportiveness

Moderate emphasis on directiveness

Focus on the present, with exploration of cognitions, behaviors, and affect, especially fears and coping skills

Numbers

Primarily individual therapy, with a few counseling sessions including Beth and her daughter

Timing

Short-term

Weekly sessions

Rapid to moderate pace

Medications Needed

None needed

Adjunct Services

Support group for women coping with breast cancer

Prognosis

Excellent

Recommended Reading

Araoz, D. L., & Carrese, M. A. (1996). *Solution oriented brief therapy for adjustment disorders: A guide for providers under managed care.* New York: Brunner/Mazel.

Despland, J. N., Monod, L., & Ferrero, F. (1995). Clinical relevance of adjustment disorder in *DSM-III-R* and *DSM-IV. Comprehensive Psychiatry, 36*(6), 454–460.

Noshpitz, J., & Coddington, R. (Eds.) (1990). *Stressors and the adjustment disorders.* New York: Wiley.

CHAPTER FOUR

Mood Disorders

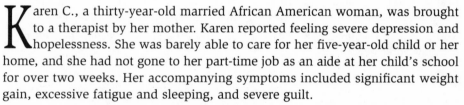aren C., a thirty-year-old married African American woman, was brought to a therapist by her mother. Karen reported feeling severe depression and hopelessness. She was barely able to care for her five-year-old child or her home, and she had not gone to her part-time job as an aide at her child's school for over two weeks. Her accompanying symptoms included significant weight gain, excessive fatigue and sleeping, and severe guilt.

Karen and her husband had been married for eight years. Karen's husband was in the military, which meant that he was frequently away from home. Karen had always found his absences difficult and had encouraged her husband to leave the service. He complained that she was too dependent on him, and he urged her to develop her own interests.

Apart from her work at their child's school, Karen had few outside activities, and she had few supports other than her mother, who had been widowed when Karen was a child (the only one). Her mother had not remarried. She told Karen that she had been so devastated by the death of Karen's father that she would never get involved with another man. The mother seemed to have experienced episodes of severe depression, although she had never received treatment for them.

Conflict had been increasing in Karen's marriage and had reached a peak about three weeks before, when Karen's husband had left for an overseas tour of duty. Karen was fearful that he would become involved with another woman and never return home, even though her husband's behavior gave her no justification for her concerns. She berated herself for not being a good wife and stated that life was not worth living without her husband. The only bright spot for Karen over the past few weeks had come when she received a letter from him. She read it again and again and did feel better for a few hours, but her depression soon returned.

Karen's developmental history was unremarkable except for her having been ill quite often. After her graduation from high school she had worked as a secretary and lived with her mother until her marriage. She had dated little before her marriage, but she did remember having felt very depressed at least once before in her life, when a young man she had dated a few times became engaged to another woman.

Karen is suffering from a severe depression that has impaired her level of functioning. A precipitant can be identified for Karen's current episode of depression, but her symptoms do not suggest either an Adjustment Disorder or a Condition: her reactions show too much dysfunction to be reflective of either one, and the precipitant—her husband's departure for an overseas tour of duty—is less disruptive than the sort of precipitant that usually would spark a Situationally-Precipitated Disorder. Instead, Karen is experiencing another prevalent condition, a Mood Disorder, characterized by depression. This chapter provides information on the diagnosis and treatment of the various types of Mood Disorders— Major Depressive Disorder, Dysthymic Disorder, Depressive Disorder Not Otherwise Specified, Bipolar I Disorder, Bipolar II Disorder, and Cyclothymic Disorder, all of which typically include significant depression. Although three of these disorders (Bipolar I and II and Cyclothymic Disorder) also include inordinately elevated moods (mania or hypomania), the focus of this section of the chapter will be on depression, the common ingredient of all these disorders.

OVERVIEW OF MOOD DISORDERS

Description of the Disorders

Primary Symptoms

Primary symptoms of depression are feelings of discouragement and hopelessness, a dysphoric mood, a loss of energy, and a sense of worthlessness and excessive guilt. Physiological symptoms are common and typically include changes in appetite and sleep, with insomnia and loss of appetite the most common. A physical examination sometimes is indicated to ascertain whether medical treatment is needed for the specific physical complaints.

Some sources (for example, Atwood & Chester, 1987) distinguish between *exogenous* or reactive depression, linked to an external event or situation, and *endogenous,* melancholic, or biochemical depression, apparently having a physiological basis. Endogenous depressions are less common than reactive ones. Severe and reversed physiological symptoms (increased appetite, early-morning awakening rather than insomnia) are more common in endogenous depression than in reactive depression. Melancholia, or an absence of pleasure or interest, typically accompanies this form of depression. Endogenous depressions are also far more likely than reactive ones to involve delusions or hallucinations, psychomotor retardation or agitation, extreme guilt, and worsening in the morning (Gotlib & Colby, 1987). Depressions beginning during the postpartum period (within four weeks of giving birth) or the involutional period (late in life) are more likely to be endogenous (Atwood & Chester, 1987).

Common Secondary or Underlying Symptoms

Suicidal ideation is a common symptom in depression, one that obviously requires attention. People suffering from depression may be in such severe emotional pain that they feel as if their symptoms will never end, and suicide may seem to be the only escape. Records reveal approximately 25,000 suicides and 200,000 suicide attempts annually in the United States; 80 percent of these seem linked to depression (Gotlib & Colby, 1987). Suicidal ideation, like depression, seems to have a genetic or familial component. Roy (1983) studied 243 people with a family history of suicide and found that 48.6 percent of them had also attempted suicide and that 84.4 percent had experienced a depressive episode. Therefore, depressed clients should be asked about suicidal thinking. If suicidal ideation is present, information should be gathered about any plans that have been formulated, as well as about the availability of means. Preventing suicide must be a first priority, and if a threat of suicide is present, consideration should be given to hospitalization, to notifying friends and relatives (ideally with the client's consent), and to developing a written agreement with the client that is designed to ensure safety and provide alternatives to self-injury.

Most people with Mood Disorders are not psychotic. They do not have hallucinations or delusions, although their reality testing is likely to be impaired. They generally will not manifest true paranoia but are likely to feel bereft of supports and to feel that even those who care about them are undermining them. The following are some other secondary symptoms common in depression (Gotlib & Colby, 1987):

- *Emotional symptoms:* anxiety, guilt, anger and hostility, irritability and agitation, social and marital distress
- *Behavioral symptoms:* crying, neglect of appearance, withdrawal, dependence, lethargy, reduced activity, poor social skills, psychomotor retardation or agitation

- *Attitudinal symptoms:* pessimism, helplessness, thoughts of death or suicide, low self-esteem

- *Cognitive symptoms:* reduced concentration, indecisiveness, distorted thinking

- *Physiological symptoms:* sleep disturbances, loss of appetite, decreased sexual interest, gastrointestinal and menstrual difficulties, muscle pains, headaches

Typical Onset, Course, and Duration of the Disorder

A first episode of depression generally occurs during young or middle adulthood but may occur at any age, as can a recurrence. The initial episode of depression tends to occur earlier in women than in men, who are more likely to have an initial episode in midlife. Depression may also begin in childhood. In this case, it is often typified by agitation rather than by overt sadness. Depression may be primary or secondary to a preexisting chronic mental or physical disorder (such as Alcohol Dependence). Depression often coexists with a Personality Disorder (most often Borderline, Histrionic, or Dependent Personality Disorders) and, in children, with Attention-Deficit and Disruptive Behavior Disorders.

Relevant Predisposing Factors

Depression can have many possible origins, dynamics, and precipitants. Familiarity with these and an ability to understand the determinants of a particular person's depression will be essential to the formulation of any treatment plan likely to be effective (Goldfried, Greenberg, & Marmar, 1990). Freud viewed depression as representing the symbolic loss of a love object, accompanied by the turning inward of anger toward the parents. In these circumstances, according to Freud, self-esteem becomes contingent on receiving constant affirmation from others, and depression can result if sufficient affirmation is not received. The social learning theorists believe that depression can become a learned response when it is rewarded and reinforced: the secondary gains it brings outweigh the negative experience of being depressed. Beck (Beck, Rush, Shaw, & Emery, 1979) and other cognitive theorists view depression as a result of faulty logic and misinterpretation, involving a negative cognitive set. Behavioral theorists hypothesize that people who become depressed have poor interpersonal skills and therefore receive little positive social reinforcement. The interpersonal model explains depression as stemming from undue dependence on others as well as from friction and poor communication in relationships. Biological approaches view depression as resulting from a dysfunctional level of serotonin, a neurotransmitter (Atwood & Chester, 1987). Developmental models suggest that people who experience depression are more likely to have had difficult childhoods with parental discord, an inappropriate level of maternal care, low cohesion or adaptability in the family, and controlling and/or rejecting parents (Gotlib & Colby, 1987).

The onset of depression often follows one or more negative and stressful life events, which frequently involve a real or threatened interpersonal loss, and the anticipation of an impending loss can trigger a return of unresolved feelings about an earlier loss. This pattern is particularly likely in people who have few social supports, no intimate confidants, and generally negative social relationships. Unfortunately, the proverbial vicious circle is likely to appear in this situation: depression is exacerbated by a lack of friends, but because people are depressed, forming new friends is very difficult. Giesler, Josephs, and Swann (1996) have identified another sort of self-perpetuating cycle as contributing to depression. They found that people who were depressed emphasized negative self-evaluations and failed to seek out or recognize positive self-evaluations, and this pattern served to maintain their depression.

Depression sometimes has a genetic or familial component, particularly for men whose mothers were depressed (Gutsch, 1988). Roy (1996) has found two common precursors of depression in women: separation from a parent for at least one year before the age of seventeen, and poor marital relationships. In addition, people with depression often have a history of early developmental difficulties. Therefore, the taking of a history should include questions about any possible familial background of depression and about childhood development. Information that reveals a family history of depression and a history of early developmental problems may help both the therapist and the client understand the nature and dynamics of the disorder.

Epidemiology

According to Kessler et al. (1994), 19.3 percent of the population of the United States has experienced a Mood Disorder at some time (23.9 percent of women and 14.7 percent of men), with approximately 11 percent experiencing a Mood Disorder during any twelve-month period. Depressive disorders are the most common and, because of suicide, probably the most lethal of the mental disorders. Although only 20 to 25 percent of those who experience clinical depression will actually receive treatment, a large percentage of the people who are seen by therapists are treated for Mood Disorders; indeed, one survey reports that people with Mood Disorders account for 27.6 percent of psychiatrists' practices (Maxmen & Ward, 1995).

Depression has a broad range of severity. Most people with depression are able to carry on with their lives and may even succeed in concealing their symptoms from others. In some people, depression may be present for many years at a subclinical level, becoming a deeply ingrained part of the personality. People with severe depression, however, typically manifest significantly impaired functioning.

Approximately one in fifty depressed clients is hospitalized, and depression accounts for 75 percent of psychiatric hospitalizations. One in one hundred people suffering from depression commits suicide (Gotlib & Colby, 1987), and 15 percent of those with chronic, recurrent depression commit suicide (Klerman, Weissman, Rounsaville, & Chevron, 1984). Young people with the combination of a Mood Disorder and a Substance-Related Disorder have particularly elevated suicide rates, as do people over the age of sixty-five who are diagnosed with Major Depressive Disorder. People with concurrent diagnoses of a Mood Disorder and a Borderline Personality Disorder, or with depression accompanied by delusions, are also particularly likely to commit suicide (Roose, Glassman, Walsh, Woodring, and Vital-Herne, 1983).

The prevalence of clinical depression seems to be increasing, and its onset appears to be occurring at an earlier age (Klerman et al., 1985). Women are much more likely to experience depression than men are, but it is unclear whether this difference suggests a causative factor that is hormonal or environmental and social. Currently and formerly married women are more likely to be depressed than those who have never married; the opposite is true for men (Gotlib & Colby, 1987). Depression seems particularly common among married women of lower socioeconomic levels who are full-time homemakers with young children.

Typical Client Characteristics

Seligman (1990) has written about the importance of what he calls "learned helplessness" in the dynamics of depression. He theorizes that many people who are depressed have long-standing motivational, interpersonal, cognitive, and affective deficits, as well as low self-esteem, resulting from a long series of uncontrollable and painful events that seem to make them depression-prone. They tend to set unrealistic goals, have little sense of competence, and view others as more powerful and capable than themselves.

People suffering from depression frequently experience marital discord. Gotlib and Colby (1987) hypothesize a connection between the course of the depression and that of the marriage and suggest that mild to moderate depression will often respond to a structural approach to family therapy. Although relationship dissatisfaction does seem to bear some causal connection to depression, other factors must also be considered in determining both the precipitant of depression and the route to resolving it (Burns, Sayers, & Moras, 1994).

Hirschfeld, Klerman, Clayton, and Keller (1983) studied a group of women who had recovered from depression and found that they tended to be introverted, submissive, passive, and interpersonally dependent but that they had normal emotional strength. Whether these traits reflected a predisposition to depression, a subclinical manifestation of the disorder, or part of the aftermath of depression remains unclear. Moreover, Gutsch (1988) reports that depressed clients tend to turn anger inward, to experience conflicts between their needs for dependence and autonomy, and to believe they have failed to live up to their goals and ideals.

Preferred Therapist Characteristics

The National Institutes of Mental Health (NIMH) Treatment of Depression Collaborative Research Program (Krupnick, 1996) indicates that the therapeutic alliance seems far more important than the intervention strategy in determining outcomes of treatment for depression. Even people in the placebo and clinical management conditions of that study demonstrated significant alleviation of depression, apparently because of the power of a positive therapeutic alliance. The quality of the alliance was important both early and late in treatment and for all groups, including those receiving psychotherapy and those receiving drug therapy. Krupnick speculates that medication alone as a treatment for depression may not be very effective because it often is not provided in the context of an ongoing positive therapeutic alliance.

Ideally, a therapist working with a person who is depressed should strongly communicate the core conditions required for effective therapy (genuineness, caring, acceptance, empathy, and others discussed in Chapter One) and should be able to provide support, structure, reality testing, optimism, reinforcement, and a strong role model. The therapist needs to intervene actively if suicide is threatened.

Schmitt (1983) emphasizes the importance of the therapist's assuming a directive role and warns that a person-centered approach, in which all the client's behaviors receive approval, can lead to a sense of helplessness in depressed clients, although their sense of responsibility may be increased. The therapist should avoid being threatened, gratified, or frustrated by the depressed client's dependence and neediness and should gradually promote the client's independence. Sometimes a person who is depressed directs anger and disappointment at the therapist and may invite rejection; the therapist should maintain objectivity despite the challenges presented by a depressed client.

Intervention Strategies

Depression takes many forms, and diagnosis of the particular form is crucial in determining the best treatment. In general, individual psychotherapy without medication is appropriate for treatment of mild to moderate depression that is uncomplicated by a bipolar pattern, by coexisting Schizophrenia, by cognitive impairment, by Mental Retardation, or by misuse of substances (Beck et al., 1979). This is particularly true if the depression is reactive or exogenous (that is, if it has arisen in response to a troubling life circumstance). For severe or complex forms of depression, the combination of medication and psychotherapy is almost always recommended. Couples therapy and family therapy can enhance treatment by providing support to the family as well as by ameliorating any family conflict that may be contributing to the depression. Group therapy generally does not seem appropriate as the primary mode of treatment for people with severe depression; their hopelessness and lack of energy make it difficult for them to engage actively in that process.

Findings by the NIMH Treatment of Depression Collaborative Research Program (Elkin et al., 1989) provide helpful information. Depressed clients were divided into four sixteen-week treatment conditions: interpersonal psychotherapy (a form of psychodynamic psychotherapy); cognitive-behavioral therapy; imipramine and clinical management; and placebo and clinical management. All four groups demonstrated a significant reduction in symptoms and an improvement in overall functioning, but the group treated with cognitive-behavioral therapy had the best overall results, with the interpersonal psychotherapy group following closely behind. Although the drug therapy group had the third best overall results, medication seemed to work best for those clients who were severely depressed, with interpersonal therapy second best.

Cognitive and Cognitive-Behavioral Therapy. A substantial body of research over the past twenty years has supported the use of cognitive and cognitive-behavioral approaches in treating depression. Emmelkamp (1986), for example, has found an approach initially focusing on behavioral and social skills and progressing to cognitive restructuring highly effective in alleviating depression. Smith, Glass, and Miller (1980) have found a behavioral approach to have a sizable impact (1.18 effect size) on depression. Rush, Beck, Kovacs, and Hollon (1977) compared cognitive-behavior therapy to imipramine over eleven weeks of treatment and found that 79 percent of clients were at least markedly improved with psychotherapy, whereas only 23 percent were markedly improved with pharmacotherapy. In addition, the medication-only group had a higher dropout rate. Jarrett and Rush (1986) have found cognitive-behavioral therapy to be associated with lower relapse rates (9 percent at one year follow-up) than short-term dynamic therapy (56 percent at one year follow-up).

Kornblith, Rehm, O'Hara, and Lamparski (1983) and Lewinsohn and Hoberman (1982), having reviewed the cognitive-behavioral approaches to the treatment of depression, find the following features of the cognitive-behavioral approaches instrumental in producing positive change:

1. They present a concrete rationale for depression and treatment, as well as a vocabulary for defining and describing the problem.

2. They are highly structured and offer clear plans for change, giving people a sense of control.

3. They provide feedback and support so that people can see change, receive reinforcement, and attribute improvement to their own efforts.

4. They teach skills that increase personal effectiveness and independence.

These features may contribute at least as much to clients' improvement as modification of cognitions.

Cognitive therapy may be more successful with some types of clients than with others. Hollon and Beck (1986), for example, suggest that people's personalities influence treatment responses; those high in self-control respond well to cognitive therapy, whereas those low in self-control do better with pharmacotherapy. Jarrett and Rush (1986) find cognitive-behavioral therapy particularly effective with young people who have a sense of mastery, view their families as supportive, and have good reading ability. Perry, Frances, and Clarkin (1985) recommend choosing candidates for cognitive therapy carefully; they believe that not all depressions are cognitively based, and that not all clients can handle either the active role required of them by the cognitive model or the relatively confrontational stance of the cognitive therapist.

The effectiveness of treatment for depression seems linked to the duration of treatment. Johnson et al. (1994) have found that eight sessions of rational-emotive therapy significantly reduced mild to moderate depression, negative and irrational thinking, and general pathology, with results well maintained at three-month follow-up. Nevertheless, Shapiro et al. (1994) have found that sixteen sessions of either cognitive-behavioral therapy or psychodynamic-interpersonal psychotherapy were needed to effect significant improvement in symptoms of severe depression.

Interpersonal Psychotherapy. Like cognitive-behavioral therapy, interpersonal psychotherapy (IPT)—based on the work of Harry Stack Sullivan and the psychodynamic therapists, and developed by Klerman et al. (1984)—has received considerable attention as an approach to treating depression. Klerman and his colleagues describe IPT as "a focused, short-term, time-limited therapy that emphasizes the current interpersonal relations of the depressed patient while recognizing the role of genetic, biochemical, developmental, and personality factors in causation and vulnerability to depression" (p. 5). Depression is thought of as usually being due to the combination of early loss of a parental figure and lack of adequate replacements.

In the IPT model, depression is viewed as having three components: symptom function, social and interpersonal relations, and personality and character problems. IPT focuses on the first two components while taking account of the third in the formulation of interventions. Proponents of IPT hold that there are essentially four problem areas playing key roles in depression: abnormal grief, nonreciprocal role expectations in significant relationships, role transitions (such as retirement or divorce), and interpersonal deficits. The IPT model has developed strategies for dealing with each of these focal problem areas and matches treatment to clients' concerns. In general, IPT concentrates on the clients' history of significant relationships, the quality and patterns of the clients' interactions, the clients' cognitions about themselves and their relationships, and the associated emotions. Attention is also paid to increasing the clients' optimism and acceptance, developing the clients' strengths and coping mechanisms, providing information, and enhancing the clients' competence. IPT differs from the cognitive-behavioral approaches in that it uses little homework and places less emphasis on planning actions and assessing progress; it places more emphasis on insight, relationships, and clarification of patterns.

Other Approaches to the Treatment of Depression. Another model that has been advanced for treating depression is self-control therapy, developed by Rehm (1984) and others. Proponents of this approach believe that people who are depressed view their failures as internally determined while seeing their successes as externally determined. This model emphasizes goal setting, self-administered rewards, and self-monitoring of levels of both depression and progress. The model seems likely to be effective in the treatment of mild to moderate depression and can be conducted in both group and individual therapy settings (Jarrett & Rush, 1986).

Lewinsohn, Sullivan, and Grosscup (1980) have advanced yet another model for treating depression. Their model incorporates many of the features of the cognitive-behavioral, self-control, and interpersonal models of treatment and includes teaching clients to take the following steps:

1. Examining feelings, actions, and thoughts that need to be changed
2. Understanding when depression emerges, and learning to anticipate and recognize antecedent events
3. Discovering and exploring reactions to antecedent events, as well as the consequences of those reactions and events
4. Developing ways to change feelings and reactions
5. Charting their progress and rewarding themselves for positive change
6. Learning when to seek help

In addition to these steps, their model incorporates such techniques as relaxation, the diffusing of negative ideas with pleasant experiences, the development of interpersonal skills, homework assignments (such as maintaining mood schedules, relaxation logs, and activity schedules).

New approaches to the treatment of depression are currently being studied. For example, some researchers have found that deprivation of one night's sleep reduces depression (Roy-Byrne, Unde, & Post, 1986). Other approaches—brief and intensive hospitalization, guided imagery, social skills training, simulated rites of passage (such as a staged funeral), and flooding—have been used effectively to help people cope with sadness and move ahead with their lives. Running and other forms of exercise have also been found to contribute to the relief of depression (Bellack, Hersen, & Himmelhoch, 1983; Mendelberg, 1995; Millman, Huber, & Diggins, 1982).

Medication, of course, is often used for severe or treatment-resistant depression, although medication is not successful in alleviating symptoms in all clients. Moreover, problems associated with medication include its acceptability to the client, its side effects, the client's adherence to treatment, incomplete remission of symptoms, and high rates of recurrence when the medication is discontinued (Thase & Kupfer, 1996). Therefore, the clinician should carefully consider whether a client should be referred for medication and, if so, should closely monitor its impact.

Common Ingredients of Treatments for Depression. Whether the therapist follows the cognitive model of Beck and his associates, the interpersonal model, Rehm's self-control model, or one of the other models, the treatments for depression discussed here include many common ingredients that are associated with their success. Therapists should promote a positive therapeutic alliance and encourage clients' active involvement in treatment, their realistic appraisal of alternatives, goal setting, a sense of mastery and improved self-esteem, better reality testing, clearer interpersonal boundaries, and a repertoire of problem-solving skills and coping mechanisms. Interventions that focus both on developmental issues (to elicit long-standing patterns and core assumptions) and on interpersonal issues are associated with alleviation of depression and maintenance of gains two years after treatment (Hayes, Castonguay, & Goldfried, 1996). Therapy should be moderately high in directiveness, at least in the early stages of treatment. Therapists should gradually decrease directiveness over the course of treatment, however, to prevent clients from becoming too dependent and to increase client self-esteem. Supportiveness will also need to be fairly high initially; people who are depressed are in considerable pain, and a probing approach runs the risk of opening new painful areas. Clients also need considerable acceptance and positive regard at the start of counseling because of the fragility of their self-concepts. Nevertheless, a pure person-centered approach is not nearly as likely to reduce depression as is a process-experiential sort of approach (Watson & Greenberg, 1996).

The focus of the initial stages of treatment usually will be on cognitive and behavioral areas of concern rather than on affective areas. Affect certainly should receive some attention, but extensive discussion of depression tends to entrench its symptoms and contributes to the client's sense of discouragement and hopelessness; a focus on the cognitive or the behavioral area is more likely to mobilize the client.

Treatment will often be multifaceted and will involve individual and family treatment. The familial nature of some forms of depression provides an important rationale for family therapy. Other family members who manifest overt or underlying depression, or who are at risk for developing such disorders, may also benefit from therapy, and their improvement in turn can help relieve the client's depression.

Treatment will typically be provided one to two times a week in an outpatient setting and will be paced fairly rapidly, but not so rapidly as to threaten or discourage the client. Inventories like the Beck Depression Inventory, as well as concrete, mutually agreed-on assignments, can give the client optimism and a sense of progress and direction. Therapy for depression tends to be short-term (twelve to twenty sessions, three to six months) and rarely takes as long as a year. The treatment of depression can also be enhanced by adjunct services to help clients establish a sense of direction and become involved in rewarding activities (such as social groups and sports) likely to increase their sense of competence and confidence.

Prognosis

The prognosis for a positive response to treatment for depression is excellent; a high percentage of people improve, regardless of which of the treatments discussed here has been used. Prognosis is correlated with many factors, which include the severity of the depression (Stewart et al., 1985), the previous level of adjustment, and the initial response to treatment (Baker & Wilson, 1985). Both the formation of new friendships during treatment and the number and severity of antecedent stressful life events are positively related to a good outcome (Monroe, Roberts, Kupfer, & Frank, 1996), whereas experiencing severe stress after seventeen weeks of sustained recovery is associated with a higher likelihood of recurrence.

Severe depression tends to be a self-limiting disorder and rarely lasts longer than six to twelve months, but depression has a high rate of relapse, especially during the first few months after treatment. Baker and Wilson (1985), for example, have found that 46 to 60 percent of clients reported depressive symptoms during a follow-up phase. This finding is due in part to a pattern in which a person who has been depressed tends to become sensitized to stressors so that progressively less severe stressors can trigger an episode of depression. In light of this finding, treatment should include a relapse-prevention component, such as Meichenbaum's (1985) stress inoculation training. Treatment should usually also involve follow-up sessions, perhaps at monthly intervals, to maintain progress and facilitate rapid treatment for relapses. The length of this continuation-phase treatment will depend on the severity of the initial depression but typically lasts four to nine months (Rush & Kupfer, 1995).

TYPES OF MOOD DISORDERS

We will now consider the nature and treatment of the following Mood Disorders as defined by the fourth edition of the *Diagnostic and Statistical Manual of Mental Disorders,* or *DSM-IV* (American Psychiatric Association, 1994a):

- Major Depressive Disorder
- Dysthymic Disorder
- Depressive Disorder Not Otherwise Specified (NOS)
- Bipolar I and II Disorders
- Cyclothymic Disorder

All these disorders typically have depression as a prominent feature, but the depression varies in its intensity, duration, and pattern of onset. Bipolar Disorders and Cyclothymic Disorder are also characterized by unpredictable shifts in mood, as well as by elevated moods. (The Mood Disorders section of *DSM-IV* also includes Bipolar Disorder NOS, Mood Disorder Due to a General Medical Condition, Substance-Induced Mood Disorder, and Mood Disorder NOS. Nearly all the major sections of *DSM-IV* include Substance-Induced Disorders, Medical Disorders Due to a General Medical Condition, and NOS variations. Substance-Induced Disorders will be discussed in Chapter Six; Impulse-Control Disorders and Mental Disorders Due to a General Medical Condition will be discussed in Chapter Seven; little attention will be paid in this book to the Not Otherwise Specified Disorders because of their variability and the lack of standard definitions.)

Major Depressive Disorder

Description of the Disorder

According to *DSM-IV,* a Major Depressive Episode is manifested by the presence of a depressed mood (dysphoria) or loss of enjoyment or interest in almost everything (anhedonia) and the presence of at least four of the following symptoms nearly every day for at least two weeks:

1. Significant weight or appetite change (found in over 70 percent of cases)
2. Insomnia or hypersomnia (found in nearly 90 percent of cases)
3. Psychomotor retardation or agitation
4. Fatigue or loss of energy (found in 78 percent of cases) (Craighead, Kennedy, Raczynski, & Dow, 1984)
5. Feelings of guilt or worthlessness

6. Reduced ability to think or concentrate

7. Recurrent thoughts of death or suicide

These symptoms are accompanied by significant distress or impairment in functioning. Although depression usually is not difficult to identify, irritability sometimes masks depression in children and adolescents. Somatic complaints also may deflect attention from depression but are frequently associated with depression, as are sexual difficulties, excessive worry and ruminating, and problems of substance use.

A Major Depressive Disorder consists of one or more Major Depressive Episodes. In diagnosing a Major Depressive Disorder, clinicians must make determinations related to the following factors:

1. *Severity:* Mild, moderate, severe, in partial remission, or in full remission (no symptoms for two months or longer).

2. *Presence of psychotic features:* Mood-congruent (consistent with the depressive attitudes), mood-incongruent, or none. (Psychotic features are found in 10 to 35 percent of people with Major Depressive Disorder.)

3. *Chronicity:* Relative consistency of episode for at least two years. (Approximately 15 to 20 percent of people with Major Depressive Disorder have chronic symptoms, according to Maxmen & Ward, 1995.)

4. *Presence of melancholic features:* Depression of endogenous or biochemical origin suggested by loss of interest or pleasure, lack of reactivity to pleasurable events, and at least three of the following symptoms: (a) characteristically different quality of depression from that associated with a bereavement, (b) worsening of symptoms in the morning, (c) awakening typically at least two hours before usual time, (d) experience of psychomotor retardation or agitation, (e) significant weight loss or loss of appetite, (f) unwarranted guilt, (g) flat rather than reactive mood, (h) good response to medication, (i) lack of a clear precipitant, and (j) absence of a Personality Disorder. The dexamethasone suppression test (a biochemical measure) and EEG sleep patterns are sometimes useful in discriminating endogenous from reactive depressions (Feinberg & Carroll, 1984).

5. *Presence of atypical features:* Depression improves in response to actual or anticipated positive events and is accompanied by at least two of the following characteristics: (a) weight gain or increase in appetite, (b) sleeping at least ten hours a day, (c) heavy feelings in arms or legs, and (d) prolonged pattern of sensitivity to rejection that is severe enough to cause impairment. This type of depression is often accompanied by anxiety and episodes of panic (Michels & Marzuk, 1993).

6. *Presence of postpartum onset:* Begins within four weeks of giving birth. Often accompanied by high anxiety, suicidal and violent thoughts, and mood lability. Needs rapid intervention and follow-up preventive treatment so as not to pose a danger to the child's life or to the parent-child relationship. Has a 30 to 50 percent likelihood of recurrence with subsequent births (American Psychiatric Association, 1994a).

7. *Presence of full interepisode recovery:* Greater likelihood of recurrence, and less likelihood of good response to treatment, in the absence of complete recovery between multiple depressive episodes. Pattern of multiple depressive episodes without full interepisode recovery often reflects an underlying Dysthymic Disorder.

8. *Presence of seasonal pattern:* Characterized by a depression, usually of moderate severity, that begins in the fall or the winter and remits in the spring for at least the previous two years. Episodes of this nature outnumber any other type of depression the person has experienced. Other signs include carbohydrate craving, headaches, fatigue, and hypersomnia (Michels & Marzuk, 1993). Remission is sometimes followed by a period of elevated mood. Recurrent summer depression is a less common variety. Related to the amount of available natural light and linked to such biological phenomena as light sensitivity and problems in melatonin secretion (Dalgleish, Rosen, & Marks, 1996). Present in 4 percent of the population of the United States (Emory, 1996). Particularly common in women and young people, as well as in people living in northern climates. Primary treatment is exposure to bright white light.

Symptoms of a Major Depressive Disorder usually begin with dysphoria and anxiety and develop over several days or weeks, although the onset may be sudden and may closely follow a loss or other stressor. Without treatment, this disorder typically runs its course in about six months to one year, but residual symptoms can be present for two years or more and reflect a chronic disorder. Overall impairment during episodes is typical and may be so severe as to prevent even minimal functioning. Constant feelings of lethargy and hopelessness may be present, and people typically have to struggle to perform daily routines or even to get dressed in the morning. Recurrence is a strong possibility with this disorder, and its likelihood increases with each subsequent recurrence.

Approximately 17 percent of women and 12 percent of men experience a Major Depressive Disorder during their lifetimes (Kessler et al., 1994), with approximately 3 percent of men and 6 percent of women having a Major Depressive Episode of sufficient severity to require hospitalization (Millman et al., 1982). As many as 15 percent of people with severe, prolonged Major Depressive Disorder commit suicide.

The typical age at which onset of Major Depressive Disorder occurs is decreasing and is currently in the middle twenties, with forty being the mean age of onset (Kaplan, Sadock, & Grebb, 1994). This disorder may begin at any point, however, from childhood to old age. Women not only are more prone to depression but also tend to have an earlier onset (Hirschfeld & Cross, 1982). Incidence peaks in both men and women at midlife.

People with Major Depressive Disorder typically have other emotional and family problems. Major Depressive Disorder is associated with a family history of depression and alcohol misuse (Boyd & Weissman, 1982). This relationship seems to hold true for women more than for men. At least 25 percent of people with Major Depressive Disorder have a preexisting Dysthymic Disorder; that combination is sometimes referred to as *double depression.* They also frequently have coexisting disorders, notably Substance-Related Disorders, Eating Disorders, Anxiety Disorders, and Personality Disorders. Children with Major Depressive Disorder are particularly likely to have a coexisting mental disorder. (Additional information on depression in children and adolescents is provided in Chapter Two.)

Typical Client Characteristics

The initial episode of a Major Depressive Disorder is often preceded by a stressor, particularly one involving an interpersonal loss, and is frequently associated with childbirth, substance misuse, or chronic and life-threatening physical illnesses, such as heart disease and cancer. Clinicians should bear in mind that drugs (both prescribed and street drugs) and alcohol also can precipitate depressive symptoms.

Several studies have found an association between personality type and incidence of Major Depressive Disorder and suggest that the combination of a stressor and a depression-prone personality has a high correlation with the onset of a Major Depressive Disorder. Cofer and Wittenborn (1980) have found that women who experience Major Depressive Episodes tend to have a sense of hopelessness, pessimism, and failure, to be self-critical and vulnerable, and to be from lower socioeconomic groups. They have also found an association between Major Depressive Disorder and having a critical mother and a dependence-fostering father. Hirschfeld and Cross (1982) describe two personality types they have found to be depression-prone: personalities characterized by low self-esteem and high obsessionality, and personalities characterized by low frustration tolerance, dependence, emotional lability, and vulnerability to the impact of stressors. Boyd and Weissman (1982) have found a personality pattern involving difficulty handling stress, low energy, insecurity, introversion, worrying, low assertiveness, dependence, and obsessional thinking to be typical of people who experience Major Depressive Episodes. Scott, Harrington, House, and Ferrier (1996) have found high scores on inventories of dysfunctional beliefs to be associated both with more severe symptoms of Major Depressive Disorder and with a less positive prognosis; high scores in autonomy were found to have the opposite associations. Thus many studies confirm a connection between severe depression and a preexisting personality pattern that includes low self-esteem, dependence, anxiety, dysfunctional thinking, and fragility.

Preferred Therapist Characteristics

The therapists most likely to be effective in treating clients with Major Depressive Disorder are those who are structured, focused on the present, and able to attend to interpersonal issues and deficits. They can establish clear and realistic goals with clients, and encourage optimism and a higher level of activity.

Intervention Strategies

As we have seen, approaches like cognitive-behavioral therapy and interpersonal therapy are the ones most likely to be effective in the treatment of depression. Many studies have demonstrated that these approaches to treatment are likely to have a significant and relatively rapid impact on the symptoms of Major Depressive Disorder. Cognitive-behavioral therapy has demonstrated a slight but not usually significant superiority to interpersonal therapy in the treatment of Major Depressive Disorder, and both approaches have demonstrated a slight superiority over treatment by medication alone. Good results have been obtained in as few as eight sessions, but at least sixteen sessions seem indicated for the treatment of severe depression.

Conte, Plutchik, Wild, and Karasu (1986) reviewed all the controlled studies of outpatient treatment for depression conducted between 1974 and 1984 and conclude that, especially for endogenous depressions, the combination of drugs and psychotherapy is "appreciably more effective than the placebo conditions but only slightly superior to psychotherapy alone, pharmacotherapy alone, or either combined with a placebo" (p. 471). These findings have been substantiated by many more recent studies (Roth & Fonagy, 1996).

A variety of medications have been used in the treatment of Major Depressive Disorder, including the tricyclic antidepressants (TCAs) and monoamine oxidase inhibitors (MAOIs), as well as the newer and extensively used selective serotonin reuptake inhibitors (SSRIs) like Prozac and Zoloft. The Agency for Health Care Policy and Research (AHCPR) has indicated that criteria for medication include severe or chronic depression, failure of psychotherapy alone to ameliorate symptoms, and dual diagnoses (Depression Guideline Panel, 1993). Although medication seems to act more quickly on symptoms than psychotherapy does, the effects of the medication are generally not as enduring unless it is continued. Social functioning is not improved by medication, although it usually responds to psychotherapy (Meyer & Deitsch, 1996). Clients also tend not to be as accepting of medication as they are of psychotherapy (Hollon & Fawcett, 1995).

Therefore, clinicians often begin treating depression with psychotherapy alone, but the AHCPR guidelines recommend the prescription of medication if improvement is not noted after several months of psychotherapeutic treatment.

Medication and therapy both have a place in the treatment of depression. The particular nature of the depression, however, and its accompanying symptoms suggest whether medication is likely to be helpful and, if so, which medication. For example, SSRIs and the combination of tricyclic and neuroleptic medication both seem effective with depression that is accompanied by delusions (Zanardi et al., 1996). SSRIs also are effective in treating Major Depressive Disorder without melancholia (Michels & Marzuk, 1993). However, clients whose depression is accompanied by Somatization Disorders or other Personality Disorders tend not to respond as well to medication (Van Valkenburg & Akiskal, 1985). Medication is particularly indicated for people with endogenous (rather than reactive) depressions that include such symptoms as biological disturbances, a family history of depression, and lack of a clear precipitant. When medication is needed, compliance with treatment and improvement in overall functioning can be enhanced by its combination with psychotherapy (Roth & Fonagy, 1996).

Electroconvulsive therapy (ECT) is also sometimes used to treat depression, particularly the severe, medication-resistant endogenous varieties. Criteria for the use of ECT include a need for rapid symptom reduction, a history of good response to ECT, the client's preference for ECT, and the inappropriateness or ineffectiveness of other treatment approaches (Weiner, 1995). Although ECT has been greatly improved in recent years (Michels & Marzuk, 1993), both ECT and antidepressant medication have side effects, and their risks need to be weighed against their possible benefits.

Daily exposure to light therapy for at least four weeks has been shown to significantly reduce symptoms in seasonally related Major Depressive Disorder (Bauer, Kurtz, Rubin, & Marcus, 1994), although some people with winter recurrences of depression benefit more from a combination of phototherapy and medication (Schwartz, Brown, Wehr, & Rosenthal, 1996) or cognitive therapy (Dalgleish et al., 1996). Dietary changes, including avoidance of caffeine and alcohol and emphasis on complex carbohydrates (bread, pasta, potatoes), together with exercise, have been found to ease symptoms of seasonally related depression (Emory, 1996). These recommendations may also be beneficial in other types of depression.

Although the hospital continues to be used as an initial setting for treating some people with severe depression, a trend toward using day treatment programs and residential crisis centers has developed. These programs typically are more cost-effective, and they seem to achieve slightly better short- and long-term outcomes for people whose depressions warrant close supervision, usually because they are suicidal, psychotic, or immobilized by depression (Sledge et al., 1996).

Prognosis

The prognosis for fairly rapid symptom relief via medication and/or psychotherapy is very good: approximately 85 percent of people treated for Major Depressive Disorder experience remission of their symptoms within one year (Maxmen & Ward, 1995). Nevertheless, 15 to 20 percent of people treated for Major Depressive Disorder do not recover fully from a given episode and have persistent symptoms. Moreover, recurrences ranging from mild, transient symptoms to full-blown Major Depressive Disorder are reported in 37 to 65 percent within the first year after treatment (Kendall & Lipman, 1991), and approximately half of those people will have yet another recurrence. Rates of recurrence are highest during the first four to six months after recovery and have a negative correlation with response to treatment. In other words, those people who have had a rapid and complete response to treatment are the ones least likely to have a recurrence. Overall, then, the prognosis for recovery from a given episode of a Major Depressive Disorder is good, but there is a high likelihood of relapse, particularly for those with preexisting mild depression and a history of dysfunction. Keller et al. (1983) have found that 25 percent of people diagnosed with a Major Depressive Disorder had a preexisting chronic mild depression (usually Dysthymic Disorder), and that among this group the chances for relapse were greater than among those who had not had a prior underlying depression: 62 percent of the group with double depression had a relapse within two years of recovery, whereas only 33 percent of those with single depression had a relapse. They have also found the duration of mild depression to be correlated with the likelihood of a recurrence. Lambert (1982) has found that the prognosis is generally worse for people with accompanying pervasive maladjustment. By contrast, a good prognosis has been found to be positively associated with the number and supportiveness of social resources, with positive life changes undertaken during treatment, and with low stress after treatment (Billings & Moos, 1985; Monroe et al., 1996). The prognosis for Major Depressive Disorder is worsened by the presence of a coexisting general medical condition and by the presence of long-standing depression prior to treatment (Depression Guideline Panel, 1993).

Several approaches to treatment have been found to improve prognosis. Treatment of both initial and residual symptoms via cognitive-behavioral therapy, either alone or in combination with medication, has been associated with a reduced rate of recurrence (Kendall & Lipman, 1991). Extended treatment and follow-up can also improve prognosis. For example, treatment may comprise six to eighteen weeks of intensive psychotherapy, four to nine months of less intensive relapse prevention, and maintenance and follow-up that may continue for years. Teaching people to recognize the early symptoms of depression, to reduce and manage stress, to increase the level of mastery and pleasure in their lives (Burns, 1990), and to make good use of support systems is also likely to reduce rates of recurrence.

Dysthymic Disorder

Description of the Disorder

Dysthymic Disorder (formerly called Dysthymia, Depressive Personality Disorder, and Depressive Neurosis) is characterized by the presence of chronic depression, usually mild to moderate in severity, on most days for at least two years. (In children and adolescents, a minimum duration of one year is required for diagnosis, and the primary manifestation of the disorder may be irritability rather than depression.) According to *DSM-IV*, at least two of the following symptoms also are present:

1. Poor appetite or overeating
2. Insomnia or hypersomnia
3. Low energy or fatigue
4. Low self-esteem
5. Difficulty in concentrating or decision making
6. A sense of hopelessness

Other common symptoms of this disorder include reduced activity and accomplishment, guilt and self-doubts, habitual complaining, withdrawal from social and other activities, and vegetative symptoms (disturbances in eating, sleeping, and weight). Suicidal ideation and thoughts of death may be present but are less common in people with Dysthymic Disorder than in those with Major Depressive Disorder.

People diagnosed with Dysthymic Disorder have not had manic or hypomanic episodes, and their symptoms are not due to substance use. They do manifest some distress or impairment as a result of their symptoms, but typically not as much as people diagnosed with Major Depressive Disorder. In establishing the diagnosis, the clinician also makes the following determinations about the disorder:

1. *Age of onset:* Most common periods of onset include late adolescence or early adulthood and middle age.
2. *Presence of atypical features:* Described in the previous section, on Major Depressive Disorder.

Dysthymic Disorder generally has no clear point of onset or obvious precipitant. People with this disorder tend to maintain an acceptable level of social and occupational functioning and often conceal their symptoms from others but may experience mild to moderate impairment or limitations that are due to their depression. Sometimes people with this disorder grow so accustomed to their symptoms that they assume the way they are feeling is normal; consequently, only a small percentage of people with this disorder seek treatment (Gwirtsman, 1994), and they often do so then only for related symptoms like a change in weight or a failure to achieve success in their careers. The possibility has been raised that Dysthymic Disorder is really a Personality Disorder rather than a Mood Disorder and is a pervasive, enduring, and potentially lifelong way of dealing with the world (Flach, 1987).

Dysthymic Disorder is common, particularly among females. In any given year, approximately 2 to 3 percent of the general adult population will experience this disorder (Kessler et al., 1994). Among people sixty years of age and older, approximately 18 percent have been found to meet the criteria for this disorder, and in this group the disorder is more common in men than in women (Margolis, 1997). Dysthymic Disorder has a lifetime prevalence of approximately 6 percent (American Psychiatric Association, 1994a).

Typical Client Characteristics

People with this disorder often have chronic environmental stressors and most commonly have a rejecting, confusing, affectionless, and controlling family background (Sacks, 1986). Men with Dysthymic Disorder are particularly likely to present accompanying situational problems, usually in the areas of work or family.

Prior, comorbid, or familial mental disorders are also common in people with Dysthymic Disorder. A coexisting or previous childhood mental disorder (such as Conduct Disorder, Attention-Deficit/Hyperactivity Disorder, or Learning Disorder) is often reported, as is a family history of depression. Dysthymic Disorder frequently is accompanied by a Personality Disorder or by another physical or mental disorder; Anxiety, Eating, and Substance Use Disorders are particularly common as comorbid disorders. People with Dysthymic Disorder are also at considerably elevated risk for development of a subsequent Major Depressive Disorder, and therapists should be alert to that possibility.

Personality patterns of people with Dysthymic Disorder tend to be similar to those of people with Major Depressive Disorder. They typically are low in self-esteem, are introverted, feel helpless and vulnerable, are focused on themselves, and overreact to stressful events or social disappointments (Sacks, 1986). Underlying hostility may be present, as well as dependence and a low tolerance for frustration (Koponen, Lepola, & Leinonen, 1995). People with Dysthymic Disorder may have a long-standing pattern of avoiding their difficulties by fleeing into overwork or excessive activity. Children with this disorder, like those with Major Depressive Disorder, often are irritable and complaining. People with Dysthymic Disorder are often divorced or separated and come from lower socioeconomic groups. Somatic and physiological complaints (such as eating and sleeping problems) are common and may be the presenting problem when treatment is sought.

In some ways, people with Dysthymic Disorder present more of a challenge to the therapist than do people with Major Depressive Disorder. People with Dysthymic Disorder have been depressed for so long that they may not know how to be anything but depressed, and they may be resistant to and apprehensive about change. Secondary gains, such as attention and reduced demands, may reinforce their sad, helpless stance, and they may hesitate to relinquish those gains without the assurance of continuing rewards and attention. These clients also present some suicidal risk. Although their depression is not as severe as in a Major Depressive Disorder, they do have the resourcefulness and the energy to make a suicide attempt, whereas a severely depressed client may be too incapacitated even to attempt suicide.

Preferred Therapist Characteristics

The type of therapist recommended for people diagnosed with Dysthymic Disorder is quite similar to the type of therapist recommended for people diagnosed with Major Depressive Disorder. The establishment and maintenance of a strong working alliance are important in motivating people to continue and to comply with treatment. The therapist working with a person who has Dysthymic Disorder can be somewhat less supportive and more confrontational, however, and can expect the client to complete more extratherapeutic tasks because these people generally are less impaired and more resilient than those with Major Depressive or Bipolar Disorders.

Intervention Strategies

The psychotherapeutic approaches discussed earlier in this chapter also are recommended for the treatment of Dysthymic Disorder. These include cognitive, cognitive-behavioral, and interpersonal therapy, particularly in combination with the client's development of such social and related skills as assertiveness and decision making (Paykel, 1994; Roth & Fonagy, 1996). Promoting the development of coping skills to address the client's sense of hopelessness and helplessness can also make a positive difference.

Although research on the treatment of Dysthymic Disorder is sparse, some information on its treatment is available. Wierzbicki and Bartlett (1987) describe one of the few studies available on the treatment of mild depression. Their study of individual and group cognitive therapy suggests that individual treatment is superior to group treatment, which in turn is superior to no treatment at all. Markowitz (1994) has obtained positive preliminary findings in the use of interpersonal psychotherapy to treat Dysthymic Disorder. Harmon, Nelson, and Hayes (1980) have found that dysthymic clients' self-monitoring of mood and activity levels reduced their depression and increased their participation in activities. They also report that these clients have benefited from help in modulating their reactions to temporary discouragement and overcoming learned helplessness. Meyer (1983) emphasizes the importance of not reinforcing the depressive and negative verbalizations of depressed clients and suggests counteracting negative thoughts with images of pleasurable and successful activities. Jacobson and McKinney (1982) recommend a treatment approach that involves identifying and resolving sources of stress, mobilizing clients' energy, and improving their self-esteem. They view the ideal treatment for Dysthymic Disorder as one that combines interpersonal and psychodynamic ingredients.

Supportive therapy and group therapy seem to play a greater role in the treatment of Dysthymic Disorder than in Major Depressive Disorder. People with Dysthymic Disorder have more energy and a better level of functioning, and so they are more able to engage and participate in group therapy and make use of purely supportive interventions.

Merikangas (1984) has found that people who are depressed often have spouses with emotional disorders, a finding that raises the question of whether difficult marriages contribute to the incidence of depression or whether people who are depressed select mates with similar traits. Regardless of the answer, family counseling in combination with individual therapy is indicated for many people with Dysthymic Disorder, as well as for people with other forms of depression.

Although people with Dysthymic Disorder have milder symptoms than people with Major Depressive Disorder, successful treatment of Dysthymic Disorder often takes longer than treatment of shorter and more severe depressive disorders. People with Dysthymic Disorder have been depressed for so long that their impaired functioning may have had a profound impact on many areas of their lives, including work, relationships, and leisure activities, and so they may need to restructure and repair their lives in these areas. Moreover, their long-standing depression probably has become so deeply entrenched that they lack the coping skills to overcome it. Some very basic education and development may need to take place before the symptoms of the depression will remit.

Current research is investigating the place of medication in the treatment of Dysthymic Disorder. MAOIs, TCAs, and SSRIs all have demonstrated effectiveness in the treatment of this disorder. Sertraline (Zoloft) has shown particular effectiveness in reducing symptoms, whereas desipramine has been effective in maintaining gains. Despite the recent increased use of pharmacotherapy in combination with psychotherapy to treat this disorder, psychotherapy is still central because of the importance of improving overall functioning, developing social and coping skills, and establishing a rewarding lifestyle.

Therapists working with people with Dysthymic Disorder seem to have a broader range of therapeutic options from which to choose than do therapists working with more severely depressed people. In general, psychotherapy aimed at treating Dysthymic Disorder is most effective if it is moderately supportive, moderately structured and directive, focused on cognitions and behavior more than on affect, and composed of an array of educational and psychotherapeutic interventions designed to modify cognitions, increase activity, and improve self-esteem and interpersonal skills. Treatment will also probably pay some attention to the past, in an effort to elucidate repetitive and self-destructive patterns and clarify the dynamics that are perpetuating the depression.

Prognosis

Viable goals for treatment of Dysthymic Disorder include relief of depression and associated anxiety, amelioration of somatic and physiological symptoms, increased optimism and sense of control, and improved social and occupational functioning. Without treatment, the prognosis for Dysthymic Disorder is poor (Koponen et al., 1995). Even with treatment, however, the prognosis for this disorder is not as good as for Major Depressive Disorder: only about 50 percent of those treated for Dysthymic Disorder benefit enough from treatment to be viewed as recovered (Maxmen & Ward, 1995). In the case of double depression—a Major Depressive Disorder superimposed on a Dysthymic Disorder—the prognosis is even worse, with only about one-third recovering from that combination of disorders. In general, people with Dysthymic Disorder who can recall a healthier way of functioning, who have some good interpersonal skills and support systems, who have maintained a reasonably rewarding lifestyle, and whose depression is not deeply entrenched are likely to respond well to treatment. For people who do not meet those criteria, therapy may be long and difficult and perhaps unsuccessful. Setting limited goals and focusing on gains may help promote optimism in both the client and the therapist, even if a full recovery cannot be obtained.

Depressive Disorder Not Otherwise Specified

Description of the Disorder

As is true of most other categories of mental disorder listed in the *DSM*, a Not Otherwise Specified (NOS) category is included at the end of the section on depression. This particular NOS category, however, unlike most others, is used often by clinicians because many manifestations of depression are not encompassed by the depressive disorders listed in the *DSM*. According to *DSM-IV*, Depressive Disorder NOS is defined as a disorder with depressive features that do not meet the criteria for any other specific depressive disorder or Adjustment Disorder. This category can be used, for example, to describe a recurrent depression with episodes briefer than two weeks, Premenstrual Dysphoric Disorder (depression associated with the menstrual cycle), depression occurring in the residual phase of a psychotic disorder, or a depression that is not severe enough to meet the criteria for Major Depressive Disorder but is too brief for a diagnosis of Dysthymic Disorder. Treatment recommendations for the other types of depression provide the basis for determining the treatment of Depressive Disorder NOS, with treatment adapted to meet the needs of the particular client.

Bipolar Disorders

Description of the Disorders

A Bipolar Disorder involves episodes of dysfunctional mood (potentially including Major Depressive Episodes, Manic Episodes, Hypomanic Episodes, and Mixed Episodes) often separated by periods of relatively normal mood. The disorder is not the result of a psychotic disorder, nor is it superimposed on a psychotic disorder.

The nature of a Major Depressive Episode was described earlier in this chapter. The depressive phase of a Bipolar Disorder closely resembles the depression associated with a Major Depressive Disorder but may have some differences. According to Smith and Winokur (1984), for example, the depression associated with a Bipolar Disorder often entails less anger and somatizing and more oversleeping and psychomotor retardation. A bipolar depression is more likely than a Major Depressive Disorder to include psychotic thinking, to feature little anxiety, and to worsen in the morning; it is also likely to be more severe than the depression associated with a Major Depressive Disorder (Maxmen & Ward, 1995).

A Manic Episode is a period of "abnormally and persistently elevated, expansive, or irritable mood lasting at least 1 week" (American Psychiatric Association, 1994a, p. 332). At least three of the following symptoms accompany the elevated mood:

1. Grandiosity
2. Reduced need for sleep
3. Increased talkativeness
4. Racing thoughts
5. Distractibility
6. Increased activity
7. Excessive pleasure-seeking, to a potentially self-destructive extent (for example, excessive spending)

A Manic Episode, like an episode of Major Depression, is typically quite severe and causes impairment in social and occupational functioning. People experiencing this phase of a Bipolar Disorder tend to view themselves as powerful and destined for great success. They disregard the potential risks of their behavior, as well as the feelings of others, and they may become hostile and threatening if challenged. Their judgment and impulse control are poor, and they typically are hyperactive and distractible. Their speech tends to be loud, pressured, and intrusive. Approximately 75 percent of people in Manic Episodes have delusions or hallucinations (usually mood-congruent), which may lead clinicians to misdiagnose them as having Schizophrenia (Kaplan et al., 1994). One person whose experience typifies the manic phase of a Bipolar Disorder is described below:

> Evelyn R. is a twenty-seven-year-old Caucasian woman with a stable marriage and work history. During a Manic Episode she slept little, staying up most of the night to make plans for her future, which was to include the purchase of several houses, not to mention love affairs with many of her co-workers and acquaintances. When her startled husband objected, she informed him that she was in the prime of her life and that he should stay out of her way. A brief period of hospitalization was required to prevent Evelyn from destroying her marriage and spending all the couple's resources.

Hypomanic Episodes resemble Manic Episodes in terms of symptoms and accompanying mood. Hypomanic Episodes have a minimum duration of four days, however, and are not severe enough to cause significant impairment in functioning. Moreover, by definition, they never include delusions or hallucinations. The therapist meeting initially with a person who is having a Hypomanic Episode may mistakenly think that the person is simply in a very good mood, but the mood's unremitting nature, its usual lack of a precipitant, and the person's history of dysfunctional mood episodes will distinguish a Hypomanic Episode from a normal cheerful mood.

Mixed Episodes may also play a part in a Bipolar Disorder. In these episodes, the criteria for both a Major Depressive Episode and a Manic Episode are met nearly every day for at least one week.

The average duration of an episode of dysfunctional mood is two and a half to four months but may be as short as a few days. The depressive phase tends to be the longest, with an average duration of six to nine months. The manic phase has an average duration of two to six weeks, shorter than an episode of Major Depression. An average of thirty-three months elapses between episodes of dysfunctional mood, but five years or more may elapse between the first and the second episode, with the time between episodes becoming shorter and the episodes themselves becoming longer as they recur. Typically, the pattern of the episodes' duration and frequency stabilizes by the fourth or fifth episode. Episodes tend to end abruptly. Without treatment, people with Bipolar Disorders typically have ten or more episodes during their lives, with the frequency of the episodes varying from three per year to one every ten years.

Three specific types of Bipolar Disorder have been identified in *DSM-IV:* Bipolar I Disorder, Bipolar II Disorder, and Cyclothymic Disorder (considered later in this chapter). A Bipolar I Disorder, by definition, includes at least one Manic Episode and can also include any or all of the other three types of episodes (Depressive, Hypomanic, and Mixed). In men, the first episode of this disorder is usually a Manic Episode; in women, it is more likely to be a Depressive Episode (American Psychiatric Association, 1994a). When the initial episode is a depressive one, the disorder may be incorrectly diagnosed as a Major Depressive Disorder. If the symptoms are treated with antidepressant medication, the mania or hypomania typically emerges, and the diagnosis is thereby clarified (Van Valkenburg & Akiskal, 1985). The nature of a person's first episode tends to reflect the nature of the person's dominant type of episode for the illness; that is, a person who has an initial episode of depression as part of a Bipolar I Disorder has a 90 percent likelihood of subsequent episodes of depression.

Bipolar II Disorder differs from Bipolar I Disorder primarily in its lack of any Manic Episodes. It includes at least one Hypomanic Episode and at least one Depressive Episode and, like the Bipolar I Disorder, causes considerable distress or impairment in functioning.

In diagnosing Bipolar I or II Disorders, the clinician should specify the nature and severity of the current episode and should make the appropriate determinations:

- *All types of episodes:* Presence or absence of a seasonal pattern and of interepisode recovery
- *Manic and Depressive Episodes:* Presence or absence of catatonic features, psychotic features, and postpartum onset
- *Depressive Episode:* Same determinations as for Major Depressive Disorder

An additional course descriptor for Bipolar I and II Disorders is determination of the presence of rapid cycling, characterized by at least four episodes of dysfunctional mood in the previous twelve months. This pattern is linked to increased dysfunction and to a poorer prognosis.

Major Depressive Disorder without a history of Manic Episodes (also known as Unipolar Depression) is much more common than Bipolar I Disorder. Only 0.5 percent to 1 percent of the population experiences a Bipolar I Disorder, with an additional 0.5 percent experiencing a Bipolar II Disorder (American Psychiatric Association, 1994a; Smith & Winokur, 1984). The genders are equally represented among people with Bipolar I Disorder, but women are more likely than men to develop Bipolar II Disorder. Onset of a Bipolar I Disorder is usually earlier than for Major Depressive Disorder, with over half experiencing onset before the age of thirty (American Psychiatric Association, 1994b; Kaplan et al., 1994). Onset may occur anytime after the age of five, although the incidence of Bipolar I Disorder peaks in the late teens and early twenties and is unlikely before the age of twelve or after the age of fifty. Glassner and Haldipur (1983) suggest that Bipolar I Disorder with early onset is more likely to be genetic and responsive to medication, whereas Bipolar I Disorder with later onset is more likely to be connected to stressful life events.

People with Bipolar I and II Disorders often have prior or comorbid mental disorders, most often Dysthymic or Cyclothymic Disorder, Substance-Related Disorders, Schizoaffective Disorder, Borderline Personality Disorder, Eating Disorders, or Anxiety Disorders. Adolescents with Bipolar Disorders tend to have interpersonal and academic problems and can be misdiagnosed as having the more common Conduct or Attention-Deficit Disorders (Bowring & Kovacs, 1992). Many people with Bipolar I Disorder have had premorbid Cyclothymic Disorder involving unstable but less severe mood changes.

Typical Client Characteristics

Research has found that people with Bipolar Disorders have underlying personality patterns that are healthier than those of people with Major Depressive Disorder and that their functioning between episodes can be quite positive (Silverman, Silverman, & Eardley, 1984). This pattern may reflect the fact that biological elements are a more important ingredient than intrapsychic and interpersonal factors in the development of Bipolar Disorders, whereas Major Depressive Disorder typically is more closely linked to environmental than to physiological disturbances. Both disorders, however, tend to begin at times of high stress, and both can result in considerable impairment. Moreover, people with Bipolar Disorders are even more likely than people with Major Depressive Disorder to commit suicide and to require hospitalization (Dunner, 1993).

Studies have looked at the personality patterns of people with Bipolar Disorders and compared them to those of people with other Mood Disorders. Perris (1982) has found that people with Bipolar Disorders are more independent and dominant, less guilty and anxious, and more prone to instability and risk taking than are people with Major Depressive Disorder. People with Bipolar Disorders tend to come from higher socioeconomic groups than do people with Major Depressive Disorder. Clients with Bipolar Disorders typically describe their families as socially inferior but upwardly striving, and these clients say that their families put pressure on them to increase the family's prestige (Gotlib & Colby, 1987). Obsessionality is often high in the personalities of these clients.

First-degree relatives of people with Bipolar I Disorder are eight to ten times more likely than the general population to have a Bipolar I Disorder and two to ten times more likely to have a Major Depressive Disorder (Kaplan et al., 1994), a finding that suggests a genetic component. Similarly, 50 percent of those with Bipolar I Disorder have a parent with a Mood Disorder. Children of one parent with a Bipolar I disorder have a 25 percent chance of developing a Mood Disorder; if both parents have Bipolar I Disorder, children have a 50 to 75 percent chance of developing a Mood Disorder. People with a Bipolar Disorder that begins at an early age are especially likely to have family members with Mood Disorders (Pauls, Morton, & Engeland, 1992).

Preferred Therapist Characteristics

The therapeutic alliance plays an important role in the successful treatment of Bipolar Disorders, just as it does in the treatment of Depressive Disorders. Rosenbaum, Fava, Nierenberg, and Sachs (1995) recommended that therapists form a true partnership with the client for the purpose of monitoring medication, charting moods, educating the client about the diagnosis and its treatment, and helping the client put a written treatment plan into action. According to Perry et al. (1985), if a therapist is treating someone who is experiencing a Manic Episode, the therapist should be empathic but should not support inappropriate behavior; the therapist should also be directive, set limits, and promote reality testing. Stability and resilience on the part of the therapist also seem important because the client is likely to be unstable and possibly hostile and resistant during the manic phase. The guidelines for the therapist's role during the depressed phase are similar to those for Major Depressive Disorder.

Intervention Strategies

Goals for the treatment of Bipolar I and II Disorders include alleviating acute symptoms, preventing future episodes of dysfunctional mood, and remedying any occupational, interpersonal, or other lifestyle problems that have resulted from the disorder. The nature and severity of the episode of dysfunctional mood, and the accompanying impairment, will guide the specific choice of treatment.

Bipolar symptoms, particularly those that are present during the manic phase, are sometimes so severe and so self-destructive for the client that hospitalization is needed. The period of hospitalization is typically brief, lasting only until medication has had an opportunity to modify the client's mood.

Medication is clearly the primary mode of treatment for Bipolar I and II Disorders. Lithium is the standard, acting primarily on manic symptoms, and is supplemented by antipsychotic, antidepressant, anticonvulsant, or other medications; the choice depends on whether rapid cycling, psychotic features, depression, or severe mania are present (Rosenbaum et al., 1995). Of clients given lithium, 75 to 80 percent improve, typically in about ten days. (Anticonvulsant medication is often effective if lithium is not.) The long-term impact of lithium seems to have been overrated, however; lithium fails to produce a sustained remission (at least three years in duration) in approximately 75 percent of people with Bipolar Disorders. Moreover, people with Bipolar Disorders often fail to maintain long-term compliance with medication regimes. Therefore, psychotherapy and supplementary medications are needed to enhance the impact of lithium. ECT also can play a role in the treatment of Bipolar Disorders, usually after other treatments have failed, as it does in the treatment of Major Depressive Disorder.

Treatment for Bipolar Disorders typically has multiple components. In addition to medication, individual psychotherapy can help people recover from the symptoms of their disorder, restore a normal mood, repair damage they have done to relationships and careers as a result of their disorder, and establish a milieu that offers structure and support.

Providing therapy during the manic phase is likely to be very difficult; people tend to enjoy the manic phase and resist the idea that they need treatment. Their flight of ideas and high activity levels make analysis and clarification of concerns all but impossible. If therapy is attempted during the manic phase, it will probably have to be very structured and concrete, involving short, frequent sessions focusing more on behavior and milieu than on introspection and exploration of affect.

By contrast, treatment during the normal or depressive phases generally can be very helpful if the guidelines discussed earlier for the treatment of depression are followed. Treatment usually will be more supportive and less confrontational than therapy for Major Depressive Disorder, however, because medication is really the primary mode of treatment for Bipolar I and II Disorders. The relatively high level of functioning experienced by many people between episodes of a Bipolar Disorder suggests that less emphasis is needed on social skills, although educating people about the nature of their disorder is an important element of the treatment. Attention should also be paid to suicide prevention, particularly during the depressed phase.

Few controlled studies have been done on the type of psychotherapy that is most likely to be helpful in the treatment of Bipolar Disorders, but several small, preliminary studies provide a promising picture of the use of cognitive-behavioral approaches (Roth & Fonagy, 1996). Encouraging people to chart the precipitants, nature, duration, frequency, and seasonality of their dysfunctional mood episodes can suggest ways of avoiding future episodes. Maintaining a stable, balanced, and healthy lifestyle and minimizing and coping with stressors can also contribute to the prevention of dysfunctional mood episodes (Rosenbaum et al., 1995). Dion and Pollack (1992) have outlined a comprehensive rehabilitation model for the treatment of Bipolar Disorder. Based on a framework of cognitive, psychoeducational, behavioral, and environmental interventions, the program includes the following components:

- An empathic and positive therapist
- Didactic education about Bipolar Disorders
- Plotting of the disorder's course
- Symptom management
- Improvement in the client's lifestyle and environment
- Assessment of the client's functioning and development of the client's coping skills and supports

Family therapy and family education are also important aspects of treating people with Bipolar Disorders. These interventions can help families understand the nature and treatment of this potentially chronic and heritable disorder and can address the marital and family difficulties that typically accompany it. Some association has also been found between relapses of Mood Disorders and family environment, with people in negative, critical environments more likely to have recurrent episodes of these disorders than are people in supportive, positive, optimistic settings (Michels & Marzuk, 1993). Therapy that improves the family environment may help prevent relapses.

Group therapy is usually not indicated for people experiencing a severe episode of a Bipolar Disorder because the nature of their symptoms makes it difficult for them to engage in the group process. Nevertheless, Klerman (1986) has found group therapy to enhance treatment compliance and suggests that it may be useful during the recovery phase. Couples group therapy has also been associated with a better course for the disorder (Roth & Fonagy, 1996). Self-help groups like the National Depressive and Manic Depressive Association are another source of support and information.

Prognosis

Bipolar Disorders present an even greater risk of recurrence than Major Depressive Disorder and, without treatment, that risk does not decline over time. Sachs, Lafer, and Truman (1994), studying one hundred people with Bipolar Disorders, have found that 90 percent had a positive response to treatment, but that 58 percent had one or more additional acute episodes, and only 10 percent had remained free of recurrences at the end of two years. Recurrences are particularly likely for people with Bipolar I Disorder characterized by Rapid Cycling or by Mixed Episodes, whereas people with pure Manic Episodes are the least likely to have recurrences (Keller, Lavori, Coryell, & Endicott, 1993).

Despite these findings, the prognosis for controlling the disorder with consistent medication and psychotherapy is fairly good. This means that people may need to be on medication for many years. Monitoring of progress, blood tests to assess the effects of lithium, and follow-up are important in obtaining treatment compliance. Although six to nine months of lithium treatment may suffice for a first episode, extended maintenance on lithium or other medication is strongly recommended for most people who have had recurrent episodes, to reduce the likelihood of future recurrences.

Preventive use of therapy is also recommended. Its efficacy has not yet been well documented, but group or individual psychotherapy, perhaps on an infrequent schedule, may play an important role in follow-up treatment of people with Bipolar Disorders. Even though medication will be provided by a psychiatrist or other physician, a nonmedical therapist can monitor progress, promote appropriate use of the medication, and facilitate the adjustment of a client with a history of Bipolar Disorder.

Cyclothymic Disorder

Description of the Disorder

Cyclothymic Disorder is, in a sense, a more consistent and milder version of Bipolar I and II Disorders, just as Dysthymic Disorder can be thought of as a longer and milder version of Major Depressive Disorder (although any biological relationship between the pairs is unclear). Cyclothymic Disorder entails a period of at least two years (one year for children and adolescents) during which a person experiences numerous periods of hypomania and dysphoria (with symptom-free periods lasting no longer than two months), and during which the episodes of mood disorder do not meet the criteria for Major Depressive Episode, Manic Episode, or Mixed Episode. The mood changes tend to be abrupt and unpredictable and to have no apparent cause.

People with Cyclothymic Disorder have continual mood cycles that are usually briefer (days or weeks rather than months) and less severe than those characteristic of Bipolar I or II Disorders. The instability and moodiness associated with Cyclothymic Disorder, however, tend to make people difficult co-workers and companions, and so some social and occupational dysfunction typically results. This disorder sometimes resembles and can be confused with a Borderline Personality Disorder.

Lifetime prevalence of this disorder ranges from 0.4 percent to 1 percent (American Psychiatric Association, 1994b). Like Dysthymic Disorder, Cyclothymic Disorder probably is underreported because the long-standing behavior becomes so familiar that it is viewed as normal. This disorder, like other Mood Disorders, most commonly begins in late adolescence or early adulthood and, without treatment, tends to have a chronic course, with no significant symptom-free periods (Howland & Thase, 1995). Data are unclear, but this disorder may be more common in females.

Typical Client Characteristics

In people with Cyclothymic Disorder and their family members, other mental disorders are often also found. First-degree relatives of people with Cyclothymic Disorder have an increased incidence of Major Depressive, Substance-Related, and Bipolar Disorders. Some clinicians have noted in people with Cyclothymic Disorder a common childhood history of poor object relations and of being sensitive, hyperactive, and moody (Kaplan et al., 1994; Van Valkenburg & Akiskal, 1985). This disorder sometimes is accompanied by Substance-Related, Personality, Somatoform, and Sleep Disorders and, in about one-third of cases, is a precursor to another Mood Disorder, most often Bipolar II Disorder. Substance misuse often reflects an effort at self-medication. People with Cyclothymic Disorder often have trouble coping effectively with stress (Goplerud & Depue, 1985). Beyond this information, little research is available on family background, personality patterns, and other antecedent variables associated with this disorder. To speak of a premorbid personality does not make sense in many cases because the affective lability characteristic of people with Cyclothymic Disorder may have been present throughout most of their lives.

Preferred Therapist Characteristics

Little information is available on the therapist's role in the treatment of Cyclothymic Disorder. Logic suggests the need for stability, patience, structure, and flexibility. Role modeling and feedback may also be useful tools for therapists because people with Cyclothymic Disorder have no stable sense of themselves and probably will need to clarify their values and direction as symptoms are reduced.

Intervention Strategies

Little information is available on the treatment of Cyclothymic Disorder because people with this disorder are not usually motivated to seek treatment for their symptoms. Treatment seems to be most effective when it includes a combination of medication and psychotherapy. Antimanic drugs typically are the first choice of medication for this disorder. Jacobsen (1993) has found that valproate (Depakene) effects significant reduction in symptoms as well as stabilization of mood in people with Cyclothymic Disorder. Howland and Thase (1995) reviewed many studies and found that most people with this disorder had a positive initial response to lithium, although remission rates varied from 26 percent to 97 percent in those studies. Lithium does not seem quite as effective in the treatment of Cyclothymic Disorder as in the treatment of Bipolar I and II Disorders, but it still seems to be an important component of treatment, particularly for people who have a family history of Mood Disorders (Howland & Thase, 1995).

Psychotherapy usually is important in the treatment of Cyclothymic Disorder. Treatment goals include education about the disorder, identification of triggers of mood shifts, mood stabilization, amelioration of any work- and family-related concerns, and overall improvement of lifestyle. Individual therapy should probably follow the cognitive-behavioral, interpersonal, and other models that have demonstrated effectiveness in treating Dysthymic Disorder because depression is a central element in Cyclothymic Disorder and because behavioral and cognitive deficits are likely to accompany the mood shifts. The depressive cycles of this disorder also tend to produce more dysfunction than the hypomanic phases do. In addition, people with Cyclothymic Disorder seem unlikely to be very introspective; therefore, affective and analytic approaches do not seem appropriate, at least in the early stages of treatment.

Family therapy is indicated, as it is for most of the disorders in this section, because the unpredictable mood shifts experienced by people with this disorder may well have damaged their family relationships, and so rebuilding the family and educating its members about the disorder will often be necessary steps. Career counseling and interpersonal skill development will usually be helpful supplements to the treatment of individuals with Cyclothymic Disorder because their mood changes will probably have made it difficult to negotiate a smooth career path and develop a repertoire of positive social skills and coping mechanisms. Group therapy may also be useful; clients with Cyclothymic Disorder are generally healthy enough to interact with other group members and may benefit from the opportunity to try out new ways of relating, receive feedback, and make use of the role models provided by others.

In general, then, psychotherapy for people with Cyclothymic Disorder will be multifaceted. Treatment will include individual psychotherapy and may also include group therapy, family therapy, career counseling, and education. If medication is indicated, the treatment will usually include lithium. Therapy will be structured and relatively directive, to keep clients focused. It will combine supportive and exploratory elements, to help clients understand their patterns of interaction, and will emphasize cognitive and behavioral strategies.

Prognosis

The combination of psychotherapy and medication has a good likelihood of reducing symptoms and effecting overall improvement in people with Cyclothymic Disorder. Nevertheless, the long-standing nature of this disorder and the chronicity of related disorders suggest that complete recovery may be difficult. Long-term treatment is usually indicated for this disorder (Kaplan et al., 1994).

TREATMENT RECOMMENDATIONS: CLIENT MAP

Five specific types of Mood Disorder have been discussed in this chapter: Major Depressive Disorder, Dysthymic Disorder, Bipolar I and II Disorders, and Cyclothymic Disorder. The information presented in this chapter about these disorders is summarized here according to the Client Map format.

Client Map

Diagnosis

Mood Disorders (Major Depressive Disorder, Dysthymic Disorder, Bipolar I and II Disorders, Cyclothymic Disorder)

Objectives of Treatment

Stabilize mood

Alleviate depression, mania, and hypomania

Prevent relapse

Improve coping mechanisms, relationships, career, and overall adjustment

Establish a consistent and healthy lifestyle

Assessments

Measures of depression and suicidal ideation, such as the Beck Depression Inventory and the Schedule of Affective Disorders and Schizophrenia (Seligman & Moore, 1995)

Medical examination for physical symptoms

Clinician Characteristics

High in core conditions

Comfortable with client's dependence and discouragement

Resilient

Able to promote motivation, independence, and optimism

Able to be structured and present-oriented

Location of Treatment

Usually outpatient setting, but inpatient setting if symptoms are severe, if risk of suicide is high, or if there is loss of contact with reality

Interventions to Be Used

Cognitive-behavioral, interpersonal, and related models of treatment

Education about disorder

Relapse prevention

Emphasis of Treatment

Emphasis on cognitions and behavior

Initial directive and supportive emphasis

Later on, less directive and more exploratory emphasis

Numbers

Primarily individual therapy

Family therapy often indicated

Group therapy useful after symptoms have abated

Timing

Medium duration (three to six months)

Moderate pace (one to two sessions per week)

Maintenance and extended follow-up phases common

Medications Needed

Often indicated in combination with psychotherapy, especially for manic symptoms or severe depression

Adjunct Services

Increased activity

Homework assignments

Career counseling

Development of social and coping skills

Homogeneous support groups

Prognosis

Good for recovery from each episode

Fair for complete remission

Relapses common

Client Map of Karen

This chapter began with a description of Karen C., a thirty-year-old woman who began experiencing severe depression after her husband's departure for a tour of duty. Karen's case reflects many of the characteristics of people suffering from depression. Karen's mother had episodes of depression, a disorder that often has a familial component. Karen herself had suffered an early loss with the death of her father, was dependent and low in self-esteem, had few resources and interests, and looked to others for structure and support. Her current depression seemed to be a reactive one, triggered by her perception that her marriage was at risk. Her symptoms were typical of Major Depressive Disorder and included both emotional features (hopelessness, guilt) and somatic features (sleep and appetite disturbances, fatigue). The following Client Map outlines the treatment for Karen.

Diagnosis

Axis I: 296.23 Major Depressive Disorder, Single Episode, Severe, Without Psychotic Features, With Atypical Features

Axis II: Dependent Personality Traits

Axis III: No known physical disorders or conditions, but weight change reported

Axis IV: Separation from husband due to his tour of duty, marital conflict

Axis V: Global assessment of functioning (GAF Scale): current GAF = 45

Objectives of Treatment

Reduce level of depression

Eliminate physiological complaints

Improve social and occupational functioning

Increase self-esteem, sense of independence, and activity level

Improve communication and differentiation in marital relationship

Reduce marital stress and conflict

Reduce cognitive distortions and unwarranted assumptions

Assessments

Beck Depression Inventory, to be used at the start of each session

Safekeeping contract, in which Karen (after discussion of her suicidal ideation) agrees not to harm herself (assumption is that client is not acutely suicidal)

Physical examination

Clinician Characteristics

Supportive and patient, yet structured

Able to model and teach effective interpersonal functioning

Able to build a working alliance rapidly with a discouraged and potentially suicidal client

Possibly female (and thereby also able to serve as a role model)

Location of Treatment

Outpatient setting

Period of inpatient treatment possible if Karen does not respond to treatment quickly and remains relatively immobilized by depression

Interventions to Be Used

Exploration of patterns in Karen's significant relationships (effects of early loss of her father, dependent and enmeshed relationship with her mother, extended conflict with her husband)

Encouragement of social interactions

Analysis of her thoughts about herself and her roles and relationships

Exploration of her associated emotions, in light of the guidelines for interpersonal psychotherapy (Klerman et al., 1984)

Primary focus on Karen's present relationship with her husband and her lack of self-direction (interpersonal role disputes and interpersonal deficits)

Attention to helping Karen clarify and communicate her expectations and wishes to her husband and renegotiate their relationship

Encouragement for Karen to review strengths and weaknesses of her past and present relationships and to try out improved ways of relating, both at home and in therapy sessions

Use of techniques like role playing, examination of logic and belief systems, communication analysis, and modeling

Emphasis of Treatment

High level of directiveness, given Karen's near-immobilization by her depression

Provision of guidance and structure by the therapist, in view of Karen's lack of a sense of how to help herself

Reduction of guidance and structure over time, to promote an increase in Karen's own sense of mastery and competence and help her take responsibility for her life

High degree of support at the outset, given Karen's relative lack of friends and confidants

Shift of focus to include more exploration and education as Karen's symptoms abate, and as she begins to develop some additional outside support systems (but support to remain relatively high)

Attention to both cognitive dysfunction (inappropriate generalizations, self-blame) and behavioral deficits (lack of activities, poor social and interpersonal skills, dependence on others)

Primary emphasis of treatment to be on Karen's relationships, even though affective symptoms are prominent (focusing on her feelings of depression would probably only further entrench her sense of hopelessness, and the precipitant of her present depression seems to be interpersonal)

Numbers

Individual therapy as the initial approach to treatment

Marital counseling once Karen's husband returns home (Karen's mother may also be invited to attend several sessions if this idea is acceptable to Karen)

Timing

Two weekly sessions initially (to facilitate reduction of Karen's depression and suicidal ideation and improve her functioning)

One weekly session after she is able to return to work

Relatively gradual and supportive pace at first (but as fast as Karen's fragile condition will allow)

Anticipated duration of three to nine months

Possible extension of treatment beyond symptom abatement (for preventive impact, given long history of Dependent Personality Traits, and for possible value in averting recurrences)

Medications Needed

Referral to a psychiatrist for determination of whether medication may be indicated (given Karen's quite severe depression and hopelessness, even though hers seems to be a reactive rather than an endogenous depression, and given that medication combined with psychotherapy seems particularly effective in treating Major Depressive Disorder)

Adjunct Services

Suggestion of some nondemanding tasks (such as reading about assertiveness; increasing and listing pleasurable activities, particularly those involving socialization)

Participation in a women's support group after depression has been reduced

Prognosis

Very good for symptom reduction in Major Depressive Disorder, Single Episode

Less optimistic for significant modification of underlying Dependent Personality Traits

About a 50 percent probability of another Major Depressive Episode (possibility should be discussed with Karen and her family and addressed via extended treatment and/or follow-up)

Recommended Reading

Beck, A. T., Rush, A. J., Shaw, B. F., & Emery, G. (1979). *Cognitive therapy of depression.* New York: Guilford Press.

Bowring, M., & Kovacs, M. (1992). Difficulties in diagnosing manic disorders among children and adolescents. *Journal of the American Academy of Child and Adolescent Psychiatry, 31,* 611–614.

Gotlib, I. H., & Colby, C. A. (1987). *Treatment of depression.* New York: Pergamon Press.

Grandin, T. (1995). *Thinking in pictures and other reports from my life with autism.* New York: Doubleday.

Klerman, G. L., Weissman, M. M., Rounsaville, B. J., & Chevron, E. S. (1984). *Interpersonal psychotherapy of depression.* New York: Basic Books.

Markowitz, J. C. (1994). Psychotherapy for dysthymia: Is it effective? *American Journal of Psychiatry, 151,* 1114–1121.

Seligman, L., & Moore, B. (1995). Diagnosis of mood disorders. *Journal of Counseling and Development, 74*(1), 65–69.

CHAPTER FIVE

Anxiety Disorders

Roberto, a twenty-seven-year-old Latino man, sought therapy at the insistence of his fiancée, Luisa. For the past four months Roberto had been experiencing nightmares and intrusive memories of having been sexually abused during his childhood by his family's housekeeper. Roberto had withdrawn from Luisa as well as from his other friends. He no longer engaged in running and other exercise, which had been a daily activity for him in the past. He refused to visit his parents, who still lived in the house where the abuse had occurred.

Luisa reported that Roberto appeared anxious and irritable. When she encouraged him to get out of the house and do something enjoyable, he became angry and told her that she just did not understand. The change in Roberto had been triggered by a visit to the dentist. Roberto, who needed extensive dental work, apparently became emotionally and physically uncomfortable during the process. When he sought to leave the dental chair in the middle of the procedure, the authoritarian dentist told Roberto that he would just have to "put up with it." The powerlessness of the situation, the attitude of the dentist, and the reclining position of the chair brought back memories that Roberto had long tried to push out of his mind.

Although he had never forgotten his mistreatment by the housekeeper, Roberto had done his best to act as if the abuse had never happened, and he had built a rewarding life for himself. When the abuse was still continuing, however, the housekeeper had told Roberto that she would harm his baby sister if he told anyone, and so he had kept it to himself. As an adult, he felt ashamed of his experiences and had continued to keep them secret. Now, however, those experiences could no longer be pushed aside.

Roberto was experiencing an Anxiety Disorder—Posttraumatic Stress Disorder (PTSD)—typified by both emotional and physiological sensations of tension and apprehension, as well as by a reexperiencing of the trauma and by withdrawal. Although the Condition Sexual Abuse of Child (discussed in Chapter Three) would also probably be used to describe Roberto's childhood experiences, the diagnosis of PTSD is used as well, to convey the emotional distress and impairment that he was experiencing. His symptoms cannot accurately be classified as an Adjustment Disorder because the precipitant happened so long ago and because the nature and severity of Roberto's symptoms do not fit the profile for an Adjustment Disorder. Roberto did have some underlying depression, but his overriding emotion was anxiety.

OVERVIEW OF ANXIETY DISORDERS

Description of the Disorders

This chapter reviews the diagnosis and treatment of five categories of anxiety disorder:

- Phobias (including Agoraphobia, Specific Phobia, and Social Phobia)
- Panic Disorder
- Obsessive-Compulsive Disorder
- The trauma-related stress disorders (Posttraumatic Stress Disorder and Acute Stress Disorder)
- Generalized Anxiety Disorder

Although these disorders differ in terms of duration, precipitants, secondary symptoms, and impact, they are all characterized primarily by anxiety.

Anxiety Disorders are among the most prevalent forms of mental illness in the United States. According to a survey conducted by Kessler and others (1994), nearly 25 percent of the population has experienced an Anxiety Disorder at some time in life, and more than 12 percent of the population experiences an Anxiety Disorder in any given year (Narrow et al., 1993). Phobias are the most commonly reported Anxiety Disorders. Anxiety is the primary symptom in 20 to 25 percent of all psychiatric disorders (Turner & Hersen, 1984), and stress related to anxiety is a significant factor in more than 30 percent of the people who consult physicians because of physical ailments (Maxmen & Ward, 1995). In fact, people are more likely to consult physicians than psychotherapists for treatment of anxiety symptoms. All of the Anxiety Disorders seem to be more prevalent in females.

Many explanations have been advanced for the causes of anxiety. These explanations differ, but all are valid for some types of anxiety and for some people. Psychoanalytic theorists, for example, suggest that anxiety is the product of experiences in which internal impulses, previously punished and repressed, evoke distress that signals danger of further punishment if the impulses are expressed. To restate this theory in cognitive-behavioral terms, a stressor is believed to produce the perception of a threat, and this perception in turn is thought to produce a dysfunctional emotional reaction (anxiety): we learn to view a particular stimulus as frightening, either through our own experiences (conditioning) or through the experiences of others (social learning), and so threats of that stimulus evoke apprehension and avoidance behavior. To mention two more examples of theories about anxiety, existentialist theory explains free-floating or generalized anxiety as reflecting discomfort with the inherent meaninglessness of life, and biological explanations of anxiety have also been advanced (indeed, many medical conditions, including endocrine disturbances and cardiovascular abnormalities, can produce symptoms that resemble those of anxiety).

Anxiety is a common and useful response inherent in everyday experiences. It can warn people of potential hazards and risky choices and can provide a stimulus to effective action. Fawzy and others (1993), for example, have found that higher initial levels of distress in response to a diagnosis of cancer enhanced coping. Anxiety becomes a disorder, however, when it is characterized by great intensity or duration and when it causes significant distress and impairment.

Anxiety, like depression, takes many forms, but anxiety usually is not severely debilitating, nor is it usually accompanied by loss of contact with reality. Anxiety may be free-floating and without obvious cause or it may be what is called *signal anxiety,* occurring in response to a fear-inducing stimulus (such as recollection of an accident or pictures of snakes). Most people with anxiety try to manage or conceal their symptoms and go about their lives.

Anxiety is characterized by both emotional and physiological symptoms. Fear and apprehension are the primary emotional symptoms but are often accompanied by others, including confusion, impaired concentration, selective attention, avoidance, and, especially in children and adolescents, behavioral problems. Anxiety-related symptoms contribute to suicide almost as often as depressive symptoms do (Allgulander & Lavonri, 1991). Common physiological symptoms of anxiety include dizziness, heart palpitations, changes in bowel and bladder functioning, perspiration, muscle tension, restlessness, headaches, and queasiness. Adolescents experiencing anxiety are particularly likely to present somatic manifestations of their anxiety (Kearney & Silverman, 1995). The symptoms of the disorder, such as heart palpitations and shortness of breath, are in themselves frightening and may lead the person who has them to believe that a heart attack is in progress or that some other serious physical ailment exists. Thus anxiety often breeds further anxiety. Again, however, because many medical conditions can be the cause of anxietylike symptoms, any unexplained physiological symptoms that accompany anxiety warrant a referral for medical evaluation.

Diagnosis of an Anxiety Disorder can be facilitated by the use of a brief inventory of anxiety symptoms. Probably the one most widely used is the Beck Anxiety Inventory, which assesses four categories of anxiety symptoms—neurophysiological, subjective, panic-related, and autonomic (Beck & Steer, 1990).

Typical Client Characteristics

The onset of severe anxiety is often preceded by financial or marital problems, a bereavement, or another aversive event that may place stress on an area in which the person is vulnerable, increase the person's responsibilities, or weaken the person's support system. Long-standing anxiety is often linked to an early trauma or a learned fear.

People who are prone to anxiety tend to see themselves as powerless and may view the world as a source of harm and threat. Those who are prone to excessive anxiety typically come from difficult backgrounds that include poverty, family conflict, dissolution of the family, separation from the mother in childhood, or critical and demanding parents (Turner & Hersen, 1984). These people seem to have few effective support systems and usually have not had a history of successfully coping with stressors. They characteristically have a high level of underlying stress (called *trait anxiety*), are pessimistic, have a need to overprotect and overcontrol, and react with elevated stress (called *state anxiety*) to even minor disturbances. Stress has been linked to a pattern of such cognitive distortions as catastrophizing, overgeneralizing, and selective attending (Meyer & Deitsch, 1996). Like depression, anxiety tends to run in families (Kearney & Silverman, 1995), although this finding is less clearly true of Generalized Anxiety Disorder than it is of Panic Disorder. More females than males seek treatment for Anxiety Disorders, perhaps because many men who are anxious turn to alcohol rather than to therapy (Gorman & Liebowitz, 1986).

Anxiety is often accompanied by secondary symptoms and disorders. When depression is also present, the result may be what has been termed an *agitated depression*. About half of those with an Anxiety Disorder also have a Personality Disorder (Van Velzen & Emmelkamp, 1996). Substance misuse and dependence on others are also common and may represent efforts to control the symptoms through self-medication and overreliance on support systems. Unfortunately, those behaviors seem more likely to worsen the anxiety than to alleviate it.

Preferred Therapist Characteristics

Although little research is available on the optimal therapist for the anxious client, that therapist is probably one who is stable and calm, untroubled by anxiety, and able to exert a calming and reassuring effect on the client. Beck and Emery (1985) suggest that the therapist be a model of patience and persistence, encouraging rather than forcing change. Horowitz, Marmar, Krupnick, et al. (1984) view the best therapist for a client with an Anxiety Disorder as an "expert and healer" who is compassionate, understanding, nonjudgmental, and genuine. According to Horowitz and colleagues, "Frequently, stress-related symptoms subside rapidly once a firm therapeutic alliance is established" (p. 42). The therapeutic relationship, then, can have a powerful impact on symptoms of anxiety.

The therapist working with an anxious client should be comfortable enough with the client's pain and tension to refrain from taking complete control of the therapeutic process. Nevertheless, the therapist should also have enough concern and compassion to keep searching for an approach that will have a beneficial impact on the client. The therapist should be flexible and able to draw from a variety of therapeutic approaches in finding an optimal balance of techniques.

Intervention Strategies

In recent years, considerable progress has been made in determining effective treatments for Anxiety Disorders (Goldfried, Greenberg, & Marmar, 1990). Optimal treatment of Anxiety Disorders involves multiple components, usually emphasizing behavioral and cognitive therapy (Kelly, 1996). Smith, Glass, and Miller's (1980) meta-analysis found cognitive-behavioral and cognitive approaches to yield the largest effect sizes (1.78 and 1.67, respectively) in the treatment of fear and anxiety. These approaches were followed by the behavioral approach (with an effect size of 1.12).

Anxiety Disorders vary considerably, and so treatment must be tailored to the specific nature of the disorder, but it usually includes the following elements:

1. *Establishment of a strong therapeutic alliance* that promotes the client's motivation and feelings of safety.

2. *Exploration of the manifestations of anxiety* and of the stimuli for fears. Although treatment of Anxiety Disorders usually does not emphasize psychodynamic interventions, an Anxiety Disorder related to a trauma may require considerable processing of affect, as well as exploration of past experiences and patterns.

3. *Referral for medical evaluation* to determine any contributing physical disorders, as well as the need for medication.

4. *The teaching of relaxation skills* and incorporation of regular relaxation into the person's lifestyle. Effective approaches to relaxation include meditation, exercise, visual imagery, and yoga.

5. *Analysis of dysfunctional cognitions* that are contributing to anxiety, and substitution of empowering, positive, more accurate cognitions.

6. *Exposure to feared objects,* which can be accomplished in many ways, including hypnotherapy, in vivo or imaginal desensitization, eye movement desensitization and reprocessing (EMDR), and flooding.

7. *Homework,* to track and increase the client's progress and to promote the client's responsibility.

8. *Solidification of efforts to cope* with anxiety and prevent a relapse.

One example of a useful short-term approach to treating anxiety disorders, presented in a manualized format, is anxiety management training (AMT) (Suinn, 1990). AMT is a relaxation-based self-control therapy in which people are taught to identify cognitive and bodily cues of the onset of anxiety and to develop responses (such as guided imagery and relaxation) that they can use to reduce or eliminate those symptoms. Homework assignments are used to promote generalization of gains, log progress, and encourage self-efficacy. AMT is especially useful in treating such forms of anxiety as Panic Disorder and Generalized Anxiety Disorder, which have no obvious precipitant, but it can also be used as an adjunct to the treatment of other Anxiety Disorders. The AMT format has demonstrated its effectiveness in both individual and group therapy.

A similar approach is described by Meichenbaum and Deffenbacher (1988). Their model, stress inoculation training (SIT), includes three phases: (1) conceptualization of the problem and building of rapport, (2) skill acquisition and rehearsal, and (3) application and follow-through. The teaching of relaxation and cognitive coping skills (such as the use of problem-oriented self-instruction, the restructuring of negative cognitions, and the use of self-reward/self-efficacy statements) is an important component of this helpful model. According to the particular client and disorder, techniques like imaginal and in vivo desensitization, relaxation, and hypnotherapy, which are designed to reduce fear and anxiety, may also be used in this model.

The therapist treating anxiety, like a therapist treating depression, will probably begin with a moderate level of directiveness and a high level of supportiveness. A person who is anxious typically feels fragile and apprehensive and needs support and encouragement for engaging in therapy. Although some directiveness on the part of the therapist is needed, to give structure to the sessions, the anxious client is in emotional pain and so will usually be eager to collaborate with the therapist in relieving the symptoms. Once the debilitating anxiety has been reduced, the therapist can assume a more probing stance. Most people with anxiety will have had a period of relatively healthy functioning before the onset of symptoms and should be able to respond to and grow from some exploration.

Group therapy is often used along with or in lieu of individual therapy in the treatment of anxiety. People with similar anxiety-related symptoms and experiences (for example, Posttraumatic Stress Disorder after a rape, or fear of social situations) can provide each other with a powerful source of encouragement, role models, and reinforcement.

Family counseling can also be a useful adjunct to treatment. A highly anxious and constricted person may have a strong impact on the life of the family. Family members may benefit from help in understanding the disorder and in learning how to respond supportively and helpfully and without providing the secondary gains that may reinforce the symptoms.

Collaboration with a physician is important in treating people with Anxiety Disorders because, as previously mentioned, anxietylike symptoms can be caused by many medical conditions, such as those in the following list:

- Cardiopulmonary disorders (mitral valve prolapse, angina pectoris, and cardiac arrhythmia)
- Endocrine disturbances (hyperthyroidism, hypoglycemia)
- Neurological disorders
- Inflammatory disorders (rheumatoid arthritis, lupus erythematosus)
- Abuse of substances (diet or cold medications, amphetamines, caffeine, nicotine, or cocaine)

The therapist and the physician must determine whether a physical symptom is causing a psychological symptom or vice versa. Medication sometimes can accelerate the treatment of certain Anxiety Disorders, among them Panic Disorder and Obsessive-Compulsive Disorder, but hospitalization is rarely necessary. Outpatient psychotherapy of medium duration (months rather than weeks or years), combining cognitive and behavioral interventions with between-session practice, will usually be the best approach to treating Anxiety Disorders.

Prognosis

Prognosis for the treatment of Anxiety Disorders varies greatly according to the specific disorder. Some Anxiety Disorders, like Phobias, respond very well to treatment; others, like Obsessive-Compulsive Disorder, are sometimes treatment-resistant. Recurrences of Anxiety Disorders, like recurrences of Mood Disorders, are common. The setting of goals that focus on measurable behavioral and affective change is integral to treatment, and procedures for assessing progress toward goals (such as observation and the use of checklists, diaries, questionnaires, inventories, and even videotapes) often play a role in the monitoring of change. Later sections of this chapter focus on specific Anxiety Disorders and provide more information on their prognoses.

PANIC DISORDER

Description of the Disorder

The hallmark of Panic Disorder, as the name suggests, is attacks of panic that are unexpected. A panic attack is a circumscribed period of intense fear or discomfort that develops suddenly, usually begins with cardiac symptoms and difficulty in breathing, and peaks within ten minutes. A full panic attack is accompanied by at least four physiological symptoms, which may include sweating, nausea, and trembling in addition to rapid heartbeat, chest pain, and difficulty in breathing. Maxmen and Ward (1995) report that panic attacks typically last three to ten minutes and rarely last longer than thirty minutes.

Three types of panic attacks have been identified: *unexpected or uncued* attacks (with no apparent trigger), *situationally bound or cued* attacks (in anticipation of or on contact with specific stimuli), and *situationally predisposed* attacks (usually but not always associated with specific triggers). As already mentioned, the panic attacks that accompany Panic Disorder are usually unexpected, but people with this disorder may have all three types of attacks.

Panic attacks are common; approximately 30 percent of adults have had at least one. Although most panic attacks occur during the waking hours, a panic attack that occurs during sleep may awaken the sleeping person. A given person may have infrequent panic attacks, with little impact, or may have many attacks each week, which result in considerable distress and impairment.

Even a small number of panic attacks can be very upsetting. The degree of upset depends on the person's interpretation of the symptoms, the person's underlying fears, and the extent of the person's anticipatory anxiety. People sometimes believe that their panic symptoms are indications of having a heart attack or going crazy. Beck and Emery (1985) hypothesize that one of the three fears is at the core of an acute attack of panic: fear of serious physical disease or illness, fear of a mental disorder, or fear of social catastrophe or public disgrace.

Craske and Barlow (1993) advance a biopsychosocial explanation of an initial panic attack, viewing it as a "misfiring of the fear system under stressful life circumstances in physiologically and psychologically vulnerable individuals" (p. 5). They view Panic Disorder as a Phobia of bodily sensations. The feelings of panic are caused by fear and stress, those bodily sensations are then misinterpreted, and the outcome is both increased fear and greater likelihood of additional panic attacks, an unfortunate and self-perpetuating cycle.

According to the fourth edition of the *Diagnostic and Statistical Manual of Mental Disorders,* or *DSM-IV* (American Psychiatric Association, 1994a), a Panic Disorder is characterized by at least two unexpected panic attacks, neither of which can be explained by medical conditions or substance use, with one or more followed by at least a month of persistent fear of another attack, worry about the implications of the attack, and/or behavioral change (usually designed to avert future attacks) in response to the attack.

DSM-IV recognizes a connection between Panic Disorder and phobic avoidance by establishing two subtypes of Panic Disorder: Panic Disorder Without Agoraphobia and Panic Disorder With Agoraphobia. (A subsequent section of this chapter discusses Agoraphobia itself, with or without Panic Disorder.) About half of all people with Panic Disorder will fall into each of the two groups. People who have Panic Disorder With Agoraphobia typically associate their panic attacks with where they have occurred and avoid those places in an effort to prevent future attacks. They also are likely to misinterpret the attacks as imminent heart attacks or other catastrophes. As the panic attacks occur in more and more places, people with this disorder tend to restrict their activities until, in severe cases, they refuse to leave home; unfortunately, this safety-seeking behavior tends to maintain these people's inaccurate cognitions. Besides Agoraphobia, additional frequent concomitants of Panic Disorder are Substance-Related Disorders (especially alcohol, used as self-medication in an effort to control panic attacks) and depression, as well as other kinds of Anxiety Disorders.

Panic Disorder typically has a sudden onset, beginning with a severe panic attack. Approximately 2 percent of males and 3.5 percent of females in the United States will experience a Panic Disorder at some time in their lives (Kessler et al., 1994). The mean age of onset for Panic Disorder ranges from twenty-three to twenty-nine, with treatment usually sought around the age of thirty-four (Craske & Barlow, 1993). Identifiable stressors typically accompany the initial attack, but the panic attacks tend to recur even after the stressor is resolved (Gorman & Liebowitz, 1986).

Typical Client Characteristics

Both Panic Disorder and its close relative, Agoraphobia, seem to be familial disorders. The risk that first-degree relatives of people with these disorders will develop an Anxiety Disorder themselves is twice as high as it is for the general population: 20 percent of people with Panic Disorder have first-degree relatives with that disorder (Harris, Noyes, Crowe, & Chaudhry, 1983; Maxmen & Ward, 1995). The risk of developing Panic Disorder is particularly high for female relatives of people with this disorder, whereas the male relatives of people with Panic Disorder are at particular risk for problems related to alcohol use (often, as mentioned, a mechanism for coping with anxiety). Some studies have also found a familial relationship between Panic Disorder and depression (Breier, Charney, & Heninger, 1985).

People with Panic Disorder have a high incidence of early separations and of very disturbed childhood environments. They have a high likelihood of having experienced episodes of Major Depressive Disorder and Separation Anxiety Disorder or other Anxiety Disorders as children (Gorman & Liebowitz, 1986). Many people with Panic Disorder were depressed, dependent, and passive even before the panic attacks began. People with this disorder typically also have pronounced preexisting beliefs and fears that specific bodily sensations reflect physical and mental disease. Relationship and occupational difficulties are often prominent in people with Panic Disorder (Barbaree & Marshall, 1985; Clum, Clum, & Surls, 1993). People with Panic Disorder are also at increased risk for developing other Anxiety Disorders, Depressive Disorders, Substance-Related Disorders, and suicidal ideation (Kaplan, Sadock, & Grebb, 1994).

Preferred Therapist Characteristics

The first session with clients experiencing Panic Disorder is critical in establishing a successful therapeutic alliance (Ballenger, Lydiard, & Turner, 1995). People with this disorder typically have a history of unsuccessful personal and professional efforts to ameliorate it and may feel demoralized as well as ashamed at not having been successful. These individuals also often feel angry at having been referred to a psychotherapist for what they believe is a medical or physical problem. Normalizing these reactions, as well as reassuring clients that effective treatments for this disorder are available, can contribute greatly to their motivation to engage in yet another treatment. The general recommendations in the preceding section, about the ideal therapist to treat Anxiety Disorder, are also pertinent here.

Intervention Strategies

Considerable research on the treatment of Panic Disorder has been conducted over the past ten years, and much more is now known about its treatment. Cognitive therapy, enhanced by behavioral interventions and sometimes combined with medication, has been found to be more effective than other interventions, including medication alone and behavior therapy alone (Clum et al., 1993). This finding makes sense because the disorder stems primarily from misinterpretations of physical symptoms. The cognitive interventions seek to change people's catastrophic and distorted thinking, and such behavioral techniques as distraction, comforting rituals, meditation, and relaxation contribute to the control of anticipatory anxiety and of any panic attacks that may occur.

Arntz and Van Den Hout (1996), having reviewed multiple studies of cognitive therapy in the treatment of Panic Disorder, find that cognitive therapy has a strong positive impact on both the frequency of attacks and the fear of future attacks. In the studies they reviewed, 75 to 90 percent of people with Panic Disorder were panic-free after treatment.

One of the challenging aspects of treating panic attacks is their unpredictable and intermittent nature. A multifaceted cognitive-behavioral treatment program for Panic Disorder has been developed by Barlow and his associates to assess this issue and present treatment recommendations (Barlow & Cerny, 1988; Craske & Barlow, 1993). A unique component of Barlow's panic-control therapy is progressive evocation of the somatic sensations of panic attacks. People are asked to spin in a chair, hyperventilate, or run up and down stairs (after receiving medical clearance, of course). Treatment interventions, including education, a combination of exposure and desensitization to the panic attacks, and cognitive restructuring, help people to recognize that these sensations are not life-threatening and to extinguish their fears. Behavioral techniques like breathing retraining and relaxation enhance people's recovery from the disorder. Inventories and logs are used to assess the severity of the disorder and to track progress.

Despite the overwhelming preponderance of studies focused on cognitive-behavioral interventions, some success has also been reported with the use of insight-oriented treatment strategies (Wiborg & Dahl, 1996). These strategies can help people understand the underlying meaning of their anxiety and the anxiety-related behaviors and attitudes they probably have manifested for many years.

Both family and group therapy in treatment of this disorder have also received some support. Family interventions, combined with specific treatments for panic attacks, can help ameliorate the impact that this disorder has on family functioning and relationships. Group therapy using cognitive-behavioral interventions has demonstrated high levels of effectiveness; so has individual therapy.

Medication is sometimes part of the treatment plan for Panic Disorder, but it can interfere with the impact of psychotherapy by artificially promoting relaxation and limiting people's ability to self-soothe and credit themselves with overcoming the disorder. Consequently, a referral for medication probably should be made only if psychotherapy alone clearly is not effective or if a person is having many severe panic attacks each week.

Tricyclic antidepressant medications (TCAs), notably clomipramine (Anafranil) and imipramine (Tofranil), have contributed to the amelioration of Panic Disorder (Kaplan et al., 1994). It has also been reported that monoamine oxidase inhibitors (MAOIs), selective serotonin reuptake inhibitors (SSRIs), and benzodiazepines have a success rate of about 70 percent in the treatment of Panic Disorder (McCarter, 1996). Barbaree and Marshall (1985) have found antidepressant medication to suppress panic attacks but not to diminish anticipatory anxiety, whereas anxiolytics have been found to reduce overall anxiety but not to affect panic attacks—a finding that provides yet another rationale for combining medication and psychotherapy in the treatment of this disorder.

Despite the demonstrated effectiveness of medication in treating this disorder, medication should almost never be the sole modality of treatment. Wiborg and Dahl (1996) have found that the combination of psychotherapy and medication yields an even higher percentage of people who are free of panic attacks after nine months of treatment. People with this disorder also tend to have concerns (such as low self-esteem and interpersonal difficulties) that precede and underlie their panic attacks, and so elimination of the panic attacks may not be sufficient; chronicity and incomplete remission are significant concerns in the treatment of this disorder. Psychotherapy, with or without medication, is necessary in helping to effect those personal changes that are likely to prevent future episodes of Anxiety Disorders. Lifestyle changes can also contribute to relief of Panic Disorder. For example, caffeine is likely to increase the frequency and severity of panic attacks, and so its use should be discouraged in people with this disorder.

Whether or not a person with Panic Disorder is referred for medication, the person almost always should be referred for overall medical evaluation so that the therapist can be sure that the symptoms are indeed of psychological origin. Because people with Panic Disorder frequently believe their symptoms to be physiological in origin, they are likely to be receptive to the suggestion of a physical examination.

Prognosis

The prognosis for successful treatment of Panic Disorder, primarily via relatively short-term cognitive-behavioral therapy, is excellent, especially if treatment is sought early in the course of the disorder. Craske and Barlow (1993) report that 80 to 100 percent of the people they treated were panic-free after approximately fifteen sessions of treatment, and 50 to 80 percent of that number were viewed as having been cured of the disorder. Not all sources present such an optimistic picture of treatment for this disorder, but most do agree that only 10 to 20 percent of people with Panic Disorder continue to have significant symptoms after treatment, and that another 50 percent continue to have only mild symptoms (Kaplan et al., 1994). Treatment of Panic Disorder Without Agoraphobia has a slightly higher rate of success than the rate for Panic Disorder With Agoraphobia (Roth & Fonagy, 1996). Advances in our understanding of this disorder's nature and treatment have led to a significant and positive change in its prognosis.

PHOBIAS

Description of the Disorders

Phobias are characterized by two ingredients: a persistent, unwarranted, and disproportionate fear of an actual or anticipated environmental stimulus (for example, snakes, heights, being alone, speaking in public), and a dysfunctional way of coping with that fear, with resulting impairment in social or occupational functioning (such as refusal to leave one's home). People with Phobias often experience limited-symptom or full panic attacks when they are confronted with or expect to encounter the objects of their fear. Unlike attacks associated with Panic Disorder, panic attacks associated with Phobias are usually cued attacks in which triggers can be identified. Anticipatory anxiety often accompanies an established Phobia and may be associated with long-standing underlying apprehension and with avoidance behavior. People with Phobias typically are aware that their reactions are unreasonable yet feel powerless to change them.

Beck and Emery (1985) believe that a core concern involving acceptance, competence, or control generally underlies extreme, unwarranted fears or Phobias. They also suggest that people react to these exaggerated and disabling fears with self-protective primal reactions (fight, flight, freeze, or faint).

DSM-IV describes three categories of Phobia: Agoraphobia, Specific Phobia (formerly known as Simple Phobia), and Social Phobia. Specific Phobia and Social Phobia are quite common. Kessler et al. (1994) report a lifetime prevalence of 13.3 percent for Social Phobia, 11.3 percent for Specific Phobia, and 5.3 percent for Agoraphobia Without Panic Disorder. (Probably an additional 2 percent will have Panic Disorder With Agoraphobia.) All three disorders are more common in females, with Specific Phobia and Agoraphobia at least twice as prevalent in females as in males. The incidence of new Phobias is highest in childhood and then decreases with maturity, although many Phobias have a chronic course. Most Phobias develop suddenly, with the exception of Agoraphobia, which tends to have a gradual onset. Phobias, particularly Agoraphobia, Social Phobia, and Phobias of the Animal Type, seem to run in families, but whether this phenomenon is due to learning or to genetics is unclear. People with Phobias usually reduce their anxiety by avoiding feared stimuli but simultaneously reinforce their fears through this phobic avoidance. As a result, Phobias that have been present for longer than one year are unlikely to remit spontaneously (Maxmen & Ward, 1995).

Several explanations of Phobias have been advanced. The psychoanalytic model suggests that they develop in situations that cause great internal conflict, and that the internal conflicts are avoided through their displacement or projection onto these external situations. Social learning theorists view Phobias as due to conditioning, stimulus generalization, and secondary gains (for example, increased attention or avoidance of challenging situations). Cognitive-behavioral theory views Phobias as a result of illogical thinking, a category that includes such cognitive distortions as overgeneralization, selective perception, and negative views of the self and the world. Biological theorists suggest that some people have a biological predisposition for avoiding certain situations (Atwood & Chester, 1987). Clearly, many explanations for Phobias exist, and, as with Panic Disorder, a conclusive explanation has not yet been found.

Typical Client Characteristics

People with Phobias typically do not to have the pervasive pessimism of most people who are depressed or of those with Generalized Anxiety Disorder. Most people with Phobias see hope for the future and do not condemn themselves for their shortcomings. Their worries and self-doubts usually have a specific rather than a general focus and do not pervade all aspects of their lives. People with Phobias do tend to be apprehensive and tentative, however, fearing failure and exposure, particularly when they are approaching new experiences (Beck & Emery, 1985). They often feel vulnerable and have deficits in social skills and coping mechanisms. The particular nature of their Phobias may limit their social and occupational opportunities and cause conflicts in their relationships. One client, for example, a successful lawyer, had a Phobia related to driving. His job was accessible by way of public transportation, but when he and his wife began to discuss buying a house in the suburbs, he told her that she would have to arrange her work hours so that she could drive him to and from work. It was the resulting marital conflict that led this client to seek therapy.

Preferred Therapist Characteristics

Contextual therapy is often used to accommodate the client's limitations and provide in vivo exposure to feared objects or situations, and so the therapist treating Phobias needs to be flexible: treatment may have to begin at the client's home, for example, or be scheduled for places (such as elevators or dentists' offices) that evoke fear. The therapist needs to be comfortable taking charge of the therapy and providing structure, direction, and suggested assignments while developing a positive working relationship with the client. Kaplan et al. (1994) report that encouragement, instruction, suggestion, exhortation, support, and modeling on the part of the therapist can all contribute to the client's improvement.

Intervention Strategies

Many approaches have been suggested to the treatment of Phobias. Most approaches are derived from behavioral models of psychotherapy and involve exposing people to feared objects or situations. Unless the therapist has reason to believe that a person's Phobia is linked to a more complex problem (such as a history of abuse), treatment will usually focus primarily on the symptom itself. A range of techniques has been designed to reduce anxiety while increasing a person's comfort with a feared stimulus. Most approaches to treating Phobias are also structured and directive and include procedures for quantifying and measuring the nature of the presenting problem and monitoring the client's progress. For example, progress in the treatment of Agoraphobia can be reflected by the distance from home that a person becomes willing to travel and by the person's degree of anxiety while away from home.

Supportive therapy, group or family counseling, and cognitive interventions can all contribute to symptom reduction as long as they are combined with behavioral approaches that provide exposure to dreaded stimuli. Maxmen and Ward (1995) describe three approaches to providing this crucial treatment ingredient: flooding, graduated exposure, and systematic desensitization. Long, continuous-exposure sessions are generally more effective than short, interrupted sessions (Craske & Barlow, 1993). Most theorists advocate exposing people to feared situations long enough for their fears to be aroused and reduced within a single session. Some studies, however, have also substantiated the value of allowing people to leave frightening situations when their anxiety becomes too uncomfortable, as long as they rapidly return to those situations. Encouraging people to focus on their anxiety and control it through coping self-statements, thought stopping, and relaxation techniques seems preferable to encouraging the reduction of fear through distraction. The determination of which approach to exposure is likely to be the most successful, as well as of exactly how that approach should be implemented, will depend on the nature and severity of the Phobia and on the particular client. For example, massed-exposure sessions and spaced-exposure sessions can both be effective, but some people prefer not to participate in massed-exposure sessions, and their preference should be respected.

Flooding or implosion, the first of the three approaches described by Maxmen and Ward (1995), involves prolonged and intensive exposure (usually thirty minutes to eight hours) to the feared object until satiation and anxiety reduction are achieved. Marshall (1985) has found that teaching people to use coping self-statements enhances the impact of implosion. This approach can cause overwhelming initial anxiety, however. If not properly implemented, it can ultimately worsen fears and related physical and emotional conditions, and it is often unappealing to clients. Therefore, it is not often used, but it is sometimes helpful if the feared situation can easily be recreated without causing any danger, and when the client can be closely monitored. Maxmen and Ward (1995), for example, describe curing a man of a pillow Phobia by having him spend two forty-five-minute sessions in a room filled with more than one hundred pillows. By contrast, flooding would be an unlikely treatment for a driving Phobia because that approach clearly could create danger.

Graduated exposure, the second of Maxmen and Ward's exposure approaches (1995), involves having a person confront the object of a Phobia for a very brief time and then increasing the duration of exposure until the person can remain reasonably calm in the presence of the feared object for approximately one hour. This approach could be very effective, for example, with a person who is able to look at cars and ride in cars while others are driving, but who has the specific fear of driving a car. Initially, the person could be encouraged to drive the car in the driveway or on his or her own street for a few minutes. The driving time would then gradually be increased as the person became more comfortable with driving.

Systematic desensitization, the third approach to exposure treatment described by Maxmen and Ward (1995), involves setting up an anxiety hierarchy—a list of the person's fears, organized according to severity. The therapist begins with the least frightening presentation of the feared object (often a picture or other image) and uses relaxation techniques to help the person become comfortable with that level of exposure. Presentations of the feared object gradually move up the hierarchy, with the person becoming acclimated to each successive level. Systematic desensitization can be imaginal (conducted in the imagination), in vivo (conducted in context), or a combination of the two. Theoretically, for example, this approach could be used with someone who feared cars in general: treatment could progress from the person's viewing pictures of cars to being in the presence of stationary cars and then to sitting in cars, to watching others drive, to riding in cars driven by others, to driving with others, and finally to driving alone. Given the nature of this fear, however, the best treatment would probably be graduated exposure. More complex fears, as well as fears that are not amenable to treatment via graduated exposure (such as the fear of thunderstorms and the fear of snakes), can often be successfully treated through systematic desensitization.

Frances, Clarkin, and Perry (1984) suggest that in vivo desensitization can be conducted as effectively in group therapy as in individual therapy, with the group setting offering the advantages of support and modeling. With in vivo treatment the number of participants does not seem critical, but the duration of treatment does seem important.

A typical approach to treating Phobias is Wolpe's reciprocal inhibition, as described by Gutsch (1988), in which "a response inhibitory of anxiety is counterpoised with anxiety-evoking stimuli to weaken the bond between the stimuli and the anxiety" (p. 7). This treatment has two phases. During the assessment phase, clients learn to use "subjective units of disturbance," or SUDS, a rating of felt anxiety and distress. The SUDS scale ranges from 0 (reflecting a state of calm) to 100 (reflecting a state of extreme anxiety). When individuals have successfully used relaxation techniques to bring their anxiety below a rating of 10, the second phase of treatment can begin. In this phase, with the therapist's assistance, the individuals construct a rank-ordered list (an anxiety hierarchy) of anxiety-provoking situations and stimuli. Beginning with the least threatening situation or stimuli, clients imagine it for five to seven seconds and then experience an interval of relaxation lasting from ten to twenty seconds. As they become acclimated to the lower-level sources of anxiety, they progress up the anxiety hierarchy and deal with anxiety-provoking situations at higher levels.

The approaches that are successful in treating Phobias include several common ingredients:

1. Development of anxiety hierarchies
2. Relaxation
3. Imaginal or in vivo systematic desensitization, possibly via modeling
4. Encouragement of expressions of feeling, a sense of responsibility, and self-confidence
5. Attention to any family-related issues that may be impinging on the Phobia or being affected by it

Cognitive therapy is another approach that has been used successfully to treat Phobias, usually in combination with behavioral therapy. This approach views inordinate fears as being maintained by mistaken or dysfunctional appraisals of situations. The goal of therapy is to help people understand, normalize, and manage their fears (Beck & Emery, 1985). Therapy is typically brief and time-limited (five to twenty sessions lasting one to two hours), structured, directive, and problem-oriented. Socratic questions, designed to elucidate cognitive distortions and encourage the testing of their validity, are the primary mode of intervention. Manageable homework assignments are another central feature of the treatment and are designed to help people face their fears and test their cognitions. These assignments include such experiences as undergoing gradual exposure to feared stimuli, telling others about fears in order to reduce shame, and testing beliefs. The approach stresses the principle of overcoming fears by confronting them.

Medication contributes to the treatment of some Phobias but not to the treatment of others. (This point will be expanded in later sections of this chapter, which deal with the three types of Phobias.) When Phobias are not accompanied by severe depression or panic attacks, however, they generally do not require referral for medication (Maxmen & Ward, 1995).

Prognosis

As already mentioned, childhood Phobias often remit without treatment, but Phobias that have been present for at least one year are unlikely to do so. Most people with Phobias do not seek treatment for their symptoms, however, but tend simply to modify their lifestyles so as to tolerate their Phobias. This tendency is unfortunate because psychotherapy usually has a very positive impact on Phobias, and the prognosis for the treatment of most Phobias is excellent. Maxmen and Ward (1995), for example, report a positive and enduring response to treatment in at least 50 percent of people who received therapy for Phobias. Nevertheless, they report only 5 percent as being totally without symptoms after treatment; indeed, complete remission of a Phobia is unusual, and people do tend to retain mild symptoms after treatment, although functioning is much improved. The improvement seems to be well maintained (Lambert, 1982), and symptom substitution is uncommon. Some people do report an increase in depression after treatment, however (Lambert, 1982), as well as in marital difficulties, perhaps because the reduction of specific fears has given them the freedom to take a broader view of their lives and acknowledge other troubling concerns. Because treatment relies heavily on homework assignments, the client's motivation is a major determinant of treatment outcome. Family and social support are other important determinants of success: the treatment can be undermined by family members who have an investment in maintaining the client's disorder or who refuse to assist in the contextual application of homework assignments.

Let us turn now to an examination of the three types of Phobia described in *DSM-IV*: Agoraphobia, Specific Phobia, and Social Phobia.

Agoraphobia

Description of the Disorder

Agoraphobia, especially in association with Panic Disorder, is the most common Phobia presented by people seeking treatment. Agoraphobia accounts for 60 percent of all phobic disorders seen in therapy (Maxmen & Ward, 1995). (Other Phobias are actually more common but are less disabling and are seen less frequently for treatment.) Agoraphobia is increasing in prevalence, perhaps as a reflection of the increased isolation, alienation, and pressure felt by many people in our urbanized, highly technical society (Meyer & Deitsch, 1996). Agoraphobia can be diagnosed as occurring With or Without Panic Disorder (which itself was discussed earlier).

Agoraphobia is defined by *DSM-IV* as "anxiety about being in places or situations from which escape might be difficult (or embarrassing) or in which help might not be available in the event of having an unexpected or situationally predisposed panic attack or panic-like symptom" (American Psychiatric Association, 1994a, p. 396). This disorder reflects "fear of the marketplace" ("marketplace" being the translation of the Greek term *agora*).

People with Agoraphobia express fear of losing control and having a limited-symptom attack (that is, developing one or a few specific symptoms—for example, loss of bladder control, chest pains, or fainting). As a result of this fear, the individuals restrict their travel and may refuse to enter certain situations without a companion. Places from which escape is difficult (such as cars, barber shops, supermarket checkout lines, and crowds) are particularly frightening. Exposure to phobic situations typically triggers intense emotional and somatic anxiety, including such symptoms as dizziness, faintness, weakness in the limbs, shortness of breath, and ringing in the ears (Liebowitz, Gorman, Fyer,

& Klein, 1985; Wolfe & Maser, 1994). In severe cases of Agoraphobia, people may become housebound for many years in an effort to avoid their fears and symptoms. This disorder typically begins in the twenties or thirties, later than other Phobias.

Typical Client Characteristics

People with Agoraphobia tend to be anxious, apprehensive, low in self-esteem, socially uncomfortable, vigilant, concerned about their health, and occasionally obsessive. Depression, anticipatory anxiety, and passivity are common as well; they not only exacerbate this disorder but are also reactions to the circumscribed lives of the people who suffer from it. Medical problems are often presented, and people with this disorder may view those problems as the reasons for their limited mobility.

People with Agoraphobia often develop substance use problems in an effort to reduce their anxiety (Barlow & Waddell, 1985). Accompanying Personality Disorders, particularly Avoidant and Dependent Personality Disorders, as well as a history of Generalized Anxiety Disorder, Separation Anxiety Disorder, and social isolation in childhood, are often reported, along with a family history of Agoraphobia (Meyer & Deitsch, 1996).

Sometimes a person with Agoraphobia feels simultaneously dominated by and dependent on a significant person. This is often the "safe person," the one with whom the person who has Agoraphobia feels most comfortable, yet who also often contributes to the dynamics of the disorder. For example, a man's "safe person" may be his wife, but she may be covertly reinforcing his fears so as to maintain his need for her. Marital difficulties may also trigger or exacerbate Agoraphobia: the disorder can provide the secondary gain of cementing a marital relationship.

Agoraphobia sometimes follows an increase in responsibility or an actual or threatened interpersonal loss (Beck & Emery, 1985). Symptoms are particularly severe for some women just before and after menstruation (Barlow & Waddell, 1985) and are worsened by caffeine consumption. Inventories like the Beck Depression Inventory and the Mobility Inventory for Agoraphobia can be useful in assessing symptoms (Thyer, 1987).

Preferred Therapist Characteristics

The provision of support, suggestions, acceptance, and empathy is essential in the treatment of Agoraphobia (Chambless, 1985). Praise and reinforcement can also help the client take risks. The therapist's comfort with providing structure and contextual therapy, as well as with the client's initial dependence, will be particularly important.

Intervention Strategies

According to Kaplan et al. (1994), Agoraphobia that is seen for treatment is usually a part of Panic Disorder, and "if the Panic Disorder is treated, the Agoraphobia often improves with time" (p. 589). If the Agoraphobia itself is the target of treatment, however, then behavioral methods in combination with cognitive therapy are generally the treatment of choice. Analytic and psychodynamic techniques do not seem at all effective in treating Agoraphobia (Millman, Huber, & Diggins, 1982).

Not surprisingly, exposure to frightening situations—in sessions and through homework assignments—is the key element of most approaches to treating Agoraphobia, and many variations on this element have been developed. The client should remain in the exposure situation long enough, and should repeat the exposure frequently enough, for the anxiety to be diminished. This procedure is called *habituation*. Fear of habituation may precipitate the client's noncompliance with treatment and his or her premature termination; therefore, a carefully paced and supportive approach is indicated.

Trull, Nietzel, and Main (1988), reviewing nineteen studies that used behavior therapy to treat Agoraphobia, assessed pre- and posttreatment levels of Phobia and found both in vivo and imaginal desensitization to have brought about large positive changes, with in vivo treatment slightly superior. Other behavioral interventions shown to reduce symptoms of Agoraphobia include training in relaxation and assertiveness (Roth & Fonagy, 1996). Cognitive therapy—using such techniques as paradoxical intention (encouragement for people to welcome and exaggerate their fears), hypnosis, thought stopping, restructuring of negative thoughts, and training in positive self-statements about coping abilities—has also contributed to symptom relief, especially in combination with exposure (Hecker & Thorpe, 1992; Mavissakalian et al., 1983). Flooding, however, has not received much support in the treatment of Agoraphobia. Logs of panic attacks and of exposure activities are helpful adjuncts to treatment and can be used to assess and reinforce progress.

Both family and group therapy can also enhance the treatment of Agoraphobia; indeed, several studies suggest that family dynamics should receive attention in the treatment of people with Agoraphobia. For example, Hafner (1984) has found that those husbands who had adapted to their wives' Agoraphobia, as well as those who tended to be critical and unsupportive, demonstrated negative reactions to their wives' improvement, whereas husbands who were supportive and involved in their wives' recovery reported concurrent marital improvement. Apparently, some spouses undermine treatment and view a partner's improvement as a threat to the marriage. As for group therapy, treatment in a group setting can help reduce dependence on the "safe person" and can offer models and support.

The client's social and environmental patterns and relationships should be considered when treatment is planned. Millman et al. (1982) note that relapse is associated with marriages in which the client has been dependent and fearful of divorce, or in which improvement in the client's symptoms focuses greater attention on the spouse's inadequacies. The effectiveness of treatment has also been improved by home visits and by partners' involvement, either as coaches or as participants in family therapy (Meyer & Deitsch, 1996).

Medication, particularly drugs designed to reduce anxiety, is sometimes combined with psychotherapy in the treatment of Agoraphobia. For example, Telch et al. (1985) have found that treatment combining imipramine with exposure to feared situations is more effective than either alone. Marks et al. (1993), however, have found exposure in combination with a placebo more effective than alprazolam (Xanax) with exposure, alprazolam with relaxation, and a placebo with relaxation. Moreover, withdrawal from medication sometimes triggers a relapse. Medication does have a role in the treatment of Agoraphobia, especially when it accompanies Panic Disorder (Hecker & Thorpe, 1992), but medication alone clearly is inferior to exposure treatment and, even as an adjunct to psychotherapy, should be used with great caution, perhaps only for severe and treatment-resistant cases.

Prognosis

Approximately two-thirds of the people treated for Agoraphobia achieve significant improvement in symptoms and functioning, and most of these people seem to maintain their gains. Many continue to have underlying fears, however, and relapse is not unusual (Barlow & Waddell, 1985). Nevertheless, a relapse seems easier to treat than the original disorder.

Specific Phobias

Description of the Disorders

DSM-IV defines a Specific Phobia as "a marked and persistent fear that is excessive or unreasonable, cued by the presence or anticipation of a specific object or situation" (American Psychiatric Association, 1994a, p. 410). Common Specific Phobias include fear of dogs, snakes, heights, thunderstorms, flying, injections, and the sight of blood, but they may also involve unusual objects or situations, such as balloons or stairs with openings between the treads.

DSM-IV classifies Phobias into five groups:

- Animal Type
- Natural Environment Type
- Blood-Injection-Injury Type
- Situational Type
- Other Type

The Situational Type (for example, Phobias involving flying, escalators, and bridges), which usually begins in the middle twenties, is most common in adults; the Animal Type and the Blood-Injection-Injury Type are most common in children. The most frequently feared objects and situations include (in descending order) animals, storms, heights, illness, injury, and death (Kaplan et al., 1994). Females are more likely to develop Phobias, particularly of the Animal Type.

Adults with Specific Phobias recognize the excessive or unreasonable nature of their reactions, but the Phobias still may interfere with activities and relationships and may cause considerable distress. Exposure to feared stimuli typically results in high anxiety and perhaps even in a situationally related (cued) panic attack. Tantrums and clinging may be manifested by children in frightening situations. A minimum duration of six months is required for the diagnosis of a Specific Phobia in a person under the age of eighteen.

Phobias in children are relatively common, and most remit spontaneously; if a Phobia persists into adulthood, however, it is unlikely to remit without treatment. A Phobia may stem from a childhood fear that has not been outgrown and has been entrenched by avoidance, or the Phobia may begin later in life. Thyer (1987) reports that 60 percent of Phobias result from frightening experiences, 20 percent from vicarious experiences or modeling, and 10 to 20 percent from frightening information. Some people present multiple Phobias, but these often involve a common underlying fear that can become the focus of treatment.

The average age of onset varies and depends on the particular Phobia; most, however, begin either in childhood (especially between the ages of five and nine) or in the twenties. Phobias involving animals and blood tend to begin during childhood; claustrophobia, at about the age of twenty. Phobias involving heights, driving, and air travel usually begin in midlife (Lars-Goran, 1987).

Specific Phobias are quite common, with a lifetime prevalence rate of over 10 percent. In fact, as Meyer (1983) states, "most individuals have at least one mild, nondisabling Phobia of one sort or another" (p. 115). As mentioned before, however, only a small percentage of people with Phobias seek treatment for their difficulties; instead, the usual responses are modifications in lifestyle and accommodation to episodic anxiety.

Typical Client Characteristics

Very little information is available about common personality patterns in people with Specific Phobias, probably because the disorder is so pervasive and diverse and tends to be linked more to experiences than to personality traits. Nevertheless, people with Specific Phobias do have a disproportionate number of first-degree relatives who have similar Phobias and who may have communicated these Phobias to other family members (Thyer, 1987).

When anticipating or confronting feared objects or situations, people with Specific Phobias typically become agitated and tearful and may experience physical symptoms of anxiety, such as shortness of breath and heart palpitations. People with Phobias of the Blood-Injection-Injury Type sometimes faint in the presence of the feared stimulus. A medical examination may be a useful safeguard with fragile or highly anxious clients, to ensure that they can handle the temporarily increased stress caused by treatment.

Phobias are often accompanied by other Anxiety Disorders and may have been preceded by traumatic experiences. Both, of course, are clinically relevant. The therapist should elicit information on antecedent events and on secondary gains that may complicate treatment of the disorder.

Preferred Therapist Characteristics

Treatment of Specific Phobias is often anxiety-provoking to clients. A therapist who is supportive and optimistic about the outcome of treatment, and who can communicate acceptance and empathy while still encouraging people to experience frightening situations, is ideal. Creativity and flexibility can be useful in planning exposure and related treatments.

Intervention Strategies

Exposure, typically involving prolonged and repeated contact with feared stimuli, is clearly the treatment of choice for Specific Phobias (Schneier et al., 1995). In this approach, a list (usually including about ten feared stimuli) is developed. To facilitate the establishment of a hierarchy, each of the listed stimuli is then rated on a scale of 1 to 100 for the level of fear and avoidance it provokes. In vivo or imaginal desensitization is then used to lessen fear. This approach to treatment involves relaxation and exposure to one item at a time until the anxiety connected to that item is reduced to a manageable level. In vivo treatment is usually preferable, but imaginal exposure involving visualization and pictures can also be very effective, especially if it is combined with carefully planned actual contact with feared stimuli outside the treatment sessions. Some use is being made of virtual reality techniques to provide exposure treatment for fear of flying and other Specific Phobias.

Combining exposure treatment with encouragement to develop a sense of mastery usually contributes to the effectiveness of treatment (Emmelkamp, 1986). Exposure treatment can also be enhanced by the following techniques:

- Imaginal flooding
- Use of positive coping statements
- Paradoxical intention (focusing on anticipatory anxiety)
- Thought stopping
- Thought switching
- Success rehearsal

- Assertiveness training
- Hypnosis
- Cognitive restructuring
- Increased exposure to and awareness of internal cues of anxiety
- Modeling by the therapist or another
- Reinforced practice
- Supportive and family therapy

Cognitive techniques can also enhance treatment but are usually ineffective by themselves in the treatment of Specific Phobias.

Circumscribed Phobias, such as Dental Phobias or Phobias of the Animal Type, can often be treated in as few as two to four sessions. More complex Phobias, as well as the Blood-Injection-Injury Type, which may cause fainting, usually need somewhat longer and more gradually paced treatment. Thyer (1987), emphasizing the importance of practice outside therapy sessions, recommends eight hours of outside homework and practice for every two hours of therapy. Clients should be encouraged to keep a diary of their efforts, rating any distress that is experienced and gradually attempting to cope with more frightening situations while controlling anxiety.

Medication is rarely indicated in the treatment of Specific Phobias, but some people who are too anxious even to participate successfully in exposure treatment may benefit from medication (usually benzodiazepines) if it is taken before an exposure session to increase relaxation during the session.

Group therapy with three to eight members, using exposure and modeling, has yielded significant improvement (Ost, 1996); groups of three to four have been found more effective than groups of seven to eight.

Prognosis

The prognosis for treatment of Specific Phobias is generally excellent, with most people (70 to 85 percent) showing significant improvement (Emmelkamp, 1994). Often, however, some residual apprehension associated with feared stimuli remains (Linden, 1981). In general, the more motivated the persons are and the more anxiety they are willing to tolerate, the faster they progress (Thyer, 1987). If noncompliance is impeding treatment, the presence of secondary gains should be investigated.

Social Phobia

Description of the Disorder

Social Phobia is a very common Anxiety Disorder. It is defined by *DSM-IV* as "a marked and persistent fear of one or more social or performance situations in which the person is exposed to unfamiliar situations or to possible scrutiny by others" (American Psychiatric Association, 1994a, p. 416). Underlying the situational fear is worry that the person will do something or act in a way that will be humiliating or embarrassing.

Situations involving evaluation are likely to be particularly threatening. Actual or threatened exposure to such situations typically produces an immediate anxiety response that may involve noticeable physical symptoms, such as blushing, perspiration, hoarseness, and tremor (Morrison, 1995). These symptoms can contribute to worsening of the original fear by exacerbating embarrassment. Typically, people with Social Phobia avoid anxiety-provoking social or occupational situations. Social Phobia sometimes leads to social isolation.

Social Phobias often focus on one or more specific situations, such as public speaking, eating in public, taking tests, writing while observed, and being interviewed. People who fear most social situations are described as having a Generalized Type of this disorder.

Considerable impairment is usually evident in people with Social Phobia. They tend to be underemployed, have a relatively low rate of marriage, and may have panic attacks and suicidal thoughts related to the Phobia. As in Specific Phobias, adolescents and adults recognize the excessive nature of their fears, and a duration of at least six months is required for the diagnosis of this disorder in a person under the age of eighteen. Social Phobia is unlikely to remit without treatment.

One client who was typical of people with Social Phobia, Generalized Type, had married the daughter of a family friend and secured stable employment, but his life had still been shaped by his Phobia. He sought treatment at the age of thirty-five because he saw himself as harming his family: he had turned down several promotions because they involved leading meetings, and he refused to attend events at his child's school, because of his fear of meeting new people. He and his wife had little social life outside their immediate families.

Several explanations have been offered for Social Phobia, including deficits in social skills, conditioned responses to painful experiences, emotional blocks, and deficits in perceptual or cognitive processing. The onset of Social Phobia may immediately follow a humiliating incident, or it may be insidious (Fyer & Klein, 1986). Males and females are equally likely to seek treatment for Social Phobia, but the disorder seems to be more common in women. For both men and women, however, Social Phobia tends to begin in adolescence; it rarely begins after the age of twenty-five and, without treatment, usually has a chronic course (Judd, 1994).

Typical Client Characteristics

Social Phobia is associated with a broad range of accompanying disorders, notably Depressive Disorders, other Anxiety Disorders, Avoidant Personality Disorder, and Substance-Related Disorders, as well as with educational, marital, occupational, financial, and interpersonal difficulties (Schneier, Johnson, & Hornig, 1992). People with Social Phobia typically have low self-esteem, are fragile and easily hurt, are uncomfortable with new and unfamiliar situations, and have deficits in social skills.

These deficits can take many forms. For example, some people with this disorder mask their anxiety with aggression; others seem shy and insecure. People with Social Phobia have difficulty maintaining conversation and eye contact, seem awkward and stiff, and may talk too much about themselves.

For many years Social Phobia was believed to be related to a rejecting, overprotective family environment that lacked emotional warmth (Judd, 1994). Recently, however, biological abnormalities have been discovered in people with Social Phobia, a finding that suggests genetic and physiological components.

Preferred Therapist Characteristics

Clients with Social Phobia typically bring their interpersonal discomfort into the therapy room and feel threatened by the perceived need to perform for the therapist. An important role for the therapist, then, is to help clients manage the initial anxiety well enough so that they do not flee therapy before the process can begin.

Intervention Strategies

The treatment of Social Phobia is more complex than the treatment of a Specific Phobia because the impact of Social Phobia is usually broader and greater. Although the repertoire of useful behavioral interventions is the same for all phobic disorders, the treatment plan for Social Phobia is typically multifaceted and is aimed both at reducing fear and at improving socialization. Cognitive interventions are almost always integrated with behavioral ones.

In vivo desensitization, training in social skills, and cognitive restructuring are typically included in the treatment of Social Phobia. Relaxation and other behavioral techniques can also enhance the impact of exposure. Mattick and Peters (1988) have found the combination of cognitive restructuring and exposure more effective in treating this disorder than either one alone. Chambless and Gillis (1994), in a review of treatments for Social Phobia, have found the combination of anxiety management, exposure, and social skills training to have a high degree of success that was well maintained. Social skills training may focus on communication skills, tone of voice, posture, eye contact, or other aspects of socialization, according to the needs of the individual client. Cognitive therapy is especially useful in improving the accuracy of people's self-ratings, the accuracy of their perceptions of the likelihood of receiving negative reactions from others, and the accuracy of their assessments of the impacts of such negative reactions (Foa, Franklin, Perry, & Herbert, 1996; Rapee & Hayman, 1996). Some form of self-monitoring is also a valuable aspect of the treatment and may involve soliciting feedback from others, role playing, and rehearsal with videotaping or audiotaping, self-ratings, and ratings by others. Homework assignments, to facilitate the application of in-session learning, are almost always part of the treatment.

Group therapy is valuable for people who are not too incapacitated by Social Phobia to participate. The group interaction gives people the opportunity to learn new skills from others, experiment in a safe setting with new ways of relating, and receive feedback from peers. Scholing and Emmelkamp (1996) have found that group treatment using in vivo exposure was more effective than individual treatment of Social Phobia, Generalized Type.

Beta-blockers and MAOIs, especially phenelzine (Nardil), have been used in combination with psychotherapy, especially to reduce performance anxiety and improve people's ability to participate in therapy. Medication does not cure Social Phobia, however, and usually is not needed in the treatment of this disorder.

Prognosis

The prognosis is excellent for effecting significant and well-maintained improvement in Social Phobia in a relatively small number of treatment sessions (five to twenty). Only about 10 percent of clients will experience no improvement from treatment. Nevertheless, another 25 percent or so will continue to have discomfort and impairment related to socialization.

OBSESSIVE-COMPULSIVE DISORDER

Description of the Disorder

As is also true of Panic Disorder, great strides have been made over the last ten years in understanding and successfully treating Obsessive-Compulsive Disorder (OCD). According to *DSM-IV*, people diagnosed with Obsessive-Compulsive Disorder have obsessions (recurrent intrusive thoughts, images, or impulses) or compulsions (repetitive, purposeful, driven behaviors or mental acts designed to reduce anxiety or avoid a feared circumstance) or a combination of the two (American Psychiatric Association, 1994a). These thoughts and behaviors are distressing and interfere with daily activities and social and occupational functioning. People with OCD typically realize that their thoughts or behaviors are excessive and unreasonable yet are unable to get rid of them. In adolescents or adults who do not see the excessive or unreasonable nature of their thoughts or actions, the disorder is described as With Poor Insight. The course of this chronic disorder is typically static or worsens without treatment, although symptoms may wax and wane in response to stressors (Morrison, 1995; Rapoport, 1989).

Specific obsessions and compulsions are the hallmarks of this disorder and distinguish it from the similarly named but unrelated Obsessive-Compulsive Personality Disorder (OCPD), in which obsessions and compulsions are not present; rather, a perfectionistic or compulsive lifestyle characterizes people with OCPD (see Chapter Eight). In OCD, obsessions typically have some content that is unacceptable to the client (because it is immoral, illegal, disgusting, or embarrassing) and creates considerable anxiety. The client may also engage in magical thinking and believe that having a thought is tantamount to acting on that thought.

Compulsions, as already mentioned, are behavioral or mental acts, often ritualized, that are designed to prevent anxiety, discomfort, or unwanted thoughts and events. People with OCD usually have both obsessions and compulsions, and these are yoked in some way. For example, a woman who had obsessions about accidentally shutting her cat in the refrigerator also had the compulsion of emptying out and replacing the contents of her refrigerator several times a day, to be sure that the cat was not in there.

Four patterns are particularly common in OCD and are listed here in descending order of prevalence (Kaplan et al., 1994):

1. *Obsessions focused on contamination* are accompanied by excessive washing and avoidance of objects viewed as carriers of germs and disease. Anxiety, shame, disgust, and extremely limited activities are common in people with these symptoms.

2. *Obsessive doubts* lead to time-consuming and sometimes ritualized and repetitive checking (for example, of appliances or of door and window locks). Guilt and worry about forgetting something important usually characterize these people.

3. *Obsessions without compulsions* sometimes occur (usually thoughts of sexual or violent acts that are horrifying to the person).

4. *A powerful need for symmetry or precision* can cause the person to perform even routine activities (such as eating and dressing) with extreme slowness.

Common compulsions in addition to those just listed include counting, hoarding, repeating, ordering, asking for reassurance, and touching in some ritualistic fashion. About half of those with compulsions have a mixture of three or more rituals, whereas about one-third confine their rituals to a single place, usually the home (Mavissakalian & Barlow, 1981).

Obsessive-Compulsive Disorder is less common than Specific Phobias or Social Phobia. Its incidence in the general population is 2 to 3 percent (Kaplan et al., 1994). OCD seems equally common in both genders, but it begins earlier in males. The disorder can begin as early as the age of two, but it most often begins in the late teens for males and in the early twenties for females. The disorder typically has a sudden onset, which often follows a stressful event.

Many explanations have been advanced for the development of OCD. Psychoanalytic theory views this disorder as representing an underlying conflict between repressed sexual and aggressive impulses and efforts to inhibit them; thus compulsive cleanliness, using the defense of reaction formation, may be a way of warding off unacceptable sexual impulses. Social learning theory hypothesizes that the obsession or compulsion is a learned response, often received from parental models, that has been reinforced because it reduced anxiety. Interpersonal theory suggests that obsessions reflect an underlying fear of humiliation or loss of control, whereas compulsions represent an effort to maintain self-esteem. Behavioral theory posits a reinforced association between a source of anxiety and an obsession, and it views compulsions as reinforced ways of reducing anxiety (Atwood & Chester, 1987; Kaplan et al., 1994). Despite the inherent appeal of all these explanations, however, current research primarily supports a biological explanation for this disorder (Riggs & Foa, 1993).

Typical Client Characteristics

Because OCD is heritable, people with this disorder often come from troubled and anxious families. On the average, 20 percent of immediate family members of people with OCD can also be diagnosed as having OCD (Rasmussen & Eisen, 1991), and the disorder in itself usually causes people to have considerable family and interpersonal difficulty. The rate of celibacy of people with OCD is unusually high (40 percent), particularly among men (Shear & Frosch, 1986), and about half of those who are married experience significant marital difficulties (Emmelkamp, de Haan, & Hoogduin, 1990).

Many characteristic personality patterns have been identified in people with OCD. About one-third have a coexisting Major Depressive Disorder (Greist & Jefferson, 1995). Common concurrent disorders also include other Anxiety Disorders, Alcohol Use Disorders, Eating Disorders (especially Bulimia), Personality Disorders, and Tourette's Disorder. People with OCD tend to have rigid consciences and strong feelings of guilt and remorse. They feel driven and pressured, ruminate excessively, doubt themselves, are concerned with control, have a high need for reassurance, and tend to be indecisive and perfectionistic. They typically conceal their symptoms for years before seeking help, and they feel shame and guilt about their symptoms. They sometimes are aggressive and avoid intimacy and affectionate feelings. The disorder seems more common among the affluent and intelligent, possibly because of its connection to the capacity for abstract thinking (Steketee, 1993; Van Oppen, Hoekstra, & Emmelkamp, 1995).

Preferred Therapist Characteristics

Riggs and Foa (1993) describe the delicate balance between support and pressure that should be maintained by the therapist working with a client who has OCD. The shame, guilt, anxiety, and reluctance to self-disclose that are common in people with this disorder require a therapist who is respectful, encouraging, and flexible. At the same time, the therapist needs to be structured, firm, specific, and able to plan, prompting the client to cooperate with treatment and using confrontation and pressure as necessary to counteract the resistance to treatment that is common in people with OCD. Resistance is especially likely to impede treatment in people who are depressed and who have poor insight, overvalued ideations, and difficulty seeing the unreasonable nature of their thoughts and behaviors (Goldfried et al., 1990).

Intervention Strategies

The literature on the treatment of OCD is quite consistent in recommending behavioral therapy as the primary intervention, with prolonged in vivo and imaginal exposure to sources of anxiety (the obsessions), and with concurrent prevention of all dysfunctional efforts to reduce anxiety (the compulsions). The first step in applying this treatment usually involves obtaining a clear idea of the nature, frequency, and severity of the obsessions, compulsions, and anxiety. Instruments such as the Yale-Brown Obsessive Compulsive Scale can facilitate the gathering of that information (Steketee, Frost, & Bogart, 1996).

Both the exposure and the response prevention need to be carefully planned and controlled. The exposure typically is graduated, beginning with situations that evoke low anxiety and then moving on to higher levels of anxiety-provoking stimuli as clients become habituated to the lower levels. Riggs and Foa (1993) emphasize the importance of not terminating the exposure while the persons' level of distress is still high; thus exposure sessions should last from forty-five minutes to two hours, to allow ample time for anxiety to rise and then fall. Once clients have developed some comfort and familiarity with this procedure, they are encouraged to continue the exposure and response prevention at home, often with the help of friends or family members. The clients' keeping a written diary of these experiences is important in maintaining and solidifying progress (Greist & Jefferson, 1995).

Although exposure and response prevention are the essential ingredients of treatment for Obsessive-Compulsive Disorder, other treatment approaches and interventions have been combined with those components and have enhanced treatment. These include cognitive approaches designed to help people challenge their irrational cognitions, stop intrusive thoughts and ruminations, and avoid relapse (Roth & Fonagy, 1996), as well as progressive relaxation, stress management, and training in assertiveness, social skills, and relationship improvement.

Therapy for OCD is typically of relatively brief duration (sometimes fewer than ten sessions). Between-session assignments, however, as well as relapse prevention, are essential in effecting and maintaining improvement (Kelly, 1996).

Several studies have found that medication can enhance the impact of exposure and response prevention (Dattilio, 1993). The drugs most commonly used include clomipramine (Anafranil, a TCA) and SSRIs, especially fluoxetine (Prozac). It may be six to ten weeks before these medications have a demonstrable impact on the symptoms of OCD, but they can accelerate improvement. Other medications may also be used, especially if severe depression or anxiety are present, to pave the way for treatment.

The negative impact of OCD on social adjustment and family life suggests that family therapy may be a useful part of the treatment plan (Sherman, Ellison, & Iwamoto, 1996). Family therapy can normalize family members' feelings of anger, guilt, and confusion. It can also promote understanding of the disorder and engage family members in helping the person with the disorder. Group therapy (usually after some individual therapy) has also been shown to be helpful in the treatment of this disorder. Group therapy can decrease isolation, offer models and support, encourage self-disclosure and compliance with treatment, improve socialization, and provide necessary feedback.

Prognosis

Christensen, Hadzi-Pavlovic, Andrews, and Mattick (1987), having conducted a meta-analysis of outcome studies on OCD, conclude that psychotherapy and medication have "produced appreciable changes in obsessive compulsive symptoms" (p. 701). Riggs and Foa (1993) arrive at a similar conclusion: they report that 90 percent of people who completed treatment for OCD showed significant improvement, and 75 percent of that group had maintained improvement at long-term follow-up.

It is important to set realistic goals for the treatment of OCD. Although a high percentage of people completing treatment do experience significant improvement, incomplete improvement is far more likely than full recovery, according to Greist and Jefferson (1995). Even the common 50 percent reduction in symptoms, however, is likely to make a considerable difference in people's lives.

Factors associated with a positive prognosis include the presence of compulsions, low anxiety and depression, brief duration of the disorder before help is sought, the client's insight into the unrealistic nature of the thoughts and actions, the client's positive social and environmental adjustment, and the presence of an identified precipitant for the onset of the disorder (Kaplan et al., 1994; Maxmen & Ward, 1995; Meyer & Deitsch, 1996). Compulsions and checking symptoms seem to respond particularly well to treatment, but ruminations are often resistant to treatment (Roth & Fonagy, 1996).

POSTTRAUMATIC STRESS DISORDER
AND ACUTE STRESS DISORDER

Description of the Disorders

Both Posttraumatic Stress Disorder (PTSD) and Acute Stress Disorder involve a reaction to an extreme stressor that has caused or threatened death or severe injury. Extreme stressors include rape, combat, automobile accidents, and natural disasters, among others. A person's contact with the stressor may involve direct experience, observation (as with a firefighter or the witness to an accident), or vicarious experience (as when a friend, family member, or close associate experiences the stressor).

DSM-IV includes the following criteria as relevant to the diagnosis of these disorders:

- Great fear and helplessness in response to the traumatic event

- Persistent reexperiencing of the event (for example, through dreams, distressing recollections, or intense distress on exposure to reminders of the event)

- Loss of general responsiveness, and at least three indications of avoiding reminders of the trauma (for example, feeling detached from others, believing that one's life is foreshortened, and dissociating from or being unable to recall major aspects of the traumatic experience)

- At least two persistent symptoms of arousal and anxiety (such as sleep disturbances, anger or irritability, severe startle responses, and difficulty concentrating) that are apparently due to the stressor and are severe enough to cause significant distress or impairment

Common additional symptoms include shame, survivor guilt or self-blame, lack of interest in usual activities (particularly sexual relationships), alexithymia (inability to identify or articulate emotions), mistrust of others, withdrawal from close relationships, difficulty in self-soothing, fear of losing control or going crazy, and psychosomatic symptoms. Individuals often feel that their previous ways of coping and making sense of the world no longer work, and they are left feeling confused and without direction. Trauma-related disorders involve symptoms of anxiety in all systems—physical, affective, cognitive, and behavioral—but they always reflect the three major characteristics of these disorders: reexperiencing, avoidance and numbing, and increased arousal (Atwood & Chester, 1987; Calhoun & Resick, 1993).

The primary differences between Posttraumatic Stress Disorder and Acute Stress Disorder are time of onset and duration. Acute Stress Disorder begins within four weeks of exposure to a traumatic stressor and lasts at least two days but no longer than four weeks; it sometimes develops into PTSD. The symptoms of PTSD, by definition, persist for more than one month. PTSD is described as Acute if it lasts for less than three months and as Chronic if the symptoms last longer. The disorder is termed PTSD With Delayed Onset if the symptoms begin more than six months after exposure to the stressor.

The incidence of PTSD in the general population is approximately 1 to 3 percent (Kaplan et al., 1994). Incidence is much higher, however, in people who have had traumatic experiences. For example, 20 to 30 percent of Vietnam veterans, over one-third of people who have been raped or assaulted, and 75 percent of concentration camp survivors have developed PTSD (Kaplan et al., 1994; Roth & Fonagy, 1996).

Onset of trauma-related disorders may occur at any age, although children often do not recognize the sources of their symptoms. In children, repetitive themes during play and persistent nightmares reflect the trauma; agitation and confusion reflect their distress. Childhood traumas are often associated with subsequent delays in development (Kaplan et al., 1994).

Although people who have been through traumas may seem initially to have recovered, they are often left with residual and underlying symptoms (such as mistrust, avoidance of close relationships, and psychic numbing). These symptoms can last for many years and may be maintained by the use of drugs or alcohol, denial, and withdrawal. Reminders of a trauma, however, as well as other stressors or negative life events, can trigger a reexperiencing of the trauma, and the residual symptoms can develop into full-blown PTSD months or even many years after the original trauma (Buckley, Blanchard, & Hickling, 1996). For example, children who are sexually abused sometimes manifest no symptoms or awareness of the experience in childhood; such prominent symptoms as nightmares, reexperiencing of the trauma, and increased arousal may surface only in adulthood, when upsetting sexual or interpersonal situations are encountered, but these people's self-images and socialization have probably been adversely affected for many years by the abuse.

The impact of a trauma seems to be particularly severe and long-lasting when it has a human cause. For example, a rape is likely to be more disturbing than a tornado. The impact also seems to be worse if an event is sudden and unexpected, if the person who experiences it has had no prior experience of dealing with such an event (Atwood & Chester, 1987), and if people involved in the event are perceived by some as having deserved their fate (for example, if an accident has occurred as a result of engaging in high-risk behavior). If a trauma involves others who did not survive (as in a war or an accident), the survivor often experiences guilt along with the other symptoms of PTSD. Suicidal ideation, depression, somatization, increased impulsivity, Substance-Related

Disorders, and other Anxiety Disorders often develop along with PTSD. Future stressors become inordinately troubling, and the individuals sometimes feel permanently damaged, with little control over their lives. Some people even seem to undergo major personality changes after a trauma (Horowitz, Marmar, Krupnick, et al., 1984).

Typical Client Characteristics

The severity of a trauma certainly bears a strong relationship to the likelihood of a person's developing PTSD. Nevertheless, the subjective meaning attached to the stressor, as well as the person's functioning prior to the trauma, will also be important factors in determining the person's response (Kaplan et al., 1994). Therefore, the therapist needs to understand the client's prior functioning and interpretation of the trauma. Exploration of the client's pretrauma history, as well as the use of inventories like the PTSD Checklist (Blanchard, Jones-Alexander, Buckley, & Forneris, 1996), can clarify the presenting concerns. Factors that predispose a client to vulnerability include childhood trauma, preexisting mental disorders, inadequate support systems, alcohol misuse, recent stressful life changes or circumstances, and an external locus of control. For example, a four-year follow-up of children involved in the Chowchilla (California) school bus kidnapping found that all had some posttraumatic symptoms, but that the severity of these symptoms was positively correlated with the children's prior vulnerability, family dysfunction, and lack of community support. The aged, who often have few support systems and a limited sense of control, and young people, who have not yet developed good coping skills, are particularly prone to trauma-related Anxiety Disorders.

Preferred Therapist Characteristics

Resistance—manifested particularly by mistrust of the therapist, noncompliance with treatment recommendations, and missed appointments—is common in the client with PTSD or Acute Stress Disorder. Therefore, the therapist must be extremely supportive and provide a safe and secure therapeutic environment. Warmth, positive regard, empathy, and consistency are essential in building the client's trust. If the trauma occurred many years before treatment, therapy may be a slow process of gradually building trust and helping the person access the troubling memories. At the same time, the therapist should not reinforce the client's sense of being a victim.

People with these disorders may have strong preferences regarding the gender of their therapists; for example, women who have been raped typically prefer to have female therapists. To maximize the development of trust, the client's preferences should be elicited and respected.

Secondary or vicarious trauma can occur in the therapist working with a client who has experienced a trauma (Calhoun & Resick, 1993). Indications of secondary or vicarious trauma might be shifts in the therapist's sense of safety, view of the world, and feelings of vulnerability. The therapist whose caseload emphasizes trauma-related work is especially prone to these reactions. Awareness of the possibility of these reactions, balance in the therapist's life and caseload, supervision, and peer consultation can help the therapist deal with secondary trauma.

Intervention Strategies

Treatment for Acute Stress Disorder and PTSD should begin as soon as possible after the trauma, and preventive treatment is recommended even before symptoms emerge. For example, Jeffrey Mitchell has developed a group intervention—critical incident stress debriefing (CISD)—to provide early help for people who have undergone traumas (Everly, 1995). Designed primarily for groups of people who have experienced the same trauma—for example, the survivors of a natural disaster, an airplane crash, or an act of terrorism—as well as for police and firefighters who are involved in the aftermath of a trauma, CISD is ideally provided twenty-four to seventy-eight hours after the event. Groups of eight to twelve participants meet with facilitators for one or more sessions of ninety minutes to three hours. The emphasis is on caring, peer support, hope, and empowerment of the participants. Typically, facilitators guide the group through the following stages:

1. Introductions, information about the process, and guidelines for participation
2. Exploration of facts and information related to the trauma
3. Discussion of thoughts about the event
4. Exploration of emotions and reactions
5. Exploration of symptoms of distress, in order to stabilize, normalize, and facilitate a return to the cognitive domain as a way of coping with overwhelming affect
6. Teaching about reactions to trauma, symptoms, and risk factors
7. Reinforcement of coping skills, provision of information about stress management, encouragement of reentry (with offer of further help, as needed), and closure

A multifaced treatment plan that emphasizes cognitive-behavioral interventions seems best for the treatment of PTSD and Acute Stress Disorder, and exposure to the memory of the trauma is an important ingredient of treatment. Other interventions, however, are equally important to the treatment of these disorders. In fact, for people with severe symptoms, or for those who are very distraught or impaired, interventions designed to rebuild a sense of safety and control should precede exposure to the trauma.

Resick and her colleagues, for example, have developed cognitive processing therapy (CPT), designed especially for survivors of sexual assault. CPT is a twelve-session structured model in which exposure is combined with cognitive restructuring to change people's disrupted cognitions. Exposure is accomplished through information about the trauma, recollection of responses, and discussion of the trauma's meaning. Exposure must be handled very carefully to ensure that people are not retraumatized. It should include frequent reminders of safety and survival, be conducted in pieces, and continue until anxiety diminishes. Development of coping skills, changes in maladaptive beliefs, and provision of a safe setting all are essential to appropriate processing of the traumatic memories. Writing about the traumatic event is used in CPT but is always paired with training in coping skills. Written-out recollections of the traumatic event are first read to the therapist, who facilitates understanding, exploration of responses, and expression of emotions. People then are instructed to read their accounts to themselves daily, to habituate themselves to the experience and increase their understanding of the traumatic events and of their reactions.

Other approaches, mentioned earlier in this chapter, in the overview of Anxiety Disorders, have also demonstrated effectiveness in treating people with trauma-related disorders. Anxiety management training (AMT), for example, typically pairs prolonged activation of traumatic memories with techniques (such as relaxation, cognitive restructuring, and biofeedback) designed to modify these memories and the associated fears (Foa, Davidson, & Rothbaum, 1995). Stress inoculation training (SIT) includes education and training in six coping skills (muscle relaxation, thought stopping, breath control, guided self-dialogue, covert modeling, and role playing). Eye movement desensitization and reprocessing (EMDR) pairs visual stimulation (eye movements), kinesthetic stimulation (taps), or auditory stimulation (tones) with a focus on traumatic memories and associated negative beliefs (Shapiro, 1989). Preliminary research suggests rapid relief of symptoms when these techniques are used in conjunction with other therapeutic interventions.

In general, effective treatments of trauma-related disorders are designed to promote the accessing and processing of the trauma, the expression of feelings, increased coping with and control over memories (to dilute pain), reduction of cognitive distortions and self-blame, and restoration of self-concept and previous level of functioning. Other useful ingredients of treatment include education about the nature of trauma-related stress disorders, encouragement for assertiveness and mastery experiences, anger management, stress management, grounding, containment of anxiety, affirmations, and expressive therapies (involving art and movement). Hypnotherapy is often used to help people retrieve and deal with dissociated memories.

Some researchers have studied the impact of brief psychodynamic interventions on PTSD. Although some improvement seems to be effected through that approach, the results are not yet clear (Greist & Jefferson, 1995).

Development of support systems is another important ingredient of treatment for Acute Stress Disorder and PTSD. Peer support and therapy groups involving others who have had similar experiences can be particularly helpful in reducing a person's feelings of being stigmatized and alone (Marmar & Freeman, 1988); for example, group therapy seems to have become the primary mode of treatment for Vietnam veterans. Nevertheless, although a group made up of trauma survivors can provide considerable help, it can also contribute to an exacerbation of the trauma; therefore, the group therapist should screen participants carefully and should closely control disclosure of and exposure to trauma experiences in the group.

If symptoms of PTSD have been present for an extended period, the disorder has probably had a negative impact on social and occupational pursuits and on family relationships. Therapy with clients in this situation should usually assume a broad focus. Vietnam veterans with PTSD, for example, have had problems involving self-disclosure and expressiveness with their partners, physical aggressiveness toward their partners, and overall adjustment (Carroll, Rueger, Foy, & Donahoe, 1985). Therefore, therapy with troubled veterans has to go beyond the exploration of their traumatic wartime experiences and must promote improvement in communication skills, socialization, and trust of others. Similarly, people who were abused as children have a higher than average likelihood of experiencing abuse as adults, and this vulnerability may have to be addressed in therapy (Messman & Long, 1996). Moreover, because the initial abuse often came at the hands of a father or a stepfather, it has of course contributed to family difficulties.

Medication is generally not indicated for people with trauma-related disorders. Nevertheless, TCAs and MAOIs have both been associated with relief of symptoms and enhancement of the impact of psychotherapy when therapy alone has not appeared to be working (Kocsis & Mann, 1986; Roth & Fonagy, 1996).

Prognosis

Symptoms of trauma-related disorders often remit spontaneously within three months after a trauma. With treatment, the prognosis usually is also very good for recovery from symptoms that have not spontaneously remitted, especially for people whose functioning was positive before exposure to trauma, whose onset of symptoms was rapid, whose symptoms have lasted less than six months, whose social supports are strong, and who have received early treatment (Kaplan et al., 1994). The prognosis for treatment of Delayed Onset PTSD does not seem to be as good because that type of PTSD is often accompanied by another psychological disorder (Roth & Fonagy, 1996). Although people's vivid memories of their traumatic experiences cannot be erased through therapy, most people can be helped to resume or even improve on their former levels of functioning. Foa et al. (1995), for example, report a 91 percent rate of significant improvement after treatment that combined exposure and stress inoculation training. Relapses are not uncommon, especially under stress, but they may be averted through extended follow-up treatment. Kaplan et al. (1994) report that, overall, 30 percent of those with trauma-related disorders recover completely, 40 percent have mild symptoms, 20 percent have moderate symptoms, and 10 percent do not improve through treatment.

GENERALIZED ANXIETY DISORDER

Description of the Disorder

Generalized Anxiety Disorder (GAD) is another pervasive disorder that affects almost every system of the body: physiological, cognitive, motivational, affective, and behavioral (Beck & Emery, 1985). According to *DSM-IV*, people diagnosed with Generalized Anxiety Disorder have had "excessive anxiety and worry" about at least two life circumstances for most days during a period of at least six months (American Psychiatric Association, 1994a, p. 435). The worry is difficult to control, causes appreciable distress and/or impairment, and is accompanied by at least three of the following physiological symptoms (at least one in children):

- Edginess or restlessness
- Tiring easily
- Difficulty in concentrating
- Irritability
- Muscle tension
- Difficulty in sleeping

The most common affective and somatic symptoms of GAD include inability to relax (experienced by 96.6 percent of those with the disorder), tension (86.2 percent), fright (79.3 percent), jumpiness (72.4 percent), and unsteadiness (62.1 percent) (Beck & Emery, 1985). Somatic symptoms such as dry mouth, intestinal discomfort, and cold hands are also common. The most prevalent cognitive and behavioral symptoms include difficulty in concentrating (86.2 percent), apprehension about losing control (75.9 percent), fear of being rejected (72.4 percent), inability to control thinking (72.4 percent), and confusion (69 percent). For the diagnosis to be made, the symptoms should not be substance-induced or due to a medical condition.

Common secondary symptoms of GAD include emotional outbursts and hypersensitivity, reduced sexual and interpersonal activity, perfectionism, hypervigilance, and an exaggerated startle response (Michels & Marzuk, 1993;

Rosenthal & Rosenthal, 1985). People with GAD typically have low self-esteem, feel insecure, indecisive, and socially inadequate, and have strong needs for affection and approval (Speilberger, Pollans, & Worden, 1984). Children with GAD typically worry a great deal about their abilities. People with GAD are also prone to anxiety-laden dreams (Atwood & Chester, 1987).

Anticipatory anxiety is a central manifestation of GAD. The diffuse, unrelenting, free-floating anxiety experienced by people with GAD has led Maxmen and Ward (1995) to refer to them as worrywarts. According to Barlow (1988), anticipatory anxiety is a future-oriented mood state in which people are in a constant state of hypervigilance and overarousal in expectation of threat-related stimuli. The term *Generalized Anxiety Disorder* is clearly not a misnomer; the anxiety expresses itself through a multitude of pervasive symptoms that typically are without obvious immediate precipitants and that leave people feeling frightened and overwhelmed by what is happening to them.

Approximately 80 to 90 percent of people with GAD have had another mental disorder (Roth & Fonagy, 1996). Depression often underlies anxiety: Anderson, Noyes, and Crowe (1984) have found 37 percent of their clients with GAD to also have had a secondary diagnosis of a depressive disorder; other writers have reported an even higher prevalence of depression in people with GAD (Maxmen & Ward, 1995). Beck and Emery (1985) report that more than 80 percent of those with GAD have also experienced Phobias or panic attacks at some time in their lives. Substance-Related Disorders are also frequent companions of GAD.

This disorder tends to have a fairly gradual onset, often beginning in childhood or adolescence. The client usually cannot identify a precipitant for the disorder or report exactly when it began. People usually seek treatment when they are in their twenties (Kaplan et al., 1994). Without treatment the disorder tends to have a chronic course, but, depending on the coexisting stressors, it may wax and wane in severity. Some theorists view GAD as similar to a Personality Disorder because of its early and insidious onset and its characterological nature.

Lifetime prevalence of GAD is approximately 5 percent of the population (Kessler et al., 1994). As with most of the other Anxiety Disorders, females are twice as likely as males to experience GAD.

Barbaree and Marshall (1985) suggest that the intake interview for a person believed to have GAD gather data about the following areas:

- Relevant cognitions (as reflected by self-statements, expectations, fears, attributions, evaluations)
- Somatic and physiological complaints
- Relevant behaviors
- Severity and generalizability of the disorder
- Antecedents and precipitants

- Consequences for relationships and for responses from others
- Family and individual history of emotional disorders
- Previous attempts to manage anxiety
- Overall lifestyle

A comprehensive interview like this one can provide important information about the dynamics of the disorder, and this information in turn can dispel some of the client's fears about the symptoms. Inventories like the Beck Anxiety Inventory, the Penn State Worry Questionnaire, and the Anxiety Disorders Interview Schedule are also helpful in diagnosing GAD. A key diagnostic question (Brown, O'Leary, & Barlow, 1993, p. 140) is "Do you worry excessively about minor matters?"

Typical Client Characteristics

Generalized Anxiety Disorder seems to be especially prevalent among young adults with long-standing feelings of nervousness and a history of physical disease or substance misuse (Beck & Emery, 1985). Some research on people with GAD suggests that they come from disrupted families and have had patterns of adjustment involving dependence and low self-esteem. Feelings of tension, vulnerability, and lack of control, common in people with GAD, are believed to result from early life experiences (Brown et al., 1993).

Both men and women with GAD were likely to have had one or more negative, important, and unexpected life events associated with the onset of the disorder. For men, the number of such events was also correlated with the likelihood of developing the disorder (Blazer, Hughes, & George, 1987).

Preferred Therapist Characteristics

Information in earlier sections dealing with the ideal therapist for a client with an Anxiety Disorder is also relevant here. The therapist should also have a wide repertoire of anxiety-management techniques so that those approaches most likely to work with a given client can be selected. People diagnosed with GAD are sometimes resistant to treatment, primarily because of the ego-syntonic nature of their symptoms, or because of their attribution of the symptoms to medical causes. Therefore, a collaborative stance and good reasoning abilities on the part of the therapist will also be helpful (Brown et al., 1993). Nonspecific therapeutic qualities like warmth, empathy, acceptance, and the ability to encourage trust and collaboration are important in addressing resistance and promoting clients' involvement in treatment (Meyer & Deitsch, 1996).

Intervention Strategies

Many studies have been conducted on the relative effectiveness of cognitive and behavioral therapy in treating GAD (Durham & Allan, 1993). For example, Durham and Turvey (1987) compared two groups of people who had chronic anxiety and had received a maximum of sixteen sessions of either behavioral or cognitive therapy. They found that both groups had made equal progress at the end of treatment, but at six-month follow-up the people who had received cognitive therapy had maintained or improved on their gains, whereas the other group showed some decline. In contrast to the treatment of most other Anxiety Disorders, then, GAD seems more amenable to cognitive than to behavioral interventions, although a combination of the two is particularly likely to be effective.

The two targets of intervention in the treatment of GAD are excessive, uncontrollable worry and the persistent overarousal that accompanies it (Brown et al., 1993). Treatment approaches tend to be active and multifaceted and to include cognitive therapy, relaxation, training in anxiety management, and other cognitive and behavioral interventions. Several structured approaches to the treatment of GAD have been developed that incorporate these elements. Butler et al. (1987), for example, describe an anxiety management package for GAD that was based on the AMT work of Suinn (1990). The treatment involved teaching people to cope with anxiety via such procedures as self-administered relaxation and distraction. People receiving this treatment were also helped to take greater control of their lives and to schedule more pleasurable activities. Butler and others report considerable improvement as an outcome of this approach. Another approach to the treatment of GAD is reported by Brown et al. (1993). It involved both exposure to worry and prevention of worry-related behavior. This approach, reminiscent of the one typically used in the treatment of Obsessive-Compulsive Disorder, was used in group and individual therapy and typically included twelve to fifteen sessions. Clients were encouraged to confront their worries, and to do so without using distraction or any of the other dysfunctional means of avoidance that tend to increase worrying in the long run. The following techniques were used to help clients deal with their worries and become habituated to and reduce anxiety:

- Self-monitoring of mood levels
- Analysis and modification of catastrophizing and other cognitive distortions
- Relaxation training, including cue-controlled relaxation
- Problem solving
- Cognitive countering
- Time management

Many other effective approaches are also available for reducing the symptoms of GAD. Clients' and therapists' preferences, clients' lifestyles, and the nature of the disorder should be considered in planning specific approaches to stress management. The cognitive and behavioral approaches, to be described shortly, can facilitate the development of individualized, multifaceted programs for treatment of GAD. Cognitive and behavioral components will probably be emphasized over affective ones in the treatment of this disorder. Nevertheless, some attention should also be paid to affect, so as to facilitate the decrease of anxiety. Beck and Emery (1985) propose a five-step process, based on the acronym AWARE, for dealing with the affective component of an Anxiety Disorder:

A: Accept feelings. Normalize, identify, and express them. People are encouraged to go on with life despite their anxiety and to learn strategies like self-talk to develop some mastery of their anxiety.

W: Watch the anxiety. Seek objectivity and distance. People are encouraged to use diaries and ratings to demonstrate that the anxiety is situational, time-limited, and controllable.

A: Act with the anxiety rather than fighting it in dysfunctional ways. People are encouraged to act against their inclinations by confronting fears rather than avoiding them, and to deliberately seek out anxiety-provoking situations in order to inoculate themselves against anxiety.

R: Repeat the steps. People are taught that doing so will establish learning and facilitate the process.

E: Expect the best. People are encouraged to maintain an optimistic outlook.

Cognitive Therapy. Beck and Emery (1985) describe a brief, time-limited approach (five to twenty sessions) for treating GAD. This approach emphasizes an inductive/Socratic method of teaching (questions are the primary form of intervention), and homework is an important component. Four stages of treatment are described:

1. Relieving the client's symptoms
2. Helping the client recognize distorted automatic thoughts
3. Teaching the client logic and reason
4. Helping the client modify long-held dysfunctional assumptions underlying major concerns

The techniques suggested by Beck and Emery include the use of logic and educational (Ericksonian) stories, systematic testing and rational restructuring of beliefs, eliciting and examination of automatic thoughts via free association and behavioral tasks, use of the active voice, emphasis on how rather than why in inquiry, reattribution, decatastrophizing, and induction and modification of visual images. This approach is active, logical, and organized, emphasizing good therapist-client rapport and collaboration as well as specific interventions.

Behavior Therapy. The primary goal of behavior therapy for GAD is stress management. The following approaches are some of those available for helping people with GAD control stress:

- Progressive muscle relaxation
- Autogenic training
- Guided imagery
- Yoga
- Self-monitoring via logs of anxiety levels and anxiety-reduction activities
- Diaphragmatic breathing
- Meditation
- Biofeedback
- Exercise
- Expressive therapy
- Systematic desensitization
- Meichenbaum's (1985) self-instruction

Medication is not often necessary in the treatment of GAD. In cases where it is indicated, benzodiazepines usually are the drug of choice (Hoehn-Saric, Borkovec, & Nemiah, 1995). Drug therapy has been found to have a negative effect on the maintenance of improvement after psychotherapy is discontinued, however; people who take medication during therapy do not have a full opportunity to experience and deal with their anxiety and so are typically less tolerant of and less able to cope with any return of the anxiety. Therefore, medication for clients experiencing GAD should be used with considerable caution and should be monitored carefully; the inherent risks may not be worth the temporary relief of anxiety. Other approaches to anxiety reduction may be safer and at least as effective, if somewhat slower.

Prognosis

Spontaneous remission of GAD is uncommon (Gorman & Liebowitz, 1986), but most people who receive cognitive-behavioral therapy for GAD show significant and consistent improvement. In fact, approximately 60 percent maintain their improvement at six-month follow-up (Roth & Fonagy, 1996), although many will not be entirely free of symptoms (as is also the case with most of the other Anxiety Disorders). Treatment design should take account of the fact that this disorder usually does not remit fully. Therefore, treatment should include training in the use of preventive and coping mechanisms so that clients can be helped to continue managing anxiety and stress effectively on their own.

TREATMENT RECOMMENDATIONS: CLIENT MAP

Treatment recommendations for the Anxiety Disorders discussed in this chapter are summarized here according to the framework of the Client Map.

Client Map

Diagnoses

Anxiety Disorders (Panic Disorder, Agoraphobia, Specific Phobia, Social Phobia, Obsessive-Compulsive Disorder, Acute Stress Disorder, Posttraumatic Stress Disorder, and Generalized Anxiety Disorder)

Objectives of Treatment

Reduce anxiety and related behavioral and somatic symptoms of the disorder

Improve stress management, social and occupational functioning, sense of mastery

Assessments

Often will include physical examination to rule out medical disorder

Measures of anxiety or fear

Clinician Characteristics

Patient

Encouraging

Supportive yet firm and flexible

Concerned but not controlling

Calming and reassuring

Comfortable with a broad range of behavioral and cognitive interventions

Location of Treatment

Generally outpatient, sometimes contextual

Interventions to Be Used

Cognitive-behavioral and behavior therapy, especially in vivo and imaginal desensitization, exposure, and response prevention

Training in anxiety management

Stress inoculation

Problem solving

Relaxation

Assertiveness training

Self-monitoring of progress

Homework assignments

Emphasis of Treatment

Usually present-oriented

Moderately directive

Supportive

Cognitive and behavioral

Numbers

Individual or group therapy, according to the nature of the disorder

Ancillary family therapy as needed, particularly for heritable disorders

Timing

Usually weekly treatment of brief to moderate duration (eight to twenty sessions)

Moderate pacing

Possibly flexible scheduling, as necessitated by contextual treatment

Medications Needed

Usually not needed unless anxiety is disabling

May supplement treatment in some forms of Anxiety Disorders, especially Obsessive-Compulsive Disorder

Adjunct Services

Hypnotherapy

Biofeedback

Meditation

Exercise

Other approaches to stress management

Planned pleasurable activities

Prognosis

Variable according to the specific disorder

Generally good for amelioration of symptoms

Fair for complete elimination of signs of the disorder

Client Map of Roberto

This chapter began with a description of Roberto, a twenty-seven-year-old man who developed symptoms of strong anxiety after a visit to the dentist reactivated memories of childhood sexual abuse. Roberto's diagnosis and treatment plan are presented here according to the format of the Client Map.

Diagnosis

Axis I: 309.81 Posttraumatic Stress Disorder, Delayed Onset

Axis II: V71.09 No diagnosis on Axis II

Axis III: Fatigue, difficulty sleeping, other physical complaints reported, but no General Medical Condition diagnosed

Axis IV: Other psychosocial and environmental problems (childhood abuse); problems with primary support group (conflict with fiancée)

Axis V: Global assessment of functioning (GAF Scale): current GAF = 55

Objectives of Treatment

Reduce level of anxiety and accompanying somatic symptoms

Increase level of self-confidence

Reduce guilt and shame

Increase productivity at work

Improve relationship with fiancée

Help Roberto cope effectively with his history of abuse

Assessments

Referral to a physician for medical examination

Clinician Characteristics

Male (at Roberto's request)

Supportive and encouraging

Skilled at empowerment

Location of Treatment

Outpatient

Interventions to Be Used

Cognitive restructuring

Encouragement for retrieval and discussion of memories at a gradual pace and in a safe fashion

Cognitive restructuring for feelings of guilt, shame, and self-blame

Training in coping skills, including progressive relaxation

Encouragement for resumption of exercise program

Writing about abuse (after some improvement in therapy) and reading account aloud to the therapist, with use of coping skills to combat anxiety created by this process

Goal setting and realistic planning for resumption of previous lifestyle

Emphasis of Treatment

Moderately directive, to mobilize Roberto's energy and give structure to the treatment in view of Roberto's feeling confused, overwhelmed, and hopeless at the start

Moderately supportive, to bolster self-esteem and avoid adding the experience of even more threat

With abatement of symptoms, increasingly collaborative emphasis

Emphasis on exploration of the past (to help Roberto cope with the abuse), but also on current successes

Numbers

Individual therapy as initial mode of treatment

With lessening of Roberto's anxiety, several joint sessions with him and his fiancée, to help her understand what he was experiencing, encourage her to provide support, and help them both resume their previously close, positive relationship

Timing

Twice a week initially, for rapid reduction of anxiety, and then weekly sessions for at least three to six months

Moderately rapid pace, in view of Roberto's previous high level of functioning and the fact that Roberto was in considerable pain

Medications Needed

Not indicated

Adjunct Services

Provision of information about the prevalence and impact of abuse, especially for males

Prognosis

Good for significant reduction of symptoms

Optimistic but less positive for elimination of long-standing mild anxiety

Recommended Reading

Beck, A. T., & Emery, G. (1985). *Anxiety disorders and phobias.* New York: Basic Books.

Chambless, D. L., & Gillis, M. M. (1994). Cognitive therapy of anxiety disorders. *Journal of Consulting and Clinical Psychology, 61,* 248–260.

Craig, K. D., & Dobson, K. S. (Eds.) (1995). *Anxiety and depression in adults and children.* Thousand Oaks, CA: Sage.

Craske, M. G., & Barlow, D. H. (1993). Panic disorder and agoraphobia. In D. H. Barlow (Ed.), *Clinical handbook of psychological disorders* (2nd ed., pp. 1–47). New York: Guilford Press.

Meichenbaum, D. H., & Deffenbacher, J. L. (1988). Stress inoculation training. *The Counseling Psychologist, 16,* 69–90.

Rapoport, J. L. (1989). *The boy who couldn't stop washing.* New York: NAL/Dutton.

Suinn, R. M. (1990). *Anxiety management training (AMT): A behavior therapy.* New York: Plenum.

CHAPTER SIX

Disorders of Behavior and Impulse Control

George W., a thirty-six-year-old white male, was referred for therapy by the courts. After his third conviction for driving while intoxicated, George had been sentenced to a six-month stay in a work-release program. Therapy was a required part of his participation in that program.

George had begun abusing alcohol when he was fourteen years old and had been drinking excessively ever since. His father, his maternal grandfather, and two of his three brothers also used alcohol in harmful ways.

George had been married to his second wife for two years, and they had a year-old child. His first marriage had ended in divorce four years before, partly because his wife would no longer tolerate George's drinking. George had maintained contact with his two children from that marriage.

George was employed as a supervisor for a construction firm. He had been with the same company for more than ten years, despite frequent absences. He consumed little alcohol during the day but would begin drinking beer as soon as he returned home from work. George reported frequent weekend episodes of binge drinking, as well as occasional blackouts. He had repeatedly tried to quit using alcohol on his own and had been alcohol-free for six months at the time of his marriage to his second wife, but he stated that financial difficulties associated with the birth of their child had led him to resume drinking. George said that his wife was unhappy about his drinking and had expressed disappointment that they never went out socially, but he believed their lack of a social life really mattered little to her because she was so absorbed in caring for their baby.

George reported some mild depression and stated that he was shy and uncomfortable around people. He reported that alcohol had helped him to feel more self-confident and establish friendships with a group of men who apparently also drank to excess.

George had been suffering for more than twenty years from Alcohol Dependence, a disorder of behavior and impulse control. As is common among people with this disorder, George reported a family history of alcohol misuse. As is also typical of people with disorders of behavior and impulse control, George's mental disorder affected most, if not all, areas of his life; he presented with impairment in interpersonal, occupational, and other areas.

The possible diagnosis of an underlying Avoidant Personality Disorder was considered. George's problems otherwise seemed related to his Alcohol Dependence, which became the focus of treatment.

OVERVIEW OF DISORDERS OF BEHAVIOR AND IMPULSE CONTROL

Description of the Disorders

This chapter focuses on disorders that are characterized primarily by behavioral concerns, behaviors that are engaged in to excess (as in Alcohol Dependence, Bulimia Nervosa, and Pathological Gambling), behaviors that are engaged in too little (as in Anorexia Nervosa), behaviors that are inappropriate (as in the Paraphilias and Kleptomania), and behaviors that are unrewarding (as in the Sexual Dysfunctions and the Dyssomnias). All these disorders can cause impairment in social and occupational functioning, and many are even life-threatening. The following five categories of disorders will be discussed in this chapter:

- Substance-Related Disorders
- Eating Disorders (Anorexia Nervosa and Bulimia Nervosa)
- Sexual and Gender Identity Disorders (Sexual Dysfunctions, Paraphilias, and Gender Identity Disorders)
- Impulse-Control Disorders Not Elsewhere Classified (Pathological Gambling, Intermittent Explosive Disorder, Pyromania, Kleptomania, and Trichotillomania)
- Sleep Disorders

This section of the chapter provides an overview of diagnosis and treatment of the entire group of disorders of behavior and impulse control. Subsequent sections of the chapter focus on the five categories of disorders.

The prevalence of the behavioral disorders varies considerably. Some of these disorders (such as Pyromania and Transvestic Fetishism) are rarely encountered by most therapists; others (such as the Alcohol Use Disorders) are frequently seen in therapy. The primary symptom of all the disorders discussed in this chapter is undesirable behavior. Because many of these disorders typically begin in adolescence, however, persisting and often worsening without treatment, people with these disorders commonly have serious developmental and social deficits. Rather than benefiting from the normal developmental experiences of adolescence and early adulthood, people with behavioral disorders sometimes focus their lives around their dysfunctional behavior. When they finally do seek help to change their behavior, their failure to have developed age-appropriate maturity, self-confidence, and life skills complicates the treatment process and becomes an important secondary focus of treatment.

For many reasons, the disorders considered in this chapter almost inevitably affect how the people who suffer from them are viewed by others. People may be able to conceal an Anxiety Disorder or a Depressive Disorder from family members, friends, and colleagues, but a behavioral disorder is more difficult to hide because of its external manifestations (for example, intoxication or weight loss). Lifestyles and behavioral disorders are interconnected, with mutual impacts. Some of the disorders discussed in this chapter are illegal (such as Pyromania and Pedophilia); others (such as the Sexual Dysfunctions) involve a partner. Thus these disorders may damage relationships, career development, and self-image.

The time of onset varies according to the specific disorder. The most common ones, Substance-Related Disorders and Eating Disorders, usually begin during adolescence. Others, such as Kleptomania, tend to begin considerably later. Course and duration also vary. Some people respond to encouragement or exhortation from others to control their behavioral difficulties and may curtail or even eliminate their dysfunctional behaviors without therapy. This pattern is unusual, however, and these disorders generally do not remit spontaneously. Without treatment, most of them tend to become deeply entrenched and often worsen.

Typical Client Characteristics

Some of these disorders, like Alcohol Dependence or Abuse, have a strong familial component; others, like Anorexia Nervosa, are often related to a characteristic pattern of family interactions and expectations that predispose a person to develop a particular set of symptoms. People who present with disorders of behavior and impulse control sometimes come from dysfunctional families in which they were not afforded models of positive relationships.

Specific information on the particular personality patterns that characterize people with the various disorders is provided in later sections. Contrary to popular belief, however, people with behavioral disorders do not all have other underlying personality or emotional disorders. Some may have preexisting conditions that have contributed to the development of their behavioral disorders, and some may develop emotional disorders secondary to their behavioral problems, but many do not have additional diagnoses, particularly people diagnosed with Sexual Dysfunctions, Gender Identity Disorders, or Sleep Disorders.

Preferred Therapist Characteristics

Therapists treating people with behavioral disorders have diverse educational and experiential backgrounds. Some have doctoral or master's degrees. Others are paraprofessionals (sometimes called *mental health technicians*) with associate degrees, many of whom have had personal experience with the behavioral difficulties presented by their clients. These treatment providers are especially likely to be involved in the treatment of people with drug and alcohol problems. The establishment of a sound collaborative relationship between professional and paraprofessional therapists is an important element in the treatment of people with Substance-Related Disorders.

Therapists working with this population need to have not only the usual expertise in relationship building and strategies of psychotherapy but also a good grasp of personal and career development, as well as of family dynamics, so that they can assess and address the impact that a behavioral disorder has had on a particular client's overall development. These therapists also should have a good understanding of the nature of the particular disorders they are treating because education is typically an important component in the treatment of behavioral disorders. Therapists should also have a style of psychotherapy that is directive and structured and involves goal setting and follow-up but is at the same time supportive and empathic.

Therapists working with people who have problems of behavior and impulse control should be skilled in conducting group and family sessions as well as individual therapy sessions. They should also feel comfortable with incorporating self-help groups into treatment plans. Coordination of a multifaceted treatment plan is typically part of the therapist's role in treating behavioral disorders.

Intervention Strategies

Not surprisingly, the treatment of disorders of behavior and impulse control emphasizes behavioral interventions, such as behavioral counts, logs, and checklists; goal setting; learning, practicing, and mastering new behaviors; reducing or eliminating dysfunctional behaviors; reinforcement, reward, and punishment; and homework assignments. Exercise, relaxation, distraction, desensitization, role playing, and other techniques may also be incorporated into the treatment plan. Information and education are almost always a part of treatment as people are taught about the negative impact of their behaviors on their physical and emotional adjustment and as they learn new and more effective behaviors to replace the old ones.

In treatment of these disorders, group therapy is at least as important as individual therapy. People with behavioral disorders usually benefit from receiving therapy along with others who have experienced similar difficulties. Group therapy allows people to learn from others' successes and failures and to receive feedback and encouragement from other group members. Group therapy also enables people to increase their social interest and involvement and to develop their social skills. It facilitates reality testing and the challenging of defenses, offers points of comparison, promotes self-understanding and self-acceptance, and is often less threatening than individual therapy. Group therapy is particularly useful in the early stages of treatment, when motivation may be uncertain, but it usually is not indicated for people who are very fragile or disturbed.

Self-help peer groups like Rational Recovery, Alcoholics Anonymous, and Overeaters Anonymous are another important component of treatment. Whenever their inclusion is feasible, they constitute part of a multifaceted treatment plan for disorders of behavior and impulse control.

Family therapy, too, is a salient component of treatment for these disorders. Clients' behavioral concerns typically have had an adverse impact on family relationships, and help may be needed in that arena. Families usually also benefit from education about the nature of these clients' concerns and about how to help these clients maintain desired behavioral changes. Moreover, family members themselves (for example, the enabling husband of a woman who misuses alcohol or the overwhelmed wife who does not know how to cope with her husband's physical abuse) are often participants in patterns that contribute to the perpetuation of these clients' behavioral disorders. When family members are helped to change patterns that maintain, reinforce, and provide secondary gains for these clients, the likelihood of these clients' improvement is increased, and their families benefit as well. Multiple family therapy groups, as well as therapy for an individual family member, can provide feedback, support, and information, ameliorating family difficulties and improving relationships.

Medication is usually not the primary mode of treatment for behavioral disorders, with the exception of several of the Sleep Disorders, but it sometimes can contribute to the treatment process. For example, Antabuse may help people diagnosed with Alcohol Dependence remain alcohol-free, and antidepressant medication may reduce hopelessness and inertia in people with Bulimia Nervosa so that they are able to benefit from psychotherapy.

Many behavioral disorders, including the Substance-Related Disorders and the Eating Disorders, are physically harmful and even life-threatening. Other disorders that have behavioral manifestations, such as the Sexual Dysfunctions, Intermittent Explosive Disorder, and Hypersomnia, sometimes have a physiological cause. For both reasons, people who have many of the disorders discussed in this section should be referred to physicians for evaluation. Medical information can be useful in determining the most appropriate treatment plan for a particular individual.

Prognosis

The prognosis for treatment of the behavioral disorders varies according to the nature of the particular disorder and the motivation and lifestyle of the client. Perhaps the greatest barrier to treatment is the inherently gratifying nature of many of these disorders. For example, even though the Eating Disorders and the Substance-Related Disorders often cause physical, social, and possibly occupational difficulties for the people diagnosed with them, the rewards of being thin or being intoxicated are very powerful and are difficult to counteract in therapy, and relapses are common. The basic course of treatment may be relatively brief, but extended aftercare is indicated (via self-help groups, intermittent psychotherapy appointments, drug testing, medical examinations, homework assignments, and family or individual therapy) for consolidation of gains, prevention of relapse, promotion of adjustment, and assistance in coping effectively with the possibility of a relapse. With appropriate treatment and follow-up, and with motivation on the part of the client, the prognosis is good for significant improvement if not for complete remission of most behavioral disorders.

SUBSTANCE-RELATED DISORDERS

Description of the Disorders

The category of Substance-Related Disorders, as listed in the fourth edition of the *Diagnostic and Statistical Manual of Mental Disorders* (*DSM-IV*) includes two Substance Use Disorders (Substance Dependence and Substance Abuse) and a wide variety of Substance-Induced Disorders. The Substance Use Disorders describe maladaptive behavioral patterns of using drugs and alcohol; the Substance-Induced Disorders label symptoms such as intoxication, mood changes, and sleep-related problems that stem directly from maladaptive patterns of using drugs or alcohol. Consequently, a Substance-Induced Disorder typically will be accompanied by the diagnosis of one or more Substance Use Disorders.

DSM-IV describes Substance Dependence as "a maladaptive pattern of substance use, leading to clinically significant impairment or distress" (American Psychiatric Association, 1994a, p. 181). According to this definition, at least three of the following seven symptoms will be manifested at any time in the same twelve-month period:

- Signs of tolerance
- Symptoms of withdrawal
- Use of more of a substance than was planned
- Enduring desire or unsuccessful efforts to reduce use of the substance
- Extensive devotion of time to substance-related activities or recovery
- Minimal or reduced involvement in career and leisure activities
- Continued use of a substance despite the awareness that it is having a negative impact

Substance Dependence can be described as being With or Without Physiological Dependence; In a Controlled Environment (such as a prison or halfway house); On Agonist Therapy (such as Antabuse or Methadone); and in Early or Sustained, Full, or Partial Remission.

Substance Abuse also involves recurrent and self-destructive use of drugs or alcohol leading to significant impairment or distress. This disorder is characterized by at least one of the following four substance-related symptoms:

- Impairment in primary roles (for example, employee, parent, spouse, student)
- Recurrent use of drugs or alcohol in hazardous situations (such as while operating machinery)
- Recurrent substance-related legal problems (such as arrests for driving while intoxicated)
- Continued use of a substance despite the awareness that it is having a negative impact

Substance Abuse is often characterized by sporadic use of substances (for example, weekend rather than daily use) and entails fewer physiological effects and less consumption of drugs or alcohol than Substance Dependence. Nevertheless, Substance Abuse can also have a profound impact on a person's lifestyle and is often a precursor of Substance Dependence. Substance Abuse can be diagnosed only in people who have never met the criteria for Substance Dependence related to the particular substance in question.

DSM-IV specifies eleven classes of psychoactive substances that often are used in maladaptive ways:

- Alcohol
- Amphetamines and amphetaminelike substances
- Caffeine
- Cannabis
- Cocaine
- Hallucinogens
- Inhalants
- Nicotine
- Opioids
- Phencyclidine (PCP) or phencyclidinelike substances
- Sedatives, hypnotics, and anxiolytics

DSM-IV also includes Other or Unknown Substance Use Disorders and Polysubstance Dependence, which involve the use of three or more categories of substances (not including caffeine), with no one substance predominating during a twelve-month period. In diagnosing a Substance Use Disorder, the clinician specifies the substance. Substance Use Disorders do not necessarily entail long-standing and pervasive impairment; in fact, most people who misuse drugs or alcohol are employed and have families. Nevertheless, Substance Use Disorders typically have a powerful negative impact on the users, as well as on the people who are close to them.

Substance-Induced Disorders vary from substance to substance; their manifestations depend on the impacts of specific substances. This category includes the following disorders:

- Substance Intoxication
- Substance Withdrawal
- Substance-Induced Delirium
- Substance-Induced Persisting Dementia
- Substance-Induced Persisting Amnestic Disorder
- Substance-Induced Psychotic Disorder
- Substance-Induced Mood Disorder
- Substance-Induced Anxiety Disorder
- Substance-Induced Sexual Dysfunction
- Substance-Induced Sleep Disorder

According to Maxmen and Ward (1995), 19.2 percent of the population of the United States will meet the criteria for a Substance-Related Disorder (not including disorders of nicotine use) at some point in their lives. Nearly 15 percent of the population will meet the criteria for an Alcohol-Related Disorder, and more than 5 percent will meet the criteria for a Drug-Related Disorder (Kaplan, Sadock, & Grebb, 1994). Substance-Related Disorders are particularly prevalent among young adults between the ages of eighteen and twenty-five, men, African Americans, people living in large urban areas, people living in the western part of the United States, and people who are unemployed. Medical professionals have an elevated incidence of Substance Use Disorders, perhaps because of their easy access to drugs.

Many causes have been suggested as explanations of Substance Use Disorders. Early views of drug and alcohol misuse (as regressive, as reflecting a defense against unacceptable impulses, and as reflecting immoral behavior) have largely been discredited. Current theories are more likely to view Substance Use Disorders as adaptive and defensive although dysfunctional (Kaplan et al., 1994).

The medical (or disease) model of addiction, developed by Jellinek, is primarily focused on explaining dysfunctional use of alcohol. This model underlies Alcoholics Anonymous and other Twelve-Step programs and has been widely accepted for many years (Fisher & Harrison, 1997).

Most theoreticians view Substance Use Disorders as having many determinants from many spheres—biological, cultural, environmental, behavioral (anxiety relief, reinforcement of positive affect), interpersonal (social, familial), and intrapersonal (developmental, cognitive, affective)—but no conclusive explanation has been found yet for these disorders.

Typical Client Characteristics

The search for an addictive personality has not been particularly fruitful, although some researchers believe that certain personality patterns predispose people toward Substance-Related Disorders. Forrest (1985) views those who misuse substances as having been hurt by significant others, as experiencing life-long anxiety, as seeking a sense of identity, and as being depressed, dependent, avoidant, suspicious, and guilt-ridden. To some extent, these characteristics may stem from people's efforts to conceal their substance use from others and to defend their use of drugs and alcohol. People who use drugs or alcohol in maladaptive ways may have learned to cope through dishonesty, placating, or abusing others, and these patterns may be carried into their therapy.

Approximately two-thirds of those with Substance Use Disorders have another coexisting disorder. A second Substance Use Disorder is most common, but other disorders that often accompany a Substance Use Disorder include Personality Disorders (especially Antisocial Personality Disorder), Depressive Disorders, Phobias, and Sexual Dysfunctions (Maxmen & Ward, 1995). The coexisting disorders may be preexisting conditions or may be initiated or worsened by substance use. Sometimes the substance use reflects an effort at self-medication for another mental disorder. People with a family history of alcohol misuse, as well as people who use opioids, are particularly likely to have coexisting mental disorders. This pattern of dual disorders is difficult to treat because it becomes a vicious cycle: the substance use worsens the coexisting disorder, which in turn increases the person's tendency to use drugs or alcohol to self-medicate. Often, moreover, the substance use masks the symptoms of the underlying disorder, further complicating the treatment picture.

Suicide and suicidal ideation are common in people with Substance-Related Disorders and seem to increase as substance use increases (Fowler, Rich, & Young, 1986). This is particularly worrisome because people who misuse substances have an available lethal weapon—drugs or alcohol—and the combination of intoxication and depression may lead a binge to become a suicide attempt. With the use of multiple drugs becoming increasingly the norm, suicide becomes even easier via a mixture of drugs (such as alcohol and tranquilizers).

Substance Use Disorders, particularly Alcohol Dependence and Alcohol Abuse, tend to run in families. Leigh (1985) has found that family members tend to use the same drugs, and in similar amounts. This pattern can affect people with Substance Use Disorders in many ways. If they have grown up in homes where using substances was modeled and accepted, this experience may have prompted and entrenched their use of substances. Such a home environment is likely to be dysfunctional and to have serious shortcomings in terms of the life skills that are demonstrated and passed on to the children. People who misuse substances also typically have a negative impact on their own partners and children and can contribute to Substance Use Disorders in the next generation. Therapy, then, will have to go beyond the immediate presenting problem and focus on addressing interpersonal and occupational impairment. It also should reach out to family members who have their own problems with substances or who are being adversely affected by the client's substance use.

Preferred Therapist Characteristics

Roher, Thomas, and Yasenchak (1992), having surveyed people in residential programs that treat Substance Use Disorders, describe the ideal therapist as understanding, concerned, caring, experienced, honest, streetwise, a good listener, easy to talk to, direct, fair, respectful, and open-minded. According to these researchers, clients with Substance Use Disorders also prefer therapists who are well educated and have appropriate professional credentials. The authors report the African American clients in these programs as especially disliking therapists they perceive as lazy, weak, or unfair, whereas females with Substance Use Disorders are reported to dislike therapists who use obscenities.

Therapists working with people who misuse substances must be prepared to deal with resistance, hostility, manipulativeness, and deception. Indeed, one challenge therapists face is reversal of resistance and deception and development of an honest relationship. Resistance certainly is not present in all people seeking help for problems with substance use, but it is common. Therapists need to find appropriate ways of handling their own reactions to clients' reluctance to change and should continue communicating empathy, optimism, and acceptance to even the most hostile and resistant clients.

Building rapport with clients who misuse substances is sometimes difficult because support, caring, and empathy have to be combined with a straightforward and realistic approach that may involve confrontation, persuasion, monitoring, and limit setting. Care should always be taken to empower and support clients and help them feel safe rather than to denigrate and humiliate them.

Clients' emphasis on therapists' experience, as well as on their own rapport with therapists who treat Substance Use Disorders (Roher et al., 1992), supports the use of paraprofessional counselors collaborating with therapists who have graduate-level training. Because of the preponderance of people providing treatment who are themselves recovering from problems with substance use, the therapist's own history is often of interest to the client. Bratter (1985) suggests that some judicious sharing of the therapist's own experiences, whether or not the therapist has had problems with substances, can promote rapport and straightforwardness in the therapeutic relationship. Nevertheless, the focus should be kept on the client's concerns, and the therapist should not assume that what has been personally helpful will necessarily be helpful to others.

Intervention Strategies

Refusal to seek treatment and denial of the severity of their symptoms is common among people who misuse substances. If a person clearly needs treatment for a Substance Use Disorder but is reluctant to obtain help, a therapist often will assist friends and family members in organizing what is called an *intervention*. Developed by Vernon Johnson (1986), founder of the Johnson Institute, this approach involves having two or more people concerned about someone's substance use meet with that person, usually along with a therapist, to present information on the negative impact of the person's use of substances and encourage the person to accept help. Typically, treatment is prearranged, and consequences (such as loss of a job or a relationship) if the person does not agree to treatment are clearly stated. Interventions have been shown to be highly successful both at involving a person in treatment and at leading to a positive outcome (Fisher & Harrison, 1997).

Because of the prevalence of dual diagnoses in people with Substance Use Disorders, careful assessment and diagnosis are essential before treatment is planned. Inventories like the Michigan Alcoholism Screening Test and the Addiction Severity Index can facilitate the assessment process (George, 1990). A urinalysis and other laboratory-analyzed tests, as well as a medical examination, can provide further information on the nature of a person's substance use and its physiological impact.

These screening procedures can help determine whether detoxification or a residential treatment program is needed or whether outpatient treatment is sufficient. People's reluctance to leave jobs and families, and cutbacks in insurance payments for inpatient treatment of Substance Use Disorders, have led to a reduction in the length and availability of residential treatment. If a person is physiologically addicted to a substance, however, or if resistance and danger to the himself or herself and to others is high, inpatient treatment may be the best first step in treatment.

Some people seem to deteriorate after detoxification. Memory problems and other mild cognitive deficits emerge, and people may develop anxiety and feelings of being out of control. If these symptoms are not dealt with through education and therapy, they can frighten people into a relapse. The early stages of recovery are tenuous, and close monitoring and support are needed.

Therapeutic communities or partial hospitalization programs are available for people who are not ready to live independently immediately after detoxification, or who have failed to respond positively to outpatient programs in the past. Such transitional programs can help people locate employment and develop the skills and resources necessary for becoming self-sufficient. Token economies, sometimes used in these programs, offer people additional motivation to change and can solidify their resolve to stop using drugs or alcohol. Therapeutic communities can be particularly helpful to people with few resources and support systems, as well as to those whose peer groups and places of residence have promoted such dysfunctional use of substances that a comprehensive life change is required in order to facilitate abstinence.

Morgenstern and McCrady (1992) organize the treatments for Substance Use Disorders into four categories:

- General psychotherapy
- Behaviorally oriented therapy
- Disease model of treatment
- Pharmacology

Programs designed to help people with Substance Use Disorders typically are behaviorally oriented, with abstinence as the goal. Contracts are useful in affirming this goal and in specifying the steps that people can take when they feel the desire for drugs or alcohol. Behavioral therapy usually is conducted in a group setting so that participants can reinforce and confront each other, as appropriate, and serve as role models and sources of support and information. Behavioral group therapy for people with Substance Use Disorders includes such approaches as relaxation training, assertiveness training, role playing, stress management, development of other sources of gratification, and offering help for people to cope with the urge to misuse substances and be involved in high-risk situations.

Programs that adopt a medical model or disease concept of treatment typically begin by educating clients about the concept. Treatment approaches associated with this model include emphasizing the importance of spirituality in recovery, encouraging people to become involved in a Twelve-Step program like Alcoholics Anonymous, linking clients with sponsors, and helping them work their way through the steps.

An example of general psychotherapy for people with Substance Use Disorders is advanced by Forrest (1985), who suggests an eclectic approach to treatment that involves behavior therapy (as already described), abstinence, and self-help groups. It also includes what Forrest calls "genetic reconstruction" to help people come to terms with the past, accept reality, and modify their defenses. Interpretation and insight are used to help people understand and manage their feelings. Other approaches that Forrest suggests as supplements to treatment include aversive conditioning, cognitive restructuring, and, in the later stages of recovery, existential therapy to promote the decision to establish a different lifestyle. Forrest reports abstinence on five-year follow-up in 50 percent of clients with six to eight months of this sort of general psychotherapy.

Psychopharmacology can enhance the treatment of Substance Use Disorders in two ways. First, it can help alleviate the symptoms of disorders like Schizophrenia or a Bipolar Disorder, which may be contributing to people's dysfunctional use of substances (for example, if they are using substances as self-medication), and which may also be causing people to have poor judgment. Second, psychopharmacology is sometimes used to help in directly modifying a person's use of substances (for example, methadone is used to modify use of heroin, and Antabuse is used to discourage a person from drinking alcohol). Although psychopharmacology does have a place in the treatment of Substance Use Disorders, drugs must be used judiciously with people who already are prone to misuse substances. Moreover, medication as the primary mode of treatment may interfere with people's ability to learn the skills they need in order to remain abstinent and improve their lives.

Education is an important component of most drug and alcohol treatment programs. Understanding the negative effects of drugs and alcohol, as well as recognizing, in themselves, the triggers and patterns of misuse, can contribute to people's motivation and enable them to deal more effectively with the challenge of abstinence.

For many people, substance use is reinforced by peer groups, and group counseling, as well as self-help programs, can counteract that influence. Self-help groups like Alcoholics Anonymous, Rational Recovery, Women for Sobriety, and Narcotics Anonymous are almost always part of the treatment plan for problems of substance use and become a central ingredient of most aftercare programs. Self-help programs also have groups for family members (for example, Al-Anon, Alateen, and Adult Children of Alcoholics) that are useful in helping them deal with the impact on them of another family member's maladaptive substance use and encourage that family member's recovery.

In addition to direct treatment for substance use, therapy should focus on any developmental or lifestyle deficits that may be present. Many people with Substance Use Disorders need assistance with career development and job seeking, socialization and communication, parenting, developing drug-free leisure activities, and improving relationships. If a coexisting disorder is present in addition to the Substance Use Disorder, treatment is most likely to be effective if both problem areas are addressed (Frances & Allen, 1986).

Substance use and relapse are associated with stressful life events. To prevent a setback when things are not going well, therapy should help people look realistically at their lives, make needed changes, and develop coping mechanisms so that they are better prepared to deal with future stress.

Therapy with people who have Substance Use Disorders typically follows a series of stages:

- Identifying the problem
- Taking a detailed history
- Providing detoxification, as needed
- Helping motivate people toward change
- Setting goals
- Providing education and interventions to develop coping mechanisms
- Offering concurrent involvement in family therapy and self-help groups
- Maintaining change via follow-up and relapse prevention.

Reid's (1983) conclusion that no single approach to treatment seems best for Substance Use Disorders still seems correct. Instead, a combination of interventions (including but not limited to detoxification, education, individual and group behavior therapy, general psychotherapy, multiple family therapy, assertiveness training, self-help groups, and psychopharmacology), individualized to meet the needs of a particular person, seems ideal.

Prognosis

Relapse, especially within the first year after treatment, is common for people who have been treated for Substance Use Disorders. George (1990) reports a 37 percent relapse rate within the first year and a 70 percent relapse rate sometime after treatment. Nevertheless, approximately one-third do remain abstinent, and another third are significantly improved after treatment (Fisher & Harrison, 1997). Treatment of Substance Use Disorders has a particularly positive prognosis for people who have stable work and family lives, who manifest little or no accompanying antisocial behavior, and who do not have family histories of alcohol problems (Frances & Allen, 1986). The prognosis is also good for people who comply with treatment, who can see the positive consequences of abstaining from drugs and alcohol, and who do not have strong guilt and low self-esteem. The prognosis is less optimistic for people with coexisting emotional disorders; in fact, the more severe the accompanying diagnosis, the worse the prognosis (O'Brien, Woody, & McLellan, 1984). The overall emotional health of the client, then, is usually a better predictor of outcome than is the severity of the Substance Use Disorder (McLellan et al., 1983).

The next two major sections of this chapter—on disorders related to alcohol and drugs, respectively—provide an overview of the nature and treatment of some of the specific Substance Use Disorders. In each section, the primary focus will be on the Use Disorders (Abuse and Dependence) rather than on the Induced Disorders, which can vary widely and often require medical intervention. (Nevertheless, the therapist must always determine whether a Substance Use Disorder is accompanied by one or more Induced Disorders, and treatment must take account of the combination of disorders that are present.)

Alcohol-Related Disorders

Description of the Disorders

Alcohol-Related Disorders represent a large and costly health problem in the United States: 10 percent of women and 20 percent of men have met the criteria for Alcohol Abuse at some point in their lives, and 10 percent of men and 3 to 5 percent of women have met the criteria for Alcohol Dependence (Kaplan et al., 1994); fewer than 5 percent of these people are stereotypical Skid Row alcohol users. Approximately two hundred thousand deaths each year are directly attributable to alcohol use, a total that comprises 25 percent of all suicides and 50 percent of homicides as well as a large percentage of automobile and other kinds of accidents. The only positive note is that for the past twenty years alcohol use has declined or remained stable for most age groups.

Alcohol-Related Disorders tend to begin in adolescence or early adulthood, especially for males; they rarely begin after the age of forty-five, and they sometimes remit spontaneously in midlife. People between the ages of twenty and thirty-five are most likely to misuse alcohol.

Men and women typically have different patterns of alcohol use. Women who consume alcohol to excess are more likely to drink alone, to feel guilty and attempt to conceal their drinking, to combine alcohol with other drugs, and to suffer from depression, anxiety, and insomnia. Alcohol problems seem to start later and progress faster in women and are more closely linked to stressful life circumstances (McDonough & Russell, 1994).

Some ethnic groups have a higher prevalence of alcohol problems than others. People from Irish, American Indian, or Eskimo cultures, for example, are overrepresented among those with alcohol problems; those from Asian and Jewish cultures are underrepresented (Atwood & Chester, 1987; Kaplan et al., 1994). Alcohol-Related Disorders typically are less prevalent in groups where alcohol is an accepted part of dining or religion rather than being used primarily for recreation. Several models, described in the paragraphs that follow, have been advanced to explain the development of Alcohol Use Disorders.

Medical or Disease Model. The medical or disease model suggests that some people have an inborn vulnerability to the physiological effects of alcohol, a vulnerability that is activated when they begin to consume alcohol. This theory is largely based on the belief that brain abnormalities, notably neurotransmitter deficits, can be inherited and may predispose people to maladaptive use of alcohol. The theory that underlies the medical or disease model has received some support from studies of twins and seems to be borne out particularly by men. People with first-degree relatives who have an Alcohol-Related Disorder are three to four times more likely than people without such a family history to develop an Alcohol-Related Disorder. This model is the most widely accepted of those discussed here.

Family Systems Model. According to this model, dysfunctional use of alcohol is passed on from one generation to the next, either through modeling or genetic transmission. Although the medical or disease model offers the most widely accepted explanation for alcohol misuse, the family systems model is also important in our current understanding of Alcohol Use Disorders.

Behavioral/Social Learning Model. According to this model, alcohol use is reinforced by its immediate social and physiological rewards. Alcohol misuse is particularly prevalent in metropolitan areas and in some college and military environments, where alcohol use is often accepted and perhaps encouraged. Like the family systems model, the behavioral/social learning model occupies an important place in current understanding of Alcohol Use Disorders.

Psychodynamic/Psychoanalytic Model. This model suggests that alcohol misuse reflects infantile oral dependence needs and unresolved conflict with parents. Alcohol reduces fear and hostility and gives a sense of power. There is little empirical support for the notion of alcohol as reflecting oral needs and unresolved early conflict, but it is clear that alcohol is widely used to reduce anxiety and stabilize mood.

Humanistic/Existential Model. Using alcohol, according to this model, is a way to receive attention, sympathy, and care and to avoid responsibility. Less research has been conducted on this model than on most of the others, so its usefulness is still unclear.

Typical Client Characteristics

People who misuse alcohol typically have significant life problems. Particularly common are interpersonal, occupational, and legal difficulties, cognitive impairment, and physical problems (McCrady, 1993). People with Alcohol-Related

Disorders often have had other mental disorders during their lives as well; the incidence of Anxiety Disorders (especially Phobias), Mood Disorders, Antisocial Personality Disorder, and other Substance-Related Disorders is particularly high (Gallant, 1995). Alcohol sometimes is used to reduce anxiety or to lessen the severity of a manic or psychotic episode (Agras, 1993). Adolescents who misuse alcohol often have comorbid diagnoses of Attention-Deficit/Hyperactivity Disorder and Conduct Disorder. As a result of all these related difficulties, people who misuse alcohol often present with concerns other than alcohol. Careful interviewing is necessary to determine that alcohol is the central difficulty, typically the one that must be addressed before the others can be ameliorated.

Some studies have found certain personality patterns to be associated with maladaptive use of alcohol. On the Minnesota Multiphasic Personality Inventory, according to Meyer (1983), people who misuse alcohol tend to receive high scores in introversion, depression, and somatization. They also tend to score high in imagination, intellectual ability, extroversion, passivity, instability, anxiety, and interpersonal undependability on the California Psychological Inventory. Leigh (1985) has found that people who misuse alcohol tend to be immature and impulsive and to have poor coping skills and low self-esteem, with men often manifesting antisocial behaviors and attitudes, and with women more likely to experience depression and Phobias. According to Yost and Mines (1985), people who use alcohol in self-destructive ways tend to be anxious, self-centered, and sensitive to stress; to have interpersonal difficulties and poor ego strength; to perceive themselves as having little control and few options; and to overreact to failure.

Women who misuse alcohol are particularly likely to experience depression and anxiety. Patterns of learned helplessness, passivity, and dependence are common in these women. They typically have difficulty in intimate relationships and often have drinking patterns that are linked to those of significant others in their lives. These women have a high incidence of rape and incest in their backgrounds and are more likely than men to attempt suicide. Unfortunately, they are less likely to seek treatment; their efforts to conceal their drinking, their family responsibilities, their passivity, and the stigma associated with women who misuse alcohol are all barriers to their seeking treatment (McDonough & Russell, 1994).

Alcohol-Related Disorders have a strong tendency to run in families; males who have grown up in families that have a history of alcohol misuse are three times as likely to develop Alcohol-Related Disorders as males from families without that pattern (Schuckit & Smith, 1996), and women who have grown up in families that misused alcohol often marry men with alcohol problems. Familial-pattern alcoholism tends to begin earlier and to be more severe than alcohol problems in people from families without a history of the disorder. Moreover, because people with alcohol-related problems commonly have had family members with similar problems, they have often grown up in dysfunctional families, where ineffective parenting and deceptive and chaotic relationships were the norm. Rates of divorce and family violence are much higher in families where alcohol misuse is present than in families in which alcohol is not a problem. Familial alcoholism also tends to be associated with poor coping and social deficits because those from alcoholic families typically have lacked positive role models. People who misuse alcohol are likely to have a range of associated difficulties; depression, anxiety, poor coping skills, interpersonal difficulties, and family dysfunction are particularly prevalent. Whether these concerns precede or are consequences of alcohol use is often unclear, but what is clear is that therapy must go beyond establishing abstinence in people with Alcohol-Related Disorders.

Preferred Therapist Characteristics

As in the treatment of other Substance-Related Disorders, therapists working with people who misuse alcohol should promote optimism, commitment, and a sense of responsibility. They should facilitate reality testing and provide structured treatment and limit setting. Therapists need to be able to tolerate these clients' anger and resistance, to be flexible and patient, to avoid power struggles and negative countertransference, and to inspire hope and motivation (Najavits & Weiss, 1994). Confrontation and self-disclosure on the part of the therapist should be used judiciously but can sometimes facilitate progress and reduce resistance to treatment. McCrady (1993) emphasizes the importance of the therapist's honesty and of the therapist's empathy for the considerable challenge that most clients face in remaining abstinent. Therapists should be prepared for clients to engage in some alcohol use while in treatment and should not be discouraged if it occurs. At the same time, a therapy session should not be held if a client arrives intoxicated.

Intervention Strategies

The first considerations in treating Alcohol-Related Disorders are to assess the extent and severity of the problem, the person's motivation, and social and other factors maintaining the current pattern of use (McCrady, 1993). Withdrawal can be dangerous if alcohol consumption is high, and hospitalization may need to be the first step in treatment. Even if hospitalization is not indicated, a medical examination almost always is because of the damaging effects of alcohol.

Although *DSM-IV* distinguishes between Alcohol Abuse and Alcohol Dependence, treatment is basically the same for the two, with the specific ingredients of the treatment plan being individualized. Current treatment of these disorders has shifted away from intensive residential and rehabilitative programs toward brief, multifaceted interventions (Roth & Fonagy, 1996). Nevertheless, longer and more intensive programs sometimes are indicated for people with long-standing misuse of alcohol, especially if they have a history of treatment failure.

Most approaches to treating Alcohol-Related Disorders take a behavioral focus. They view maladaptive consumption of alcohol as triggered by a stimulus, as mediated by cognitive, affective, and physiological responses, and as providing immediate reinforcement despite subsequent negative consequences. McCrady (1993) summarizes these assumptions in the SORC model, which assesses environmental *stimuli* (S) that elicit cognitive, affective, behavioral, and physiological *organismic* (O) reactions leading to a drinking *response* (R) and the positive *consequences* (C) of that behavior. Treatment seeks to modify the stimuli as well as the responses that are promoting the substance use.

The typical multifaceted approach to treating Alcohol-Related Disorders includes many of the following elements:

- A treatment contract specifying the goals, duration, and ingredients of therapy
- Detoxification
- Promotion of insight into situations and motives that contribute to drinking behavior
- Behavior therapy, usually provided in a group setting and emphasizing decision making, assertiveness training, communication skills, reduction of anxiety and stress, control and redirection of impulses, identification and reduction of cues for drinking, monitoring of drinking behavior, and reinforcement for abstinence (Monti, Abrams, Kadden, & Cooney, 1989)
- Couples and family therapy, to enhance the impact of behavior therapy and help family members with their own alcohol-related difficulties
- Self-help groups
- Disulfiram (Antabuse), naltrexone, or other drugs
- Change in the client's social context through residence in a halfway house or through distancing from and assertiveness with the peer group that encourages substance use
- Nutritional and recreational counseling

The treatments that have demonstrated the most effectiveness for Alcohol-Related Disorders are primarily behavioral in nature and include social skills training, coping skills training, self-control training, brief motivational interviewing, behavioral marital therapy, community reinforcement, and stress management. Studies of the use of disulfiram, naltrexone, medications to reduce depression and mania, and cognitive therapy are promising but so far inconclusive (Emmelkamp, 1986; Roth & Fonagy, 1996; Schuckit, 1996). Research has not supported the use of an analytic or insight-oriented approach, the use of chemical or electrical aversion therapy, or antianxiety medication. Supportive therapy, as a primary intervention, also has not proved effective in the treatment of Alcohol-Related Disorders.

It is clear that some types of interventions for treating these disorders are unlikely to be effective, but no one ideal treatment approach has emerged. One large-scale study, Project MATCH, funded by the National Institute on Alcohol Abuse and Alcoholism, studied three different treatment approaches, each of which lasted twelve weeks:

- Twelve-Step facilitation, which introduced people to the first three steps of Alcoholics Anonymous and promoted active participation in that organization
- Cognitive-behavioral therapy, designed to help people manage their thoughts and behaviors, recognize high-risk situations, refuse alcohol, and maintain sobriety
- Motivational-enhancement therapy

At one year follow-up, all three treatments had demonstrated a positive impact: drinking had decreased, and abstinence had increased. Careful matching of clients to treatments was not supported by the outcomes of the research, but each of the approaches did seem best for particular types of people. The Twelve-Step approach was best for those with few psychological problems but severe alcohol use that was encouraged by the social environment. Women, especially those with other significant mental disorders, responded best to the cognitive-behavioral approach. The motivational approach was helpful to those who had low motivation but who had neither social pressure to drink nor significant psychological difficulties ("Tailoring treatment," 1997).

One of the controversies in the field of alcohol treatment concerns the question of whether controlled drinking can be a viable alternative to abstinence. Those who accept the disease concept of Alcohol-Related Disorders generally believe that controlled drinking does not work, and most research suggests that therapy with abstinence as a goal is more effective. Atwood and Chester (1987) report a success rate of only 5 percent in controlled-drinking programs. Sanchez-Craig, Annis, Bornet, and MacDonald (1984), by contrast, have found brief treatment of people in the early stages of problem alcohol use to be equally effective whether the goal is abstinence or controlled drinking. They also report that most people in both groups become controlled drinkers in any case, and that people find the idea of controlled drinking more acceptable than abstinence. Emmelkamp (1986) suggests that controlled drinking is most likely to be effective with younger clients who have brief and mild drinking histories and little coexisting pathology, but this issue has not yet been resolved.

For maximum effectiveness, peer support groups should be part of a multifaceted treatment plan. Participation in Alcoholics Anonymous is strongly correlated with treatment success: 70 percent of those who are in Alcoholics Anonymous for at least a year "have good sobriety" (McCrady, 1985, p. 247). Alcoholics Anonymous currently has more than ten thousand groups in the

United States. Its primary tenets are that alcoholism is a progressive disease and that once someone has become an alcoholic, he or she will always be an alcoholic and cannot stop drinking without help. Some people are uncomfortable with Alcoholics Anonymous because of its strong spiritual component, and dealing with this issue beforehand in therapy may facilitate people's involvement with the program. Rational Recovery, a self-help group based on Ellis's rational-emotive behavior therapy (Ellis & George, 1986), is an alternative to Alcoholics Anonymous that deemphasizes religious and spiritual elements and does not insist on abstinence as a goal.

Antabuse (disulfiram) is sometimes part of the treatment of Alcohol-Related Disorders, particularly for people who have a long history of alcohol problems and who have failed at efforts to maintain sobriety in the past. Antabuse is an alcohol antagonist. If taken regularly, it acts as an emetic when combined with alcohol. Antabuse is most commonly prescribed only for the first ninety to one hundred twenty days of treatment. Integrated with other treatment approaches, it has yielded recovery rates of 60 to 80 percent (Forrest, 1985) but often does not have an enduring impact (Seligman, 1995). Antabuse can worsen depression and should be used cautiously, particularly with people who are depressed. Naltrexone, an opiate antagonist, is currently under study as a promising alternative to Antabuse.

As with most forms of Substance-Related Disorders, treatment of Alcohol Abuse or Dependence should go beyond abstinence and focus on career development, social and family relationships, and leisure activities. Treatment should encourage development of those skills that are needed to establish a rewarding and alcohol-free lifestyle. People seem to go through a particularly difficult phase during the early months of abstinence, when they are struggling to adjust to sobriety. Halfway houses, day treatment programs, and other follow-up or aftercare programs can facilitate the transition from severe alcohol use to self-sufficiency. Women who misuse alcohol often need help with parenting skills, past physical and sexual abuse, social support systems, and feelings of low self-esteem (McDonough & Russell, 1994).

Families in which alcohol is misused typically have more than one person who has a strong need for therapy. The children may be suffering the impact of the parents' inconsistent and negative behavior and may manifest emotional and behavioral disorders and early alcohol use themselves, as well as low self-esteem and confused goals and aspirations. Spouses or partners of those who misuse alcohol are sometimes enablers, who indirectly encourage the alcohol use because of their own dependence needs. Therefore, therapy should also address the needs of family members, both to treat their immediate problems and to help them avoid the continuation of patterns that promote Alcohol-Related Disorders. Involving the family in the therapy can also increase the accuracy of the available information on the client's drinking. Al-Anon, Alateen, and Adult Children of Alcoholics are programs that can further enhance the treatment of family members.

Prognosis

Many factors have been linked to prognosis for Alcohol-Related Disorders. Prognosis is better if the alcohol use started late and developed slowly and if the client has strong relationships, is active in work and other pursuits, has a history of accomplishments, and has sought treatment voluntarily (Atwood & Chester, 1987; Kaplan et al., 1994). Vaillant and Milofsky (1982) have found abstinence to be associated with the discovery of substitutes for alcohol, such as activities, jobs, new relationships, or involvement in spiritual or self-help groups. Rounsaville, Dolinsky, Babor, and Meyer (1987) observe that, for men, having an Antisocial Personality Disorder or a problem with drug use in addition to an Alcohol-Related Disorder is associated with a poorer outcome, but having a treatment-responsive Major Depressive Disorder is associated with a better outcome. In general, older people and women seem to respond better to treatment.

The likelihood of a relapse after treatment is very high. Maxmen and Ward (1995) report that 70 to 90 percent of people who have been treated for alcohol use relapse within the first year after treatment. Therefore, relapse prevention is an essential element of treatment. Treatment failure certainly should not become a self-fulfilling prophecy, but therapists and clients must recognize that many people will not succeed in maintaining long-term abstinence after initial treatment and may need additional treatment, particularly during the first year of abstinence, in addition to long-term follow-up. Thus the prognosis is good for improvement of Alcohol-Related Disorders but fair at best for total abstinence, although approximately 20 percent do achieve long-term sobriety, some even without treatment (American Psychiatric Association, 1994a).

Drug-Related Disorders

Description of the Disorders

Leigh (1985) has identified two groups of people who misuse drugs: troubled people in emotional or physical pain, who are using drugs as a form of self-medication; and people who use drugs recreationally and enjoy the sensations afforded by the drugs. Kessler et al. (1994) report the lifetime prevalence of Drug Abuse without dependence as 4.4 percent and of Drug Dependence as 7.5 percent. Approximately 20 percent of people with a drug-related disorder misuse drugs that originally were prescribed for them; for example, approximately 5 percent of people who are prescribed anxiolytics like alprazolam (Xanax) become addicted to those drugs (Maxmen & Ward, 1995).

Although most people have a drug of choice, studies have noted an increasing tendency for people to misuse more than one drug. This tendency complicates the treatment picture and makes accidental overdoses more likely. People with comorbid Substance Use Disorders also have a particularly high incidence of suicidal and homicidal behavior.

An important difference between people who misuse drugs and those who misuse alcohol is the illegality of many drugs. People who misuse alcohol may also have legal difficulties, typically due to their having driven while intoxicated, but those who misuse other substances are often involved in felonies and devote extensive time and energy to obtaining the funds needed to purchase drugs. Many people with problems of drug use (and some of those with alcohol problems) come to therapy involuntarily, having been ordered into therapy by the courts, and may be suspicious, guarded, and resentful. With these clients, therapists need to confront issues of criminality and anger as well as those of substance misuse.

DSM-IV includes the following categories of drugs among the Substance-Related Disorders: Amphetamines, Caffeine, Cannabis, Hallucinogens, Inhalants, Nicotine, Opioids, Phencyclidine, and Sedatives, Hypnotics, or Anxiolytics. In addition, this section of the *DSM* includes Other (or Unknown) Substance-Related Disorders, involving substances such as anabolic steroids or nitrous oxide, and also includes Polysubstance Dependence. Specific criteria for the Use and Induced Disorders can be found in the *DSM* and are beyond the scope of this book.

Typical Client Characteristics

Like people with Alcohol-Related Disorders, people who misuse drugs have a broad range of physical and emotional symptoms and often present with social and occupational impairment. Many people who misuse drugs have a generalized difficulty with impulse control. In particular, adolescents who misuse drugs seem to be highly susceptible to boredom and have a high need to take risks and seek excitement (Leigh, 1985). Men are more likely to misuse illicit drugs; women are more likely to misuse prescription drugs. People who misuse prescription drugs tend to be dependent, shy, anxious, and socially isolated (Meyer, 1983).

Research has indicated a possible association between personality traits and preferred drug. These findings should be viewed as tentative rather than conclusive at present, and overgeneralization should be avoided. Nevertheless, research on the association between personality and drug of choice can help clinicians understand the personality patterns and choices of their clients.

Amphetamines typically increase energy and performance and suppress appetite. People who misuse amphetamines often are coping with underlying depression and suicidal ideation. People using amphetamines also tend to be agitated and suspicious, aggressive and violent, and frequently have little sense of direction. The amphetamines themselves can produce psychotic symptoms. Amphetamine use is most common among men in their late teens and their twenties, but the growing number of young people treated for Attention-Deficit/Hyperactivity Disorder with methylphenidate (Ritalin) or pemoline (Cylert) has increased the availability and misuse of amphetaminelike drugs among children and adolescents.

Although no Caffeine Use Disorders per se are included in the *DSM*, Caffeine-Induced Disorders are listed and are characterized by anxiety, restlessness, and sleep disturbances. A cycle can evolve in which a person does not get restful sleep because of caffeine but perpetuates the problem by using caffeine to stay awake during the day. Because two-thirds to three-quarters of adults regularly consume beverages with caffeine, they tend to overlook both its negative side effects and the effects of a sudden withdrawal from caffeine (Morrison, 1995), which include headaches, fatigue, irritability, mild depression, mild anxiety, nausea, and muscle pain; tapering off the use of caffeine over seven to fourteen days is recommended for people who make heavy use of caffeine (Kaplan et al., 1994).

People who use cannabis (including marijuana and hashish) typically value the relaxation, increased sensory awareness, and elevated mood it provides. Chronic users of cannabis tend to be passive, lacking in ambition, and prone to depression, suspiciousness, panic or anxiety attacks, and impaired judgment. Long-term use of cannabis can cause neurological impairment and problems in fertility and sexual functioning (George, 1990). Cannabis often is used along with other substances, especially nicotine, alcohol, and cocaine (American Psychiatric Association, 1994a). Cannabis probably is the most commonly used illegal drug, and its use is particularly prevalent in young adult males, but its use has declined since the 1970s.

Cocaine seems initially to boost self-esteem and optimism, increase mental and physical abilities, and convey feelings of power (Glauser, 1995), but extended use leads to many negative symptoms, including anxiety, depression, suicidal ideation, weight loss, aggressiveness, sexual dysfunction, sleeping problems, and paranoid delusions and hallucinations. People who misuse cocaine are often seeking ways to affirm themselves and increase their sense of accomplishment. In reality, however, they more often sacrifice themselves and their potential successes to the drug. Cocaine dependence is particularly likely to be found in young adult men who are Hispanic or African American (Kaplan et al., 1994). Depressive, Bipolar, and Anxiety Disorders and Antisocial Personality Disorder often are comorbid with use of cocaine. Because this drug is highly addictive and can be lethal, detoxification and inpatient treatment are usually indicated.

Hallucinogens like lysergic acid diethylamide (LSD) can sharpen perceptions and promote insight, introspection, and feelings of euphoria, but the negative effects of hallucinogens include psychosis, mood changes, illusions (not usually hallucinations), and cognitive impairment. People who misuse hallucinogens often have accompanying interpersonal, academic, and occupational problems. Hallucinogen Persisting Perception Disorder—that is, Flashbacks, which can occur intermittently for years—is a particularly distressing consequence of hallucinogen use. Hallucinogens are most commonly taken by young white males (Kaplan et al., 1994).

Although use of amphetamines and hallucinogens is declining, use of inhalants is increasing (Hegarty, 1997). Misuse of inhalants tends to begin early, typically between the ages of seven and seventeen, because of the ready availability of these substances. Commonly used inhalants include lighter fluid, glue, nail polish remover, gasoline, spray paint, and anesthetic gases. These substances produce euphoria and an out-of-body sensation. They also have many short- and long-term side effects ranging from headaches and nausea to irreversible brain damage and death. The use of inhalants is often associated with family, social, and school-related difficulties, depression, anxiety, hostility, suicide attempts, and physiological damage to nerves, organs, and muscles. People typically use inhalants only briefly and then move on to other substances.

Nicotine can increase learning and attention, improve mood, and promote relaxation. For many years, the negative effects of nicotine, like those of caffeine, were minimized, but awareness of the addictive and lethal properties of nicotine, as well as of the difficulty of quitting smoking, has increased over the past twenty-five years. Correspondingly, the number of people in the United States who smoke declined from 44 percent to 27 percent between 1964 and 1991 (Kaplan et al., 1994). Tobacco continues to be associated with 25 percent of all deaths in the United States, however. Lifetime prevalence of Nicotine Dependence is approximately 20 percent and characterizes 50 to 80 percent of people who currently smoke. Nicotine use is much higher among people with mental disorders than it is in the general population (American Psychiatric Association, 1994a) and often coexists with Alcohol Dependence, Schizophrenia, Mood Disorders, and Anxiety Disorders.

Opioids, including heroin and morphine, produce a rapid sense of euphoria. Opioid use typically is preceded by use of other drugs. Opioid tolerance develops rapidly, and use of this substance often leads to theft and other illegal behaviors, so that the person using opioids can pay for them. Use of this substance can lead to a wide range of negative symptoms, which include psychosis, sleep and sexual difficulties, depression, mania, and such medical conditions as hepatitis, skin infections, and damage to the heart and lungs (George, 1990). Meyer (1983) observes that people who use opioids tend to be apathetic, egocentric, narcissistic, and easily bored and frustrated and to have difficulty dealing with authority. Rounsaville, Weissman, Kleber, and Wilber (1982) have found approximately 90 percent of people dependent on opioids to have at least one coexisting mental disorder, most often Major Depressive Disorder, an Alcohol Use Disorder, Antisocial Personality Disorder, or an Anxiety Disorder (especially Posttraumatic Stress Disorder). According to Morrison (1995), approximately 50 percent of people who inject opioids are seropositive for human immunodeficiency virus (HIV). Methadone, used as a less harmful but still addictive opioid, is sometimes substituted for heroin in drug treatment. People who misuse opioids are likely to come from lower socioeconomic urban settings; about 50 percent come from single-parent or divorced families (Kaplan et al., 1994).

Use of phencyclidines (PCP) and related substances can produce euphoria. These drugs also cause many severe psychological problems, however, including rage, disinhibition, panic, mania, unpredictability, psychosis, and flashbacks, as well as such physical problems as seizures and death from respiratory arrest. Aggressive behavior and poor judgment are particularly likely consequences of PCP use.

Sedatives, hypnotics, and anxiolytics, including barbiturates, benzodiazepines (such as Xanax and Valium), and other prescription sleeping and antianxiety medications, tend to be misused by people who feel tense, anxious, and inadequate. These substances have often been prescribed for the people who ultimately abuse them, the sense of well-being and relaxation provided by the drugs having led people to persist in their use. Many of these substances are highly addictive brain depressants. They cause a range of symptoms, among them delirium, psychosis, and amnesia. These substances are potentially lethal, especially in combination with alcohol.

Polysubstance Dependence is defined as the use of at least three groups of substances (not including nicotine and caffeine) within a twelve-month period in which the criteria for Substance Dependence were not met by any one substance but were met by the group of drugs as a whole. Meyer (1983) notes that people who have Polysubstance Dependence tend to be young, adventurous, apathetic, and depressed, to have social problems, and to engage in antisocial behavior. They often are dependent and have confused values and poor problem-solving skills. Hostility and aggression are also likely to be prominent in people who can be diagnosed with Polysubstance Dependence (McCormick & Smith, 1995).

Families of people who misuse drugs seem to have a high incidence of impulse-control problems and interpersonal conflict. Antisocial behavior, as well as Alcohol and other Substance-Related Disorders, are often found in these families, as are high levels of marital disruption, inconsistency, and emotional disorders (Cadoret, Troughton, O'Gorman, & Heywood, 1986). The person who misuses drugs often has an important role in holding the family together (Stanton, 1985). Dysfunctional use of drugs is particularly prevalent among immigrant youth, possibly as a route to acceptance by a peer group.

Preferred Therapist Characteristics

The guidelines for therapists working with people who misuse drugs are similar to those given in the sections on Alcohol- and Substance-Related Disorders. Therapists working with this population also need a solid understanding of drugs, their current nicknames, their symptoms and prevalence, and the environments that promote their use, as well as an understanding of the legal and medical issues pertinent to people who misuse drugs (Lewis, 1994).

Intervention Strategies

Treatment goals for people who misuse drugs include abstinence, improved well-being (physical, emotional, social, and occupational), and, as necessary, improved family functioning. Treatment for people who misuse drugs is similar to treatment for people with Alcohol Use Disorders and usually includes the following components:

- Medical and psychological assessment
- Detoxification and, as necessary, treatment for symptoms of withdrawal
- Drug education
- Behavior therapy designed to eliminate drug use
- Psychotherapy to improve coping and interpersonal skills and to address any coexisting mental disorders
- Self-help groups
- Family therapy
- Relapse prevention

Although behavior therapy has been the most common approach to treating problems of drug use, supportive therapy (promoting impulse control and environmental change) and psychodynamic therapy (focusing on insight), in combination with behavior therapy, have also been used with some success.

Improving interpersonal skills to promote development of a peer group that does not misuse drugs can be an important treatment ingredient for people who may not know how to relate to others without using drugs. Developing leisure activities to fill time previously spent in drug-related activities can also be helpful. People with the typical personality patterns (shyness, anxiety) of those who misuse prescription drugs are particularly likely to benefit from relaxation and assertiveness training.

Group and individual therapy are both often part of the treatment plan, as is involvement in self-help groups, notably Narcotics Anonymous, Cocaine Anonymous, and Alcoholics Anonymous. Participation in structured smoking-cessation programs like those offered by the American Cancer Society has also been effective in helping a substantial number of people stop smoking.

Therapists who have had drug problems themselves can provide helpful role models for some people who misuse drugs. O'Brien et al. (1984) have found that, for people with mild drug use problems, counseling by paraprofessionals can be as effective as cognitive-behavioral therapy and psychodynamic (supportive-expressive) therapy provided by professionals, although therapy provided by professionals is more effective for people with moderate to severe drug use problems.

Family therapy is another important part of the treatment plan. Many people begin to use drugs like inhalants and cannabis while still in childhood or adolescence. Family therapy can help empower parents to establish sound values and rules in the home, as well as rewards and consequences that discourage drug use.

Methadone maintenance, a heroin-antagonist treatment, as well as other drug antagonists, will sometimes become part of the treatment program for opioid users. Methadone programs have had good success rates; for example, O'Brien et al. (1984) have found that people who were misusing drugs and also suffering from severe pathology benefited more from methadone maintenance than from therapeutic communities because their social difficulties led them to feel uncomfortable in close interpersonal situations. Methadone maintenance is controversial, however, because it involves substituting one drug for another.

Drugs can also facilitate smoking cessation. The use of nicotine transdermal patches, especially combined with behavioral therapy, has produced abstinence rates of approximately 60 percent (Heather & Richmond, 1992; Kaplan et al., 1994).

Other medications, such as antidepressants and lithium, can be helpful in controlling underlying symptoms and thereby facilitating the treatment of drug problems. However, medication should be used cautiously with people who tend to misuse drugs.

Therapeutic communities are another avenue to treatment, particularly for those with a long history of opioid use. Many of these communities have adopted a highly confrontational model, popularized many years ago by the Synanon program. They encourage responsibility, insist on honesty and self-examination, and exert peer pressure to effect change. People recovering from problems with drugs provide valuable role models. The focus of these communities is on the present, on unlearning and new learning based on education and feedback, and on building responsibility and competence (Bratter et al., 1985). This approach to treatment has yielded mixed results. Bale and colleagues (1984) have found therapeutic communities to be most effective if they offer program clarity, order, staff control, and a focus on residents' personal problems.

People who misuse drugs seem to respond strongly to life crises, especially those involving arguments and losses (Kinnunen, Doherty, Militello, & Garvey, 1996; Kosten, Rounsaville, & Kleber, 1986). Such events often precipitate a relapse, and so therapy should help people who misuse drugs to find effective ways of coping with negative events. Extended aftercare, as well as monitoring and building on people's coping mechanisms, will be useful in preventing relapses. Periodic blood or urine testing can also be helpful in motivating people to remain drug-free and in keeping therapists informed of relapses. Environmental change is yet another aspect of aftercare, especially for people whose families and peer groups encourage their drug use. Simpson, Joe, and Bracy (1982) have found that it takes about three years of abstinence for recovery to be well established, and this finding suggests the need for an equivalent period of aftercare, follow-up, and attendance at meetings of self-help groups.

Prognosis

High relapse rates, often more than 50 percent, are reported for problems of drug use. People with stable family backgrounds, intact marriages, jobs, minimal criminal activity, less use of drugs and alcohol, and less severe coexisting mental disorders have the best prognosis (Hser, 1995). A positive prognosis is also associated with the client's attributing the improvement to himself or herself rather than to a program, with the client's involvement in maintenance treatment, and with the client's having social support for the effort to stop misusing drugs.

Use of many drugs, such as the opioids, seems to decline with age whether treatment is provided or not. Therefore, middle adulthood may be a time when people who misuse drugs are especially receptive to treatment.

EATING DISORDERS

Description of the Disorders

This section focuses on the two eating disorders, Anorexia Nervosa and Bulimia Nervosa, that are most likely to be found in adolescents and adults. Other Eating Disorders, found primarily in children, were described in Chapter Two.

Anorexia Nervosa and Bulimia Nervosa, like Substance-Related Disorders, are disorders of behavior and impulse control that can be physically harmful and even life-threatening. Overall prevalence rates of 0.5 to 2 percent have been reported for Anorexia Nervosa, with rates of 1 to 3 percent reported for Bulimia Nervosa (Roth & Fonagy, 1996), and the incidence of these Eating Disorders is increasing. People in professions where low weight is desirable (for example, ballet, modeling, and sports) are particularly prone to these disorders.

The onset of Anorexia Nervosa is typically between the ages of ten and thirty; for 85 percent of people with this disorder, onset comes between the ages of thirteen and twenty (Kaplan et al., 1994). Bulimia Nervosa typically has a somewhat later onset and is often preceded by Anorexia Nervosa, which then evolves into Bulimia Nervosa.

Both Anorexia Nervosa and Bulimia Nervosa are most common in young women. These disorders are being reported with increasing frequency, however, in males and older women. Approximately 10 percent of the people with Eating Disorders are men (Andersen, 1987a). Males with Anorexia Nervosa usually explain their eating behavior as a way to achieve better muscle definition rather than as a way to lose weight. Herzog, Norman, Gordon, and Pepose (1984) have found men with Eating Disorders to manifest more severe pathology than women with these disorders.

Anorexia Nervosa, according to *DSM-IV,* involves a person's refusal to maintain normal body weight. As a result, body weight is less than 85 percent of what would be expected for the person's age and height. Other symptoms of the disorder include great fear of becoming fat (even though the individuals are underweight), a disturbed body image (whereby the persons see themselves as fat even though they are underweight), dread of loss of control, and, in females, amenorrhea (absence of at least three consecutive expected menstrual cycles). In some very young women the disorder is associated with apprehension about puberty and seems to represent an effort to delay development. Leaving home, as well as other triggers related to separation and maturation, sometimes precipitate this disorder, although it more often has an insidious onset that may begin with poor eating in childhood.

Common physiological symptoms of Anorexia Nervosa include cold intolerance, dry skin, an increase in fine body hair, low blood pressure, and edema (Agras, 1987; Maxmen & Ward, 1995). Metabolic changes, potassium loss, and cardiac damage can result from this disorder and can be lethal. Approximately 5 percent of people with Anorexia Nervosa die as a result of the disorder (Morrison, 1995).

Two types of Anorexia Nervosa have been identified. People with the Restricting Type of the disorder (the more common type) do not engage in binge eating or purging but do maintain low weight by severely limiting their intake of food. People with the Binge-Eating/Purging Type habitually engage in binge eating and/or purging behavior (such as self-induced vomiting or inappropriate use of laxatives, diuretics, or enemas).

People with Bulimia Nervosa engage in behaviors similar to those of people with Anorexia Nervosa, Binge-Eating/Purging Type, but do not meet the full criteria for that disorder, usually because their weight is more than 85 percent of normal body weight. Bulimia Nervosa, according to *DSM-IV,* involves an average of at least two episodes per week of binge eating and associated compensatory behavior (such as self-induced vomiting, fasting, laxative use, or extreme involvement in exercise) for at least three months, as well as a sense of being out of control during these episodes. Binges may last anywhere from a few minutes to a few hours. They tend to occur late in the day and typically coincide with dysphoric moods and stressful or unstructured times. People usually binge when they are alone and, on average, consume approximately three thousand calories in a single binge (Maxmen & Ward, 1995). People give many reasons for their binges. These reasons include (in descending order) tension and anxiety, food cravings, unhappiness, inability to control appetite, hunger, and insomnia.

Dieting is often a precursor to the development of Bulimia Nervosa. People who binge have many ways of controlling their weight, including purging, fasting, exercising excessively, spitting out food, and using diuretics or laxatives. Combinations of these compensatory behaviors are common. Purging is often learned from friends and seems to have some support among adolescent girls as an acceptable way to control weight. The self-induced vomiting seems to increase feelings of self-control and to reduce anxiety, and these secondary gains often make it a difficult behavior to extinguish.

Physical signs usually accompany the self-induced vomiting often associated binge eating. These signs include swelling of the parotid glands, which produces a chipmunklike appearance; scars on the back of the hand (from the hand's contact with the teeth while vomiting is being induced); chronic hoarseness; and dryness of the mouth. Physiological reactions to purging include dental cavities and enamel loss, electrolyte imbalance, cardiac and renal problems, and esophageal tears (Agras, 1987).

Typical Client Characteristics

Low self-esteem, denial, shame, depression, and problems related to socialization, sleeping, and sexual desire are commonly found in people with Anorexia Nervosa, as are obsessive-compulsive features, especially those related to a preoccupation with food (Rogers & Petrie, 1996). People with Anorexia Nervosa often cook for their families but refuse to eat what they have prepared because of their intense fear of gaining weight. They tend to be resistant to treatment because their disorder is ego-syntonic, and they typically do not want to change their eating behavior.

People with the Restricting Type of Anorexia Nervosa typically are dependent, introverted, compulsive, stubborn, perfectionistic, asexual, and shy. They have low self-esteem and feel ineffectual. They tend to come from affluent homes where food had an important role. They also tend to have been very well-behaved children and often have played an important part in holding the family together. Many have been parentified children in enmeshed families and were overprotected, constricted, and overregulated. They lack autonomy and a clear sense of their own identity. They have often had eating problems as children and tend to be strongly attached to their mothers (Atwood & Chester, 1987; Gutsch, 1988). At the same time, these people often resent the control that they perceive their parents as having, and they want more independence and separation. In many cases, the Anorexia Nervosa seems to represent people's efforts to resolve their separation-enmeshment conflict.

Most people with bulimic symptoms report problems with interpersonal relationships (70 percent), family relationships (61 percent), finances (53 percent), and work (50 percent) (Hudson, Pope, Yurgelun-Todd, & Jonas, 1987). They tend to be anxious, depressed, demoralized, self-critical, and secretive about their eating behaviors. People who binge typically feel angry, powerless, and out of control. They have difficulty handling pain, loss, and conflict (Gutsch, 1988), are preoccupied with their bodies, and tend to have many physical complaints. Although they usually are sexually active, they tend to have sexual difficulties, as well as conflicted feelings about intimate relationships. They tend to be slightly older, more likely to act out, more extroverted, more emotional, less rigid, more anxious, more guilty, and more depressed than those people with eating disorders who do not habitually binge (Andersen, 1987b). They also tend to have a high incidence of other difficulties involving impulse control, including self-mutilation. Thus people who engage in binge eating and purging seem to present more associated emotional and behavioral disorders than do people with Anorexia Nervosa, Restricting Type.

People with bulimic disorders tend to see their families as low in cohesiveness and as discouraging of intellectual and recreational activities, independence, assertiveness, and open expression of feelings. These families tend to have high levels of conflict and often are enmeshed yet disengaged (Johnson & Flach, 1985).

Bulimic behavior, unlike restriction of food intake, tends to be ego-dystonic, and people with this symptom experience considerable hunger and disappointment in connection with their need to binge and purge. As a result, they are more likely to seek treatment than are those with Anorexia Nervosa, Restricting Type.

People with Bulimia Nervosa and those with Anorexia Nervosa both tend to have suicidal ideation. Both do have some friends and have fairly successful lifestyles, but they also tend to isolate themselves and to have social difficulties. Characteristics associated with both groups include a low sense of well-being, problems with intimacy and separation, high negative affectivity, considerable stress, and feelings of alienation (Pryor & Wiederman, 1996).

People with Anorexia Nervosa, Binge-Eating/Purging Type, are particularly likely to have had troubled and chaotic families (Foreyt & Kondo, 1985). People with bulimic symptoms are also particularly likely to have first-degree relatives with Mood Disorders, Substance Use Disorders, and obesity. Many women with Eating Disorders have mothers who doubt themselves and are unresponsive to their daughters, and fathers who are distant and who have high expectations for their daughters (Atwood & Chester, 1987). Their siblings and parents have an unusually high incidence of Eating Disorders and of Major Depressive Disorders (Agras, 1987).

Other mental disorders are highly likely to accompany Anorexia Nervosa and Bulimia Nervosa. Most people with these disorders have also experienced a Major Depressive Disorder, and many have met the diagnostic criteria for Anxiety Disorders, Substance Use Disorders, and Obsessive-Compulsive Disorder (Kennedy & Garfinkel, 1992). At least half have accompanying Personality

Disorders (Van Velzen & Emmelkamp, 1996), most commonly Borderline, Histrionic, or Narcissistic Personality Disorder. People with Eating Disorders, particularly those with a coexisting diagnosis of Borderline Personality Disorder, have a higher than average prevalence of childhood sexual abuse (Waller, 1994).

Preferred Therapist Characteristics

Developing strong therapist-client rapport seems integral to treatment. People with Eating Disorders typically are very sensitive to any hint of rejection or disapproval (Wilson & Pike, 1993). Consequently, they need considerable support and approval in therapy, to help them disclose symptoms that typically seem shameful to them and make the potentially frightening behavioral changes that will be asked of them. As Bruch (1982) observes, the individuality of these clients has often been denied in their families, and this situation should not be re-created in therapy. They must be heard and encouraged to develop separateness and autonomy. Therapists will need to handle these clients' strong dependence needs by gently encouraging self-control, independence, and active involvement in treatment. At the same time, therapists will also need to be structured, to provide stability and constancy, and to set limits for these clients' protection, even hospitalizing them if that measure becomes necessary (Rogers & Petrie, 1996). Women with Eating Disorders are sometimes uncomfortable with men and often work better with a female therapist or with a male/female cotherapist team. Because of the high likelihood that people with Eating Disorders will have at least one other mental disorder, therapists treating these clients need to be knowledgeable not only about Eating Disorders but also about the many other disorders that may also be present.

Intervention Strategies

Both Anorexia Nervosa and Bulimia Nervosa are physically damaging and potentially lethal disorders. Therefore, the first step in treatment is to assess the client's eating behaviors and any physiological damage by taking a careful history and referring the client for examination by a physician. Inventories like the Eating Disorder Examination (Wilson & Pike, 1993) or the Questionnaire for Eating Disorder Diagnoses (Mintz, O'Halloran, Mulholland, & Schneider, 1997) can be useful in obtaining an accurate assessment of the disorder's severity. If weight loss has been great (25 percent or more), if the person's medical condition is precarious, or if the eating behaviors seem unlikely to respond to outpatient treatment, hospitalization may be needed to supervise eating, prevent vomiting and abuse of laxatives, and promote weight gain. Hospitalization does restore about two-thirds of people with Eating Disorders to normal weight, but most continue to have eating problems after discharge, a finding that indicates the need for continued outpatient treatment (Agras, 1987). If the client does not seem to be in immediate danger, however, outpatient treatment may be adequate as long as steps are taken to restore normal weight and to curtail other self-damaging behaviors.

Therapy for people with Eating Disorders, as for most people with behavioral and impulse-control disorders, typically has several components. The core of treatment is behavior therapy, to promote healthy eating and eliminate purging. This approach usually entails the gathering of baseline data on the client's weight and related compensatory behaviors (such as laxative use), the establishment of goals, contingency contracting, the client's self-monitoring (usually through a diary of eating and related behaviors), reinforcement and rewards for positive change, and relaxation strategies for reducing anxiety and improving self-image and sense of control. Other behavioral techniques, such as training in assertiveness and in communication and social skills, can enhance treatment, as can development of leisure activities and improved relationships so that there will be alternatives to dysfunctional eating.

Exposure and response prevention are important components of treatment for people who binge and purge (Carter & Bulik, 1994). Presenting people with both prebinging and purging cues in multiple settings while preventing or delaying those behaviors can enhance treatment, although this approach should also be combined with other treatment interventions.

Cognitive therapy in combination with behavioral treatment can help the client gain an understanding of the dynamics of the disorder, improve self-esteem and sense of control, and contribute to the development of better eating. Cognitive approaches may include provision of information; teaching strategies for the client's self-monitoring, self-regulation, and positive self-talk; imagery; identification and reduction of fears; and exploration and modification of dysfunctional attitudes toward eating and body image (Brouwers & Wiggum, 1993; Wilson & Pike, 1993). Training in problem-solving and decision-making skills also seems likely to enhance treatment and promote adjustment. Education and dietary advice about establishing sound nutrition and weight management can also contribute significantly to the success of treatment (Roth & Fonagy, 1996). These interventions are particularly important for promoting weight gain in people with Anorexia Nervosa.

Fairburn (1985) has developed a structured manual that describes a cognitive-behavioral approach to treating Eating Disorders. That manual has been widely adopted. The approach it describes consists of nineteen sessions of individual therapy that span approximately twenty weeks. The approach emphasizes problem solving and is both present- and future-oriented. The treatment is divided into three stages. The first stage includes information on the treatment approach, on eating disorders, and on nutrition. Self-monitoring is begun, and behavioral techniques to modify behavior are taught, in an effort to restore healthy patterns of eating. Cognitive interventions are emphasized in the second stage, where people are helped to identify and modify their dysfunctional thoughts about eating, weight, and body size. The third stage emphasizes the maintenance of gains and the prevention of relapses.

Boskind-White and White (1983) suggest that group therapy with a male/female leadership team can be particularly helpful to women who binge. These authors' approach to treating bulimic behaviors has the following elements:

- Exploring affect (including shame, hostility, isolation, and self-esteem) as a way of clarifying the connection between emotions and eating
- Promoting an understanding of relationships and the connection between intimacy and responsibility
- Promoting improvement of social skills
- Promoting awareness of eating patterns and of cues to dysfunctional eating and purging
- Role-playing as a way of developing assertiveness and communication skills, in addition to other skills
- Developing strategies for coping and for making behavioral changes

Autobiographies, feedback, values clarification, and self-disclosure were also used to help people establish and work toward goals.

The treatment program developed by Fairburn and the one developed by Boskind-White and White are typical of those used to treat Eating Disorders. Both programs combine cognitive and behavioral interventions, with some attention to affect, into a structured format that can be used either with individuals or with groups.

Although little support has been given to psychodynamic approaches in the treatment of Eating Disorders, one comparative study of cognitive-behavioral therapy, behavioral therapy, and interpersonal psychotherapy has indicated that posttreatment improvement was greatest for the group of clients receiving interpersonal therapy (Fairburn et al., 1993). That group did show the least progress immediately after treatment, but at twelve-month posttreatment follow-up those clients' gains had outstripped those of the other two groups (the group that had received cognitive-behavioral therapy had the second-best showing). These findings are not surprising in light of the prevalence of depression among people with Eating Disorders, and given the effectiveness of both interpersonal therapy and cognitive-behavioral therapy in treating Mood Disorders.

Although research has not established the superiority of group over individual therapy in the treatment of people with Eating Disorders, group therapy for these clients offers many benefits. These include mutual support, reduction of shame, diffusion of power struggles, feedback from multiple sources, and the opportunity to practice interpersonal skills. At the same time, group therapists must ensure that group members have sufficient empathy to participate successfully in the group and that the group does not encourage competitive weight loss.

Family therapy may be a useful adjunct in the treatment of Eating Disorders, particularly for adolescents. Family members of people with Eating Disorders commonly are coping with their own mental disorders, and family therapy may help them in addition to improving the overall functioning of the family. People with Eating Disorders also often have issues related to separation and individuation from their families of origin, and these, too, can be addressed through family therapy.

Antidepressant medication has been found to reduce binge eating and purging (Wilson & Pike, 1993), but relapse is highly likely when medication is withdrawn. Therefore, most researchers agree that medication usually adds little to psychotherapy with this population (Roth & Fonagy, 1996), although in conjunction with psychotherapy it may reduce the severity of depression or of other coexisting mental disorders (Maxmen & Ward, 1995). Medication should be used with care and should not be routinely recommended for people with Eating Disorders.

Duration seems to be an important variable in the treatment of Eating Disorders. Longer treatments, typically lasting at least four to six months, are usually more successful. People with severe Eating Disorders may need treatment of at least a year in duration.

Prognosis

Improvement of Eating Disorders has been reported in terms of reductions in binge eating and purging and in terms of the cessation of all disordered eating patterns. Treatment that follows recommended guidelines is likely to have a considerable impact on eating patterns, typically reducing binge eating and purging by a rate of at least 75 percent. Nevertheless, the prognosis is less favorable for complete remission of the Eating Disorder. Maxmen and Ward (1995) report that 44 percent of people with Anorexia Nervosa recover completely through treatment, 28 percent are significantly improved, 24 percent are unimproved or significantly impaired, and 5 percent die prematurely as a result of the disorder. The prognosis for Bulimia Nervosa is somewhat better (Kaplan et al., 1994). A positive prognosis for treatment of this disorder is associated with the following factors:

- Good premorbid functioning
- A positive family environment
- The client's acknowledgment of hunger
- Greater maturity (including psychosexual maturity) and self-esteem
- High educational level
- Early age of onset
- Less weight loss
- Shorter duration of the disorder

- Less denial of the disorder
- Overactivity
- Absence of coexisting mental disorders

As with most of the other behavioral disorders, relapses of Eating Disorders are common and are often triggered by stressful life events. Moreover, even if people no longer meet the full criteria for an Eating Disorder, many continue to experience dysphoric moods and to engage in unhealthy eating. Treatment should be extended through follow-up or support groups to prevent and address setbacks. Follow-up treatment should also be helpful in reducing the family, social, and occupational difficulties that often persist after the Eating Disorder has been eliminated.

SEXUAL AND GENDER IDENTITY DISORDERS

Most Sexual Disorders, like Substance-Related Disorders and Eating Disorders, involve behavioral patterns that are dysfunctional or self-destructive. Sexual Disorders, however, unlike Eating Disorders or Substance Use Disorders, are usually not physically self-injurious, nor do they usually cause pervasive dysfunction. Nevertheless, they are often closely linked to people's satisfaction with their relationships, and these disorders may both reflect and cause impairment in relationships. Some Paraphilias may also lead people to break the law in an effort to find sexual gratification.

DSM-IV divides Sexual and Gender Identity Disorders into three categories: Sexual Dysfunctions, Paraphilias, and Gender Identity Disorders. In a sense, all three are disorders of behavior involving dysfunctional and inappropriate responses to stimuli, but the people with these three disorders tend to be very different in terms of lifestyle and personality patterns, motivation for treatment, and interactions with their therapists. Their disorders also differ in terms of duration, severity, and impact. The treatments for all three categories have some common ingredients (the primary one being the facilitation of expressions of normal, healthy sexuality), but the three will be discussed separately here because of the important differences among them.

Sexual Dysfunctions

Description of the Disorders

This category of disorders involves disturbances in sexual desire or functioning that cause significant distress and interpersonal difficulties. *DSM-IV* organizes this category according to stages in the sexual response cycle and lists the following disorders:

Sexual Desire Disorders: Hypoactive (deficient) Sexual Desire Disorder, and Sexual Aversion Disorder. These disorders are experienced by as many as 20 percent of the population and are more common in women (Morrison, 1995).

Sexual Arousal Disorders: Female Sexual Arousal Disorder, and Male Erectile Disorder. Both reflect a lack of physiological arousal and sexual excitement. Sexual Arousal Disorders are very common, affecting approximately one-third of all women and 10 to 20 percent of men (Kaplan et al., 1994). Male Erectile Disorder is almost always a disorder of the Acquired Type rather than of the Lifelong Type.

Orgasmic Disorder: Female Orgasmic Disorder, Male Orgasmic Disorder, and Premature Ejaculation. Female Orgasmic Disorder is more much common than Male Orgasmic Disorder and affects approximately 30 percent of women. Premature Ejaculation, by contrast, is very prevalent; together, Premature Ejaculation and Male Erectile Disorder comprise nearly all the Sexual Dysfunctions treated in men.

Sexual Pain Disorders: Dyspareunia (genital pain, usually diagnosed in females), and Vaginismus (involuntary vaginal contractions). Vaginismus is often associated with sexual trauma.

Sexual Dysfunctions Due to a General Medical Condition. Approximately 50 percent of Sexual Dysfunctions in men are caused by medical conditions or substances. Diabetes, endocrine disorders, vascular disease, and injuries are some of the more common medical causes of these dysfunctions. Gynecological surgery, vaginitis, and menopause are some of the medical conditions that can cause Sexual Dysfunctions in women.

Substance-Induced Sexual Dysfunction. Many substances, including alcohol, opioids, anxiolytics, antidepressants (especially Prozac), and some medications for hypertension, also can cause Sexual Dysfunction.

To warrant a diagnosis of a Sexual Dysfunction, symptoms must be recurrent and persistent and must cause considerable distress and interpersonal difficulty. The symptoms are not attributable to another Axis I disorder (such as Posttraumatic Stress Disorder). In making the diagnosis, the clinician specifies the disorder and indicates whether it is of the Lifelong or Acquired Type, of the Generalized or Situational Type, and Due to Psychological Factors or Due to Combined Factors (psychological and physiological).

Most Sexual Dysfunctions begin in early adulthood, although some, particularly Male Erectile Disorder, tend to begin later. Treatment for Sexual Dysfunctions typically is not sought until people are in their late twenties or early thirties (Skinner & Becker, 1985).

The course of these disorders is quite variable. Some are situationally related, precipitated by stress or relationship difficulties, and remit spontaneously once the situation has improved. Others are chronic or progressive, worsening as anxiety about the disorder increases.

Kaplan (1986) suggests that 50 percent of the population suffers from a sexual problem at some time. Sexual Dysfunctions have many possible determinants. Substances or medical conditions should be investigated first. However, approximately 75 percent of Sexual Dysfunctions have a psychological rather than a physiological origin (Atwood & Chester, 1987). Therefore, in making the diagnosis of a Sexual Dysfunction, the therapist should also explore the client's cultural and family background, knowledge about sexuality, sexual and relationship history, the possibility of a history of sexual abuse, self-image, and the possibility that the client has a coexisting mental disorder. McCabe (1994) has found Sexual Dysfunctions particularly likely to be associated with negative attitudes toward sex on the part of clients and their parents, clients' dissatisfaction with and instability in their intimate relationships, and clients' discomfort with their sexual identities. A history of abuse in childhood and a dysfunctional family background also contribute to the development of these disorders (Kinzl, Mangweth, Traweger, & Biebl, 1996). Other factors associated with Sexual Dysfunction include fear of rejection and abandonment, difficulty sharing control and trusting others, poor communication skills, anger and hostility, guilt about sexual thoughts and behaviors, impaired self-esteem, anxiety (especially about sexual performance), depression, and inaccurate information about sexual functioning. These symptoms may be either causes or consequences of Sexual Dysfunctions.

Typical Client Characteristics

A clear association has not been found between particular personality traits or backgrounds and Sexual Dysfunctions. However, anxiety is almost always a component of these disorders.

Preferred Therapist Characteristics

Treating Sexual Dysfunctions can be challenging to therapists because they must have expertise in the specific techniques of sex therapy and must also be skilled at providing support and encouragement, communicating empathy, and establishing a relationship with a client who is likely to feel uncomfortable, embarrassed, and exposed. Many people have never talked openly about their sexual attitudes and behaviors before seeking therapy and will have difficulty doing so with a therapist. The client may avoid specific details, minimize the problem, and display unfamiliarity with terminology. The therapist must be sure to conduct a detailed inquiry in terms that are comprehensible to the client and that reduce threat and anxiety as much as possible. Maintaining a nonjudgmental stance is particularly important. Orienting the client quickly to the nature of the treatment may also be useful because the client may be apprehensive about what will be required.

Transference reactions, sometimes of an erotic nature, are frequent in the treatment of Sexual Dysfunctions because of the intimate nature of the discussions (Kaplan, 1995). The therapist should be aware of the development of transference; addressing, discussing, normalizing, interpreting, and diffusing the transference will usually prevent it from undermining psychotherapy.

Intervention Strategies

The first step in treating a Sexual Dysfunction is to determine the cause of the difficulty by taking a history and referring the client for examination by a physician. Although most Sexual Dysfunctions are psychological in origin, many do have a physiological basis. Prescription medications, for example, as well as other drugs and alcohol, are common physiological causes of Sexual Dysfunction. Whatever the cause, psychotherapy may still be indicated, but medical treatment may also need to be part of the plan.

People often experience sexual difficulties for years before seeking treatment. By the time a client seeks help, the disorder may have been exacerbated by multiple disappointing sexual experiences, avoidance of sexual contact, and longstanding self-blame, all of which may complicate treatment.

A repertoire of techniques for treating these disorders have been developed by Masters and Johnson (1970), Kaplan (1995), Lo Piccolo (Lo Piccolo & Stock, 1986), and others. Discussion of the specific techniques designed for particular disorders is beyond the scope of this book—the reader is referred to these authors for that information—but some elements are common to most treatment of Sexual Dysfunctions, and these elements will be reviewed here. Treatment of these disorders tends to be primarily behavioral. Nevertheless, cognitive and psychodynamic interventions can also be useful in modifying self-damaging thoughts and resolving such long-standing problems as abuse, family dysfunction, and mistrust.

Sexual Dysfunctions are often exacerbated by inadequate or incorrect information about the process of sexual arousal and about what is considered normal sexual functioning. For example, attitudes about the inappropriateness of sexual activity for older people, or erroneous beliefs about differences between types of female orgasm, can inhibit sexual functioning and cause people to feel uncomfortable with healthy feelings and behaviors. Educating people about sexuality and sexual functioning can help dispel some of their self-blame and modify unrealistic expectations.

If the person with a Sexual Dysfunction has a consistent sexual partner, that partner should almost always be involved in the therapy. Sexual Dysfunctions grow out of relationships and affect relationships, and so they must be considered in context. Information should be gathered on the couple's interpersonal and sexual relationship, to determine whether any difficulties in their interaction have a bearing on the Sexual Dysfunction. Data should be gathered from the partners while they are together and while they are apart because they will often have discrepant perceptions of their sexual relationship. In most cases, some amount of couples therapy is helpful, focusing on communication (both verbal and nonverbal), expectations, assertiveness, and sexual desires and behaviors.

Many people develop or exacerbate Sexual Dysfunctions because of what has been called *spectatoring:* the process of watching and monitoring their own sexual performance as well as their partners' responses during sexual relations. Typically, the tension and the anxiety associated with this self-monitoring prevent relaxation and comfortable involvement in sexual behaviors, worsening the Sexual Dysfunction and leading to a vicious cycle in which the Sexual Dysfunction promotes spectatoring, which in turn increases the severity of the Sexual Dysfunction.

The first step in the behavioral treatment of a Sexual Dysfunction, then, is reduction of spectatoring and its accompanying anxiety. To accomplish this step, the couple may be taught nonthreatening relaxation techniques (such as progressive relaxation or nonsexual massage) and may be asked to refrain from overt sexual activity. Reducing pressure and demands in this way can help people gradually resume a more rewarding sexual relationship and apply specific techniques, taught in therapy, that can improve sexual functioning.

Sensate focusing is a common technique used early in treatment. It is designed to help the couple enjoy closeness and intimacy without intercourse, in order to reduce pressure and demands. Other specific techniques that may play a role in the treatment of Sexual Dysfunction include systematic desensitization, masturbation for women with inhibited orgasm, bridging (making the transition from masturbation or manual stimulation to intercourse), the squeeze technique (to teach control for men with premature ejaculation), and imagery and fantasy to enhance sexual arousal.

Friedman and Hogan (1985) suggest four components of effective therapy for Sexual Dysfunctions:

1. Experiential/sensory awareness exercises
2. Insight, to promote awareness of factors that cause and maintain the disorder
3. Cognitive restructuring, to increase flexibility in attitudes and promote commitment to change
4. Behavioral interventions focused on interpersonal as well as sexual concerns

They emphasize the importance of homework assignments for practicing the techniques that have been taught, and they stress the need for posttreatment follow-up to deal with any relapses. This is a typical and appropriate model for treating most Sexual Dysfunctions.

Therapy for Sexual Dysfunctions tends to be relatively brief, although a history of sexual victimization may necessitate longer treatment. Masters and

Johnson often conducted their therapy sessions on an intensive, daily basis, but weekly therapy does not seem to yield inferior results and is the norm (Emmelkamp, 1986).

Masters and Johnson (1970) established a model for doing sex therapy that involved a male/female treatment team working with a couple experiencing a Sexual Dysfunction. This model allows considerable flexibility and does seem ideal—but, of course, it often is not feasible. In general, therapy for Sexual Dysfunction is conducted with a couple or, if necessary, with an individual. Nevertheless, some Sexual Dysfunctions also seem to benefit from group therapy that is designed to provide support as well as education, role models, and reduction of guilt and anxiety (Kaplan et al., 1994). Therapy groups have been used for women with Orgasmic Disorders and for men with Erectile Disorders. Groups for couples have also been used successfully.

Medication usually is not necessary in the treatment of Sexual Dysfunction, but occasionally it can enhance treatment. A short course of treatment with benzodiazepines, for example, can be useful to people who have considerable anxiety associated with sexual behavior. Penile implants and intracavernosal injection therapy for Male Erectile Disorder are other medical treatments that show promise. Most people with Sexual Dysfunctions will be referred for medical examination, and so in those few cases where medication seems likely to enhance treatment, the possibility can be raised when the referral is made.

Although therapy for Sexual Dysfunctions focuses primarily on the couple and on the partners' relationship and sexual difficulties, sometimes a Sexual Dysfunction is of intrapsychic origin and is linked to other emotional disorders or to underlying pathology. Kaplan (1995), for example, suggests that Sexual Desire Disorders are sometimes associated with hostility and parental transferences in relationships, as well as with guilt and intimacy-related conflicts. In such cases, a treatment plan that combines couples behavioral therapy with some individual cognitive, interpersonal, or psychodynamic therapy may facilitate change. The therapist needs to determine the best combination of interventions for treating a person who has both a Sexual Dysfunction and another mental disorder or emotional difficulty.

Prognosis

In their early research, Masters and Johnson (1970) reported an 80 percent overall success rate for 733 cases in which clients received two weeks of intensive treatment for Sexual Dysfunction, with only 5 percent having a recurrence within five years. Current research, however, suggests that these figures may be too optimistic. Approximately half of all Sexual Dysfunctions show improvement in response to treatment, but these gains tend not to be fully maintained (Roth & Fonagy, 1996). Prognosis is particularly good for treatment of Vaginismus but fair to poor for treatment of Sexual Desire Disorders. Therefore, therapists working with people who have Sexual Dysfunctions should communicate realistic expectations (improvement rather than cure; likelihood of setbacks) and should plan for follow-up visits and relapse prevention.

A positive prognosis is associated with the following factors (Lambert, 1982):

- A stable and rewarding relationship with a partner
- Good communication and problem-solving abilities
- Brief duration and low severity of the impairment
- Specificity of the dysfunction
- Initial lack of information on sexual functioning
- Absence of coexisting mental disorders
- Openness and flexibility on the part of the client
- The client's motivation and follow-through on assignments
- The client's interest in sexual activity

The treatment of a Sexual Dysfunction often has a ripple effect, improving the client's relationship and reducing anxiety (Kaplan, 1986).

Paraphilias

Description of the Disorders

DSM-IV gives the essential features of a Paraphilia as "recurrent, intense, sexually arousing fantasies, sexual urges, or behaviors generally involving 1) nonhuman objects, 2) the suffering or humiliation of oneself or one's partner, or 3) children or other nonconsenting persons" (American Psychiatric Association, 1994a, pp. 522–523). These urges or behaviors persist for at least six months and typically lead to impairment in social and sexual relationships and in other important areas of functioning, as well as to considerable distress. *DSM-IV*'s extensive list includes the following Paraphilias:

- Exhibitionism (exposing one's genitals to an unsuspecting stranger)
- Fetishism (sexual activity focused on objects)
- Frotteurism (touching and rubbing against others without their consent)
- Pedophilia (sexual activity with children)
- Sexual Masochism (enjoyment of humiliation or suffering during sexual activity)
- Sexual Sadism (deriving pleasure from causing others to suffer)
- Transvestic Fetishism (cross-dressing)
- Voyeurism (covert observation of people who are disrobed or engaged in sexual activity)

- Paraphilia Not Otherwise Specified, including such behaviors as telephone scatologia (lewd phone calls), necrophilia (sexual interest in corpses), partialism (a focus on part of the body), zoophilia (sexual behavior involving animals), coprophilia (sexual behavior involving feces), klismaphilia (sexual behavior involving enemas), and urophilia (sexual behavior involving urine)

Specific criteria are provided in *DSM-IV* for each of these disorders, but discussion of these criteria is beyond the scope of this book. Here, the Paraphilias will be considered as an entire class of disorders.

Paraphilias are far more prevalent in males than in females, although both Sexual Masochism and Sexual Sadism are diagnosed with some frequency in females (Person, 1986). The most common Paraphilias (in descending order) are Pedophilia, Exhibitionism, Voyeurism, and Frotteurism (Morrison, 1995). The diagnosis of two or more Paraphilias in one person is not unusual. Paraphilias are believed to be quite prevalent (Berlin, Malin, & Thomas, 1995), although only a small percentage of people with these disorders will seek help. People with Paraphilias typically commit large numbers of paraphilic acts: according to Bradford, Boulet, and Pawlak (1992), for example, 274 men diagnosed with Paraphilias acknowledged committing a total of 7,677 paraphilic acts. This pattern has led to difficulty in estimating the prevalence of this disorder.

In general, people with Paraphilias do not see themselves as having emotional disorders and tend not to seek treatment on their own initiative; rather, they come into treatment at the urging of a friend or family member (usually the spouse) or because actions associated with their Paraphilia have led to their arrest.

Paraphilias vary widely in terms of severity. One client, a successful thirty-two-year-old lawyer, had rewarding intimate relationships with women but fantasized a great deal about causing women to suffer. He bought pornographic magazines with sadistic themes and enjoyed films in which women were injured, raped, or killed. He had never hurt a woman, but he sought therapy because he was afraid he would lose control of his fantasies and would injure someone. This client had a mild Paraphilia. By contrast, another client, an accountant, had a severe Paraphilia: Pedophilia. His only sexual experiences had been with young boys. He had been arrested three times and had received treatment while in prison. Although he, like the other client, also had a professional career, he had lost his job because of his imprisonment, and he feared that his prison record would prevent him from locating future employment in his field.

Expression of paraphilic impulses often follows a cycle that is also common in other disorders of impulse control. Tension builds in the person until it is relieved by a paraphilic act; then guilt and regret ensue, with the person often promising a change in behavior. In time, however, tension builds up again, and it is once again released through the undesirable behavior.

Paraphilias rarely seem to have a biological cause, but they are often linked to early childhood sexual experiences, such as being tied up or forced to cross-dress. Over half of adults who commit sexual offenses report having first begun illegal sexual behavior as children or adolescents (Gelman et al., 1992). Paraphilic behavior reportedly peaks between the ages of fifteen and twenty-five and typically declines greatly by midlife (Kaplan et al., 1994).

Typical Client Characteristics

Although about half of all people with Paraphilias are married, most have some impairment in their capacity for intimate relationships, according to DSM-IV (American Psychiatric Association, 1994a). Their sexual activities tend to be ritualized and unspontaneous. Most experience some distress and anxiety connected to their disorder, as well as interpersonal difficulties and social rejection. Nevertheless, most continue to deny that their paraphilic impulses are a problem (Person, 1986). For example, some men who rape go so far as to allege that their victims enjoy the experience (Arndt, 1991).

Marshall (1993) has found people diagnosed with Paraphilias typically to be characterized by vulnerability, low self-confidence, little empathy and insight, poor social skills, and inadequate attachment to their parents. They also tend to be lonely, angry, and self-centered (Fisher & Howells, 1993). People with Paraphilias often have been victims of sexual abuse themselves; Paraphilias sometimes can be directly attributed to these experiences.

Pedophilia, often taking the form of incest, is one of the most common Paraphilias treated by psychotherapists. Men who are attracted to young girls typically have marital difficulties, are anxious and immature, and have problems with impulse control. Men who molest young boys tend to avoid any adult sexual experiences and are attracted only to children. Their Paraphilia is especially likely to be chronic.

Preferred Therapist Characteristics

Therapists will have to deal with the reluctance of many people diagnosed with Paraphilias to engage in treatment. People with Paraphilias, like those with drug and alcohol problems, generally enjoy the behaviors involved in their disorder. It is typically the negative consequences rather than the behaviors themselves that lead these people to accept treatment. As a result, they may be ambivalent toward or resistant to treatment and, especially if their treatment is court-ordered, may be guarded and suspicious. Thus it may be difficult to establish a positive therapeutic relationship with these clients.

Some therapists find that they have strong countertransference reactions to people with Paraphilias, particularly Paraphilias that involve children. One of the challenges for therapists is to manage their own feelings so that these do not undermine the therapeutic relationship and increase the clients' guilt and distress.

Intervention Strategies

Although treatments for specific Paraphilias vary to some extent, the therapeutic principles and techniques used to modify erotic responses are generally the same for all Paraphilias (Berlin et al., 1995). Three categories of treatment have been identified for this disorder.

Psychodynamic or insight-oriented treatment is a common approach (Kaplan et al., 1994). This model attributes the development of Paraphilias to early childhood experiences and seeks to resolve the conflicts that maintain paraphilic behaviors. Clarification of the impact of those past events, as well as identification of current triggers for the undesirable behavior, can help people improve their impulse control. This treatment model also seeks to improve interpersonal skills and self-esteem so that healthier routes to sexual gratification can be developed. A variation on this model is the approach of Money (Money & Lamacz, 1989), who has sought to uncover traumas and developmental problems that damaged people's "lovemaps" and led to paraphilic behavior.

Cognitive-behavioral therapy is also widely used in the treatment of Paraphilias. Various techniques have been incorporated into this approach:

- Identification of triggers and substitution of alternative behaviors
- Stress reduction
- Aversion therapy that pairs paraphilic urges and fantasies with negative experiences, such as electric shocks or noxious odors
- Covert sensitization, which uses images (such as images of imprisonment or humiliation) to discourage paraphilic behavior
- Covert extinction, in which the paraphilic behavior is imagined, but without the anticipated reinforcement or positive feeling
- Orgasmic reconditioning
- Thought stopping
- Cognitive restructuring
- Encouragement of empathy for the victim

Some people with Paraphilias engage in sexual activities with children, animals, or objects because they are afraid of rejection if they seek sexual relationships with adults. Improvement of social and assertiveness skills and education about sexuality can encourage those people to engage in sexual activities involving peers.

Carnes (1990) views Paraphilias as sexual addictions and recommends treatment with a Twelve-Step model like the one used in Alcoholics Anonymous. Carnes has used cognitive restructuring to replace such core beliefs as "Sex is my most important need" and "No one can love me as I am" with beliefs that promote responsibility and positive, intimate relationships. He has also promoted behavioral changes, following the Twelve-Step model.

Antiandrogenic medication, such as medroxyprogesterone acetate (Depo-Provera), which lowers testosterone, has also been used, particularly in the treatment of people who are sexually attracted to children and who are hypersexual. This medication produces a general reduction in sexuality, however, and so it is resisted by many clients. Surgical interventions, including brain surgery and removal of the testes, have also been used, but their use is still experimental.

Group therapy is a particularly appropriate vehicle for treating Paraphilias. People with Paraphilias can help one another to modify their behaviors, learn and practice better interpersonal skills, and prevent relapse. Family therapy also can be helpful, especially if the paraphilic behaviors have damaged current family relationships or if sexual abuse has occurred in the family of origin.

Prognosis

Paraphilias tend to be treatment-resistant, although coexisting adjustment and relationship difficulties may improve through therapy (McGrath, 1991). Relapses are also common, and so short-term improvement does not provide any assurance of continuing change (Person, 1986). Long-term treatment and supervision may be needed for these clients. The prognosis seems better for people with good ego strength and flexibility, intrinsic motivation for treatment, and normal adult sexual experiences. The prognosis is worse for people with coexisting mental disorders, early onset and high frequency of paraphilic behaviors, substance misuse, and lack of remorse for their behavior (Kaplan et al., 1994; Person, 1986).

Gender Identity Disorder

Description of the Disorder

Gender Identity Disorder (GID), according to DSM-IV, is characterized by a strong and enduring cross-gender identification, along with discomfort about one's assigned gender. These symptoms are not due to a physical condition. They are of sufficient severity to cause considerable distress or impairment in functioning. The age of the client determines whether the diagnosis is Gender Identity Disorder in Children or Gender Identity Disorder in Adolescents or Adults.

Two theories have been advanced to explain GID, also known as Transsexualism (Schafer, Wheeler, & Futterweit, 1995). Some believe this disorder is a birth phenomenon; others view GID as a conditioned response. Each of these theories may explain the disorder in some people.

Family dynamics have received particular attention from researchers attempting to understand how GID may be conditioned. Green (1995) observes that boys with GID sometimes come from families in which the son has replaced the father as the mother's sensitive and supportive confidant, thereby incurring the resentment of the father. This pattern encourages the child to reject the male role and become more feminine. Girls with this disorder tend to be distant from their mothers and to view their fathers as their role models. Other family dynamics may also contribute to GID (Kaplan et al., 1994). For example, children who are rejected or abused may believe that they will be more appreciated if they are more like the other gender. A hostile and critical parent, especially a mother, can also lead children to devalue themselves and their assigned gender.

Gender Identity Disorder is relatively rare. Morrison (1995) reports a prevalence of three males out of one hundred thousand and one female out of one hundred thousand. The disorder begins early, typically by the age of four (Green, 1995).

Typical Client Characteristics

People with a Gender Identity Disorder typically prefer activities, occupations, and dress associated with the gender opposite to their own. Among children with GID, boys typically appear effeminate, whereas girls may be thought of as tomboys. These children prefer toys associated with the other gender (dolls for boys and sports for girls), as well as playmates of the other gender. Cross-dressing is common, often beginning during the preschool years, and typically leads to teasing and rejection by peers, especially for boys. Parents, too, may be viewed as rejecting if they manifest concern about the child's behaviors.

Similarly, adolescents and adults with GID tend to adopt behaviors, clothing, and roles that are stereotypically associated with the gender they would like to be rather than with their assigned gender. If sexual desire is present, it often is directed toward people of the same gender, particularly for males, although most people with GID do not view themselves as homosexual (Kaplan et al., 1994).

Considerable social and occupational impairment is associated with GID, at least in part because of societal attitudes and reactions. Depression and anxiety are often presented by people with this disorder. Adolescents typically present with acting-out behavior and particularly severe identity confusion. People with GID are more likely to present for treatment because of these associated symptoms than because of their gender discomfort. They also may seek psychotherapy as a condition of being accepted for sex-reassignment surgery.

Preferred Therapist Characteristics

People with GID sometimes are angry and resistant clients, blaming others for their difficulties and refusing to discuss their gender-related issues. They typically are not interested in changing their feelings about their gender. Resistance may be complicated if they have been brought to therapy by their parents or if they have come as a requirement for sex-reassignment surgery.

Therapists will need to deal with this resistance and find ways for these clients to use therapy productively. An emphasis on relieving depression and anxiety and exploring options is usually more successful than focusing treatment on changing the gender dysphoria (Schafer et al., 1995). Therapists also will need to be aware of and deal with their own countertransference reactions and any discomfort they may have with these clients and with the surgery they may be seeking. Whether or not therapists agree with these clients' choices, the clients' right to make their own choices has to be respected.

Intervention Strategies

Setting realistic goals is essential to the effective treatment of GID. Promoting adjustment or helping people make decisions about biological treatment are usually more viable goals than eliminating the symptoms of GID.

According to Green (1995), family therapy is the primary approach to helping children with GID. Because GID in children often does remit, efforts to change gender-related attitudes are appropriate. At the same time, Green encourages a present-oriented focus and suggests that parents focus on alleviating children's current distress rather than on worrying about problems the children will encounter in adulthood. Green's approach involves reducing enmeshment, especially in mother-son relationships, while strengthening father-son, mother-daughter, and husband-wife relationships. Parents are advised to curtail children's involvement in cross-gender activities and to reinforce gender-appropriate behaviors. Involving children in activities that are not strongly associated with either gender, such as board games, can offer them new and rewarding social opportunities that will not elicit ridicule. Play therapy can be a useful vehicle for introducing children to new activities and role models.

If GID persists into adolescence and adulthood, the likelihood of changing gender-related attitudes and identifications is low. Therefore, goals should focus on choosing ways to improve adjustment and life satisfaction. In making choices, people should be encouraged to reflect not only on their own preferences but also on the reactions of family members, colleagues, friends, and society at large, and on the clients' own responses to those reactions.

Lifestyle and relationship changes, which may involve clients' living in their preferred gender roles, are an avenue to improved adjustment and satisfaction. Other avenues include hormonal therapy and sex-reassignment surgery. In hormonal therapy, biological males take estrogen, and biological females take testosterone. These hormones not only effect physiological changes that are gratifying to some people with GID but also improve their sense of well-being. Sex reassignment is a controversial, complex, and multifaceted process that involves trial cross-gender living before surgery, hormone treatments, and eventual surgery. Only a small percentage of people with GID pursue this treatment option.

Prognosis

Few controlled studies have been conducted on the treatment of GID, but the prognosis for treatment of children with GID seems excellent, especially for girls. Green (1995) reports that few people who were treated for GID in childhood continue to manifest the disorder when they are older. For adolescents and adults, outcome research has focused primarily on the results of sex-reassignment surgery. Approximately 70 percent of those with male-to-female reassignment, and 80 percent of those with female-to-male reassignment, report satisfaction with outcomes (Kaplan et al., 1994). Many continue to have significant problems of adjustment, however, and 2 percent of those who undergo this surgery commit suicide. The likelihood of a negative treatment outcome is greatest in people who have coexisting mental disorders.

IMPULSE-CONTROL DISORDERS
NOT ELSEWHERE CLASSIFIED

Description of the Disorders

Substance-Related Disorders, Paraphilias, and Eating Disorders have already been discussed in this chapter. The remaining Impulse-Control Disorders listed in *DSM-IV* are included in the present section. This group of disorders includes the following varied array, all characterized by repeated failure to resist an impulse to perform a behavior that is harmful to oneself or to others:

- Intermittent Explosive Disorder
- Kleptomania
- Pyromania
- Pathological Gambling
- Trichotillomania

These disorders typically are characterized by increasing tension or arousal before the harmful behavior is engaged in, and by feelings of release or pleasure after the act has been completed. The behavior, although it may be followed by feelings of guilt and remorse, is itself usually ego-syntonic.

Although the behaviors associated with the disorders in this section vary considerably, most are similar in terms of age at onset and course (usually chronic but episodic, and worsening under stress). These disorders are also strongly associated with comorbid diagnoses of Obsessive-Compulsive Disorder, Substance-Related Disorders, and Mood Disorders (Lion & Scheinberg, 1995).

Some believe that Impulse-Control Disorders have a common underlying dynamic or cause. Possible explanations for these disorders include a biological cause (organic impairment), a psychodynamic cause (an oral fixation, a weak ego and superego, a response to childhood trauma, or use of actions to avoid painful emotions), and a psychosocial cause (reflection of dysfunctional role models) (Kaplan et al., 1994). All these possibilities should be considered in seeking to understand a particular person's impulsive behavior.

Intermittent Explosive Disorder. According to *DSM-IV*, this disorder involves "several discrete episodes of failure to resist aggressive impulses that result in serious assaultive acts or destruction of property" (American Psychiatric Association, 1994a, p. 612) The symptoms are not due to another mental disorder, a medical condition, or drug or alcohol use, although use of disinhibiting substances often does accompany the aggressive episodes.

Intermittent Explosive Disorder is much more common in males than in females, usually begins in adolescence or early adulthood, abates in midlife, and is more common in first-degree relatives of people with this disorder. Intermittent Explosive Disorder is particularly likely to be found in men who have concerns about their masculine identity, as well as strong dependence needs, and who feel powerless and useless (Kaplan et al., 1994). Episodes of this disorder are often triggered by strong feelings of powerlessness or by stressful situations.

As children, people with Intermittent Explosive Disorder typically were hyperactive and had assaultive, hostile, and frustrating parents. People with this disorder often have a history of job loss, relationship conflict, and legal difficulties that are due to their angry outbursts. They may be self-destructive as well as harmful to others and may experience suicidal ideation. A history of reckless behavior and other Impulse-Control Disorders frequently is also present (Lion & Scheinberg, 1995).

Kleptomania. This disorder is characterized by unplanned, solitary, recurrent theft of unneeded objects. The person's goal is the act of stealing, not the objects that are taken.

Although this relatively rare disorder sometimes begins in childhood, it is most often diagnosed in middle-aged women who are mildly depressed and experiencing interpersonal losses and who feel a sense of injustice and deprivation in their lives (Frosch, Frosch, & Frosch, 1986). Depression, anxiety, and guilt are common in people with Kleptomania. Many have concomitant Eating Disorders (especially Bulimia Nervosa), Obsessive-Compulsive Disorder, Substance-Related Disorders, and Personality Disorders (Maxmen & Ward, 1995).

Fewer than 5 percent of people who shoplift can accurately be diagnosed as having Kleptomania (Morrison, 1995). Conduct Disorder or Antisocial Personality Disorder are more common diagnoses for people who frequently steal.

Pyromania. This disorder affects a small percentage of people who engage in the harmful setting of fires. It specifically describes those who repeatedly set fires for the purposes of pleasure and tension relief rather than for financial gain or revenge. People with this disorder not only set fires but have an interest in anything associated with fires. They set off false fire alarms and associate themselves with fire departments, sometimes becoming firefighters themselves.

This rare disorder usually begins in childhood and is found primarily in males who feel powerless. Their involvement with fire can provide a sense of power and social prestige. Pyromania is often associated with a dysfunctional family background (especially characterized by an absent father and misuse of alcohol), poor social skills, interpersonal difficulties, low self-esteem, alcohol intoxication, sexual dysfunction, depression, antisocial behaviors, cruelty to animals, and childhood mental disorders (such as Attention-Deficit/Hyperactivity Disorder, Learning Disorders, and mild Mental Retardation) (Kaplan et al., 1994; Maxmen & Ward, 1995).

Pathological Gambling. The primary feature of this disorder is persistent preoccupation with self-destructive gambling. This relatively common disorder is found in 1 to 3 percent of the population, is twice as common in males as in females, and usually begins in adolescence for males but later for females. Pathological Gambling is sometimes accompanied by other mental disorders, notably Substance-Related Disorders, Attention-Deficit/Hyperactivity Disorder, other Impulse-Control Disorders, Anxiety Disorders, Mood Disorders (especially a Major Depressive Disorder), and Personality Disorders (Specker, Carlson, Christenson, & Marcotte, 1995).

People who gamble excessively tend to be intelligent, overconfident, energetic, competitive, industrious, restless, and prone to take risks (Custer, 1984). Family, financial, occupational, and legal problems are common in people with this disorder, as is difficulty in sustaining intimate, emotionally expressive relationships (McGurrin, 1992). The families of origin of people with this disorder commonly manifest dysfunctional substance use, Mood Disorders, antisocial behavior, gambling, and an emphasis on material gain. Often people diagnosed with Pathological Gambling have as children experienced harsh and inappropriate discipline and significant losses.

Pathological Gambling typically has three phases (Kaplan et al., 1994):

- Winning, which promotes overconfidence and further involvement in gambling
- Losing, in which undue risks are taken and financial resources are depleted
- Desperation, in which gambling becomes frenzied and people borrow large sums of money, write bad checks, and engage in other kinds of nonviolent criminal behavior

These phases may extend over as many as fifteen years.

Trichotillomania. This disorder is characterized by recurrent plucking of hair from one's own head and body. The practice results in perceptible hair loss, usually from the scalp. Mouthing or eating the hairs is a common feature of the disorder.

Trichotillomania is more common in females and tends to be linked to early losses and disturbances in the mother-child relationship (Kaplan et al., 1994). The hair pulling typically provides feelings of tension release and gratification and perhaps also of stimulation. This disorder typically begins within five years of puberty and is chronic, although its severity changes, usually in response to changes in stressors (Christenson, Mackenzie, & Mitchell, 1991). Other physically self-damaging behavior is common in people with this disorder. Most people diagnosed with Trichotillomania also have at least one concurrent mental disorder, most often Mood or Anxiety Disorders, although Substance-Related Disorders, Obsessive-Compulsive Disorder, Eating Disorders, and Personality Disorders (most often Borderline Personality Disorder) are also common. Although Trichotillomania is not often presented in treatment, it may be found in as many as 3 percent of the population (Morrison, 1995).

Typical Client Characteristics

In addition to the information already provided about the common characteristics of people with these disorders, it should be noted that, overall, Impulse-Control Disorders are typically associated with other mental disorders, including Personality Disorders, Depressive Disorders, Anxiety Disorders, Eating Disorders, and Substance-Related Disorders. Suicidal ideation is common, especially among people with Pathological Gambling. Alcohol may be used to reduce self-control and allow people to act on destructive impulses. The impulsive behavior itself is typically used to relieve anxiety and depression.

Although people with Impulse-Control Disorders generally are not severely troubled by their symptoms, they recognize that others find these symptoms unacceptable, and so they frequently take steps to conceal their behaviors. These disorders commonly have a negative impact on interpersonal relationships and occupational functioning. People with these disorders typically have limited, conflicted, or unrewarding patterns of socialization. Except for those who engage in dysfunctional gambling, people with these disorders tend to be passive and have difficulty expressing their feelings.

The backgrounds of people with Impulse-Control Disorders often reveal failure to have learned to defer gratification (Frosch et al., 1986). People with these disorders frequently come from dysfunctional and impulsive families, have had important early losses, felt powerless as children, and did not do well in school. The Impulse-Control Disorder seems to be a way both to express feelings of anger and frustration and to feel more powerful.

Preferred Therapist Characteristics

People with Impulse-Control Disorders, like those with Substance-Related Disorders and Paraphilias, typically are resistant to treatment. They may seek therapy only as a result of a court order or because of pressure from friends and family members.

People with Impulse-Control Disorders tend to be defensive, to engage in denial and avoidance, and to resist taking responsibility for the consequences of their behavior. They may perceive others as forcing them to act as they have, and they may view themselves as blameless. In most cases their insight is limited, and so engaging them in therapy is likely to present quite a challenge to therapists.

As with Paraphilias, some of the behaviors of people with Impulse-Control Disorders (such as fire setting or physical abuse of their partners) may be viewed as distasteful and reprehensible. Another challenge to therapists, then, is managing their own feelings about these clients' behaviors and remaining objective while communicating acceptance and support.

Intervention Strategies

Little research is available on the treatment of many of these Impulse-Control Disorders, and so treatment recommendations are tentative and based primarily on theory and on what has been effective in treating individual cases and related disorders. Developing an appropriate treatment plan involves exploring the behavioral, cognitive, and affective components of the disorder, as well as the impact of the disorder on the person's lifestyle.

Behavioral techniques usually will form the core of treatment for people with Impulse-Control Disorders. Such techniques as stress management, impulse management, distraction, systematic desensitization, contingency contracting, and aversive conditioning commonly are used to discourage impulsive behavior. Overcorrection via public confession and restitution has also been part of the treatment of these clients.

Because these disorders typically worsen under stress, raising awareness of stressful triggers (such as anniversary dates and family visits) is important, as is an accompanying effort to assist in stress reduction. Reinforcement with praise and tangible rewards can also help modify dysfunctional behaviors. Assertiveness training and improvement of communication skills can help alleviate interpersonal difficulties and increase people's sense of control and power. If an impulsive behavior has reached addictive proportions, people may experience symptoms of withdrawal after its cessation. This withdrawal will also require attention so that a relapse can be prevented.

The specific choice of behavioral intervention depends on the nature of the disorder, of course. For example, social skills training focused on anger management has been effective in treating people with problems involving anger and explosiveness (Deffenbacher et al., 1987). With Trichotillomania, a topical cream that enhances sensitivity to pain has been used successfully to decrease hair pulling (Ristvedt & Christenson, 1996), as has hypnotherapy to heighten skin sensitivity. In a different approach to this disorder, fist clenching has been successfully substituted for hair pulling (Lion & Scheinberg, 1995). People who engage in Pathological Gambling usually need help in coping with their high need for stimulation. People diagnosed with Kleptomania should be prevented from shopping alone.

Limit setting is an important component of treatment for these disorders. People must deal with the consequences of their behavior, whether these consequences are legal or interpersonal. Bailing people out of trouble seems to reinforce and perpetuate the behavior (Custer, 1984).

Exploration of cognitions can help clients and therapists understand the thinking that promotes these disorders—thoughts like "Setting fires will show people I'm not really a weakling" or "If I can only gamble a little longer, I'm sure I'll get that big win." An understanding of the adverse consequences of their behavior can also help people with Impulse-Control Disorders modify their actions. Underlying depression and anxiety, as well as other coexisting symptoms, also need to be relieved, typically through cognitive therapy, since the impulsive behavior is often a way to manage those feelings.

Some people with these Impulse-Control Disorders benefit from psychodynamic treatment designed to help them deal with childhood losses and abuse and to help them gain an understanding of the underlying reasons for their behavior. People who are high in insight and motivation are particularly likely to benefit from therapy with a psychodynamic component. People who have been diagnosed with Kleptomania typically are responsive to insight-oriented therapy (Kaplan et al., 1994).

Therapy also needs to attend to the correlates of the disorder, including legal, financial, occupational, and family difficulties. Development of leisure activities and increased involvement with career responsibilities and family members can help replace impulsive behavior. Family therapy is often indicated as well, particularly for people with Pathological Gambling or Kleptomania, those who abuse family members, and adolescents engaged in Pyromania.

In most Impulse-Control Disorders, the negative behavior is inherently gratifying, and so it reinforces itself and makes treatment difficult. Group therapy with other people who share the same problems can often reduce the attraction of an impulse by providing peer confrontation and support. This approach to treatment is particularly useful for people who engage in Pathological Gambling and for those who have been diagnosed with Intermittent Explosive Disorder. Gamblers Anonymous, modeled after Alcoholics Anonymous, offers an important avenue to peer support and is viewed as the most important intervention for treatment of Pathological Gambling (Kaplan et al., 1994). Support groups can help fill the void left when an impulsive behavior is stopped and can offer understanding, concern, role models, peer pressure, inspiration, motivation, and new behaviors.

Medication is sometimes useful in the treatment of Impulse-Control Disorders. Impulsive behaviors sometimes have a neurological component that can be modified by such drugs as lithium, anticonvulsant medication, or fluoxetine (Prozac). Selective serotonin reuptake inhibitors, including Prozac, Zoloft, and Paxil, have been helpful to people with Kleptomania and Trichotillomania. Antidepressant and other medication can also have an indirect beneficial impact on Impulse-Control Disorders by alleviating accompanying depression and other symptoms.

Prognosis

As with most other Impulse-Control Disorders, the prognosis for the disorders reviewed here is uncertain. Relapse is common, especially at times of stress, loss, or disappointment, and it should be addressed in treatment. Few figures are available on success rates for treatment of these disorders, although research suggests that children treated for Pyromania have a good prognosis, and that people with late-onset Trichotillomania have a poor prognosis (Kaplan et al., 1994). Even after eighteen months of abstinence, people with Pathological Gambling have a 25 to 85 percent likelihood of relapse (Lewis, 1994). Several of the disorders, however, among them Intermittent Explosive Disorder, tend to diminish spontaneously over time.

SLEEP DISORDERS

Description of the Disorders

Sleep Disorders are a very different type of behavioral disorder from those discussed earlier in this chapter. Unlike most of the others, Sleep Disorders provide few secondary gains and rewards, and people clearly want to be free of their symptoms. As described in *DSM-IV,* Sleep Disorders are reflected by disturbances in the restorativeness and continuity of sleep. They include four major subgroups:

- Primary Sleep Disorders (not caused by a medical condition, a substance, or another mental disorder)
- Sleep Disorder Related to Another Mental Disorder
- Sleep Disorder Due to a General Medical Condition
- Substance-Induced Sleep Disorder

A review of the specific disorders encompassed by the category of Primary Sleep Disorders will provide familiarity with the major clusters of symptoms included among all the Sleep Disorders.

Primary Insomnia. This disorder is described by *DSM-IV* as "difficulty initiating or maintaining sleep or of nonrestorative sleep that lasts for at least 1 month and causes clinically significant distress or impairment" (American Psychiatric Association, 1994a, p. 553). This fairly common disorder is more prevalent in later life and among women (Morrison, 1995). Difficulty falling asleep is its most common manifestation. Secondary symptoms, including fatigue, mild anxiety, depression, and difficulty concentrating, may interfere with daytime functioning.

Primary Hypersomnia. This disorder is characterized by prolonged sleep (more than nine hours per day), excessive daytime sleepiness (despite adequate sleep), or sometimes both, for more than one month. It is more common in men than in women, tends to begin in young adulthood, and, without treatment, usually has a chronic course. The tiredness, as well as the napping and the lengthy periods of sleep that characterize the disorder, can have an adverse impact on a person's social or occupational activities.

Narcolepsy. This disorder is characterized by at least three months of daily irresistible attacks of sleeping that typically last ten to twenty minutes. Upon awakening, the person is refreshed but may have another attack in two to three hours. Cataplexy or paralysis of voluntary muscles occurs in about 50 percent of those with this disorder and may cause them to fall or collapse. Sleep paralysis, the inability to move, is another troubling symptom of this disorder. Hallucinations, usually visual, are sometimes the first symptom of this disorder, and they indicate that REM sleep is intruding on the waking state. Symptoms of Narcolepsy often are precipitated by intense arousal or boredom (Maxmen & Ward, 1995). This disorder has a hereditary component, as does Breathing-Related Sleep Disorder. Narcolepsy affects approximately five hundred thousand people in the United States, with males and females equally represented among those with this disorder. It usually begins in puberty but always before the age of thirty. This chronic disorder can contribute to accidents, depression, and work problems.

Breathing-Related Sleep Disorder (Sleep Apnea). Abnormal respiration during sleep can lead to the excessive sleepiness that is often the presenting problem for this disorder. Loud snoring and gasping during sleep are other clues to the presence of this disorder, although shallow breathing may be present instead. Typically, people with this disorder have as many as three hundred episodes a night in which air flow ceases for ten seconds or longer and is restarted with accompanying arousal. People with this disorder may be unaware of their repeated awakenings, but their bed partners can describe the characteristic breathing and snoring patterns. If left untreated, this disorder can contribute to the development of hypertension and heart failure. This disorder is particularly prevalent among overweight men in midlife. Breathing-Related Sleep Disorders have increased in children since routine removal of children's tonsils and adenoids was discontinued.

Circadian Rhythm Sleep Disorder. This disorder results from a mismatch between people's natural biological clocks and the demands of their lifestyles. Subtypes—including Delayed Sleep Phase Type, in which people have preferred times for sleeping and waking that are significantly later than those of most people; Jet Lag Type; and Shift Work Type—reflect common examples of such mismatches. Difficulty falling asleep leads to daytime sleepiness, which in turn often leads to irregular sleeping patterns and use of caffeine and other stimulants, and these then exacerbate the disorder.

Parasomnias. Parasomnias are characterized by undesirable physical happenings during sleep and include Nightmare Disorder, Sleep Terror Disorder, and Sleepwalking Disorder. All three disorders are particularly common in children. The first two both involve upsetting dreams but are distinguished by the point in the sleep cycle when they occur and by people's reactions upon awakening. Sleep Terror Disorder, which usually begins between the ages of four and twelve, is characterized by repeated awakening from dreams with a loud scream or cry and accompanying disorientation. People with Nightmare Disorder, by contrast, are alert upon awakening and can clearly report details of their frightening dreams. Sleepwalking affects 1 to 5 percent of children, with onset typically between the ages of six and twelve and elimination of sleepwalking by the age of fifteen; 1 percent of adults experience Sleepwalking (Morrison, 1995). All three of the Parasomnias typically worsen under stress or fatigue (Anders, 1996).

A Sleep Disorder can also be related to another mental disorder (most often a Mood or Anxiety Disorder) or may be caused by a medical condition (such as pain, asthma, fever, or a neurological disorder). Substance-Induced Sleep Disorders can be caused by alcohol, caffeine, amphetamines, and other substances.

A diagnostic sleep laboratory, which can provide polysomnographic studies of sleep patterns, is invaluable in diagnosing most of these Sleep Disorders, especially Breathing-Related Sleep Disorder, Primary Insomnia, and Narcolepsy. These studies should be conducted before a diagnosis of these disorders is finalized. A sleep diary kept by the client can also provide useful information on sleeping patterns.

Typical Client Characteristics

Sleep Disorders are quite varied, as are the people who experience them. Buchholz (1988) reports that 10 to 20 percent of the population have chronic sleep complaints, with Primary Insomnia and Primary Hypersomnia being the most common of these disorders. People with Sleep Disorders are more likely to be female, older, and experiencing health problems (Mellinger, Balter, & Uhlenhuth, 1985) as well as undergoing considerable stress.

People with a Sleep Disorder Related to Another Mental Disorder typically have difficulty expressing their feelings directly and tend to channel their emotional difficulties into somatic symptoms. Presentation of the Sleep Disorder may be a way to seek help for underlying concerns that they are reluctant to acknowledge.

Kales, Soldatos, and Kales (1982) have found that adults with Parasomnias tend to appear active, outwardly directed, hostile, aggressive, and easily frustrated. Underneath this facade, however, they are often anxious, depressed, or phobic and tend to have negative views of themselves. The possibility of abuse or other aversive events should be explored in people with persistent upsetting dreams; memories of the negative events may be breaking though during sleep.

Preferred Therapist Characteristics

Therapists treating people with Sleep Disorders seem to be most successful if they assume an active, directive, yet supportive stance. People with these disorders often have deferred seeking help until the problems felt overwhelming, and they need reassurance and active intervention to modify the symptoms quickly. People with Sleep Disorders are sometimes resistant to engaging in exploration of their lifestyles and possible underlying concerns, and this resistance must be addressed and reduced by therapists.

Intervention Strategies

Insomnia and Hypersomnia are often related to or caused by other disorders or situations that require attention, such as depression, stress reactions, and Substance-Related Disorders. People with Sleep Disorders also may have life circumstances that interfere with their obtaining restful sleep, such as a noisy environment or an uncomfortable living situation. Therefore, when a person presents with symptoms of a Sleep Disorder, a careful assessment, often including polysomnographic studies, is indicated for ascertaining the dynamics of the disorder. Detailed interviewing is particularly indicated with people who present Circadian Rhythm Sleep Disorders because their lifestyle and their work schedules often contribute to the disorder. Another reason for thorough interviewing is the finding that up to 30 percent of those who complain of difficulty falling or remaining asleep actually do sleep well (Buchholz, 1988).

If a disorder such as Major Depressive Disorder or a Substance-Related Disorder seems to be causing the Sleep Disorder, focusing on the underlying disorder usually will take priority. Successful treatment of that disorder may automatically relieve the Sleep Disorder. The therapist will often have difficulty shifting the client's focus from the sleeping difficulties to the concerns that underlie them, however.

Research on the use of psychotherapy to treat Sleep Disorders is limited. Most of the relevant research has been done by medical researchers working in sleep laboratories. Nevertheless, the literature does provide some guidelines for using psychotherapy to treat Sleep Disorders once medical causes have been ruled out. If it has been determined that the focus of treatment will be on the Sleep Disorder, the first steps usually will be to ensure that the person has a sleeping environment conducive to restful sleep and to stabilize the sleep schedule as much as possible, eliminating naps and caffeine and establishing healthy patterns of eating, drinking, and exercising.

As a general rule, people who clearly are not getting enough sleep, typically people with Insomnia or Circadian Rhythm Sleep Disorder, can be treated primarily via behavioral therapy. People who are sleeping too much, however, or who are exhausted even though they seem to have had enough sleep (typically people with Narcolepsy, Breathing-Related Sleep Disorder, and Hypersomnia), require medication or medical treatment. People with Parasomnias, especially children, require primarily reassurance and help in reducing any stress and anxiety that may be contributing to the disorder.

A variety of behavioral techniques have been used successfully in the treatment of Insomnia, which often has a self-perpetuating course: the difficulty in sleeping causes worry about not sleeping, and the worry in turn exacerbates the difficulty in sleeping. Breaking the cycle is important in reducing the symptoms. People should be discouraged from lying in bed for long periods and worrying about not sleeping, and they should not use their beds for reading or watching television. Instead, they should get up and engage in a restful activity until they feel tired. Borkovec (1982) has found relaxation and biofeedback consistently effective in the treatment of Insomnia, yielding an average reduction of 45 percent in latency of sleep onset. Meditation, use of positive imagery, and light therapy are other sleep-enhancing techniques. Sleep restriction, another approach that has been effective, is a behavioral shaping procedure in which people are instructed not to go to sleep until the time they usually fall asleep. This bedtime is then gradually modified in increments of fifteen to thirty minutes (from, say, 11:30 P.M. to 11:15 P.M. to 11:00 P.M.) until people are going to sleep at an appropriate time. Sedative-hypnotic medication can also alleviate Insomnia but is potentially addictive and should probably be viewed as a treatment of last resort. Some people use melatonin and other over-the-counter remedies to help them fall asleep. The long-term impact of these substances has not been fully documented, and so these remedies should be used with great care, if at all.

Circadian Rhythm Sleep Disorder, Jet Lag Type and Shift Work Type, are best treated through lifestyle modification that stabilizes sleeping patterns. Chronotherapy, or resetting of the biological clock, is another approach to treatment of this disorder (Anders, 1996). The Delayed Sleep Phase Type of this disorder, for example, can be treated through phase advancing, which systematically, gradually, and progressively schedules earlier bedtimes for people with this disorder. Light therapy, stress management, relaxation, avoidance of alcohol and caffeine, and improved sleep habits can enhance treatment (Emory, 1996).

Unlike Insomnia, excessive sleeping or fatigue usually has a physical or genetic rather than a psychological basis (Buchholz, 1988). Consequently, treatment of these symptoms should always include a medical evaluation. The recommended treatment usually will be primarily medical, although psychotherapy can help people cope with the diagnosis and any impact it has on their lives.

Medical treatments vary according to the disorder. For example, Primary Hypersomnia and Narcolepsy can be treated successfully with stimulant medication, such as amphetamines. Narcolepsy also benefits from two or three scheduled daily naps of twenty to thirty minutes each (Anders, 1996). Antidepressant medications can relieve the cataplexy that often accompanies Narcolepsy. Breathing-Related Sleep Disorders can be treated with weight loss, nasal continuous positive airway pressure (via CPAP machines) that regulates breathing, and, if all else fails, by surgery. People with fatigue and chronic sleepiness can also usually benefit from the establishment of a regular sleeping schedule and healthy eating and exercise. Psychotherapy, addressing both underlying stressors and the stress introduced by the sleepiness, is often indicated, to facilitate accomplishment of those goals.

In children, the Parasomnias usually do not reflect underlying pathology and are usually outgrown without any intervention, although they may reflect a stress reaction (Anders, 1996). In adults, however, Parasomnias sometimes are linked to underlying emotional disorders. If the Parasomnia reflects an aversive or traumatic experience, of course, this will need to be addressed through psychotherapy.

In addition to specific treatments for the Sleep Disorders, people with these disorders also usually benefit from education and attention to any underlying conflicts or sources of excessive arousal. Education as part of treatment can provide people with needed reassurance, for example, informing them that no permanent damage will result from missed sleep (Buchholz, 1988) and that people need less sleep when they are older. If the Sleep Disorder has been long-standing and chronic, it may have damaged a person's career and relationships, and these too may need to be addressed in therapy.

Prognosis

The prognosis for reducing Sleep Disorders is quite good, but an accurate assessment of etiology is critical in determining outcome. Those with a medically or physiologically caused Sleep Disorder usually respond well to medical treatment or to alleviation of the cause. Those with a psychologically determined Sleep Disorder are likely to respond well to behavioral psychotherapy as long as any underlying disorders are also addressed. The Parasomnias have a high probability of spontaneous remission. Breathing-Related Sleep Disorders and Narcolepsy may need lifelong treatment but usually can be well controlled through that treatment. The prognosis for both Primary Insomnia and Circadian Rhythm Sleep Disorder is uncertain and depends primarily on the person's lifestyle and ability to stabilize his or her life and to reduce stress and change.

TREATMENT RECOMMENDATIONS: CLIENT MAP

This chapter has focused on the diagnosis and treatment of five groups of Disorders of Behavior and Impulse Control: Substance-Related Disorders, Eating Disorders, Sexual and Gender Identity Disorders, Impulse-Control Disorders Not Elsewhere Classified, and Sleep Disorders. Although the symptoms of these disorders vary widely, they do have an underlying commonality: behavioral dysfunction. The following general treatment recommendations, organized according to the format of the Client Map, are provided for Disorders of Behavior and Impulse Control.

Client Map

Diagnosis

Disorders of Behavior and Impulse Control

Objectives of Treatment

Increased knowledge of the disorder

Reduction of dysfunctional behaviors

Acquisition of new and more positive behaviors

Stress reduction

Lifestyle improvement

Relapse prevention

Assessments

Physical examination (especially important for Sleep and Sexual Disorders)

Symptom inventories

Establishment of baseline severity of symptoms

Determination of presence of coexisting mental disorders

Clinician Characteristics

Knowledgeable about individual, group, and family therapy

Well informed about specific disorder

Able to be structured and directive yet supportive

Able to manage potential negative feelings about client's behavior

Able to work effectively with client's resistance and hostility

Location of Treatment

Usually outpatient setting

Short-term inpatient treatment possible for severe cases of Substance-Related Disorders and Eating Disorders

Therapeutic communities, day treatment programs also possible

Interventions to Be Used

Multifaceted program emphasizing behavioral therapy

Measurement of change

Education

Improvement of communication and relationship skills

Stress management

Impulse-control strategies

Emphasis of Treatment

Highly directive

Moderately supportive

Primary focus on current behaviors and coping mechanisms

Some attention to past patterns and history

Numbers

Group therapy particularly important when resistance is high

Individual and family therapy also important

Timing

Rapid pace

Short to medium duration

Medications Needed

Usually not the primary mode of treatment

Antabuse, methadone, and stimulant and antidepressant medication can accelerate progress in some cases

Adjunct Services

Peer support groups such as Alcoholics Anonymous, Narcotics Anonymous, Overeaters Anonymous, Gamblers Anonymous, Rational Recovery

Prognosis

Good prognosis for significant improvement if client is (or becomes) motivated to change

Relapse is common

Client Map of George

This chapter began with a description of George W., a thirty-six-year-old male with a twenty-two-year history of maladaptive alcohol use. George was also experiencing legal, interpersonal, occupational, and marital problems. He reported some underlying depression and social discomfort. George was seen in therapy after his arrest for driving while intoxicated (DWI). The following client map outlines the treatment provided to George, a course of treatment typical of what is recommended for people who misuse alcohol or have other disorders of behavior and impulse control.

Diagnosis

Axis I: 303.90 Alcohol Dependence, Severe

Axis II: 799.90 Diagnosis deferred on Axis II. Rule out Avoidant Personality Disorder or Avoidant Personality Traits

Axis III: High blood pressure, intestinal discomfort reported

Axis IV: Incarceration for third DWI conviction, marital conflict, occupational problems

Axis V: Global Assessment of Functioning (GAF Scale): current GAF = 55

Objectives of Treatment

Establish and maintain abstinence from alcohol

Improve marital relationship

Improve social skills

Obtain diagnosis and treatment for medical complaints

Assessments

Thorough medical evaluation to determine impact of alcohol use on his physical condition and obtain treatment for physical complaints

Minnesota Alcoholism Screening Test

Clinician Characteristics

Knowledgeable about the development and symptoms of Alcohol Dependence

Structured and directive

Skilled at setting limits

Location of Treatment

Outpatient setting (rather than inpatient setting with concurrent medical evaluation and supervision), given that client had been alcohol-free for several weeks as a result of incarceration

Interventions to Be Used

Group behavior therapy as primary approach

Individual therapy, later family therapy and marital therapy as needed

Encouragement for abstinence

Education about stress management, problem solving, communication skills, impact of alcohol, and maladaptive patterns of alcohol use

Development of leisure and social activities not focused on drinking

Emphasis of Treatment

Directive

Focused on current behavior

Elements of both support and exploration

Numbers

Individual, group, family, and marital therapy

Timing

Rapid pace

Medium duration

Extended follow-up and participation in Alcoholics Anonymous

Medications Needed

None

Antabuse to be considered in case of early relapse

Adjunct Services

Alcoholics Anonymous (at least three meetings per week)

Later participation in Adult Children of Alcoholics

Al-Anon for client's wife

Prognosis

Fair (client internally and externally motivated, acknowledges need to reduce or eliminate drinking, aware that job and marriage are in jeopardy, but reluctant to make the commitment to long-term abstinence)

Better with long-term follow-up and continued participation in Alcoholics Anonymous

Relapse common

Recommended Reading

Anders, T. F. (1996). Sleep disorders. In G. O. Gabbard & S. D. Atkinson (Eds.), *Synopsis of treatments of psychiatric disorders* (pp. 167–176). Washington, DC: American Psychiatric Press.

Arndt, W. (1991). *Gender disorders and the paraphilias.* Madison, CT: International Universities Press.

Fisher, G. L., & Harrison, T. C. (1997). *Substance abuse.* Needham Heights, MA: Allyn & Bacon.

Lewis, J. A. (1994). *Addictions.* Gaithersburg, MD: Aspen.

Lion, J. R., & Scheinberg, A. W. (1995). Disorders of impulse control. In G. O. Gabbard (Ed.), *Treatments of psychiatric disorders* (pp. 2457–2468). Washington, DC: American Psychiatric Press.

Wilson, G. T., & Pike, K. M. (1993). Eating disorders. In D. H. Barlow (Ed.), *Clinical handbook of psychological disorders* (2nd ed., pp. 278–317). New York: Guilford Press.

CHAPTER SEVEN

Disorders in Which Physical and Psychological Factors Combine

D r. Martin C., a sixty-two-year-old African American male, was referred for therapy by his physician. Martin had sought medical help for intestinal discomfort. He believed that he had cancer of the small intestine. His father had died of that form of cancer when Martin was a teenager, and when his father had been in his sixties. Martin had seen three physicians (including an oncologist), had undergone a thorough medical evaluation, and was found to have nothing more than frequent indigestion and constipation due to poor eating habits. Because Martin had difficulty accepting this diagnosis, his physician referred him for therapy.

Martin had been a history professor for almost thirty-five years. He had been promoted to associate professor about twenty-five years before, after the publication of an influential book he had written on the history of war, but he had never been able to equal that accomplishment, and his efforts to achieve promotion to full professor had been unsuccessful. Martin was also experiencing stress at home. He had been divorced fifteen years before and had been remarried for eight years to a woman twenty years younger than he. Martin felt that she was disappointed in him because of his lack of professional success, and he was worried about the future of his marriage. He coped with this worry by working long hours and taking a great deal of nonprescription medication for his gastric symptoms. He was rarely home, had few friends and leisure activities, and had considerable difficulty verbalizing his feelings.

Martin initially sought help for a physical problem—intestinal discomfort and gastric distress—but his physician believed that Martin's complaints had an emotional cause. Martin was experiencing a disorder called *Hypochondriasis*, one of four groups of disorders considered in this chapter, in which physical complaints are intertwined with emotional difficulties, and in which attention must be paid to both groups of symptoms.

OVERVIEW OF DISORDERS IN WHICH PHYSICAL AND PSYCHOLOGICAL FACTORS COMBINE

Description of the Disorders

This chapter begins with an overview of disorders involving an interrelationship of physical and psychological concerns. The chapter goes on to provide information on the diagnosis and treatment of the four groups of disorders that fit this description:

- Somatoform Disorders
- Factitious Disorders
- Delirium, Dementia, and Amnestic and Other Cognitive Disorders
- Mental Disorders Due to a General Medical Condition

People with these disorders often present for treatment with concerns about a physical or medical complaint or cause. They sometimes seek therapy after referral from a physician who has not been able to find a medical cause for their complaints or who believes that the clients' emotional difficulties, even though they may stem from a medical condition, would be helped by psychotherapy. These clients may or may not be aware of the dynamics of their disorders. In either case, their focus is often on their physical concerns, and they may be surprised by and resistant to the suggestion that they would benefit from psychotherapy.

Typical Client Characteristics

People with disorders in which physical and psychological factors combine typically have difficulty expressing emotions directly and so may channel concerns into the physiological realm. People with Factitious Disorders or Somatoform Disorders typically were sickly as children or had close contact with people who suffered long illnesses, and they learned that having medical complaints is a way to get attention. They often are having trouble managing environmental stress and tend not to be insightful or psychologically minded. Sometimes people with these disorders have strong dependence needs and want others to take care of them. They typically have impairment in both the interpersonal and the occupational aspects of their lives.

Preferred Therapist Characteristics

Therapists treating people with these disorders benefit from having information on medical conditions and should be comfortable collaborating with physicians. These therapists need to be skilled at developing rapport and communicating support and interest so that a helpful therapeutic relationship is established fairly rapidly. Clients will often be resistant and will often dispute the importance of psychological variables.

If the therapist is harshly confrontational or unsympathetic, the client may well terminate treatment, but if the therapist overemphasizes the physical complaints, little progress will be made. Therefore, the therapist must carefully control discussion of the presenting complaints. Therapy is most likely to be successful if the therapist is concrete and structured as well as comfortable using styles of intervention that are flexible and involve little in-depth analysis.

Intervention Strategies

Few controlled studies exist on the treatment of the disorders covered in this section. Nevertheless, case studies and theoretical articles provide a good indication of approaches to treatment that are likely to be effective.

The first step in treating people who present with interrelated physical and psychological complaints is to obtain a medical consultation (or to confer with physicians whom the client has already consulted) to determine whether a physical disorder really is present. If so, the therapist should become familiar with the impact of the medical condition on the client and should ensure that appropriate medical treatment is provided if it is needed. Clients should be kept informed about their medical condition and should be involved in decisions about treatment whenever that is possible. Clients who feel that their medical symptoms are being ignored may manifest an increase in somatization, in an effort to obtain the medical attention believed to be necessary.

Therapy for people with interrelated physical and psychological complaints generally deemphasizes interpretation and analysis because of the resistance that those approaches may provoke and because of the typical lack of psychological-mindedness in these clients. Therapy is usually eclectic, focusing on affective, cognitive, and behavioral areas, to build up the person's coping mechanisms, reduce accompanying depression and anxiety, modify cognitions promoting hopelessness and dependence, and help people meet their needs more effectively so that they do not need to somatize or use illness to gain attention. Leisure and career counseling can facilitate that process, and family counseling can prevent reinforcement of secondary gains (such as the extra attention that the clients receive when they feel ill). Cognitive-behavioral therapy, stress management, and hypnotherapy are useful in helping people integrate the physical and emotional aspects of themselves and maximize their strengths. If the client is experiencing significant impairment, either cognitive or physical, psychotherapy will need to take that impairment into account.

Prognosis

The prognosis for treating disorders in which physical and psychological factors combine varies greatly according to the nature and dynamics of the client's concerns and the client's receptivity to therapy. If the client can acknowledge having emotional concerns that could benefit from therapy, the client may well derive considerable benefit from that process: not only can therapy reduce people's focus on their perceived physical complaints, it can also increase their self-confidence and self-esteem and improve the quality of their lives. Nevertheless, the presence of cognitive impairment or a medical illness may limit the progress of therapy.

Somatoform Disorders

Description of the Disorders

Somatoform Disorders are characterized by physical complaints or symptoms that are not fully explained by a medical condition or by another mental disorder and are believed to be caused (at least in part) by psychological factors. People who have these disorders, however, genuinely believe that they are afflicted with the symptoms and physical illnesses they are presenting. They are not deliberately producing these symptoms, and so they are typically very distressed about their physical complaints and about the failure of the medical community to find and address a medical cause for their symptoms. The fourth edition of the *Diagnostic and Statistical Manual of Mental Disorders* (*DSM-IV*) lists the following six types of Somatoform Disorders (American Psychiatric Association, 1994a).

Somatization Disorder. This disorder is also known as Briquet's syndrome. It is characterized by multiple medically unexplained physical complaints, beginning before the age of thirty and lasting for at least several years, for which a person seeks medical treatment and because of which he or she makes modifications in lifestyle. Over the course of the disorder, by definition, the person has experienced at least four pain symptoms, two gastrointestinal symptoms (usually nausea and bloating), one symptom related to sexual or reproductive activity, and one neurological or conversion symptom. Common symptoms of this disorder include shortness of breath, menstrual complaints, nausea and vomiting, burning sensations in the genitals, limb pain, amnesia, and a sensation of having a lump in the throat (Othmer & De Souza, 1985). This disorder causes considerable distress and social and occupational impairment; men who have this disorder are particularly likely to be work-impaired (Golding, Smith, & Kashner, 1991).

This relatively rare disorder is present in 0.1 to 0.5 percent of the population and is far more common in women than in men (Kaplan, Sadock, & Grebb, 1994). It often is accompanied by Anxiety, Mood, and Personality Disorders as well as by Alcohol Use Disorders and attentional difficulties. Somatization Disorder usually follows a chronic course, beginning in adolescence, although symptoms may wax and wane. This disorder has a familial component, with female relatives often having Somatization Disorder and males having Antisocial Personality Disorder and Alcohol Use Disorders (Maxmen & Ward, 1995).

Undifferentiated Somatoform Disorder. This disorder involves the presence, for at least six months, of one or more somatic symptoms, not attributable to a medical condition, that cause significant upset or dysfunction. Common complaints include persistent fatigue, loss of appetite, gastrointestinal symptoms, and genitourinary symptoms (American Psychiatric Association, 1994a). The diagnosis of Undifferentiated Somatoform Disorder can be used to describe symptoms that resemble but do not meet the full criteria for Somatization Disorder (Martin & Yutzy, 1994). People with Undifferentiated Somatoform Disorder tend not to be as impaired as those with Somatization Disorder, but their symptoms often evolve into Somatization Disorder.

Conversion Disorder. This disorder was well known in Freud's time but is relatively rare today. It is present in approximately one out of every ten thousand people (Morrison, 1995). Conversion Disorder involves a loss or change in voluntary motor or sensory functioning, and it results in such symptoms as blindness, paralysis of a limb, impaired balance, mutism, or seizures. The physical symptom has no medical cause but is typically associated with and symbolic of a conflict, a stressor, or a psychological difficulty. For example, disability associated with Conversion Disorder is often localized in body parts previously affected by injury or illness or that have some special significance. The symptoms often provide secondary gains. Conversion Disorder is most common in adolescents and women who are not medically or psychologically sophisticated and who may have limited education and intellectual ability. This disorder is rarely diagnosed before the age of ten or after the age of thirty-five (Martin & Yutzy, 1994) and is sometimes associated with childhood sexual abuse (Martin, 1994).

Pain Disorder. This disorder entails either an excessive reaction to an existing physical pain (Pain Disorder Associated With Both Psychological Factors and a General Medical Condition) or preoccupation with a pain that is not shown to have any medical origin (Pain Disorder Associated With Psychological Factors).

Secondary gains, including attention or avoidance of unpleasant experiences, are often important determinants of this disorder. Depression and anxiety sometimes accompany this relatively common disorder, as does impairment in functioning. Pain Disorder is most often diagnosed in adolescence and young adulthood and is more prevalent among women than among men (Maxmen & Ward, 1995). The disorder typically begins abruptly and worsens over time. When Pain Disorder is associated with a medically diagnosed physical condition, it sometimes stems from physicians' minimization or inadequate treatment of pain (Arntz, 1996).

Hypochondriasis. This is probably the best known variant of Somatoform Disorder. It is characterized by the belief that minor physical complaints (such as chest pain or a headache) are symptoms of serious conditions like a heart attack or a brain tumor. This fear of having a serious medical condition lasts for at least six months, typically begins in early adulthood, and causes marked distress or dysfunction, although the belief is not of sufficient intensity to be described as delusional. Men and women are equally affected by this disorder, which is often accompanied by Depressive and Anxiety Disorders (Noyes et al., 1994). Hypochondriasis is fairly common and is believed to affect 4 to 6 percent of people in a general medical clinic (Kaplan et al., 1994).

Body Dysmorphic Disorder. This disorder involves preoccupation with an imagined or slight flaw in physical appearance. Facial flaws are most likely to concern the person with this disorder, but he or she typically has more than one concern; genitalia, hair, and breasts are other common areas of focus. People with this disorder are not delusional and can acknowledge that they may be exaggerating, but they do not have a realistic image of themselves. This disorder typically causes marked distress or dysfunction. People's self-consciousness can lead them to engage in prolonged grooming and staring into mirrors, to dress in concealing garments, and to avoid public situations (sometimes to the point of becoming housebound). Body Dysmorphic Disorder is most likely to begin in adolescence, usually has a gradual onset (American Psychiatric Association, 1994a), and is somewhat more common in females (Meyer & Deitsch, 1996). It has high comorbidity with other mental disorders, including Mood, Anxiety, and Psychotic Disorders. Suicidal ideation is also common. People with this disorder are more likely to seek help from dermatologists and surgeons than from therapists.

Typical Client Characteristics

Somatoform Disorders typically begin in adolescence or young adulthood and follows a chronic but often inconsistent course (Gutsch, 1988). Most types of Somatoform Disorder are more common in women and in people who live in rural areas, are not well educated, have below-average intellectual functioning and socioeconomic status, are not psychologically minded or insightful, and have difficulty identifying and expressing their feelings. People with these disorders tend to become preoccupied with their illnesses and medical histories and to deemphasize other areas of their lives, often experiencing social or occupational impairment as a result. They tend to feel dependent and helpless and use their physical complaints as a way to relate to others and to gain attention. Use of both prescription and nonprescription medication to relieve symptoms is common, and these people's lives may revolve around medication schedules and medical appointments and tests. Some become dependent on analgesics.

People with Somatoform Disorders usually restrict their activities, movement, and levels of stimulation in the belief that if they protect themselves in this way, they may prevent a worsening of their pain or other symptoms (Philips, 1987). Their preoccupation with and amplification of their bodily symptoms often leads to social isolation and depression, which in turn precipitate an intensification of the symptoms. People with Somatoform Disorders often manifest attitudes of learned helplessness, reinforced by early family and social experiences, and they tend to be discouraged, worried, angry, and low in self-esteem. They commonly have a sense of emptiness, lack positive emotions and energy, and believe that they cannot build rewarding lives until their physical complaints have been alleviated. Underlying depression may be reflected in sleeping and eating patterns.

Many people with Somatoform Disorders report a family history of illness, and clients' symptoms may mirror those experienced by family members when the clients were children. The clients themselves may have been sickly when they were younger and may have learned that, in their families, physical illness gained more attention than verbal expressions of emotional discomfort.

In addition to the research already mentioned on the overall relationship between Somatoform Disorders and personality patterns, research also has been conducted on the personality patterns of people with specific types of Somatoform Disorders. Alexithymia, the inability to experience and express emotions, sometimes contributes to and coexists with Somatoform Disorders, notably Pain Disorder (Bach & Bach, 1995). Gutsch (1988) notes that people with Pain Disorder have often had early exposure to people experiencing pain, tend to be in strenuous, routinized, difficult jobs where the experience of pain is common, and reject the idea that their pain has a psychological origin. Their experience of pain is often connected to a threatened loss or unresolved conflict that raises negative feelings, which are then expressed through somatization (Kaufman & Aronoff, 1983). Pain Disorder often reflects masked depression. Families of people with this disorder also have a high incidence of chronic pain, dysfunctional alcohol use, and depression.

People with Hypochondriasis are particularly likely to have low self-esteem and feelings of guilt (Maxmen & Ward, 1995). Hypochondriasis is often associated with an early bereavement, a history of illness in the family, and overprotective parents. Hypochondriasis commonly is accompanied by anxiety, depression, mistrust, underlying anger and hostility, obsessive-compulsive traits, fear of disease, a low pain threshold, Personality Disorders, and disturbed early relationships. This disorder may be situational or chronic, typically worsening during times of stress or emotional arousal (Kellner, 1985).

People with Somatization Disorder tend to view themselves as always having been sickly and unhappy. They commonly have had problems of adjustment as children and may have been abused. As adults, people with Somatization Disorder are often manipulative, suicidal, dependent, overemotional, exhibitionistic, narcissistic, disorganized, dependent, and self-centered (Kaplan et al., 1994).

Somatization Disorder seems to have a familial component. The families of origin of people with Somatization Disorder tend to be disorganized. Lilienfeld, Van Valkenburg, Larntz, and Akiskal (1986) suggest that Somatization Disorder and Histrionic and Antisocial Personality Disorders are different stages of the same disorder and share an underlying structure. The three often overlap, co-exist, and are found in the same families. The female relatives of people with a Somatoform Disorder often have that same disorder or Histrionic Personality Disorder, whereas their male relatives, particularly their husbands or fathers, are more likely to manifest Substance-Related Disorders or antisocial behavior.

Preferred Therapist Characteristics

Therapists generally should assume a warm, positive, optimistic stance in treating people with Somatoform Disorders. These clients need a stable relationship that inspires confidence and provides acceptance, approval, and empathy. This requirement may present a challenge because some people with Somatoform Disorders are frustrated and angry with the medical community's inability to resolve their physical complaints. They may be resentful of a referral for psychotherapy, viewing the referral as a statement that others think their complaints are "all in their mind." These negative feelings are often displaced onto the therapist, who may bear the brunt of these clients' discouragement and unhappiness.

Some therapists experience annoyance and even anger with these clients if the clients refuse to let go of the belief that they have serious physical disorders or if the clients view therapists and physicians as adversaries who are refusing to find physical causes for the symptoms. Therapists need to be aware of their own reactions to these clients' behaviors and attitudes so that they can prevent countertransference reactions from harming the therapeutic relationship.

Viederman (1986) suggests communicating admiration for the suffering these clients have endured. That may be helpful, but the therapist needs to be careful not to reinforce the client's role as a sick person; rather, the therapist should gradually shift the focus off the physical illness and encourage stress management, increased activities and socialization, and positive verbalization. Reinforcement should be used when the client does not dwell on the bodily symptoms but instead takes an active role in self-help.

Intervention Strategies

As with all the disorders in this section, a team approach to treatment is indicated, with the physician and the therapist working together. The therapist can even be presented as a consultant who will help alleviate the impact of stress on the client's physical complaints while the physician focuses on the medical aspects of those complaints. This stance reassures the client that the physical complaints are being taken seriously and treated appropriately. A collaborative approach also allows the therapist to monitor the client's medical care and discourage unnecessary tests or medical consultations while making sure that the physician does indeed take the client seriously. Presenting both the physiological and the psychological component of treatment as an integrated package can promote treatment compliance and increase the chances of a successful outcome.

The overall treatment goals should focus on improving functioning rather than on reducing physical symptoms; if functioning is improved, in most cases, the symptoms will spontaneously decrease. Clients' tendency toward selective perception and exaggeration of physiological symptoms, as well as their withdrawal from relationships and activities, can be reduced through cognitive-behavioral therapy. The focus of therapy should be on the present rather than on the past and should seek to increase skills in stress management and coping, facilitate verbal expression of feelings, promote empowerment, and encourage healthy cognitions as well as increased activity and socialization. Confrontation and emphasis on insight, if used at all, should be reserved for later phases of treatment with these clients.

Medical complaints should be deemphasized, but the therapist should avoid taking a position on the veracity of the medical complaints and certainly should not engage in arguments with the client. People with Somatoform Disorders genuinely experience and believe in the symptoms they present, and therapists should treat those beliefs gently. Understanding and addressing the social context of people with this disorder is essential because context typically reinforces and explains the presence of the symptoms.

The empirical research on effective treatment of Somatoform Disorders is limited, but many approaches and techniques have been suggested and have demonstrated success, such as the following three-stage treatment process. In stage one, therapy begins with a concrete focus on physical symptoms, teaching people strategies for reducing them. Techniques like biofeedback and relaxation training are usually well received because of their emphasis on the body. Stage two emphasizes supportive discussion of symptoms and lifestyle and helps the client make connections between the two, raising awareness of difficulties that may be experienced in the interpersonal, occupational, and leisure areas as well as in self-expression. Stage three employs cognitive and emotive approaches, enabling the client to gain deeper awareness of cognitive distortions and make changes in thoughts, feelings, relationships, and lifestyle.

Kellner (1982) suggests a comprehensive approach to treating Hypochondriasis that has application to the other types of Somatoform Disorders. Therapy begins with a physical examination and the gathering of information and then focuses on helping the client understand how distress can aggravate symptoms. Once that goal has been accomplished, therapy typically includes the following five steps:

1. Exploration of the client's attitudes toward illness

2. Presentation of information on the client's medical condition

3. Perceptual retraining to help the client focus more on external information and less on internal cues

4. Ericksonian suggestions that the client's symptoms will be reduced

5. Encouragement of self-talk and internal dialogue to reduce stress and anxiety

Many other approaches also seem likely to be useful in the treatment of specific types of Somatoform Disorders. Spelic (1997) suggests that a client with Somatization Disorder or Hypochondriasis may benefit from keeping a journal of physical symptoms and associated stressors so that the connection can be emphasized. Viederman (1995) has found the combination of a therapeutic environment emphasizing levity and good fellowship with the use of metaphors and dramatic interpretations to be helpful in promoting understanding and symptom relief in people with Conversion Disorder. Hypnosis, in addition to relaxation, has also contributed to the treatment of that disorder and of Pain Disorder.

An informal 1 to 10 rating scale of pain's severity can be useful in assessing progress that has been made in the treatment of Pain Disorder. Omer (1994) has found that pain symptoms can be reduced through the combining of techniques for pain management (such as biofeedback and relaxation) with techniques designed to reduce negative self-talk, increase activity, and promote emotional stability and perceptions of the meaningfulness of life. Pain Disorder generally responds better to family, group, or activity therapy than to individual therapy (Maxmen & Ward, 1995).

Some hospitals have pain treatment units that facilitate the treatment of people with Pain Disorder. These programs typically aim at decreasing people's experience of pain as well as their reliance on medication while increasing their activity levels, their cognitive control over the pain, and their effective use of coping mechanisms (King & Stoudemire, 1995). Such programs usually offer a multidisciplinary approach to treatment and include the following elements:

- Detoxification from medication (if needed)
- Physical, occupational, and recreational therapy
- Acupuncture
- Trigger-point injections
- Transcutaneous electrical nerve stimulation (TENS)
- Group, individual, and family therapy
- Various forms of relaxation

Obsessive features in both Body Dysmorphic Disorder and Hypochondriasis have responded well to behavior therapy. Gomez-Perez, Marks, and Gutierrez-Fisac (1994) have seen marked improvement in people with Body Dysmorphic Disorder when these clients were given controlled exposure to their own perceived physical flaws while social avoidance, mirror checking, and other dysfunctional behaviors were also prevented.

Group therapy is often an important component of treatment for Somatoform Disorders, particularly for Hypochondriasis and Pain Disorder. It can promote socialization, provide support, and facilitate direct expression of emotions. Group therapy can also change people's expression of symptoms, reduce depression, modify avoidance behaviors, help people assume responsibility for their symptoms, enhance their ability to enjoy life, provide information and support as well as reinforcement, and teach relaxation and other positive behaviors.

Family members usually should be involved in the treatment of Somatoform Disorders. They can learn to reinforce positive behavior and, as appropriate, to ignore or deemphasize the client's physical complaints. People diagnosed with Somatoform Disorders need to learn to get attention and affection through means other than physical illness; for most people, this learning is best gained and reinforced in the family environment. Getto and Ochitill (1982) have found people with Somatoform Disorders to be more receptive to therapy when it was endorsed not only by a professional whose opinion was valued but also by a friend or a family member—yet another reason for involving the client's significant others in treatment. If the client has a history of conflicted and dysfunctional family relationships or is still troubled by the illness or death of a family member, therapy may need to pay some attention to those issues in an effort to reduce their present impact.

Because many people with Somatoform Disorders have neglected the social and occupational areas of their lives, those should receive attention through therapy. People will often need to build support systems, develop leisure activities that may have been avoided before, and establish and work toward realistic and rewarding career goals. Environmental modifications, such as walking to work with a neighbor, may encourage some of these lifestyle changes by reducing secondary gains and altering patterns of activity.

Increasingly, medication has been used to treat Somatoform Disorders. Although analgesic medication usually does not reduce the pain associated with these disorders, antidepressant medication is often recommended to alleviate the underlying depression and often leads to reduction in the somatic symptoms. For example, clomipramine (Anafranil) and fluoxetine (Prozac) generally reduce symptoms of Body Dysmorphic Disorder by at least 50 percent (Kaplan et al., 1994). Pain Disorder, too, shows significant improvement in response to antidepressant medication. Nevertheless, the medication does not teach people to develop coping skills and rebuild their lives. Thus, even if medication is helpful, psychotherapy also seems essential to effecting and maintaining a positive response to treatment. Whatever approach to the treatment of Somatoform Disorders is used, what should be encouraged is healthy, independent, responsible behavior.

Prognosis

Somatoform Disorders tend to be persistent and resistant to treatment. Factors associated with a good prognosis are the presence of a stressful precipitant for the symptoms, the presence of brief and circumscribed symptoms, the ability to form stable relationships, the capacity to feel and express emotions directly, the ability to form a therapeutic alliance, and the ability to be introspective. A negative prognosis seems most likely when people fail to recognize that their concerns are probably excessive.

Prognosis varies according to the specific disorder and the individual client. Somatization Disorder, for example, has a particularly poor prognosis and often results in severe debilitation (Viederman, 1986), whereas Conversion Disorder almost always spontaneously disappears within a few days or weeks but may recur and tend to be difficult to treat once it becomes entrenched (Kaplan et al., 1994). Conversion symptoms of blindness, aphonia, and paralysis usually respond well to treatment, but seizures and tremors are less likely to remit (Toone, 1990). Pain symptoms can be chronic and disabling, but pain-treatment centers report a 60 to 80 percent rate of significant improvement among people with Pain Disorder, and that improvement is well maintained after discharge. Hypochondriasis can be a chronic and fluctuating disorder, although one-third to two-thirds of people with this disorder do improve significantly (Kaplan et al., 1994). Kellner (1985) reports a positive prognosis for treatment of Hypochondriasis among young clients from upper socioeconomic levels who did not have coexisting Personality Disorders or medical conditions, had few previous medical problems, and had disorders that were of sudden onset and relatively brief duration. Body Dysmorphic Disorder tends to be a chronic and stable disorder, although success has been reported with exposure treatment (Hollander et al., 1992).

Factitious Disorders

Description of the Disorder

Factitious Disorders are "characterized by physical or psychological symptoms that are intentionally produced or feigned in order to assume the sick role" (American Psychiatric Association, 1994a, p. 471). Unlike people with Somatoform Disorders, who really experience and believe in their physical complaints, people with Factitious Disorders purposely simulate symptoms in order to be treated as though they were ill. They are not feigning the symptoms in order to escape work or other obligations, however; rather, their primary goal is to assume the role of patient and to receive care, nurturance, and attention.

Factitious Disorders, also known as Munchausen's syndrome, are among the most difficult disorders to diagnose because of the person's untruthfulness and hidden agendas (Meyer, 1983). People with this disorder typically present severe physical or psychological symptoms (for example, psychosis or abnormal bleeding). Their affect tends to be incongruent with these symptoms, often reflecting indifference or lack of concern. They are eager to undergo invasive medical procedures but will not allow communication with previous physicians. They avoid accurate diagnosis by changes of residence, physicians, and symptoms.

The onset of a Factitious Disorder is usually in early adulthood, but the disorder may begin in childhood, often following a medically verified physical illness that places these people in the patient role, which they find rewarding. Sometimes people with Factitious Disorders have worked in medical settings or are otherwise familiar with medical personnel and illnesses, and this familiarity facilitates their simulation of the symptoms of illness. This disorder is more common in males (American Psychiatric Association, 1994a) and is severe in that it typically prevents people's involvement in normal social and occupational activities. Although the prevalence of this disorder is unknown, it seems to be relatively rare (Maxmen & Ward, 1995). Factitious Disorders are often accompanied by a Personality Disorder, particularly one involving instability, self-destructive and acting-out behavior, dependence, and manipulation (Bauer & Boegner, 1996).

In a variation on this disorder, Factitious Disorder by Proxy (diagnosed as Factitious Disorder Not Otherwise Specified), parents or caretakers deliberately create or exaggerate physical or psychological symptoms in people under their care (children, for example, or people who are disabled). The caretaker may coach the person in his or her care to confirm or present signs of the illness. The symptoms bring attention, support, and sympathy to the caretaker. Approximately 9 percent of children involved in this pattern die; many others are disfigured or impaired, as a result either of harm from their caretakers or of harm from unnecessary medical procedures (Rappaport & Hochstadt, 1993).

Typical Client Characteristics

People with Factitious Disorders tend to be immature, dramatic, grandiose, and demanding and to insist on attention while often refusing to comply with prescribed treatments. Common motivators are self-punishment, the desire to obtain compensation for past suffering and perceived wrongs, and the desire to obtain drugs, in addition to wishes for attention and nurturing (Folks, 1995). People with Factitious Disorders typically had parents who were normally harsh and demanding but who became caring and loving when their children were ill (Brodsky, 1984). People with this disorder also typically derive great pleasure from manipulating the medical system.

Males with Factitious Disorders tend to be unstable and egocentric, whereas females tend to be younger, more stable, and more likely to be in the medical field (Viederman, 1986). As children, many of the people with this disorder were abused or neglected, and illness may have been the only way for them to get attention. They also may have developed positive early relationships with physicians. First-degree relatives often have mental disorders (Pope, Jones, & Jones, 1982), chronic medical problems, and poor coping skills (Brodsky, 1984). People with Factitious Disorders may have undergone many surgical procedures and other medical tests and treatments that produced genuine physical complaints and now complicate the treatment picture.

People with Factitious Disorder by Proxy usually are young mothers who, on the surface, appear devoted to their children but are actually using their children to gain access to the medical community. They typically are experiencing marital discord and have symbiotic relationships with their children (Rappaport & Hochstadt, 1993). Their backgrounds often include a history of family dysfunction and abuse. Medical settings may be familiar and comfortable to them because of their own illnesses or work experiences.

Preferred Therapist Characteristics

Establishing a therapeutic alliance with a person diagnosed as having Factitious Disorders will usually be extremely difficult. The therapist should be supportive and empathic but should also gently confront the deception. Strong confrontation should be avoided because it typically will be met with denial and hostility. Folks (1995) suggests that a partnership of physician and therapist can be especially effective in working with these clients: the physician confronts the client, and the therapist provides support. The therapist should avoid power struggles, open conflict, and humiliation of people with Factitious Disorders and must manage his or her own feelings of anger and frustration in dealing with these clients' deceptions and manipulations. Viewing the symptoms as a cry for help rather than as hostile or manipulative behavior can be helpful to both therapist and client.

Intervention Strategies

People with Factitious Disorders are rarely seen for psychotherapy because they typically are not motivated to address their disorder, but they may appear in treatment as a result of pressure from a family member, or after their dissembling has been discovered. Some may remain in treatment if attention is paid to their feigned complaints and if the treatment meets some of their dependence needs, although most will leave treatment once they realize that they have been found out. While in treatment, people with Factitious Disorders are likely to be hostile and to resist the formation of a positive therapeutic relationship.

It is important to set realistic treatment goals with these clients. Personality reconstruction through therapy is unlikely; nevertheless, improvement in coping skills, reduction in self-injurious behavior and dangerous medical procedures, and symptom reduction are all realistic goals.

The available information on the treatment of this disorder is nearly all anecdotal or theoretical: it is extremely difficult to obtain a large enough sample size of people with Factitious Disorders to conduct controlled research. No interventions are now known to be consistently effective in treating Factitious Disorders (Maxmen & Ward, 1995), and so treatment recommendations are based on theory rather than on data. Folks (1995), having reviewed the existing reports on successful treatment of Factitious Disorders, concludes that all the successful treatments contained three common elements: reinforcement of positive health behaviors, the presence of a primary therapist, and a collaborative relationship between the therapist and a physician.

Several authors provide specific suggestions for treating Factitious Disorders. Meyer (1983) suggests reality therapy as an approach to treating people with this disorder, so that they can be helped to see that their current behavior is not meeting their needs and to find more rewarding ways of behaving. Jefferson and Ochitill (1982) recommend focusing on stressors that may have precipitated the disorder, providing support, and encouraging the development of more effective mechanisms for managing and coping with stress. Maxmen and Ward (1995) encourage hospitalization of people with Factitious Disorders, to give therapists greater access and control. (Children whose caretakers can be diagnosed with Factitious Disorder by Proxy also may need to be hospitalized for their own protection.) Eisendrath (1995) suggests a double-bind approach to treatment. In this approach, clients are offered a benign medical intervention (such as biofeedback) and are told that failure of the treatment will confirm a diagnosis of a Factitious Disorder. This apparently leads some people to choose recovery. One reason for the success of this approach is that it allows the person to give up factitious behaviors without embarrassment—an important element of treatment. Family therapy may be particularly useful for people with Factitious Disorder by Proxy.

Prognosis

In some cases a Factitious Disorder that develops in response to environmental stress will remit spontaneously when the stressor has passed. Once a Factitious Disorder becomes chronic and part of a person's lifestyle, however, the prognosis for treatment is poor (Maxmen & Ward, 1995). Factors associated with responsiveness to treatment include coexisting Axis I mental disorders (such as depression, anxiety, or substance use), compulsive or histrionic personality traits, and the ability to establish a therapeutic alliance. The presence of severe Personality Disorders reduces the likelihood of a successful treatment outcome (Folks & Houck, 1993).

Delirium, Dementia, and Amnestic and Other Cognitive Disorders

Description of the Disorders

According to *DSM-IV*, all the Cognitive Disorders are characterized by "a clinically significant deficit in cognition or memory that represents a significant change from a previous level of functioning" (American Psychiatric Association, 1994a, p. 123). Common symptoms of Cognitive Disorders include not only impairments in memory (especially of recent memory) but also impairments in the following areas:

- Abstract thinking
- Perception
- Language
- Ability to concentrate and perform new tasks
- Overall intellectual performance
- Judgment
- Attention
- Spatiotemporal orientation
- Calculating ability
- Ability to grasp meaning and recognize or identify objects
- Perceptions of body and environment

The Cognitive Disorders are a heterogeneous group with diverse symptoms and origins. Common causes include Alzheimer's disease, a systemic illness, a head injury, or deleterious exposure to a psychoactive or toxic substance (such as alcohol).

The symptoms of a Cognitive Disorder encompass many of the symptoms associated with other mental disorders such as depression, anxiety, personality change, paranoia, and confusion. Consequently, other mental disorders may be mistaken for the Cognitive Disorders that they resemble, and Cognitive Disorders also can be mistaken for other mental disorders (for example, some people diagnosed as having Alzheimer's disease actually have pseudodementia, a form of depression that has similar symptoms). This error is unfortunate because there are effective treatments for depression, but an effective treatment for Alzheimer's disease has yet to be found.

In light of the diagnostic challenge presented by the Cognitive Disorders, their diagnosis must take account of symptoms as well as of possible causes. The clinician should obtain a psychiatric or neurological evaluation when one of these disorders is suspected. Electroencephalograms and other medical tests, as well as psychological tests like the Wechsler Adult Intelligence Scales and the Halstead-Reitan, can determine the likelihood of a Cognitive Disorder's being present. The therapist may also find the Mini–Mental State Exam useful in making a preliminary diagnosis of a Cognitive Disorder (Kaplan et al., 1994).

DSM-IV defines three Cognitive Disorders—Delirium, Dementia, and Amnestic Disorder. Cognitive Disorders are present in approximately 1 percent of the adult population and are expected to increase their prevalence with the lengthening of the life span (Maxmen & Ward, 1995). Discussion of specific etiologies and related presentations of these disorders is beyond the scope of this book; clinicians treating people with Cognitive Disorders will want to consult the *DSM* for the detailed descriptions and diagnostic criteria provided there.

Delirium. This disorder is typified by abrupt onset and clouded consciousness, as well as by impairment of recent memory and attention, with accompanying disorientation. Emotional, perceptual, and psychomotor disturbances and disturbances of the sleep-wake cycle often accompany this disorder, which is most common in children and the elderly. Possible causes of Delirium include central nervous system disease (such as epilepsy), cardiac failure, electrolyte imbalance, and postoperative states. Excessive exposure to substances like anesthetics, opioids, cocaine, lithium, antihistamines, carbon monoxide, and insecticides, as well as withdrawal from those substances, can produce symptoms of Delirium (Lipowski, 1989; Gustafson et al., 1988). This disorder typically has an inconsistent course and a positive response to appropriate treatment, although it is a sign of impending death for approximately one-third of those with this disorder (Davison & Neale, 1996).

Dementia. This disorder is more likely to have an insidious onset and a progressive and pervasive course. It is characterized by multiple cognitive deficits, including memory impairment. Common symptoms of this disorder are decline in language functioning, difficulty in recognizing even familiar people and objects, and impairment in abstract thinking, judgment, and insight. An overall decline in social and occupational functioning nearly always accompanies this disorder. Delusions, especially those of persecution, often are symptoms of this disorder and may lead to aggressive and destructive behavior. Hallucinations and depression also often accompany Dementia. Level of consciousness and alertness may be unaffected. The most common causes of Dementia are Alzheimer's disease and vascular disease, but there are many other causes as well, including traumatic brain injury, brain tumors, human immunodeficiency virus (HIV), substances (such as alcohol, inhalants, and sedatives), neurological and endocrine conditions, and vitamin deficiencies. This disorder is most prevalent among people over the age of eighty-five: at least 20 percent of people in this age group have severe Dementia (American Psychiatric Association, 1994a).

Amnestic Disorder. This disorder is characterized by memory impairment, especially learning and recall of new information, without other significant accompanying cognitive deficits. This disorder, too, has multiple possible etiologies, including head trauma, encephalitis, alcohol use with accompanying vitamin B1 (thiamine) deficiency, sedative misuse, and brain tumors.

Typical Client Characteristics

Few generalizations can be drawn about people with Cognitive Disorders because the causes and symptoms of these disorders vary so greatly. Most people with Cognitive Disorders will be past midlife, and many will have coexisting medical or Substance Use Disorders. Additional client characteristics are linked to specific disorders.

Dementia is one of the most common Cognitive Disorders. Dementia of the Alzheimer's Type affects 5 percent of people over the age of sixty-five and encompasses 50 to 60 percent of people with Dementia (Kaplan et al., 1994). That disorder has a genetic component and is more likely to occur in first-degree relatives of those with the disorder, in women, and in those with low educational and occupational levels (Andreasen & Black, 1995). Vascular Dementia is more common among people with a history of diabetes and hypertension and often coexists with depression. Many forms of Cognitive Disorder have an external cause, such as excessive use of drugs or alcohol, a blow to the head, or exposure to a toxic substance, and will often be associated with habits or lifestyle. For example, Substance-Induced Cognitive Disorders usually will be accompanied by concurrent diagnosis of a Substance Use Disorder.

Preferred Therapist Characteristics

Therapists treating people with Cognitive Disorders should either have training in the physiological and neurological aspects of these disorders or collaborate with someone who does have that training. The therapeutic relationship that is established with a person who has a Cognitive Disorder will depend to a large extent on the person's level of functioning. In general, a therapist working with a person who has one of these disorders will have to be directive, supportive, and reassuring. The therapist will have to take charge of the therapy and determine what psychological and medical interventions are necessary. Promoting awareness of reality usually will be an important part of the therapist's role, as will provision of information, family education and intervention, and assistance in obtaining adjunct services like family support groups, residential treatment facilities, respite care, and medical care. The therapist will also need to deal with his or her own feelings about treating people who may have a poor prognosis and limited prospects for improvement.

Intervention Strategies

Treatment of Cognitive Disorders usually involves a multifaceted approach. Medical and neurological treatment, including drugs or surgery, may be needed to assess and arrest or reduce the cognitive impairment. Medication may target such symptoms as depression, anxiety, psychosis, and aggressiveness or it may address the disorder itself. New medications, such as tacrine (Cognex), are being approved to treat Dementia of the Alzheimer's Type and other Cognitive Disorders. Environmental manipulation may be indicated to help people cope more effectively with their living situations despite their impairment and to maintain some form of employment as long as possible. Change, stress, and external stimuli should be reduced so as not to exacerbate symptoms. A person in the advanced stages of one of these disorders may need to be placed in a supervised living situation.

Family members of those diagnosed as having long-standing and progressive Cognitive Disorders are often overwhelmed with worry, guilt, and the responsibility of caring for their affected relatives. Counseling, information, support, and help with making decisions, expressing feelings, and setting goals can enable family members to cope more effectively with the difficulties of dealing with someone with a Cognitive Disorder. Family members may also benefit from help in identifying and making use of community resources, such as respite care and in-home help, that are available to them.

Although psychotherapy typically plays a secondary role in direct treatment of most Cognitive Disorders, it can be an important complementary part of the medical treatment. Therapy seems particularly helpful to people in the early or mild stages of Dementia of the Alzheimer's Type and of Vascular Dementia. Therapy probably will be most useful if it emphasizes behavioral interventions, encouraging people to remain as active and independent as possible and helping them to compensate for changes in their capacities by building on any coping mechanisms that are still accessible to them. Behaviorally oriented therapy can also help these people to control their destructive impulses and their emotional lability. Attention should be paid to keeping people appropriately informed about the nature of their disorders, helping them express their feelings about the changes they are experiencing, and maximizing their contact with reality via family pictures, clocks, and other visual and verbal reminders. These therapeutic interventions can help to reduce such secondary symptoms as depression, denial, fear, confusion, and negative feelings about themselves that are common in people in the early stages of Cognitive Disorders (Shamoian & Teusink, 1987).

People with Cognitive Disorders caused by psychoactive substances often will have a coexisting diagnosis of a Substance Use Disorder. Psychotherapy will play an important role in these people's treatment, helping them eliminate their self-destructive use of drugs or alcohol, a modification that in turn will probably ameliorate the accompanying Cognitive Disorder and greatly reduce the chances of a recurrence.

Prognosis

The prognosis for recovery from a Cognitive Disorder is as variable as the disorders themselves and is usually determined by the cause of the disorder. Those disorders stemming from psychoactive substances, metabolic abnormalities, and systemic illnesses tend to be time-limited and usually are followed by full recovery or significant improvement. Dementia of the Alzheimer's Type, however, currently has no known cure and is the fourth or fifth leading cause of death (Shamoian & Teusink, 1987).

Mental Disorders Due to a General Medical Condition

According to *DSM-IV,* a "Mental Disorder Due to a General Medical Condition is characterized by the presence of mental symptoms that are judged to be the direct physiological consequence of a medical condition" (American Psychiatric Association, 1994a, p. 165). The causative medical condition should be listed on Axis III of the multiaxial assessment.

Nonpsychiatric medical conditions can be direct or physiological causes of a broad range of mental disorders, including not only Delirium, Dementia, and Amnestic Disorder but also Psychotic Disorders, Mood Disorders, Anxiety Disorders, Sexual Dysfunction, and Sleep Disorders. Specific diagnoses cited in this section of the *DSM* include Catatonic Disorder Due to a General Medical Condition (such as neurological and metabolic abnormalities), Personality Change Due to a General Medical Condition (such as endocrine and autoimmune conditions), and Mental Disorder Not Otherwise Specified Due to a General Medical Condition. Diagnosis of disorders such as these is usually made by a psychiatrist or a neurologist. Psychotherapists may well collaborate in the treatment of people with these disorders, as well as in the treatment of their family members, but medical treatment that targets the medical condition will generally be the primary intervention. Because of the scope and diversity of these disorders and their etiologies, further discussion of their diagnosis and treatment will not be provided here. Nevertheless, clinicians should keep these disorders in mind when making diagnoses.

TREATMENT RECOMMENDATIONS: CLIENT MAP

This chapter has discussed the category of Disorders in Which Physical and Psychological Factors Combine. The following summary of treatment recommendations is organized according to the format of the Client Map.

Client Map

Diagnoses

Disorders in Which Physical and Psychological Factors Combine (Somatoform Disorders; Factitious Disorders; Delirium, Dementia, and Amnestic and Other Cognitive Disorders; Mental Disorders Due to a General Medical Condition)

Objectives of Treatment

Reduce somatization

Promote more constructive expression of feelings

Maximize functioning and coping skills

Improve socialization and use of leisure time

Assessments

Physical examination

Clinician Characteristics

Knowledgeable about physical disorders

Willing to collaborate with physicians

Skilled at handling resistance

Structured and concrete

Warm and optimistic

High in tolerance of frustration

Location of Treatment

Usually outpatient setting

Interventions to Be Used

Team approach to treatment

Holistic approach

Teaching of stress management and coping skills

Use of relaxation techniques

Improvement in socialization

Behavioral strategies to improve functioning

Emphasis of Treatment

Supportive emphasis

Moderately directive emphasis

Some attention to history, with primary orientation toward the present

Integrated focus on cognitive, behavioral, and affective areas (with behavioral interventions usually predominating)

Numbers

Primarily individual therapy

Family therapy to reduce secondary gains and help family members understand and cope with disorder

Group therapy, as functioning permits, to promote socialization

Timing

Geared to readiness of client

May need to be gradual and long-term

Medications Needed

As indicated by the physical disorders and specific emotional symptoms

Adjunct Services

Leisure and career counseling

Prognosis

Fair in general, but widely variable according to disorder

Client Map of Dr. Martin C.

This chapter began with a description of Dr. Martin C., a sixty-two-year-old African American male who was referred for psychotherapy by his physician after seeking medical help for what he was convinced was cancer.

Diagnosis

Axis I: 300.7 Hypochondriasis, Moderate

Axis II: V71.09 No diagnosis on Axis II

Axis III: No known physical disorders or conditions, but symptoms of gastric distress reported

Axis IV: Occupational and financial dissatisfaction, marital conflict, physical problems

Axis V: Global assessment of functioning (GAF Scale): current GAF = 65

Objectives of Treatment

Improve skills related to stress management and coping

Improve marital relationship

Facilitate development of realistic occupational and financial goals

Improve medical condition

Assessments

Physical evaluation

Clinician Characteristics

Warm, optimistic

Skilled at handling resistance

Knowledgeable about medical concerns

Mature and experienced

Supportive and accepting throughout, yet directive and structured

Location of Treatment

Outpatient setting

Interventions to Be Used

Multifaceted collaboration between therapist and physician, with therapist as primary engineer of treatment (to ensure compatibility of physical and psychological treatments and give client a sense of control missing from other areas of life)

Education about the impact of stress on gastric functioning

Education about dietary approaches to reducing gastrointestinal discomfort

Supportive and reflective counseling designed to promote awareness of feelings and ability to verbalize them

Techniques of stress management, including progressive relaxation and expansion of leisure activities

Exploration of career-related attitudes, abilities, and opportunities, with goal of establishing more realistic and rewarding career goals

Discussion of partial retirement combined with consulting and half-time teaching (to reduce stress and stabilize but perhaps not improve client's financial situation)

Marital therapy (to improve communication between client and his wife, help them understand each other's feelings, and define a realistic and mutually acceptable lifestyle)

Emphasis of Treatment

Structured, relatively directive but encouraging

Client to take appropriate responsibility for his own treatment and his lifestyle

Numbers

Individual and couples therapy

Timing

Weekly sessions, rapid pace, medium duration

Medications Needed

Carefully monitored medication as needed for gastrointestinal distress

Adjunct Services

Financial and retirement planning

Leisure counseling

Prognosis

Fair to good

Recommended Reading

Bass, C. (Ed.). (1990). *Physical symptoms and psychological illness.* Oxford, England: Blackwell.

Folks, D. G., & Houck, C. A. (1993). Somatoform disorders, factitious disorders, and malingering. In A. Stoudemire & B. S. Fogel (Eds.), *Psychiatric care of the medical patient* (pp. 267–287). New York: Oxford University Press.

Personality Disorders

Joanne, a twenty-five-year-old Caucasian woman, was referred to a psychotherapist by the hospital where she had been treated after her eighth suicide attempt. The therapist to whom she was referred would be her fourth one; nevertheless, she responded with initial optimism to the new therapist and provided an extensive narration of her long-standing difficulties.

Joanne was the fourth and last child born to her parents within the first six years of their marriage. Her father abandoned the family a year after Joanne's birth, and she had had no contact with him since that time. Joanne's mother had remarried about five years later, and she and her children had moved into a three-bedroom apartment with her new husband and his two teenaged sons.

The elder boy, fifteen, soon began to abuse Joanne sexually. He won her silence and cooperation by telling her that he loved her best and by threatening to harm her pets if she did not do what he wanted. The first time Joanne balked at complying with his demands, he proved the seriousness of his threats by killing her canary.

After about a year, Joanne's stepfather found her undressed in her stepbrother's room. The stepfather became enraged with Joanne, now seven years old, and accused her of trying to ruin his family. He also blamed Joanne's mother and became increasingly abusive, both emotionally and physically, toward both Joanne and her mother.

When Joanne was ten years old, her mother committed suicide. Joanne and her siblings were separated and put in foster homes. Joanne remained in her foster home until she dropped out of high school and married, at seventeen.

At the time she provided this information, Joanne was married to her second husband. Her first husband had been physically abusive, particularly when he was intoxicated. Her current husband was also physically abusive. ("At least he doesn't drink" was Joanne's comment on the situation.)

Joanne herself presented with many difficulties. She reported having been depressed for as long as she could remember, with frequent episodes of suicidal ideation and behavior. She often plucked out her eyebrows and eyelashes, as well as the hair on her head, and reportedly spent a great deal of time each day putting on makeup and styling her hair to disguise the hair loss. She was nearly 100 pounds overweight and often consumed alcohol to excess, a behavior that she blamed on her first husband. She had little contact with her siblings and had no close women friends, but she had engaged in several brief but intense extramarital relationships, one with her husband's brother. She had a spotty employment history, with some computer skills and intermittent work for temporary agencies, but she reported that her depression made it difficult for her to get to work consistently and on time. Joanne's principal diagnosis was Borderline Personality Disorder.

OVERVIEW OF PERSONALITY DISORDERS

Description of the Disorders

Personality Disorders are very long-standing and are deeply ingrained. They are characterized by maladaptive attitudes and behaviors that show up in at least two of the following areas:

- Perceptions and understanding of oneself and one's environment
- Expression, nature, range, and appropriateness of emotions
- Interpersonal skills and relationships
- Impulse control

These attitudes and behaviors typically are rigid and inflexible, causing distress and/or impairment in important areas of a person's life (American Psychiatric Association, 1994a). According to Gunderson and Gabbard (1995), a high proportion of people involved in acrimonious divorces, abandonments, violence, and self-destructive substance use have Personality Disorders.

Most people with Personality Disorders have trouble accepting appropriate responsibility for their difficulties; they usually blame others for their problems, but sometimes they blame themselves too much. People with Personality Disorders also have poor coping mechanisms and relationship skills. Because their disorders are so enduring and deeply entrenched, and because people with Personality Disorders typically have little insight and tend to externalize their difficulties, their disorders are difficult to treat (Beck & Freeman, 1990).

Presenting concerns generally focus on symptoms of depression or anxiety, reflecting a disorder listed on Axis I of a *DSM-IV* (American Psychiatric Association, 1994a) multiaxial assessment. These clients typically have little awareness of their underlying dysfunctional personality patterns. Those personality styles are ego-syntonic and acceptable to these clients, who are rarely able to grasp the effect of their personalities on others. Even for people whose Personality Disorders are ego-dystonic or in conflict with self-image, change is difficult because typically they have never manifested healthy personality patterns.

In the past, Personality Disorders were explained almost exclusively from a psychodynamic perspective, but they are now viewed as resulting from a combination of biological and social factors (Sperry, 1995). For example, one model (Cloninger, Svrakic, & Przybeck, 1993) views personality as a combination of *temperament* (made up of innate, genetic, and constitutional factors such as harm avoidance and reward needs) and *character* (self-directedness, cooperativeness, and self-transcendence). According to this model, Personality Disorders are reflected in deficits or negative attributes in both character and temperament. According to Kaplan, Sadock, and Grebb (1994), a poor match between temperament and family environment is particularly likely to contribute to the development of a Personality Disorder.

Millon (1996) provides further insight into Personality Disorders and their interactive nature. Using a medical model, he views presenting problems (usually anxiety and depression) as analogous to symptoms of disease (such as fever or cough), and he sees a Personality Disorder as comparable to an impaired immune system whose condition increases a person's vulnerability to disease. Millon also views psychological stressors as infectious agents, which are especially able to produce symptoms in a person with a Personality Disorder because that person's overall psychological "immune system" is compromised.

Personality Disorders are evident by adolescence or early adulthood, if not earlier, and tend to continue throughout life. Diagnosis of a Personality Disorder in a person under the age of eighteen is made only if symptoms have been present for at least one year.

Personality Disorders vary considerably in terms of degree of impairment. Researchers have viewed the Borderline, Paranoid, and Schizotypal Personality Disorders as the most dysfunctional (Gunderson, 1988; Millon, 1996). These disorders are characterized by very poor social skills, hostility, and fragility. The Obsessive-Compulsive, Dependent, Histrionic, Narcissistic, and Avoidant Personality Disorders typically involve the least dysfunction. People with these disorders are able to seek out and deal with others in a relatively coherent fashion and can adapt to or control their environments in meaningful ways. Although all Personality Disorders tend to wax and wane in severity, according to life circumstances and stressors, some (for example, Histrionic and Narcissistic Personality Disorders) worsen with age, whereas others (such as Borderline and Antisocial Personality Disorders) tend to improve (Edell & McGlashan, 1993; Perry, 1995).

Personality Disorders are very prevalent, although they are often overlooked in clinical settings. Roth and Fonagy (1996) report a prevalence of 10 to 13 percent in community samples, and an incidence of 36 percent has been reported in clinical samples (Koeningsberg, Kaplan, Gilmore, & Cooper, 1985). According to Gunderson (1988), Personality Disorders are present in approximately 15 percent of the general population and in 30 to 50 percent of clinical populations.

Diagnostic tools can be helpful in identifying Personality Disorders that sometimes are obscured by other disorders. A number of inventories—the Millon Clinical Multiaxial Inventory (MCMI), the Minnesota Multiphasic Personality Inventory (MMPI), the Structured Interview for *DSM* Personality Inventories, and projective tests—can be useful in diagnosing these sometimes overlooked disorders (Millon, 1996).

In *DSM-IV,* the Personality Disorders are grouped into the following three clusters:

1. Cluster A (guarded or eccentric): Paranoid, Schizoid, and Schizotypal Personality Disorders

2. Cluster B (dramatic, emotional, or unpredictable): Antisocial, Borderline, Histrionic, and Narcissistic Personality Disorders

3. Cluster C (anxious and fearful): Avoidant, Dependent, and Obsessive-Compulsive Personality Disorders

DSM-IV also includes the category of Personality Disorder Not Otherwise Specified. This category encompasses Mixed Personality Disorders. These do not completely fit the criteria for any one disorder but have symptoms of two or more, which in combination meet the criteria for diagnosis of a Personality Disorder. Personality Disorder Not Otherwise Specified also includes other Personality Disorders that are currently under consideration but not yet viewed as warranting full-fledged diagnosis (such as Depressive Personality Disorder or Passive-Aggressive Personality Disorder).

Although these clusters do help to organize the array of Personality Disorders, their usefulness is controversial, and the literature typically focuses on the specific Personality Disorders rather than on the clusters. Therefore, although this chapter follows the order of the clusters, it discusses the Personality Disorders individually rather than in groups.

Typical Client Characteristics

People with Personality Disorders tend to come from troubled families (Beck & Freeman, 1990). Their families commonly have offered little sense of support or security and did not encourage development of self-esteem or an appropriate degree of independence. The families usually also failed to model healthy interpersonal and coping skills, and so identification with family members perpetuates a pattern of impaired functioning. The form taken by a person's Personality Disorder often makes sense in light of what the parental messages have been.

Personality Disorders tend to be proportionally overrepresented among lower socioeconomic and disadvantaged groups (Gunderson, 1988). Whether those circumstances predispose people to develop Personality Disorders or whether the dysfunction of people with Personality Disorders has limited their socioeconomic advancement is unclear.

Personality Disorders are often accompanied by other, more transient mental disorders and symptoms. Common examples are Mood, Anxiety, and Substance-Related Disorders. Suicidal ideation is also frequently reported by people with Personality Disorders. The presence of a Personality Disorder usually makes the treatment of a coexisting mental disorder more difficult (Roth & Fonagy, 1996). Long-standing patterns of pervasive dysfunction affecting the social and occupational areas are usually also present in people with Personality Disorders.

Achieving intimacy seems particularly difficult for these people. The strong sense of entitlement and the lack of empathy characteristic of people with Personality Disorders lead them to violate interpersonal boundaries and behave in socially inappropriate ways. People with Personality Disorders also tend to have poor self-esteem, weak ego strength, and poor impulse control. They typically are dependent, self-absorbed, and pessimistic. Underlying fear and rage are also often present. All these traits impair functioning in many areas.

Each Personality Disorder seems to be strongly associated with a particular defense mechanism. For example, Borderline Personality Disorder is associated with splitting (viewing people as extremely good or extremely bad), whereas Paranoid Personality Disorder is associated with projection. An understanding of their defenses is essential to an understanding of these clients; helping them manage and modify their defenses is usually necessary for successful treatment.

People with Personality Disorders also usually have dysfunctional and distorted schemas or belief systems, as well as maladaptive coping strategies (Beck & Freeman, 1990), and so they have great difficulty successfully managing stressors and life problems. As a result, people with these disorders typically have a long history of disappointments and come to see the world as a hostile environment. Without help, they are rarely able to make the cognitive shifts and develop the skills that would enable them to manage their lives more successfully.

Preferred Therapist Characteristics

The establishment of a sound therapeutic alliance is essential to the successful treatment of people with Personality Disorders (Meissner, 1992). The therapist should manifest those conditions that have been shown to be integral to the development of an effective, collaborative therapeutic alliance: empathy, warmth, compassion, acceptance, respect, and genuineness. Strong confrontation, punishment, or expressions of negative feelings can destroy the often fragile therapeutic bond established with a person who has a Personality Disorders. The therapist should not take sides or argue with the client but should remain supportive while maintaining control of the session.

Patience seems to be an essential ingredient because the treatment of these disorders tends to be long-term, with progress and the building of trust often very gradual. Time spent discussing the client's daily activities and relationships is not wasted; rather, it builds rapport, familiarizes the therapist with the client's life, and paves the way for subsequent treatment (Beck & Freeman, 1990).

Many people who can be diagnosed with Personality Disorders are not motivated to examine themselves or change; what they really want is to have the therapist fix their lives for them or take care of them. These clients' motivation tends to be external rather than internal. Therefore, therapists must be skilled at minimizing these clients' manipulation and resistance while developing the clients' motivation and maintaining a productive focus in therapeutic sessions.

Apparent resistance often stems from fear of change or from hopelessness, and the therapist should keep those possibilities in mind when the client fails to keep appointments or to complete agreed-upon activities between sessions. The therapist should avoid feeling hurt or angered by these behaviors and should try instead to view them as self-protection on the part of the client.

People with Personality Disorders tend to have strong transference reactions to their therapists. Some become hostile and resistant; others become needy and dependent. The therapist must monitor and manage any countertransference reactions so as to become neither overinvolved nor rejecting toward the client but instead appropriately available. Judicious use of limit setting, gentle interpretation, rewards, and modeling also help elicit positive behavior from these clients. Using humor, anecdotes, metaphors, and limited self-disclosure can also help the therapist seem genuine and human.

Intervention Strategies

Despite the prevalence of Personality Disorders in both the general and clinical populations, empirical studies on the treatment of these disorders are limited. Personality Disorders received little attention in the research literature until the mid-1980s. The writing and personality inventories developed by Millon, along with the *Journal of Personality Disorders,* initially edited by Millon, spurred interest in the study of Personality Disorders, but most of the relevant literature still consists of case studies and theoretical discussions.

Several treatment approaches have received support for use with people who have Personality Disorders. During the 1970s and the 1980s, psychodynamic psychotherapy was generally was the preferred approach to treatment. The recent literature, however, has focused increasingly on cognitive approaches to intervention (Gunderson & Gabbard, 1995).

In general, therapy for a person with a Personality Disorder will be multifaceted, with a psychodynamic or cognitive basis, so as to address the person's core difficulties. Specific interventions are selected to address the client's defenses and individual concerns. The long-standing nature of these disorders, their apparent relationship to family dynamics, and their relatively early origin all suggest an approach that will not only relieve symptoms but also effect change in overall functioning and in the person's view of self and the world.

Beck and Freeman (1990) and their associates report success in treating Personality Disorders via cognitive therapy, although case studies provide their primary substantiation. Their approach begins with standard cognitive therapy, to elicit and modify dysfunctional automatic thoughts that are contributing to anxiety and depression. Once affective changes begin, the therapist gradually shifts focus from immediate concerns to dysfunctional core schemas that underlie the Personality Disorder. Guided discovery helps clients see the impact of these core schemas on their lives. Techniques like deliberate exaggeration, labeling of distortions, decatastrophizing, and reattribution of responsibility for actions and outcomes gradually help clients with Personality Disorders identify and modify their schemas. Concurrent attention is paid to helping people learn coping, communication, decision-making, and other important life skills. Behavioral techniques, such as relaxation and role playing, along with exploration of childhood experiences that may have entrenched the schemas, enhance treatment. This kind of integrated treatment, with clear goals and treatment strategies, is especially likely to effect positive change in a Personality Disorder.

Another approach that has been successful in treating Personality Disorders has been developed by Millon (1996), who advances four goals in the treatment of Personality Disorders: "modifying the Pain-Pleasure Polarity, Balancing the Passive-Active Polarity, Altering the Other-Self Polarity, and Rebuilding the Personality Structure" (p. 191). A thorough assessment of a person and of that person's Personality Disorder determines which of these polarities may need particular attention. Using an integrated model that draws on a broad range of expressive, cognitive, and behavioral interventions, Millon seeks to modify the dysfunctional polarities. A careful treatment plan gives both the clinician and the client a sense of direction and allows for systematic selection of interventions.

Behavior therapy has also been used successfully in treating Personality Disorders, particularly in the initial stages of treatment. Behavior therapy is especially helpful and appealing to people who are resistant to long-term treatment or who have severely dysfunctional and self-destructive behavioral patterns that require rapid modification. Through behavior therapy, they can learn new social and occupational skills, as well as practical approaches to coping and stress management. Generally, behavior therapy is used to address the Axis I disorders (such as Substance-Related or Mood Disorders) and to effect fairly rapid improvement, which in turn often increases clients' motivation and confidence in psychotherapy and encourages them to continue treatment, with a focus on underlying personality patterns. Even if these clients do terminate treatment prematurely, at least they are left with positive feelings about their treatment and may return for help if symptoms recur.

People with Personality Disorders typically have deficits in many areas of their lives. Therefore, adjunct services like career counseling and Alcoholics Anonymous are often important parts of the treatment package.

In severe forms or exacerbations of Personality Disorders, brief hospitalization may be indicated, especially for people with Borderline or Schizotypal Personality Disorders. Low doses of medication have also been helpful to people with Personality Disorders. Pimozide (Orap) has reduced paranoid ideation, and antidepressant or antianxiety medication has helped reduce the affective symptoms that accompany many of the Personality Disorders. Low doses of antipsychotic medications have alleviated the anger, resentment, mistrust, and anxiety that characterizes some Personality Disorders (Meyer & Deitsch, 1996). Drugs do not cure Personality Disorders, however; they only reduce the severity of their accompanying symptoms (Roth & Fonagy, 1996) and perhaps facilitate a person's involvement in psychotherapy. Moreover, many people with Personality Disorders are susceptible to becoming dependent on external sources of help and so tend to misuse drugs. Therefore, care must be taken in recommending medication as part of treatment.

Family therapy can be a useful adjunct to individual therapy for a person with a Personality Disorder. Family members themselves often present disorders that merit attention, and they can also be helped to understand and react helpfully to the client's Personality Disorder, thereby reducing the secondary gains of the disorder. The client's social and occupational dysfunctions have probably already damaged family relationships, and family therapy can offer the person an opportunity to improve those relationships and develop new ways of relating to family members. Nevertheless, as Harbin (1981) cautions, the therapist should not form separate alliances with family members; doing so could jeopardize the client's tenuous trust in the therapeutic process and could be perceived as a rejection.

Group therapy can be another useful adjunct to individual therapy for people with Personality Disorders, although it should generally be initiated only after some progress has been made in individual therapy. Otherwise, these clients' poor social skills, strong mistrust, and dependence needs can turn group therapy into another disappointing interpersonal experience for them. Once clients are ready for group involvement, the feedback and support they receive from others can provide encouragement for positive change, as well as a safe place for experimenting with new ways of relating both to peers and to authority figures.

Prognosis

The prognosis for effecting major change in a Personality Disorder seems fair at best because of the deeply ingrained and pervasive nature of these disorders. Nevertheless, the prognosis for reducing symptoms and improving social and occupational functioning is fair to good if the client can be persuaded to remain in and cooperate with treatment. Unfortunately, however, people with Personality Disorders often are not motivated to change and may leave treatment abruptly and prematurely.

It is unclear whether the prognosis is determined more by the specific Personality Disorder itself or by the severity and dynamics of a particular instance of the disorder. At least one study has found the specific diagnosis not to be predictive of treatment outcome (Millon & Klerman, 1986).

New and more comprehensive approaches to treatment, such as those developed by Beck and Millon, may yield better outcomes than the earlier treatment approaches were able to produce. The setting of realistic goals—for example, goals involving symptom reduction, improvement in coping skills, and creation of a more rewarding lifestyle—can also increase the chances of a good prognosis (Maxmen & Ward, 1995).

PARANOID PERSONALITY DISORDER

Description of the Disorder

People with Paranoid Personality Disorder have a persistent suspiciousness and expectation that they will be treated badly by others. According to *DSM-IV*, they manifest at least four of the following patterns:

- Unjustly suspecting others of seeking to harm or take advantage of them
- Continually questioning the trustworthiness of others
- Rarely disclosing information about themselves because they believe it will be used against them
- Interpreting benign comments or behaviors as intended to harm them
- Being unforgiving and maintaining long-standing grudges
- Often perceiving themselves, without justification, as under attack
- Being easily motivated to anger or attack
- Frequently questioning the faithfulness of their partners

People with Paranoid Personality Disorder often misinterpret the behavior of others and tend to personalize experiences. As a result of their apprehension about being exploited or made to feel helpless, they are constantly on guard. They have little tenderness or sense of humor and tend to be critical, moralistic, grandiose, insecure, resentful, suspicious, defensive, and jealous. They share little of themselves with others and are typically rigid and controlling. They are more interested in things than in people or ideas and have little empathy or understanding of others. These clients have a strong sense of hierarchy and typically appear fiercely independent. They crave power and envy those with more influence and success than they have. Sometimes they achieve a sense of authority by becoming leaders of fringe religious or political groups. Under stress, they may experience brief psychotic episodes.

The behavioral dynamics of people with Paranoid Personality Disorder contain elements of self-defeat and self-fulfilling prophecy. These people believe that others dislike them and treat them badly; consequently, they protect themselves by treating others badly. Therefore, others often respond with disapproval and rejection, giving people with this Personality Disorder the responses that they have feared and yet invited.

People with Paranoid Personality Disorder often have concurrent disorders. The most common are other Personality Disorders (including Narcissistic, Avoidant, or Obsessive-Compulsive Personality Disorders) and Anxiety or Mood Disorders (Millon, 1996). Relatives of people with this disorder have an increased incidence of chronic Schizophrenia and Delusional Disorder, Persecutory Type (American Psychiatric Association, 1994a). Therefore, the symptoms of a Paranoid Personality Disorder actually may be the premorbid phase of one of these other disorders.

Approximately 5 percent of people with Personality Disorders have Paranoid Personality Disorder, whereas 0.5 to 2.5 percent of the general population can be diagnosed with this disorder (Kaplan et al., 1994). It is more common among men than among women (Millon, 1996). The disorder also has a higher prevalence among people from minority groups, recent immigrants, and people who are deaf, perhaps because of these groups' increased feelings of vulnerability, their cultural differences, and their problems in adaptation.

Typical Client Characteristics

Millon (1996) describes five subtypes of people with Paranoid Personality Disorder: fanatic, malignant, obdurate, querulous, and insular. The family backgrounds of people with this disorder also vary considerably, although some common antecedents to the disorder have been identified. Turkat and Maisto (1985), for example, suggest that most people with Paranoid Personality Disorder have had at least one parent who was perfectionistic. According to Sperry (1995), people with this disorder "are likely to have grown up in an atmosphere charged with criticism, blame, and hostility, and to have identified with a critical parent" (pp. 158–159). Abuse is not unusual in their histories.

People with Paranoid Personality Disorder are rarely self-referred for treatment and have great difficulty acknowledging a need for help. They externalize blame for their difficulties and insist that they do not need to make changes. People with Paranoid Personality Disorder may take pride in what they perceive as their independence and objectivity, and they may criticize those who express feelings more easily as being weak or troubled.

These clients typically have both interpersonal and occupational difficulties, particularly conflict with family and co-workers. People with Paranoid Personality Disorder typically expect obedience and rigid organization in their family lives and may experience considerable stress when children and partners resist their control. Some can establish a comfortable work or family situation for themselves, as long as they are in charge and do not need to cooperate with others, but that stability may be a tenuous one.

People with this disorder do tend to be fairly consistent and predictable, unlike people with many of the other Personality Disorders. This consistency can help family members and therapists identify and deal with patterns of relating and reacting. At the same time, however, these clients have considerable difficulty handling stress, and their symptoms are likely to worsen under pressure, failure, or humiliation. Brief psychotic symptoms may even occur in those circumstances.

Preferred Therapist Characteristics

Perhaps the most fundamental goal of therapy for people with Paranoid Personality Disorder is the establishment of trust so that they can become less resistant and engage in therapy. To establish a trusting therapeutic alliance, the therapist should assume a respectful, courteous, and professional stance, be honest although tactful, and not intrude on the client's privacy and independence. Soloff (1985) suggests that therapists working with these clients should be emotionally visible and responsive, offering a mild, gentle, interested presence.

Beck and Freeman (1990) have found it helpful to give these clients considerable control over the nature of their treatment, particularly the frequency of their sessions and their between-session tasks. Infrequent sessions, perhaps one every three weeks, were found to reduce the threat of the therapeutic process for these clients. These clients have little respect for people who seem weak or inept, however, and so therapists need to communicate confidence and knowledge, but without demeaning these clients.

Because people with Paranoid Personality Disorder are often hostile and abrasive, therapists need to monitor their own reactions and resist being intimidated or angered. Limits may need to be set if clients behave in threatening or aggressive ways. Therapists should avoid arguing with these clients, communicating excessive warmth and concern, and developing therapeutic plans that may evoke suspicion (such as meeting with a client's family when the client is not present). Clients' questionable beliefs should be accepted but not confirmed (Meissner, 1995).

Intervention Strategies

Individual therapy is usually the treatment of choice for people with Paranoid Personality Disorder. Therapy should not emphasize either interpretation or reflection of feelings; both are likely to be threatening. Rather, a behavioral approach that emphasizes the client's rather than the therapist's control, and that focuses on problem solving, stress management, and development of assertiveness and other interpersonal skills, is most likely to engage the client in the therapeutic process and effect some positive change. People with Paranoid Personality Disorder often appreciate the logic and organization of behavior therapy. They tend to be more trusting of therapists who focus on actions and experiences than of those who focus on inner dynamics and feelings. Reinforcement, modeling, and education can help these clients develop more effective coping mechanisms and social skills and promote a greater sense of self-efficacy, which in turn should help them engage in the next phase of treatment.

Once progress has been made in establishing a collaborative therapeutic relationship and effecting some behavioral change, cognitive therapy can be introduced (Beck & Freeman, 1990). This model, too, offers the appeal of a logical and clear approach. Cognitive therapy may focus on issues of shame, self-esteem, blame and self-blame, and overgeneralization. Cognitive therapy can help these clients consider alternative explanations, which can modify their pervasively defensive stance, encourage them to take more responsibility for the impact they have on others, and reduce their anger and hostility. In this stage of treatment, paranoia often evolves into depression, and cognitive approaches can also be used to reduce those symptoms (Meissner, 1995). Behavior therapy, integrated with cognitive therapy, can enhance treatment outcome by helping reduce people's exposure to humiliation while desensitizing them to uncomfortable situations.

Gentle reality testing can contribute to therapy with these clients. People facing the legal, professional, or marital consequences of their behavior may need help to appreciate how important it is for them to modify their behavior and attitudes so as to avert negative consequences.

Some clinicians have reported successful use of psychodynamic psychotherapy in treating people with Paranoid Personality Disorder (Millon, 1996). The research on that approach is limited, however, and it seems best reserved for the later stages of treatment or for unusually receptive clients.

Group therapy is rarely indicated for people with Paranoid Personality Disorder. Unless they are in charge, they are acutely uncomfortable in group settings, particularly those that are intimate or confrontational, and they tend to sabotage or flee group therapy.

Although family problems are common for people with Paranoid Personality Disorder, family therapy usually is not indicated until considerable progress has been made in individual therapy. Only when people have some awareness of the impact of their behavior and attitudes on others are they ready to talk about family issues and interact productively with family members.

Transient psychotic symptoms and severe anxiety are sometimes present in these clients. Antianxiety agents, such as diazepam (Valium), and antipsychotic agents, including haloperidol (Haldol), can ameliorate those symptoms (Kaplan et al., 1994). Pimozide (Orap) and fluoxetine (Prozac) have been found useful in reducing paranoid ideation (Sperry, 1995). A referral for medication should be presented cautiously, however, lest people feel insulted, manipulated, or controlled.

Prognosis

Therapy for people with Paranoid Personality Disorder is a long, slow process. If they can be engaged in that process, some clients will make positive changes (Meissner, 1995). Because of their resistance to treatment, however, people with this disorder often refuse to engage in the therapeutic process, and they terminate therapy prematurely. Even if they do cooperate with therapy and manifest some positive change, treatment is not likely to result in extensive modification of their pervasive patterns of relating. Therefore, limited goals should be set at the outset of treatment so that therapist and client alike have a clear direction and can feel a sense of accomplishment even if treatment is not completed. If treatment continues after the initial goals have been achieved, goals can be revised.

SCHIZOID PERSONALITY DISORDER

Description of the Disorder

According to *DSM-IV*, the primary feature of Schizoid Personality Disorder is "a pervasive pattern of detachment from social relationships and a restricted range of expression of emotions in interpersonal settings" (American Psychiatric Association, 1994a, p. 638). This pattern is evident by early adulthood, and in all or nearly all contexts it characterizes the behavior and attitudes of people with this disorder. They tend to prefer solitary activities, shun family and social activities, and are usually perceived as cold and detached. People with Schizoid Personality Disorder report few if any sources of pleasure. Interest in sexual or interpersonal closeness is minimal or absent. People with this disorder typically have great difficulty expressing their feelings, may deny having strong emotions, and seem preoccupied and indecisive. When with others, they tend to be guarded and tactless and often alienate others (Gutsch, 1988). Most are unaffected by people's reactions to them, although some do acknowledge underlying pain related to their unrewarding social interactions and perceive themselves as social misfits (Beck & Freeman, 1990). Although their reality testing usually is unimpaired, people with Schizoid Personality Disorder often act or dress in inappropriate ways because of their lack of information on current styles and socially accepted behaviors.

Inventories like the MCMI and the MMPI can be helpful in making a diagnosis and in understanding people with Schizoid Personality Disorder. Written responses may be more comfortable for these clients and more informative to therapists than oral responses, especially in the early stages of treatment.

Schizoid Personality Disorder is not commonly seen in clinical settings, although it may be present in as many as 7.5 percent of the general population (Kaplan et al., 1994). This disorder seems to be more common among males than among females.

Typical Client Characteristics

From childhood on, people with Schizoid Personality Disorder have few good interpersonal experiences and have the expectation that relationships will be frustrating and disappointing. Rather than expose themselves to what they perceive as more negative experiences, they shun socialization and develop private, isolated lives. Males generally do not date or marry. Females may engage in more social and family activities, but they tend to assume a passive role and allow others to make their social decisions. Both men and women with this disorder have poor social skills and few if any close friends. Their capacity for empathy and introspection seems to be severely constricted.

People with Schizoid Personality Disorder have considerable occupational impairment, particularly if their chosen occupations involve interpersonal contact. Some shun employment and continue to live with their parents. Others manage to find stable, secure occupational roles that are congruent with their need for solitude. They may become skilled at scientific, theoretical, creative, or mechanical pursuits, or in endeavors that involve animals rather than people, and may have relatively successful careers. They also may become involved with philosophical or social movements or with extreme health regimes, as long as these pursuits require little interpersonal contact. Although people with Schizoid Personality Disorder typically are not interested in becoming successful or in competing for recognition, they may gain recognition or become successful by accident, as a result of being totally immersed in their work or hobbies and having no social interests to distract them.

In general, people with Schizoid Personality Disorder have a relatively stable existence as long as outside pressures do not intrude. For example, one client with Schizoid Personality Disorder devoted his energy to raising pit bulls and collecting poisonous snakes. He had no social life and saw others only for business transactions. He was referred to counseling after his neighbors, feeling endangered by his activities, complained to the police. The client reported contentment with his life; his only concern was his neighbors.

People with this disorder tend to fantasize extensively but almost never lose contact with reality, even though they may prefer fantasy to reality (Meyer, 1983). Their affect is typically flat, and their behavior is lethargic. They tend to be relatively satisfied with their lives, although some engage in considerable intellectualization and denial to justify their lives to themselves and others.

People with Schizoid Personality Disorder typically have experienced inadequate, neglectful, and unreliable parenting, with impaired attachment (Siever & Kendler, 1986). Because this disorder often manifests itself in unresponsive early childhood behavior, the poor parenting may be, at least in part, a reaction to having a child who is unaffectionate and unrewarding.

Schizoid Personality Disorder usually is not accompanied by other prominent disorders, but some people with this disorder exhibit symptoms of depression, anxiety, depersonalization, obsessional thinking, somatic complaints, or brief manic states (Millon, 1996). This disorder, like Paranoid Personality Disorder, may also be a precursor of a Psychotic Disorder. Coexisting Personality Disorders may be present, especially Schizotypal, Antisocial, and Avoidant Personality Disorders.

Preferred Therapist Characteristics

Building trust is a critical ingredient of treatment with people who have Schizoid Personality Disorder, as it is with those who have Paranoid Personality Disorder. People with Schizoid Personality Disorder have little experience of expressing their feelings, engaging in close and collaborative relationships, or trusting others. Confrontation or scrutiny of their emotions generally makes them very uncomfortable and may lead to their premature termination of the therapeutic relationship. What they need instead is what Siever and Kendler (1986) call a "reconstructive relationship," to decrease their withdrawal and increase their optimism about relationships. The therapist needs to take an active and encouraging stance with this type of client and yet avoid being threatening. A gentle, consistent, patient, accepting, optimistic, available, and supportive therapist is needed to establish a therapeutic alliance.

On occasion, people with Schizoid Personality Disorder do take the initiative in seeking therapy—usually when someone breaks through their reserve and increases their anxiety—but they rarely experience an internal wish to change. Most of the time, people with Schizoid Personality Disorder are not self-referred. They are typically encouraged to seek help by concerned family members or employers who are hoping for a change in these people's ability to relate to others. Therefore, they are likely to see little need for therapy and to manifest passive resistance. Their eye contact is poor, and they rarely volunteer information, responding only minimally to questions.

Getting past this initial resistance will be challenging. The therapist will need a high tolerance for distance, for silence, and possibly even for some acting-out behavior. The therapist may also need to manage his or her own feelings of boredom, irritation, and frustration with this kind of client. If the nature and value of psychotherapy can be clarified for these clients, and if they can be assured that therapists will respect their privacy, they may be able to engage in the therapeutic process. People with Schizoid Personality Disorder do present a challenge; under the proper conditions, however, they may become "devoted if distant" clients (Kaplan et al., 1994, p. 736).

Intervention Strategies

Little research exists on therapy for people with Schizoid Personality Disorder, but some cautious generalizations can be made. The recommended treatment is similar to that for people with Paranoid Personality Disorder (Kaplan et al., 1994). If people with Schizoid Personality Disorder can be engaged in psychotherapy, treatment is likely to be a long, slow process involving an integrated approach (Sperry, 1995). Typical ingredients of psychotherapy for these clients include supportive, cognitive, behavioral, and group therapy.

A supportive therapeutic relationship can provide a corrective emotional experience for clients with Schizoid Personality Disorder, helping them to appreciate the value of relationships and to experience acceptance by another person. Empathic listening, education about daily living, advice and assistance in problem solving, and encouragement to try new activities can also have positive impacts (Stone, 1995).

Cognitive therapy can address clients' underlying assumptions and dysfunctional thoughts. These typically include the perception that life is bland and unfulfilling and that human relationships are not worth the trouble (Beck & Freeman, 1990). Clients' fantasies and their apprehension about dependence are other areas that can be productively explored through cognitive therapy. Inventories like Beck's Dysfunctional Thought Record can facilitate identification and modification of such thoughts, as can guided discovery, which helps clients determine their interests and increase their involvement in pleasurable activities. Building on interests that are already present can facilitate clients' involvement in additional activities.

Behavioral techniques can help people with Schizoid Personality Disorder improve their social and communication skills and increase their empathy for others. Therapists should keep in mind, however, that people with Schizoid Personality Disorder generally do not respond well to reinforcement, given their lack of reactivity and the limited importance they attach to interpersonal relationships. They may also resent the intrusive and manipulative aspects of some behavioral approaches. An intellectual approach to behavioral change, such as education to increase assertiveness, self-expression, and social skills, is most likely to succeed. Some clients also respond well to environmental changes that afford clients increased but still limited exposure to other people and provide them a natural laboratory for practicing their new skills.

The sequencing of the components of a treatment plan for people with Schizoid Personality Disorder is critical. These clients should not be overwhelmed by a multifaceted treatment strategy, nor should they be pushed into group or family therapy before they are ready. A stable therapeutic alliance should first be established through individual therapy. Only when the person is ready should group or family therapy, assertiveness training, career counseling, or other more active and more threatening interventions be introduced.

Group therapy can be helpful to these clients, but therapists must assume a protective stance toward them, especially during the initial stages, when they are likely to say little and to appear detached from the group. Intrusive interpretations and forced interactions should be avoided. Other group members must also be carefully selected, to ensure that these clients will not feel pressured or attacked. Sperry (1995) recommends a group that is homogeneous in terms of overall functioning but heterogeneous in terms of personality styles. If accepted by the client, group therapy can provide a socialization experience and offer gentle feedback. In time, the group may become very important to a person with Schizoid Personality Disorder (Kaplan et al., 1994).

Those who are in regular contact with people who have Schizoid Personality Disorder typically have trouble dealing with them because of these clients' limited social interests and skills. Some family or worksite meetings can help others accept the special characteristics of people with Schizoid Personality Disorder, appreciate their strengths, and deal with them more effectively. Pressure from family members or co-workers for the person to date or to socialize more at work, even though the pressure may be the product of good intentions, is likely to exacerbate the person's condition. At the same time, gentle encouragement and increased acceptance on the part of family members and colleagues can help people with Schizoid Personality Disorder socialize more comfortably.

Medication and psychoanalytic therapy are rarely effective in treating Schizoid Personality Disorder. In some cases, however, medication to reduce severe anxiety or depression can facilitate therapy (Gunderson, 1988).

Relapse prevention is another important ingredient of treatment for people with Schizoid Personality Disorder (Beck & Freeman, 1990). Without help in identifying the signs of a relapse, and without periodic follow-up sessions, people with this disorder have a high likelihood of reverting to their previous isolated behaviors.

Prognosis

The prognosis for treating Schizoid Personality Disorder is not promising. Premature termination of treatment and failure to benefit or maintain gains from therapy are common (Millon, 1996). Many of these clients have established a relatively stable lifestyle and are not motivated to participate in treatment. They may increase their socialization somewhat, especially if required by their employers to do so, but fundamental change is unlikely. With these clients, as with those who have Paranoid Personality Disorder, setting limited goals can lead to the establishment of a more rewarding therapeutic relationship.

SCHIZOTYPAL PERSONALITY DISORDER

Description of the Disorder

People with Schizotypal Personality Disorder, like those with Paranoid and Schizoid Personality Disorders, have pervasive deficits in interpersonal relations and social skills. They tend to be guarded, suspicious, and hypersensitive. They have few close friends other than first-degree relatives, manifest flat and inappropriate affect, and are uncomfortable and awkward in social situations. In addition, this disorder is characterized by "cognitive or perceptual distortions and eccentricities of behavior" (American Psychiatric Association, 1994a, p. 641) that may involve ideas of reference, magical thinking, unusual beliefs or perceptual experiences, prominent superstitions, eccentric actions or grooming, and idiosyncratic speech patterns. People with Schizotypal Personality Disorder typically are more dysfunctional and unusual in presentation than are those with Paranoid or Schizoid Personality Disorders.

Schizotypal Personality Disorder is found in approximately 3 percent of the general population and usually begins in early childhood (Kaplan et al., 1994). Clear information is not available on gender distribution of this disorder.

Typical Client Characteristics

People with Schizotypal Personality Disorder almost always have significant social and occupational impairment. They usually do not marry or have children but tend to drift from one endeavor to another, with little investment in or enthusiasm for anything. Sometimes they become involved with cults or other groups with unusual beliefs. Their peculiar habits and attitudes generally are evident to those around them, and people with Schizotypal Personality Disorder are viewed as strange and troubled. They seem to experience more discomfort than do those with Schizoid or Paranoid Personality Disorders and sometimes appear distraught, agitated, chaotic, and emotionally labile, although they are more likely to present as cold and aloof.

Schizotypal Personality Disorder seems to have both genetic and environmental components. People with this Personality Disorder have a higher percentage of first-degree biological relatives with Schizophrenia than does the general population (American Psychiatric Association, 1994a). The parenting received by people with this disorder was commonly deficient, often fragmented and hypercritical or distant and disinterested. Humiliation and abuse are common in these people's backgrounds, as is discouragement of social involvement (Sperry, 1995).

Torgersen (1984) has found more than half of people with Schizotypal Personality Disorder to have coexisting affective disorders (usually Major Depressive Disorder), with anxiety and transient, stress-related psychotic symptoms also often accompanying this disorder. People with Schizotypal Personality Disorder tend to somatize and may present vague physical complaints (Siever & Kendler, 1986). Suicidal ideation and behavior often accompany this disorder, particularly if a Mood Disorder is also present. Other personality disorders, including Schizoid, Paranoid, Avoidant, and Borderline Personality Disorders, may be present. In some cases, Schizotypal Personality Disorder is a precursor of Schizophrenia.

Preferred Therapist Characteristics

People with Schizotypal Personality Disorder, like those with Schizoid and Paranoid Personality Disorders, are likely to be resistant to treatment. Building trust is a challenging yet critical ingredient in engaging the person in the therapeutic process. An available, reliable, encouraging, warm, empathic, positive, and non-intrusive stance can help therapists interact effectively with these clients (Sperry, 1995). Because people with Schizotypal Personality Disorder tend to ramble and have difficulty making meaningful use of therapy, clinicians will have to be structured and focused and to teach these clients about psychotherapy. Frequent sessions or telephone calls between sessions can keep clients connected to and involved with treatment. Allowing them to determine the degree of intimacy also can increase their sense of control over and comfort with therapy and can provide a corrective emotional experience.

Therapists sometimes will function as auxiliary egos, providing clients with basic information and advice on taking care of themselves and dealing with the world (Stone, 1995). Although some therapists may not be comfortable with this role, it can help clients see the value in therapy.

People with Schizotypal Personality Disorder have particular difficulty expressing their feelings and dealing appropriately with interpersonal situations. Therefore, therapists should be prepared for unusual reactions and behaviors on the part of these clients. Therapists will need to manage their own discomfort with the strange and possibly offensive mannerisms of these people, as well as with their lack of motivation for treatment. Therapists should communicate acceptance and support while providing some reality testing and education.

On the positive side, these clients are usually willing to talk about themselves and their experiences and do not tend to be manipulative; they generally will be sincere, if guarded and cautious (Gunderson, 1984).

Intervention Strategies

The research on treatment of Schizotypal Personality Disorder is limited, but treatment usually resembles the treatment for Schizoid Personality Disorder, with the addition of medication. People with Schizotypal Personality Disorder are unlikely to seek out treatment on their own. Most people with this disorder seem to accept their lifestyles. As a result, Siever and Kendler (1986) report, they are seen more often in inpatient than in outpatient settings, seeking treatment only when their symptoms become so severe that they can no longer function on their own.

Therapy for people with Schizotypal Personality Disorder typically is supportive, lengthy, and slow-paced, beginning with supportive interventions and medication and subsequently making gentle use of cognitive and behavioral strategies to promote self-awareness, self-esteem, reality testing, and more socially acceptable behavior. The focus of therapy with these people is likely to be very basic, dealing with personal hygiene and daily activities, seeking to prevent isolation and total dysfunction, and establishing some independence and pleasure in their lives (Benjamin, 1993). Cognitive therapy can focus on superstitious and magical thoughts and encourage these clients to determine whether evidence is available for their beliefs. Cognitive therapy can also help them cope more effectively with perceived criticism. Behavioral therapy can improve speech patterns and personal hygiene as well as social skills. Group therapy may also be useful for milder cases of this disorder, but the group members must be carefully chosen, and these clients must be carefully prepared, so that the experience does not prove too threatening.

Medication, particularly neuroleptics, is sometimes needed to treat the psychotic symptoms of people with Schizotypal Personality Disorder (Stone, 1995). Serban and Siegel (1984), for example, found that 84 percent of a sample of people who had Schizotypal Personality Disorder were markedly improved after three months of treatment with neuroleptic medication; reductions were effected in cognitive disturbance, derealization, ideas of reference, anxiety, depression, social dysfunction, and negative self-image. Anxiolytics can also be useful in reducing the anxiety that often accompanies this disorder. Nevertheless, although medication may reduce the degree of impairment of people with Schizotypal Personality Disorder, it does not change basic personality patterns.

Case management is often an important component of treatment for these clients. They sometimes are seen in treatment programs for the chronically mentally ill, where long-term oversight of their functioning can be provided. These clients often benefit from help in locating housing, finding employment that provides support and supervision and is not emotionally stressful, and obtaining needed medication on a regular basis. It is also helpful for them to have a place to turn to in times of crisis.

Prognosis

McGlashan's (1986b) long-term follow-up of people with Schizotypal Personality Disorder who were treated in an inpatient setting indicates relatively poor social adjustment at follow-up, as well as an average of 2.5 additional hospitalizations in the fifteen years after initial treatment. The prognosis was worst for those with Schizophrenia-type symptoms and best for those with some capacity for warmth and empathy. Despite the poor prognosis for significant positive change, however, most people with this disorder do not deteriorate into Schizophrenia and do manage to achieve a stable if marginal existence. Realistic goals, focused on improved adaptive functioning and enjoyment of life rather than on personality restructuring, can help both therapist and client view their work as a success.

ANTISOCIAL PERSONALITY DISORDER

Description of the Disorder

The symptoms of Antisocial Personality Disorder (APD), by definition, begin before the age of fifteen with a pattern of behavior that reflects a diagnosis of Conduct Disorder (see Chapter Two). This pattern is typified by impulsive and aggressive behavior, such as theft, lying, truancy, cruelty to people and animals, vandalism, fighting, and running away from home.

APD is the only Personality Disorder that, by definition, cannot be diagnosed before the age of eighteen. In people with APD, the symptoms of Conduct Disorder have persisted beyond the age of eighteen via a pervasive pattern of irresponsible behavior that violates and shows disregard for the rights and feelings of others. Symptoms of the disorder are likely to be most severe in early adulthood and to diminish spontaneously in midlife.

People with APD are typically unable to sustain employment or monogamous relationships. They are egocentric, impulsive, reckless, angry, irritable, deceptive, and aggressive. They fail to abide by social and legal guidelines for behavior, are often in financial difficulty, behave irresponsibly as employees and parents, and feel no guilt or remorse for their actions. Rather, they justify their behavior, perceiving themselves as superior and infallible, and project blame for their difficulties onto others, who are devalued. They are easily bored, have a high need for excitement and stimulation, and typically enjoy life, although they do not want to bear the consequences of their actions. They have difficulty with rejection and delayed gratification and want to impress others despite their professed need for independence (Soloff, 1985). They have faith only in themselves and tend to attack in anticipation of being attacked. They are often shrewd judges of others and can use their verbal and interpersonal skills in manipulative ways. At the same time, they rarely engage in introspection and have little sense of themselves.

People with APD embrace a socially deviant lifestyle and disdain generally accepted values and behaviors, although not all actually engage in criminal behavior. Millon (1996) reports that many find a place for themselves in business, politics, or other settings where a focus on self-interest and accumulation of material goods is rewarded.

Antisocial Personality Disorder is approximately three times more common among males than it is among females: approximately 3 percent of men and fewer than 1 percent of women can be diagnosed with this disorder. It is particularly prevalent at low socioeconomic levels and in urban areas (Gunderson, 1988). Up to 75 percent of people in prison may have Antisocial Personality Disorder (Kaplan et al., 1994).

Typical Client Characteristics

Genetic and environmental influences both seem to be factors in the development of APD, as they are with many of the Personality Disorders. People with this Personality Disorder typically lacked secure and stable parenting and grew up in inconsistent, excessively punitive, contentious, and disrupted families with others who manifested antisocial behavior (Gunderson, 1988). Fathers of people with this disorder typically have manifested antisocial and alcoholic behaviors and often left their families or were otherwise unavailable. Mothers characteristically were overburdened (Millon, 1996). Therefore, as children, people later diagnosed with APD failed to develop positive attachments and learned that they had to look out for themselves. They were typically undeterred by punishment, engaged in challenging and dangerous activities, and manifested behavioral problems.

People with APD often have painful underlying symptoms, typically depression and anxiety (Gunderson, 1988). They also are prone to Substance-Related Disorders and may develop Somatic Disorders. APD is sometimes accompanied by other Personality Disorders, notably Narcissistic, Paranoid, and Histrionic Personality Disorders, as well as by sadistic and negativistic personality patterns (Millon, 1996).

Occupational and interpersonal dysfunction is almost always present. People with Antisocial Personality Disorder have considerable difficulty sustaining warm, intimate relationships and tend to change partners and jobs frequently.

Preferred Therapist Characteristics

People with APD rarely seek therapy on their own initiative, because they attribute their difficulties to others. They are often seen in therapy anyway, having been ordered into treatment by the courts as a result of breaking the law. Therapy may be a condition of their parole or probation, or they may be treated while incarcerated.

These clients tend to be very resistant to therapy, although some are manipulative and appear superficially cooperative in order to avoid negative consequences. They may afford therapists an initial "honeymoon" phase, but their resistance is likely to surface once therapy progresses beyond superficial interactions (Lion, 1981a). These clients typically resent authority figures and may see therapists as part of that group. To reduce the likelihood of being seen in this way, therapists should avoid assuming judgmental and punitive roles, even if they are working in correctional settings. Instead, they should present themselves as specialists and collaborative partners in psychotherapy.

Therapists working with people diagnosed with APD typically encounter a considerable challenge. Once again the development of trust will be a critical ingredient of successful treatment. Despite these clients' hostility and resistance, however, therapists need to be genuine, accepting, and empathic. They also should be self-assured, relaxed, and straightforward and should have a sense of humor. As appropriate, therapists can increase their likelihood of becoming role models by playing chess with clients or helping them with their budgets or with other practical problems.

Directive techniques are often necessary in persuading people with APD to engage in treatment. Beck and Freeman (1990) advise providing these clients with clear explanations of this disorder and setting explicit guidelines and limits for their involvement in therapy. Clear limits in the therapeutic relationship can help prevent clients from becoming hostile and abusive and attempting to engage their therapists in battles; power struggles will only undermine treatment. Therapy should be continued only if clients give some evidence of benefiting from the process.

Therapists may be angered or threatened by the histories of clients with APD, as well as frustrated and discouraged by their lack of progress in treatment. These countertransference reactions must be monitored and managed.

Intervention Strategies

A structured and active approach to therapy is indicated for people with Antisocial Personality Disorder, although research has yet to identify a treatment approach that has a high degree of effectiveness (Maxmen & Ward, 1995). The failure to find an effective treatment has not been due to any lack of research; APD is one of the most studied of the Personality Disorders (Turkat & Maisto, 1985). Rather, the discouraging results of outcome research reflect the guarded prognosis for treatment of this disorder.

Milieu and residential approaches, as well as group therapy, have achieved some success in strengthening interpersonal skills and prosocial behaviors in people with APD (Meloy, 1995). Therapeutic communities, institutional settings that use token economies, and wilderness programs that involve peer pressure and clear consequences sometimes succeed in breaking through resistance and effecting some change in these clients. For those who are incarcerated, prerelease or halfway programs can also be helpful in facilitating the transition to a more socially acceptable lifestyle. Residential therapeutic programs established specifically for offenders typically focus on increasing these clients' responsibility, increasing their trust in themselves and others, increasing their sense of mastery, and inculcating an understanding of their behavior's consequences. An important benefit of these residential programs is that they remove people from their former environments, where their antisocial behavior may have been reinforced by peers. Developing new support systems and a sense of belonging through employment or self-help groups (such as Narcotics Anonymous) can accomplish a similar end.

Individual therapy is also an essential ingredient of treatment for people with APD. The first steps in individual therapy include establishing a collaborative therapeutic relationship and setting clear and mutually agreed-upon goals. Once those steps have been accomplished, behavioral, reality, and cognitive therapy can be helpful. Reality therapy can enable people to see the self-destructive nature of their actions and to make a commitment to change. Behavioral therapy can promote positive change by improving problem-solving and decision-making skills, anger management, and impulse control. Beck and Freeman (1990) recommend cognitive interventions that are designed to promote moral development, abstract thinking, and appreciation for the rights and feelings of others, as well as analysis and modification of dysfunctional thoughts.

Although the focus of treatment is generally on current behavior, people with APD are sometimes less defensive when they are talking about the past, and this tendency may provide a useful bridge to a discussion of current activities. Person-centered and insight-oriented therapies are not indicated with these clients, however, even if discussion does focus on past experiences.

An early sign of progress is the emergence of underlying depression (Reid, 1986). This development can be upsetting and may precipitate a resumption of old patterns of behavior. To encourage these clients' persistence in treatment if depression does surface, therapists may increase support and empathy.

Medication is sometimes combined with therapy in the treatment of people with APD. Lithium carbonate, fluoxetine (Prozac), and sertraline (Zoloft) have all demonstrated some effectiveness in controlling anger and impulsivity (Sperry, 1995). Medication should be prescribed cautiously, however, because of the clients' tendency to misuse drugs and because of their reliance on external rather than internal solutions to problems.

Family therapy has also been suggested, especially when clients are young, in an effort to reverse familial patterns that are being transmitted. Therapy may also help family members separate from and set limits for the client and deal with their own guilt and anger toward the client.

Treatment specifically for coexisting Substance-Related Disorders can also be helpful to people with APD and can reduce their motivation to engage in antisocial behavior. Reduction of substance use seems to improve the prognosis for treatment of APD (Reid, 1986).

One issue that often arises in the treatment of people diagnosed with APD is the relationship between therapy and punishment, given that many of these clients come into therapy as a consequence of breaking the law. Millon (1996) recommends separating therapy and punishment to increase the likelihood of clients' using therapy constructively and not manipulating or deceiving the therapist. At the same time, the threat of punishment can have a powerful coercive effect and can promote initial involvement in therapy. This issue has not been definitively resolved but must be considered by therapists working with people diagnosed as having APD.

Prognosis

The prognosis for treating Antisocial Personality Disorder is not good, primarily because of clients' lack of motivation (Gunderson, 1988). Nevertheless, therapy does seem to be helpful to some people with APD. The likelihood of successful treatment is higher with people over the age of forty and who manifest some remorse for their actions, have a history of some attachments, have not been sadistic or violent, are neither very high nor very low in intelligence, and do not create fear in clinicians (Meloy, 1995). As with most of the other Personality Disorders, realistic and circumscribed goals (such as improvement in prosocial behavior) are likely to lead to a better outcome (Beck & Freeman, 1990).

BORDERLINE PERSONALITY DISORDER

Description of the Disorder

People with Borderline Personality Disorder are characterized primarily by pervasive instability in mood, relationships, behavior, and self-image, as well as impulsivity (American Psychiatric Association, 1994a). This instability affects all or nearly all areas of their lives. The very name of this disorder reflects the precariousness of people with this condition. (The name was originally intended to indicate that they were on the border between psychosis and neurosis.) By definition, Borderline Personality Disorder is characterized by five (or more) of the following patterns:

- Intense and fluctuating interpersonal relationships
- Self-destructive and impulsive behavior (for example, substance misuse, binge eating, excessive spending, promiscuity)

- Labile moods
- Self-mutilation (usually cutting or burning) or suicidal threats and behavior
- Lack of a stable, internalized sense of self
- Persistent sense of emptiness and boredom
- Frantic efforts to avoid loneliness or abandonment
- Inappropriate anger
- Transient stress-related dissociation or paranoid ideation

According to Millon (1986), Borderline Personality Disorder is second only to Dependent Personality Disorder in prevalence and is present in 12 percent of the people who have Personality Disorders. Borderline Personality Disorder can be found in about 2 percent of the general population, 10 percent of people seen in outpatient mental health clinics, and 20 percent of people receiving inpatient psychotherapy. Approximately 75 percent of people with this disorder are females (American Psychiatric Association, 1994a).

People with Borderline Personality Disorder often have coexisting disorders. Common are Mood, Anxiety, Somatoform, Dissociative, Substance-Related, and Schizoaffective Disorders, as well as other Personality Disorders (McGlashan, 1983; Millon, 1996). Sleeping, eating, and grooming habits are often erratic (Gutsch, 1988). In addition, people with this disorder almost always experience occupational and social impairment.

Typical Client Characteristics

Parents of people with Borderline Personality Disorder typically were troubled themselves and were inconsistent in their behavior and availability (Sperry, 1995). Dysfunctional alcohol use is very prevalent in the families of these clients, as are Borderline Personality Disorder, Substance-Related Disorders, Mood Disorders, and Antisocial Personality Disorder (American Psychiatric Association, 1994a). Loranger and Tulis (1985) have found one-third of fathers of people with Borderline Personality Disorder to have misused alcohol.

A history of incest, brutality, early loss, and neglect is also common among people with Borderline Personality Disorder (Gunderson, 1988). Some people with this disorder are amnesiac with respect to much of their childhoods, a circumstance that usually reflects their experience of early traumas (Searles, 1986).

Mothers of people with Borderline Personality Disorder often had mental disorders themselves, most often Borderline Personality Disorder, a Depressive Disorder, or Psychosis. The mothers typically tried to prevent the individuation of their children by threatening withdrawal, thereby producing in the children a fear of abandonment and an impaired development (Masterson, 1981).

Issues around separation and individuation persist from childhood into adulthood for these clients. People with Borderline Personality Disorder tend to have little sense of themselves and an external locus of control. They seek to avoid individuation by attaining a symbiotic relationship with another, typically a romantic partner or a therapist. They have considerable difficulty expressing feelings because they often are uncertain of what they are feeling or of how they are expected to be feeling and are fearful of incurring anger and rejection if they make a mistake. They seem to have a sort of false self, built around an effort to please others (Masterson, 1981). Fantasy and reality often become confused for them.

People with Borderline Personality Disorder seem to have a great deal of underlying anger combined with vengeful impulses (which are another source of self-doubt and interpersonal difficulties). Sometimes these feelings are denied and suppressed lest their expression precipitate abandonment; at other times these feelings are expressed in self-destructive ways that provoke considerable anger in others. This emotional chaos typically leaves people with Borderline Personality Disorder in a near-constant state of crisis, which they usually attribute to the actions of other people.

Borderline Personality Disorder tends to be particularly severe in late adolescence and early adulthood (Gunderson, 1988). Like many of the other Personality Disorders, it sometimes declines in severity with age.

Preferred Therapist Characteristics

Masterson (1981) describes two ways in which people with Borderline Personality Disorder are likely to relate to their therapists. The higher-functioning clients with this disorder have a strong fear of abandonment and so tend to cling to their therapists, making constant demands for extra time and attention. Those who are functioning less well are more fearful of engulfment and tend to use distancing maneuvers to avoid being overwhelmed by the therapeutic relationship. Some clients seem to alternate between the two fears. Regardless of which stance predominates, these clients are challenging, and many therapists perceive them as their most difficult clients.

Therapists working with these clients need to maintain a careful balance. Too much attention can promote dependence or flight, but too little can promote suicidal threats, panic, anger, and failure to develop a therapeutic alliance. Therapists should remain calm and nonjudgmental and maintain control in the face of these clients' manipulative endeavors. Therapists must be active and involving, providing a stable and safe therapeutic environment. Although therapists should communicate availability, reliability, interest, acceptance, support, genuineness, and empathy to these clients, they must also establish and adhere to clear and consistent limits and guidelines. Extra sessions and supportive telephone calls can be given when they are therapeutically advisable, but they should not be offered as capitulation to these clients' manipulations or threats.

Therapists need to make clear that they cannot take responsibility for the lives of these clients and should not become their rescuers. At the same time, clients need to feel secure and trusting of their therapists. Steps must be taken to protect the safety of these clients, perhaps by providing them with emergency resources, other sources of therapeutic support, and outside contacts to whom they can turn in times of crisis.

Splitting is a common dynamic in the self-images and relationships of people with Borderline Personality Disorder. They tend to perceive people in extremes, as either idealized or devalued. They may alternate in viewing the same person in both ways, or they may idealize one helping figure while devaluing another. The devaluation sometimes has elements of projective identification as clients perceive unacceptable aspects of themselves in others. The client with Borderline Personality Disorder typically begins a therapeutic relationship by idealizing the therapist. When the therapist has failed to yield to demands for special attention, the idealistic view shifts, and the client then harshly criticizes the therapist, often terminating treatment and moving on to the next idealized therapist.

Noncompliance with treatment is a common problem that therapists face in working with people with Borderline Personality Disorder. Instead of blaming these clients or pressuring them to cooperate, therapists need to recognize these clients' underlying fear of change. By acknowledging this fear and helping them see the benefits that treatment has to offer, therapists can encourage these clients' compliance.

Therapists will need to deal with their own reactions to these often frustrating and complicated clients and should not be lulled into confidence by positive phases of therapy. Because countertransference reactions can be a useful route to understanding these clients, they should be examined. Inevitably, if therapy is to succeed, therapists will need to find gentle and supportive ways to deal with the resistance and transference manifested by people with this disorder. Consultation with colleagues or supervisors is recommended, to help therapists maintain their objectivity and equilibrium with these clients.

Intervention Strategies

There are very few systematic studies of the treatment of Borderline Personality Disorder (Gunderson & Links, 1995; Waldinger, 1986). However, several approaches have demonstrated some success with people who have this disorder.

One of the few approaches to yield empirical evidence of success is Dialectical Behavior Therapy (DBT), developed by Linehan and her colleagues (Linehan & Kehrer, 1993). A manualized version of DBT (Linehan, 1993) has been used, primarily to treat people with Borderline Personality Disorder who were chronically suicidal and severely dysfunctional. Goals of DBT are grouped into four stages: (1) development of commitment to therapy; (2) establishment of stability, connection, and safety; (3) exposure to and emotional processing of the past; and (4) synthesis (increasing self-respect, achieving individual goals). DBT takes a holistic, biosocial perspective, emphasizing the use of persuasive dialogue to promote new understanding and change and incorporating many techniques (including skills training, use of metaphors, and playing devil's advocate). Clients are asked to make a commitment of at least six to twelve months to a combination of individual and group therapy. Follow-up of clients who had at least one year of DBT reflected considerable reduction in suicidal ideation and hospitalization. Improved work and social adjustment were also reported, as well as less anxiety and anger (Linehan & Kehrer, 1993).

Cognitive therapy has also been reported as successful with these clients, who typically harbor many strong and maladaptive schemas: "I'll be alone forever"; "I'm a bad person. I deserve to be punished"; "I must subjugate my wants to the desires of others or they'll abandon me or attack me" (Beck & Freeman, 1990, p. 185). The strategies of cognitive therapy can effect modification in these dysfunctional thoughts. Standard cognitive therapy needs to be adapted to these clients, however, with initial attention paid to the development of a collaborative therapeutic relationship and subsequent attention placed not only on modifying these schemas but also on reducing dichotomous thinking, teaching adaptive ways to express emotions, and promoting a sense of self.

Gunderson (1984) recommends a supportive-expressive approach to therapy with these clients that integrates many of the ingredients found effective in their treatment. He outlines a long-term plan of treatment that includes the following five phases:

1. Establishment of boundaries through clarification of anger, demands, and manipulativeness

2. Exploration of the therapeutic relationship and the client's history, to provide corrective emotional experiences and promote appropriate expression of feeling, and to shift the client from acting-out behavior to verbalization

3. Separation and individuation

4. Development of new feelings, interests, and social skills

5. Termination, carefully planned

Gunderson's approach uses inquiry more than interpretation in treating people with Borderline Personality Disorder and seeks to promote an observing and moderating self rather than unlimited expression of feeling. Adjuncts to treatment (such as group and family therapy, hospitalization, medication, art therapy) are used as needed.

Supportive therapy is particularly appropriate for people with Borderline Personality Disorder who are not high-functioning. Dawson and MacMillan's Relationship Management Psychotherapy (1993), a supportive approach to treating these clients, emphasizes the importance of the therapeutic relationship in bringing about change. Indeed, research has shown that several years of supportive treatment can effect basic personality changes in people with Borderline Personality Disorder (Sperry, 1995).

For many years, long-term psychodynamic or modified psychoanalytic psychotherapy was viewed as most effective in treating people with this disorder. According to Dorr, Barley, Gard, and Webb (1983), however, "A passive classical analytic approach is not recommended. Rather, the psychotherapist is advised to be more direct, real, confrontive and, in some cases, even more directive than he or she would be with a neurotic patient" (p. 403). Stevenson and Meares (1992), following the progress of thirty clients with Borderline Personality Disorder who received one year of twice-weekly psychodynamic psychotherapy treatment, report 30 percent as no longer meeting the diagnostic criteria for the disorder, with many others showing reductions in impulsivity, affective instability, anger, suicidal behavior, and substance use.

Although all approaches to treating these clients pay some attention to past issues, the primary focus of therapy is usually on the present because for most of these clients the present mirrors the past. The therapeutic relationship typically serves as a vehicle to help people work through concerns of separation and individuation and early losses dating back to childhood. Reality testing, rage neutralization, and management of the transference relationship are other important ingredients of therapy with these clients.

Approximately 10 percent of people with Borderline Personality Disorder commit suicide (Gunderson & Links, 1995). Because of the self-destructive and potentially lethal behavior of these clients, any approach to therapy that is used with these clients must make an effort to reduce acting out and promote more effective functioning and reality testing. Many people with Borderline Personality Disorder need to be seen several times a week so that stability can be maintained in their lives, suicide can be averted, and the therapeutic alliance can be ensured.

In general, the self-destructive behaviors of people with Borderline Personality Disorder are ego-dystonic and evoke considerable shame, guilt, and anxiety, as well as the wish to be forgiven and to change. For most of these clients, acting out is a defense against boredom and depression and a way of preventing abandonment, and so dealing with those concerns can reduce the pressure toward self-destructive behavior. Clients must be helped to link their actions with their emotions and to reduce the gratification they receive from self-destructive behavior.

Group therapy, combined with individual therapy, can be a useful adjunct to treatment of Borderline Personality Disorder after some progress has been made in individual therapy. Homogeneous groups, with co-therapists, seem most likely to be effective (Gunderson & Links, 1995; Sperry, 1995). These groups can dilute transference reactions, afford support and friendship, encourage change of manipulative and dysfunctional behaviors, and model coping skills.

Antidepressant, antiseizure, antianxiety, and antipsychotic medications sometimes can be useful in treating the secondary symptoms of Borderline Personality Disorder. Fluoxetine (Prozac) has been especially helpful in reducing aggression and impulsivity (Coccaro, Astill, & Herbert, 1990). Again, however, medication does not eliminate the basic Personality Disorder. Use of medication should be closely monitored, given the high suicide risk of these clients, their frequent noncompliance with treatment, and their fear that improvement may lead to abandonment.

Hospitalization, too, may be indicated when clients are experiencing psychotic or suicidal ideation. Typically, hospitalization will be a brief but frequent component of treatment, although some people may require long-term psychiatric hospitalization, particularly if they have been living in a destructive home environment (Kaplan et al., 1994).

Family therapy is another useful treatment component for many of these clients. They typically have dysfunctional families of origin and are likely to be in current relationships that are also dysfunctional. Family therapy can have a positive impact on other troubled family members as well and can improve family dynamics and communication.

Prognosis

Pope et al. (1983) report a prognosis for treatment of Borderline Personality Disorder that is somewhat better than that for treatment of Schizophrenia but not as good as that for treatment of Schizoaffective and Bipolar Disorders. McGlashan (1986a) conducted a long-term follow-up of eighty-one inpatients diagnosed as having Borderline Personality Disorder who were seen for an average of two years of intensive treatment. Although they typically had one or two subsequent hospitalizations, most were living independently at follow-up and functioning fairly well. According to Gunderson (1988), treatment of people with Borderline Personality Disorder may require as long as five years. He has found those who complete treatment to be much improved but still vulnerable. Gunderson sees reduced acting out and more direct expression of hostility and dependence needs as signals of improvement. According to Marziali (1992), 50 percent of people with Borderline Personality Disorder leave treatment prematurely, with only 10 percent of those who remain in treatment having a successful outcome. The prognosis is better for those with histrionic, depressive, obsessive, or phobic features and worse for those with paranoid or narcissistic features, although the suicide rate is very high for those with depression or alcohol-related disorders (Stone, 1990). Increased use of medication and cognitive-behavioral approaches seems likely to yield more encouraging data in the future.

HISTRIONIC PERSONALITY DISORDER

Description of the Disorder

DSM-IV describes Histrionic Personality Disorder as being characterized by "a pervasive pattern of excessive emotionality and attention seeking, beginning by early adulthood and present in a variety of contexts" (American Psychiatric Association, 1994a, p. 657). This pattern is characterized by the following features, among others:

- Constant demands for praise or reassurance
- Inappropriate seductiveness
- A need to be the center of attention
- Overemphasis on physical attractiveness
- Exaggerated, shallow, and labile expressions of emotion
- Self-centeredness
- Poor impulse control
- Self-dramatization
- Suggestibility
- A vague, disjointed, general way of speaking

People with this disorder readily become impatient, jealous, manipulative, and volatile. Repression and denial are common defenses. These people also tend to be gullible, to trust others too easily, and to exaggerate the depth of their involvement in their intimate relationships. They usually appear affected and flighty, but their vivacity, imagination, and attractiveness can be engaging. They can also be charming, energetic, and entertaining, especially early in relationships.

People with Histrionic Personality Disorder tend to be other-directed; their moods as well as their feelings about themselves come largely from the reactions they receive from others (Millon & Klerman, 1986). They tend to avoid responsibility, feel helpless, and want others to take care of them. Intimate relationships and friendships are both typically impaired. Suicidal threats, although common, are part of these people's exaggerated emotionality and are rarely fatal but should nevertheless be taken seriously (Maxmen & Ward, 1995).

Approximately 2 to 3 percent of the general population and 10 to 15 percent of people in clinical settings meet the criteria for this disorder. Approximately 9 percent of those with Personality Disorders will be diagnosed as Histrionic (Millon, 1986). Histrionic Personality Disorder is more commonly presented by females than males in clinical settings, but gender distribution may not differ greatly in the general population (American Psychiatric Association, 1994a).

Histrionic Personality Disorder is often accompanied by other disorders. A particularly strong connection has been found between Histrionic Personality Disorder and Somatoform, Depressive, Dissociative, Anxiety, and Substance-Related Disorders, as well as other Personality Disorders (Millon, 1996). Bipolar and Cyclothymic Disorders have also been reported in people with Histrionic Personality Disorder (Millon, 1981). Males with Histrionic Personality Disorder sometimes have a concurrent diagnosis of Antisocial Personality Disorder (Maxmen & Ward, 1995). Lilienfeld, Van Valkenburg, Larntz, and Akiskal (1986) suggest that Histrionic and Antisocial Personality Disorders and Somatoform Disorders represent different stages or manifestations of the same disorder and often coexist.

Typical Client Characteristics

Histrionic Personality Disorder tends to run in families (Maxmen & Ward, 1995). People with Histrionic Personality Disorder typically grew up in families that were dramatic and chaotic but not dangerous (unlike the families of those with Borderline Personality Disorder). These families frequently have a history of antisocial behavior, other Personality Disorders, and Alcohol-Related Disorders. They typically provide nurturing only when children are ill and give approval primarily for children's attractiveness, talent, and charm. As children, then, people with this disorder were valued for their external presentation rather than for their inner selves.

Gunderson (1988) reports that females with Histrionic Personality Disorder often have experienced insufficiency, conflict, and disapproval in their early interactions with their mothers and so have sought attention primarily from their fathers. Consequently, as they mature, these women overemphasize the importance of heterosexual relationships.

People with Histrionic Personality Disorder usually are sexually and socially active but may experience sexual difficulties. They tend to be easily bored and typically, just as they achieve the commitment they seem to be seeking, shift partners in their quest for the ideal mate. This pattern is exacerbated by the tendency of people with Histrionic Personality Disorder to choose partners who are detached and unemotional and who cannot give them the strong responses they crave (Bergner, 1977).

The tendency of people with this disorder to seek out new sources of challenge and stimulation can also interfere with their occupational and social adjustment, and they may have unstable work histories. Their lack of attention to detail and their illogical thinking can also contribute to poor occupational adjustment. If they choose fields that can make accommodations to their unstable temperaments, however, they may be quite successful because they can be driven and energetic in their pursuits.

Preferred Therapist Characteristics

People with Histrionic Personality Disorder tend to be sociable and outgoing and may appear to be charming, ingratiating, expressive, and motivated clients, eager to please their therapists. These people usually seek therapy voluntarily, often as a result of the real or threatened loss of relationship or a decline in affection for their partners. Therefore, treatment usually begins on a positive note, but these clients often want the therapist to fix their problems, retrieve their relationships, or make others (usually a spouse or a partner) change.

As therapy progresses, their manipulative and seductive patterns will probably become more evident. They may be annoyed that the therapist has not rescued them, but the secondary gains of therapy—the attention paid by the therapist, and the opportunity to talk about themselves—are often reason enough for them to continue. Their strong need for approval and attention may lead them to seek a romantic relationship with an opposite-sex therapist or to compete with a same-sex therapist.

The therapist must monitor countertransference reactions to these clients, remaining warm, genuine, and accepting yet professional. Clarity and consistency can help to build and maintain trust. The therapist can also make productive therapeutic use of these clients' transference reactions to help clients gain an understanding of how they relate to others and to appreciate the negative impact that their behavior can have.

The therapist should quickly set limits with these clients and must maintain a professional relationship at all times. The clinician should avoid reinforcing dramatic behavior with attention. Soloff (1985) suggests focusing on process and on the facts of the person's history as a way of setting limits and maintaining appropriate distance. Gentle confrontation also seems to help people with Histrionic Personality Disorder look at the self-destructive nature of their behavior. Guided discovery also can facilitate establishment of a collaborative relationship. Keeping these clients on task will be a challenge because they tend to be distractible and to talk at length in vague, general terms. They may resist being introspective and specific, tasks that tend to be difficult for them. They are also unable to recall much of their past, including emotionally upsetting experiences, and have poor reality testing (Kaplan et al., 1994).

Persuading people with Histrionic Personality Disorder to engage in long-term therapy may be difficult in light of their high need for change, challenge, and stimulation. Such therapeutic strategies as limit setting and confrontation may also make people with Histrionic Personality Disorder feel rejected and unappreciated, and they may become reproachful and demanding, threatening to leave treatment if their demands are not met. Setting a series of clear short-term goals that are meaningful to the client can facilitate extended therapy, as can initiating therapy in an active and engaging fashion and reinforcing even small gains.

Intervention Strategies

As with most of the other Personality Disorders, few systematic studies exist on the treatment of Histrionic Personality Disorder (Sperry, 1995). Nevertheless, the literature does point to the use of long-term individual psychodynamic or cognitive-behavioral therapy as the core of treatment. People with Histrionic Personality Disorder need help in thinking more systematically, reducing emotional reactivity, improving reality testing, increasing self-reliance, promoting appropriate expression of feeling, and increasing their awareness of the impact of their behavior on others; thus Maxmen and Ward (1995) recommend that therapy be systematic and goal-directed, providing an external structure.

Gabbard (1990) reports success in using psychoanalytically oriented psychotherapy to treat higher-functioning clients with Histrionic Personality Disorder. He has found that they readily develop a positive therapeutic alliance and are amenable to exploring both the origins of their difficulties and their wishes for others to meet all their needs. The most challenging aspect of treatment with these clients, according to Gabbard, is managing the erotic transference.

Beck and Freeman (1990) have found that people with Histrionic Personality Disorder respond well to cognitive therapy, although modifications have to be made to that treatment approach. A sound therapeutic relationship, meaningful goals, and clear limits have to be established before these clients feel comfortable engaging in cognitive exploration, which is typically antithetical to their usual style. According to Beck and Freeman, therapists who take an active role and make extensive use of collaborative and guided discovery are particularly likely to be successful. One way to encourage cooperation is to combine structured tools, such as the Dysfunctional Thoughts Record, with more creative activities. Once the therapeutic process is well under way, clients should be encouraged to challenge such basic assumptions as "I am inadequate and have to rely on others to survive" (Beck & Freeman, 1990, p. 230). Training clients in assertiveness and problem solving, increasing clients' awareness of others' feelings, and promoting clients' self-awareness have all been helpful and have contributed to reducing clients' impulsivity. Helping them find new, safer means of stimulation can also be helpful.

Accompanying disorders also should receive attention. Unless depression, anxiety, or somatic symptoms are relieved, these clients may not be able or willing to modify their pervasive dysfunctional patterns.

Couples and group therapy can be very useful in treating people with Histrionic Personality Disorder (Gunderson, 1988). Those therapeutic experiences can provide helpful feedback, enable people to see that their behavior is not getting them the approval and affection they seek, and provide them with an opportunity to try new ways of establishing both casual and intimate relationships. Group therapy can dilute transference reactions and offer feedback while still providing attention and support to these clients, but they should be carefully screened for group participation, to ensure that they do not monopolize the group.

Family therapy is often is indicated because people with Histrionic Personality Disorder usually have partners with emotional difficulties; obsessive-compulsive patterns are especially common in the partners of women with these disorders (Sperry, 1995). Family therapy can ameliorate the emotional difficulties of both client and partner and can improve their communication and stabilize their relationship.

Medication is sometimes needed for treatment of the symptoms of people with Histrionic Personality Disorder. Monoamine oxidase inhibitors (MAOIs), for example, can successfully reduce depression, demanding behavior, and somatic complaints in these clients. If medication is recommended, considerable caution should be exercised because these clients are prone to suicidal threats and gestures.

Prognosis

Histrionic Personality Disorder is one of the milder Personality Disorders. People with this disorder are likely to benefit from therapy if they can be persuaded to remain in treatment (but persuading them to do so is often a considerable challenge). Unlike most people with Paranoid, Schizoid, Schizotypal, or Antisocial Personality Disorders, people with Histrionic Personality Disorder are motivated to make some changes, and their interpersonal skills are good enough to allow them to engage in therapy.

NARCISSISTIC PERSONALITY DISORDER

Description of the Disorder

Narcissistic Personality Disorder, according to *DSM-IV*, is characterized by "a pervasive pattern of grandiosity (in fantasy or behavior), need for admiration, and lack of empathy, beginning by early adulthood and present in a variety of contexts" (American Psychiatric Association, 1994a, p. 661). The disorder is characterized by the following features:

- Strong negative reactions to criticism
- Exploitation of others to accomplish one's own goals
- An exaggerated sense of self-importance
- A sense of entitlement
- Constant seeking of attention and praise
- Little appreciation for the feelings of others
- Enviousness, as well as the belief that one inspires envy in others

- Persistent fantasies of high achievement and special endowments, both personally and professionally
- The belief that one can be understood only by special people
- Arrogance and devaluing of others and their accomplishments
- Shallowness and unstable moods

Extensive use of rationalization, denial, and projection is common in people with this disorder. They have trouble seeing the part they play in their own difficulties (Millon & Klerman, 1986).

Although most people with this disorder appear arrogant and boastful, some are shy and hypersensitive (Groopman & Cooper, 1995). Despite their veneer of superiority, many people with Narcissistic Personality Disorder feel very vulnerable and may react even to minor criticisms with depression or rage. People with Narcissistic Personality Disorder tend to have low self-esteem. They often feel like frauds and failures, concealing their real selves from others lest their fraudulence and failure be discovered. They are frequently troubled by an underlying sense of emptiness.

Narcissistic Personality Disorder is probably more common among men than among women. This disorder is found in less than 1 percent of the general population and in 2 to 16 percent of clinical populations, although the prevalence of the disorder is increasing (Kaplan et al., 1994).

Narcissistic Personality Disorder is often accompanied by other disorders, most commonly Dysthymic Disorder (Millon, 1996). Symptoms of Somatoform Disorders sometimes follow experiences that evoke shame.

Typical Client Characteristics

Narcissistic Personality Disorder seems particularly prevalent in only children. Their families typically pampered and overindulged them and rarely set limits or disciplined them (Sperry, 1995). At the same time, these families typically conveyed the message that imperfection is cause for rejection (Meyer & Deitsch, 1996). As a result, people with Narcissistic Personality Disorder have internalized the message that they are superior and deserve special treatment, but that they will be rejected if they cease to be so exceptional.

People with Narcissistic Personality Disorder tend to avoid intimacy and seek to control and manipulate others. They may become contentious, arrogant, and demanding if they do not receive the treatment they feel they deserve. Thus their interpersonal relationships typically are impaired. Their quest for the perfect partner to affirm their own perfection can also be extremely damaging to their relationships and can lead to problems later in relationships, when these clients become competitive with their "perfect" partners. A dissatisfied partner is often the motivation for these clients to seek treatment.

Some people with Narcissistic Personality Disorder manifest occupational impairment. Fear of rejection or humiliation can inhibit their occupational success, as can their poor interpersonal skills, their intolerance of others' successes, and their disregard of rules or the requests of their supervisors. Some, however, driven by their self-absorption and their fantasies of unlimited success, have an impressive occupational history. Their tendency to be self-reliant and to take control of their own lives contributes to their sense of direction.

People with Narcissistic Personality Disorder tend to deteriorate with age; their loss of youthful vitality and good looks may be extremely painful for them. Nevertheless, as Kernberg (1986) observes, the aging process may weaken their grandiose facade and lead them to be more receptive to therapy.

Preferred Therapist Characteristics

People with Narcissistic Personality Disorder typically are quite resistant to treatment. They typically feel too fragile to acknowledge that they have any problems and too special to believe that anyone else can help them. Therefore, as in the treatment of most of the other Personality Disorders, the therapist working with a client who has Narcissistic Personality Disorder needs to communicate acceptance, warmth, genuineness, and understanding in order to engage the client in treatment; any hint of criticism may provoke premature termination.

The therapist should not underestimate the fragility of people with Narcissistic Personality Disorder. These clients may appear powerful, but they must be handled gently. Loss of their defenses can precipitate transient psychotic symptoms and regression.

Although the therapist should not be judgmental, indifference can be as painful to these clients as rejection. It may be wise for the therapist to engage in some cautious sharing of positive reactions to the client, as well as in extensive use of empathy.

People with this disorder tend to be very conscious of authority and are fearful of losing self-determination. These qualities can be used to the therapist's advantage. The therapeutic relationship should be a professional one, with clients accepted as experts on their own concerns and the therapist as the expert on psychotherapy. This collaborative relationship can facilitate clients' acceptance of help and their engagement in a working alliance. Kernberg (1985) emphasizes the importance of giving these clients full credit for any positive changes, to prevent their sabotaging the therapy so as to avoid admitting that another person has helped them.

People with Narcissistic Personality Disorder tend to be concerned with perfection and to seek it in themselves and their relationships. They frequently alternate between idealizing and devaluing others, including the therapist. The development of an idealizing transference, in which the therapist is viewed as an extension of the client or an admiring mirror, is not unusual and will need to be dealt with lest the client subsequently become disillusioned with the therapist's lack of perfection and leave therapy (Groopman & Cooper, 1995).

The therapist should avoid being either seduced by the client's flattery or discouraged by the client's deprecating remarks. Instead, the therapist needs to view these transference reactions as therapeutic material and make use of them. With patience, persistence, and the establishment of clear and appropriate limits, the therapist can sometimes succeed in establishing a positive therapeutic relationship with this type of client (Beck & Freeman, 1990).

Intervention Strategies

Little conclusive information is available on the treatment of this disorder. As with most of the other Personality Disorders, however, inferences can be drawn about the types of treatment that are most likely to be successful.

Kernberg (1985), Kohut (1971), and others have used a modified psychoanalytic approach, with some success, to help people with Narcissistic Personality Disorder develop a more accurate sense of reality and to make positive personality changes. Kernberg has focused on such basic issues as anger, envy, self-sufficiency, and demands on the self and others, in reality and in transference. Kohut has made use of the transference relationship to explore the client's early development and the client's wish for a perfect relationship and an ideal self. In an empathic context, both have explored defenses as well as needs and frustrations.

A psychodynamic approach seems to have a fair chance of succeeding with people who have Narcissistic Personality Disorder and mild dysfunction and who are motivated to engage in therapy. However, this approach seems not to be indicated for those who have significant disturbances of affect or impulse control; these clients seem to respond better to expressive, cognitive, and supportive forms of therapy than they do to analytic approaches (Kernberg, 1986).

Cognitive-behavioral approaches have also shown some success with these clients. Beck and Freeman (1990) recommend that treatment begin with the building of a collaborative relationship, the effort to help clients understand how therapy can help them, and the establishing of goals. A focus on behavioral change typically would be the next phase in this kind of treatment. Behavioral interventions that do not require much self-disclosure or discussion of weaknesses are usually more acceptable to these clients than cognitive interventions. Behavior therapy can alleviate depression and other affective symptoms while beginning to modify the Personality Disorder; cognitive interventions can subsequently be used to reduce grandiosity and hypersensitivity and increase empathy.

Significant change in people with Narcissistic Personality Disorder will usually require long-term treatment, but it is difficult to engage people with this disorder in lengthy, intensive treatment because of their resistance, their limited insight, and their extensive rationalization. Therefore, some therapists advocate a model of brief therapy, which sets limited goals and focuses on symptoms and current crises rather than on the underlying disorder itself. Gutsch (1988), for example, describes a present-oriented therapy for people with Narcissistic Personality Disorder. This treatment focuses on rapport, cognitive reorientation, reality testing, improvement in communication skills, rehearsal of new behaviors, and application of the new behaviors outside the therapeutic setting. Clients with Narcissistic Personality Disorder often have difficulty with loss and failure and may be particularly amenable to therapy focusing on those issues.

Group therapy, consisting exclusively of people diagnosed with Narcissistic Personality Disorder, can be useful to these clients if they are able to tolerate the exposure and negative feedback of the group experience and do not become disruptive (Sperry, 1995). Group therapy can help these clients develop a more realistic sense of themselves, deal with others in less abrasive ways, and stabilize their functioning, but it should always be combined with individual therapy for these clients (Groopman & Cooper, 1995).

People with Narcissistic Personality Disorder often come into treatment at the urging of an unhappy partner. In such a case, marital therapy may help the partners understand their roles and patterns of interacting and learn more effective ways of communicating with each other. Relationship enhancement therapy (Snyder, 1994), for example, combines object relations, social learning, interpersonal, and systems theories and offers psychoeducation and skills training geared to the needs of people with narcissistic personality patterns.

No medication has been found that really modifies Narcissistic Personality Disorder, but medication can treat the symptoms of this disorder in addition to any underlying disorders. Selective serotonin reuptake inhibitors (SSRIs), for example, have been shown to decrease vulnerability and reactivity in people with Narcissistic Personality Disorders (Sperry, 1995).

Prognosis

People with Narcissistic Personality Disorder are very difficult to treat. Meyer and Deitsch (1996) view the prognosis for their treatment as being fair at best. Nevertheless, despite the challenges presented by these clients, Beck, Kohut, Kernberg, and others all report some success. Kernberg (1986), for example, reports a favorable prognosis unless clients have strong features of Borderline or Antisocial Personality Disorders, and he suggests (1985) that the prognosis for treatment is particularly good for those who are creative and have some capacity to establish and work toward their desired goals.

AVOIDANT PERSONALITY DISORDER

Description of the Disorder

DSM-IV describes Avoidant Personality Disorder as characterized by "a pervasive pattern of social inhibition, feelings of inadequacy, and hypersensitivity to negative evaluation that begins by early adulthood and is present in a variety of contexts" (American Psychiatric Association, 1994a, p. 662). Typical manifestations of this disorder include emotional fragility, reluctance to become involved in interpersonal contact without guarantees of acceptance, fear of being embarrassed by doing something inappropriate or foolish in public, and avoidance of new and challenging activities that might lead to humiliation. People with this disorder typically view themselves as having poor interpersonal skills and as being inferior and unattractive to others.

Unlike people with Schizoid Personality Disorder, those with Avoidant Personality Disorder generally long for companionship and involvement in social activities, but their great anxiety and shyness inhibit their socialization. These people tend to have low self-esteem, to be self-effacing, and to berate themselves for their refusal to take risks in social situations. They fantasize about having a different lifestyle and anguish over their inability to change. Without assistance, however, they typically remain alienated, introverted, mistrustful, and guarded in social situations and avoid them whenever possible. Their need for control and self-protection outweighs their need for companionship.

Males and females are affected by this disorder in approximately equal numbers. About 0.5 to 1 percent of the general population can be diagnosed with Avoidant Personality Disorder, as can about 10 percent of people seen in clinical settings. Millon (1986) has found Avoidant Personality Disorder to be one of the more prevalent personality disorders, representing over 10 percent of those with Personality Disorders.

Gunderson (1988) has found that when people with this disorder are seen in treatment, another disorder, frequently one involving anxiety and depression, is usually the initial focus. Anxiety Disorders seem closely related to Avoidant Personality Disorder; Dissociative Disorder, Somatoform Disorders, and Schizophrenia have also been reported in combination with this disorder (Millon, 1996), as have Dependent, Borderline, Paranoid, Schizoid, and Schizotypal Personality Disorders.

Typical Client Characteristics

People with Avoidant Personality Disorder typically come from families that did afford some appropriate nurturing and bonding, but these families were also controlling and critical and very concerned with their children's presenting a positive social image (Benjamin, 1993). This combination led these people as children to value and desire relationships but to simultaneously fear and avoid them, believing that others would inevitably reject them. Even as children, people with Avoidant Personality Disorder had limited social experiences and poor peer relationships, and so they have had little opportunity to learn the skills needed for appropriate adult socialization.

By definition, people with Avoidant Personality Disorder have considerable social impairment, which is typically accompanied by occupational impairment.

People with this disorder often have jobs well below their abilities, usually because their fear of risk, rejection, and embarrassment prevents them from seeking promotions, taking an active part in meetings, attending business-related social events, and calling attention to their accomplishments.

Females with Avoidant Personality Disorder often have a strongly traditional gender identification. They tend to be passive, insecure, and dependent and look to others to direct their lives. Although they may have underlying anger about the situation in which they find themselves, they are afraid of the consequences of change.

The life of a person with Avoidant Personality Disorder is unsatisfying and disappointing, even if the person does manage to achieve a comfortable occupational situation. Some people with this disorder marry or develop a few close relationships. Typically, however, their friends tend to be distant, shy, and unstable, providing little help to these clients (Meyer, 1983). Although this disorder tends to improve somewhat with age, the avoidant patterns rarely remit significantly without help.

Preferred Therapist Characteristics

People with Avoidant Personality Disorder rarely seek treatment specifically for the symptoms of this disorder because that process in itself feels threatening and potentially embarrassing. If they do enter treatment, they often have one foot out the door, testing whether the therapist can be trusted, and may leave at any hint of ridicule, disapproval, or embarrassment.

These people typically are seen in treatment as a result of another disorder (such as Agoraphobia or depression), particularly at the urging of a family member or an employer. Therapists should proceed gradually in light of the apprehension that people with Avoidant Personality Disorder have about treatment, and given the fragile equilibrium they have established. Therapists should communicate concern, availability, empathy, acceptance, support, and protection. Building trust may be slow but is integral to the establishment of an effective therapeutic relationship with these clients. Focusing on their strengths, at least initially, can build self-confidence and contribute to the establishment of rapport. Contracting for a specific number of sessions may increase their commitment to treatment and prevent them from using therapy to avoid confronting real situations.

One advantage that therapists have in working with these clients is that they are in pain, are not happy with themselves, and want to change. Moreover, these clients typically appreciate safe attention and have a capacity for introspection. If they can be convinced that therapy can help them and is unlikely to embarrass them, they may have the motivation they need to benefit from treatment and may welcome the opportunity to discuss their concerns.

Therapists may feel frustrated with the apprehensions and slow progress of these clients. Beck and Freeman (1990) suggest that therapists and clients alike will benefit from focusing on progress, no matter how slight. In addition, signs of avoidance can be viewed positively, as offering opportunities to elicit information on impaired behavior and dysfunctional thoughts.

Sperry (1995) has observed two common types of countertransference in therapists working with people who have Avoidant Personality Disorder: overprotectiveness and unrealistic expectations for rapid change. Pacing is important in the treatment of these clients, and therapists should be sure that they are nudging clients forward but not forcing premature confrontation of frightening situations. A gradual shift from general support to selective reinforcement of assertive behavior and positive self-statements can promote progress.

Intervention Strategies

Little empirical research is available to guide treatment of Avoidant Personality Disorder, but guidelines can be drawn from case studies and from research on Social Phobia. Adler (1992) recommends an integrated approach, consisting of four treatment stages:

1. Building trust and a positive therapeutic relationship, and bringing clients to the point where they are willing to discuss their social anxieties

2. Promoting self-awareness and observational skills so that clients become aware of their self-destructive thoughts and behaviors

3. Helping clients learn alternative responses and behaviors

4. Modifying clients' automatic dysfunctional thoughts while clients implement their learning in the real world

Behavioral interventions are clearly essential to successful treatment of Avoidant Personality Disorder. Behavioral therapy can begin with fairly safe relaxation exercises and then progress to such techniques as training in assertiveness and social skills, modeling, various kinds of role playing and psychodrama, anxiety management, and graduated exposure or desensitization (using a hierarchy of feared situations). Between-session assignments can accelerate behavioral change as long as they do not cause feelings of failure and humiliation.

Beck and Freeman (1990) suggest incorporating a focus on cognitions after some behavioral change has been made. Changes in clients' emotions can be used as opportunities to elicit automatic thoughts. Using prediction logs to point out any discrepancies between expectations and reality, positive-experience logs, and lists of evidence for and against automatic thoughts (such as "I am not a likable person") can promote changes in self-critical cognitions.

Sutherland and Frances (1995) support the use of cognitive as well as behavioral techniques in the treatment of people diagnosed with Avoidant Personality Disorder but also suggest that these techniques are not sufficient to enable clients to reach a rewarding level of functioning. The addition of psychodynamic therapy to the treatment plan can promote further gains and help people address issues related to their harsh superegos, underlying shame, and projection of unrealistic self-expectations onto others. Interpretations should be made with caution, however, because these clients sometimes perceive them as criticisms.

As people with Avoidant Personality Disorder improve, group therapy can be a very important addition to treatment. It can help clients learn and practice new social skills in a safe context, receive feedback and encouragement, and increase their comfort with others. Nevertheless, people with Avoidant Personality Disorder should not be placed in group therapy prematurely. Inappropriate placement in a therapy group can be very threatening and lead these clients to terminate treatment abruptly.

Family therapy can be useful, too, if clients are actively involved with family members. The families of people with Avoidant Personality Disorder typically either try to be helpful by protecting these clients or try to effect change by insisting on the clients' greater involvement with others. Clients and family members alike can be helped if family members are able to learn ways of remaining supportive while still encouraging these clients to increase their socialization (Sutherland & Frances, 1995). These clients also often have marital relationships that are characterized by interpersonal distance, and family therapy can modify that pattern, facilitating the establishment of a marriage that is more rewarding to both partners.

Medication usually is not needed in the treatment of Avoidant Personality Disorder, and people with this disorder seem uncomfortable with the idea of taking medication (probably because they fear loss of control). These clients also benefit from taking credit for positive changes rather than attributing them to medication. Nevertheless, sometimes medications (such as MAOIs and benzodiazepines) that have been helpful in the treatment of people with Social Phobia can also reduce anxiety, shyness, and sensitivity to rejection in people with Avoidant Personality Disorder (Sutherland & Frances, 1995).

According to Beck and Freeman (1990), relapse prevention is an important element of treatment for these clients because their avoidant behavior often returns after therapy. Relapse prevention can include infrequent but ongoing sessions and may include the agreement that the client will continue using assertive behaviors and pursuing new friendships and challenging tasks.

Prognosis

As with most of the other Personality Disorders, prognosis depends on the setting of realistic goals and on clients' finding interpersonal and occupational environments that meet their needs. Most people with Avoidant Personality

Disorder can make meaningful changes as long as they are willing to invest in therapy, but they probably always will tend to have self-doubts, as well as some discomfort in new interpersonal situations.

DEPENDENT PERSONALITY DISORDER

Description of the Disorder

Dependent Personality Disorder, according to *DSM-IV*, is characterized by "a pervasive and excessive need to be taken care of that leads to submissive and clinging behavior and fears of separation" (American Psychiatric Association, 1994a, p. 665). People with this disorder typically have great difficulty making decisions independently and without reassurance. They look to others to make major decisions for them, and they avoid disagreeing with others lest they be rejected. They feel uncomfortable, frightened, and helpless when they are alone or when they are required to take initiative. They go out of their way to be helpful in order to be liked, are hypersensitive to criticism or disapproval, fear abandonment, and, if a close relationship ends, feel devastated and driven to quickly find another relationship that provides care and nurturance.

People with Dependent Personality Disorder have very low self-esteem and are frequently self-critical. They believe that they have little to offer and so must assume a secondary, even subservient, position with respect to others in order to be accepted. They tend to be inordinately tolerant of destructive relationships and unreasonable requests. They typically are other-directed, and their gratifications and disappointments hinge on the reactions they receive from others. At the same time, they are egocentric in that they are pleasing others to gain appreciation. They tend to think in dichotomous ways and to believe in absolutes, viewing things as either right or wrong (Sperry, 1995).

According to Millon (1986), Dependent Personality Disorder is the most commonly diagnosed Personality Disorder, found in approximately 14 percent of those with Personality Disorders and at least 2.5 percent of the general population (Sperry, 1995). People with Dependent Personality Disorder are frequently seen in treatment. This disorder seems to be more commonly diagnosed among females than among males, but this apparent pattern has raised the question of whether some women who embrace traditional female roles are being discriminated against by being inappropriately diagnosed as having Dependent Personality Disorder. Gender, age, and cultural factors should be taken into account before this diagnosis is made.

The seeds of Dependent Personality Disorder are often seen in an early history of Separation Anxiety Disorder or chronic illness. Other disorders, such as Mood and Anxiety Disorders, Somatoform Disorders, Substance Use Disorders, and other Personality Disorders, are often diagnosed along with Dependent Personality Disorder (Beck & Freeman, 1990; Millon, 1996). Symptoms are especially likely to emerge or worsen after a loss or anticipated abandonment.

Typical Client Characteristics

Not surprisingly, many people with Dependent Personality Disorder report a history of having been overprotected (Meyer & Deitsch, 1996). They were pampered as children and were expected to behave perfectly and to maintain strong family ties and loyalties. As Millon (1981) puts it, their home lives were often "too good." Youngest children are particularly susceptible to Dependent Personality Disorder, perhaps because their upbringing has encouraged them to depend on older family members and did not lead to sufficient independence (Maxmen & Ward, 1995).

People with Dependent Personality Disorder tend to have a small number of significant others on whom they are dependent, and who seem to accept their passive and submissive attitudes. They bind those significant others to them through guilt and service and rarely seek to broaden their social circles.

People with this disorder may function satisfactorily in occupations that are consistent with their need to be told what to do and to receive approval. They have difficulty with tasks that require independent action and decisions, however, and may appear fragile, indecisive, placating, inept, and immature to those around them (Millon & Klerman, 1986).

Even when these people's lives seem to be going well, they experience little happiness and seem to have a pervasive underlying pessimistic and dysphoric mood. They typically appear rigid, judgmental, and moralistic, especially under stress. In crisis, despondency and suicidal ideation may surface.

Preferred Therapist Characteristics

People with Dependent Personality Disorder may seek therapy voluntarily after an experienced or threatened loss of a relationship (particularly via bereavement or divorce), or they may seek therapy at the suggestion of a spouse, another relative, or an employer. These clients also may ask for help with secondary symptoms, such as depression and substance use (Gunderson, 1988). They typically are apprehensive about therapy but want help in averting any threatened loss. Nevertheless, they are unlikely to have much initial interest in becoming more assertive and independent. They tend to be passive clients, waiting for their therapists to ask them questions or give direction to the sessions. They tend to view the therapist as someone else on whom to depend—a magic helper—and probably will work hard to please the therapist rather than themselves.

The challenge for the therapist is to use these dynamics constructively. The client's wish to please may be used to develop rapport and encourage increased independence. Changes made only to please the therapist are not likely to persist outside the sessions, however, and do not reflect internal change.

In working with a person who has Dependent Personality Disorder, the therapist should probably begin in a directive and structured way, to give focus to the sessions. In order to establish rapport, the therapist will also need to communicate a great deal of support, acceptance, and empathy and should guard against appearing critical. Some initial dependence on the part of the client should be allowed as part of the rapport-building process. With the development of a therapeutic alliance, however, the therapist should gradually assume less responsibility and encourage the client to take more control of the sessions. The therapist should continue to convey empathy, appreciation, and optimism but should also ask the client to make a commitment to working on his or her own concerns. The therapist should not give the client feedback on dependence needs, however, or offer interpretations of the transference until less threatening approaches have effected some improvement. The overall goal of treatment will be to promote the client's self-reliance, self-expression, and autonomy in a safe context and then facilitate the transfer of those experiences to settings outside the therapy room. Termination is likely to be particularly difficult, and the therapist will need to be cautious lest the client feel abandoned.

It is common for a client with Dependent Personality Disorder to develop a romantic attachment to the therapist (Beck & Freeman, 1990). The therapist should set clear limits on the relationship with the client, avoid any physical contact, and explain that such romantic feelings are not unusual in therapeutic relationships but that this relationship will remain a professional one. Some have recommended that women with Dependent Personality Disorder be seen by women therapists so as to have positive role models and be at less risk for growing dependent on or romantically attached to their therapists (Hill, 1970), and this recommendation could be considered when treatment is planned.

Strong countertransference reactions to these clients are common (Perry, 1995). The therapist may find this type of client frustrating and annoying or may want to protect the client from mistreatment. The therapist needs to manage these feelings and be sure that these feelings do not damage the therapeutic relationship.

Intervention Strategies

Both long-term and short-term psychodynamic approaches have demonstrated effectiveness with people who have Dependent Personality Disorder (Perry, 1995). Psychodynamic approaches involve allowing the emergence of a dependent transference that is then dealt with in growth-promoting ways. In addition, encouragement and support are used to promote autonomy and improved communication and problem solving. These interventions can help improve clients' self-esteem, increase their sense of autonomy and individuation, teach them to manage their own lives and ask for help and support without being manipulative, and relieve their fears of harming others or being devastated by rejection. Short-term psychodynamic approaches typically involve weekly therapy for three to nine months. These approaches are most likely to succeed when the client presents a clear and circumscribed focal conflict or issue, can rapidly form a therapeutic alliance, and is unlikely to act out or regress (Sperry, 1995). A psychodynamic approach requires both commitment to therapy and introspection and will not be right for everyone with Dependent Personality Disorder; for example, some people respond to insight-oriented therapy with increased dependence (McDaniel, 1981).

Cognitive-behavioral therapy has also been used effectively to ameliorate some of the symptoms of Dependent Personality Disorder (Perry, 1995; Sperry, 1995). The treatment is similar to that recommended for Avoidant Personality Disorder. It usually includes relaxation and desensitization, to help the client handle challenging interpersonal situations, and provides training in assertiveness and communication skills, to help the client identify and express feelings and wants in more functional ways. Standard behavioral techniques, such as modeling, reinforcement, and rehearsal, can all contribute to the client's improvement. Homework assignments should be practiced in sessions initially, to reduce the fear of failure. Properly handled, homework tasks are likely to be completed because these clients typically follow directions and want to please.

Cognitive therapy is generally used to treat Dependent Personality Disorder only after a therapeutic relationship has been formed and some gains have been made through supportive and behavioral interventions. Cognitive therapy can challenge those dichotomous and dysfunctional beliefs that limit clients' autonomy and impair their self-esteem. It can be empowering and reinforcing for clients to gather evidence of their competence and learn to use coping and problem-solving skills. As clients gain experience in these and other skills (such as self-monitoring, accurate self-evaluation, and reinforcement), they can assume greater responsibility for their sessions.

Practical issues like housing and employment sometimes require attention because many people with Dependent Personality Disorder seek therapy after the end of a marriage. Helping them successfully reestablish themselves can promote behavioral changes, and the tasks involved in their getting reestablished can serve as vehicles for applying what they have learned in therapy.

Family and group therapy is often indicated for these clients. Those treatment settings will afford them the opportunity to try out new ways of expressing themselves and relating to others while receiving support and encouragement along the way. Family therapy may be difficult if the client has a resistant partner, but, as Turkat (1990) suggests, the family's collaboration can both facilitate progress and improve familial relationships. Therapeutic groups need to be chosen carefully for these clients so as not to overwhelm and threaten them or expose them to undue pressure to leave a harmful relationship. At the same time, shifting a client from individual to group treatment can reduce transference and facilitate termination.

People with Dependent Personality Disorder sometimes request medication (Gutsch, 1988). It rarely is needed except in cases of severe depression or anxiety. These clients also sometimes misuse drugs, and the belief that they need medication can detract from their growing sense of competence.

Prognosis

Treatment of Dependent Personality Disorder is difficult; the patterns are deeply entrenched, and the clients really want to be saved rather than changed (Esman, 1986). Nevertheless, treatment of this disorder has a relatively good prognosis (Perry, 1995). People with this disorder are trusting. They can form relationships and make commitments. They want to please, and they can ask for help. All of these attributes lead to a somewhat better prognosis and a shorter and more rewarding course of therapy than is found in treating most of the other Personality Disorders.

OBSESSIVE-COMPULSIVE PERSONALITY DISORDER

Description of the Disorder

Perfectionism and inflexibility characterize Obsessive-Compulsive Personality Disorder (OCPD). The following manifestations are typical of this pervasive pattern (American Psychiatric Association, 1994a):

- Impaired performance on tasks and activities because of preoccupation with details, rules, order, duties, and perfection
- A strong need to control others
- Avoidance of delegating tasks for fear that they will not be done correctly
- Overinvolvement in work, accompanied by minimal attention to leisure and social activities
- Indecisiveness
- Rigid moral and ethical beliefs
- Restricted expression of emotion
- Reluctance to give to others without the promise of personal gain
- Harsh self-criticism
- Difficulty discarding objects that no longer have value

Although people with OCPD seem indifferent to the feelings of others, they are very sensitive to slights themselves and typically overreact to real or imagined insults. These clients tend to be well defended, typically using sublimation, intellectualization, isolation, reaction formation, displacement, and regression (McCullough & Maltsberger, 1995). Rules are used to insulate them from their emotions.

Oldham and Frosch (1986) identify the three major characteristics of OCPD as orderliness, stinginess, and obstinacy. This disorder differs from Obsessive-Compulsive Disorder, an Anxiety Disorder, in that OCPD is pervasive and ego-syntonic and typically does not include specific unwanted and intrusive obsessions or compulsions.

OCPD is approximately twice as common among males as females and is diagnosed most often in eldest children (American Psychiatric Association, 1994a; Kaplan et al., 1994). This disorder is present in approximately 1 percent of the general population and in 3 to 10 percent of people seen at mental health clinics.

Anxiety and depression are frequent accompaniments of OCPD (Millon, 1996). In people with this disorder, depression often follows a perceived loss or failure and is particularly common in later life (Gutsch, 1988; Kaplan et al., 1994). Paranoia also has been reported (Oldham & Frosch, 1986).

Typical Client Characteristics

People diagnosed with OCPD typically experienced strict and punitive parenting that was designed to ensure that they did not cause trouble (Sperry, 1995). The home environments of people with this disorder have usually been rigid, emphasizing the work ethic (Turkat & Maisto, 1985), and guilt was inculcated when people failed to live up to expectations or to meet their responsibilities. OCPD is more common among first-degree relatives of those with the same disorder than it is in the general population. Parents' punitive and authoritarian behavior may be a reflection of their own OCPD.

People with this disorder almost inevitably have interpersonal and social difficulties, although many achieve stable but rigid marriages (Gutsch, 1988). People with OCPD tend to be cold, mistrustful, demanding, and uninteresting and put little time or effort into building relationships and communicating feelings. They are typically angry and competitive toward others, have difficulty expressing emotions or affection, and are most comfortable in the intellectual realm. Their lives tend to be joyless and focused on work and obligations.

Their occupational development may or may not be impaired, and they typically have greater occupational success than people with other Personality Disorders because they are tireless and dedicated workers (Oldham & Frosch, 1986). Nevertheless, people with OCPD have difficulty delegating, collaborating, and supervising. They tend to be self-righteous and domineering, and they usually have poor relationships with co-workers, whom they tend to view as incompetent and irresponsible. People with OCPD also tend to have difficulty bringing projects to closure because of their indecisiveness, poor planning, and perfectionism, and this pattern may cause them to miss deadlines and have work-related difficulties.

Preferred Therapist Characteristics

People with OCPD tend to be difficult clients. They have trouble giving up control and accepting help from others, and they have little facility with insight and self-expression. They often focus on external events and physical rather than psychological complaints in treatment. New situations make them anxious, and they are likely to become even more obstinate and resistant in therapy than they usually are (Gunderson, 1988). If they can become engaged in conversation, they tend to complain bitterly about others' incompetence and how unappreciated they feel. Their interest is in changing others rather than in changing themselves, and they may attack therapists who suggest that they need to make changes. They also may feel competitive with their therapists and may have an investment in sabotaging therapy or proving their therapists incompetent.

Involving people with this disorder in a productive therapeutic relationship clearly presents a considerable challenge. These clients are respectful of authority, however, as well as persevering, and they usually comply with rules and directions (although they may feel inwardly defiant). Therapists may initially be able to use the authority of their education and position to elicit a short-term commitment to therapy from these clients.

Therapists should be sure not to engage in power struggles and arguments with these clients. Other ways for therapists to earn the admiration of these people and enable them to accept help are to treat them in a respectful and professional way, to refrain from violating their defenses and their need for privacy, to collaborate with them on therapeutic decisions, and to be prompt, organized, and efficient. Too much attention to emotion can be upsetting to these clients, but acceptance, support, and empathy can help convince them that their therapists are not their enemies.

Intervention Strategies

Little clear research exists on effective treatment of Obsessive-Compulsive Personality Disorder (McCullough & Maltsberger, 1995). Although long-term psychodynamic or modified psychoanalytic therapy may be ideal for people with this disorder, it is difficult to involve them in therapy that is extended, intensive, and introspective. Therefore, more present- and action-oriented approaches, consistent with these clients' limited insight and intolerance of yielding control, will often have to be used if these clients are to be helped in establishing more realistic expectations for themselves and others.

Gunderson (1988) suggests short-term psychodynamic therapy for those who are reluctant to become involved in lengthier therapy. Brief psychotherapy with these clients can be especially well received if it helps them deal with specific and current issues or crises and validates their feelings. Treatment may focus on such issues as their need for control, their perfectionism, and conflicts in their relationships. According to Oldham and Frosch (1986), a fundamental goal of treatment is to make the obsessive-compulsive behaviors and attitudes ego-dystonic so that people are motivated to change. Gentle confrontation and education can help people take a realistic view of their current difficulties and promote expression of affect. Likely gains include increases in positive self-references and decreases in procrastination and egocentrism (Primac, 1993).

Several authors have suggested that cognitive-behavioral therapy is likely to be well received by people with OCPD because that approach is structured, problem-centered, and present-oriented, requiring only limited analysis and expression of emotions. Behavior therapy can be useful in reducing some of the dysfunctional behaviors of these clients. It can also increase their ability to plan and make decisions, their involvement in leisure and social activities, and their facility with communicating their feelings and reactions positively and assertively. Meyer (1983) recommends a behavioral approach to treating these clients, using such techniques as covert conditioning, in which the image of an aversive event is paired with a dysfunctional behavior, in an effort to motivate people to make some behavioral changes. Meyer also recommends paradoxical interventions as a way to give people choices and a sense of control. Having a mutually agreed list of prioritized goals can keep these clients working productively and can minimize complaining and oppositional tactics. Modeling humor and spontaneity in controlled ways can teach these clients new ways of behaving. Techniques for stress management can also contribute to the improvement of OCPD, as can thought stopping, social skills training, desensitization, and response prevention (Salzman, 1989).

Beck and Freeman (1990) report success in using a modified version of cognitive therapy with these clients. In this approach, behavioral experiments rather than direct disputation were used to change such characteristic automatic thoughts as "I must avoid mistakes to be worthwhile" (p. 315). Inventories like the Weekly Activity Schedule and the Dysfunctional Thought Record increased structure and, correspondingly, clients' cooperation.

People with Obsessive-Compulsive Personality Disorder typically are resistant to participation in group and family therapy because of their reluctance to disclose their feelings to others and their fear of humiliation. If their commitment to individual therapy can be sustained long enough for them to make some positive changes, however, they may later be able to make productive use of group or family therapy. Those approaches can offer them feedback, as well as the opportunity to learn and experiment with new interpersonal behaviors and improve relationships. Nevertheless, therapists should be sure that these clients do not monopolize group or family sessions and are ready to listen to others.

Medication generally is not necessary for treatment of people with OCPD, but some medications, such as clomipramine (Anafranil), have demonstrated effectiveness in treating Obsessive-Compulsive Disorder and may be beneficial in the treatment of OCPD as well (Kaplan et al., 1994). Medication is also occasionally indicated for relief of severe anxiety and depression accompanying OCPD (Sperry, 1995).

Relapse prevention can be helpful to people with OCPD, just as it can be to people with most of the other Personality Disorders. Beck and Freeman (1990) suggest teaching people to monitor their own progress and scheduling periodic booster sessions.

Prognosis

Without treatment, OCPD usually is relatively stable over time, neither improving nor worsening. Gutsch (1988) reports that some people with OCPD do seek therapy voluntarily and respond well to treatment. Many case studies report improvement, if not major personality changes, in people with OCPD. As with most of the other Personality Disorders, a small number of these clients probably make major changes as a result of therapy. A larger number make some important behavioral and attitudinal changes, and another large number either leave therapy prematurely or remain resistant to help. Overall, then, the prognosis is probably only fair for treatment of Obsessive-Compulsive Personality Disorder.

TREATMENT RECOMMENDATIONS: CLIENT MAP

Recommendations on treating Personality Disorders are summarized below according to the framework of the Client Map.

Client Map

Diagnosis

Personality Disorders (Paranoid, Schizoid, Schizotypal, Antisocial, Borderline, Histrionic, Narcissistic, Avoidant, Dependent, and Obsessive-Compulsive)

Objectives of Treatment

Short- to medium-term objectives: improve social and occupational functioning, communication skills, self-esteem, empathy, and coping mechanisms; develop appropriate sense of responsibility

Long-term objectives: modify underlying dysfunctional personality patterns

Assessments

Broad-based personality inventory (for example, the Millon Clinical Multiaxial Inventory)

Measures of specific symptoms (for example, substance use, depression, anxiety)

Clinician Characteristics

Consistent

Able to set limits

Able to communicate acceptance and empathy in the face of resistance, hostility, or dependence

Good ability to manage transference and countertransference reactions

Patient and comfortable with slow progress

Location

Usually outpatient setting

Emergency and inpatient settings, as necessary, to deal with suicidal ideation or regression

Interventions to Be Used

Usually psychodynamic (to modify dysfunctional personality)

Behavioral and cognitive (to effect change in coping skills and relationships and to address presenting problems)

Emphasis of Treatment

Strong emphasis on establishing a therapeutic relationship

Fairly strong emphasis on structure and directiveness

Simultaneous emphasis on fostering client's responsibility

Emphasis balanced between supportive and exploratory elements

Numbers

Individual therapy usually primary, combined later with family or couples therapy

Group therapy often very useful in combination with individual therapy after client is able to tolerate group without becoming frightened or destructive

Timing

Usually long-term, but with development of short-term goals to discourage premature termination

Gradual but steady pace

More than one session per week possible, especially when client is in crisis

Medications Needed

Not effective in modifying basic Personality Disorder

May sometimes help alleviate depression, anxiety, or psychotic symptoms

Should be used with caution in light of any tendency to misuse substances or attempt suicide

Adjunct Services

Possibly Alcoholics Anonymous, Narcotics Anonymous, social groups

Career counseling

Assertiveness training

Prognosis

Usually fair, but variable

Can be good for short-term behavioral changes

Fair for underlying personality changes

Client Map of Joanne

This chapter opened with a description of Joanne, a twenty-five-year-old woman who was seen for therapy after a suicide attempt. Joanne's background included emotional and physical abuse and loss of both biological parents. She presented a long history of depression, maladaptive substance use, and instability in relationships and employment. Joanne was a challenging client because of her multiple diagnoses, her previous unsuccessful treatments, her suicidal behavior, her limited sense of self, and her lack of support systems. She initially idealized her therapists, made excessive demands on them, and then left treatment when they failed to meet her demands. Her principal diagnosis was Borderline Personality Disorder. The following Client Map presents recommendations for treating Joanne.

Diagnosis

Axis I: 296.33 Major Depressive Disorder, Recurrent, Severe
300.4 Dysthymic Disorder, Severe
305.00 Alcohol Abuse, Moderate
312.39 Trichotillomania, Moderate

Axis II: 301.83 Borderline Personality Disorder

Axis III: 278.0 Obesity

Axis IV: Marital conflict and abuse, history of childhood sexual, emotional, and physical abuse

Axis V: Global assessment of functioning (GAF Scale): current GAF = 25

Objectives of Treatment

Reduction of depression and suicidal ideation

Improved coping mechanisms (stress management, verbal self-expression)

Abstinence from alcohol

Reduction of hair pulling

Improved support systems and safety

Establishment of rewarding and realistic goals and direction

Increased stability and sense of competence

Assessments

Millon Clinical Multiaxial Inventory

Michigan Alcoholism Screening Test

Beck Depression Inventory

Medical examination

Clinician Characteristics

Stable

Structured

Accepting and supportive

Able to set and maintain clear limits

Able to manage transference and countertransference reactions

Location of Treatment

Outpatient setting

Inpatient and day treatment settings as needed

Interventions to Be Used

Supportive and behavioral therapy at first (to build a therapeutic relationship and enable client to see that therapy could be useful)

Contracts specifying alternative coping behaviors (to prevent suicidal behavior and reduce alcohol consumption)

Development of a safety plan (to protect client from abuse by her husband)

Rewarding activities and between-session tasks (to promote motivation, begin to build feelings of competence, and reduce depression)

Later integration of cognitive and psychodynamic approaches (to help client deal with past losses and profound feelings of hopelessness, emptiness, and worthlessness)

Emphasis of Treatment

Supportive and structured emphasis (but promoting client's responsibility)

Initial emphasis on the present and on behavior

Later emphasis on past issues and underlying dysfunction and dynamics

Numbers

Primarily individual therapy at first

Marital therapy (to help client and her husband improve their relationship and eliminate abuse)

Group therapy (after amelioration of client's immediate difficulties, and with client's growing ability to participate effectively and benefit from feedback, support, and opportunities for socialization and practice of interpersonal skills)

Timing

Long-term (if client willing)

Steady pace, with communication of clear expectations

Medications Needed

Antidepressant medication probably useful, but with careful monitoring in light of client's suicidal ideation

Adjunct Services

Alcoholics Anonymous

Nutritional counseling

Exercise and weight-control programs

Education about the physiology of alcohol use, stress management, assertiveness, and job seeking

Prognosis

Fair at best, in light of client's history of treatment failures

Recommended Reading

Beck, A. T., & Freeman, A. (1990). *Cognitive therapy of personality disorders.* New York: Guilford Press.

Benjamin, L. (1993). *Interpersonal diagnosis and treatment of personality disorders.* New York: Guilford Press.

Gunderson, J. G. (1988). Personality disorders. In A. M. Nicholi Jr. (Ed.), *The new Harvard guide to psychiatry* (pp. 337–357). Cambridge, MA: Harvard University Press.

Gunderson, J. G., & Gabbard, G. O. (1995). Personality disorders: Introduction. In G. O. Gabbard (Ed.), *Treatments of psychiatric disorders* (pp. 2243–2247). Washington, DC: American Psychiatric Press.

Lion, J. R. (Ed.). (1981). *Personality disorders: Diagnosis and management.* Baltimore: Williams & Wilkins.

Millon, T. (1996). *Disorders of personality: DSM-IV and beyond.* New York: Wiley.

Sperry, L. (1995). *Handbook of diagnosis and treatment of the DSM-IV personality disorders.* New York: Brunner/Mazel.

CHAPTER NINE

Disorders Involving Impairment in Awareness of Reality: Psychotic and Dissociative Disorders

Victor J., a twenty-two-year-old college senior, was brought to the psychologist in the college counseling center by his roommate, Arnold, who expressed great concern about Victor's thoughts and behaviors. Several months earlier, Victor had spent the winter break in New York City with Arnold and his divorced mother, Vanessa. During that time, Vanessa, a well-known writer of romance novels, had gone out of her way to entertain Victor. She took Victor and Arnold out to dinner and to the theater, introduced them to her friends, and took them shopping.

Upon returning to college, Victor told Arnold that Vanessa and he were in love and would marry in the spring, after graduation. He began writing impassioned letters to Vanessa, called her frequently, and spent most of his free time reading her novels.

At first Vanessa was amused and teased Victor about his interest in "an older woman." The teasing only prompted more passionate and graphic letters, however. Vanessa tried repeatedly to let Victor know that she was not romantically interested in him, but even when she returned his letters unopened, he continued his avowals of love. He told Arnold that his mother was concealing her real feelings because she did not want to upset her son.

The week before Victor was brought for counseling, he had borrowed money and traveled to New York, where he had appeared at Vanessa's office. When she told him she was busy and did not want to see him, he refused to leave for several hours and reappeared at her office for the next few days. Vanessa believed that Victor had taken some notes from her desk and had rummaged through her files and her wastebasket.

Victor had dated little in college and generally seemed uncomfortable around women his own age. He had grown up in a lower-middle-class family. His father owned an automobile repair business and had been opposed to Victor's attending college. He expected Victor to join him in the business after graduation. Although Victor's grades had declined somewhat, he was passing all his courses and was due to graduate in two months. Interviews with Victor indicated that he was experiencing Delusional Disorder, a mental disorder that involves loss of contact with reality.

OVERVIEW OF PSYCHOTIC AND DISSOCIATIVE DISORDERS

Description of the Disorders

This chapter considers a diverse array of disorders that are characterized by impairment in awareness of reality. They include Schizophrenia and Other Psychotic Disorders, as well as Dissociative Disorders. All these disorders differ considerably in terms of origin, duration, treatment, and prognosis. What connects them is similarity in their symptoms: these disorders typically involve a distortion or impairment in memory, awareness of reality, or both. Most have significant impacts on people's lives, usually producing marked dysfunction in at least one area. People with these disorders are often unable or unwilling to present a clear picture of their symptoms. Therefore, these disorders can offer a challenge to the diagnostician and are sometimes misdiagnosed as Cognitive, Mood, or Substance-Induced Disorders. Misdiagnosis is an unfortunate possibility, of course, because it can lead to inappropriate treatment.

Psychotic Disorders

DSM-IV (American Psychiatric Association, 1994a) lists the following Psychotic Disorders:

- Schizophrenia
- Brief Psychotic Disorder
- Schizophreniform Disorder
- Delusional Disorder
- Schizoaffective Disorder
- Shared Psychotic Disorder

The first five are considered in detail in later sections of this chapter. Like the other psychotic disorders, Brief Psychotic Disorder and Schizophreniform Disorder are described separately, but they are discussed together in terms of typical client characteristics, preferred therapist characteristics, intervention strategies, and prognosis. Shared Psychotic Disorder, which involves one or more people adopting the psychotic beliefs of another person, is not discussed here because it is rarely presented in clinical settings and because the dominant member of the dyad or group usually meets the criteria for a diagnosis of Schizophrenia.

Dissociative Disorders

The Dissociative Disorders present a very different picture from that of the Psychotic Disorders, although they too involve changes in awareness of reality, memory, consciousness, perceptions, and personality integration. Nemiah (1988) describes the Dissociative Disorders as involving a "sudden alteration in mental functioning leading either to an altered state of consciousness or to a change in identity, or both" (p. 246). These disorders seem to serve the purpose of "removing painful mental events from consciousness" (p. 249). Examples of benign episodes of dissociation are the hypnotic states or momentary lapses in awareness that may occur, for example, when people are driving familiar routes. Dissociative Disorders, however, involve episodes that are severe enough to cause distress and, sometimes, an accompanying impairment in functioning.

Dissociative Disorders are believed to be uncommon, although they do seem to be increasing (Morrison, 1995). These disorders are associated with traumatic, conflicted, or highly stressful experiences, which also seem to be on the rise and are perhaps contributing to the apparent increase in these disorders. Most Dissociative Disorders begin and end suddenly, although recurrent episodes are common. They tend to make their initial appearance in childhood or adolescence.

DSM-IV defines four types of Dissociative Disorders, in addition to Dissociative Disorder Not Otherwise Specified:

- Dissociative Identity Disorder
- Dissociative Fugue
- Dissociative Amnesia
- Depersonalization Disorder

Dissociative Fugue and Dissociative Amnesia involve a person's temporarily forgetting important components of his or her life, to a more extensive or more extreme degree than would be due to ordinary forgetfulness. By definition, neither disorder is caused by substances or by a general medical condition. Both tend to occur suddenly at times of trauma or unusual stress, are typically of brief duration, and usually remit without recurrence. Both disorders are also rare but increase in circumstances of natural disaster, accidents, or warfare.

Diagnosis of any disorder reflected by impaired memory should involve neurological, medical, and psychiatric evaluation. Because many general medical conditions, as well as substance use, can cause memory impairment, those causes should be ruled out before any diagnosis of a Dissociative Disorder is made. Clouded consciousness and disorientation, particularly in a person past middle age, suggest that a Cognitive Disorder or a medical condition rather than a Dissociative Disorder may be present.

All the Dissociative Disorders are described separately in later sections of this chapter, but Dissociative Fugue, Dissociative Amnesia, and Depersonalization Disorder are discussed together in terms of typical client characteristics, preferred therapist characteristics, intervention strategies, and prognosis.

Typical Client Characteristics

Just as the disorders in this chapter vary considerably, so do the people who present them. The premorbid functioning of people with Psychotic and Dissociative Disorders varies widely. Some have poor prior adjustment; others previously manifested positive social skills and sound coping mechanisms. The disorders discussed in this chapter also differ in terms of their development. Some people experience gradual deterioration, whereas others suffer a rapid alteration in consciousness in response to an immediate stressor.

People with these disorders typically are aware that something is wrong but may not understand what is happening, may conceal their symptoms for fear of being harmed or hospitalized, and may not be receptive to help that is offered. While their symptoms are present, their social and occupational adjustment is almost invariably affected, although the degree of disturbance ranges from mild and circumscribed to severe and pervasive, according to the particular disorder and its manifestation. Disturbed family relationships are especially common.

Preferred Therapist Characteristics

With the exception of Dissociative Identity Disorder and Depersonalization Disorder, treatment of these disorders generally requires medical as well as psychological intervention. Nevertheless, psychologists, counselors, and other nonmedical mental health professionals often collaborate with physicians and social service professionals to treat clients with all the disorders in this chapter.

Therapists will need to employ a variety of approaches, including long-term intensive psychodynamic psychotherapy, hypnotherapy, and cognitive-behavioral treatment. They will need to be comfortable dealing with people who typically do not present a clear and coherent picture of their symptoms or history and who may be resistant. They also need to be able to deal with chronic mental disorders, as well as those that respond rapidly to treatment.

Intervention Strategies

The nature of the treatment indicated for the disorders discussed in this chapter varies with respect to duration and approach to treatment. Specifics are provided in the sections on the individual disorders.

Prognosis

Prognosis for these disorders is uncertain but bears some relationship to duration. Those disorders that are of shorter duration, such as Brief Psychotic Disorder and Dissociative Amnesia, typically respond well to relatively brief treatment. Those of longer duration, especially those of insidious onset, such as Schizophrenia and Dissociative Identity Disorder, have a less favorable prognosis and usually require long-term treatment.

PSYCHOTIC DISORDERS

Schizophrenia

Description of the Disorder

Schizophrenia is by definition a relatively long-standing and pervasive disorder. *DSM-IV* lists the following symptoms as characteristic of this disorder:

- Bizarre delusions
- Hallucinations (usually auditory and threatening)
- Disorganized speech and behavior
- Flat or very inappropriate affect
- Markedly impaired social and occupational functioning
- A confused sense of self
- Limited insight
- Dependence conflicts
- Loose associations
- Concrete thinking
- Physical awkwardness
- Psychomotor disturbances (for example, catatonic symptoms)
- Dysphoric mood

Schizophrenia typically involves a *prodromal* (initial) phase, when functioning declines and symptoms begin; an *active* phase, when such so-called *positive* symptoms as delusions, hallucinations, and incoherence typically are present; and a *residual* phase, in which severe symptoms have abated but signs of the disorder are still evident. These signs include such symptoms as flattened affect, restricted thought and speech patterns, and lack of goals or motivation, which have been referred to as the *negative* symptoms of psychosis. To warrant a diagnosis of Schizophrenia, the course of the disorder must be at least six months in duration, including at least one month of the positive symptoms (unless it can be assumed that those symptoms would have persisted for that length of time had treatment not been provided).

DSM-IV describes three major types of Schizophrenia. The Paranoid Type seems to be the most common type in the United States. It typically is characterized by systematized delusions and hallucinations that are related to a theme of grandiosity and persecution. Anger and suspiciousness are usually also present (Meyer, 1983). Schizophrenia, Paranoid Type, tends to involve less evidence of incoherence, disorganization, catatonia, and inappropriate affect, as well as a later onset and a better prognosis than the other types of Schizophrenia. The Disorganized Type, formerly known as the Hebephrenic Type, is associated with poor previous functioning, an early and insidious onset, extreme impairment, confusion and disorganization in speech and behavior, and flat or inappropriate affect. The Catatonic Type is uncommon in the United States. It is characterized by some form of catatonia (stupor, rigidity, excitement, or posturing) and by negativity and repetitive imitation of others' words and gestures.

Undifferentiated and Residual Types of Schizophrenia also are included in *DSM-IV*. The Undifferentiated Type includes the positive symptoms of Schizophrenia but does not meet the criteria for any one of the three types just described. The Residual Type either follows a full-blown episode of Schizophrenia and reflects only the negative symptoms of the disorder or is a circumscribed presentation of at least two positive symptoms.

Schizophrenia usually begins in early adulthood and starts earlier in males than in females. Initial episodes of this disorder are unlikely to occur after the age of fifty or before adolescence (Kaplan, Sadock, & Grebb, 1994). Women with Schizophrenia tend to have less severe forms of the disorder and a better prognosis than do men (Loranger, 1984; Morrison, 1995). Schizophrenia has a prevalence of approximately 1 percent (Tsuang, Farone, & Day, 1988). Incidence of this disorder is approximately equal in both genders.

Research on the causes of Schizophrenia has implicated brain dysfunction, particularly in the limbic system, as well as excessive dopaminergic activity. Studies have demonstrated differences between brains of people diagnosed with Schizophrenia and those without the disorder. A high incidence of eye-movement dysfunction and immunological abnormalities has also been noted in people with Schizophrenia. These findings have led theorists to discredit the early belief that family dysfunction causes Schizophrenia. Beyond attributing the disorder to a combination of abnormal brain functioning and stress, researchers have been unable to point to any clear cause of Schizophrenia, although many explanations have been advanced.

Typical Client Characteristics

Environmental and other patterns have been observed in the lives of people diagnosed with Schizophrenia. People with this disorder are likely to come from lower socioeconomic groups and urban environments. They also are likely to have been born during the winter and early spring. The latter correlation may have to do with those months' increased risk of infectious diseases, exposure to which in utero contributes to the development of this disorder (Kaplan et al., 1994). People with Schizophrenia are unusually likely to have experienced stressful events in the three weeks prior to onset of the disorder (Bebbington, 1986). This pattern, rather than being interpreted as meaning that stress is causative, has been interpreted as suggesting a stress-diathesis model for the disorder's onset, whereby biological (physical) or psychological (emotional) stress activates a predisposition toward the disorder.

Schizophrenia tends to run in families; most research suggests that people with this disorder are unusually likely to have first-degree relatives who also can be diagnosed with Schizophrenia (Kendell, 1986). The chances of developing Schizophrenia are two in five for those with two parents who have Schizophrenia, and one in two for monozygotic twins of those with Schizophrenia. At the same time, factors other than genetics are clearly relevant; only about 10 percent of those with Schizophrenia have a parent who also manifests the symptoms of the disorder.

Prior adjustment often reflects precursors of the disorder. People with Schizophrenia tend to have been socially awkward and isolated, passive, mildly eccentric, impulsive, uncomfortable with competition, and absorbed with fantasy (Kendell, 1986). An unstable employment history is also common. Personality Disorders, especially Paranoid, Schizoid, or Schizotypal Personality Disorders, sometimes precede the diagnosis of Schizophrenia (American Psychiatric Association, 1994a).

People with Schizophrenia typically have comorbid mental and medical disorders. Substance-Related Disorders are common, in part because some substances apparently reduce psychotic, neurological, and affective symptoms of Schizophrenia. Most people with Schizophrenia smoke cigarettes, up to 50 percent meet the criteria for an Alcohol Use Disorder, and the incidence of cannabis use also is high. The presence of coexisting Substance Use Disorders is associated with poor prognosis for the treatment of Schizophrenia (Kaplan et al., 1994). Most people with this disorder have significant medical illnesses. Suicidal ideation is also common: about half of all those with Schizophrenia make suicide attempts, and for at least 10 percent of that group the attempts are successful. Depression, usually most severe immediately after a psychotic episode, has a strong association with suicide risk in people with Schizophrenia (Taiminen, 1994).

Preferred Therapist Characteristics

The quality of these clients' relationships with their physicians and therapists has been found to be an important determinant of treatment outcome (Fenton & Cole, 1995). A therapeutic alliance that reduces anxiety and enhances treatment compliance can be integral to recovery. Therapists working with people with Schizophrenia should be available, consistent, patient, and straightforward. Warmth, reassurance, optimism, empathy, genuineness, stability, support, and acceptance on the part of the therapist are all important in forming a positive and trusting working relationship with people diagnosed as having Schizophrenia, many of whom are suspicious, guarded, and withdrawn. Limits also need to be established for the protection of these clients and their therapists. Beyond all these requirements, flexibility and creativity are needed because these clients often will be unable or unwilling to discuss their concerns in any clear fashion. Simply sitting with a distraught client, taking a walk, discussing neutral topics of interest like a movie, or providing practical assistance can promote a therapeutic alliance and offer support and comfort.

Retterstøl (1986) suggests that therapists working with people who have Schizophrenia help them regain contact with reality. At the same time, arguing with or interrogating these clients about their delusions or hallucinations is likely to be nonproductive and harmful to the therapeutic relationship. Perry, Frances, and Clarkin (1985) present a case in which the therapist labeled hallucinations tricks of the mind. This kind of perspective avoids the need to debate the veracity of clients' experiences and can increase understanding and appropriate discussion of the phenomena.

Therapists must find a balance between overwhelming and undersupporting these vulnerable clients. Too much closeness can lead to regression, but too much distance can result in alienation. Therapists should respect clients' privacy and need for distance and should individualize treatment, reducing interpretations and being flexible as the need arises.

Intervention Strategies

Treatment for Schizophrenia usually entails a combination of interventions. Without accompanying medication, psychotherapy is unlikely to be effective, but the combination of psychotherapy, family intervention, and medication will usually ameliorate if not eliminate the symptoms of the disorder (Roth & Fonagy, 1996).

Medication is almost always a component of treatment and is beneficial to most but not all who are diagnosed with Schizophrenia. Neuroleptic drugs can effectively alleviate symptoms, particularly the positive symptoms of psychosis (delusions and hallucinations). Medication is less effective in treating the negative symptoms (flat affect, depression, withdrawal). Until recent years, the classic antipsychotic drugs, such as Thorazine and Mellaril, were the primary treatment for Schizophrenia, but their continued use poses serious risks, including the development of tardive dyskinesia. Newer drugs, including risperidone (Risperdal), olanzapine (Zyprexa), and clozapine (Clozaril), are also effective and have fewer aversive side effects (Kaplan et al., 1994).

Medication is important as well in reducing the risk of relapse. Most people treated for Schizophrenia need continued medication after their symptoms have been alleviated. Without medication, 50 to 75 percent relapse within four years, whereas only 20 percent relapse when they are maintained on medication (Tsuang et al., 1988). Medication groups, with meetings held regularly during the maintenance phase of treatment, can promote treatment compliance as well as providing support, socialization, and practical help.

Hospitalization is often required for people with Schizophrenia, particularly during the active phase of the disorder. The average hospital stay for these clients has declined in length and typically is now shorter than two weeks (Klerman, 1986). Day treatment centers, partial hospitalization, and halfway houses can also be helpful once recovery has begun and acute symptoms have subsided (Atwood & Chester, 1987). These transitional settings can promote socialization, ease people's return to independent living, and, as necessary, provide long-term maintenance. Use of these treatment facilities is increasing as the length of hospital stays is decreasing.

Psychotherapy is another common component of treatment for people diagnosed with Schizophrenia. Fenton and Cole (1995) recommend an approach called *flexible psychotherapy* for these clients. The goals of this approach are "to minimize the effect of vulnerabilities, strengthen adaptive capacities, and reduce the extent and effects of stress" (p. 427). This multifaceted, individualized treatment approach recognizes that people with Schizophrenia, as well as the manifestations of the disorder itself, vary widely and will therefore benefit from a broad repertoire of interventions. In this model, individual therapy is generally present-oriented. It focuses on life issues and relationships, explores feelings, clarifies ego boundaries, and promotes readjustment via cognitive and behavioral techniques. Short, frequent therapeutic contacts are often particularly useful. Group therapy can be helpful in providing information, promoting appropriate use of medication, improving skills (such as communication, problem solving, and socialization), encouraging constructive activities, facilitating reality testing, and providing support and encouragement. Family therapy is also integral to this treatment approach, as are psychoeducation and rehabilitation. Careful attention to the therapeutic relationship, facilitated by mutual goal setting when that activity is possible, is another important element of flexible psychotherapy.

Behavioral therapy is the primary approach to psychotherapy for people with Schizophrenia. This approach typically focuses on providing the information and skills necessary to reducing bizarre and destructive behavior and improving functioning. Social skills training (for example, learning how to maintain eye contact and use appropriate facial expressions) has been used for people with Schizophrenia, although only modest gains have been reported (Benton & Schroeder, 1990). Development of practical life skills can also be beneficial in facilitating people's resocialization and their adjustment to living with their families or on their own after a period of hospitalization. Adjustment can also be facilitated by training in useful occupational skills and by increased involvement in recreational activities. Behavioral therapy can be provided via inpatient or outpatient treatment in individual or group formats. Hospitals and day treatment centers sometimes use behavioral models, such as milieu therapy or token economies, to reinforce desirable behaviors.

Cognitive-behavioral therapy has also received support in the treatment of Schizophrenia (Tarrier, Sharpe, & Beckett, 1993). Such techniques as challenging and modifying delusional beliefs, enhancing skills for problem solving and coping, increasing meaningful activities, and encouraging family support have shown effectiveness in reducing both positive and negative symptoms of Schizophrenia.

Psychodynamic psychotherapy has not received much support in the treatment of Schizophrenia. In fact, Roth and Fonagy (1996) raise the possibility that the emotional intensity of that approach may even be harmful to some people with Schizophrenia.

Education and counseling for the family are a particularly important component of treatment for Schizophrenia. Family members are often confused and angered by the delusions and hallucinations of the person with Schizophrenia and may benefit from understanding the nature of this disorder. In addition, what has been called high expressed emotion (EE) in the families of people with Schizophrenia seems to be a significant factor, as is stress, in provoking a reemergence of acute symptoms (Bellack & Hersen, 1993). High EE is reflected in the tendency of the family to be critical of, emotionally overinvolved with, and hostile toward the person with Schizophrenia. Vaughn and Leff (1976) have found the single best predictor of relapse during the nine months following discharge to be the number of critical comments made by family members about a person with Schizophrenia at the time of admission to the hospital, and research over the years has supported this connection. McCreadie (1992), for example, conducted a five-year follow-up study of people diagnosed with Schizophrenia and found that those from families characterized by high EE had three times as many relapses as those from families with low EE. Family treatment to reduce high EE has shown beneficial effects on the course of the disorder (Goldfried, Greenberg, & Marmar, 1990). Hogarty et al. (1986) conclude that only a combination of treatments, including social skills training, family treatment, and medication, is likely to "sustain a remission in households that remain high in EE" (p. 633); none of the people in their study who received that combination of treatments relapsed over a two-year period, whereas 41 percent who received only support and medication did relapse.

Extended contact with helping professionals, often via treatment programs for the chronically mentally ill, also contributes to long-term reduction in relapse rates (Roth & Fonagy, 1996). Similarly, extended involvement with support groups, such as the National Alliance for the Mentally Ill, can be useful to families of people with Schizophrenia.

Prognosis

A return to full and healthy functioning after an episode of Schizophrenia is unusual. Although the acute symptoms of this disorder may be controlled with medication, people are frequently left feeling apathetic, socially uncomfortable, depressed, and uneasy in handling emotions. Tsuang et al. (1988) report that 20 percent of people with Schizophrenia seem to recover completely, 33 percent remain only mildly impaired after treatment, and 47 percent stay severely impaired. Approximately 50 percent are hospitalized again within two years of an initial episode of this disorder. The risk of personality deterioration increases greatly after the second relapse and worsens with each successive episode, as does the risk of another relapse. The prognosis is particularly poor if the disorder begins with a gradual deterioration that has extended over many years, or if the person with Schizophrenia has extensive exposure to a high EE family. The following factors (Kaplan et al., 1994; Maxmen & Ward, 1995) are some of those associated with a more positive prognosis for the treatment of Schizophrenia (and for Schizophreniform Disorder, discussed later):

- *Premorbid factors:* positive premorbid functioning, especially in social areas; positive work history; intelligence that is average or higher; being married

- *Factors related to characteristics of the disorder:* abrupt onset, particularly when there is an identifiable precipitant; midlife onset; symptoms of confusion and perplexity; depression; absence of flattened affect, psychotic assaultiveness, or Schizoid Personality Disorder

- *Family and environmental factors:* family history of depression and mania; positive and supportive environment to which client will return; absence of a family history of Schizophrenia

A positive prognosis also is associated with compliance with recommended medication and aftercare, an adequate financial and living situation, and having social and recreational activities.

In addition to relapses and residual symptoms, people with Schizophrenia often must cope with severe and sometimes permanent side effects of neuroleptic antipsychotic medication. Tardive dyskinesia, for example, resulting from long-term use of antipsychotic medications, is primarily characterized by involuntary smacking and sucking movements of the lips and tongue. This gives people an unusual appearance and can interfere with their social and occupational adjustment.

Brief Psychotic Disorder

Description of the Disorder

Brief Psychotic Disorder may resemble Schizophrenia, as well as Delusional Disorder (discussed later). According to *DSM-IV,* the essential feature of Brief Psychotic Disorder is "the sudden onset of at least one of the following positive psychotic symptoms: delusions, hallucinations, disorganized speech . . . , or grossly disorganized or catatonic behavior" (American Psychiatric Association, 1994a, p. 302). This disorder lasts at least one day but less than one month, and the person eventually has a full return to premorbid levels of functioning.

Three subtypes of this disorder are described in *DSM-IV.* In the type described as With Marked Stressor(s), the onset of symptoms is preceded by an identifiable and prominent stressor (for example, loss of a loved one, rape, or combat experience) and typically is accompanied by extreme and rapid emotional shifts and a strong feeling of confusion. Multiple concurrent stressors are particularly likely to precipitate this disorder. The second type, With Postpartum Onset, begins within four weeks of giving birth. The disorder typically is characterized by depression and thoughts of suicide or infanticide (Kaplan et al., 1994). The third type, Without Marked Stressor(s), does not fit either of the other two patterns.

Unlike Schizophrenia, Brief Psychotic Disorder usually is not preceded by evidence of prodromal symptoms. This relatively uncommon disorder may begin in adolescence but is more likely to begin in the late twenties or early thirties.

Schizophreniform Disorder

Description of the Disorder

Schizophreniform Disorder is usually characterized by symptoms that may be indistinguishable from the most prominent symptoms of Schizophrenia. These include impaired reality testing, extremely inappropriate behavior, bizarre delusions and hallucinations, incoherence, and catatonia. Schizophreniform Disorder is more like Schizophrenia than Brief Psychotic Disorder is, in that it may include a prodromal phase, does not usually have an identifiable precipitant, and includes passive as well as active features of Schizophrenia. Agitation and high anxiety are common in Schizophreniform Disorder, but flat affect is unusual (Tsuang & Loyd, 1986). Unlike Schizophrenia, impaired social or occupational functioning is not an essential feature of the disorder but often will be present.

Schizophreniform Disorder is distinguished from Schizophrenia primarily in terms of duration. Schizophreniform Disorder, by definition, has a duration of at least one month but less than six months (including prodromal, active, and residual phases). Schizophreniform Disorder is also much less common than Schizophrenia and is particularly likely to occur in adolescents and young adults (Kaplan et al., 1994). Although Schizophreniform Disorder probably is closely related to Schizophrenia, and although both reflect abnormalities in brain functioning, Schizophreniform Disorder is currently categorized as a separate disorder, partly because it seems to have a superior prognosis to that for Schizophrenia.

Schizophreniform Disorder and Brief Psychotic Disorder clearly seem to differ from Schizophrenia in terms of development, cause, treatment, and prognosis. Schizophreniform Disorder may be viewed as a sort of bridge between Brief Psychotic Disorder and Schizophrenia, with Brief Psychotic Disorder having the best prognosis and Schizophrenia the worst. Schizophreniform Disorder can be diagnosed when symptoms originally thought to be Brief Psychotic Disorder persist for at least one month but less than six months.

If diagnosis of either Brief Psychotic Disorder or Schizophreniform Disorder is made before recovery, the diagnosis is viewed as provisional and as subject to change if the disorder lasts longer than anticipated. Thus both disorders are sometimes actually the early stages of Schizophrenia.

Typical Client Characteristics

Like Schizophrenia, both Brief Psychotic Disorder and Schizophreniform Disorder are more common in people who have had preexisting emotional disorders, particularly Personality Disorders typified by emotional instability, suspiciousness, and impaired socialization. Depression and suicidal ideation also often coexist with both Brief Psychotic Disorder and Schizophreniform Disorder. The immediate aftermath of a severe psychotic episode is the most common time for these symptoms to emerge.

The risk of developing a psychotic disorder for first-degree relatives of those with Schizophreniform Disorder seems to be less than for relatives of those with Schizophrenia, but the risk of developing a Mood Disorder is higher. Relatives of those with Brief Psychotic Disorder seem to be at increased risk for both Mood Disorders and for Brief Psychotic Disorder but not for Schizophrenia (Tsuang & Loyd, 1986).

Preferred Therapist Characteristics

People diagnosed with Brief Psychotic Disorder or Schizophreniform Disorder typically benefit from supportive, safe, and structured therapeutic relationships that avoid casting them in a sick role. Acceptance, respect, genuineness, and empathy can be instrumental in helping these people come to terms with the events that have triggered their disorders and in restoring their awareness of reality. Modeling by therapists and identification with therapists can increase clients' use of effective coping mechanisms, as well as their efforts to take control of their lives.

Intervention Strategies

Initial treatments of Brief Psychotic Disorder and Schizophreniform Disorder have many similarities to the treatment of Schizophrenia. People with these disorders may be so severely incapacitated, aggressive, or disoriented and out of touch with reality that hospitalization and medication are required to protect them, calm them down, and alleviate acute symptoms. Long-term medication or extended inpatient treatment are unusual, however, unless a comorbid mental disorder is present. Most people with Schizophreniform Disorder, for example, respond to medication within eight days and need a course of medication lasting only three to six months (Kaplan et al., 1994).

Once the psychotic symptoms have subsided, the focus of treatment usually will shift quickly, with psychotherapy rather than medication being the primary ingredient of treatment. In this second phase of treatment, attention should be paid to the nature of any precipitants, and interventions should be used to help people deal with the events that have triggered their symptoms. People with these disorders often are in crisis, and so a crisis-intervention approach to therapy can provide useful direction. According to that model, people are assisted in taking a realistic look at their circumstances, becoming aware of and expressing their feelings and reactions, identifying and mobilizing the coping mechanisms that they have used effectively in the past, and applying them to the current circumstances. Specific additional interventions are determined by the nature of the precipitant, but those interventions generally are short-term and symptom-focused, emphasizing cognitive, behavioral, and supportive approaches rather than long-term exploratory ones.

Often people with Schizophreniform Disorder and Brief Psychotic Disorder experience guilt, loss of self-esteem and self-confidence, and confusion related to their symptoms. They may be troubled by their own reactions and may need help to accept and integrate their symptoms into their view of themselves and their lives. Both supportive and educational interventions can facilitate that process (McGlashan & Krystal, 1995).

Group and family treatment also may help clients and their families to deal with the aftermath of these disorders, as well as to promote effective resolution of any precipitants and restore positive social and occupational functioning. Encouraging people to draw on support systems also can facilitate recovery, crisis resolution, and abatement of residual symptoms.

Prognosis

Some clinicians distinguish between *process* and *reactive* psychotic disorders, with reactive disorders having a rapid onset and a clear precipitant and process disorders more likely to have an insidious onset, a genetic component, and no identifiable precipitant. In general, the prognosis is better for those disorders that follow a reactive pattern: more than 90 percent recover from reactive psychoses, but only 50 percent recover from process conditions (Atwood & Chester, 1987). Accordingly, people who are diagnosed with Brief Psychotic Disorder or Schizophreniform Disorder, and whose disorders seem to be reactive in nature, have a good prognosis. Even if a precipitant cannot be identified, psychotic disorders that are brief in nature have a better prognosis than those that are lengthy or recurrent.

The prognosis for a Brief Psychotic Disorder that does not progress to another disorder is by definition excellent. Symptoms of such a disorder typically remit within a few days. Nevertheless, the active phase may be followed by temporary symptoms of depression, confusion, and anxiety as the client deals with the stressors that precipitated the disorder and with the experience of having had his or her functioning severely impaired. The client often feels embarrassed at having had psychotic symptoms and fears a recurrence and its accompanying loss of control.

The prognosis for Schizophreniform Disorder is not as good as for Brief Psychotic Disorder but is better than the prognosis for Schizophrenia (Coryell & Tsuang, 1986). According to *DSM-IV*, features associated with a positive prognosis for recovery from Schizophreniform Disorder are a brief prodromal period (four weeks or less), confusion and perplexity during the active phase of the disorder, good previous functioning, and affect that is depressed rather than flat or blunted. The ability to maintain good eye contact and speak with examiners also suggests a positive prognosis (Kaplan et al., 1994).

Delusional Disorder

Description of the Disorder

Delusional Disorder typically is less pervasive and disabling than Schizophreniform Disorder or Schizophrenia but may have some similar symptoms. According to *DSM-IV*, a Delusional Disorder is characterized by the presence of nonbizarre (possible or believable) delusions of at least one month's duration. The delusions typically are circumscribed, and the person's overall behavior, apart from the delusions, usually does not seem odd or severely impaired. This is a disorder of thoughts rather than of perceptual experiences. Hallucinations are absent or minimal. A history of Schizophrenia rules out the diagnosis of this disorder.

The type of Delusional Disorder experienced by a person should be indicated when this diagnosis is made. The *DSM* identifies the following five types of Delusional Disorder, in addition to Mixed and Unspecified Types:

1. *Erotomanic Type:* unrealistic beliefs about a romantic relationship, often with a stranger or a person in a higher position, and sometimes associated with stalking behavior

2. *Grandiose Type:* typically, the inaccurate belief that one has a special talent or has made an important discovery

3. *Jealous Type:* unfounded belief that one's partner is unfaithful

4. *Persecutory Type:* the most common type of Delusional Disorder, involving the incorrect belief that others are seeking to harm one, and sometimes associated with violent retaliation or lawsuits based on perceived wrongs

5. *Somatic Type:* intense, unrealistic beliefs focused on the body, such as thinking that one emits a foul odor or is infested with insects

The onset of a Delusional Disorder typically occurs in middle or late adulthood and may be acute, chronic, or recurrent (Kaplan et al., 1994). Delusional Disorder is fairly rare, occurring in approximately 0.03 percent of the population. It occurs with approximately equal frequency in both genders, but the Jealous Type is more common in men (American Psychiatric Association, 1994a).

Typical Client Characteristics

People with Delusional Disorder typically demonstrate satisfactory premorbid functioning, although they tend to be excessively sensitive, below average in intelligence and insight, and prone to manifest patterns of underachievement. As with Schizophrenia, people who are recent immigrants and who come from lower socioeconomic backgrounds are more likely to develop a Delusional Disorder, as are people who are isolated.

Delusional Disorder is often preceded by a period of stress and by an experience that evokes strong feelings of insecurity, distrust, and self-doubt (Retterstøl, 1986). The delusion sometimes is a defense mechanism, particularly one involving denial, projection, or reaction formation, and provides the person a way to preserve self-esteem and be protected from feelings of rejection and inadequacy.

A genetic basis for this disorder has not been well established, although first-degree relatives of people with this disorder are more likely to have Avoidant or Paranoid Personality Disorders or Delusional Disorder (Day & Manschreck, 1988; American Psychiatric Association, 1994a). Delusional Disorder does not seem to be closely related to or an early manifestation of a Mood Disorder or of Schizophrenia, although, as in Schizophrenia, pathology of the limbic system sometimes is diagnosed.

According to Retterstøl (1986), people with Delusional Disorder commonly had difficult childhoods characterized by concerns around developing trust. They may have had conflicted home environments or may have lost a parent when they were young. Kaplan et al. (1994) believe that people with Delusional Disorder come from a characteristic family-of-origin environment that was both demanding and punitive, involving one parent who was distant while the other was overinvolved.

People with Delusional Disorder tend to be low in self-esteem, isolated, easily frustrated, mistrustful, and fearful of intimacy. Irritability and a dysphoric mood are common in people with Delusional Disorder, although moods vary according to the nature of the delusions to which they are linked. These people view the world as a hostile and unfriendly place. They are very concerned with how they are perceived by others, often feel taken advantage of, and tend to overreact to criticism. People with Delusional Disorder tend to be defensive and argumentative, particularly with authority figures. They typically project blame for their own failures and shortcomings onto others, sometimes have ideas of reference, and may be perceived as hostile, suspicious, and excessively critical of themselves and others. Their social and sexual adjustment is often flawed, although their occupational adjustment may be satisfactory. People with Delusional Disorder sometimes have physical problems (for example, a hearing or visual loss) that contribute to their feeling different and isolated. Litigious and aggressive behavior may be manifested in response to delusions.

People with Delusional Disorder rarely are self-referred for treatment; rather, they present at the instigation of a family member, an employer, or the legal system. Consequently, they typically are resistant to treatment and do not see how it could help them. They tend to deny affective symptoms, resist acceptance of the idea that stress may have precipitated their symptoms, have little empathy and insight, and often block attempts to reassure them and modify their typically ego-syntonic delusions (Retterstøl, 1986).

Preferred Therapist Characteristics

Therapists should deal gently with people with Delusional Disorder, respecting their need for privacy and not arguing with them about their delusional beliefs. Instead, therapists should be stable and structured, reliable, reassuring, genuine, supportive, accepting, empathic, fair, and professional, serving as positive role models in an effort to engage these people in treatment and encourage more effective coping methods.

Therapists should discuss the delusions enough to understand their nature and possible functions but should not participate in clients' delusional belief systems (McGlashan & Krystal, 1995). At the same time, confrontation should be avoided. If clients demand to know whether therapists believe their delusions, therapists can respond, "I don't know, but I know it is very important to you and is having a great impact on your life." The therapeutic focus, then, should be on the immediate precursors and consequences of the delusions and on the personality traits that may have contributed to the development of the delusions rather than on the unrealistic beliefs themselves.

These conditions of the therapeutic relationship are particularly important in treating people with Delusional Disorder. Without a positive relationship, therapy is not likely to take place, but with a positive relationship, much can be accomplished.

Intervention Strategies

People with Delusional Disorder rarely seek treatment of their own volition and typically function well enough to avoid involuntary treatment. As a result, they rarely are seen in treatment, and little research is available on the effective treatment of this disorder. Some inferences can be drawn from the literature, however.

Medication and hospitalization are less likely to be needed in treating this disorder than in the treatment of Schizophrenia. Most people with Delusional Disorder can be treated on an outpatient basis, although a day treatment center may provide a helpful change in environment. The suspiciousness that is typical of people with Delusional Disorder may lead them to refuse medication or fail to comply with prescribed treatments and to mistrust those who recommend medication. Nevertheless, antipsychotic and antidepressant medication sometimes are helpful in reducing delusions and accompanying symptoms (Manschreck, 1992; McGlashan & Krystal, 1995). Drugs that have shown some effectiveness include pimozide (Orap), clomipramine (Anafranil), and haloperidol (Haldol). Medication is most likely to be effective in the treatment of somatic delusions and in cases where there has been an apparent precipitant and early diagnosis (Kaplan et al., 1994; Simpson & May, 1982).

Typically, the amelioration of environmental stressors and the encouragement of improved coping mechanisms will be more essential than medication to effective treatment of Delusional Disorder. It is also essential to establish a supportive therapeutic relationship, which is sometimes sufficient to give these people the courage they need to deal more effectively with their lives. Treatment should be present-oriented and should focus on maximizing adjustment, helping people deal with loss and frustration, and improving reality testing (Day & Manschreck, 1988; McGlashan & Krystal, 1995). It can also be helpful to encourage independence and the expression of feelings. An emphasis on clients' strengths, positive behaviors, and improvements can contribute to both establishment of a positive therapeutic alliance and to clients' growth.

Clients' motivation for treatment can be increased with an initial focus on distressing secondary symptoms (such as insomnia or occupational concerns) rather than on delusions, their precipitants, and their consequences, but some attention should also be paid to the delusions themselves because they typically serve a symbolic function that, if understood, could facilitate treatment (Retterstøl, 1986).

As people begin to improve, depression and anxiety that were masked by delusional symptoms may emerge. Therapists and clients alike should be prepared for this development and should view it as a sign of progress. If depression and anxiety do emerge, the focus of treatment should be shifted to amelioration of these affective symptoms.

Family therapy is often an important ingredient of treatment. Because these clients continue to function relatively well, family members may not understand that the clients are experiencing a mental disorder. Particularly if family members have been cast in an unfavorable light by a delusional belief system, they may feel angry and unsympathetic and may benefit from help in understanding the nature of the disorder. Reducing any family-related stress and conflict that are contributing to the Delusional Disorder can also help alleviate symptoms. Nevertheless, family therapy should be undertaken only with clients' permission, and clients should be reassured that family sessions will be discussed with them.

Although people diagnosed with Delusional Disorder often need to improve their social skills and relationships, they typically do not derive much benefit from group therapy (Retterstøl, 1986). They tend to use their delusions to protect themselves from the group and wind up alienating other group members.

Prognosis

Although Delusional Disorder has a somewhat better prognosis than Schizophrenia and does not have the same pervasive impact on functioning as that disorder does, the prognosis for treatment of Delusional Disorder is uncertain. Some people—particularly women, people with good premorbid functioning, and those for whom the disorder has had a rapid onset, brief duration, and an apparent precipitant—recover quickly. For others, however, the disorder has a chronic course, and these people may experience alternating periods of remission and relapse over many years. Still others develop Schizophrenia. At follow-up, approximately 50 percent of people with this disorder have recovered, another 20 percent have experienced a decrease in symptoms, and 30 percent have continued to manifest the disorder (Kaplan et al., 1994). Those with Delusional Disorder of the Persecutory, Somatic, and Erotomanic Types seem to have better prospects for recovery than those with Delusional Disorder of the Grandiose and Jealous Types.

Schizoaffective Disorder

Description of the Disorder

Schizoaffective Disorder is one of the most complicated diagnoses listed in *DSM-IV*. By definition, it meets the criteria for a significant Mood Disorder (either Major Depressive Disorder or Bipolar I or II Disorder) and for the active phase of Schizophrenia. The disorder includes at least two weeks of delusions or hallucinations that are not accompanied by prominent mood symptoms, although depression or mania are present throughout most of the course of the disorder. Minimum duration for this disorder is one month. Some view Schizoaffective Disorder as two discrete disorders—Schizophrenia and a Mood Disorder—or as an atypical form of mania or depression; others believe it is a separate diagnostic entity, a sort of hybrid with its own distinguishing features. Fewer than 1 percent of the population are diagnosed as having this disorder, which is less common than Schizophrenia and much less common than Mood Disorders.

Disorders observed to precede or accompany Schizoaffective Disorder include Substance-Related Disorders and Schizoid, Schizotypal, Paranoid, and Borderline Personality Disorders. Mood Disorders, Schizophreniform Disorder, and Schizophrenia may develop later (American Psychiatric Association, 1994a).

Typical Client Characteristics

Two types of Schizoaffective Disorder have been identified. Schizoaffective Disorder, Bipolar Type, most often appears in early adulthood; Schizoaffective Disorder, Depressive Type, usually begins later. The age of onset of Schizoaffective Disorder is later for women than for men, with men particularly likely to manifest flat or inappropriate affect and antisocial behavior (Kaplan et al., 1994). This disorder is more prevalent among married women and among those with first-degree relatives who have been diagnosed as having Schizophrenia or a major Mood Disorder (Rice & McGuffin, 1986).

Williams and McGlashan (1987) have found that the demographic backgrounds and premorbid patterns of adjustment for those with Schizoaffective Disorder are more like the backgrounds and patterns of people with Major Depressive Disorder than like those of people with Schizophrenia or a Bipolar Disorder. Overall, social and occupational impairment typically accompany Schizoaffective Disorder. Poor self-care and suicidal ideation often are present, and at least 10 percent of people affected by this disorder commit suicide (Kaplan et al., 1994).

Little clear information is available about the cause of Schizoaffective Disorder, although the disorder sometimes appears in relatively healthy people after a stressful precipitant; in these cases, onset is usually sudden and is accompanied by marked turmoil and confusion. This disorder seems more likely to follow a chronic and insidious pattern, however (Tsuang & Loyd, 1986).

Preferred Therapist Characteristics

Therapist variables discussed in the section on Schizophrenia probably also are applicable to Schizoaffective Disorder. Therapists should provide support, structure, reality testing, empathy, acceptance, and reassurance to allay the resistance and suspiciousness that often accompany psychotic symptoms. Establishing realistic goals and avoiding situations that lead clients to feel demoralized and to blame themselves are important (Bartels & Drake, 1989). The relatively strong motivation for treatment that is often found in people with Schizoaffective Disorder (as it is in people with Mood Disorders), together with these people's relatively positive previous functioning, may make it easier to form a therapeutic alliance with them than it is to form a therapeutic alliance with people who have a diagnosis of Schizophrenia.

Intervention Strategies

Treatment of Schizoaffective Disorder should focus on affective as well as psychotic symptoms and must be individualized because the symptom picture associated with this disorder can vary widely. Tsuang and Loyd (1986) suggest basing treatment on the most prominent symptoms.

Psychotherapy for people diagnosed with Schizoaffective Disorder usually resembles approaches used to treat Schizophrenia. Research on the components of the disorder suggests an interpersonal, cognitive, or cognitive-behavioral approach for the affective symptoms and a supportive and behavioral approach for the psychotic symptoms. Some mix of the two approaches—emphasizing the supportive and the behavioral, with the balance determined by the nature of a particular person's symptoms—is usually a reasonable choice, but caution should be exercised in planning psychotherapy with these clients because of the limited research. Psychoeducation, rehabilitation, and social skills training also usually enhance treatment. Maniacci (1991) reports success in increasing clients' social interests via a structured program designed to develop life skills and promote insight and motivation; family involvement in this program also contributed to its positive outcome. Family therapy can be helpful in promoting family members' understanding of the disorder and in improving the family environment.

Medication is often useful in reducing both psychotic and affective symptoms, and a referral for medical evaluation should almost always be made for people with Schizoaffective Disorder. Determining the appropriate drugs can be challenging, however, because multiple medications may be needed and because the side effects of a medication designed to ameliorate one facet of this disorder may exacerbate symptoms involved in another facet. Therefore, a trial-and-error approach is often necessary in determining the best combination of medications for this disorder. Lithium, antidepressants, and neuroleptics all have been found useful in treating some cases of Schizoaffective Disorder (McGlashan & Krystal, 1995). Lithium has been particularly helpful in the maintenance of people with the Bipolar Type of this disorder. Maintenance on clozapine has also yielded positive results, with 65 percent in one study having no further hospitalizations or mood episodes (Zarate, Tohen, Banov, & Weiss, 1995). Electroconvulsive therapy has been used, especially for people who do not have a good response to medication.

Many people diagnosed as having a Schizoaffective Disorder require some period of hospitalization in addition to medication. Extensive treatment after hospitalization is often needed for people with severe forms of the disorder.

Prognosis

The prognosis for Schizoaffective Disorder, not surprisingly, seems to be better than that for Schizophrenia but not as good as that for a Mood Disorder (Morrison, 1995). The Bipolar Type of this disorder has a better prognosis than the Depressive Type. Mood-incongruent psychotic features are associated with a poor prognosis, as are impaired premorbid functioning, early onset, unremitting course, a family history of Schizophrenia, and a predominance of psychotic symptoms (Kaplan et al., 1994).

DISSOCIATIVE DISORDERS

Dissociative Identity Disorder

Description of the Disorder

The Dissociative Disorder that has received the most attention is Dissociative Identity Disorder (DID), which was called Multiple Personality Disorder in *DSM-III-R*. According to *DSM-IV*, "the essential feature of Dissociative Identity Disorder is the presence of two or more distinct identities or personality states" that repeatedly assume control of the person's behavior (American Psychiatric Association, 1994a, p. 484). People with this disorder cannot integrate aspects of their identity, memory, and awareness and often are unable to recall important personal information.

Cases ranging from two to over two hundred personalities (alters) have been reported, with an average of thirteen personalities (Kluft, 1995). Most people with DID have fewer than ten personalities, which can vary widely. Some, usually the more aggressive and protective personalities, have full or partial awareness; others have amnesia for times when they are not the personality in control. Typically, personalities associated with this disorder shift in ascendancy under stress.

Treatment usually is sought by a primary or host personality that tends to be rigid, depressed, dependent, guilty, and moralistic. A principal secondary personality typically exists that is less inhibited and has greater awareness of all the changing personalities (Nemiah, 1988).

Onset of DID usually is in childhood, after a severe trauma or accompanying negative and abusive experiences in a context involving few support systems. Females are far more likely to be diagnosed with this disorder than are males, although some believe that men with this disorder are more likely to be in prisons than in mental health settings.

Because of the long-standing and deeply ingrained nature of this disorder, the limited awareness that people with DID have of their condition, and their tendency to conceal their symptoms, this disorder can be mistaken for other

Dissociative Disorders, Personality Disorders, or Psychotic Disorders. Diagnosis is also difficult because approximately 80 percent of people with this disorder have only occasional episodes (Kaplan et al., 1994), and few present their symptoms openly at initial treatment. Consequently, people often spend years in the mental health system before an accurate diagnosis is made. Inventories such as the Dissociative Experiences Scale and the Dissociative Disorders Interview Schedule can facilitate diagnosis (Kluft, 1995).

DID once was thought to be very rare but is being diagnosed with increasing frequency as clinicians become more familiar with its symptoms. As many as 2 percent of people admitted to psychiatric hospitals meet the criteria for this disorder (Kaplan et al., 1994). DID remains a controversial diagnosis, however.

Typical Client Characteristics

Discussion of preexisting personality patterns and accompanying disorders has little relevance with respect to people diagnosed as having DID. The onset of the disorder usually is so early that no period can be identified when only one intact, mature personality was present.

The degree of impairment of people with DID varies widely. Symptoms that frequently accompany this disorder include substance misuse, self-mutilation, suicidal and aggressive impulses, eating and sexual difficulties, sleeping problems, time lapses, disorientation, phobias, hallucinatory experiences, feelings of being influenced or changed, and mood swings (Kluft, 1987). A history of severe sexual and physical abuse in childhood is common, as are somatic symptoms, especially migraine headaches and intestinal disturbances.

Accompanying disorders can include almost any mental disorder; within a given person with DID, some personalities may be relatively well adjusted, whereas others may manifest severe emotional disorders in addition to DID. Typically, people with DID have at least two additional mental disorders, with Mood Disorders, Posttraumatic Stress Disorder, and Personality Disorders (especially Borderline Personality Disorder) being particularly common (Ross, 1989).

Two symptom patterns have been identified in adolescents with DID. One is characterized by a chaotic and impulsive lifestyle, often including promiscuity and substance misuse. The other is characterized by fearful, withdrawn, and childlike behavior (Kaplan et al., 1994). Poor judgment, inadequate support systems, and interpersonal and family difficulties characterize both types. These patterns can continue into adulthood.

Preferred Therapist Characteristics

People with Dissociative Disorders typically are coping with considerable stress and anxiety. They may be confused and frightened by their disorders and fear that they are going insane. They need a warm, supportive therapeutic relationship that provides them clear information on the nature, course, and treatment of their disorders and reassures them that deterioration is unlikely, and that the prognosis for improvement is good.

The importance of a strong therapeutic relationship is especially critical for people with DID, who usually have been abused and violated by their caretakers, a fact that makes trust and self-disclosure difficult. Therapists should strive to instill realistic hope and promote clients' active participation in recovery but at the same time protect them from moving too quickly or dealing with material that may retraumatize them.

Clients' reports of their abuse can be particularly troubling to therapists. Countertransference may occur in which therapists become enraged with the abusers and want to care for and rescue their clients. This reaction is understandable, but it is of course countertherapeutic and can detract from clients' growing self-confidence. Moreover, people's reports of abuse cannot always be proved and may not always be accurate. Therapists should not take on the role of either validating or discrediting clients' stories; rather, they are advised to assume what Kluft (1995) calls "informed uncertainty," whereby they convey to clients that "healing and recovery are the business of therapy and that getting well does not necessitate discovering the absolute truth . . . honesty and truth are important but . . . the determination of what is . . . true may prove impossible" (p. 1604).

Intervention Strategies

Treatment of DID typically is a long, slow, challenging process that requires years of therapy and a skillful therapist. General psychotherapy that is not geared to the special needs of this disorder is unlikely to promote improvement (Kluft, 1995). By contrast, Coons (1986) has found that, after an average of thirty-nine months of treatment specific to DID, 25 percent of the clients who were studied had integrated their personalities, and 67 percent were considerably improved.

Psychotherapy for DID usually is psychodynamic and typically has two thrusts, which Kluft terms "adaptationalism" and "strategic integrationalism." Adaptationalism seeks to help people improve their functioning, resolve life issues, enhance social relationships, and manage their activities in positive ways. Integrationalism, often begun later in treatment, uses interpretation, hypnosis, abreaction, imagery, rituals, and other techniques to elicit, join, and blend the personalities into one healthy, well-integrated personality. According to Kluft (1995), approaches that focus on improving the functioning of the personalities without facilitating their integration are usually not successful and sometimes are harmful. Careful pacing, consistent treatment of all personalities, and safeguarding the client throughout this process is also essential.

Treatment of traumatic memories is important in helping people recover from DID, as well as from other disorders in which underlying traumatic memories are present (Kluft, 1996). The early age at which the traumas occurred, the fear induced by the traumatic experiences, and neural changes during stress can all interfere with recall and accuracy of memories (Bremner, Krystal, Charney, & Southwick, 1996). Nevertheless, because the memories are real for the client, regardless of their historical accuracy, they must be addressed in treatment.

Adjunct modes of treatment can be helpful to people with DID. Homogeneous group therapy with a present-oriented focus can be particularly beneficial. Expressive therapy can facilitate awareness of emotions, personalities, and past experiences. Family therapy, focused on the current family, can promote understanding and improve relationships, although therapy with a family of origin that was abusive is generally contraindicated.

Prognosis

Despite its severity, DID has an excellent prognosis with appropriate treatment. Clients typically continue in long-term treatment and usually are rewarded by considerable improvement. Kluft (1996) reports that 68 percent of 117 people with DID whom he treated achieved integration of their personalities.

A need for very lengthy treatment, as well as a less optimistic prognosis, will be associated with DID that began very early and involves many personalities, although a positive outcome to treatment is still likely for these clients if they are motivated to make positive changes.

Dissociative Fugue

Description of the Disorder

Dissociative Fugue (and Dissociative Amnesia, discussed in the next section) involves temporary forgetting of important components of a person's life. The forgetting is more extensive or extreme than would be due to ordinary forgetfulness. Dissociative Fugue (as well as Dissociative Amnesia) is not caused by substances or a general medical condition.

Dissociative Fugue most often occurs in adults who have undergone a traumatic or very upsetting experience, such as a natural disaster or a severe interpersonal conflict with a loved one. People with Dissociative Fugue typically develop sudden confusion about their identity and travel to other places, sometimes for only a few hours but sometimes for months. In a small percentage of cases, a new identity develops, typically that of a more energetic, outgoing, and adventurous personality. Awareness of the old personality and of the amnesia usually is absent.

The behaviors of people with Dissociative Fugue generally are unremarkable, although their memory loss may cause others to pay attention to them and try to help them. When the fugue state is gone (usually suddenly and spontaneously), people with this disorder typically are confused by what has happened to them, may have amnesia for troubling past events, and cannot recall the details of the fugue state. This is the most common time for them to seek treatment (Gilmore & Kaufman, 1986). People with Dissociative Fugue may experience depression, remorse, anger, and suicidal impulses during this postfugue period and may need to repair the social and occupational consequences of their absence. Dissociative Fugue has been associated with alcohol misuse, Mood Disorders, and Personality Disorders, as well as with highly stressful experiences.

Dissociative Amnesia

Description of the Disorder

Dissociative Amnesia involves partial amnesia or forgetting of important personal information, such as the names and identities of significant family members, one's place of employment, or events during a circumscribed period of time. *DSM-IV* describes five types of amnesia that can characterize this disorder:

1. *Localized amnesia,* focused on events during a limited period
2. *Selective amnesia,* involving recall of some but not all events during a certain period
3. *Generalized amnesia,* or inability to recall one's entire life
4. *Continuous amnesia,* which involves the inability to recall events up to a specific point
5. *Systematized amnesia,* or failure to recall certain categories of events or information

The first two represent the most common types of this disorder. This diagnosis has been used for some people who report having recovered memories of traumatic childhood experiences.

Like those who have experienced Dissociative Fugue, people with Dissociative Amnesia sometimes report a broad range of symptoms after memory has been regained, including depression, aggressive and suicidal impulses, impaired functioning, sexual dysfunction, self-mutilation, trance states, and Ganser's syndrome (presenting approximate answers to questions) (American Psychiatric Association, 1994a).

Dissociative Amnesia, like Dissociative Fugue, tends to occur suddenly at times of traumatic events or unusual stress, is typically of brief duration, and usually remits without recurrence. Both disorders are rare but increase under circumstances of natural disaster, accidents, or warfare. Research on the characteristics of people who experience Dissociative Fugue or Amnesia is limited, but Dissociative Amnesia seems to be more prevalent among adolescents and females, whereas Dissociative Fugue is more common among adults and those with a history of abuse. Dissociative Amnesia is particularly common among people who are immature, suggestible, and rigid, who look to authority figures for direction, who have had traumatic experiences, and who are experiencing depression or anxiety (Kaplan et al., 1994; Meyer, 1983).

Depersonalization Disorder

Description of the Disorder

DSM-IV describes Depersonalization Disorder as characterized by "a feeling of detachment and estrangement from one's self" (American Psychiatric Association, 1994a, p. 488). People with this disorder report feeling like robots, experiencing parts of their bodies as foreign or changed, or feeling as though they are outside their bodies, observing themselves. Despite these unusual sensations, delusions and hallucinations are not present, and reality testing is intact. Nevertheless, the symptoms are severe and persistent enough to cause considerable distress or impairment. Symptoms of depression, anxiety, and somatic distress often accompany this disorder, and people sometimes believe that these symptoms are signs that they are "crazy."

Onset of Depersonalization Disorder tends to be rapid, usually is associated with severe stress or trauma, and can occur at any age, including the childhood years, although it is most common between the ages of fifteen and thirty. This disorder may be brief or chronic, persistent or episodic. It is more common among females than among males (Kaplan et al., 1994).

Typical Client Characteristics

Depersonalization Disorder is particularly common among adolescents. It also seems more prevalent among people with Substance-Related, Anxiety, and Somatization Disorders (Meyer, 1983). Cultural variables should be considered when diagnosing Dissociative Disorders; culturally sanctioned trance experiences should not be mistaken for Depersonalization Disorder.

Preferred Therapist Characteristics

For many people with Dissociative Fugue, Dissociative Amnesia, or Depersonalization Disorder, a helpful therapeutic relationship is sufficient to promote spontaneous remission. Therefore, therapists working with these clients need to be warm, supportive, consistent, and straightforward. They should be able to establish a safe environment for their clients and able to draw on a broad range of techniques to help them.

Intervention Strategies

The treatments for Dissociative Fugue and Dissociative Amnesia are quite similar (Lowenstein, 1995). Typically, the first step is to build a positive therapeutic relationship while helping people achieve a safe and stable life situation.

Once those goals have been accomplished, the second step is to help people regain any memories that may not yet have been recovered and deal with the traumas or stressors that may have precipitated memory loss or flight. The third step in treatment is to help people integrate their upsetting experiences into their lives, reorder and move on with their lives, and develop coping skills that seem likely to help them manage future stressors more successfully.

Although this process sounds straightforward, it can be challenging to come to terms with traumatic experiences and their consequences (such as flashbacks and withdrawal), as well as to deal with the feelings (such as shame, self-blame, rage, fear, and hopelessness) that often result not just from traumas but also from having had a Dissociative Disorder. Careful pacing, grounding, and considerable support are needed to control people's exposure to upsetting material, as well as to the recognition, for some, that they may never be ready to fully process their traumatic experiences. Dissociative Disorders often function as defense mechanisms and should not be stripped away before people have developed other ways of taking care of themselves. Maintaining control and a sense of self is usually important to people with Dissociative Disorders, and that need should be respected.

Many types of interventions can contribute to treatment. In Dissociative Fugue and Dissociative Amnesia, hypnosis can facilitate the controlled uncovering of memories, as well as the working through and integration of those memories (Nemiah, 1988). Medication, including barbiturates and benzodiazepines, can also be helpful in restoring lost memories and reducing anxiety (Kaplan et al., 1994). Expressive-supportive psychodynamic psychotherapy, encouraging exploration, coping, the building of confidence, and the expression of feelings, can also help reduce anxiety. Once memory has been regained, psychotherapy can be useful in helping people deal with the precipitants of amnesia. Family therapy, free association, environmental change, cognitive therapy, and behavior therapy also can help ameliorate Dissociative Fugue and Dissociative Amnesia and can help people cope with stress-related precipitants (Combs & Ludwig, 1982). Group therapy, particularly with others who have survived similar traumatic experiences, can be helpful as long as caution is exercised in pacing.

Little is known about the treatment of Depersonalization Disorder, partly because people usually do not seek treatment for its symptoms. The overall goal of treatment for Depersonalization Disorder is to help people regain their sense of reality and develop a feeling of personality integration. A first step toward this goal is to provide education on the nature of Depersonalization Disorder. Clarifying and normalizing the symptoms of this disorder can often be very therapeutic and can reduce fear about the meaning of the symptoms. The choice of subsequent interventions depends primarily on other disorders and experiences that are associated with the depersonalization.

Many forms of treatment have been used successfully with Depersonalization Disorder, including cognitive and behavioral therapy, hypnosis, group and family therapy, and antidepressant and antianxiety medications (Steinberg, 1995). All have helped some clients and been ineffective with others. Few data-based studies are available to provide general guidance for treatment of this disorder. Consequently, therapists should determine as accurately as possible what symptoms and past experiences need attention and what treatment approaches are most likely to have a positive impact on those associated difficulties. Finally, improvement of coping skills, life and stress management, and integration of self and experiences almost always are indicated as part of treatment for these clients.

Prognosis

The prognosis is excellent for a rapid and complete recovery from initial episodes of Dissociative Fugue and Dissociative Amnesia, particularly if they are linked to specific precipitants (Spiegel, 1996). Recovery is often spontaneous, although it can be facilitated by treatment, but recurrences are common, particularly for Dissociative Amnesia associated with secondary gains (Gilmore & Kaufman, 1986).

Although some do recover from Depersonalization Disorder, that disorder is more likely to have a chronic course (American Psychiatric Association, 1994a). Symptoms may be fairly stable or may wax and wane in response to stressors (Kaplan et al., 1994).

SUMMARY OF TREATMENT RECOMMENDATIONS: CLIENT MAP

Treatment recommendations for disorders involving impairment in awareness of reality are summarized below according to the Client Map format. Because these disorders do vary widely, readers are also encouraged to review the preceding sections on the specific disorders.

Client Map

Diagnosis

Disorders involving impairment in awareness of reality (Schizophrenia, Brief Psychotic Disorder, Schizophreniform Disorder, Delusional Disorder, Schizoaffective Disorder, Dissociative Identity Disorder, Dissociative Fugue, Dissociative Amnesia, Depersonalization Disorder)

Objectives of Treatment

As possible, reduce or eliminate prominent symptoms

Restore client's awareness of reality

Maximize client's coping abilities and emotional and behavioral adjustment to the disorder

Help client deal with any precipitating stressors or traumatic experiences

Prevent relapse

Enable family members to develop understanding of the disorder, deal with their own related needs and feelings, and learn how to help the affected family member

Assessments

Usually medical, neurological, or psychological evaluations, or all three

Inventories of specific symptoms (dissociation, substance use, stress, depression), to clarify diagnosis and provide useful information on level of functioning and secondary symptoms

Clinician Characteristics

Able to communicate caring, consistency, and optimism

Able to establish a trusting and sometimes long-term therapeutic relationship

Knowledgeable about usual nature and course of disorder

Able to collaborate with medical personnel, family and individual psychotherapists, and rehabilitation counselors

Able to provide support and, as necessary, long-term treatment to client and family

Location of Treatment

For Psychotic Disorders, often inpatient setting initially, with later outpatient setting (sometimes day treatment)

For Dissociative Disorders, usually outpatient setting, with hospitalization as necessary if client in crisis or overwhelmed by traumatic memories

Interventions to Be Used

Supportive psychotherapy

Family therapy, to promote family members' understanding and client adjustment

Education on the disorder

Medication (especially for the Psychotic Disorders)

Behavioral therapy, to promote development of coping mechanisms and stress management

Hypnotherapy, psychodynamic psychotherapy as indicated for specific disorders

Emphasis of Treatment

Variable according to nature of disorder (for example, focus on behavior and symptom alleviation for Psychotic Disorders; focus on exploration of dynamics for Dissociative Identity Disorder)

Emphasis on supportiveness and structure typical

Numbers

Primarily individual treatment

Family therapy also useful

Group therapy only in specialized forms (milieu therapy for Schizophrenia; homogeneous group therapy for survivors of abuse diagnosed with Dissociative Identity Disorder)

Timing

Long-term, with some exceptions including Brief Psychotic Disorder and Dissociative Amnesia

Sometimes several sessions per week

Medications Needed

Almost always indicated for Psychotic Disorders

Sometimes indicated for Dissociative Disorders

Should be monitored carefully to minimize side effects and prevent misuse or suicide

Adjunct Services

Rehabilitation counseling

Socialization and development of activities

Respite care for families

Prognosis

Variable, depending on the disorder (for example, excellent for Brief Psychotic Disorder, good for Dissociative Amnesia, fair for Schizophrenia)

Client Map of Victor

This chapter began with a description of Victor J., a twenty-two-year-old college senior who believed that his roommate's mother was in love with him. Victor's poor coping and social skills, his apprehension about graduating from college, and his apparent wish to escape from his family environment all probably contributed to the development of his Delusional Disorder. Treatment had a rapid effect on Victor's symptoms. His delusional beliefs began to fade in intensity and quickly ceased to become a dominant theme. Victor was then able to invest energy into completing his college studies and seeking employment. Victor made many positive changes within about six months, and his medication was stopped, although he was expected to need continued psychotherapy after the initial interventions. The following Client Map outlines the treatment recommended for Victor.

Diagnosis

Axis I:297.1 Delusional Disorder, Erotomanic Type, Moderate

Axis II: Avoidant Personality Traits

Axis III: No medical problems

Axis IV: Impending college graduation, conflict with family

Axis V: Global assessment of functioning (GAF Scale): current GAF = 52

Objectives of Treatment

Eliminate delusional symptoms

Improve relationship skills

Improve communication skills

Establish realistic and rewarding postgraduation plans

Improve socialization, leisure activities, coping mechanisms, support systems, self-confidence, and self-reliance

Facilitate exploration, understanding, and resolution of family issues

Assessments

Referral for medical and neurological tests, to rule out the possibility of cognitive impairment

Clinician Characteristics

Supportive

Empathic

Skilled at reducing resistance and restoring contact with reality

Preferably male, to serve as a role model for client

Knowledgeable about family dynamics

Location of Treatment

Outpatient setting

Interventions to Be Used

Individual therapy combining supportive, cognitive, and behavioral elements

Emphasis on development of strong therapeutic alliance

Behavior therapy, to build up client's coping mechanisms

Education about problem appraisal, communication of concerns, development of alternative solutions to problems, and effective decision making

Training in stress management

Assistance in developing plans for after graduation

Validation of client's feelings, but with minimum discussion of client's delusional beliefs

Emphasis of Treatment

Emphasis on structure

Relatively directive emphasis, with supportiveness and orientation to the present

Focus on behavioral and affective elements, in holistic context

Numbers

Individual therapy, perhaps followed by group therapy with sufficient abatement of symptoms to permit client to benefit from group feedback and opportunity to practice communication skills

Timing

Gentle yet steady pace, to quickly develop commitment to treatment and reduce symptoms

Moderate duration

Medications Needed

Medication prescribed as short-term aid to reducing client's thought disorder and anxiety and facilitating his involvement in therapy

Adjunct Services

Cycling group (to promote client's present enjoyment of biking and facilitate his involvement in a nondemanding, rewarding activity likely to offer increased contact with other young people but unlikely to create discomfort or embarrassment)

Prognosis

Excellent, with combination of medication and psychotherapy

Extended follow-up psychotherapy anticipated

Recommended Readings

Kluft, R. P. (1996). Treating the traumatic memories of patients with dissociative identity disorder. *American Journal of Psychiatry, 153*(7), 103–110.

Manschreck, T. C. (1992). Delusional disorders: Clinical concepts and diagnostic strategies. *Psychiatric Annals, 22*(5), 241–251.

McGlashan, T. H., & Krystal, J. H. (1995). Schizophrenia-related disorders and dual diagnosis. In G. O. Gabbard (Ed.), *Treatments of psychiatric disorders* (pp. 1039–1074). Washington, DC: American Psychiatric Press.

Spiegel, D. (1996). Dissociative disorders. In R. E. Hales & S. C. Yudofsky (Eds.), *The American Psychiatric Press synopsis of psychiatry* (pp. 583–604).Washington, DC: American Psychiatric Press.

CHAPTER TEN

The Future of Diagnosis and Treatment Planning

This book has sought to provide greater understanding about the mental disorders affecting people of all ages and about these disorders' effective treatment. The book has also presented a systematic and comprehensive approach to treatment planning, as represented by the acronym DO A CLIENT MAP, an approach designed to lead clinicians through a series of decisions culminating in a complete treatment plan.

Although the information in this book should enhance clinicians' ability to diagnose and treat their clients' mental disorders, the book can only shape and refine the skills that clinicians already possess. The therapist's personality, style, knowledge, background, and experience are essential ingredients of treatment, and no book can turn a weak therapist into a strong one unless the basic ingredients of a good therapist are already present. This book, then, is to be used by therapists to help them refine their existing knowledge of diagnosis and treatment; it is not to be used as a source of definitive "recipes" for treatment.

THE ART AND SCIENCE OF PSYCHOTHERAPY

Scientific research can assess the impact of various treatment approaches on a particular disorder and can provide invaluable guidelines for treatment planning. Two striking examples of the contribution that data-based research can make to psychotherapy are the research conducted at the National Institutes of Mental Health on the treatment of Major Depressive Disorder and Obsessive-

Compulsive Disorder and the research conducted by Brown, O'Leary, and Barlow (1993) on the treatment of Anxiety Disorders; both bodies of research are discussed elsewhere in this volume. At the same time, because psychotherapy involves a relationship of at least two people, each of whom brings unique qualities to the relationship, and because it involves an interaction that will be different from any other interaction that has ever occurred, psychotherapy is an art as well as a science.

This mixture of art and science contains strengths as well as pitfalls. Psychotherapy at its best is a rich process of recovery and growth, with both client and therapist benefiting from the interaction. Ideally, psychotherapy is a weaving together of empirically validated treatment approaches with creative and individualized interventions; reasoned innovation often is just what is needed to change a deeply entrenched and dysfunctional personality pattern. Nevertheless, because psychotherapy is not an exact science, no recipe or formula is available to remedy each mental disorder. This inexactness allows room for error and failure.

Many disorders are difficult to diagnose and may be mistaken for other, similar disorders. (For example, the diagnostic challenges presented by Dissociative Identity Disorder, Cognitive Mental Disorders, Schizoaffective Disorder, and most of the Personality Disorders have been discussed elsewhere in this book.) Misdiagnosis is only one possible reason for a treatment failure. Others include lack of expertise on the part of the therapist, inappropriate choice of treatment, a challenging client, or a treatment-resistant disorder.

Occasional treatment failures or setbacks are probably inevitable, but therapists can take steps to maximize the likelihood of a successful treatment. Consulting with other mental health practitioners is one important step. Therapists should not hesitate to refer clients for evaluation by someone from a related discipline (perhaps a neurologist or a psychiatrist) to confirm or clarify a diagnosis. Discussion of a case with colleagues also can be useful in gaining ideas for diagnosis and treatment. Frequent evaluation of the progress attained in meeting the goals established in a client map is imperative in monitoring a treatment's effectiveness. As indicated in Chapter One, people typically manifest progress fairly early in therapy; if even slight progress is not made in the first few months of treatment, reevaluation and modification probably is needed of the goals themselves, the treatment plan, or the therapist-client interaction.

SOURCES OF INFLUENCE ON DIAGNOSIS AND TREATMENT PLANNING

The diagnosis and treatment of mental disorders are fields that are constantly changing and evolving. No sooner had the third edition of the *Diagnostic and Statistical Manual of Mental Disorders (DSM-III)* been published, for example, than work was begun on the fourth edition, and work is currently under way on the next edition. Changes in our understanding of diagnosis and treatment come from many sources as well—clinical, biological, social, historical, political, legislative, and economic. Given these multiple influences and the constancy of change, it is probably true that the major source of error in diagnosis and treatment is inadequate information.

Clinical Influences

Clinical experience commonly provides the basis for scientific research and often leads to changes in treatments even before they are scientifically validated. For example, *DSM-IV* contains several diagnoses that have been proposed but that need further study. These include Premenstrual Dysphoric Disorder (emotional and physiological concomitants of premenstrual syndrome), Depressive Personality Disorder, Caffeine Withdrawal, and Mixed Anxiety-Depressive Disorder, among others; data are being gathered on these disorders to determine whether they should be included in the next edition of the *DSM*. Moreover, questions have been raised about the absence from *DSM-IV* of certain diagnoses, such as one that addresses the impact of maladaptive substance use on families. As one consequence, people who can be described as Adult Children of Alcoholics, codependent, or enabling must be diagnosed according to the nature of their symptoms rather than according to a combination of symptoms and interpersonal dynamics. Thus many people who could be perceived as codependent or enabling are diagnosed as having a Dependent Personality Disorder, a diagnosis that does not reflect the familial/genetic component of the disorder, which might be better captured by a new diagnosis encompassing both the dependence needs and the family origins of those needs.

Clinical research like that conducted at the National Institutes of Mental Health has also greatly modified the treatment of several disorders in recent years. For instance, studies have led to a deemphasis on medication in the treatment of Panic Disorder and to an increasing emphasis on medication in the treatment of Obsessive-Compulsive Disorder.

In short, clinical work provides a limitless source of information. This information will modify and alter diagnostic categories and criteria as well as treatments for mental disorders.

Biological Influences

Biological findings play an increasing role in the diagnosis and treatment of mental disorders. Genetic or familial factors have a part in the development of many mental disorders, including Schizophrenia, Obsessive-Compulsive Disorder, Dementia of the Alzheimer's Type, and most Mood Disorders. This biological link does not diminish the value of psychotherapy in the amelioration of these disorders, but it often suggests the importance of adding medication to the treatment plan.

Social Influences

Social changes also have an impact on diagnosis and treatment. In the 1950s, for example, when *DSM-II* was developed, homosexuality was viewed as a mental disorder. That diagnosis had become controversial by 1980, when *DSM-III* was published, and it was eliminated altogether from the revised edition of *DSM-III* (known as *DSM-III-R*), published in 1987. Homosexuality itself has not changed, but social understanding and acceptance of homosexuality have changed greatly, and those changes are reflected in the newer diagnostic manuals. Growing awareness of the impact of gender and cultural background on personality has also led to the inclusion in *DSM-IV* of extensive narrative material on the relationship of those variables to many of the diagnoses (for example, particular caution must be exercised in the diagnosis of disorders like Dependent Personality Disorder that are found much more in one gender or cultural group than in others). The inclusion of this narrative material is indicative of an effort to help clinicians distinguish patterns reflecting cultural influences from those reflecting pathology.

Historical Influences

Historical change is another force that shapes our understanding of the diagnosis and treatment of mental disorders. In the 1960s and the 1970s, for example, the antiwar movement, with its associated emphasis on individuality and freedom of expression, led to the growth of encounter groups, rebirthing, and Gestalt therapy. The 1980s and the 1990s have witnessed a considerable decline of interest in these experiential approaches and a corresponding growth of interest in structured and rational approaches that emphasize cognitive and behavioral interventions. The impact that historical change will have on future diagnosis and treatment planning, although difficult to predict, is certain to be considerable.

Political, Legislative, and Economic Influences

It is also difficult to predict the impact of political, legislative, and economic change on the funding of programs and on attitudes toward mental illness, but these kinds of change are just as important and just as inevitable as historical change. For example, during the Kennedy-Johnson era, funds were made available to develop a nationwide network of community mental health centers. In more recent years we have seen a decrease in funding for these programs, and this decrease has contributed to a growing emphasis on brief therapy and group treatment.

Rapid growth of health maintenance organizations, preferred provider organizations, and employee assistance programs, which are very concerned with cost containment, have further contributed to the emphasis on brief treatment of mental disorders. Some third-party payers offer clients very little choice over who the treatment provider will be and pay little attention to the need for extended treatment for amelioration and prevention of certain mental disorders. Therefore, many people make the choice either to pay large bills themselves for psychotherapy or not receive the treatment they need.

Legislation has also contributed to a shift in who provides mental health services. For example, the number of psychiatrists has been declining, and the number of doctoral-level psychologists has not grown rapidly; at the same time, the number of mental health counselors and social workers has grown considerably, and legislation has both reflected and facilitated these trends. In 1976, Virginia became the first state to pass legislation licensing counselors; some twenty years later, nearly all states have legislation providing for licensure or certification of independently practicing counselors and social workers, and more than one-fifth of the states have passed what has been called "freedom of choice" legislation, which mandates that insurance companies provide third-party payments to any mental health treatment providers credentialed in those states. Moreover, although a long-considered national health insurance plan has been on the drawing board for years and has not yet taken legislative form, there has been a legislative mandate for third-party payers to furnish more equal treatment of mental and physical disorders. These examples of legislation have made psychotherapy increasingly available.

The future of diagnosis and treatment clearly will be affected by many factors and will continue to evolve through research and practice as well as through clinical, biological, social, historical, legal, political, and economic learning and change. It is to be hoped that most of this change will lead to more accurate diagnosis and more effective treatment. We have already learned a great deal, but the field of psychotherapy is in its late adolescence at best; this book alone probably covers more options for treatment than could be explored in all the doctoral dissertations and research projects that will be conducted in the next decade.

The rapid and often unpredictable changes in the field are both exciting and disconcerting. The challenge to mental health therapists is to stay aware of change, incorporate it wisely and selectively into their own therapeutic practices, and promote positive change in their professions. In so doing, they will be able to maximize the rewards that they receive from the practice of their profession, as well as the benefits that psychotherapy can bring to their clients.

Recommended Reading

Andreasen, N. C., & Black, D. W. (1995). *Introductory textbook of psychiatry* (2nd ed.). Washington, DC: American Psychiatric Press.

Barlow, D. H. (Ed.). (1993). *Clinical handbook of psychological disorders* (2nd ed.) New York: Guilford Press.

Beck, A. T., & Freeman, A. (1990). *Cognitive therapy of personality disorders.* New York: Guilford Press.

Gabbard, G. O. (Ed.) (1995). *Treatments of psychiatric disorders.* Washington, DC: American Psychiatric Press.

Kaplan, H., Sadock, B., & Grebb, J. (1994). *Synopsis of psychiatry* (7th ed.). Baltimore: Williams & Wilkins.

Maxmen, J. S., & Ward, N. G. (1995). *Essential psychopathology and its treatment* (2nd ed.). New York: Norton.

Millon, T. (1996). *Disorders of personality: DSM-IV and beyond.* New York: Wiley.

Roth, A., & Fonagy, P. (1996). *What works for whom?* New York: Guilford Press.

Seligman, L. (1996). *Diagnosis and treatment planning in counseling* (2nd ed.). San Francisco: Jossey-Bass.

Sperry, L. (1995). *Handbook of diagnosis and treatment of the DSM-IV personality disorders.* New York: Brunner/Mazel.

Walker, C. E., & Roberts, M. C. (1992). *Handbook of clinical child psychology.* New York: Wiley.

Wiener, J. M. (Ed.). (1996). *Diagnosis and psychopharmacology of childhood and adolescent disorders.* New York: Wiley.

REFERENCES

Abikoff, H., & Klein, R. G. (1992). Attention-deficit hyperactivity and conduct disorder: Comorbidity and implications for treatment. *Journal of Consulting and Clinical Psychology, 60*(6), 881–892.

Abrahamian, R. P., & Lloyd-Still, J. D. (1984). Chronic constipation in childhood: A longitudinal study of 186 patients. *Journal of Pediatric Gastroenterology and Nutrition, 3,* 460–467.

Abramowitz, A. J., & O'Leary, S. G. (1991). Behavioral interventions for the classroom: Implications for students with ADHD. *School Psychology Review, 20*(2), 220–234.

Achenbach, T. (1991). *Manual for the Child Behavior Checklist.* Burlington: Department of Psychiatry, University of Vermont.

Agras, W. S. (1987). *Eating disorders.* New York: Pergamon Press.

Agras, W. S. (1993). The diagnosis and treatment of panic disorder. *Annual Review of Medicine, 44,* 39–51.

Albano, A. M., Chorpita, B. F., & Barlow, D. H. (1996). Childhood anxiety disorders. In E. J. Mash and R. A. Barkley (Eds.), *Child psychopathology* (pp. 196–241). New York: Guilford Press.

Alden, L. (1992). Cognitive-interpersonal treatment of avoidant personality disorder. In P. Keller and S. Heyman (Eds.), *Innovations in clinical practice: A source book* (Vol. 11, pp. 5–22). Sarasota, FL: Professional Resource Exchange.

Alexander, J. F., & Parsons, B. V. (1982). *Functional family therapy.* Pacific Grove, CA: Brooks/Cole.

Allen, J. G., Coyne, L., Colson, D. B., & Horwitz, L. (1996). Pattern of therapist interventions associated with patient collaboration. *Psychotherapy, 38*(32), 254–261.

Allgulander, C., & Lavonri, P. (1991). Excess mortality among 3302 patients with "pure" anxiety neurosis. *Archives of General Psychiatry, 48,* 599–602.

American Psychiatric Association. (1980). *Diagnostic and statistical manual of mental disorders* (3rd ed.). Washington, DC: American Psychiatric Association.

American Psychiatric Association. (1987). *Diagnostic and statistical manual of mental disorders* (3rd ed., rev.). Washington, DC: American Psychiatric Association.

American Psychiatric Association. (1994a). *Diagnostic and statistical manual of mental disorders* (4th ed.). Washington, DC: American Psychiatric Association.

American Psychiatric Association. (1994b). Practice guidelines for the treatment of patients with bipolar disorder. *American Journal of Psychiatry, 151* (Suppl. 12), 1–35.

Anastopoulos, A. D., Shelton, T., Du Paul, G. J., & Guevremont, D. C. (1993). Parent training for attention-deficit hyperactivity disorder: Its impact on parent functioning. *Journal of Abnormal Child Psychology, 21*(5), 581–596.

Anders, T. F. (1996). Sleep disorders. In G. O. Gabbard and S. D. Atkinson (Eds.), *Synopsis of treatments of psychiatric disorders* (pp. 167–176). Washington, DC: American Psychiatric Press.

Andersen, A. E. (1987a). Anorexia nervosa, bulimia, and depression: Multiple interactions. In F. Flach (Ed.), *Diagnostics and psychopathology* (pp. 131–139). New York: Norton.

Andersen, A. E. (1987b). Psychiatric aspects of bulimia. In F. Flach (Ed.), *Diagnostics and psychopathology* (pp. 121–130). New York: Norton.

Anderson, D. J., Noyes, R. J., & Crowe, R. R. (1984). A comparison of panic disorder and generalized anxiety disorder. *American Journal of Psychiatry, 141,* 572–575.

Andreasen, N. C., & Black, D. W. (1995). *Introductory textbook of psychiatry* (2nd ed.). Washington, DC: American Psychiatric Press.

Andreasen, N. C., & Hoenk, P. R. (1983). The predictive value of adjustment disorders: A follow-up study. *American Journal of Psychiatry, 139,* 584–590.

Andrews, G., & Harvey, R. (1981). Does psychotherapy benefit neurotic patients? *Archives of General Psychiatry, 38,* 1203–1208.

Araoz, D. L., & Carrese, M. A. (1996). *Solution oriented brief therapy for adjustment disorders: A guide for providers under managed care.* New York: Brunner/Mazel.

Arndt, W. (1991). *Gender disorders and the paraphilias.* Madison, CT: International Universities Press.

Arnold, L., & Jensen, P. S. (1995). Attention deficit disorders. In H. Kaplan, B. Sadock, & J. Grebb (Eds.), *Comprehensive textbook of psychiatry* (6th ed., pp. 2295–2310). Baltimore: Williams & Wilkins.

Arntz, A. (1996). Why do people tend to overpredict pain? On the asymmetries between underpredictions and overpredictions of pain. *Behaviour Research and Therapy, 34*(7), 545–554.

Arntz, A., & Van Den Hout, M. (1996). Psychological treatments of panic disorder without agoraphobia: Cognitive therapy versus applied relaxation. *Behaviour Research and Therapy, 34*(2), 113–122.

Arredondo, D. E., & Butler, S. F. (1994). Affective comorbidity in psychiatrically hospitalized adolescents with conduct disorder or oppositional defiant disorder: Should conduct disorder be treated with mood stabilizers? *Journal of Child and Adolescent Psychopharmacology, 4*(3), 151–158.

Atwood, J. D., & Chester, R. (1987). *Treatment techniques for common mental disorders.* Northvale, NJ: Aronson.

Awad, G. A. (1995). An outpatient treatment program for young children with pervasive developmental disorder. *American Journal of Psychotherapy, 49*(1), 28–46.

Azrin, N. H., & Peterson, A. L. (1988). Habit reversal for the treatment of Tourette syndrome. *Behaviour Research and Therapy, 11,* 347–355.

Azrin, N. H., & Peterson, A. L. (1990). Treatment of Tourette syndrome by habit reversal: A waiting-list control group comparison. *Behavior Therapy, 21,* 305–318.

Azrin, N. H., & Peterson, A. L. (1992). An evaluation of behavioral treatment for Tourette syndrome. *Behaviour Research and Therapy, 30*(2), 167–174.

Azrin, N. H., Sneed, T. J., & Foxx, R. M. (1973). Dry bed: A rapid method of eliminating bedwetting (enuresis) of the retarded. *Behaviour Research and Therapy, 11*(3), 427–434.

Bach, M., & Bach, D. (1995). Predictive value of alexithymia: A prospective study in somatizing patients. *Psychotherapy and Psychosomatics, 64*(1), 43–48.

Bagenholm, A., & Gillberg, C. (1991). Psychosocial effects on siblings of children with autism and mental retardation: A population-based study. *Journal of Mental Deficiency Research, 35*(4), 291–307.

Baker, A. L., & Wilson, P. H. (1985). Cognitive-behavior therapy for depression: The effects of booster sessions on relapse. *Behavior Therapy, 16,* 335–344.

Bale, R. M., Zarcone, V. P., Van Stone, W. W., Kuldau, J. M., Engelsing, T.M.J., & Elashoff, R. M. (1984). Three therapeutic communities. *Archives of General Psychiatry, 41,* 185–191.

Ballenger, J. C., Lydiard, R. B., & Turner, S. M. (1995). Panic disorder and agoraphobia. In G. O. Gabbard (Ed.), *Treatments of psychiatric disorders* (pp. 1421–1452). Washington, DC: American Psychiatric Press.

Barbaree, H. E., & Marshall, W. E. (1985). Anxiety-based disorders. In M. Hersen and S. M. Turner (Eds.), *Diagnostic interviewing* (pp. 55–77). New York: Plenum.

Barkley, R. A. (1990). *Attention deficit hyperactivity disorder: A handbook for diagnosis and treatment* (2nd ed.). New York: Guilford Press.

Barkley, R. A. (1996). Attention-deficit hyperactivity disorder. In E. J. Mash and R. A. Barkley (Eds.), *Child psychopathology* (pp. 63–112). New York: Guilford Press.

Barkley, R. A., Anastopoulos, A. D., Guevremont, D. C., & Fletcher, K. E. (1991). Adolescents with ADHD: Patterns of behavioral adjustment, academic functioning, and treatment utilization. *Journal of the American Academy of Child and Adolescent Psychiatry, 30*(5), 752–761.

Barlow, D. H. (1988). *Anxiety and its disorders: The nature and treatment of anxiety and panic.* New York: Guilford Press.

Barlow, D. H. (Ed.). (1993). *Clinical handbook of psychological disorders* (2nd ed.). New York: Guilford Press.

Barlow, D. H., & Cerny, J. A. (1988). *Psychological treatment of panic.* New York: Guilford Press.

Barlow, D. H., & Waddell, M. T. (1985). Agoraphobia. In D. H. Barlow (Ed.), *Clinical handbook of psychological disorders* (pp. 1–68). New York: Guilford Press.

Baron-Cohen, S., Allen, J., & Gillberg, C. (1992). Can autism be detected at 18 months? The needle, the haystack, and the CHAT. *British Journal of Psychiatry, 161,* 839–843.

Bartels, S. J., & Drake, R. E. (1989). Depression in schizophrenia: Current guidelines to treatment. *Psychiatric Quarterly, 60,* 337–357.

Bass, C. (Ed.). (1990). *Physical symptoms and psychological illness.* Oxford, England: Blackwell.

Bauer, M., & Boegner, F. (1996). Neurological syndromes in factitious disorder. *Journal of Nervous and Mental Disease, 184*(5), 281–288.

Bauer, M. S., Kurtz, J. W., Rubin, L. B., & Marcus, J. G. (1994). Mood and behavioral effects of four-week light treatment in winter depressives and controls. *Journal of Psychiatric Research, 28*(2), 135–145.

Baumeister, A. A., & Baumeister, A. A. (1995). Mental retardation. In M. Hersen and R. T. Ammerman (Eds.), *Advanced abnormal child psychology* (pp. 283–304). Hillsdale, NJ: Erlbaum.

Bebbington, P. E. (1986). Psychosocial etiology of schizophrenia and affective disorders. In J. E. Helzer and S. B. Guze (Eds.), *Psychoses, affective disorders, and dementia* (pp. 171–192). New York: Basic Books.

Beck, A. T., & Emery, G. (1985). *Anxiety disorders and phobias.* New York: Basic Books.

Beck, A. T., & Freeman, A. (1990). *Cognitive therapy of personality disorders.* New York: Guilford Press.

Beck, A. T., Rush, A. J., Shaw, B. F., & Emery, G. (1979). *Cognitive therapy of depression.* New York: Guilford Press.

Beck, A. T., & Steer, R. A. (1990). *Manual for the Beck Anxiety Inventory.* San Antonio, TX: Psychological Corporation.

Beck, D. F. (1988). *Counselor characteristics: How they affect outcome.* Milwaukee: Family Service America.

Bellack, A. S., & Hersen, M. (1993). *Psychopathology in adulthood.* Needham Heights, MA: Allyn & Bacon.

Bellack, A. S., Hersen, M., & Himmelhoch, J. M. (1983). A comparison of social-skills training, pharmacotherapy and psychotherapy for depression. *Behaviour Research and Therapy, 21,* 101–107.

Bellack, A., & Mueser, K. T. (1993). Psychosocial treatment for schizophrenia. *Schizophrenia Bulletin, 19*(2), 317–336.

Benjamin, L. (1993). *Interpersonal diagnosis and treatment of personality disorders.* New York: Guilford Press.

Benton, M. K., & Schroeder, H. E. (1990). Social skills training with schizophrenics: A meta-analytic evaluation. *Journal of Consulting and Clinical Psychology, 58,* 741–747.

Berg, I., & Jackson, A. (1985). Teenage school refusers grow up: A follow-up study of 168 subjects ten years on average after in-patient treatment. *British Journal of Psychiatry, 147,* 366–370.

Bergner, R. M. (1977). The marital system of the hysterical individual. *Family Process, 16,* 85–95.

Berlin, F. S., Malin, H. M., & Thomas, K. (1995). Nonpedophilic and nontransvestic paraphilias. In G. O. Gabbard (Ed.), *Treatments of psychiatric disorders* (pp. 1941–1958). Washington, DC: American Psychiatric Press.

Berman, J. S., & Norton, N. C. (1985). Does professional training make a therapist more effective? *Psychological Bulletin, 98,* 401–407.

Beutler, L. E. (1991). Have all won and must all have prizes? Revisiting Luborsky et al.'s verdict. *Journal of Consulting and Clinical Psychology, 59*(2), 226–232.

Beutler, L. E., & Consoli, A. J. (1993). Matching the therapist's interpersonal stance to clients' characteristics: Contributions from systematic eclectic psychotherapy. *Psychotherapy, 30*(3), 417–422.

Beutler, L. E., Crago, M., & Arizmendi, T. G. (1986). Therapist variables in psychotherapy process. In S. L. Garfield and A. E. Bergin (Eds.), *Handbook of psychotherapy and behavior change* (pp. 257–310). New York: Wiley.

Biederman, J., Faraone, S., Mick, E., Wozniak, J., Chen, L., Ouellette, C., Marrs, A., Moore, P., Garcia, J., Mennin, D., & Lelon, E. (1996). Attention-deficit hyperactivity disorder and juvenile mania: An overlooked comorbidity? *Journal of the American Academy of Child and Adolescent Psychiatry, 35*(8), 997–1009.

Biederman, J., Newcorn, J., & Sprich, S. (1991). Comorbidity of attention deficit hyperactivity disorder with conduct, depressive, anxiety, and other disorders. *American Journal of Psychiatry, 148,* 564–577.

Billings, A. G., & Moos, R. H. (1985). Life stressors and social resources affect post-treatment outcomes among depressed patients. *Journal of Abnormal Psychology, 94,* 140–155.

Birmaher, B., Ryan, N. D., Williamson, D. E., Brent, D. A., & Kaufman, J. (1996). Childhood and adolescent depression: A review of the past 10 years: Part II. *Journal of the American Academy of Child and Adolescent Psychiatry, 35*(12), 1575–1583.

Black, B., & Uhde, T. W. (1994). Treatment of elective mutism with fluoxetine: A double blind placebo controlled study. *Journal of American Academy of Child and Adolescent Psychiatry, 33,* 1000–1006.

Black, B., & Uhde, T. W. (1995). Psychiatric characteristics of children with selective mutism: A pilot study. *Journal of the American Academy of Child and Adolescent Psychiatry, 34*(7), 847–856.

Blanchard, E. B., Jones-Alexander, J., Buckley, T. C., & Forneris, C. A. (1996). Psychometric properties of the PTSD checklist (PCL). *Behaviour Research and Therapy, 34*(8), 669–673.

Blazer, D., Hughes, D., & George, L. K. (1987). Stressful life events and the onset of a generalized anxiety syndrome. *American Journal of Psychiatry, 144,* 1178–1183.

Bloch, C., Crouch, E., & Reibstein, J. (1981). Therapeutic factors in group psychotherapy. *Archives of General Psychiatry, 38,* 519–526.

Bloom, B. L. (1981). Focused single-session therapy: Initial development and evaluation. In S. H. Budman (Ed.), *Forms of brief therapy* (pp. 167–216). New York: Guilford Press.

Boggs, S. R., Geffken, G. R., Johnson, S. B., & Silverstein, J. (1992). Behavioral treatment of nocturnal enuresis in children with insulin-dependent diabetes mellitus. *Journal of Pediatric Psychology, 17*(1), 111–118.

Bolles, R. N. (1996). *What color is your parachute?* Berkeley: Ten Speed Press.

Boon, F. F., & Singh, N. N. (1991). A model for the treatment of encopresis. *Behavior Modification, 15*(3), 355–371.

Borkovec, T. D. (1982). Insomnia. *Journal of Consulting and Clinical Psychology, 50,* 880–895.

Boskind-White, M., & White, W. C., Jr. (1983). *Bulimarexia: The binge-purge cycle.* New York: Norton.

Bourg, S., Connor, E. J., & Landis, E. E. (1995). The impact of expertise and sufficient information on psychologists' ability to detect malingering. *Behavioral Sciences and the Law, 13*(4), 505–515.

Bowlby, J. (1982). *Attachment and loss.* Vol. 1: *Attachment.* New York: Basic Books. (Originally published 1969.)

Bowring, M., & Kovacs, M. (1992). Difficulties in diagnosing manic disorders among children and adolescents. *Journal of the American Academy of Child and Adolescent Psychiatry, 31,* 611–614.

Boyd, J. H., & Weissman, M. M. (1982). Epidemiology. In E. S. Paykel (Ed.), *Handbook of affective disorders* (pp. 109–125). New York: Guilford.

Bradford, J. M., Boulet, J., & Pawlak, A. (1992). The paraphilias: A multiplicity of deviant behaviours. *Canadian Journal of Psychiatry, 37*(2), 104–108.

Brammer, L. M., Shostrom, E. L., & Abrego, P. J. (1989). *Therapeutic psychology: Fundamentals of counseling and psychotherapy* (5th ed.). Upper Saddle River, NJ: Prentice Hall.

Brandenburg, N. A., Friedman, R. M., & Silver, S. F. (1990). The epidemiology of childhood psychiatric disorders: Prevalence findings from recent studies. *Journal of the American Academy of Child and Adolescent Psychiatry, 29,* 76–83.

Bratter, T. E. (1985). Special clinical psychotherapeutic concerns for alcoholic and drug-addicted individuals. In T. E. Bratter and E. G. Forrest (Eds.), *Alcoholism and substance abuse* (pp. 523–574). New York: Free Press.

Bratter, T. E., Collabolletta, E. A., Fossbender, A. J., Pennacchia, M. C., & Rubel, J. R. (1985). The American self-help residential therapeutic community. In T. E. Bratter and G. G. Forrest (Eds.), *Alcoholism and substance abuse* (pp. 461–507). New York: Free Press.

Bregman, J. D., & Gerdtz, J. (1995). Psychiatry. In B. A. Thyer and N. P. Kropf (Eds.), *Developmental disabilities: A handbook for interdisciplinary practice* (pp. 160–171). Cambridge, MA: Brookline Books.

Breier, A., Charney, D. S., & Heninger, G. R. (1985). The diagnostic validity of anxiety disorders and their relationship to depressive illness. *American Journal of Psychiatry, 142,* 787–797.

Bremner, J. D., Krystal, J. H., Charney, D. S., & Southwick, S. M. (1996). Neural mechanisms in dissociative amnesia for childhood abuse: Relevance to the current controversy surrounding the "false memory syndrome." *American Journal of Psychiatry, 153* (Suppl.), 71–82.

Breslau, N., Schultz, L., & Peterson, E. (1995). Sex differences in depression: A role for preexisting anxiety. *Psychiatry Research, 58,* 1–12.

Brodsky, C. M. (1984). Sociocultural and interactional influences on somatization. *Psychosomatics, 25,* 573–680.

Brouwers, M., & Wiggum, C. D. (1993). Bulimia and perfectionism: Developing the courage to be imperfect. *Journal of Mental Health Counseling, 15*(2), 141–149.

Brown, T. A., O'Leary, T. A., & Barlow, D. H. (1993). Generalized anxiety disorder. In D. H. Barlow (Ed.), *Clinical handbook of psychological disorders* (2nd ed., pp. 137–188). New York: Guilford Press.

Bruch, H. (1982). Anorexia nervosa: Therapy and theory. *American Journal of Psychiatry, 139,* 1531–1538.

Buchholz, D. (1988). Sleep disorders. *Treatment Trends, 3,* 1–9.

Buckley, T. C., Blanchard, E. B., & Hickling, E. J. (1996). A prospective examination of delayed onset PTSD secondary to motor vehicle accidents. *Journal of Abnormal Psychology, 105*(4), 617–625.

Budman, S. H. (Ed.). (1981). *Forms of brief therapy.* New York: Guilford Press.

Burns, D. B., Sayers, S. L., & Moras, K. (1994). Intimate relationships and depression: Is there a causal connection? *Journal of Consulting and Clinical Psychology, 62,* 1033–1043.

Burns, D. D. (1990). *The feeling good handbook.* New York: Penguin Books.

Butler, G., Cullington, A., Hibbert, G., Klimes, I., & Gelder, M. (1987). Anxiety management for persistent generalized anxiety. *British Journal of Psychiatry, 151,* 535–542.

Butler, R., Brewin, C. R., & Forsythe, I. (1990). Relapse in children treated for nocturnal enuresis: Prediction of response using pre-treatment variables. *Behavioural Psychotherapy, 18*(1), 65–72.

Cadoret, R. J., Troughton, E., O'Gorman, T. W., & Heywood, E. (1986). An adoption study of genetic and environmental factors in drug abuse. *Archives of General Psychiatry, 43,* 1131–1136.

Calhoun, K. S., & Resick, P. A. (1993). Post-traumatic stress disorder. In D. H. Barlow (Ed.), *Clinical handbook of psychological disorders* (2nd ed., pp. 48–98). New York: Guilford Press.

Campbell, J., Cueva, J. E., & Hallin, A. (1996). Autism and pervasive developmental disorders. In J. M. Wiener (Ed.), *Diagnosis and psychopharmacology of childhood and adolescent disorders* (2nd ed., pp. 151–192). New York: Wiley.

Campbell, M., Schopler, E., Cueva, J. E., & Hallin, A. (1996). Treatment of autistic disorder. *Journal of the American Academy of Child and Adolescent Psychiatry, 35*(2), 134–141.

Campbell, M., Schopler, E., Mesibov, G. B., & Sanchez, L. E. (1995). Pervasive developmental disorders. In G. O. Gabbard (Ed.), *Treatments of psychiatric disorders* (pp. 141–166). Washington, DC: American Psychiatric Press.

Cantwell, D. P. (1996). Attention deficit disorder: A review of the past 10 years. *Journal of the American Academy of Child and Adolescent Psychiatry, 35*(8), 978–987.

Cantwell, E. P., & Baker, L. (1989). Stability and natural history of *DSM-III* childhood diagnoses. *Journal of the American Academy of Child and Adolescent Psychiatry, 29,* 691–700.

Carkhuff, R. R., & Berenson, B. G. (1977). *Beyond counseling and therapy.* Austin, TX: Holt, Rinehart and Winston.

Carlson, G. A., & Kashani, J. H. (1988). Phenomenology of major depression from childhood through adulthood: Analysis of three studies. *American Journal of Psychiatry, 145*(10), 1222–1225.

Carnegie Council on Adolescent Development. (1995). *Great transitions: Preparing adolescents for a new century.* Waldorf, MD: Carnegie Corporation.

Carnes, P. J. (1990). Sexual addiction: Progress, criticism, challenges. *American Journal of Preventive Psychiatry and Neurology, 2,* 1–8.

Carroll, E. M., Rueger, D. B., Foy, D. W., & Donahoe, C. P., Jr. (1985). Vietnam combat veterans with post-traumatic stress disorder: Analysis of marital and cohabiting adjustment. *Journal of Abnormal Psychology, 94,* 329–337.

Carter, C., Urbanowicz, M., Hemsley, R., Mantilla, L., Strobel, S., Graham, P., & Taylor, E. (1993). Effects of a new food diet in attention deficit disorder. *Archives of Disease in Childhood, 69*(5), 564–568.

Carter, E. A., & McGoldrick, M. (1988). *The changing family life cycle.* Lake Worth, FL: Gardner Press.

Carter, F. A., & Bulik, C. M. (1994). Exposure treatments for bulimia nervosa: Procedure, efficacy, and mechanisms. *Advances in Behavior Research and Therapy, 16,* 77–129.

Cartwright, R. D., & Wood, E. (1991). Adjustment disorders of sleep: The sleep effects of a major stressful event and its resolution. *Psychiatry Research, 39*(3), 199–209.

Cassidy, J. (1988). Child-mother attachment and the self in six-year olds. *Child Development, 59*(1), 121–134.

Chambless, D. (1985). The relationship of severity of agoraphobia to associated psychopathology. *Behavior Research and Therapy, 23,* 305–310.

Chambless, D. L., & Gillis, M. M. (1994). Cognitive therapy of anxiety disorders. *Journal of Consulting and Clinical Psychology, 61,* 248–260.

Christensen, H., Hadzi-Pavlovic, D., Andrews, G., & Mattick, R. (1987). Behavior therapy and tricyclic medication in the treatment of obsessive-compulsive disorder: A quantitative review. *Journal of Consulting and Clinical Psychology, 55,* 701–711.

Christenson, G. A., Mackenzie, T. B., & Mitchell, J. E. (1991). Characteristics of 60 adult chronic hair pullers. *American Journal of Psychiatry, 148,* 365–370.

Christopherson, E. R., & Rapoff, M. A. (1992). Toileting problems in children. In C. E. Walker and M. C. Roberts (Eds.), *Handbook of clinical child psychology* (pp. 399–412). New York: Wiley.

Clarkin, J. F., Frances, A. J., & Perry, S. (1992). Differential therapeutics: Macro and micro levels of treatment planning. In J. C. Norcross and M. R. Goldfried (Eds.), *Handbook of psychotherapy integration* (pp. 463–502). New York: Basic Books.

Cloninger, C., Svrakic, D., & Przybeck, R. (1993). A psychobiological model of temperament and character. *Archives of General Psychiatry, 50,* 975–990.

Clum, G. A., Clum, G. A., & Surls, R. (1993). A meta-analysis of treatments for panic disorder. *Journal of Consulting and Clinical Psychology, 61,* 317–326.

Coccaro, E. F., Astill, J. L., & Herbert, J. A. (1990). Fluoxetine treatment of impulsive aggression in *DSM-III-R* personality disorder patients. *Journal of Clinical Psychopharmacology, 10,* 373–375.

Cofer, D., & Wittenborn, J. (1980). Personality characteristics of formerly depressed women. *Journal of Abnormal Psychology, 89,* 309–315.

Cohen, D., Ort, S., Leckman, J. F., & Hardin, M. (1988). Family functioning in Tourette's syndrome. In D. J. Cohen, R. Brunn, & J. Leckman (Eds.), *Tourette's syndrome and tic disorders: Clinical understanding and treatment* (pp. 179–196). New York: Wiley.

Coleman, H.K.L., Wampold, B. E., & Casali, S. L. (1995). Ethnic minorities' ratings of ethnically similar and European American counselors: A meta-analysis. *Journal of Counseling Psychology, 42,* 55–64.

Combs, G., Jr., & Ludwig, A. M. (1982). Dissociative disorders. In J. H. Greist, J. W. Jefferson, & R. L. Spitzer (Eds.), *Treatment of mental disorders* (pp. 309–319). New York: Oxford University Press.

Comings, D. E., Himes, J. A., & Comings, B. G. (1990). An epidemiologic study of Tourette's syndrome in a single school district. *Journal of Clinical Psychiatry, 51*(11), 463–469.

Conners, C. K. (1990). *Conners' Rating Scale Manual.* North Tonawanda, NY: Mental Health Systems.

Conte, H. R., Plutchik, R., Wild, K. V., & Karasu, T. B. (1986). Combined psychotherapy and pharmacotherapy for depression. *Archives of General Psychiatry, 43,* 471–479.

Coons, P. M. (1986). Treatment progress in 20 patients with multiple personality disorder. *Journal of Nervous and Mental Disease, 174,* 715–721.

Coryell, W., & Tsuang, M. T. (1986). Outcome after 40 years in *DSM-III* schizophreniform disorder. *Archives of General Psychiatry, 43,* 324–328.

Cousins, L., & Weiss, G. (1993). Parent training and social skills training for children with attention-deficit hyperactivity disorder: How can they be combined for greater effectiveness? *Canadian Journal of Psychiatry–Revue Canadienne de Psychiatrie, 38*(6), 449–457.

Cowan, P. A., Cohn, D. A., Cowan, C. P., & Pearson, J. L. (1996). Parents' attachment histories and children's externalizing and internalizing behaviors: Exploring family systems models of linkage. *Journal of Consulting and Clinical Psychology, 64*(1), 53–64.

Craig, K. D., & Dobson, K. S. (Eds.) (1995). *Anxiety and depression in adults and children.* Thousand Oaks, CA: Sage.

Craighead, W. E., Kennedy, R. E., Raczynski, J. M., & Dow, M. G. (1984). Affective disorders–unipolar. In S. M. Turner and M. Hersen (Eds.), *Adult psychopathology and diagnosis* (pp. 184–244). New York: Wiley.

Craske, M. G., & Barlow, D. H. (1993). Panic disorder and agoraphobia. In D. H. Barlow (Ed.), *Clinical handbook of psychological disorders* (2nd ed., pp. 1–47). New York: Guilford Press.

Crits-Christoph, P. (1992). The efficacy of brief dynamic psychotherapy: A meta-analysis. *American Journal of Psychiatry, 149*(2), 151–158.

Cuddy-Casey, M. (1997). A case study using a child-centered play therapy approach to treat enuresis and encopresis. *Elementary School Guidance and Counseling, 31*(3), 220–223.

Custer, R. L. (1984). Profile of the pathological gambler. *Journal of Clinical Psychiatry, 45,* 35–38.

Dalgleish, T., Rosen, K., & Marks, M. (1996). Rhythm and blues: The theory and treatment of seasonal affective disorder. *British Journal of Clinical Psychology, 35*(2), 163–182.

Dattilio, F. (1993). A practical update on the treatment of obsessive-compulsive disorder. *Journal of Mental Health Counseling, 15*(3), 244–259.

Davison, G. C., & Neale, J. M. (1996). *Abnormal psychology.* New York: Wiley.

Dawson, D., & MacMillan, H. (1993). *Relationship management of the borderline patient: From understanding to treatment.* New York: Brunner/Mazel.

Day, M., & Manschreck, T. C. (1988). Delusional (paranoid) disorders. In A. M. Nicholi Jr. (Ed.), *The new Harvard guide to psychiatry* (pp. 296–308). Cambridge, MA: Harvard University Press.

De Angelis, T. (1997). New research reveals who may molest again. *APA Monitor, 28*(4), 46.

Deblinger, E., McLeer, S. V., Atkins, M. S., Ralphe, D., & Foa, E. B. (1989). Posttraumatic stress in sexually abused, physically abused and nonabused children. *Child Abuse and Neglect, 13,* 403–408.

Deffenbacher, J. L., Story, D. S., Stark, R. S., Hogg, J. A., & Brandon, A. D. (1987). Cognitive-relaxation and social skills interventions in the treatment of general anger. *Journal of Counseling Psychology, 34,* 171–176.

Depression Guideline Panel. (1993). *Depression in primary care.* Vol. 1: *Detection and diagnosis* (Clinical practice guideline No. 5; AHCPR Publication No. 93–0550). Rockville, MD: Agency for Health Care Policy and Research, Public Health Service, U.S. Department of Health and Human Services.

de Shazer, S. (1991). *Putting difference to work.* New York: Norton.

Despland, J. N., Monod, L., & Ferrero, F. (1995). Clinical relevance of adjustment disorder in *DSM-III-R* and *DSM-IV. Comprehensive Psychiatry, 36*(6), 454–460.

Diamond, G. S., Serrano, A. C., Dickey, M., & Sonis, W. (1996). Current status of family-based outcome and process research. *Journal of the American Academy of Child and Adolescent Psychiatry, 35*(1), 6–17.

Di Lalla, D. L., & Rogers, S. J. (1994, April). Domains of the Childhood Autism Rating Scale: Relevance for diagnosis and treatment. *Journal of Autism and Developmental Disorders,* pp. 115–128.

Dinkmeyer, D. (1975). *Systematic training for effective parenting.* Circle Pines, MN: American Guidance Service.

Dinkmeyer, D., & Carlson, J. (1984). *Time for a better marriage.* Circle Pines, MN: American Guidance Service.

Dion, G. L., & Pollack, W. S. (1992). A rehabilitation model for persons with bipolar disorder. *Comprehensive Mental Health Care, 2*(2), 87–102.

Dishion, T., & Andrews, D. W. (1995). Preventing escalation in problem behaviors with high-risk young adolescents: Immediate and 1–year outcomes. *Journal of Consulting and Clinical Psychology, 63*(4), 538–548.

Dittman, R. W., & Wolter, S. (1996). Primary nocturnal enuresis and desmopressin treatment: Do psychosocial factors affect outcome? *European Child and Adolescent Psychiatry, 5*(2), 101–109.

Dodge, K. A., & Frame, C. L. (1982). Social cognitive biases and deficits in aggressive boys. *Child Development, 51,* 620–635.

Dodge, K. A., & Newman, J. P. (1981). Biased decision-making processes in aggressive boys. *Journal of Abnormal Psychology, 90,* 375–379.

Don, A., & Rourke, B. P. (1995). Fetal alcohol syndrome. In B. P. Rourke (Ed.), *Syndrome of nonverbal learning disabilities: Neurodevelopmental manifestations* (pp. 372–406). New York: Guilford Press.

Dorr, D., Barley, W. D., Gard, B., & Webb, C. (1983). Understanding and treating borderline personality organization. *Psychotherapy: Theory, Research and Practice, 20,* 397–407.

Drtilkova, I., Balastikova, B., Lemanova, H., & Zak, J. (1994). Therapeutical effects of clonidine and clonazepam in children with tic syndrome. *Homeostasis in Health and Disease, 35*(6), 296.

Dulmus, C. N., & Wodarski, J. S. (1996). Assessment and effective treatments of childhood psychopathology: Responsibilities and implications for practice. *Journal of Child and Adolescent Group Therapy, 6*(2), 75–99.

Dunner, D. L. (1993). A review of the diagnostic status of "bipolar II" for the *DSM-IV* work group on mood disorders. *Depression, 1,* 2–10.

Du Paul, G. J., Guevremont, D. C., & Barkley, R. A. (1992). Behavioral treatment of attention-deficit hyperactivity disorder in the classroom: The use of the attention training system. *Behavior Modification, 16*(2), 204–225.

Durham, A. C., & Allan, T. (1993). Psychological treatment of generalized anxiety disorder: A review of the clinical significance of outcome studies since 1980. *British Journal of Psychiatry, 163,* 19–26.

Durham, R. C., & Turvey, A. A. (1987). Cognitive therapy vs. behavior therapy in the treatment of chronic general anxiety. *Behaviour Research and Therapy, 25,* 229–234.

Durlak, J. A., Fuhrman, T., & Lampman, C. (1991). Effectiveness of cognitive-behavior therapy for maladapting children: A meta-analysis. *Psychological Bulletin, 110*(2), 204–214.

Edell, W., & McGlashan, T. H. (1993). *Instability of personality disorder diagnoses in adolescents.* Paper presented at the conference of the International Society for the Study of Personality Disorders, Cambridge, MA.

Egami, Y., Ford, D. E., Greenfield, S. F., & Crum, R. M. (1996). Psychiatric profile and sociodemographic characteristics of adults who report physically abusing or neglecting children. *American Journal of Psychiatry, 153*(7), 921–928.

Eisendrath, S. J. (1995). Factitious disorders and malingering. In G. O. Gabbard (Ed.), *Treatments of psychiatric disorders* (pp. 1803–1818). Washington, DC: American Psychiatric Press.

Eisenstadt, T. H., Eyberg, S., McNeil, C. B., & Newcomb, K. (1993). Parent-child interaction therapy with behavior problem children: Relative effectiveness of two stages and overall treatment outcome. *Journal of Clinical Child Psychology, 22*(1), 42–51.

Elkin, I., Shea, T., Watkins, J. T., Imber, S. D., Sotsky, S. M., Collins, J. F., Glass, D. R., Pilkonis, P. A., Leber, W. R., Docherty, J. P., Feister, S. J., & Parloff, M. B. (1989). National Institutes of Mental Health Treatment of Depression Collaborative Research Program. *Archives of General Psychiatry, 46,* 971–982.

Ellis, A., & Greiger, R. (1986). *What is rational-emotive therapy?* Baltimore: Johns Hopkins University Press.

Emmelkamp, P.M.G. (1986). Behavior therapy with adults. In S. L. Garfield and A. E. Bergin (Eds.), *Handbook of psychotherapy and behavior change* (pp. 385–442). New York: Wiley.

Emmelkamp, P.M.G. (1994). Behavior therapy with adults. In A. E. Bergin and S. L. Garfield (Eds.), *Handbook of psychotherapy and behavior change* (4th ed., pp. 247–379). New York: Wiley.

Emmelkamp, P.M.G., de Haan, E., & Hoogduin, C.A.L. (1990). Marital adjustment and obsessive-compulsive disorder. *British Journal of Psychiatry, 156,* 55–60.

Emory, D. (1996). Coping with seasonal affective disorder. *The Advocate, 20*(2), 12.

Erenberg, G. (1992). Treatment of Tourette's syndrome with neuroleptic drugs. In T. Chase, A. Friedhoff, & D. Cohen (Eds.), *Tourette's syndrome: Genetics, neurobiology and treatment advances in neurology* (pp. 241–243). New York: Raven Press.

Erk, R. R. (1997). Multidimensional treatment of attention deficit disorder: A family oriented approach. *Journal of Mental Health Counseling, 19*(1), 1830–1930.

Esman, A. H. (1986). Dependent and passive-aggressive personality disorders. In A. M. Cooper, A. J. Frances, & M. H. Sacks (Eds.), *The personality disorders and neuroses* (pp. 283–289). Philadelphia: Lippincott.

Everly, G., Jr. (1995). The role of the critical incident stress debriefing (CISD) process in disaster counseling. *Journal of Mental Health Counseling, 17*(3), 278–290.

Eysenck, H. J. (1952). The effects of psychotherapy: An evaluation. *Journal of Consulting Psychology, 16,* 319–324.

Eysenck, H. J. (1966). *The effects of psychotherapy.* New York: International Science Press.

Fairburn, C. G. (1985). Cognitive-behavioral treatment for bulimia. In D. M. Garner and P. E. Garfinkel (Eds.), *Handbook of psychotherapy for anorexia and bulimia* (pp. 160–192). New York: Guilford Press.

Fairburn, C. G., Jones, R., Peveler, R., Carr, S., Hope, R., & O'Connor, M. (1993). Psychotherapy and bulimia nervosa: Longer term effects of interpersonal psychotherapy, behavior therapy, and cognitive behavior therapy. *Archives of General Psychiatry, 50,* 421–428.

Famularo, R., Kinscherff, R., & Fenton, T. (1990). Symptom differences in acute and chronic presentation of childhood posttraumatic stress disorder. *Child Abuse and Neglect, 14,* 439–444.

Fawzy, F. I., Fawzy, N. W., Hyun, C. S., Elashoff, R., Guthrie, D., Fahey, J. L., & Morton, D. L. (1993). Malignant melanoma. *Archives of General Psychiatry, 50*(9), 681–689.

Feinberg, M., & Carroll, B. J. (1984). Biological "markers" for endogenous depression. *Archives of General Psychiatry, 41,* 1080–1085.

Fenster, A. (1993). Reflections on using group therapy as a treatment modality—why, how, for whom and when: A guide to clinicians, supervisors and instructors. *Group, 17*(2), 84–101.

Fenton, W. S., & Cole, S. A. (1995). Psychosocial therapies of schizophrenia: Individual, group, and family. In G. O. Gabbard (Ed.), *Treatments of psychiatric disorders* (pp. 987–1018). Washington, DC: American Psychiatric Press.

Fisher, D., & Howells, K. (1993). Social relationships in sexual offenders. *Sexual and Marital Therapy, 8*(2), 123–136.

Fisher, G. L., & Harrison, T. C. (1997). *Substance abuse.* Needham Heights, MA: Allyn & Bacon.

Flach, F. (Ed.). (1987). *Diagnostics and psychopathology.* New York: Norton.

Foa, E. B., Davidson, J., & Rothbaum, B. O. (1995). Posttraumatic stress disorder. In G. O. Gabbard (Ed.), *Treatments of psychiatric disorders* (pp. 1499–1520). Washington, DC: American Psychiatric Press.

Foa, E. B., Franklin, M. E., Perry, K. J., & Herbert, J. D. (1996). Cognitive biases in generalized social phobia. *Journal of Abnormal Psychology, 105*(3), 433–439.

Foa, E. B., Hearst-Ikeda, D., & Perry, K. J. (1995). Evaluation of a brief cognitive-behavioral program for the prevention of chronic PTSD in recent assault victims. *Journal of Consulting and Clinical Psychology, 63,* 948–995.

Folks, D. G. (1995). Munchausen's syndrome and other factitious disorders. *Neurologic Clinics, 13*(2), 267–281.

Folks, D. G., & Houck, C. A. (1993). Somatoform disorders, factitious disorders, and malingering. In A. Stoudemire and B. S. Fogel (Eds.), *Psychiatric care of the medical patient* (pp. 267–287). New York: Oxford University Press.

Fonagy, P., & Target, M. (1994). The efficacy of psychoanalysis for children with disruptive disorders. *Journal of the American Academy of Child and Adolescent Psychiatry, 33*(1), 45–55.

Foreyt, J. P., & Kondo, A. T. (1985). Eating disorders. In M. Hersen and S. M. Turner (Eds.), *Diagnostic interviewing* (pp. 243–259). New York: Plenum.

Forrest, G. G. (1985). Psychodynamically oriented treatment of alcoholism and substance abuse. In T. E. Bratter and G. G. Forrest (Eds.), *Alcoholism and substance abuse* (pp. 307–336). New York: Free Press.

Fowler, R. C., Rich, C. L., & Young, D. (1986). Substance abuse in young cases. *Archives of General Psychiatry, 43,* 962–965.

Frances, A. J., Clarkin, J. F., & Perry, S. (1984). *Differential therapeutics in psychiatry.* New York: Brunner/Mazel.

Frances, R. J., & Allen, M. J. (1986). The interaction of substance-use disorders with nonpsychotic psychiatric disorders. In A. M. Cooper, A. J. Frances, & M. H. Sacks (Eds.), *The personality disorders and neuroses* (pp. 425–437). Philadelphia: Lippincott.

Frank, D., & Ziesel, S. H. (1988). Failure to thrive. *Pediatric Clinics of North America, 35*(6), 1187–1206.

Friedman, J. M., & Hogan, D. R. (1985). Sexual dysfunction: Low sexual desire. In D. H. Barlow (Ed.), *Clinical handbook of psychological disorders* (pp. 417–461). New York: Guilford Press.

Frosch, W. A., Frosch, J. P., & Frosch, J. (1986). The impulse disorders. In A. M. Cooper, A. J. Frances, & M. H. Sacks (Eds.), *The personality disorders and neuroses* (pp. 275–282). Philadelphia: Lippincott.

Fyer, A. J., & Klein, D. F. (1986). Agoraphobia, social phobia, and simple phobia. In A. M. Cooper, A. J. Frances, & M. H. Sacks (Eds.), *The personality disorders and neuroses* (pp. 339–352). Philadelphia: Lippincott.

Gabbard, G. O. (1990). *Psychodynamic psychiatry in clinical practice.* Washington, DC: American Psychiatric Press.

Gabbard, G. O. (Ed.). (1995). *Treatments of psychiatric disorders.* Washington, DC: American Psychiatric Press.

Gallant, D. (1995). Alcoholism. In G. O. Gabbard (Ed.), *Treatments of psychiatric disorders* (pp. 662–672). Washington, DC: American Psychiatric Press.

Garfield, S. L. (1986). Research on client variables in psychotherapy. In S. L. Garfield and A. E. Bergin (Eds.), *Handbook of psychotherapy and behavior change* (pp. 213–256). New York: Wiley.

Gelman, D., Gordon, J., Christian, J., Talbot, M., & Snow, K. (1992, March 10). When kids molest kids. *Newsweek,* pp. 29–31.

George, R. L. (1990). *Counseling the chemically dependent.* Upper Saddle River, NJ: Prentice Hall.

Getto, C. J., & Ochitill, H. (1982). Psychogenic pain disorder. In J. H. Greist, J. W. Jefferson, & R. L. Spitzer (Eds.), *Treatment of mental disorders* (pp. 277–286). New York: Oxford University Press.

Giesler, R. B., Josephs, R. A., & Swann, W. B., Jr. (1996). Self-verification in clinical depression: The desire for negative evaluation. *Journal of Abnormal Psychology, 105*(3), 358–368.

Gillberg, C. (1991). Outcome in autism and autistic-like conditions. Special Section: Longitudinal research. *Journal of the American Academy of Child and Adolescent Psychiatry, 30*(3), 375–382.

Gillberg, C., Gillberg, I. C., & Steffenberg, S. (1992). Siblings and parents of children with autism: A controlled population-based study. *Developmental Medicine & Child Neurology, 34*(5), 389–398.

Gilmore, M. M., & Kaufman, C. (1986). Dissociative disorders. In A. M. Cooper, A. J. Frances, & M. H. Sacks (Eds.), *The personality disorders and neuroses* (pp. 383–394). Philadelphia: Lippincott.

Glasser, W. (1990). *The control theory–reality therapy workbook.* Canoga Park, CA: Institute for Reality Therapy.

Glassner, B., & Haldipur, C. V. (1983). Life events and early and late onset of bipolar disorder. *American Journal of Psychiatry, 140*, 215–217.

Glauser, A. S. (1995). Cocaine use: Glimpses of heaven. *Journal of Mental Health Counseling, 17*(2), 230–237.

Glick, B., & Goldstein, A. P. (1987). Aggression replacement training. Special Issue: Counseling and violence. *Journal of Counseling and Development, 65*(7), 356–362.

Goldfried, M. R., Greenberg, L. S., & Marmar, C. R. (1990). Individual psychotherapy: Process and outcome. *Annual Review of Psychology, 41*, 659–688.

Golding, J. M., Smith, R., Jr., & Kashner, M. (1991). Does somatization disorder occur in men? *Archives of General Psychiatry, 48*, 231–235.

Goldstein, S. (1997). *Managing attention and learning disorders in late adolescence and adulthood: A guide for practitioners.* New York: Wiley.

Gomez-Perez, J. C., Marks, I. M., & Guttierrez-Fisac, J. L. (1994). Dysmorphophobia: Clinical features and outcomes with behavior therapy. *European Psychiatry, 9*, 229–235.

Goplerud, E., & Depue, R. A. (1985). Behavioral response to naturally occurring stress in cyclothymia and dysthymia. *Journal of Abnormal Psychology, 94*, 128–139.

Gorman, J. M., & Liebowitz, M. R. (1986). Panic and anxiety disorders. In A. M. Cooper, A. J. Frances, & M. H. Sacks (Eds.), *The personality disorders and neurosis* (pp. 325–337). Philadelphia: Lippincott.

Gotlib, I. H., & Colby, C. A. (1987). *Treatment of depression.* New York: Pergamon Press.

Grandin, T. (1995). *Thinking in pictures and other reports from my life with autism.* New York: Doubleday.

Green, R. (1995). Gender identity disorder in children. In G. O. Gabbard (Ed.), *Treatments of psychiatric disorders* (pp. 2001–2014). Washington, DC: American Psychiatric Press.

Green, R., & Herget, M. (1991). Outcomes of systemic/strategic team consultation. III: The importance of therapist warmth and active structuring. *Family Process, 30*, 321–336.

Greenspan, M., & Kulish, N. M. (1985). Factors in premature termination in long-term psychotherapy. *Psychotherapy: Theory, Research and Practice, 22*, 75–82.

Greist, J. H., & Jefferson, J. W. (1996). Obsessive-compulsive disorder. In G. O. Gabbard and S. D. Atkinson (Eds.), *Synopsis of treatments of psychiatric disorders* (pp. 627–635). Washington, DC: American Psychiatric Press.

Grizenko, N., Papineau, D., & Sayegh, L. (1993). Effectiveness of a multimodal day treatment program for children with disruptive behavior problems. *Journal of the American Academy of Child and Adolescent Psychiatry, 32*(1), 127–134.

Groopman, L. C., & Cooper, A. M. (1995). Narcissistic personality disorder. In G. O. Gabbard (Ed.), *Treatments of psychiatric disorders* (pp. 2327–2347). Washington, DC: American Psychiatric Press.

Guerney, L. (1993). Two by two: A filial therapy case study. In T. Kottman and C. Schaefer (Eds.), *Play therapy in action: A casebook for practitioners.* Northvale, NJ: Aronson.

Gunderson, J. G. (1984). *Borderline personality disorder.* Washington, DC: American Psychiatric Press.

Gunderson, J. G. (1988). Personality disorders. In A. M. Nicholi Jr. (Ed.), *The new Harvard guide to psychiatry* (pp. 337–357). Cambridge, MA: Harvard University Press.

Gunderson, J. G., & Gabbard, G. O. (1995). Personality disorders: Introduction. In G. O. Gabbard (Ed.), *Treatments of psychiatric disorders* (pp. 2243–2247). Washington, DC: American Psychiatric Press.

Gunderson, J. G., & Links, P. (1995). Borderline personality disorders. In G. O. Gabbard (Ed.), *Treatments of psychiatric disorders* (pp. 2291–2309). Washington, DC: American Psychiatric Press.

Gustafson, Y., Berggren, D., Bucht, B., Norberf, A., Hansson, L. I., & Winblad, B. (1988). Acute confusional states in elderly patients treated for femoral neck fracture. *Journal of the American Geriatrics Society, 36,* 525–530.

Gutsch, K. U. (1988). *Psychotherapeutic approaches to specific DSM-III-R categories.* Springfield, IL: Thomas.

Gwirtsman, H. E. (1994). Dysthymia and chronic depressive states: Diagnosis and pharmacotherapeutic considerations. *Psychopharmacology Bulletin, 30*(1), 45–51.

Hadley, N. H. (1994). *Elective mutism: A handbook for educators, counselors and health care professionals.* Norwell, MA: Kluwer.

Hafner, R. J. (1984). Predicting the effects on husbands of behaviour therapy for wives' agoraphobia. *Behaviour Research and Therapy, 22,* 217–226.

Hallowell, E. M., & Ratey, J. J. (1994). *Driven to distraction.* New York: Pantheon Books.

Harbeck-Weber, C., & Peterson, L. (1996). Health-related disorders. In E. J. Mash and R. A. Barkley (Eds.), *Child psychopathology.* New York: Guilford Press.

Harbin, H. T. (1981). Family therapy with personality disorders. In J. R. Lion (Ed.), *Personality disorders: Diagnosis and management.* Baltimore: Williams & Wilkins.

Harmon, T., Nelson, R., & Hayes, S. (1980). Self-monitoring of mood versus activity by depressed clients. *Journal of Consulting and Clinical Psychology, 48,* 30–38.

Harris, E. L., Noyes, R., Jr., Crowe, R. R., & Chaudhry, D. R. (1983). Family study of agoraphobia. *Archives of General Psychiatry, 40,* 1061–1064.

Harris, J. C. (1995). Psychiatric disorders in mentally retarded persons. In G. O. Gabbard (Ed.), *Treatments of psychiatric disorders* (pp. 95–122). Washington, DC: American Psychiatric Press.

Hart, E. L., Lahey, B. B., Loeber, R., & Hanson, K. S. (1994). Criterion validity of informants in the diagnosis of disruptive behavior disorders in children: A preliminary study. *Journal of Consulting and Clinical Psychology, 62*(2), 410–414.

Hayes, A. M., Castonguay, L. G., & Goldfried, M. R. (1996). Effectiveness of targeting the vulnerability factors of depression in cognitive therapy. *Journal of Consulting and Clinical Psychology, 64*(3), 623–627.

Heather, N., & Richmond, R. (1992). Research into brief interventions for excessive alcohol consumers and cigarette smokers in Australia. *The Journal of Drug Issues, 22*(3), 641–660.

Hecker, J., & Thorpe, G. (1992). *Agoraphobia and panic.* Needham Heights, MA: Allyn & Bacon.

Hegarty, M. P. (1997, April). Use of inhalants among teens on the rise. *Counseling Today,* pp. 10, 13.

Henggeler, S., & Borduin, C. M. (1990). *Family therapy and beyond: A multisystemic approach to teaching the behavior problems of children and adolescents.* Pacific Grove, CA: Brooks/Cole.

Hersen, M., & Ammerman, R. T. (1995). *Advanced abnormal child psychology.* Hillsdale, NJ: Erlbaum.

Herzog, D. B., Norman, D. K., Gordon, C., & Pepose, M. (1984). Sexual conflict and eating disorders in 27 males. *American Journal of Psychiatry, 141,* 989–990.

Hess, R. S., & Street, E. M. (1991). The effect of acculturation on the relationship of counselor ethnicity and client ratings. *Journal of Counseling Psychology, 38*(1), 71–75.

Hill, D. (1970). Outpatient management of passive-dependent women. *Hospital and Community Psychiatry, 21,* 402–405.

Hirschfeld, M. A., & Cross, C. K. (1982). Epidemiology of affective disorders. *Archives of General Psychiatry, 39,* 35–46.

Hirschfeld, R.M.A., Klerman, G. L., Clayton, P. J., & Keller, M. B. (1983). Personality and depression. *Archives of General Psychiatry, 40,* 993–998.

Hoehn-Saric, R., Borkovec, T. D., & Nemiah, J. C. (1995). Generalized anxiety disorder. In G. O. Gabbard (Ed.), *Treatments of psychiatric disorders* (pp. 1537–1568). Washington, DC: American Psychiatric Press.

Hoffman, J. J. (1985). Client factors related to premature termination of psychotherapy. *Psychotherapy: Theory, Research and Practice, 22,* 83–85.

Hogarty, G. E., Anderson, C. M., Reiss, D. J., Kornblith, S. J., Greenwald, D. P., & Javna, C. D. (1986). Family psychoeducation, social skills training, and maintenance chemotherapy in the aftercare treatment of schizophrenia. *Archives of General Psychiatry, 43,* 633–642.

Hoglend, P., Sorlie, T., Heyerdahl, O., Sorbye, O., & Amlo, S. (1993). Brief dynamic psychotherapy: Patient suitability, treatment length and outcome. *Journal of Psychotherapy: Practice and Research, 2,* 230–241.

Holland, R., Moretti, M. M., Verlaan, V., & Peterson, S. (1993). Attachment and conduct disorder: The response program. *Canadian Journal of Psychiatry, 38*(6), 420–431.

Hollander, E., Neville, D., Frenkel, M., Josephson, S., & Liebowitz, M. R. (1992). Body dysmorphic disorder: Diagnostic issues and related disorders. *Psychosomatics 33*(2), 156–165.

Hollon, S. D., & Beck, A. T. (1986). Cognitive and cognitive-behavioral therapies. In S. L. Garfield and A. E. Bergin (Eds.), *Handbook of psychotherapy and behavior change* (pp. 443–482). New York: Wiley.

Hollon, S. D., & Fawcett, J. (1995). Combined medication and psychotherapy. In G. O. Gabbard (Ed.), *Treatments of psychiatric disorders* (pp. 1222–1236). Washington, DC: American Psychiatric Press.

Horowitz, M. J., Marmar, C. R., Krupnick, J. L., Wilner, N., Kaltreider, N., & Wallerstein, R. S. (1984). *Personality styles and brief psychotherapy.* New York: Basic Books.

Horowitz, M. J., Marmar, C. R., Weiss, D. S., De Witt, K. N., & Rosenbaum, R. (1984). Brief psychotherapy of bereavement reactions. *Archives of General Psychiatry, 41,* 438–448.

Horvath, A. O., & Symonds, B. D. (1991). Relation between working alliance and outcome in psychotherapy: A meta-analysis. *Journal of Counseling Psychology, 38*(2), 139–149.

Howard, G. S., Nance, D. W., & Myers, P. (1987). *Adaptive counseling and therapy.* San Francisco: Jossey-Bass.

Howard, K. I., Kopta, S. M., Krause, M. S., & Orlinsky, D. E. (1986). The dose-effect relationship in psychotherapy. *American Psychologist, 41,* 159–164.

Howland, R. H., & Thase, M. E. (1995). A comprehensive review of cyclothymic disorder. *Journal of Nervous and Mental Disease, 181*(8), 485–493.

Hser, Y. (1995). Drug treatment counselor practices and effectiveness. *Evaluation Review, 19*(4), 389–408.

Hudson, J. I., Pope, H. G., Yurgelun-Todd, D., & Jonas, J. M. (1987). A controlled study of lifetime prevalence of affective and other psychiatric disorders in bulimic outpatients. *American Journal of Psychiatry, 144,* 1283–1287.

Hurley, A. D. (1989). Individual psychotherapy with mentally retarded individuals: A review and call for research. *Research in Developmental Disabilities, 10*(3), 261–275.

Hyman, R. B., & Woog, P. (1989). Flexibility, the dominant characteristic of effective helpers: A factor analytic study. *Measurement and Evaluation in Counseling and Development, 22*(3), 151–157.

Ialongo, N., Horn, W., Pascoe, J., Greenberg, G., Packard, T., Lopez, M., Wagner, A., & Puttler, L. (1993). The effects of a multimodal intervention with attention-deficit hyperactivity disorder children: A 9–month follow-up. *Journal of the American Academy of Child and Adolescent Psychiatry, 32*(1), 182–189.

Ivey, A. E., & Rigazio-Digilio, S. A. (1991). Toward a developmental practice of mental health counseling: Strategies for training, practice, and political unity. *Journal of Mental Health Counseling, 13*(1), 21–36.

Jacobsen, F. M. (1993). Low-dose valproate: A new treatment for cyclothymia, mild rapid cycling disorders, and premenstrual syndrome. *Journal of Clinical Psychiatry, 54*(6), 229–234.

Jacobson, A., & McKinney, W. T. (1982). Affective disorders. In J. H. Greist, J. W. Jefferson, & R. L. Spitzer (Eds.), *Treatment of mental disorders* (pp.184–233). New York: Oxford University Press.

Jarrett, R. B., & Rush, A. J. (1986). Psychotherapeutic approaches for depression. In J. E. Helzer and S. B. Guze (Eds.), *Psychoses, affective disorders, and dementia* (pp. 209–243). New York: Basic Books.

Jefferson, J. W., & Ochitill, H. (1982). Factitious disorders. In J. H. Greist, J. W. Jefferson, & R. L. Spitzer (Eds.), *Treatment of mental disorders* (pp. 387–397). New York: Oxford University Press.

Johnson, C., & Flach, A. (1985). Family characteristics of 105 patients with bulimia. *American Journal of Psychiatry, 142,* 1321–1324.

Johnson, D. (1995). Specific developmental disorders. In M. Hersen and R. T. Ammerman (Eds.), *Treatments of psychiatric disorders* (pp. 95–122). Washington, DC: American Psychiatric Press.

Johnson, J. H., Rasbury, W. C., & Siegel, L. J. (1986). *Approaches to child treatment: Introduction to theory, research, and practice.* New York: Pergamon Press.

Johnson, V. E. (1986). *Intervention: How to help someone who doesn't want help. A step-by-step guide for families and friends of chemically dependent persons.* Minneapolis: Johnson Institute.

Johnson, W. B., Devries, R., Ridley, C. R., Pettorini, D., & Peterson, D. R. (1994). The comparative efficacy of Christian and secular rational-emotive therapy with Christian clients. *Journal of Psychology and Theology, 2,* 130–140.

Judd, L. L. (1994). Social phobia: A clinical overview. *Journal of Clinical Psychiatry, 55*(6), 5–9.

Kadera, S. W., Lambert, M. J., & Andrews, A. A. (1996). How much therapy is really enough? *Journal of Psychotherapy Practice and Research, 5,* 132–151.

Kales, J. D., Soldatos, C. R., & Kales, A. (1982). Diagnosis and treatment of sleep disorders. In J. H. Greist, J. W. Jefferson, & R. L. Spitzer (Eds.), *Treatment of mental disorders* (pp. 473–500). New York: Oxford University Press.

Kaplan, H., Sadock, B., & Grebb, J. (1994). *Synopsis of psychiatry* (7th ed.). Baltimore: Williams & Wilkins.

Kaplan, H. S. (1986). Psychosexual dysfunctions. In A. M. Cooper, A. J. Frances, & M. H. Sacks (Eds.), *The personality disorders and neuroses* (pp. 467–479). Philadelphia: Lippincott.

Kaplan, H. S. (1995). Sexual desire disorders. In G. O. Gabbard (Ed.), *Treatments of psychiatric disorders* (pp. 1843–1866). Washington, DC: American Psychiatric Press.

Karasu, T. (1982). Psychotherapy and pharmacotherapy: Toward an integrative model. *American Journal of Psychiatry, 139,* 1102–1113.

Karasu, T. (1986). The specificity versus nonspecifity dilemma: Toward identifying therapeutic change agents. *American Journal of Psychiatry, 143,* 687–695.

Kaufman, G. B., Jr., & Aronoff, G. M. (1983). The use of psychomotor therapy in the treatment of chronic pain. *Psychotherapy: Theory, Research, and Practice, 20,* 449–456.

Kazdin, A. E. (1986). The evaluation of psychotherapy: Research design and methodology. In S. L. Garfield and A. E. Bergin (Eds.), *Handbook of psychotherapy and behavior change* (3rd ed., pp. 23–68). New York: Wiley.

Kazdin, A. E. (1989). Conduct disorder. *Psychiatric Hospital, 20*(4), 153–158.

Kazdin, A. E. (1990). Premature termination from treatment among children referred for antisocial behavior. *Journal of Child Psychology and Psychiatry, 3,* 412–425.

Kazdin, A. E. (1993). Psychotherapy for children and adolescents: Current progress and future research directions. *American Psychologist, 48*(6), 644–657.

Kazdin, A. E. (1995). *Conduct disorders in childhood and adolescence.* Thousand Oaks, CA: Sage.

Kazdin, A. E. (1997). Psychosocial treatments for conduct disorder in children. *Journal of Child Psychology and Psychiatry and Allied Professions, 38*(2), 161–178.

Kazdin, A. E., Siegel, T. C., & Bass, D. (1992). Cognitive problem-solving skills training and parent management training in the treatment of antisocial behavior in children. *Journal of Consulting and Clinical Psychology, 60*(5), 733–747.

Kearney, C. A., & Silverman, W. K. (1995). Anxiety disorders. In V. B. Van Hasselt and M. Hersen (Eds.), *Handbook of adolescent psychopathology* (pp. 435–465). San Francisco: New Lexington Press.

Kellam, S. G., Werthamer-Larsson, L., Dolan, L. J., Brown, C. H., Mayer, L. S., Rebok, G. W., Anthony, J. C., Laudolff, J., & Edelsohn, G. (1991). Developmental epidemiologically based preventive trials: Baseline modeling of early target behaviors and depressive symptoms. *American Journal of Community Psychology, 19*(4), 563–584.

Keller, M. B., Lavori, P. W., Coryell, W., & Endicott, J. (1993). Bipolar I: A five-year prospective follow-up. *Journal of Nervous and Mental Disease, 181*(4), 238–245.

Keller, M. B., Lavori, P. W., Endicott, J., Coryell, W., & Klerman, G. L. (1983). "Double depression": Two-year follow-up. *American Journal of Psychiatry, 140,* 689–694.

Kellner, R. (1982). Psychotherapeutic strategies in hypochondriasis: A clinical study. *American Journal of Psychotherapy, 36,* 146–157.

Kellner, R. (1985). Functional somatic symptoms and hypochondriasis. *Archives of General Psychiatry, 42,* 821–833.

Kelly, K. R. (1996). Review of clinical mental health counseling process and outcome research. *Journal of Mental Health Counseling, 18*(4), 358–375.

Kendall, P. (1993). Cognitive-behavioral therapies with youth: Guiding theory, current status, and emerging developments. *Journal of Consulting and Clinical Psychology, 61*(2), 235–247.

Kendall, P. C., & Lipman, A. J. (1991). Psychological and pharmacological therapy: Methods and modes for comparative outcome research. *Journal of Consulting and Clinical Psychology, 59*(1), 78–87.

Kendell, R. E. (1986). Schizophrenia: Clinical features. In J. E. Helzer and S. B. Guze (Eds.), *Psychoses, affective disorders, and dementia* (pp. 25–44). New York: Basic Books.

Kennedy, S. H., & Garfinkel, P. E. (1992). Advances in diagnosis and treatment of anorexia nervosa and bulimia nervosa. *Canadian Journal of Psychiatry, 37*(5), 309–315.

Kernberg, O. F. (1985). *Borderline conditions and pathological narcissism.* Northvale, NJ: Aronson.

Kernberg, O. F. (1986). Hysterical and histrionic personality disorders. In A. M. Cooper, A. J. Frances, & M. H. Sacks (Eds.), *The personality disorders and neuroses* (pp. 231–241). Philadelphia: Lippincott.

Kessler, R. C., McGonagle, K. A., Zhao, S., Nelson, C. B., Hughes, M., Eshleman, S., Wittchen, H., & Kendles, K. S. (1994). Lifetime and 12–month prevalence of *DSM-III-R* psychiatric disorders in the United States. *Archives of General Psychiatry, 51,* 8–18.

King, R. A., & Noshpitz, J. D. (1991). *Pathways of growth: Essentials of child psychiatry.* New York: Wiley.

King, S. A., & Stoudemire, A. (1995). Pain disorders. In G. O. Gabbard (Ed.), *Treatments of psychiatric disorders* (pp. 1755–1782). Washington, DC: American Psychiatric Press.

Kinnunen, T., Doherty, K., Militello, F. S., & Garvey, A. J. (1996). Depression and smoking cessation: Characteristics of depressed smokers and effects of nicotine replacement. *Journal of Consulting and Clinical Psychology, 64*(4), 791–798.

Kinzl, J. F., Mangweth, B., Traweger, C., & Biebl, W. (1996). Sexual dysfunction in males: Significance of adverse childhood experiences. *Child Abuse and Neglect, 20*(8), 759–766.

Klein, R. G. (1993). Clinical efficacy of methylphenidate in children and adolescents. *Encephale, 19*(2), 89–93.

Klein, R. G. (1994). Anxiety disorders. In M. Rutter, E. Taylor, & L. Hersov (Eds.), *Child and adolescent psychiatry: Modern approaches* (pp. 351–374). Cambridge, MA: Blackwell.

Klein, R. G., Koplewicz, H. S., & Kanner, A. (1992). Imipramine treatment of children with separation anxiety disorder. Special Section: New developments in pediatric psychopharmacology. *Journal of the American Academy of Child and Adolescent Psychiatry, 31*(1), 21–28.

Klein, R. G., & Last, C. G. (1989). *Anxiety disorders in children.* Thousand Oaks, CA: Sage.

Klerman, G. L. (1986). Drugs and psychotherapy. In S. L. Garfield and A. E. Bergin (Eds.), *Handbook of psychotherapy and behavior change* (pp. 777–818). New York: Wiley.

Klerman, G. L., Dimascio, A., & Weissman, M. M. (1974). Treatment of depression by drugs and psychotherapy. *American Journal of Psychiatry, 131,* 186–191.

Klerman, G. L., Lavori, P. W., Rice, J., Reich, T., Endicott, J., Andreasen, N. C., Keller, M. B., & Hirschfield, R.M.A. (1985). Birth-cohort trends in rates of major depressive disorder among relatives of patients with affective disorders. *Archives of General Psychiatry, 42,* 689–693.

Klerman, G. L., Weissman, M. M., Rounsaville, B. J., & Chevron, E. S. (1984). *Interpersonal psychotherapy of depression.* New York: Basic Books.

Kluft, R. P. (1987). Making the diagnosis of multiple personality disorder. In F. Flach (Ed.), *Diagnostics and psychopathology* (pp. 207–225). New York: Norton.

Kluft, R. P. (1995). Dissociative identity disorder. In G. O. Gabbard (Ed.), *Treatments of psychiatric disorders* (pp. 1599–1632). Washington, DC: American Psychiatric Press.

Kluft, R. P. (1996). Treating the traumatic memories of patients with dissociative identity disorder. *American Journal of Psychiatry, 153*(7), 103–110.

Kocsis, J. H., & Mann, J. J. (1986). Drug treatment of personality disorders and neuroses. In A. M. Cooper, A. J. Frances, & M. H. Sacks (Eds.), *The personality disorders and neuroses* (pp. 129–137). Philadelphia: Lippincott.

Koeningsberg, H. W., Kaplan, R. D., Gilmore, M. M., & Cooper, A. M. (1985). The relationship between syndrome and personality disorder in *DSM-III:* Experience with 2,462 patients. *American Journal of Psychiatry, 142,* 207–212.

Kohut, H. (1971). *The analysis of self.* Madison, CT: International Universities Press.

Koponen, H., Lepola, U., & Leinonen, E. (1995). Dysthymia: A review. *Nordic Journal of Psychiatry, 49*(2), 129–132.

Kopta, S. M., Howard, K. I., Lowry, J. L., & Beutler, L. E. (1994). Patterns of symptomatic recovery in psychotherapy. *Journal of Consulting and Clinical Psychology, 62,* 1009–1016.

Kornblith, S. H., Rehm, L. P., O'Hara, M. W., & Lamparski, D. M. (1983). The contribution of self-reinforcement training and behavioral assignments to the efficacy of self-control therapy for depression. *Cognitive Therapy and Research, 7,* 499–528.

Koss, M. P., & Butcher, J. N. (1986). Research on brief psychotherapy. In S. L. Garfield and A. E. Bergin (Eds.), *Handbook of psychotherapy and behavior change* (pp. 627–670). New York: Wiley.

Kosten, T. R., Rounsaville, B. J., & Kleber, H. D. (1986). A 2.5-year follow-up of depression, life crises, and treatment effects on abstinence among opioid addicts. *Archives of General Psychiatry, 43,* 733–738.

Kottman, T., & Schaefer, C. (Eds). (1993). *Play therapy in action: A casebook for practitioners.* Northvale, NJ: Aronson.

Kovacs, M. (1992). *Children's Depression Inventory.* North Tonawanda, NY: Multi-Health Systems.

Kovacs, M., Akiskal, S., Gatsonis, C., & Parrone, P. (1994). Childhood-onset dysthymic disorder. *Archives of General Psychiatry, 51,* 365–374.

Kronenberger, W. G., & Meyer, R. G. (1996). *The child clinician's handbook.* Needham Heights, MA: Allyn & Bacon.

Krupnick, J. L. (1996). The role of therapeutic alliance in psychotherapy and pharmacotherapy outcome: Findings in the National Institutes of Mental Health treatment of depression collaborative research program. *Journal of Consulting and Clinical Psychology, 64,* 532–539.

Lambert, M. J. (1982). *The effects of psychotherapy.* New York: Human Sciences Press.

Lambert, M. J., & Bergin, A. E. (1994). The effectiveness of psychotherapy. In A. E. Bergin and S. L. Garfield (Eds.), *Handbook of psychotherapy and behavior change* (4th ed., pp. 143–189). New York: Wiley.

Lambert, M. J., & Cattani-Thompson, K. (1996). Current findings regarding the effectiveness of counseling: Implications for practice. *Journal of Counseling and Development, 74,* 601–608.

Lambert, M. J., Shapiro, D. A., & Bergin, A. E. (1986). The effectiveness of psychotherapy. In S. L. Garfield and A. E. Bergin (Eds.), *Handbook of psychotherapy and behavior change* (pp. 157–211). New York: Wiley.

Lars-Goran, O. (1987). Age of onset in different phobias. *Journal of Abnormal Psychology, 96,* 223–229.

Last, C. G., Perrin, S., Hersen, M., & Kazdin, A. E. (1992). *DSM-III-R* anxiety disorders in children: Sociodemographic and clinical characteristics. *Journal of the American Academy of Child and Adolescent Psychiatry, 31,* 1070–1076.

Last, C. G., Strauss, C., & Francis, G. (1987). Comorbidity among childhood anxiety disorders. *Journal of Nervous and Mental Disease, 175,* 726–730.

Lavin, M., & Rifkin, A. (1993). Diagnosis and pharmacotherapy of conduct disorder. *Progress in Neuro-psychopharmacology and Biological Psychiatry, 17*(6), 875–885.

Lazarus, A. A. (1989). *The practice of multimodal therapy.* Baltimore: Johns Hopkins University Press.

Leckman, J. F., & Cohen, D. J. (1994). Tic disorders. In M. Rutter, E. Taylor, & L. Hersov (Eds.), *Child and adolescent psychiatry: Modern approaches* (pp. 455–466). Cambridge, MA: Blackwell.

Leigh, G. (1985). Psychosocial factors in the etiology of substance abuse. In T. E. Bratter and G. G. Forrest (Eds.), *Alcoholism and substance abuse* (pp. 3–48). New York: Free Press.

Levine, M. D. (1975). Children with encopresis: A descriptive analysis. *Pediatrics, 56,* 412–416.

Lewinsohn, P. M., Clarke, G. N., Hops, H., & Andrews, J. (1990). Cognitive behavioral group treatment of depression in adolescents. *Behavior Therapy, 21,* 385–401.

Lewinsohn, P. M., & Hoberman, H. M. (1982). Behavioural and cognitive approaches. In E. S. Paykel (Ed.), *Handbook of affective disorders* (pp. 338–345). New York: Guilford Press.

Lewinsohn, P. M., Sullivan, M., & Grosscup, S. (1980). Changing reinforcing events: An approach to the treatment of depression. *Psychotherapy: Theory, Research and Practice, 17,* 322–334.

Lewis, J. A. (1994). *Addictions.* Gaithersburg, MD: Aspen.

Lewis, M. (1991). *Child and adolescent psychiatry.* Baltimore: Williams & Wilkins.

Lieberman, A. F., & Zeanah, C. H. (1995). Disorders of attachment in infancy. *Child and Adolescent Psychiatric Clinics of North America, 4,* 571–587.

Liebowitz, M. R., Gorman, J. M., Fyer, A. J., & Klein, D. F. (1985). Social phobia: Review of a neglected anxiety disorder. *Archives of General Psychiatry, 41,* 729–736.

Lilienfeld, S. O., Van Valkenburg, C., Larntz, K., & Akiskal, H. S. (1986). The relation of histrionic personality disorder to antisocial personality and somatization disorders. *American Journal of Psychiatry, 143,* 718–722.

Linden, W. (1981). Exposure treatments for focal phobias. *Archives of General Psychiatry, 38,* 769–775.

Linehan, M. M. (1993). *Skills training manual for treating borderline personality disorder.* New York: Guilford Press.

Linehan, M. M., & Kehrer, C. A. (1993). Borderline personality disorder. In D. A. Barlow (Ed.), *Clinical handbook of psychological disorders* (2nd ed., pp. 396–441). New York: Guilford Press.

Linscheid, T. R. (1992). Eating problems in children. In C. E. Walker and M. C. Roberts (Eds.), *Handbook of clinical child psychology* (pp. 451–473). New York: Wiley.

Lion, J. R. (1981a). Countertransference and other psychotherapy issues. In W. H. Reid (Ed.), *The treatment of antisocial syndromes.* New York: Van Nostrand Reinhold.

Lion, J. R. (Ed.) (1981b). *Personality disorders: Diagnosis and management.* Baltimore: Williams & Wilkins.

Lion, J. R., & Scheinberg, A. W. (1995). Disorders of impulse control. In G. O. Gabbard (Ed.), *Treatments of psychiatric disorders* (pp. 2457–2468). Washington, DC: American Psychiatric Press.

Lipowski, Z. J. (1989). Current concepts-geriatrics: Delirium in the elderly patient. *New England Journal of Medicine, 320*(9), 578–582.

Lipsitz, J. D., Martin, L. Y., Mannuzza, S., Chapman, T. F., Liebowitz, M. R., Klein, D. F., & Fyer, A. J. (1994). Childhood separation anxiety disorder in patients with adult anxiety disorders. *American Journal of Psychiatry, 151*(6), 927–929.

Littrell, J. M., Malia, J. A., & Vanderwood, J. (1995). Single session brief counseling in a high school. *Journal of Counseling and Development, 73,* 451–458.

Livingston, R. (1991). Anxiety disorders. In M. Lewis (Ed.), *Child and adolescent psychiatry: A comprehensive textbook* (pp. 673–685). Baltimore: Williams & Wilkins.

Lochman, J. E., White, K. J., & Wayland, K. W. (1991). Cognitive-behavioral assessment and treatment with aggressive children. In P. C. Kendall (Ed.), *Child and adolescent therapy: Cognitive behavioral procedures* (pp. 25–65). New York: Guilford Press.

Loeber, R., Green, S. M., Keenan, L., & Lahey, B. B. (1995). Which boys will fare worse? Early predictors of the onset of conduct disorder in a six-year longitudinal study. *Journal of the American Academy of Child and Adolescent Psychiatry, 34*(4), 499–509.

Loening-Baucke, V., Desch, L., & Wolraich, M. (1988). Biofeedback training for patients with myelomeningocele and fecal incontinence. *Developmental Medicine and Child Neurology, 30*(6), 781–790.

Loge, D., Staton, R. D., & Beatty, W. W. (1990). Performance of children with ADHD on tests sensitive to frontal lobe dysfunction. *Journal of the American Academy of Child and Adolescent Psychiatry, 29*(4), 540–545.

Longabough, R., Fowler, D. R., Stout, R., & Kriebel, G., Jr. (1983). Validation of a problem-focused nomenclature. *Archives of General Psychiatry, 40*, 453–461.

Lonigan, C. J., Shannon, M. P., Finch, A. J., Daugherty, T. K., & Taylor, C. M. (1991). Children's reactions to a natural disaster: Symptom severity and degree of exposure. *Advances in Behavior Research and Therapy, 13*(3), 135–154.

Lo Piccolo, J., & Stock, W. E. (1986). Treatment of sexual dysfunctions. *Journal of Consulting and Clinical Psychology, 54*, 158–167.

Loranger, A. W. (1984). Sex difference in age at onset of schizophrenia. *Archives of General Psychiatry, 41*, 157–161.

Loranger, A. W., & Tulis, E. H. (1985). Family history of alcoholism in borderline personality disorder. *Archives of General Psychiatry, 42*, 153–157.

Lord, C., & Rutter, M. (1994). Autism and pervasive developmental disorders. In M. Rutter, E. Taylor, & L. Hersov (Eds.), *Child and adolescent psychiatry: Modern approaches* (pp. 569–593). Cambridge, MA: Blackwell.

Lovaas, O. I. (1987). Behavioral treatment and normal educational and intellectual functioning in young autistic children. *Journal of Abnormal Child Psychology, 20*, 555–566.

Lowenstein, R. J. (1995). Dissociative amnesia and dissociative fugue. In G. O. Gabbard (Ed.), *Treatments of psychiatric disorders* (pp. 1569–1598). Washington, DC: American Psychiatric Press.

Luborsky, L., Barber, J. P., & Crits-Cristoph, P. (1990). Theory based research for understanding the process of dynamic psychotherapy. *Journal of Consulting and Clinical Psychology, 58*, 281–287.

Luborsky, L., Diguer, L., Cacciola, J., Barber, J. P., Moras, K., Schmidt, K., & De Rubeis, R. J. (1996). Factors in outcomes of short-term dynamic psychotherapy for chronic depression versus nonchronic depression. *Journal of Psychotherapy Practice and Research, 5*, 152–159.

Luborsky, L., McLellan, A. T., Woody, G. E., O'Brien, C. P., & Auerbach, A. (1985). Therapist success and its determinants. *Archives of General Psychiatry, 42*, 602–611.

Luborsky, L., Singer, B., & Luborsky, L. (1975). Comparative studies of psychotherapies. *Archives of General Psychiatry, 32*, 995–1008.

Lyddon, W. J. (1989). Personal epistemology and preference of counseling. *Journal of Counseling Psychology, 36*(4), 423–429.

Lyons-Ruth, K., Zeanah, C. H., & Benoit, D. (1996). Disorder and risk for disorder during infancy and toddlerhood. In E. J. Mash and R. A. Barkley (Eds.), *Child psychopathology* (pp. 457–491). New York: Guilford Press.

Maloney, M. J., McGuire, J. B., & Daniels, S. R. (1988). Reliability testing of a children's version of the Eating Attitude Test. *Journal of the American Academy of Child and Adolescent Psychiatry, 27*(5), 541–543.

Maniacci, M. P. (1991). Guidelines for developing social interest with clients in psychiatric day hospitals. *Individual Psychology Journal of Adlerian Theory Research and Practice, 47*(2), 177–188.

Mannuzza, S., Klein, R. G., Bessler, A., Malloy, P., & La Padula, M. (1993). Adult outcome of hyperactive boys: Educational achievement, occupational rank, and psychiatric status. *Archives of General Psychiatry, 50*(7), 565–576.

Manschreck, T. C. (1992). Delusional disorders: Clinical concepts and diagnostic strategies. *Psychiatric Annals, 22*(5), 241–251.

March, J. S., & Leonard, H. L. (1996). Obsessive-compulsive disorder in children and adolescents: A review of the past 10 years. *Journal of the American Academy of Child and Adolescent Psychiatry, 34*(10), 1265–1273.

Marchi, M., & Cohen, P. (1990). Early childhood eating behaviors and adolescent eating disorders. *Journal of the American Academy of Child and Adolescent Psychiatry, 29*, 112–117.

Margolis, S. (1997). The depression that won't quit. *Health After 50, 8*(12), 3.

Markowitz, J. C. (1994). Psychotherapy for dysthymia: Is it effective? *American Journal of Psychiatry, 151*, 1114–1121.

Marks, I. M., Swinton, R. P., Basoglu, M., Kuch, K., Noshirvani, H., Kuch, K., O'Sullivan, G., Lellio, P. T., Kirby, M., McNamee, G., Sengun, S., & Wickwire, K. (1993). Alprazolam and exposure alone and combined in panic disorder with agoraphobia. *Journal of Psychiatry, 162*, 776–787.

Marmar, C. R., & Freeman, M. (1988). Brief dynamic psychotherapy of post-traumatic stress disorders: Management of narcissistic regression. *Journal of Traumatic Stress, 1*, 323–337.

Marshall, W. L. (1985). The effects of variable exposure in flooding therapy. *Behavior Therapy, 16*, 117–135.

Marshall, W. L. (1993). The role of attachments, intimacy, and loneliness in the etiology and maintenance of sexual offending. *Sexual and Marital Therapy, 8*(2), 109–121.

Martin, R. L. (1994). *DSM-IV* diagnostic options for conversion disorder: Proposed autonomic arousal disorder and pseudocyesis. In T. A. Widiger, A. J. Frances, & H. A. Pincus (Eds.), *DSM-IV sourcebook* (pp. 892–914). Washington, DC: American Psychiatric Press.

Martin, R. L., & Yutzy, S. H. (1994). Somatoform disorders. In R. E. Hales, S. C. Yudofsky, & J. A. Talbott (Eds.), *Textbook of Psychiatry* (2nd ed., pp. 591–622).Washington, DC: American Psychiatric Press.

Martin-Causey, T., & Hinkle, J. C. (1995). Multimodal therapy with an aggressive preadolescent: A demonstration of effectiveness and accountability. *Journal of Counseling and Development, 73*(3), 305–310.

Marttunen, M. J., Aro, H. M., Henriksson, M. M., & Lonnqvist, J. K. (1994). Adolescent suicides with adjustment disorders or no psychiatric diagnosis. *European Child and Adolescent Psychiatry, 3*(2), 101–110.

Marziali, E. (1992). Borderline personality disorder: Diagnosis, etiology, and treatment. *Smith College Studies in Social Work, 62*(3), 205–227.

Mash, E. J., & Barkley, R. A. (1996). *Child psychopathology.* New York: Guilford Press.

Massie, M. J., & Holland, J. C. (1990). Depression and the cancer patient. *Journal of Clinical Psychiatry, 51,* 12–19.

Masters, W. H., & Johnson, V. E. (1970). *Human sexual inadequacy.* Boston: Little, Brown.

Masterson, J. F. (1981). *The narcissistic and borderline disorders.* New York: Brunner/Mazel.

Mattick, R. P., & Peters, L. (1988). Treatment of severe social phobia: Effects of guided exposure with and without cognitive restructuring. *Journal of Consulting and Clinical Psychology, 56,* 251–260.

Maughan, B., & Yule, W. (1994). Reading and other learning disabilities. In M. Rutter, E. Taylor, & L. Hersov (Eds.), *Child and adolescent psychiatry: Modern approaches.* Cambridge, MA: Blackwell.

Mavissakalian, M. R., & Barlow, D. H. (1981). Assessment of obsessive-compulsive disorders. In D. H. Barlow (Ed.), *Behavioral assessment of adult disorders* (pp. 209–238). New York: Guilford Press.

Mavissakalian, M. R., Michelson, L., Greenwald, D. P., Kornblith, S., & Greenwald, M. (1983). Cognitive-behavioral treatment of agoraphobia: Paradoxical intention vs. self-statement training. *Behaviour Research and Therapy, 21,* 75–86.

Maxmen, J. S., & Ward, N. G. (1995). *Essential psychopathology and its treatment* (2nd ed.). New York: Norton.

May, P.R.A., Tuma, A. H., & Dixon, W. J. (1976). Schizophrenia: A follow-up study of results of treatment. *Archives of General Psychiatry, 33,* 474–478.

McCabe, M. P. (1994). Childhood, adolescent and current psychological factors associated with sexual dysfunction. *Sexual and Marital Therapy, 9*(3), 267–276.

McCarroll, J. E., Orman, D. T., & Lundy, A. D. (1993). Clients, problems and diagnoses in a military community mental health clinic: A 20-month study. *Military Medicine, 158*(11), 701–705.

McCarter, R. H. (1996). Panic disorder: Cognitive-behavioral treatment and its integration with pharmacotherapy. In J. M. Ellison (Ed.), *Integrative treatment of anxiety disorders* (pp. 77–112). Washington, DC: American Psychiatric Press.

McCormick, R., & Smith, M. (1995). Aggression and hostility in substance abusers: The relationship to abuse patterns, coping style, and relapse triggers. *Addictive Behaviors, 20*(5), 555–562.

McCrady, B. S. (1985). Alcoholism. In D. H. Barlow (Ed.), *Clinical handbook of psychological disorders.* New York: Guilford Press.

McCrady, B. S. (1993). Alcoholism. In D. H. Barlow (Ed.), *Clinical handbook of psychological disorders* (2nd ed., pp. 362–395). New York: Guilford Press.

McCreadie, R. G. (1992). The Nithsdale schizophrenia surveys: An overview. *Social Psychiatry and Psychiatric Epidemiology, 27*(1), 40–45.

McCullough, P. K., & Maltsberger, J. T. (1995). Obsessive-compulsive personality disorder. In G. O. Gabbard (Ed.), *Treatments of psychiatric disorders* (pp. 2367–2376). Washington, DC: American Psychiatric Press.

McDaniel, E. (1981). Personality disorders in private practice. In J. R. Lion (Ed.), *Personality disorders: Diagnosis and management.* Baltimore: Williams & Wilkins.

McDonough, R. L., & Russell, L. (1994). Alcoholism in women: A holistic, comprehensive case model. *Journal of Mental Health Counseling, 16*(4), 459–474.

McEachin, J. J., Smith, T., & Lovaas, O. I. (1993). Long-term outcome for children with autism who received early intensive behavioral treatment. *American Journal on Mental Retardation, 97*(4), 359–372.

McGlashan, T. H. (1983). The borderline syndrome. *Archives of General Psychiatry, 40,* 1319–1323.

McGlashan, T. H. (1986a). Long-term outcome of borderline personalities. *Archives of General Psychiatry, 43,* 20–30.

McGlashan, T. H. (1986b). Schizotypal personality disorder. *Archives of General Psychiatry, 43,* 329–334.

McGlashan, T. H., & Krystal, J. H. (1995). Schizophrenia-related disorders and dual diagnosis. In G. O. Gabbard (Ed.), *Treatments of psychiatric disorders* (pp. 1039–1074). Washington, DC: American Psychiatric Press.

McGrath, R. (1991). Sex offender risk assessment and disposition planning: A review of empirical and clinical findings. *The International Journal of Offender Therapy and Comparative Criminology, 35*(4), 328–350.

McGurrin, M. C. (1992). *Pathological gambling: Conceptual, diagnostic, and treatment issues.* Sarasota, FL: Professional Resources Press.

McLellan, A. T., Luborsky, L., Woody, G. E., O'Brien, C. P., & Druley, K. A. (1983). Predicting response to alcohol and drug abuse treatments. *Archives of General Psychiatry, 40,* 620–625.

McLeod, J., & McLeod, J. (1993). The relationship between personal philosophy and effectiveness in counsellors. *Counselling Psychology Quarterly, 6*(2), 121–129.

McMahon, R. J. (1994). Diagnosis, assessment, and treatment of externalizing problems in children: The role of longitudinal data. Special Section: Childhood psychopathology. *Journal of Consulting and Clinical Psychology, 62*(5), 901–907.

Meichenbaum, D. H. (1985). *Stress inoculation training.* Elmsford, NY: Pergamon Press.

Meichenbaum, D. H., & Deffenbacher, J. L. (1988). Stress inoculation training. *The Counseling Psychologist, 16,* 69–90.

Meissner, W. W. (1992). The concept of the therapeutic alliance. *Journal of the American Psychoanalytic Association, 40,* 1059–1087.

Meissner, W. W. (1995). Paranoid personality disorder. In G. O. Gabbard (Ed.), *Treatments of psychiatric disorders* (pp. 2249–2259). Washington, DC: American Psychiatric Press.

Mellinger, G. D., Balter, M. B., & Uhlenhuth, E. H. (1985). Insomnia and its treatment. *Archives of General Psychiatry, 42,* 225–232.

Meloy, J. R. (1995). Antisocial personality disorder. In G. O. Gabbard (Ed.), *Treatments of psychiatric disorders* (pp. 2273–2290). Washington, DC: American Psychiatric Press.

Meltzoll, J., & Kornreich, M. (1970). *Research in psychotherapy.* Hawthorne, NY: Aldine de Gruyter.

Mendel, S. (1995). An adolescent group within a milieu setting. *Journal of Child and Adolescent Group Therapy, 5*(1), 47–51.

Mendelberg, H. E. (1995). Inpatient treatment of mood disorders. *Psychological Reports, 76,* 819–824.

Menta, M., Ito, K., Okuma, H., & Nakano, T. (1995). Development and outcome of the Hizen parenting skills training program for mothers of children with mental retardation. *Japanese Journal of Behavior Therapy, 21*(1), 25–38.

Merikangas, K. R. (1984). Divorce and assortive mating among depressed patients. *American Journal of Psychiatry, 141,* 74–76.

Mesibov, G. (1984). Social skills training with verbal autistic adolescents and adults: A program model. *Journal of Autism and Developmental Disorders, 14,* 395–404.

Mesibov, G. (1995). Facilitated communication: A warning for pediatric psychologists. *Journal of Pediatric Psychology, 20*(1), 127–130.

Messman, T. L., & Long, P. J. (1996). Child sexual abuse and its relationship to revictimization in adult women: A review. *Clinical Psychology Review, 16*(5), 397–420.

Meyer, R. G. (1983). *The clinician's handbook.* Needham Heights, MA: Allyn & Bacon.

Meyer, R. G., & Deitsch, S. E. (1996). *The clinician's handbook* (2nd ed.). Needham Heights, MA: Allyn & Bacon.

Michels, R., & Marzuk, P. M. (1993). Progress in psychiatry: Part I. *New England Journal of Medicine, 329*(8), 552–560.

Miller, S. D., Hubble, M. A., & Duncan, B. L. (1997). Counseling for change. *Professional Counselor, 12*(1), 15–16, 52–53.

Millman, H. L., Huber, J. T., & Diggins, D. R. (1982). *Therapies for adults.* San Francisco: Jossey-Bass.

Millon, T. (1981). *Disorders of personality: DSM-III, Axis II.* New York: Wiley.

Millon, T. (1986). The avoidant personality. In A. M. Cooper, A. J. Frances, & M. H. Sacks (Eds.), *The personality disorders and neuroses* (pp. 263–273). Philadelphia: Lippincott.

Millon, T. (1996). *Disorders of personality: DSM-IV and beyond.* New York: Wiley.

Millon, T., & Klerman, G. L. (1986). *Contemporary directions in psychopathology.* New York: Guilford Press.

Mintz, L. B., O'Halloran, M. S., Mulholland, A. M., & Schneider, P. A. (1997). Questionnaire for eating disorder diagnoses: Reliability and validity for operationalizing *DSM-IV* into a self-report format. *Journal of Counseling Psychology, 44*(1), 63–79.

Moffatt, M. E., Kato, C., & Pless, I. B. (1987). Improvements in self-concept after treatment of nocturnal enuresis: Randomized control trial. *Journal of Pediatrics, 110,* 647–652.

Mogul, K. M. (1982). Overview: The sex of the therapist. *American Journal of Psychiatry, 139,* 1–11.

Money, J., & Lamacz, M. (1989). *Vandalized lovemaps.* Amherst, NY: Prometheus Books.

Monroe, S. M., Roberts, J. E., Kupfer, D. J., & Frank, E. (1996). Life stress and treatment course of recurrent depression. II: Postrecovery associations with attribution, symptom course, and recurrence over three years. *Journal of Abnormal Psychology, 105*(3), 313–328.

Monti, P. M., Abrams, D. B., Kadden, R. M., & Cooney, N. L. (1989). *Treating alcohol dependence: A coping skills training guide.* New York: Guilford Press.

Moretti, M. M., Feldman, L. A., & Shaw, B. F. (1990). Cognitive therapy: Current issues in theory and practice. In R. Wells and V. Giannetti (Eds.), *Handbook of the brief psychotherapies.* New York: Plenum.

Morgan, R., Luborsky, L., Crits-Cristoph, P., Curtis, H., & Solomon, J. (1982). Predicting the outcomes of psychotherapy by the Penn Helping Alliance Rating Method. *Archives of General Psychiatry, 39,* 397–402.

Morgenstern, J., & McCrady, B. S. (1992). Curative factors in alcohol and drug treatment: Behavioral and disease model perspectives. *British Journal of Addiction, 87,* 901–912.

Morrison, J. (1995). *DSM-IV made easy.* New York: Guilford Press.

Myers, I. B., & McCauley, M. H. (1985). *A guide to the development and use of the Myers-Briggs Type Indicator.* Palo Alto, CA: Consulting Psychologists Press.

Myers, R. A. (1986). Research on educational and vocational counseling. In S. L. Garfield and A. E. Bergin (Eds.), *Handbook of psychotherapy and behavior change* (pp. 715–738). New York: Wiley.

Najavits, L. M., & Weiss, R. D. (1994). Variations in therapist effectiveness in the treatment of patients with substance use disorders: An empirical view. *Addiction, 89,* 679–688.

Narrow, W. E., Regier, D. A., Rae, D. S., Marderscheid, R. W., & Locke, B. Z. (1993). Use of services by persons with mental and addictive disorders. *Archives of General Psychiatry, 50*(2), 95–107.

National Institutes of Mental Health. (1990). *Research on children and adolescents with mental, behavioral and developmental disorders.* Rockville, MD: National Institutes of Mental Health.

National Wellness Institute. (1983). *Lifestyle assessment questionnaire* (2nd ed.). Stevens Point: University of Wisconsin–Stevens Point Institute for Lifestyle Improvement.

Nelson, M. L., & Neufeldt, S. A. (1996). Building on an empirical foundation: Strategies to enhance good practice. *Journal of Counseling and Development, 74,* 609–615.

Nemiah, J. C. (1988). Psychoneurotic disorders. In A. M. Nicholi Jr. (Ed.), *The new Harvard guide to psychiatry* (pp. 234–258). Cambridge, MA: Harvard University Press.

Newby, R. F., Fischer, M., & Roman, M. (1991). Parent training for families of children with ADHD. *School Psychology Review, 20,* 252–265.

Nezu, C. M., & Nezu, A. M. (1994). Outpatient psychotherapy for adults with mental retardation and concomitant psychopathology: Research and clinical imperatives. *Journal of Consulting and Clinical Psychology, 62*(1), 34–42.

Niccols, G. A. (1994). Fetal alcohol syndrome: Implications for psychologists. *Clinical Psychology Review, 14*(2), 91–111.

Nolan, T., Debelle, G., Oberflaid, F., & Coffey, C. (1991). Randomised trial of laxatives in treatment of childhood encopresis. *Lancet, 338,* 523–527.

Noshpitz, J. D., & Coddington, R. (Eds.). (1990). *Stressors and the adjustment disorders.* New York: Wiley.

Noyes, R., Kathol, R. G., Fisher, M. M., Phillips, B. M., Suelzer, M. T., & Woodman, C. L. (1994). Psychiatric comorbidity among patients with hypochondriasis. *General Hospital Psychiatry, 16,* 78–87.

O'Brien, C. P., Woody, G. E., & McLellan, A. T. (1984). Psychiatric disorders in opioid-dependent patients. *Journal of Clinical Psychiatry, 45,* 9–13.

Offord, D. R., & Bennett, K. J. (1994). Conduct disorder: Long-term outcomes and intervention effectiveness. *Journal of the American Academy of Child and Adolescent Psychiatry, 33*(8), 1069–1079.

Offord, D. R., & Fleming, J. E. (1991). Epidemiology. In M. Lewis (Ed.), *Child and adolescent psychiatry: A comprehensive textbook* (pp. 1156–1196). Baltimore: Williams & Wilkins.

Oldham, J. M., & Frosch, W. A. (1986). The compulsive personality disorder. In A. M. Cooper, A. J. Frances, & M. H. Sacks (Eds.), *The personality disorders and neuroses* (pp. 243–250). Philadelphia: Lippincott.

Ollendick, T. H., & Mayer, J. A. (1984). School phobia. In S. M. Turner (Ed.), *Behavioral theories and treatment of anxiety* (pp. 367–411). New York: Plenum.

Olson, R., Rack, J. P., Conners, F. A., De Fries, J., & Fulker, D. (1991). Genetic etiology of individual differences in reading disability. In L. V. Feagans, E. J. Short, & L. Meltzer (Eds.), *Subtypes of learning disabilities* (pp. 113–135). Hillsdale, NJ: Erlbaum.

Omer, H. (1994). *Critical interventions in psychotherapy.* New York: Norton.

Orlinsky, D. E., & Howard, K. I. (1978). The relation of process to outcome in psychotherapy. In S. L. Garfield and A. E. Bergin (Eds.), *Handbook of psychotherapy and behavior change* (2nd ed., pp. 283–329). New York: Wiley.

Orlinsky, D. E., & Howard, K. I. (1986). Process and outcome in psychotherapy. In S. L. Garfield and A. E. Bergin (Eds.), *Handbook of psychotherapy and behavior change* (pp. 311–381). New York: Wiley.

Ost, L. (1996). One-session group treatment of spider phobia. *Behaviour Research and Therapy, 34*(9), 707–715.

Othmer, E., & De Souza, C. (1985). A screening test for somatization disorder (hysteria). *American Journal of Psychiatry, 142,* 1146–1149.

Oxman, T., Barrett, J., Freeman, J., & Manheimer, E. (1994). Frequency and correlates of adjustment disorder related to cardiac surgery in older patients. *Psychosomatics, 35*(6), 557–568.

Parloff, M. B. (1986). Psychotherapy outcome research. In A. M. Cooper, A. J. Frances, & M. H. Sacks (Eds.), *The personality disorders and neuroses.* Philadelphia: Lippincott.

Patterson, G. R. (1982). *A social learning approach to family intervention.* Eugene, OR: Castalia.

Pauls, D. L., Morton, L. A., & Engeland, J. A. (1992). Risks of affective illness among first-degree relatives of bipolar I old-order Amish probands. *Archives of General Psychiatry, 49*(9), 703–708.

Paxon, J. E. (1995). Relapse prevention for individuals with developmental disabilities, borderline intellectual functioning, or illiteracy. *Journal of Psychoactive Drugs, 27*(2), 167–172.

Paykel, E. S. (1994). Psychological therapies. *Acta Psychiatrica Scandinavica, 383*(98), 35–41.

Pelham, W. E. (1994). *Attention deficit hyperactivity disorder: A clinician's guide.* New York: Plenum.

Pelham, W. E., Carlson, C. L., Sams, S. E., Vallano, G., Dixon, M. J., & Hoza, B. (1993). Separate and combined effects of methylphenidate and behavior modification on boys with attention-deficit hyperactivity disorder in the classroom. *Journal of Consulting and Clinical Psychology, 61*(3), 506–515.

Pelham, W. E., Swanson, J. M., Furman, M. B., & Schwindt, H. (1995). Pemoline effects on children with ADHD: A time-response by dose-response analysis on classroom measures. *Journal of the American Academy of Child and Adolescent Psychiatry, 34*(11), 1504–1513.

Perris, C. (1982). The distinction between bipolar and unipolar affective disorders. In E. S. Paykel (Ed.), *Handbook of affective disorders* (pp. 45–58). New York: Guilford Press.

Perry, J. D. (1995). Dependent personality disorder. In G. O. Gabbard (Ed.), *Treatments of psychiatric disorders* (pp. 2355–2366). Washington, DC: American Psychiatric Press.

Perry, S., Frances, A. J., & Clarkin, J. F. (1985). *A DSM-III casebook of differential therapeutics.* New York: Brunner/Mazel.

Person, E. S. (1986). Paraphilias and gender identity disorders. In A. M. Cooper, A. J. Frances, & M. H. Sacks (Eds.), *The personality disorders and neuroses* (pp. 447–465). Philadelphia: Lippincott.

Peterson, A. A., Campise, R. L., & Azrin, N. H. (1994). Behavioral and pharmacological treatments for tic and habit disorders: A review. *Journal of Developmental and Behavioral Pediatrics, 15*(16), 430–441.

Pettei, M., & Davidson, M. (1988). Constipation. In M. Silverberg and F. Daum (Eds.), *Textbook of gastroenterology* (pp. 180–188). St. Louis, MO: Mosby–Year Book.

Philips, H. C. (1987). Avoidance behaviour and its role in sustaining chronic pain. *Behaviour Research and Therapy, 25,* 273–279.

Pilkonis, P. A., Imber, S. D., Lewis, P., & Rubinsky, P. (1984). A comparative outcome study of individual, group, and conjoint psychotherapy. *Archives of General Psychiatry, 41,* 431–437.

Pinsof, W. M., Wynne, L. C., & Hambright, A. B. (1996). The outcome of couple and family therapy: Findings, conclusions, and recommendations. *Psychotherapy, 33*(2), 321–331.

Piper, W. E., Azim, H. F., McCallum, M., & Joyce, A. S. (1990). Patient suitability and outcome in short-term individual psychotherapy. *Journal of Consulting and Clinical Psychology, 58,* 475–481.

Piper, W. E., Debbane, E. G., Bienvenu, J. P., & Garant, J. (1984). A comparative study of four forms of psychotherapy. *Journal of Consulting and Clinical Psychology, 52,* 268–279.

Poal, P., & Weisz, J. R. (1989). Therapists' own childhood problems as predictors of their effectiveness in child psychotherapy. *Journal of Clinical Child Psychology, 18*(3), 202–205.

Pope, H. G., Jr., Jones, J. M., Hudson, J. I., Cohen, B. M., & Gunderson, J. G. (1983). The validity of *DSM-III* borderline personality disorder. *Archives of General Psychiatry, 40,* 23–30.

Pope, H. G., Jr., Jones, J. M., & Jones, B. (1982). Factitious psychosis: Phenomenology, family history, and long-term outcome of nine patients. *American Journal of Psychiatry, 139,* 1480–1483.

Popper, C. W., & Gherardi, P. C. (1996). Anxiety disorders. In J. M. Wiener (Ed.), *Diagnosis and psychopharmacology of childhood and adolescent disorders* (2nd ed., pp. 294–348). New York: Wiley.

Powell, M. P., & Wagner, W. G. (1991). Psychological evaluation of sexually abused children. *Journal of Mental Health Counseling, 13*(4), 473–485.

Primac, D. W. (1993). Measuring change in a brief therapy of a compulsive personality. *Psychological Report, 72,* 309–310.

Prinz, R. J., & Miller, G. (1994). Family based treatment for childhood antisocial behavior: Experimental influences on dropout and engagement. *Journal of Consulting and Clinical Psychology, 62*(3), 645–650.

Pryor, T., & Wiederman, M. W. (1996). Measurement of nonclinical personality characteristics of women with anorexia nervosa or bulimia nervosa. *Journal of Personality Assessment, 67*(2), 414–421.

Quinn, M. (1997, May). *Attention deficit disorder treatment dilemma: To medicate or not to medicate.* Unpublished manuscript.

Rabin, A. S., Kaslow, N. J., & Rehm, L. P. (1985). Factors influencing continuation in a behavioral therapy. *Behaviour Research and Therapy, 23,* 695–698.

Rapee, R. M., & Hayman, K. (1996). The effects of video feedback on the self-evaluation of performance in socially anxious subjects. *Behaviour Research Therapy, 34*(4), 315–322.

Rapoport, J. L. (1989). *The boy who couldn't stop washing.* New York: NAL/Dutton.

Rapoport, J. L., & Castellanos, F. X. (1996). Attention-deficit/hyperactivity disorder. In J. M. Wiener (Ed.), *Diagnosis and psychopharmacology of childhood and adolescent disorders* (2nd ed., pp. 265–292). New York: Wiley.

Rapoport, J. L., & Ismond, D. R. (1996). *DSM-IV training guide for diagnosis of childhood disorders.* New York: Brunner/Mazel.

Rapoport, J. L., Leonard, H., Swedo, S. E., & Lenane, M. C. (1993). Obsessive compulsive disorder in children and adolescents: Issues in management. *Journal of Clinical Psychiatry, 54*(6), 27–29.

Rapoport, J. L., Mikkelsen, E. J., Zavardil, A., Nee, L., Gruenau, C., Mendelson, W., & Gillin, C. (1980). Childhood enuresis II: Psychopathology, tricyclic concentration in plasma and antienuretic effect. *Archives of General Psychiatry, 37,* 1146–1152.

Rappaport, S. R., & Hochstadt, N. J. (1993). Munchausen syndrome by proxy (MSBP): An intergenerational perspective. *Journal of Mental Health Counseling, 15*(3), 278–288.

Rapport, M. D. (1995). Attention-deficit hyperactivity disorder. In M. Hersen and R. T. Ammerman (Eds.), *Advanced abnormal child psychology* (pp. 353–375). Hillsdale, NJ: Erlbaum.

Rapport, M. D., Denney, C., Du Paul, G. J., & Gardner, M. (1994). Attention deficit disorder and methylphenidate: Normalization rates, clinical effectiveness, and response prediction in 76 children. *Journal of the American Academy of Child and Adolescent Psychiatry, 33*(6), 882–893.

Rasmussen, S. A., & Eisen, J. L. (1991). Clinical features and genetics of obsessive-compulsive disorder. In M. A. Jenike and M. Asberg (Eds.), *Understanding obsessive-compulsive behavior* (pp. 17–23). Toronto: Hogrefe & Huber.

Rasmussen, S. A., & Eisen, J. L. (1994). The epidemiology and differential diagnosis of obsessive compulsive disorder. *Journal of Clinical Psychiatry, 55,* 5–14.

Rehm, L. P. (1984). Self-management therapy for depression. *Advances in Behaviour Research and Therapy, 6,* 83–98.

Reid, W. H. (1983). *Treatment of the DSM-III personality disorders.* New York: Brunner/Mazel.

Reid, W. H. (1986). Antisocial personality. In A. M. Cooper, A. J. Frances, & M. H. Sacks (Eds.), *The personality disorders and neuroses* (pp. 251–261). Philadelphia: Lippincott.

Remschmidt, H. E., Schulz, E., Martin, M., & Warnke, A. (1994). Childhood-onset schizophrenia: History of the concept and recent studies. *Schizophrenia Bulletin, 20*(4), 727–745.

Rett Syndrome Diagnostic Criteria Work Group. (1988). Diagnostic criteria for Rett syndrome. *Annals of Neurology, 23,* 425–428.

Retterstøl, N. (1986). Paranoid disorders. In J. E. Helzer and S. B. Guze (Eds.), *Psychoses, affective disorders, and dementia* (pp. 245–263). New York: Basic Books.

Rey, J. M. (1993). Oppositional defiant disorder. *American Journal of Psychiatry, 150*(12), 1769–1778.

Reyes, C. J., Kokotovic, A. M., & Cosden, M. A. (1996). Sexually abused children's perceptions: How they may change treatment focus. *Professional Psychology: Research and Practice, 27*(6), 588–591.

Reynolds, C. R., & Kamphaus, R. W. (1992). *Behavior Assessment System for Children.* Circle Pines, MN: American Guidance Service.

Reynolds, C. R., & Richmond, B. O. (1978). Revised Children's Manifest Anxiety Scale. *Journal of Abnormal Psychology, 6,* 271–280.

Rice, J. P., & McGuffin, P. (1986). Genetic etiology of schizophrenia and affective disorders. In J. E. Helzer and S. B. Guze (Eds.), *Psychoses, affective disorders, and dementia* (pp. 63–90). New York: Basic Books.

Riggs, D. S., & Foa, E. B. (1993). Obsessive compulsive disorder. In D. H. Barlow (Ed.), *Clinical handbook of psychological disorders* (2nd ed., pp. 189–239). New York: Guilford Press.

Ristvedt, S. L., & Christenson, G. A. (1996). The use of pharmacologic pain sensitization in the treatment of repetitive hair-pulling. *Behaviour Research and Therapy, 34*(8), 647–648.

Rockney, R. M., McQuade, W. H., Days, A. L., Linn, H. E., & Alario, A. J. (1996). Encopresis treatment outcome: Long-term follow-up of 45 cases. *Journal of Developmental and Behavioral Pediatrics, 17*(6), 380–385.

Rogers, C. R. (1951). *Client-centered therapy.* Boston: Houghton Mifflin.

Rogers, R., Kropp, P. R., Bagby, R. M., & Dickens, S. E. (1992). Faking specific disorders: A study of the Structured Interview of Reported Symptoms (SIRS). *Journal of Clinical Psychology, 48,* 643–648.

Rogers, R. L., & Petrie, T. L. (1996). Personality correlates of anorexic symptomatology in female undergraduates. *Journal of Counseling and Development, 75,* 138–144.

Roher, G. E., Thomas, M., & Yasenchak, M. B. (1992). Client perceptions of the ideal addictions counselor. *International Journal of the Addictions, 27,* 727–733.

Ronen, T., & Wozner, Y. (1995). A self-control intervention package for the treatment of primary nocturnal enuresis. *Child and Family Behavior Therapy, 17*(1), 1–20.

Roose, S. P., Glassman, A. H., Walsh, B. T., Woodring, S., & Vital-Herne, J. (1983). Depression, delusions, and suicide. *American Journal of Psychiatry, 140,* 1159–1162.

Rosenbaum, J. F., Fava, M., Nierenberg, A., & Sachs, G. S. (1995). Treatment-resistant mood disorders. In G. O. Gabbard (Ed.), *Treatments of psychiatric disorders* (pp. 1275–1328). Washington, DC: American Psychiatric Press.

Rosenthal, T. L., & Rosenthal, R. H. (1985). Clinical stress management. In D. H. Barlow (Ed.), *Clinical handbook of psychological disorders* (pp. 145–205). New York: Guilford Press.

Ross, C. A. (1989). *Multiple personality disorder: Diagnosis, clinical features, and treatment.* New York: Wiley.

Roth, A., & Fonagy, P. (1996). *What works for whom?* New York: Guilford Press.

Rounsaville, B. J., Dolinsky, Z. S., Babor, T. F., & Meyer, R. E. (1987). Psychopathology as a predictor of treatment outcome in alcoholics. *Archives of General Psychiatry, 44,* 505–513.

Rounsaville, B. J., Weissman, M. M., Kleber, H., & Wilber, E. (1982). Heterogeneity of psychiatry diagnosis in treated opiate addicts. *Archives of General Psychiatry, 39,* 161–166.

Roy, A. (1983). Family history of suicide. *Archives of General Psychiatry, 40,* 971–974.

Roy, A. (1996). Psychosocial factors and chronic depression. *Journal of Nervous and Mental Disease, 184*(8), 509–510.

Roy-Byrne, P. P., Unde, T. W., & Post, R. M. (1986). Effects of one night's sleep deprivation on mood and behavior in panic disorder. *Archives of General Psychiatry, 43,* 895–899.

Rush, A. J., Beck, A. T., Kovacs, M., & Hollon, S. D. (1977). Comparative efficacy of cognitive therapy and pharmacotherapy in the treatment of depressed outpatients. *Cognitive Therapy and Research, 1,* 17–37.

Rush, A. J., & Kupfer, D. J. (1995). Strategies and tactics in the treatment of depression. In G. O. Gabbard (Ed.), *Treatments of psychiatric disorders* (pp. 1349–1368). Washington, DC: American Psychiatric Press.

Rutter, M., Bailey, A., Bolton, P., & Le Couteur, A. (1993). Autism: Syndrome definition and possible genetic mechanisms. In R. Plomin and V. McClearn (Eds.), *Nature, nurture, and psychology* (pp. 269–284). Washington, DC: American Psychological Association.

Rutter, M., Taylor, E., & Hersov, L. (Eds.). *Child and adolescent psychiatry: Modern approaches.* Cambridge, MA: Blackwell.

Sachs, G. S., Lafer, B., & Truman, C. J. (1994). Lithium monotherapy: Miracle, myth and misunderstanding. *Psychiatric Annals, 24,* 299–306.

Sacks, M. H. (1986). Depressive neurosis. In A. M. Cooper, A. J. Frances, & M. H. Sacks (Eds.), *The personality disorders and neuroses* (pp. 395–408). Philadelphia: Lippincott.

Salzman, L. (1989). Compulsive personality disorder. In T. Karasu (Ed.), *Treatments of psychiatric disorders* (pp. 2771–2782). Washington, DC: American Psychiatric Press.

Sanchez-Craig, M., Annis, H. M., Bornet, A. R., & MacDonald, K. R. (1984). Random assignment to abstinence and controlled drinking: Evaluation of a cognitive-behavioral program for problem drinkers. *Journal of Consulting and Clinical Psychology, 52,* 390–403.

Schachar, R., & Wachsmuth, R. (1990). Oppositional disorder in children: A validation study comparing conduct disorder, oppositional disorder and normal control children. *Journal of Child Psychology and Psychiatry, 31*(7), 1089–1102.

Schafer, L. C., Wheeler, C. C., & Futterweit, W. (1995). Gender identity disorders. In G. O. Gabbard (Ed.), *Treatments of psychiatric disorders* (pp. 2015–2048). Washington, DC: American Psychiatric Press.

Schlossberg, N. K., & Robinson, S. P. (1996). *Going to plan B: How you can cope, regroup, and start your life on a new path.* New York: Simon & Schuster.

Schmitt, J. P. (1983). Focus of attention in the treatment of depression. *Psychotherapy: Theory, Research, and Practice, 20,* 457–463.

Schneider, K. J. (1992). Therapists' personal maturity and therapeutic success: How strong is the link? *The Psychotherapy Patient, 8*(3–4), 71–91.

Schneier, F. R., Johnson, J., & Hornig, C. D. (1992). Social phobia: Comorbidity and morbidity in an epidemiologic sample. *Archives of General Psychiatry, 49,* 282–288.

Schneier, F. R., Marshall, R. D., Street, L., Heimberg, R. G., & Juster, H. R. (1995). Social phobia and specific phobia. In G. O. Gabbard (Ed.), *Treatments of psychiatric disorders* (pp. 1453–1476). Washington, DC: American Psychiatric Press.

Scholing, A., & Emmelkamp, P.M.G. (1996). Treatment of generalized social phobia: Results at long-term follow-up. *Behaviour Research and Therapy, 34*(5–6), 447–452.

Schopler, E., Reichler, R. J., De Vellis, R. F., & Daly, K. (1991). *Childhood Autism Rating Scale.* Los Angeles: Western Psychological Services.

Schuckit, M. A. (1996). Recent developments in the pharmacotherapy of alcohol dependence. *Journal of Consulting and Clinical Psychology, 64*(4), 669–676.

Schuckit, M. A., & Smith, T. L. (1996). An 8-year follow-up of 450 sons of alcoholic and control subjects. *Archives of General Psychiatry, 53*(3), 202–210.

Schwartz, A. H., & Schwartzburg, M. (1976). Hospital care. In B. B. Wolman (Ed.), *The therapist's handbook* (pp. 199–226). New York: Van Nostrand Reinhold.

Schwartz, P. J., Brown, C., Wehr, T. A., & Rosenthal, N. E. (1996). Winter seasonal affective disorder: A follow-up study of the first 59 patients of the National Institutes of Mental Health Seasonal Studies Program. *American Journal of Psychiatry, 153*(8), 1028–1036.

Scott, J., Harrington, J., House, R., & Ferrier, I. N. (1996). A preliminary study of the relationship among personality, cognitive vulnerability, symptom profile, and outcome in major depressive disorder. *Journal of Nervous and Mental Disease, 184*(8), 503–505.

Scotti, J. R., Evans, I. M., Meyer, L. H., & Walker, P. (1991). A meta-analysis of intervention research with problem behavior: Treatment validity and standards of practice. *American Journal on Mental Retardation, 96,* 233–256.

Searles, H. F. (1986). *My work with borderline patients.* Northvale, NJ: Aronson.

Seligman, L. (1994). *Developmental career counseling and assessment.* Thousand Oaks, CA: Sage.

Seligman, L. (1996a). *Diagnosis and treatment planning in counseling* (2nd ed.). San Francisco: Jossey-Bass.

Seligman, L. (1996b). *Promoting a fighting spirit: Psychotherapy for cancer patients, survivors, and their families.* San Francisco: Jossey-Bass.

Seligman, L., & Moore, B. (1995). Diagnosis of mood disorders. *Journal of Counseling and Development, 74*(1), 65–69.

Seligman, M.E.P. (1990). *Learned optimism.* New York: Pocket Books.

Seligman, M.E.P. (1995). The effectiveness of psychotherapy. *American Psychologist, 50*(12), 965–974.

Semrud-Clikeman, M., Filipek, P. A., Biederman, J., Steingard, R., Kennedy, D., Renshaw, P., & Bekken, K. (1994). Attention-deficit hyperactivity disorder: Magnetic resonance imaging morphometric analysis of the corpus callosum. *Journal of the American Academy of Child and Adolescent Psychiatry, 33*(6), 875–881.

Serban, G., & Siegel, S. (1984). Response of borderline and schizotypal patients to small doses of thiothixene and haloperidol. *American Journal of Psychiatry, 141,* 1455–1458.

Serketich, W. J., & Dumas, J. E. (1996). The effectiveness of behavioral parent training to modify antisocial behavior in children: A meta-analysis. *Behavior Therapy, 27*(2), 171–186.

Sexton, T. L. (1995). Competency survey results. In M. K. Altekruse & T. L. Sexton (Eds.), *Mental health counseling in the '90s* (pp. 25–44). Tampa, FL: National Commission for Mental Health Counseling.

Shaffer, D. (1994). Enuresis. In M. Rutter, E. Taylor, & L. Hersov (Eds.), *Child and adolescent psychiatry: Modern approaches* (pp. 505–519). Cambridge, MA: Blackwell.

Shaffer, D., & Waslick, B. (1995). Elimination disorders. In G. O. Gabbard (Ed.), *Treatments of psychiatric disorders* (pp. 219–228). Washington, DC: American Psychiatric Press.

Shaffer, D., & Waslick, B. (1996). Elimination and sleep disorders. In J. M. Wiener (Ed.), *Diagnosis and psychopharmacology of childhood and adolescent disorders* (2nd ed., pp. 471–486). New York: Wiley.

Shamoian, C. A., & Teusink, J. P. (1987). Presenile and senile dementia. In F. Flach (Ed.), *Diagnostics and psychopathology* (pp. 171–185). New York: Norton.

Shapiro, D. A., Baskham, M., Rees, A., Hardy, G. E., Reynolds, S., & Startup, M. (1994). Effects of treatment duration and severity of depression on the effectiveness of cognitive-behavioral and psychodynamic-interpersonal psychotherapy. *Journal of Consulting and Clinical Psychology, 62,* 522–534.

Shapiro, D. A., & Shapiro, D. (1982). Meta-analysis of comparative therapy outcome research: A critical appraisal. *Behavioral Psychotherapy, 10,* 4–25.

Shapiro, E. S., Shapiro, A. K., Young, J. G., & Feinberg, T. E. (1988). *Gilles de la Tourette syndrome.* New York: Raven Press.

Shapiro, F. (1989). Efficacy of the eye movement desensitization procedure in the treatment of traumatic memories. *Journal of Traumatic Stress, 2,* 199–223.

Shear, M. K., & Frosch, W. A. (1986). Obsessive-compulsive disorder. In A. M. Cooper, A. J. Frances, & M. H. Sacks (Eds.), *The personality disorders and neuroses* (pp. 353–362). Philadelphia: Lippincott.

Sherman, A., Ellison, J. M., & Iwamoto, S. (1996). Obsessive-compulsive disorder: Integration of cognitive-behavioral therapy with pharmacotherapy. In J. M. Ellison (Ed.), *Integrative treatment of anxiety disorders* (pp. 153–198). Washington, DC: American Psychiatric Press.

Siever, L. J., & Kendler, K. S. (1986). Schizoid/schizotypal/paranoid personality disorders. In A. M. Cooper, A. J. Frances, & M. H. Sacks (Eds.), *The personality disorders and neuroses* (pp. 191–201). Philadelphia: Lippincott.

Sigman, M., & Capps, L. (1997). *Children with autism: A developmental perspective.* Cambridge, MA: Harvard University Press.

Silliman, E. R., Campbell, M., & Mitchell, R. (1989). Genetic influences in autism and assessment of metalinguistic performance in siblings of autistic children. In G. Dawson (Ed.), *Autism: Nature, diagnosis and treatment* (pp. 225–259). New York: Guilford Press.

Silva, R. R., Magee, H. J., & Friedhoff, A. J. (1993). Persistent tardive dyskinesia and other neuroleptic-related dyskinesias in Tourette's disorder. *Journal of Child and Adolescent Psychopharmacology, 3*(3), 137–144.

Silver, L. B. (1989). Elective mutism. In H. Kaplan and B. Sadock (Eds.), *Comprehensive textbook of psychiatry* (5th ed., pp. 1887–1889). Baltimore: Williams & Wilkins.

Silver, L. B. (1991). Developmental learning disorders. In M. Lewis (Ed.), *Child and adolescent psychiatry: A comprehensive textbook* (pp. 522–528). Baltimore: Williams & Wilkins.

Silver, L. B. (1992). *The misunderstood child: A guide for parents of children with learning disabilities* (2nd ed.). Blue Ridge Summit, PA: TAB Books.

Silver, L. B. (1995). Learning disorders. In G. O. Gabbard (Ed.), *Treatments of psychiatric disorders* (pp. 123–140). Washington, DC: American Psychiatric Press.

Silverman, J. S., Silverman, J. A., & Eardley, D. A. (1984). Do maladaptive attitudes cause depression? *Archives of General Psychiatry, 41,* 28–30.

Simpson, D. D., Joe, G. W., & Bracy, S. A. (1982). Six-year follow-up of opioid addicts after admission to treatment. *Archives of General Psychiatry, 39,* 1318–1323.

Simpson, G. M., & May, P.R.A. (1982). Schizophrenic disorders. In J. H. Greist, J. W. Jefferson, & R. L. Spitzer, (Eds.), *Treatment of mental disorders* (pp. 143–183). New York: Oxford University Press.

Singer, H., Reiss, A. L., Brown, J., Aylward, E. H., Shih, B., Chee, E., & Harris, E. L. (1993). Volumetric MRI changes in basal ganglia of children with Tourette syndrome. *Neurology, 43,* 950–956.

Skinner, L. J., & Becker, J. V. (1985). Sexual dysfunctions and deviations. In M. Hersen and S. M. Turner (Eds.), *Diagnostic interviewing* (pp. 205–242). New York: Plenum.

Skuse, D. (1994). Feeding and sleeping disorders. In M. Rutter, E. Taylor, & L. Hersov (Eds.), *Child and adolescent psychiatry: Modern approaches* (pp. 467–489). Cambridge, MA: Blackwell.

Sledge, W. H., Tebes, J., Rakfeldt, J., Davidson, L., Lyons, L., & Druss, B. (1996). Day hospital/crisis respite care versus inpatient care. I: Clinical outcomes. *Journal of Psychiatry, 153*(8), 1065–1073.

Smalley, S. L. (1991). Genetic influences in autism. *Psychiatric Clinics of North America, 14,* 125–139.

Smith, M. L., Glass, G. V., & Miller, T. I. (1980). *The benefits of psychotherapy.* Baltimore: Johns Hopkins University Press.

Smith, R. E., & Winokur, G. (1984). Affective disorders. In S. M. Turner and M. Hersen (Eds.), *Adult psychopathology and diagnosis* (pp. 245–262). New York: Wiley.

Snyder, M. (1994). Couples therapy with narcissistically vulnerable clients: Using the relationship enhancement model. *Family Journal: Counseling and Therapy for Couples and Families, 2,* 27–35.

Soloff, P. H. (1985). Personality disorders. In M. Hersen and S. M. Turner (Eds.), *Diagnostic interviewing* (pp. 131–159). New York: Plenum.

Sparrow, S. S., Balla, D. A., & Cicchetti, D. V. (1984). *Vineland adaptive behavior scales.* Circle Pines, MN: American Guidance Service.

Specker, S. M., Carlson, G. A., Christenson, G. A., & Marcotte, M. (1995). Impulse control disorders and attention deficit disorder in pathological gamblers. *Annals of Clinical Psychiatry, 7*(4), 175–179.

Speilberger, C. D., Pollans, C. H., & Worden, T. J. (1984). Anxiety disorders. In S. M. Turner and M. Hersen (Eds.) *Adult psychopathology and diagnosis* (pp. 263–303). New York: Wiley.

Spelic, S. S. (1997). Somatization and hypochondriasis. *Treatment Today, 9*(1), 30–31, 34.

Speltz, M. (1990). The treatment of preschool conduct problems: An integration of behavioral and attachment concepts. In M. Greenburg, D. Cicchetti, & E. M. Cummings (Eds.), *Attachment in the preschool years* (pp. 399–426). Chicago: University of Chicago Press.

Sperry, L. (1995). *Handbook of diagnosis and treatment of the DSM-IV personality disorders.* New York: Brunner/Mazel.

Spiegel, D. (1993). *Living beyond limits.* New York: Random House.

Spiegel, D. (1996). Dissociative disorders. In R. E. Hales & S. C. Yudofsky (Eds.), *The American Psychiatric Press synopsis of psychiatry* (pp. 583–604).Washington, DC: American Psychiatric Press.

Stanton, M. D. (1985). The family and drug abuse. In T. E. Bratter & G. G. Forrest (Eds.), *Alcoholism and substance abuse* (pp. 398–430). New York: Free Press.

Stavrakaki, C., & Klein, J. (1986). Psychotherapies with the mentally retarded. *Psychiatric Clinics of North America, 9*(4), 733–743.

Steinberg, M. (1995). Depersonalization. In G. O. Gabbard (Ed.), *Treatments of psychiatric disorders* (pp. 1633–1654). Washington, DC: American Psychiatric Press.

Steketee, G. (1993). *The treatment of obsessive compulsive disorder.* New York: Guilford Press.

Steketee, G., Frost, R., & Bogart, K. (1996). The Yale-Brown obsessive compulsive scale: Interview versus self-report. *Behaviour Research and Therapy, 34*(8), 675–684.

Stevenson, J., & Meares, R. J. (1992). An outcome study of psychotherapy for patients with borderline personality disorder. *American Journal of Psychiatry, 149,* 358–362.

Stewart, J. T., Myers, W. C., Burket, R. C., & Lyles, W. B. (1990). A review of pharmacotherapy of aggression in children and adolescents. *Journal of the American Academy of Child and Adolescent Psychiatry, 29*(2), 269–277.

Stewart, J. W., McGrath, P. J., Liebowitz, M. R., Harrison, W., Quitkin, F., & Rabkin, J. G. (1985). Treatment outcome validation of *DSM-III* subtypes. *Archives of General Psychiatry, 42,* 1148–1153.

Stiles, W. B., Shapiro, D. A., & Elliott, R. (1986). Are all psychotherapies equivalent? *American Psychologist, 41,* 165–180.

Stone, M. H. (1990). *The fate of borderline patients: Successful outcome and psychiatric practice.* New York: Guilford Press.

Stone, M. H. (1995). Schizoid and Schizotypal personality disorders. In G. O. Gabbard (Ed.), *Treatments of psychiatric disorders* (pp. 2261–2272). Washington, DC: American Psychiatric Press.

Strain, J. J. (1995). Adjustment disorder. In G. O. Gabbard (Ed.), *Treatments of psychiatric disorders* (pp. 1655–1666). Washington, DC: American Psychiatric Press.

Strupp, H. H. (1981). Toward the refinement of time-limited dynamic psychotherapy. In S. H. Budman (Ed.), *Forms of brief therapy* (pp. 219–242). New York: Guilford Press.

Sturmey, P. (1995). Evaluating and improving residential treatment during group leisure situations: An independent replication. *Behavioral Interventions, 10*(2), 59–67.

Sue, D. W., Ivey, A. E., & Pedersen, P. B. (1996). *A theory of multicultural counseling and therapy.* Pacific Grove, CA: Brooks/Cole.

Suinn, R. M. (1990). *Anxiety management training (AMT): A behavior therapy.* New York: Plenum.

Sutherland, S. M., & Frances, A. J. (1995). Avoidant personality disorder. In G. O. Gabbard (Ed.), *Treatments of psychiatric disorders* (pp. 2345–2353). Washington, DC: American Psychiatric Press.

Svartberg, M., & Stiles, T. C. (1994). Therapeutic alliance, therapist competence, and client charge in short-term anxiety-provoking psychotherapy. *Psychotherapy Research, 4*(1), 20–33.

Tailoring treatment for alcoholics is not the answer. (1997). *APA Monitor, 28*(2), 6.

Taiminen, R. (1994). Depression among schizophrenic patients: A selective review. *Psychiatria Fennica, 25,* 185–194.

Talley, J. E. (1992). *The predictors of successful very brief psychotherapy: A study of differences by gender, age, and treatment variables.* Springfield, IL: Thomas.

Tansey, M. (1993). Ten-year stability of EEG biofeedback results for a hyperactive boy who failed fourth grade perceptually impaired class. *Biofeedback and Self Regulation, 18*(1), 33–44.

Tarrier, N., Sharpe, L., & Beckett, R. (1993). A trial of two cognitive-behavioral methods of treating drug-resistant residual psychotic symptoms in schizophrenic patients. II: Treatment specific changes in coping and problem solving skills. *Social Psychiatry and Psychiatric Epidemiology, 28,* 5–10.

Telch, M. J., Agras, W. S., Taylor, C. B., Roth, W. T., & Gallen, C. C. (1985). Combined pharmacological and behavioral treatment for agoraphobia. *Behaviour Research and Therapy, 23,* 325–335.

Thase, M. E., & Kupfer, D. J. (1996). Recent developments in the pharmacotherapy of mood disorders. *Journal of Consulting and Clinical Psychology, 64*(4), 646–659.

Thyer, B. A. (1987). *Treating anxiety disorders.* Thousand Oaks, CA: Sage.

Toone, B. K. (1990). Disorders of hysterical conversion. In C. Bass (Ed.), *Physical symptoms and psychological illness* (pp. 207–234). Oxford, England: Blackwell.

Torgersen, S. (1984). Genetic and nosological aspects of schizotypal and borderline personality disorders. *Archives of General Psychiatry, 41,* 546–554.

Towbin, K. E., & Cohen, D. J. (1996). Tic Disorders. In J. M. Wiener (Ed.), *Diagnosis and psychopharmacology of childhood and adolescent disorders* (2nd ed., pp. 349–369). New York: Wiley.

Towbin, K. E., Cohen, D. J., & Leckman, J. F. (1995). Tic Disorders. In G. O. Gabbard (Ed.), *Treatments of psychiatric disorders* (pp. 201–218). Washington, DC: American Psychiatric Press.

Towbin, K. E., Riddle, M., Leckman, J. F., Brunn, R., & Cohen, D. J. (1988). The clinical care of individuals with Tourette's syndrome. In D. J. Cohen, R. Brunn, & J. F. Leckman (Eds.), *Tourette's syndrome and tic disorders: Clinical understanding and treatment* (pp. 329–352). New York: Wiley.

Trull, T. J., Nietzel, M. T., & Main, A. (1988). The use of meta-analysis to assess the clinical significance of behavior therapy for agoraphobia. *Behavior Therapy, 19,* 527–538.

Tsuang, M. T., Farone, S. V., & Day, M. (1988). Schizophrenic disorders. In A. M. Nicholi Jr. (Ed.), *The new Harvard guide to psychiatry* (pp. 259–295). Cambridge, MA: Harvard University Press.

Tsuang, M. T., & Loyd, D. W. (1986). Other psychotic disorders. In J. E. Helzer and S. B. Guze (Eds.), *Psychoses, affective disorders, and dementia* (pp. 20–39). New York: Basic Books.

Turkat, I. D. (1990). The personality disorders: A psychological approach to clinical management. *Journal of Psychopathology and Behavioral Assessment, 9,* 295–304.

Turkat, I. D., & Maisto, S. A. (1985). Personality disorders: Application of the experimental method to the formulation and modification of personality disorders. In D. H. Barlow (Ed.), *Clinical handbook of psychological disorders* (pp. 502–570). New York: Guilford Press.

Turner, S. M., & Hersen, M. (Eds.). (1984). *Adult psychopathology and diagnosis.* New York: Wiley.

Vaillant, G. E., & Milofsky, E. S. (1982). Natural history of male alcoholism: Paths to recovery. *Archives of General Psychiatry, 39,* 127–133.

Vanden Bos, G. R. (1986). Psychotherapy research: A special issue. *American Psychologist, 41,* 111–112.

Van Oppen, P., Hoekstra, R., & Emmelkamp, P.M.G. (1995). The structure of obsessive-compulsive symptoms. *Behavior Research and Therapy, 33,* 15–23.

Van Valkenburg, C., & Akiskal, H. S. (1985). Affective disorders. In M. Hersen and S. M. Turner (Eds.), *Diagnostic interviewing* (pp. 79–110). New York: Plenum.

Van Velzen, C.J.M., & Emmelkamp, P.M.G. (1996). The assessment of personality disorders: Implications for cognitive and behavior therapy. *Behaviour Research and Therapy, 34*(8), 655–668.

Vaughn, C. E., & Leff, J. P. (1976). The influence of family and social factors on the course of psychiatric illness. *British Journal of Psychiatry, 129,* 125–137.

Viederman, M. (1986). Somatoform and factitious disorders. In A. M. Cooper, A. J. Frances, & M. H. Sacks (Eds.), *The personality disorders and neuroses* (pp. 363–382). Philadelphia: Lippincott.

Viederman, M. (1995). Metaphor and meaning in conversion disorder: A brief active therapy. *Psychosomatic Medicine, 57,* 403–409.

Viorst, J. (1986). *Necessary losses.* New York: Fawcett.

Volkmar, F. R. (1991). Autism and the pervasive developmental disorders. In M. Lewis (Ed.), *Child and adolescent psychiatry: A comprehensive textbook* (pp. 449–508). Baltimore: Williams & Wilkins.

Volkmar, F. R. (1996). Childhood and adolescent psychosis: A review of the past 10 years. *Journal of the American Academy of Child and Adolescent Psychiatry, 35*(7), 843–851.

Wald, A., & Handen, B. L. (1987). Behavioral aspects of disorders of defecation and fecal continence. *Annals of Behavioral Medicine, 9*(3), 19–23.

Waldinger, R. (1986). Intensive psychodynamic psychotherapy with borderline patients: An overview. *American Journal of Psychiatry, 144,* 267–274.

Walker, C. E., & Roberts, M. C. (1992). *Handbook of clinical child psychology.* New York: Wiley.

Walker, J. L., Lahey, B. B., Russo, M. F., Christ, M.A.G., McBurnett, K., Loeber, R., Stouthamer-Loeber, M., & Green, S. M. (1991). Anxiety, inhibition and conduct disorder in children. I: Relation to social impairment. *Journal of the American Academy of Child and Adolescent Psychiatry, 30,* 187–191.

Waller, G. (1994). Childhood sexual abuse and borderline personality disorder in the eating disorders. *Child Abuse and Neglect, 18*(1), 97–101.

Wallerstein, R. S. (1986). *Forty-two lives in treatment.* New York: Guilford Press.

Warr-Leeper, G., Wright, N. A., & Mack, A. (1994). Language disabilities of antisocial boys in residential treatment. *Behavioral-Disorders, 19*(3), 159–169.

Waterhouse, G. J., & Strupp, H. H. (1984). The patient-therapist relationship: Research from the psychodynamic perspective. *Clinical Psychology Review, 4,* 77–92.

Watson, J. C., & Greenberg, L. S. (1996). Pathways to change in the psychotherapy of depression: Relating process to session change and outcome. *Psychotherapy, 33*(2), 262–274.

Watts, R. E., Trusty, J., Canada, R., & Harvill, R. L. (1995). Perceived early childhood family influence and counselor effectiveness: An exploratory study. *Counselor Education and Supervision, 35*(2), 104–110.

Webster-Stratton, C. (1989). *The advanced videotape parent training programs.* Seattle, WA: Seth Enterprises.

Webster-Stratton, C., & Dahl, R. W. (1995). Conduct disorders. In M. Hersen and R. T. Ammerman (Eds.), *Advanced abnormal child psychology* (pp. 333–352). Hillsdale, NJ: Erlbaum.

Webster-Stratton, C., & Hammond, M. (1997). Treating children with early-onset conduct problems: A comparison of child and parent training interventions. *Journal of Consulting and Clinical Psychology, 65*(1), 93–109.

Wechsler, D. (1992). *Wechsler Individual Achievement Test.* San Antonio, TX: Psychological Corporation.

Weiner, R. D. (1995). Electroconvulsive therapy. In G. O. Gabbard (Ed.), *Treatments of psychiatric disorders* (pp. 1238–1262). Washington, DC: American Psychiatric Press.

Weiner-Davis, M. (1992). *Divorce busting.* New York: Simon & Schuster.

Weiss, G., & Hechtman, L. T. (1986). *Hyperactive children grown up.* New York: Guilford Press.

Weisz, J. R., Weiss, B., Han, S. S., Granger, D. A., & Morton, T. (1995). Effects of psychotherapy with children and adolescents revisited: A meta-analysis of treatment outcome studies. *Psychological Bulletin, 117*(3), 450–468.

Wells, R., & Giannetti, V. (Eds.). (1990). *Handbook of the brief psychotherapies.* New York: Plenum.

Wender, P. H. (1987). *The hyperactive child, adolescent and adult.* Oxford, England: Oxford University Press.

Werry, J. (1996). Childhood schizophrenia. In F. R. Volkmar (Ed.), *Psychoses and pervasive developmental disorders in childhood and adolescence* (pp. 1–56). Washington, DC: American Psychiatric Press.

Whalen, C. K., & Henker, B. (1991). Therapies for hyperactive children: Comparisons, combinations, and compromises. *Journal of Consulting and Clinical Psychology, 59*(1), 126–137.

Wiborg, I. M., & Dahl, A. A. (1996). Does brief dynamic psychotherapy reduce the relapse rate of panic disorder? *Archives of General Psychiatry, 53*(8), 689–694.

Wiener, J. M. (Ed.). (1996). *Diagnosis and psychopharmacology of childhood and adolescent disorders.* New York: Wiley.

Wierzbicki, M., & Bartlett, T. S. (1987). The efficacy of group and individual cognitive therapy for mild depression. *Cognitive Therapy and Research, 11,* 337–342.

Williams, P. V., & McGlashan, T. H. (1987). Schizoaffective psychosis: Comparative long-term outcome. *Archives of General Psychiatry, 44,* 130–137.

Wilson, G. T. (1981). Behavior therapy as a short-term therapeutic approach. In S. H. Budman (Ed.), *Forms of brief therapy* (pp. 131–166). New York: Guilford Press.

Wilson, G. T., & Pike, K. M. (1993). Eating disorders. In D. H. Barlow (Ed.), *Clinical handbook of psychological disorders* (2nd ed., pp. 278–317). New York: Guilford Press.

Wittchen, H. U., Knauper, B., & Kessler, R. C. (1994). Lifetime risk of depression. *British Journal of Psychiatry, 165*(26), 16–22.

Wogan, M., & Norcross, J. C. (1983). Dimensions of psychotherapists' activity: A replication and extension of earlier findings. *Psychotherapy: Theory, Research, and Practice, 20,* 67–74.

Wolfe, B., & Maser, J. (Eds.). (1994). *Treatment of panic disorder.* Washington, DC: American Psychiatric Press.

Wolraich, M. L., Hannah, J. N., Pinnock, T. Y., Baumgaertel, A., & Brown, J. (1996). Comparison of diagnostic criteria for attention-deficit hyperactivity disorder in a county-wide sample. *Journal of the American Academy of Child and Adolescent Psychiatry, 35*(3), 319–324.

Woodcock, R. W., & Johnson, M. B. (1989). *Woodcock-Johnson Psycho-Educational Battery–Revised.* Allen, TX: DLM Teaching Resources.

Yalom, I. D. (1995). *The theory and practice of group psychotherapy* (4th ed.). New York: Basic Books.

Yost, J. K., & Mines, R. A. (1985). Stress and alcoholism. In T. E. Bratter and G. G. Forrest (Eds.), *Alcoholism and substance abuse* (pp. 74–103). New York: Free Press.

Yule, W. (1994). Posttraumatic stress disorders. In M. Rutter, E. Taylor, & L. Hersov (Eds.), *Child and adolescent psychiatry: Modern approaches* (pp. 392–406). Cambridge, MA: Blackwell.

Zanardi, R., Franchini, L., Gasperini, M., Perez, J., & Smeraldi, E. (1996). Double-blind controlled trial of sertraline versus paroxeton in the treatment of delusional depression. *American Journal of Psychiatry, 153*(12), 1631–1633.

Zarate, C. A., Tohen, M., Banov, M. D., & Weiss, M. K. (1995). Is clozapine a mood stabilizer? *Journal of Clinical Psychiatry, 56*(3), 108–112.

Zeanah, C. H., & Emde, R. N. (1994). Attachment disorders in infancy and childhood. In M. Rutter, E. Taylor, & L. Hersov (Eds.), *Child and adolescent psychiatry: Modern approaches* (pp. 490–504). Cambridge, MA: Blackwell.

Zigler, E., Taussig, C., & Black, K. (1992). Early childhood intervention: A promising preventative for juvenile delinquency. *American Psychologist, 47*(8), 997–1006.

THE AUTHOR

Linda Seligman is a professor of counseling and development at George Mason University, Fairfax, Virginia, where she is in charge of the Community Agency Counseling Program. She is also director of the Center for Counseling and Consultation, a private practice in Fairfax. She received her A.B. degree in English and American literature from Brandeis University, her M.A. degree in guidance and counseling from Teachers College of Columbia University, and her Ph.D. degree in counseling psychology from Columbia University.

Seligman is licensed as a psychologist in Virginia and Maryland and as a professional counselor in Virginia. Her primary research interests include the diagnosis and treatment of mental disorders and the investigation of how people cope with cancer. Her previous books are *Assessment in Developmental Career Counseling* (1980), *Diagnosis and Treatment Planning in Counseling* (1986, 1996), *Developmental Career Counseling and Assessment* (1994), *Promoting a Fighting Spirit: Psychotherapy for Cancer Patients, Survivors, and Their Families* (1996), and the first edition of the present volume. She has also published more than fifty book chapters and professional articles.

Seligman is a past president of the Virginia Mental Health Counselors Association and from 1984 to 1987 was editor of the *Journal of Mental Health Counseling*. She has also served on the editorial boards of the *Journal of Counseling and Development* and the *Virginia Counselors Journal*. She was selected as a Distinguished Professor by George Mason University in 1986 and was named

Researcher of the Year in 1990 by the American Mental Health Counselors Association. She has consulted to many governmental and human service agencies and has given over one hundred lectures and workshops on diagnosis and treatment planning.

NAME INDEX

A

Abikoff, H., 89
Abrahamian, R. P., 101
Abramowitz, A. J., 79
Abrams, D. B., 256
Abrego, P. J., 15
Achenbach, T., 53, 75, 85
Agras, W. S., 254, 267, 268, 269, 270
Akiskal, H. S., 167, 176, 181, 311, 360
Akiskal, S., 117
Albano, A. M., 106, 107
Alden, L., 370
Alexander, J. F., 88
Allen, J., 68
Allen, J. G., 25
Allen, M. J., 251, 252
Allen, T., 229
Allgulander, C., 192
Ammerman, R. T., 52
Anastopoulos, A. D., 76, 78
Anders, T. F., 295, 298, 303
Andersen, A. E., 266, 269
Anderson, D. J., 228
Andreasen, N. C., 137, 321, 424
Andrews, A. A., 30

Andrews, D. W., 56, 87, 90, 91
Andrews, G., 4, 30, 220
Andrews, J., 116–117
Anne, 24, 26, 35–36
Annis, H. M., 257
Araoz, D. L., 149
Arizmendi, T. G., 38
Arndt, W., 282, 303
Arnold, L., 74
Arntz, A., 199, 309
Aro, H. M., 132
Aronoff, G. M., 310
Arredondo, D. E., 81
Astill, J. L., 358
Atwood, J. D., 151, 152, 153, 202, 218, 221, 222, 228, 253, 257, 259, 268, 269, 276, 394, 400
Awad, G. A., 71
Azim, H. F., 31
Azrin, H. H., 99, 104–105

B

Babor, T. F., 259
Bach, D., 310
Bach, M., 310
Bagby, R. M., 140

Bagenholm, A., 71
Bailey, A., 69
Baker, A. L., 161
Baker, L., 106
Balastikova, B., 100
Bale, R. M., 265
Balla, D. A., 58
Ballenger, J. C., 199
Balter, M. B., 296
Banov, M. D., 406
Barbaree, H. E., 199, 200, 228
Barber, J. P., 48
Barkley, R. A., 75, 76, 77, 78, 79, 84, 125
Barley, W. D., 357
Barlow, D. H., 106, 197, 198, 200, 201, 204, 208, 210, 217, 228, 229, 237, 421, 424
Baron-Cohen, S., 68
Barrett, J., 132
Bartels, S. J., 406
Bartlett, T. S., 171
Bass, C., 327
Bass, D., 56
Bauer, M. S., 167, 316
Baumeister, A. A., 59, 60, 61, 62
Beatty, W. W., 75

SUBJECT INDEX